Lecture Notes in Computer Science 6104

Commenced Publication in 1973
Founding and Former Series Editors:
Gerhard Goos, Juris Hartmanis, and Jan van Leeuwen

Paolo Bellavista   Ruay-Shiung Chang
Han-Chieh Chao   Shin-Feng Lin
Peter M.A. Sloot (Eds.)

Advances in Grid and Pervasive Computing

5th International Conference, GPC 2010
Hualien, Taiwan, May 10-13, 2010
Proceedings

 Springer

Volume Editors

Paolo Bellavista
Università di Bologna, Dipartimento di Informatica,
Elettronica e Sistemistica (DEIS) 40136 Bologna, Italy
E-mail: paolo.bellavista@unibo.it

Ruay-Shiung Chang
National Dong Hwa University
Department of Computer Science and Information Engineering
Hualien, Taiwan 974, Republic of China
E-mail: rschang@mail.ndhu.edu.tw

Han-Chieh Chao
National Ilan University
Department of Electronic Engineering, Ilan, Taiwan 260, Republic of China
E-mail: hcc@niu.edu.tw

Shin-Feng Lin
National Dong Hwa University, Hualien, Taiwan 974, Republic of China
E-mail: david@mail.ndhu.edu.tw

Peter M.A. Sloot
University of Amsterdam, Faculty of Science Informatics Institute
1098 XG Amsterdam, The Netherlands
E-mail: p.m.a.sloot@uva.nl

Library of Congress Control Number: 2010926404

CR Subject Classification (1998): F.2, C.2, H.4, D.2, D.4, C.2.4

LNCS Sublibrary: SL 1 – Theoretical Computer Science and General Issues

ISSN   0302-9743
ISBN-10   3-642-13066-6 Springer Berlin Heidelberg New York
ISBN-13   978-3-642-13066-3 Springer Berlin Heidelberg New York

Typesetting: Camera-ready by author, data conversion by Scientific Publishing Services, Chennai, India
Printed on acid-free paper   06/3180

Preface

Grid and Pervasive Computing (GPC) is an annual international conference on the emerging areas of grid computing and pervasive computing, aimed at providing an exciting platform and paradigm for all-the-time, everywhere services. GPC 2010 provided a high-profile, leading-edge forum for researchers and developers from industry and academia to present their latest research in the field of grid and pervasive computing.

Three workshops were held in conjunction with the GPC 2010 conference:

- The First International Workshop on Intelligent Management of Networked Environment (IMNE 2010)
- International Workshop on Multimedia Applications for Cloud (MAC 2010)
- The 6th International Workshop on Mobile Commerce and Services (WMCS 2010)

The proceedings of these workshop are also included in this volume. We received 184 papers originating from 22 countries. The Program Committee finally selected 67 papers for presentation at the conference and inclusion in this LNCS volume. At GPC 2010, we were very pleased to have four distinguished invited speakers, who delivered state-of-the-art information on the conference topics:

- A grid based virtual laboratory for HIV drugranking by Peter Sloot (University of Amsterdam, The Netherlands)
- Solving the scalability dilemma with clouds, crowds, and algorithms by Michael J. Franklin (University of California, Berkeley, USA)
- The trend of cloud computing — from industry's perspective by Enwei Xie (Microsoft Greater China Region, China)
- Towards ubiquitous affective learning by Bin Hu (The Birmingham City University, UK)

The conference would not have been possible without the support of many people and organizations that helped in various ways to make it a success. In particular, we would like to thank the National Science Council and the Computer Center of MOE for their financial support and we therefore gratefully acknowledge their help in the realization of this conference.

May 2010

Paolo Bellavista
Ruay-Shiung Chang
Han-Chieh Chao
Shin-Feng Lin
Peter Sloot

Organization

Steering Committee

Hai Jin (Chair)   Huazhong University of Science and
Technology, China

Nabil Abdennadher   University of Applied Sciences,
Western Switzerland

Switzerland Christophe Cerin   University of Paris XIII, France
Sajal K. Das   The University of Texas at Arlington, USA
Jean-Luc Gaudiot   University of California - Irvine, USA
Kuan-Ching Li   Providence University, Taiwan
Cho-Li Wang   The University of Hong Kong, China
Chao-Tung Yang   Tunghai University, Taiwan

Conference Chairs

Ruay-Shiung Chang   National Dong Hwa University, Taiwan
Han-Chieh Chao   National Ilan University, Taiwan
Peter Sloot   University of Amsterdam, The Netherlands

Program Chair

Paolo Bellavista   Universitá degli Studi di Bologna, Italy
Shin-Feng Lin   National Dong Hwa University, Taiwan

Tutorial Chairs

Jiann-Liang Chen   NTUST, Taiwan
Shiow-Yang Wu   National Dong Hwa University, Taiwan

Exhibition Chairs

Cheng-Chin Chiang   National Dong Hwa University, Taiwan
Shih-Chien Chou   National Dong Hwa University, Taiwan

Publicity Chairs

Nabil Abdennadher   University of Applied Sciences,
Western Switzerland

Wen-Kai Tai   National Dong Hwa University, Taiwan
Chung Yung   National Dong Hwa University, Taiwan

Workshops Chairs

Ching-Hsien Hsu	Chung Hua University, Taiwan
Shi-Jim Yen	National Dong Hwa University, Taiwan

Finance Chair

Sheng-Lung Peng	National Dong Hwa University, Taiwan

Publication Chairs

I-Cheng Chang	National Dong Hwa University, Taiwan
Chenn-Jung Huang	National Dong Hwa University, Taiwan
Pao-Lien Lai	National Dong Hwa University, Taiwan
Ching-Nung Yang	National Dong Hwa University, Taiwan

Registration Chairs

Guanling Lee	National Dong Hwa University, Taiwan
Mau-Tsuen Yang	National Dong Hwa University, Taiwan

Web Chairs

Hsin-Chou Chi	National Dong Hwa University, Taiwan
Reen-Cheng Wang	National Taitung University, Taiwan

Local Arrangements Chairs

Min-Xiou Chen	National Dong Hwa University, Taiwan
Shou-Chih Lo	National Dong Hwa University, Taiwan

Program Committee

Pautasso Cesare	University of Lugano, Switzerland
Hsi-Ya Chang	NCHC, Taiwan
I-Cheng Chang	National Dong Hwa University, Taiwan
Tao-Ku Chang	National Dong Hwa University, Taiwan
Yao-Chung Chang	National Taitung University, Taiwan
Jiann-Liang Chen	NTUST, Taiwan
Min-Xiou Chen	National Dong Hwa University, Taiwan
Yuh-Shyan Chen	National Taipei University, Taiwan
Hisn-Chou Chi	National Dong Hwa University, Taiwan
Cheng-Chin Chiang	National Dong Hwa University, Taiwan
Shih-Chien Chou	National Dong Hwa University, Taiwan

Yeh-Ching Chung	National Tsing Hua University, Taiwan
Grigoras Dan	University College Cork, Ireland
Petcu Dana	Western University of Timisoara, Romania
Olmedilla Daniel	Telefonica R&D, Spain
Der-Jiunn Deng	National Changhua University of Education, Taiwan
Belli Fevzi	University Paderborn, Germany
Yong Guan	Iowa State University, USA
Jiang Hai	University of Alberta, Canada
Stockinger Heinz	University of Vienna, Austria
Muller Henning	University of Applied Sciences, Western Switzerland
Michael Hobbs	Deakin University, Australia
Hung-Chang Hsiao	National Cheng Kung University, Taiwan
Sun-Yuan Hsieh	National Cheng Kung University, Taiwan
Chenn-Jung Huang	National Dong Hwa University, Taiwan
Chung-Ming Huang	National Cheng Kung University, Taiwan
Kuo-Chan Huang	National Taichung University, Taiwan
Panetta Jairo	INPE, Brazil
Abawajy Jemal	Deakin University, Australia
Young-Sik Jeong	Wonkwang University, Korea
Han-Ying Kao	National Dong Hwa University, Taiwan
Chih-Hong Lai	National Dong Hwa University, Taiwan
Fei-Pei Lai	National Taiwan University, Taiwan
Pao-Lein Lai	National Dong Hwa University, Taiwan
Guanling Lee	National Dong Hwa University, Taiwan
Hai Liu	Hong Kong Baptist University, Hong Kong SAR
Pang-Feng Liu	National Taiwan University, Taiwan
Shing-Min Liu	National Chung Cheng University, Taiwan
Shou-Chih Lo	National Dong Hwa University, Taiwan
Arantes Luciana	LIP6, France
Jianhua Ma	Hosei University, Japan
Baker Mark	The University of Reading, UK
Beniamino Di Martino	Second University of Naples, Italy
Sato Mitsuhisa	University of Tsukuba, Japan
Jong Hyuk Park	Kyungnam University, Korea
Sheng-Lung Peng	National Dong Hwa University, Taiwan
Manneback Pierre	Faculty of Engineering, Mons, Belgium
Won-Woo Ro	Yonsei University, Korea
F. de Mello Rodrigo	University of Sao Paulo, Brazil
K. Thulasiram Ruppa	University of Manitoba, Canada
Hussain Sajid	Acadia University, Canada
Ranka Sanjay	University of Florida, USA
Zeadally Sherali	University of the District of Columbia, USA
Wen-Kai Tai	National Dong Hwa University, Taiwan

El-ghazali Talbi	University of Science and Technologies of Lille, France
Parimala Thulasiraman	University of Manitoba, Canada
Chang-Hsiung Tsai	National Dong Hwa University, Taiwan
Frank Zhigang Wang	Cranfield University, UK
Reen-Cheng Wang	National Taitung University, Taiwan
Jia Weijia	City University of Hong Kong, China
Jan-Jan Wu	Academia Sinica, Taiwan
Shiow-Yang Wu	National Dong Hwa University, Taiwan
Jingling Xue	University of New South Wales, Australia
Ching-Nung Yang	National Dong Hwa University, Taiwan
Mau-Tsuen Yang	National Dong Hwa University, Taiwan
Shi-Jim Yen	National Dong Hwa University, Taiwan
Zhiwen Yu	Northwestern Polytechnical University, China
Zhou Yuezhi	Tsinghua University, China

Additional Reviewers

Jen-Chun Chang	National Taipei University, Taiwan
Ming-Chiao Chen	National Taitung University, Taiwan
Rung-Shiang Cheng	Kun Shan University, Taiwan
Cheng-Fu Chou	National Taiwan University, Taiwan
Francesco Lelli	University of Lugano, Switzerland
Jian-Wei Li	Chaoyang University of Technology, Taiwan
Chun-Cheng Lin	Taipei Municipal University of Education, Taiwan
Man-Kwan Shan	National Chengchi University, Taiwan
Yun-Sheng Yen	Fo Guang University, Taiwan

Table of Contents

Keynote Speeches

Track 1: Cloud and Grid Computing

Track 2: Peer-to-Peer and Pervasive Computing

Track 3: Sensor and Mobile Networks

Track 4: Service-Oriented Computing

Track 5: Resource Management and Scheduling

Track 6: Grid and Pervasive Applications

Track 7: Semantic Grid and Ontologies

Track 8: Mobile Commerce and Services

Track 9: Multimedia Applications for Cloud

Track 10: Intelligent Network Management

A Grid Based Virtual Laboratory for HIV Drugranking

Peter Sloot

University of Amsterdam, Netherlands

Abstract. The virtual laboratory is a set of integrated components that, used together, form a distributed and collaborative space for science. Multiple, geographically-dispersed laboratories and institutes use the virtual laboratory to plan, and perform experiments as well as share their results. The term experiment in this context means a so-called in-silico experiment - that is, a process that combines data and computations in order to obtain new knowledge on the subject of an experiment. Here we introduce a virtual laboratory that is built for the ViroLab Project. In this scope the laboratory is prepared to support virologists, epidemiologists and clinicians investigating the HIV virus and the possibilities of treating HIV-positive patients. Although the ViroLab Virtual Laboratory is built specifically for this domain of science, the conceptual solutions and the technology developed can be reused for other domains.

R.-S. Chang et al. (Eds.): GPC 2010, LNCS 6104, p. 1, 2010.
© Springer-Verlag Berlin Heidelberg 2010

Solving the Scalability Dilemma with Clouds, Crowds, and Algorithms

Michael J. Franklin

University of California, Berkeley

Abstract. The creation, analysis, and dissemination of data have become profoundly democratized. Social networks spanning 100/per day of millions of users enable instantaneous discussion, debate, and information sharing. Streams of tweets, blogs, photos, and videos identify breaking events faster and in more detail than ever before. Deep, on-line datasets enable analysis of previously unreachable information. This sea change is the result of a confluence of Information Technology advances such as: intensively networked systems, cloud computing, social computing, and pervasive devices and communication. The key challenge is that the massive scale and diversity of this continuous flood of information breaks our existing technologies. State-of-the-art Machine Learning algorithms do not scale to massive data sets. Existing data analytics frameworks cope poorly with incomplete and dirty data and cannot process heterogeneous multi-format information. Current large-scale processing architectures struggle with diversity of programming models and job types and do not support the rapid marshalling and unmarshalling of resources to solve specific problems. All of these limitations lead to a Scalability Dilemma: beyond a point, our current systems tend to perform worse as they are given more data, more processing resources, and involve more people exactly the opposite of what should happen.

The Berkeley RADLab is a collaborative effort focused on cloud computing, involving nearly a dozen faculty members and postdocs, several dozen students and fifteen industrial sponsors. The lab is in the final year of a five-year effort to develop the software infrastructure to enable rapid deployment of robust, scalable, data-intensive internet services. In this talk I will give an overview of the RADLab effort and do a deeper dive on several projects, including: PIQL, a performance insightful query language for interactive applications, and SCADS, a self-managing, scalable key value store. I will also give an overview of a new effort we are starting on next generation cloud computing architectures (called the "AMPLab" - for Algorithms, Machines, and People) focused on large-scale data analytics, machine learning, and hybrid cloud/crowd computing. In a nutshell, the RADLab approach has been to use Statistical Machine Learning in the service of building large-scale systems. The AMPLab is exploring the other side of this relationship, namely, using large-scale systems to support Statistical Machine Learning and other analysis techniques for data-intensive applications. And given the central role of the cloud in a world of pervasive connectivity, a key part of the research agenda is to support collaborative efforts of huge populations of users connected through cloud resources.

R.-S. Chang et al. (Eds.): GPC 2010, LNCS 6104, p. 2, 2010.
© Springer-Verlag Berlin Heidelberg 2010

The Trend of Cloud Computing – From Industry's Perspective

Enwei Xie

Developer & Platform Evangelism, Microsoft Greater China Region

Abstract. Over the past decade, the world we live in has been transformed by the Web. It connects us to nearly everything we dobe it economic or social. It holds the potential to make the real world smaller, more relevant, more digestible and more personal. At the same time, the PC, mobile phones and smart devices have grown geometrically in power with rich applications unimaginable just a few years ago. Microsoft envisions a world where Software plus Services is the next logical step in the evolution of computing. It represents an industry shift toward a design approach that is neither exclusively software-centric nor browser-centric. By deeply and genuinely combining the best aspects of software with the best aspects of cloud-based services, we can deliver more compelling solutions for consumers, developers and businesses. This presentation aims to address Microsoft vision of Three Screens and a Cloud and the R&D investments and transformation in response to the industry trend of cloud computing.

R.-S. Chang et al. (Eds.): GPC 2010, LNCS 6104, p. 3, 2010.
© Springer-Verlag Berlin Heidelberg 2010

Towards to Ubiquitous Affective Learning

Bin Hu

The Birmingham City University, UK

Abstract. With the development of computer science, cognitive science and psychology, a new paradigm, affective learning, has emerged into e-learning/ubiquitous learning domain. Although scientists and researchers have achieved fruitful outcomes in exploring the ways of detecting and understanding learners affect, e.g. eyes motion, facial expression etc. in ubiquitous environment, it sounds still necessary to deepen the recognition of learners affect in learning procedure with innovative methodologies. Our research focused on using bio-signals based methodology to explore learner's affect and the study was primarily made on Electroencephalography (EEG). For the purpose of evaluating our findings, we also developed an ubiquitous affective learning prototype. The result of experiment was encouraging and more theoretical and practical work should be investigated in this subject.

R.-S. Chang et al. (Eds.): GPC 2010, LNCS 6104, p. 4, 2010.
© Springer-Verlag Berlin Heidelberg 2010

Collaboration of Reconfigurable Processors in Grid Computing for Multimedia Kernels

Mahmood Ahmadi[1], Asadollah Shahbahrami[2], and Stephan Wong[1]

[1] Computer Engineering Laboratory, Delft University of Technology,
The Netherlands
[2] Department of Computer Engineering, Faculty of Engineering,
University of Guilan, Rasht, Iran
{m.ahmadi,a.shahbahrami,j.s.s.m.wong}@tudelft.nl

Abstract. Multimedia applications are multi-standard, multi-format, and compute-intensive. These features in addition to a large set of input and output data lead to that some architectures such as application-specific integrated circuits and general-purpose processors are less suitable to process multimedia applications. Therefore, reconfigurable processors are considered as an alternative approach to develop systems to process multimedia applications efficiently. In this paper, we propose and simulate collaboration of reconfigurable processors in grid computing. Collaborative Reconfigurable Grid Computing (CRGC) employs the availability of any reconfigurable processor to accelerate compute-intensive applications such as multimedia kernels. We explore the mapping of some compute-intensive multimedia kernels such as the 2D DWT and the co-occurrence matrix in CRGC. These multimedia kernels are simulated as a set of gridlets submitted to a software simulator called CR-GridSim. In addition, the behavior of multimedia kernels in the CRGC environment is presented. The experimental results show that the CRGC approach improves performance of up to 7.2x and 2.5x compared to a GPP and the collaboration of GPPs, respectively, when assuming the speedup of reconfigurable processors 10.

Keywords: Reconfigurable processors, grid computing, multimedia kernels, high-performance computing.

1 Introduction

Multimedia standards such MPEG-1/2/3, JPEG 2000, and H.263/264 continually put increased strain on the performance of current and future processor architectures as new (usually more compute-intensive) algorithms are being introduced and the amount of data is increasing continuously. Examples of these architectures range from application-specific to domain-specific to multimedia-extended general-purpose processors (GPPs). Examples of complex algorithms that were recently introduced are 3D video rendering and real-time stereo vision processing. In essence, the major drawback is that the mentioned architectures are not able to fully marry high performance with high flexibility that is required in multimedia

R.-S. Chang et al. (Eds.): GPC 2010, LNCS 6104, pp. 5–14, 2010.

processing. A promising candidate to overcome this drawback are reconfigurable processors that contain a reconfigurable hardware fabric capable of changing its own functionality (static or dynamic) and execute at high speed (when enough parallelism is inherent in the algorithms). A logical "next step" in utilizing reconfigurable processors is combining them in a distributed grid computing environment to improve the performance and flexibility of the grid itself.

In this paper, we proposed the approach of collaborative reconfigurable grid computing (CRGC) that introduces reconfigurable processors in processing (grid) nodes and a scheme that allows for different nodes to cooperate together in processing a single application [13]. The main concept lies is the fact that the reconfigurable processors adapt themselves to the needed processing requirements (and functionality) without the need to introduce fixed hardware accelerators to improve the overall grid performance. Furthermore, we introduced the neighborhood concept as the collaboration concept between neighboring nodes in order to limit the communication throughout the whole grid. To investigate this concept, we introduced a set primitives (in which the communication could be simulated) and adapted the grid simulator GridSim v4 to simulate the CRGC concept together with the neighborhood concept. We termed the adapted simulator CRGridSim. To obtain results of real cases, we explored the mapping two computationally intensive multimedia kernels: the discrete wavelet transform (DWT) and the co-occurrence matric. These kernels were subdivided into gridlets for simulation in the CRGridSim simulator. Our experimental results show that speed-ups of up to 7.2 can be achieved when comparing to a grid with only general-purpose processor and assuming a per-processor speedup of a factor of 10 when comparing executing the same kernel in a GPP or a reconfigurable processor.

This paper is organized as follows. Section 2 presents related work. We describe the collaboration of reconfigurable processors (elements) in a grid environment in Section 3. In Section 4, we explain the chosen compute-intensive multimedia kernels in more detail. Simulation environment and tools are described in Section 5 followed by a discussion of the evaluation results in Section 6. Finally, conclusions are drawn in Section 7.

2   Related Work

In this section, we take a brief look at the previous work regarding high-performance reconfigurable computing. In [6], the design and implementation of a metacomputer based on reconfigurable hardware was presented. The Distributed Reconfigurable Metacomputing (DRMC) is defined as "the use of powerful computing resources transparently available to the user via a networked environment". The DRMC provides an environment in which computations can be constructed in a high-level manner and executed on clusters containing reconfigurable hardware. In the DRMC architecture, applications are executed on clusters using the condensed graphs model of computation that allows the parallelism inherent in applications to be executed by representing them as set of graphs.

In [8], a performance model for fork-join class and Synchronous Iterative Algorithm (SIA) was presented. They considered the division of computation between the workstation processor and the reconfigurable processor. They focused on algorithms and applications that fit into the fork-join class and SIAs types.

In [12], the 2D-FFT application has been implemented on both the standard cluster and the prototype Adaptable Computing Cluster (ACC). The ACC is an architecture that attempts to improve high-performance cluster computing with FPGAs, but not by merely adding reconfigurable computing resources to each node. Rather, by merging cluster and reconfigurable technologies and enhancing the commodity network interface. In [11], performance of single reconfigurable processor for grey level co-occurrence matrix (GLCM) and Haralick texture feature for image sizes 512*512, 1024*1024 and 2048*2048 was presented. Speedups of 4.75 and 7.3 were obtained when compared with a general-purpose processor for GCLM and Haralick co-occurrence matrix, respectively. The target hardware for this work was Celoxica RC1000-PP PCI-based FPGA development board equipped with a Xilinx XCV2000E Virtex FPGA. In addition, a co-occurrence matrix media kernel has been implemented on the various FPGA devices such as Virtex2 and Spartan3 and on a media-enhanced GPPs using MMX technology in [5]. Speedups of 20 were obtained using FPGA implementations over media-enhanced GPPs, for an image size $512 * 512$.

In [13], we investigated the concept of collaboration of reconfigurable processors in grid computing. In this paper, we simulate several computationally intensive media kernels and map on the proposed architecture. The experimental results show that collaboration of reconfigurable processors in grid computing achieves much more performance than the collaboration of GPPs.

In current work, we further investigate the performance of CRGC by looking at realistic loads and real kernels execution characteristics.

3 Collaboration of Reconfigurable Processors in Grid Computing

In this section, we present the concept of collaboration of reconfigurable processors and their properties. In grid computing, a large pool of heterogeneous computing resources is geographically dispersed over a large network, e.g., the Internet. Our approach to achieve high-performance and flexibility is to utilize reconfigurable processors in grid computing. We termed the utilization of reconfigurable processors that collaborate together in grid environment Collaboration Reconfigurable Grid Computing (CRGC). The general platform of CRGC is depicted in Figure 1. Reconfigurable elements are a part of the resources in grid computing.

Processing processors offload part of their computational workload to reconfigurable computing resources. In this type of computing, various software codes targeting different processing architectures are stored either in a centralized or a decentralized manner and must be distributed to the computing resources when needed. In CRGC, processing elements communicate and collaborate together based on the *neighborhood concept*. Each grid processing element requests assistance from neighboring processing elements. The tasks can be inserted into the

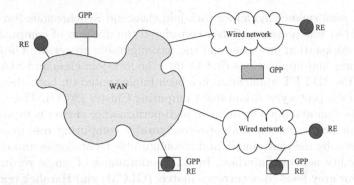

Fig. 1. A general view of a collaboration of reconfigurable elements in grid environment. RE shows reconfigurable elements (processors).

grid through existing grid elements. In our implementation of the neighborhood concept, the neighbor processing elements are a direct neighbor to a requesting grid element. The direct neighbor is defined as a grid element that is physically (or geographically closely) located next to the current requesting grid element. The neighborhood concept is defined by some primitives. A primitive is defined as a processing element with related communication link and its equipments, e.g., routers and switches, to the main processing element. The network backbone can be seen as a collection of primitives. Some important primitives are depicted in Figure 2.

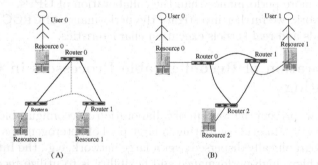

Fig. 2. Basic primitives that are utilized in neighborhood concept

Figure 2 (A) depicts a primitive with one requesting processing element and n collaborating processing elements. A primitive with two requesting processing elements and one collaborating processing element is depicted in Figure 2 (B). The neighborhood concept with active primitives in the real grid is depicted in Figure 3.

Based on Figure 3, we can observe that each user and the related requesting processing element can find the correspondent neighbor processing element. For example, user 0 and resource 0 can operate based on primitive in Figure 2 (A). From Figure 3, in the first scenario, resource 0 is assisted by resource 1 and

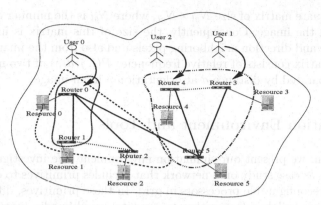

Fig. 3. Active primitives in the sample network

in the second scenario, resource 0 is assisted by resources 1 and 2. We have a similar condition for user 1, in this case resource 3 gets help from resource 5.

4   Multimedia Kernels

In this section, we explain the two chosen compute-intensive multimedia kernels, discrete wavelet transform and co-occurrence matrix. We have selected these multimedia kernels because they are compute-intensive [7].

4.1   Discrete Wavelet Transform

The digital wavelet representation of a discrete signal X consisting of N samples can be calculated by convolving X with the lowpass and highpass filters and down-sampling the output results by 2, so that the two frequency bands each contains $N/2$ samples. With the correct choice of filters, this operation is reversible. This process decomposes the original image into two sub-bands: the lower and the higher band [9][7]. This transform can be extended to multiple dimensions by using separable filters. A 2D DWT can be performed by first performing a 1D DWT on each row (*horizontal filtering*) of the image followed by a 1D DWT on each column (*vertical filtering*).

4.2   Co-occurrence Matrix

Texture features are usually used in image and video processing. Texture features determine the dependencies between neighboring pixels within region of interest in an image [3]. The co-occurrence matrix captures second order gray level information, which is a well known tool for texture analysis. Haralick et. al [4] have defined some texture features which use co-occurrence matrices. The features are related to neighboring pixels at different directions and distance. The number of occurrences of two neighboring pixels with a distance d and with a certain direction is stored in co-occurrence matrix. The co-occurrence matrix is always a square matrix of size $N_{gl} \times N_{gl}$, where N_{gl} is the number of available gray levels in the image. Consequently, the size of this matrix is independent from distance and direction neighboring pixels and also from the image size. Co-occurrence matrix consists of relative frequencies $P(i, j; d, \delta)$ of two neighboring pixels i, j separated by distance d at orientation δ in an image.

5 Simulation Environment and Tools

In this section, we present our simulation environment. We investigated multi-media kernels as case study on a network that includes primitives to construct a backbone of reconfigurable processors in grid. In these primitives, different processing elements collaborate together to execute a multimedia kernel in a grid environment. Each processing element can be a GPP or a reconfigurable processor (Reconfigurable Element (RE)). The specification of processing elements is defined in the form of Million Instructions Per Second (MIPS) for the Standard Performance Evaluation Corporation (SPEC) benchmark. In this paper, we have used 30, 35, 40 and 50 MIPS for processing elements.

In order to understand how many instructions are required to execute the discussed multimedia kernels, we have executed both the 2D DWT and co-occurrence matrix kernels using the SimpleScalar toolset [1] for an image of size 1024×1024. The number of committed instructions for the 2D DWT kernel is 46160416, while the number of committed instructions for the second kernel is 83899404. This means that in order to provide each value for the first decomposition level of 2D DWT, 44 instructions should be processed, while for the second kernel 80 instructions should be processed.

The simulation environment is an extended version of the GridSim (a traditional Java-based discrete-event grid simulator) [2][10]. We configured and prepared the GriSim simulator based on the multimedia kernels properties to support the collaborative processing between reconfigurable processors. This extension of the GridSim is called CRGridSim. In CRGridsim, each application can be broken down to different subtasks called *gridlets*. Each application is packaged as gridlets whose contents include the task length in Millions of Instructions (MI). The task length is expressed in terms of the time it takes to run on a standard GPP. To simplify the simulation of the proposed approach, we assumed that reconfigurable processors do not support partial reconfiguration.

The multimedia kernels were simulated using the primitive in Figure 2 (A) with 3 and 2 collaborator processing elements. The specifications of the simulated environment and primitives are depicted in Table 1. The speedup of reconfigurable processors over GPPs for multimedia kernels has been set to 10. This is because, as we mentioned in Section 2 the average speedup for the multimedia kernels in single reconfigurable processor is $(4.75 + 7.3 + 20)/3$.

The images size and specification of the processing elements are presented in Table 2 and Table 3, respectively. In Table 2, 4 groups of different images with various sizes have been collected. Each image is sent in the uncompressed form to the processing elements. The required instructions to process each image is packed

Table 1. Specifications of the simulated environment

Parameter	Value
Maximum packet size	32 and 65 KBytes
User-router bandwidth	100 Mb/sec
Router-router bandwidth	1000 Mb/sec
Number of images	40 (Table 2)
Number of users	1
Size of images	Based on Table 2
PE specification (MIPS)	Based on Table 3
Speedup for RE	10 in compared to a GPP
Reconfiguration file size	3 Mb
Reconfiguration speed	3 Mb/sec
Reconfiguration time	1 sec
Number of bits per pixel	24 bit

Table 2. Images and their correspondence gridlets specifications for different multimedia kernels

Image			# of instructions	
Group	Size	# of images	2D DWT	Co-occ. matrix
1	768 × 1024	10	35	64
2	1024 × 1024	10	46	84
3	1200 × 1600	10	84	156
4	2134 × 2848	10	267	493

Table 3. The specification of processing elements in terms of MIPS

Processing elements	MIPS
Main GPP	30
Collaborator 1 (GPP or RE)	35
Collaborator 2 (GPP or RE)	50
Collaborator 3 (GPP or RE)	40

up as a gridlet and is submitted to the related processing elements either a GPP or a RE. Table 3 depicts the specification of processing elements in terms of MIPS.

In the simulation environment using CRGridsim, the following steps should be considered in order to execute an application using CRGC. First, a network topology based on the availability of neighbor processing elements is defined and parameters such as network bandwidth and packet size are configured. Second, the processing elements are defined and reconfigurable processing elements are configured based on the application characteristics. Third, an application mapping policy and the number of subtasks (gridlets) for each application are determined. Finally, the main processing element packetizes the subtasks and send them to the appropriate REs. Additionally, the collaborator

REs depacketizes the received packets and process them and send back the calculated results to the main processing element. Finally, the main processing element receives the final results and send the remaining other subtasks to the idle REs.

6   Experimental Results

In this section, we present the experimental results which have been obtained using the CRGridSim simulator for the 2D DWT, co-occurrence matrix, and combination of both kernels.

In order to evaluate the proposed approach, we considered two packet sizes, 32 KBytes and 65 KBytes (the largest packet sizes in the networks). Our results show that using larger packet sizes lead to higher performance than smaller packet sizes. Larger packet sizes decreases the communication overhead due to sending less packets. In our case, we utilized 40 images with a total size of 294 MBytes. These images translate into 4539 packets of 65 KBytes or 9219 packets of 32 KBytes. In addition, we considered four different configurations, collaboration of 3 GPPs, a GPP with 2 REs, 4 GPPs, and a GPP with 3 REs. The configuration of 3 GPPs means that 2 GPPs are collaborating with a main GPP. The star topology has been used for the collaboration mechanism that a structure of this topology was depicted in Figure 2 (A).

Figure 4 depicts the speedups of the first two configurations, 3 GPPs and a GPP with 2 REs over a GPP. Figure 5 depicts the speedups of the last two configurations, 4 GPPs and a GPP with 3 REs, over a GPP.

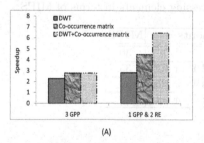
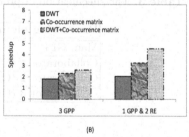

Fig. 4. Speedup for different configurations with 2 collaborator processing elements over one GPP. (A) Maximum packet size is 65 KBytes. (B) Maximum packet size is 32 KBytes.

The packet size for the Figures 4 (A) and 5 (A) is 65 KBytes, and the packet size for the Figures 4 (B) and 5 (B) is 32 KBytes. Our observations from these figures are the following. First, increasing the packet size from 32 KBytes to 65 KBytes improves the performance. As can be seen that the speedups of the left side figures are larger than the speedups of the right side figures. This is due to the fact that larger packet sizes decreases the communication overhead. Second, the collaboration of reconfigurable processors improves the performance

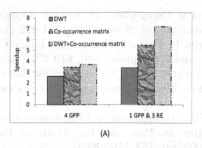 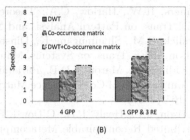

(A)   (B)

Fig. 5. Speedup for different configurations with 3 collaborator processing elements over one GPP.(A) Maximum packet size is 65 KBytes. (B) Maximum packet size is 32 KBytes.

more than the collaboration of GPPs. For our configuration, the performance improvement of the collaboration of reconfigurable processors over the collaboration of GPPs is of up to 2.5. Finally, executing computationally intensive applications yields much more performance than non-computationally intensive applications. This is because the impact of the communication overhead will be reduced compared to the computational time. As can be seen in those figures, a combination of both kernels obtains more speedups than the execution of each kernel separately. Additionally, increasing the number of collaborator processing elements improves the performance. This is because the submitted subtasks to each collaborator are decreased. This reduces the number of processed instructions by each processing element.

7 Conclusions

Multimedia kernels are compute-intensive tasks. In order to increase the performance of multimedia kernels, we have proposed and simulated the collaboration of reconfigurable processors in grid computing. The Collaborative Reconfigurable Grid Computing (CRGC) utilizes reconfigurable processing elements capabilities in the grid environment. We studied and mapped some multimedia kernels in a grid environment. This environment was simulated using CRGridSim simulator. The results show that the utilization of CRGC improves performance of up to 7.2 in comparison to a GPP when assuming the speedup of reconfigurable processors 10. The results show that the proposed CRGC approach is capable of improving the performance of compute-intensive multimedia kernels more than none compute-intensive kernels due to communication overhead.

References

1. Austin, T., Larson, E., Ernst, D.: SimpleScalar: An Infrastructure for Computer System Modeling. IEEE Computer 35(2), 59–67 (2002)
2. Buyya, R., Murshed, M.M.: GridSim: A Toolkit for the Modeling and Simulation of Distributed Resource Management and Scheduling for Grid Computing. Concurrency and Computation: Practice and Experience 14(13-15), 1175–1220 (2002)

3. Conners, R.W., Harlow, C.A.: Theoretical Comparison of Texture Algorithms. IEEE Trans. on Pattern Analysis and Machine Intelligence 2(3), 204–222 (1980)
4. Haralick, R.M., Shanmugam, K., Dinstein, I.: Textural Features for Image Classification. IEEE Trans. on Systems, Man, and Cybernetics 3(6), 610–621 (1973)
5. Iakovidis, D.K., Maroulis, D.E., Bariamis, D.G.: FPGA Architecture for Fast Parallel Computation of Co-occurrence Matrices. Microprocessors and Microsystems 31, 160–165 (2007)
6. Morrison, J.P., Healy, P.D., O'Dowd, P.J.: Architecture and Implementation of a Distributed Reconfigurable Metacomputer. In: Proc. 2nd Int. Symp. on Parallel and Distributed Computing, October 2003, pp. 153–158 (2003)
7. Shahbahrami, A., Ahmadi, M., Wong, S., Bertels, K.L.M.: A New Approach to Implement Discrete Wavelet Transform using Collaboration of Reconfigurable Elements. In: Proc. of Int. Conf. on ReConFigurable Computing and FPGAs (2009)
8. Smith, M., Peterson, G.D.: Parallel Application Performance on Shared High Performance Reconfigurable Computing resources. Performance Evaluation 60(1-4), 107–125 (2005)
9. Stollnitz, E.J., Derose, T.D., Salesin, D.H.: Wavelets for Computer Graphics: Theory and Applications. Morgan Kaufmann, San Francisco (1996)
10. Sulistio, A., Poduval, G., Buyya, R., Tham, C.K.: On Incorporating Differentiated Levels of Network Service into GridSim. Future Generation Computer Systems 23(4), 606–615 (2007)
11. Tahir, M.A., Bouridane, A., Kurugollu, F., Amira, A.: Accelerating the Computation of GLCM and Haralick Texture Features on Reconfigurable Hardware. In: Proc. of the Int. Conf. on Image Processing, pp. 2857–2860 (2004)
12. Underwood, K.D., Sass, R.R., Ligon, W.B.: Acceleration of a 2D-FFT on an Adaptable Computing Cluster. In: 9th Annual IEEE Symp. on Field Programmable Custom Computing Machines (FFCM 2001), pp. 180–189 (2001)
13. Wong, S., Ahmadi, M.: Reconfigurable Architectures in Collaborative Grid Computing: An Approach. In: Proc. 2nd Int. Conf. on Networks for Grid Applications (2008)

Multi-core Code in a Cluster – A Meaningful Option?

Martin Štava and Pavel Tvrdík

Czech Technical University in Prague
Prague, Czech Republic

Abstract. In this paper we investigate whether parallelization of an application code for multi-core machines can bring any benefit for clustering systems, especially those based on opportunistic usage of idle resources. Previous research has shown that transformation of shared memory applications into clustered applications is complicated. At the moment, there is no practical solution available. Therefore, we instead focus on message passing applications as possible candidates for parallelization. We demonstrate a low effort approach that allows programmers to transform a multi-core Erlang code into a code that can run in a cluster environment. We provide scalability measurements of the solution in small clusters of commodity computers and identify weak points of the solution.

1 Introduction

Technical barriers in scaling processor frequency recently gave rise to multi-core CPUs. Models with up to 4 cores are common now and the count of cores is expected to grow further [1]. While this approach helped manufacturers to keep up the performance growth with the so called *Moore's Law*, the problem arises on the software side. Developers of the server side applications were partly prepared for such a change, since they were already programming for multiprocessor (SMP) machines for many years and the server side applications are often well suited for parallelization. On the other hand, applications designed to run on client single CPU personal computers were not programmed in a way that would automatically benefit from additional cores. Since the introduction of multi-core CPUs, a lot of research effort was devoted to find out the best way how to utilize them.

A different often used approach to application parallelization is cluster computing. There are already many techniques how to write scientific and enterprise server-side applications for clusters. There was, however, not much motivation and hence effort to make desktop applications scale across multiple machines. Indeed, the additional effort for the parallelization of those applications would hardly pay off especially in a situation when a typical user did not have multiple computers available. Exceptions to this situation were recent versions of clustering systems like Mosix (http://www.mosix.org/) or Clondike [2] that can easily transform a small network of machines into a cluster at the operating system level. Users of those systems need their applications to be scalable as much as

R.-S. Chang et al. (Eds.): GPC 2010, LNCS 6104, pp. 15–26, 2010.
© Springer-Verlag Berlin Heidelberg 2010

possible, but since only a minority of users use such systems, they did not have any significant impact on the way how the desktop applications are written.

Due to the multi-core CPU evolution, programmers are now forced to think about parallelization of all applications. In this paper, we are investigating whether making the applications scale on multi-core machines has any real world impact on their scalability across the machine boundary. We do not specifically limit our research on desktop applications only, but rather in general we are interested in transformation of multi-core scalability into cluster scalability.

The paper is primarily focused on small-scale computer networks, designed not specifically as clusters, but rather as set of computing nodes connected ad-hoc via a standard (local) network. Such networks are typical at homes of people, but appear in business work environments and school laboratories as well. A well known attribute of those networks is low utilization of their total computing power. Scalability requirements on algorithms intended to run in those clusters are lower than on algorithms designed for a specialized dedicated clusters. The specialized clusters require a big financial investment and so there is a lot of effort devoted to achieve a maximum possible efficiency and the best outcome from the investment. In the environment not primarily built as a cluster, even a low efficiency cluster deployment is a plus, as long as it results in application speed-up.

2   Erlang

A lot of effort was devoted to attempts to effectively distribute shared memory applications on clusters, but due to the problem complexity, there is no widely adopted practical solution at the moment. Therefore, we decided to focus only on message passing languages.

Important representatives of message passing languages are pure functional languages, since in those languages there is actually no state to be shared. In this paper. we will discuss Erlang [3, 4] programming language only, but there are as well others, for example parallelization effort in Haskell language [5] is closely related.

Erlang programming language was developed internally in the Erickson company for programming highly reliable massively parallel network components. Later, the language became publicly available and open-source. It is gaining popularity and the language is used in many real-world applications. Since our paper is more oriented on practical aspects of multi-core and cluster programming, Erlang is a better suited language for our study than some other more theoretical languages.

Erlang is a pure functional dynamically typed language executed in its own virtual machine. Sequential programming in Erlang is similar to other functional languages, it heavily uses recursion and list manipulation operations. It is out of the scope of this paper to give a detailed description of the Erlang programming language, an interested reader can find a lot of information on the Erlang official site http://www.erlang.org/.

Concurrency-related aspects of the language are distinguishing features of Erlang and they are the most interesting aspects of the language for the topic of this paper. Erlang concurrency is based on the actor model [6,7]. Execution units are called *processes* in Erlang, even though they are just lightweight processes not related to the operating system processes. Instead, they are directly managed by the Erlang virtual machine. Every process has its own unique identifier called *pid*. An often stressed feature of Erlang is a low cost of process creation, it is possible to create hundreds of thousands of processes in a single second [4] on a commodity hardware. A new process is started by calling system function *spawn*, passing in a function to be executed by the new process and optional arguments. Every process executes sequentially its code and does not share any data with other processes. The only way how two processes can interact with each other is by build-in message-passing operations.

It is possible to interconnect multiple Erlang virtual machines to form a distributed environment for running Erlang programs. In this case, each of the virtual machines is called a *node*. Every node has its own unique identifier formed by a name given at start-up and the name of the machine it was started on. The *spawn* function used for creation of new processes accepts an optional argument that specifies a node where a new process should be started. If the argument is not specified, a new process is started on the same virtual machine where the *spawn* function was called. A return value of the *spawn* function is a tuple representing a newly created process identifier. This tuple is later used as an argument of a send message function. Hence, the syntax of sending messages locally or remotely is exactly the same, the virtual machine automatically detects a type of an exchange.

3 Transformations of Erlang Programs

In this section, we will describe our approach that allows to transform Erlang programs written for a non-clustered environment into programs that are able to utilize multi-computer cluster environments.

3.1 Scheduling

In this paper, we assume that the processing costs of individual tasks and their distribution are completely unknown. In addition, the computing power of all processing units can be arbitrary and change over time. The assumptions about the environment make more sophisticated scheduling strategies like those studied in [8,9,10] unusable. In our demonstrations, we will use only a simple strategy that is suitable for a computationally imbalanced environment and does not require much information about the environment or tasks. The strategy is called *self scheduling* [11] and its key idea is that every computing unit controls its workload assignment. In the simplest form of the strategy, processing units could just ask for a new task whenever they are done with their current work. In a higher latency distributed environment, it is more efficient when each node asks for more tasks that is the number of its processing units so that network transfers can be overlapped with the computation of other tasks. In our experiments, each node asks for twice as many tasks than is the number of its processing units (CPU cores).

3.2   Program Communication Structure

The actor model of communication does not impose any restrictions on the message exchange patterns. Theoretically, every actor could talk to each other. However, the more complex are the communication patterns, the more difficult is the program behavior to understand. As a result, it is difficult to make such programs efficient. In order to make readable and efficient programs, developers have to apply some restrictions on the used communication patterns.

One of the easiest communication structure to understand and use is the *master-worker* model where a single execution unit, the *master*, is responsible for generating work subtasks and for distributing them to other execution units, called *workers*. Due to its simplicity, it is often used to control concurrency in clusters as well as in multi-core processors. In a multi-core environment, it could have a form of a single shared work-queue from which execution units fetch their work. This model naturally transforms into a distributed case in Erlang, it is only required to start some workers on remote nodes. Due to the model simplicity, we will use this model in our transformation examples.

While many algorithms fit nicely into the master-worker pattern, not all programs can be or are structured in this way. One of common reasons why the programs are not structured in a master-worker pattern is the requirement to perform parallel reduction at the end of a computation. Such programs can still be easily transformed into the master-worker model, by performing only the calculation in the workers and the resulting reduction step can be performed on the master. A similar idea can be used for other programs whose structure is based on some larger blocks of sequential calculations and the results of those calculations are exchanged and combined in any other way. Performing reductions, data exchanges, and combinations on a single machine running the master execution unit limits scalability of algorithms, but as we will show, it is still possible to scale up to several machines with this approach.

3.3   Practical Transformation

The message passing mechanism from the syntax point of view is the same for local exchanges and for remote message passing. What needs to be modified is creation of processes performed by the *spawn* function. The standard *spawn* function creates processes locally only, but in order to distribute an application on multiple machines, we need the *spawn* function to start processes on remote Erlang nodes. This can be achieved simply by replacing *spawn* calls by a custom function, let us call it *distributed_spawn*. This is a very small change in a code and the code still remains completely decoupled from distributed environment specifics. The implementation of the *distributed_spawn* function has to decide where to place a newly spawned process. In our implementation, we have used the self-scheduling strategy described earlier in the paper, but the strategy can be easily changed without touching the application code. In case some more advanced scheduling strategies are required, it may be necessary to modify the *distributed_spawn* function signature and add parameters like, for example, estimated task size or a preferred partitioning. Some of those changes, however, would require more modification in the application code, as all replaced *spawn* calls may need to be extended by the specific arguments. Moreover, the programmers would need to be aware of those attributes and be able to properly fill them, so for the transformation simplicity we prefer not to use them.

Since we want to transform the program into a master worker model, we replace only the *spawn* function calls that are going to perform some non-trivial operation so that the overhead of distribution is negligible with respect to the performed work. Just by doing this we have transformed the program into a master worker model, because the *distributed_spawn* function sends a work into a scheduler that acts as a master, and then is the work distributed to the workers. If there are some nested *spawn* calls within the remotely spawned subtask, we do not replace those spawns any more, because we regard everything behind the *distributed_spawn* call as a single unit of work that is not further clustered (even if it is performed with some parallelization on its worker).

4   Examples

In order to demonstrate the approach and evaluate its performance, we will show a few examples. The demonstration code was selected not because it is the best candidate for scalability, but rather because it is most relevant in the real world.

4.1   Tests Setup and Methodology

We have performed all measurements in a test environment consisting of 3 heterogeneous machines. It is more difficult to achieve good speedups in a heterogeneous environment, because the scheduling is complicated by unequal computing power of machines. Table 1 summarizes basic numbers about the machine configurations. We do not show the CPU frequencies, since with current CPUs, this attribute could be misleading. Instead, we will show a single core performance of machines in each test. Machine Alpha is slowest in most operations, while Gamma is the fastest machine in our test setup.

Table 1. Parameters of the test machines. Memory is in Gigabytes

Name	Cores	Mem.	Vendor	OS
Alpha	2	4	AMD	Linux
Beta	2	4	Intel	Linux
Gamma	3	4	AMD	Windows

Every measurement was performed 10 times and the values presented in the result tables are the best results achieved of all runs. For each case, we measure single core performance, multi-core scalability, and finally scalability in a cluster environment. In the cluster environment, we track the scalability per core, i.e., we start with a single core of one machine and then take measurements after adding every single core. Due to the heterogeneity of machine CPUs, the results depend heavily on the order how the cores have been added, so we always perform 2 sets of measurements. In the first one, we start from the slowest machine and progress towards the fastest one. In the second one, we start from the fastest machine and progress to the slowest one.

In graphs of cluster algorithm performance, we show not only achieved times but also efficiency. The standard definition of algorithmic efficiency is not valid in heterogeneous environments and so we use a generalized definition of efficiency defined in [12]. The *heterogeneous efficiency* is defined as the optimal achievable time divided by the actual response time, where the optimal achievable time is calculated as the time of a sequential task on a hypothetical machine of the total computing power equal to the sum of the cluster computing power. As a basis for the computation of optimal achievable time, we use parallel versions of algorithms run on a SMP-enabled Erlang virtual machines restricted to run on a single core.

4.2   Sorting

In the first example, we will demonstrate the parallelization approach on the QuickSort algorithm. It is not the best algorithm that can be used in a multi-core environment. For example, a specifically developed MapSort [13] algorithm is shown to scale better. Nonetheless, the QuickSort algorithm is still often used in practice. The algorithm is interesting, because its parallelization is not in the class of *embarrassingly parallel* algorithms.

A sequential recursive implementation of the QuickSort algorithm in Erlang is just 5 lines of code. It is possible to directly parallelize this algorithm by spawning a new process for each recursive call and then merge the results. This approach gives enough parallelism, but it is too fine-grained and so, the over-head of message passing slows down the algorithm. A better way to modify the algorithm is to stop spawning of new processes when the length of a sublist to be sorted falls under a certain threshold. The larger the threshold is, the lower the overhead of the parallelization will be. On the other hand, the threshold must be small enough so that there is still enough parallelism. In our experiments, we used a static threshold of 250,000 items and we were sorting lists of 2,500,000 elements, but the threshold could be dynamically selected based on the input size. We will call the second parallelization method *the block based parallelization*.

As Figure 1 illustrates, both full and block-based parallelizations are slower than the sequential version in nearly all cases, except the 3-core machine. This is both due to a synchronization and scheduling overhead, but there are as well hardware factors like cache and bus contention, contributing to this limited scalability. If we run 2 independent sort operations concurrently, even in different

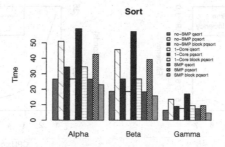

Fig. 1. Non-clustered sorting performed with disabled SMP (no-SMP), enabled SMP but with restriction on 1 core only, and with a unrestricted SMP enabled. Qsort stands for the standard sequential QuickSort, pqsort is a parallelized QuickSort with a full parallelization up to a single element and block pqsort is a block based parallelization. The no-SMP measurements were just taken to illustrate that enabling of SMP features in the Erlang VM itself has sometimes quite significant effect on the program speed.

Erlang virtual machines, there is still some overhead and each of those sorts runs about 30% longer than when run alone. Nevertheless, as demonstrated on the Gamma machine, with more cores, the algorithm eventually becomes faster than the sequential version. The Figure 1 as well demonstrates that the very fine-grained algorithm performs much worse than the coarser-grained version and even on a 3-core CPU it is still more than 25% slower than a sequential version and more than 2 times slower than the block-based version.

We perform the transformation of a multi-core code into a clustered code as we described earlier. We replace the *spawn* calls that are not going to spawn any more subtasks by the *distributed_spawn* function calls. If we would like to effectively distribute the fine grained version of the algorithm, we would have to perform *distributed_spawn* at some level before reaching the minimum task size, that is a single element list, because it would be too late to perform an efficient work distribution.

Figures 2(a) and 2(b) show the speed and efficiency of the algorithm running in a cluster. The effect of heterogeneity is well seen on the graphs. When the calculation is started from the fastest machine 2(a), we do not achieve high speedups and after involving the slowest machine, the total execution time starts increasing. However, we could not expect high speedups in this case, because based on Figure 1 the Gamma machine is 2 times faster than both Alpha and Beta together, so the speedup when only Gamma and Beta are involved, can be considered good (the absolute best speedup we can get is 22% while we got 10% speedup). The worse performance with the third machine involved is caused by a suboptimal scheduling when slower machines get too much work to do. We have to wait for the slowest machine to finish with its work at the end of the calculation, so smarter scheduling algorithms avoiding this problem could possibly resolve this limitation. When the calculation is started on the slowest machine Alpha 2(b), the speedups are better. The Alpha and Beta machines are comparable in speed and when only those 2 machines are involved, we have 52%

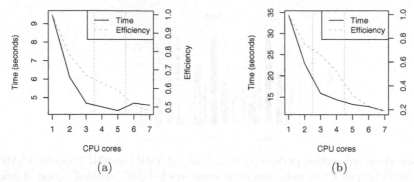

Fig. 2. (a) Coarse-grained parallelized QuickSort running in a cluster started on the Gamma machine. (b) Coarse-grained parallelized QuickSort running in a cluster started on the Alpha machine.

efficiency, that is quite a good number compared to 75% efficiency in a non-clustered 2 core version. While speeds still increase considerably after involving the machine Gamma, the efficiency drops rapidly. The problem here is due to a performance bottleneck on the machine Alpha. Since it is responsible for all the work generation and then merging of all sort results (as it acts as a master), it gets overloaded with its work, because combined computing power of Beta and Gamma is much larger than the computing power of Alpha.

It is interesting to compare best times in both cases when all machines are involved. The calculation is 2.5 faster when started from the Alpha machine than in the other case. We can get a better number if the calculation started on Alpha is immediately remotely transferred on Gamma and then performed there. In this case, the algorithm is about 70% faster than when run directly from Alpha. Our scheduler does not support such optimizations, because it is not aware of performance capabilities of individual machines, but this certainly looks like a promising way of further research for optimization.

4.3   Map Operation

An often used operation in functional languages is so called *map* function. This function applies a user-defined function on each element of a list. Standard implementation in Erlang is sequential, but since Erlang is a side-effect-free functional language, the operation can be parallelized. Indeed, this function is so obvious candidate for parallelization that many people already wrote their own simple parallel version for multi-core computers and there is even an open source project that tries to extend the parallelization into a cluster (http://code.google.com/p/plists/). We use a similar approach to provide parallel equivalent of the *map* function, let us call it as people usually do *pmap*, but under the hood we use our *distributed_spawn* function for work distribution. The idea is simple. The list is recursively iterated and in each iteration, we spawn a new process using the *distributed_spawn* function and apply the user-defined function on the element. However, this case can again suffer from the too fine-grained work problem, because the operation to be performed on elements

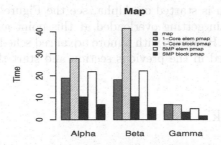

Fig. 3. Non-clustered *map* operation performed with enabled SMP but with restriction on 1 core only and with a unrestricted SMP enabled. Map is the standard *map* operation in Erlang, elem *pmap* is the parallelized version performed on a single element basis, and block *pmap* is the version where the list is split into blocks of size 10,000 elements.

can be just a simple number transformation taking a very short time. For that reason, we add a new parameter to the *pmap* function, specifying how the input list shall be split. For example, filling 10,000 means that the input list is to be split into blocks of 10,000 elements and those blocks are to be scheduled as units of work by the scheduler.

Figure 3 captures times of standard *map* and parallelized *map* operations on each of the machine. The input list contained 2.5 million elements and the block size was 10,000. The performed operation was a power 2 operator. Since this type of operation falls into an embarrassingly parallel applications class, it is no surprise that the speedups are very good.

Since we have used the *distributed_spawn* function in the *pmap* function implementation, it will be automatically clustered when some machine connects, there is no more work required from the programmer. Figures 4(a) and 4(b) present again total run times and efficiencies. The results are similar as in the previous case, but this time with a higher efficiency due to easier parallelization of the task. The most interesting is a slight slowdown after addition of the latest core

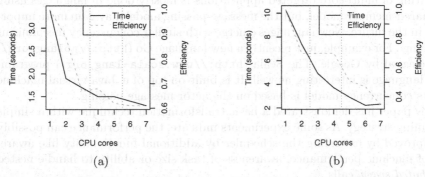

Fig. 4. (a) Block-based parallelized *pmap* running in a cluster started on the Gamma machine. (b) Block-based parallelized *pmap* running in a cluster started on the Alpha machine.

in case the calculation is started on Alpha, see the Figure 4(b). This suggests that Alpha is yet again getting overloaded at this point and a further scaling might be problematic. However, with a more advanced scheduler, we can use the same trick as suggested in the previous section and start the work directly on the Gamma machine.

5   Related Work

A relation between multi-core machines and clusters is being investigated by many authors. Typically, the focus of the research is a way how to write the most efficient applications for multi-core-based clusters. Results indicate that message passing for inter-machine communication and shared-memory model for intra-machine communication are performing best with current languages [14,15]. In this direction of research, applications are directly written for the multi-core cluster environment, while in ours, we start with a cluster-unaware application and we try to make it running in a cluster.

Closer to our approach is the research of methods to make pure message-passing applications running best in a multi-core cluster environment [16, 17]. Since the message passing was formerly used only for cluster environments, this area is still focused on applications directly written for a cluster environment.

A research in parallelization of another functional language Haskell is more focused on message passing multi-core parallelism [5], but this is already a core feature of Erlang language.

6   Conclusions and Future Work

In this paper, we have investigated a way how a cluster environment can benefit from a multi-core-aware programming. We have demonstrated that for a message passing data exchange model there exists a language where applications scale across machine boundaries with a minimum effort.

Writing of multi-core targeted applications is mostly done in languages using the shared-memory model, but the message-passing model may gain more importance in the future. New languages emerge with similar concurrency mechanisms as Erlang . For example, just recently a new language Go (`http://golang.org/`) was released by Google. The Scala (`http://www.scala-lang.org/`) programming language is interesting as well. It is built on top of a Java virtual machine and its concurrency model is based on the actor message passing.

This paper has demonstrated a basic transformation technique with a simple scheduling strategy. As some experiments indicate, the performance can possibly be improved by extending the scheduler by additional functionality like awareness of machine performance, awareness of task size or ability to handle nested *distributed_spawn* calls.

Acknowledgements

This research has been supported by MŠMT under research program MSM 6840770014 and by The Grant Agency of the Czech Technical University in Prague.

References

1. Borkar, S.Y., Dubey, P., Kahn, K.C., Kuck, D.J., Mulder, H., Ramanathan, E.R.M., Thomas, V., Corporation, I., Pawlowski, S.S.: Intel ® processor and platform evolution for the next decade executive summary
2. Kacer, M., Langr, D., Tvrdik, P.: Clondike: Linux cluster of non-dedicated workstations. In: CCGRID 2005: Proceedings of the Fifth IEEE International Symposium on Cluster Computing and the Grid (CCGrid 2005), Washington, DC, USA, vol. 1, pp. 574–581. IEEE Computer Society, Los Alamitos (2005)
3. Vinoski, S.: Concurrency with erlang. IEEE Internet Computing 11(5), 90–93 (2007)
4. Larson, J.: Erlang for concurrent programming. Queue 6(5), 18–23 (2008)
5. Al Zain, A.D.I., Hammond, K., Berthold, J., Trinder, P., Michaelson, G., Aswad, M.: Low-pain, high-gain multicore programming in haskell: coordinating irregular symbolic computations on multicore architectures (abstract only). SIGPLAN Not. 44(5), 8–9 (2009)
6. Hewitt, C., Bishop, P., Steiger, R.: A universal modular actor formalism for artificial intelligence. In: IJCAI 1973: Proceedings of the 3rd international joint conference on Artificial intelligence, San Francisco, CA, USA, pp. 235–245. Morgan Kaufmann Publishers Inc., San Francisco (1973)
7. Agha, G.: Actors: a model of concurrent computation in distributed systems. MIT Press, Cambridge (1986)
8. Task assignment with unknown duration. J. ACM 49(2), 260–288 (2002)
9. Hamidzadeh, B., Lilja, D.J., Atif, Y.: Dynamic scheduling techniques for heterogeneous computing systems. Concurrency: Practice and Experience 7(7), 633–652 (1995)
10. Oh, H., Ha, S.: A static scheduling heuristic for heterogeneous processors. In: Fraigniaud, P., Mignotte, A., Robert, Y., Bougé, L. (eds.) Euro-Par 1996. LNCS, vol. 1124, pp. 573–577. Springer, Heidelberg (1996)
11. Tang, P., Yew, P.C.: Processor self-scheduling for multiple-nested parallel loops. In: ICPP, pp. 528–535 (1986)
12. Pastor, L., Bosque, J.L.: An efficiency and scalability model for heterogeneous clusters. In: IEEE International Conference on Cluster Computing, p. 427 (2001)
13. Edahiro, M.: Parallelizing fundamental algorithms such as sorting on multi-core processors for eda acceleration. In: ASP-DAC 2009: Proceedings of the 2009 Asia and South Pacific Design Automation Conference, Piscataway, NJ, USA, pp. 230–233. IEEE Press, Los Alamitos (2009)
14. Wu, C.C., Lai, L.F., Chiu, P.H.: Parallel loop self-scheduling for heterogeneous cluster systems with multi-core computers. In: APSCC 2008: Proceedings of the 2008 IEEE Asia-Pacific Services Computing Conference, Washington, DC, USA, pp. 251–256. IEEE Computer Society, Los Alamitos (2008)

15. Drosinos, N., Koziris, N.: Performance comparison of pure mpi vs hybrid mpi-openmp parallelization models on smp clusters. In: 18th Int. Parallel & Distributed Symposium, p. 15 (2004)
16. Mamidala, A.R., Kumar, R., De, D., Panda, D.K.: Mpi collectives on modern multicore clusters: Performance optimizations and communication characteristics. In: CCGRID 2008: Proceedings of the 2008 Eighth IEEE International Symposium on Cluster Computing and the Grid, Washington, DC, USA, pp. 130–137. IEEE Computer Society, Los Alamitos (2008)
17. Tu, B., Zou, M., Zhan, J., Zhao, X., Fan, J.: Multi-core aware optimization for mpi collectives. In: CLUSTER, pp. 322–325 (2008)

A New Heuristic for Broadcasting
in Cluster of Clusters

Hazem Fkaier[1,2], Christophe Cérin[2],
Luiz Angelo Steffenel[3], and Mohamed Jemni[1]

[1] Unité de recherche UTIC/ESSTT
5, Av. Taha Hussein, B.P. 56, Bab Mnara, Tunis, Tunisia
hazem.fkaier@esstt.rnu.tn, mohamed.jemni@fst.rnu.tn
[2] LIPN, UMR 7030, CNRS, Université Paris-Nord
99, avenue J.B Clément, 93430 Villetaneuse, France
christophe.cerin@lipn.univ-paris13.fr
[3] Université de Reims Champagne-Ardenne
CReSTIC - Équipe SysCom, Département de Mathématiques et Informatique
Bâtiment 3, "Moulin de la Housse" - BP 1039, 51687 REIMS CEDEX 2, France
Luiz-Angelo.Steffenel@univ-reims.fr

Abstract. This paper deals with the problem of broadcasting for cluster of clusters. The construction of partial minimum spanning trees being
NP-complete, several heuristic algorithms have been already formulated.
Many of these heuristics (like the heuristic of Kruskal) use the shortest
path to connect the components of the tree. They are not relevant in
case of forwarding or overlapping communication during a step of the
algorithm. In this paper, we study a new heuristic for the minimum
broadcasting tree and we evaluate it through simulations with different
communication parameters and also through real experimentation over
the Grid'5000 testbed.

Keywords: scheduling in grids, resource management, collective primitives for communication in grids.

1 Introduction

It is well known that communication affects significantly the performance of applications deployed on large-scale architectures. Large-scale platforms are characterized by a collection of a great number of computing resources that are geographically distributed over sites from institutions and connected with a wide
heterogeneous dedicated network. Since data sizes in Grid applications may be
large as well as the number of nodes, the collective communication inherent to
the applications is a critical bottleneck.

In this paper we study the problem of broadcasting, i.e., sending a message
from one node to all the others in such environments. Collective communications
are central elements in real life distributed applications, and most improvements
to the broadcast problem (also known as *one-to-many* communication pattern)
are also valid for other collective communication patterns.

R.-S. Chang et al. (Eds.): GPC 2010, LNCS 6104, pp. 27–36, 2010.

Contrarily to heterogeneous clusters, optimal broadcast trees cannot be computed in advance and must therefore be determined accordingly to each network characteristics, a problem that is known to be NP-complete. Several approaches have been proposed to approximate the best way to broadcast a message in a cluster and in a cluster of clusters [1,2,8,3], mostly by decomposing the network in a two-layered structure: inter-cluster (heterogeneous communications) and intra-cluster (homogeneous communications). These works focus on different aspects of the network heterogeneity and therefore behave accordingly to specific situations. In our work we tried to encompass most of these situations, proposing a new heuristic that combines the advantages of the previous heuristics and adaptive techniques to reach the best performance in every situation.

We shall emphasize the fact that optimal broadcast tree is fundamentally different from the minimal spanning tree (MST) problem. In the optimal broadcast problem the issue is to minimize the time to reach the last node that minimizes the longest path in the tree. In the MST, the issue is to minimize the whole 'weight' of the tree. The two constructions may lead to very different trees.

The paper is organized as follows. In section 2, we describe the environment and we recall related works dealing with the problem of achieving efficient broadcast operation. In section 3, we propose a new heuristic to fulfill this task. In section 4, we present the results of our simulation and experiments. Section 5 concludes the paper.

2   Our Environment and Related Work

2.1   Description of the Environment

Heterogeneity Model: We assume a generic platform composed by heterogeneous clusters. The platform studied enjoys heterogeneity along three orthogonal axes: *(i)* the processors that populate the clusters may differ in computational powers, even within the same cluster; *(ii)* the clusters are organized hierarchically and are interconnected via a hierarchy of networks of possibly differing latencies and bandwidths. At the level of physical clusters, the interconnection networks are assumed to be heterogeneous; *(iii)* the clusters at each level of the hierarchy may differ in sizes.

Communication Model: We assume that the network is fully connected. The links between pairs of processes are bidirectional, and each process can transmit data on at most one link and receive data on at most one link at any given time. This model is well known in the literature as *1-port full-duplex*.

Transmission Model: The literature contains several parallel communication models that differ on the computational and network assumptions, such as latency, heterogeneity, network contention, etc. In this work we adopted the *parametrized LogP* model (*pLogP*) [6]. Our choice on the *pLogP* model comes from the fact that we can experience different transmission rates according to the message size, as a consequence of transport protocols and hardware policies. Hence, all along this paper we shall use L as the communication latency between

two nodes, **P** as the number of nodes and **g(m)** for the gap of a message of size
m. The gap of a message m represents the time required to transmit a message
through the network (excluding the latency), which is inversely proportional to
the bandwidth of the link. In the case of inter-cluster communications, $L_{i,j}$ and
$g_{i,j}(m)$ designate the specific latency and gap between two nodes i and j.

2.2 Related Work

One of the earliest papers, to our knowledge, dealing with communication in a wide
sense and in a grid is certainly the paper of Ian foster [4]. In that paper authors
investigated the need for a communication library for the framework of parallel
programming on a distributed multi-site architecture where heterogeneity of network is an intrinsic property. Authors proposed a version of MPICH dedicated to
grids and they called it MPICH-G. This version is built upon MPICH and Globus.
Other studies with implementations have been elaborated. Most of them consider
the MPI communication library or one of its variant such as MPICH-G2, PACX-
MPI, GridMPI and they use a variant of the Van de Gejin [2] algorithm.

We can also cite the works achieved in " The Grid Technology Research Center,
AIST " by M. Matsuda & al. In [8,9], they studied collective operations on
multi-site architectures with MPI library. The paper   [7] considers especially
the broadcast operation in the case where nodes have 2 lane NIC's. The main
contribution of that paper is the way of splitting the message to broadcast: it is
broken into two pieces then they are broadcasted independently following two
binary trees; then, nodes of the two trees exchange the two parts of the message.

Approaches for heterogeneous clusters. We assume that the network is
heterogeneous in one cluster. To calculate the broadcast tree we must determine
at each step which nodes will participate in the communication. Therefore, a set
A represents the set of nodes already having the message at a given time, while
the set B represents the set of nodes that have not yet received the message. We
introduce now only one example in this category.

Early Completion Edge First - ECEF [3]: a couple of nodes, P_i in set A and
P_j in set B, is chosen in such a way that P_j becomes ready to send the message
as early as possible. This time is computed by:

$$RT_i + g_{ij}(m) + L_{ij}$$

where RT_i is the ready time of P_i, $g_{ij}(m)$ is the latency gap between P_i and P_j
and L_{ij} is communication cost between P_i and P_j. Note that this heuristic aims
at increasing the number of nodes in set A as fast as possible.

Early Completion Edge First with look-ahead - ECEF-LA: the ECEF heuristic
allows to increase the number of nodes in set A which is yet a good fact. But
it also important to choose the next destination to be itself a good sender in
remainder steps. As an enhancement of the latter heuristic, Bhat & al. [3]propose
to estimate the efficiency of each node throughout a function that takes into
consideration the speed of forwarding the message to another node of set B.

Grid aware heuristics. We suppose, now, that we have a cluster of clusters environment and a coordinator (proxy) on each cluster. All communications between clusters are performed through the coordinators. Subsequently, global communications are ordered in two levels: inter-cluster and intra-cluster communications. Hence, if we have a message to broadcast in a grid architecture, then it is broadcasted between coordinators, and then each coordinator broadcasts the message locally. In the works elaborated by Steffenel [1], the local communication load is represented by one virtual node that is connected to a specific coordinator. Thus, the local communication load is depicted by

$$L_{kk'} + g_{kk'} = \begin{cases} T_k & \text{if } k' \text{ is associated to node } k \\ \infty & \text{if } k' \text{ is not associated to node } k \end{cases}$$

where P_k is a coordinator and $P_{k'}$ is a virtual node simulating a cluster. Under this framework, Steffenel proposed three heuristics to broadcast a message in a grid environment.

We also found in the literature the following variants: ECEF-LAt, ECEF-LAT: and BottomUp that starts by contacting the most loaded coordinator. The heuristic needs to contact it through the 'shortest path'. BottomUp uses a min-max approach to find the *'shortest path'* to contact the most loaded coordinator. For details about the heuristics, please refer to [1].

Another interesting work to mention here is the one achieved by Ching-Hsien Hsu [5]. Hsu proposed to consider the problem according to two patterns: graph pattern and tree pattern. In the graph pattern case, the author proposed the Nearest Neighbor First (*G-NNF*) and the Maximum Degree Neighbor First (*G-MDNF*) algorithms. For the tree pattern case, he proposed *T-NNF*, *T-MDNF*, the Maximum Height Subtree First (*T-MHSF*), the Maximum Subtree First (*T-MSF*) and finally the Maximum Weight Subtree First (*T-MWSF*) algorithms. The definitions of all these algorithms should be very intuitive and we will not detail them here.

3   A New Approach for Broadcasting in Clusters and Cluster of Clusters

According to previous heuristics, to reduce global broadcast time, three factors impact the performance. First, we need to increase the size of set A with clusters, in the quickest possible way. Second, the availability of numerous senders give us more chance to perform next communication in a better way, since we have more choices to consider.

The second factor is to give an advantage to communication-efficient clusters when choosing a receiver. As we explained above, it is important to communicate with the cluster that can forward the message, in the next steps, within a short time. This means that we want to augment set A with good senders.

The third factor is to begin by contacting the most loaded clusters, so that we insure the maximum of overlap between intra and inter-cluster broadcast. This strategy is the key of success of BottomUp and ECEF-LAT heuristics since, according to measured parameters, in most cases local broadcast needs more time than inter-cluster communication.

3.1 The MostCrit Heuristic

The previous heuristics try to optimize one of these 'criteria' or to combine two or all of them at each iteration. And the better we consider these factors, the better the result is.

Each heuristic has a function to optimize. This function contains parameters linked to one or two of aforementioned factors. Hence all factors are merged in only one formula to be minimized at each iteration.

Merging all factors in one may give us a compromised solution. But compromise is not always a good solution. To explain this idea let us imagine the situation where we have, at a given iteration, a 'very' loaded cluster. Then we should contact it in priority otherwise it will delay the ending time.

If we combine all factors and look for a compromise, then previous heuristics may lead us to choose another cluster, not the most loaded and subsequently we do not achieve the best performance.

The same reasoning can be applied if we have a very good forwarder cluster or a very communication efficient cluster at a given iteration. The conclusion of this example is to say that considering a single factor at a time can also be very efficient and even more efficient then combining several factors in one.

Following this idea we developed a new heuristic that considers each factor in a separate way. We proceed as follows:

We consider our two sets A and B. At each iteration we choose one sender from set A and one receiver from set B. Then at each iteration we shall decide which factor we need to satisfy. Either (1) to choose the fastest-to-communicate cluster from set B, or (2) best forwarder cluster from set B or (3) the most loaded cluster from set B.

Condition (1) implies to minimize $RT_i + g_{ij}(m) + L_{ij}$ which is to say to apply one iteration of ECEF heuristic.

Condition (2) implies to minimize $RT_i + g_{ij}(m) + L_{ij} + F_j$ which is to say applying one iteration of ECEF-LA heuristic.

And condition (3) implies to choose the most loaded cluster in set B and then to find the best sender in set A which is to say to apply one iteration of BottomUp heuristic, i.e., we apply $\max_{P_j \in B}(\min_{P_i \in A}(g_{ij}(m) + L_{ij} + T_j))$.

The question now is "How to choose the factor to satisfy?" To answer this question, we examine what would happen if we do not satisfy a given factor $fact_i$ i.e. we do not choose the best cluster according to this factor:

a- Either the chosen cluster (the optimal cluster according to another factor) behaves well with the factor $fact_i$ then $fact_i$ is not strongly violated. Then we estimate that the chosen cluster and the optimal one according to $fact_i$ behaves in relatively similar way according to $fact_i$.

b- Or the chosen cluster behaves badly with the factor $fact_i$ and then it violates it strongly. Then we estimate that the chosen cluster and the optimal one according to $fact_i$ are relatively different for $fact_i$.

At the end, it is important to choose the cluster that satisfies one factor and behaves well with the other ones, or at least does not violate them strongly.

We propose to compute the set of values associated to each factor as follows:

For factor (1), we compute set $E_1 = \min_{P_i \in A} (RT_i + g_{ij}(m) + L_{ij})/P_j \in B$
For factor (2), we compute set $E_2 = \min_{P_i \in A} (RT_i + g_{ij}(m) + L_{ij} + F_j)/P_j \in B$
For factor (3), we compute set $E_3 = \min_{P_i \in A} (RT_i + g_{ij}(m) + L_{ij} + T_j)/P_j \in B$

With dispersed value in a given set, we say that clusters are very different according to the associated factor, then factor may be strongly violated if we do not satisfy it. Whereas, if a set contains close values, then it means that clusters behave in a quite similar way. Subsequently, choosing one cluster or another one will not be decisive.

Finally we choose to satisfy the factor which has the associated set with the most dispersed values i.e. we compute the mean deviation of each set values and we choose to satisfy the factor having the greatest mean deviation.

3.2   Simulation

In our simulations, we rely on works done by Steffenel [1] for the different parameters measured on a real grid environment. He measured values of different communications parameters (L, g, T) over French **Grid'5000**[1] infrastructure. He found out a lowest value and highest value for each parameter. In his simulation, he set randomly the values of L (in μs), g (in ms), T (in ms) in the corresponding interval and then he applied the different heuristics. In our simulation we proceed in the same way. The values that we introduced now are the mean of 100 iterations.

In the first simulation, we set L, g and T in intervals measured over Grid'5000 see Table 1. As seen in Figure 1, all heuristics give almost the same completion time. Then we cannot evaluate the efficiency or compare them. The second remark we shall note is that our new heuristic (noted MostCrit) gives exactly the same values as BottomUp, which is the best heuristics at present time and to our knowledge. We can conclude that both heuristics behave exactly in the same

Table 1. Grid'5000 settings

param	First simulation fig. 1		Second simulation left part of fig. 2		Third simulation right part of fig. 2	
	min	max	min	max	min	max
L	1	15	5	75	10	150
g	100	600	500	3000	1000	6000
T	200	3000	40	600	20	300

[1] For details, refer to https://www.grid5000.fr

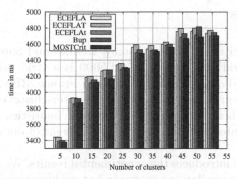

Fig. 1. Broadcasting time vs clusters number with Grid'5000 settings

way and it can be obtained only if our new heuristic chooses to apply bottomUp at each iteration. By observing parameters values we can expect this fact since the interval of T_j is much larger then intervals of L_{ij} and g_{ij}. This means that values of T_j will be sparser than values of L_{ij} and g_{ij} and consequently values in E_3 will be sparser than those in E_1 and those in E_2. And finally factor (3) (choosing the most loaded cluster) will be retained.

To evaluate the efficiency of our new heuristics, we propose to achieve simulations with other settings. We changed the ratio of L and g (parameters linked to inter-cluster broadcast) and T (parameter associated to the local broadcast).

In the second simulation, left part of Figure 2, we multiplied L and g by 5 and divided T by 5, see left part of table 1. In the third simulation, right part of Figure 2, we multiplied L and g by 10 and divided T by 10, see right part of Table 1.

Simulation represented in Figure 1 show that bottomUp keeps giving good performances as well as our new heuristic 'MostCrit' even though they do not give exactly the same values. Other heuristics behave worse.

The conclusion of our simulations is that BottomUp and MostCrit heuristics give evenly good results independently of the ratio of inter-cluster communication performances over intra-cluster communication performances. This point has never been observed before to our knowledge.

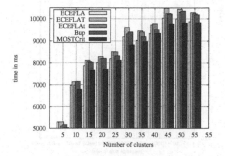
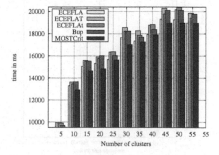

Fig. 2. Broadcasting time vs clusters number with other setting

4   Experiments

We selected 3 sites/cities in France (Nancy, Rennes and Sophia-Antipolis) and 126 nodes on the Grid'5000 testbed. Grid'5000 is a Grid testbed composed of processors distributed over clusters in 9 sites in France. RENATER, the French Educational and Research Network provides the inter-cluster connection through a 10Gbits/s "dark fiber" backbone. The different heuristics introduced in this paper were implemented in MPI, using the `MPI_send()` operation as the basic building block.

Figure 3 (left part) introduces the experimental results. We notice that the different curves are quite similar and confirm what we have found with simulations. We notice that the time to broadcast 32MB is about 5s... which is important and are probably due to the 'MPI stack' which slowdown the performance! We notice also some perturbation around 10kB and they should be due to TCP sliding windows. Perturbation around 300KB should be due to a change in MPI policy to send data, as already reported by Steffenel.

Figure 3 (right part) introduces another experimental result, on two clusters located in Rennes and Nancy again but with a new one in Sophia-Antipolis (*Sol* cluster instead of *Azur* cluster) and with new nodes. We also went further in the message sizes. We observe the same phenomena than those observed on Figure 3. We conclude that what we observe is reproducible and inherent to the tools and algorithms we used.

Figure 4 focus on larger message sizes and the scales are no more logarithmic. We observe that in this case our MostCrit heuristic behaves well compared to BottomUp for instance and justify our work to optimize the broadcast operation.

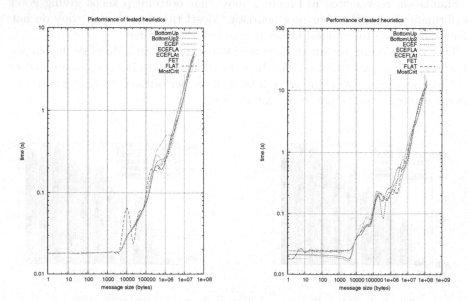

Fig. 3. First (left) and second (right) experiments on Grid'5000

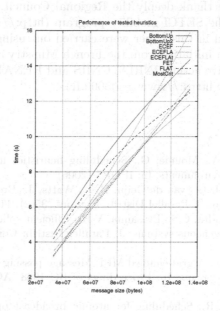

Fig. 4. A focus on messages size from 32MB to 128MB

5   Conclusions

In this paper, we investigated heuristics to achieve broadcast in a cluster of clusters. We developed a new heuristic inspired from other works in order to combine the 'best' of each solution. Our idea is not to combine different elementary factors as it is done with previous published heuristics, but to apply only one factor at ech iteration. We proved the efficiency of our approach by simulation and by real experimentation. We made simulation according to varying communication parameters and hence we cover a wide range of platforms. We also made effective experiments to prove the efficiency of our new heuristic in practice. Experiments have been carried out over Grid'5000 testbed through 126 nodes spread over 3 sites. Another important work in experiments could be to increase the input size of the problem and to observe if curves will saturate.

Concerning the experiments, since the network link is shared among the Grid'5000 sites (but the nodes are dedicated) we also need to model congestion phenomena or shared bandwidth. From a technical point of view, we could modify on the fly the matrix containing L, g and T parameters, but the problem is to have a realistic model for traffic in clusters of clusters. Finally, instead of injecting perturbations in the network, we could use the Wrekavoc tool[2] able to slowdown the delivering of messages by modifying the TCP stack. Again in this case, we need a realistic model for inter sites communication.

---

[2] See: http://wrekavoc.gforge.inria.fr/

Acknowledgement. We thank deeply the Regional Council of Ile-de-France for its support through the SETCI mobility program (http://www.iledefrance.fr). Experiments presented in this paper were carried out using the Grid'5000 experimental testbed, an initiative from the French Ministry of Research through the ACI GRID incentive action, INRIA, CNRS and RENATER and other contributing partners (see https://www.grid5000.fr).

References

1. Barchet-Steffenel, L.A., Mounie, G.: Scheduling heuristics for efficient broadcast operations on grid environments. In: IPDPS (2006)
2. Barnett, M., Payne, D.G., van de Geijn, R.A., Watts, J.: Broadcasting on meshes with wormhole routing. J. Parallel Distrib. Comput. 35(2), 111–122 (1996)
3. Bhat, P.B., Raghavendra, C.S., Prasanna, V.K.: Efficient collective communication in distributed heterogeneous systems. J. Parallel Distrib. Comput. 63(3), 251–263 (2003)
4. Foster, I., Karonis, N.: A grid-enabled MPI: Message passing in heterogeneous distributed computing systems. In: Proceedings of SC 1998. ACM Press, New York (1998)
5. Hsu, C.-H., Tsai, B.-R.: Scheduling for atomic broadcast operation in heterogeneous networks with one port model. The Journal of Supercomputing 50(3), 269–288 (2009)
6. Kielmann, T., Bal, H., Gorlatch, S., Verstoep, K., Hofman, R.: Network performance-aware collective communication for clustered wide area systems. Parallel Computing 27(11), 1431–1456 (2001)
7. Tatsuhiro, C., Toshio, E., Satochi, M.: High-performance mpi. In: IPDPS (2004)
8. Kodama, Y., Takano, R., Matsuda, M., Kudoh, T., Ishikawa, Y.: Efficient mpi collective operations for clusters in long-and-fast networks. In: Cluster 2006 (2006)
9. Matsuda, M., Kudoh, T., Tazuka, H., Ishikawa, Y.: The design and implementation of an asynchronous communication mechanism for the MPI communication model. In: CLUSTER, pp. 13–22. IEEE Computer Society, Los Alamitos (2004)

SLA-Driven Automatic Bottleneck Detection and Resolution for Read Intensive Multi-tier Applications Hosted on a Cloud

Waheed Iqbal[1], Matthew N. Dailey[1], David Carrera[2], and Paul Janecek[1]

[1] Computer Science and Information Management,
Asian Institute of Technology, Thailand
[2] Technical University of Catalonia (UPC),
Barcelona Supercomputing Center (BSC), Spain

Abstract. A Service-Level Agreement (SLA) provides surety for specific quality attributes to the consumers of services. However, the current SLAs offered by cloud providers do not address *response time*, which, from the user's point of view, is the most important quality attribute for Web applications. Satisfying a maximum average response time guarantee for Web applications is difficult for two main reasons: first, traffic patterns are unpredictable; second, the complex nature of multi-tier Web applications increases the difficulty of identifying bottlenecks and resolving them automatically. This paper presents a working prototype system that automatically detects and resolves bottlenecks in a multi-tier Web application hosted on a EUCALYPTUS-based cloud in order to satisfy specific maximum response time requirements. We demonstrate the feasibility of the approach in an experimental evaluation with a testbed cloud and a synthetic workload. Automatic bottleneck detection and resolution under dynamic resource management has the potential to enable cloud providers to provide SLAs for Web applications that guarantee specific response time requirements.

1 Introduction

Cloud service providers allow consumers to rent computational and storage resources on demand and according to their usage. Cloud service providers maximize their profits by fulfilling their obligations to consumers with minimal infrastructure and maximal resource utilization.

Although most cloud providers provide service-level agreements (SLAs) for availability or other quality attributes, the most important quality attribute for Web applications from the user's point of view, *response time*, is not addressed by current SLAs. Guaranteeing response time is a difficult problem for two main reasons. First, web application traffic is highly unpredictable. Second, the complex nature of multi-tier Web applications, in which bottlenecks can occur at multiple points, means response time violations may not be easy to diagnose or remedy. If a cloud provider is to guarantee a particular maximum response time for any traffic level, it must automatically detect bottleneck tiers and allocate additional resources to those tiers as traffic grows.

R.-S. Chang et al. (Eds.): GPC 2010, LNCS 6104, pp. 37–46, 2010.

In this paper, we take steps toward eliminating this limitation of current cloud-based Web application hosting SLAs. We present a working prototype system running on a EUCALYPTUS-based [1] cloud that actively monitors the response times for requests to a multi-tier Web application, gathers CPU usage statistics, and uses heuristics to identify the bottlenecks. When bottlenecks are identified, the system dynamically allocates the resources required by the application to resolve the identified bottlenecks and maintain response time requirements. We consider a two-tier Web application consisting of a Web server tier and a database tier to evaluate our proposed approach.

There have been several efforts to perform dynamic scaling of applications based on workload monitoring. In previous work [2] we considered single-tier Web applications, used log-based monitoring to identify SLA violations along, and used dynamic resource allocation to satisfy the SLA. Amazon Auto Scaling [3] allows consumers to scale up or down according to criteria such as average CPU utilization across a group of compute instances. [4] presents a statistical machine learning approach to predict system performance and minimize the number of resources required to maintain the performance of an application hosted on a cloud. [5] dynamically switches between different virtual machine configurations to satisfy changing workloads on an Amazon EC2 cloud. However, none of these solutions address the issues of multi-tier Web applications.

To the best of our knowledge, our system is the first SLA-driven resource manager for clouds based on open source technology. Our working prototype, built on top of a EUCALYPTUS-based compute cloud, provides dynamic resource allocation and load balancing for multi-tier Web applications in order to satisfy a SLA that enforces specific response time requirements. In this paper, we describe our prototype, the heuristics we have developed for multi-tier Web applications, and an evaluation of the prototype on a testbed cloud. We find that the system is able to detect bottlenecks, resolve them using dynamic resource allocation, and satisfy the SLA.

There are a few limitations to this preliminary work. We only address scaling of the application server tier and a read-only database tier. Our prototype is only able to scale up, although it would also be easy to enable the system to scale down by detecting the ends of traffic spikes. Our proposed system is also not capable of reversing scaling operations that turn out not to be helpful for bottleneck resolution. We plan to address some of these limitations in future work. In the rest of this paper, we describe our approach, the prototype implementation, and an experimental evaluation of the prototype.

2   System Design and Implementation

To manage cloud resources dynamically based on response time requirements, we developed three components: VLBCoordinator, VLBManager, and VMProfiler. We use Nginx [6] as a load balancer because it offers detailed logging and allows reloading of its configuration file without termination of existing client sessions.

VLBCoordinator interacts with a EUCALYPTUS cloud using Typica [7]. Typica is a simple API written in Java to access a variety of Amazon Web services such as EC2, SimpleDB, and DevPay. The core functions of VLBCoordinator are instantiateVirtualMachine and getVMIP, which are accessible through XML-RPC. VLBManager monitors the traces of the load balancer and detects violations of response time requirements. It clusters the requests into static and dynamic resource requests and calculates the average response time for each type of request. VMProfiler is used to log the CPU utilization of each virtual machine. It exposes XML-RPC functions to obtain the CPU utilization of specific virtual machine for the last n minutes.

RUBiS [8] is an open-source benchmark Web application for auctions. It provides core functionality of an auction site such as browsing, selling, and bidding for items, and provides three user roles: visitor, buyer, and seller. Visitors are not required to register and are allowed to browse items that are available for auction. We used the PHP implementation of RUBiS as a sample Web application to evaluate our system. Since RUBiS does not currently support load balancing over a database tier, we modified it to use round-robin balancing over a set of database servers listed in a database connection settings file, and we developed a server-side component, DbConfigAgent, to update the database connection settings file after a scaling operation has modified the configuration of the database tier. The entire benchmark system consists of the physical machines supporting the EUCALYPTUS cloud, a virtual Web server acting as a proxying load balancer for the entire Web application, a tier of virtual Web servers running the RUBiS application software, and a tier of virtual database servers. Figure 1 shows the deployment of our components along with the main interactions.

We use heuristics and active profiling of the CPUs of virtual machine-hosted application tiers for identification of bottlenecks. Our system reads the Web server proxy logs for 60 seconds and clusters the log entries into dynamic content requests and static content requests. Requests to resources (Web pages) containing server-side scripts (PHP, JSP, ASP, etc.) are considered as dynamic content requests. Requests to the static resources (HTML, JPG, PNG, TXT, etc.) are considered as static content requests. Dynamic resources are generated through utilization of the CPU and may depend on other tiers, while static resources are pre-generated flat files available in the Web server tier. Each type of request has different characteristics and is monitored separately for purposes of bottleneck detection. The system calculates the 95th percentile of the average response time. When static

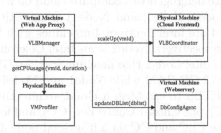

Fig. 1. Component deployment diagram for system components including main interactions

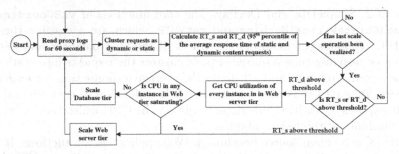

Fig. 2. Flow diagram for prototype system that detects the bottleneck tier in a two-tier Web application hosted on a heterogeneous cloud and dynamically scales the tier to satisfy a SLA that defines response time requirements

content response time indicates saturation, the system scales the Web server tier. When the system determines that dynamic content response time indicates saturation, it obtains the CPU utilization across the Web server tier. If the CPU utilization of any instance in the Web server tier has reached a saturation threshold, the system scales up the Web server tier; otherwise, it scales up the database tier. Each scale operation adds exactly one server to a specific tier. Our focus is on read-intensive applications, and we assume that a mechanism such as [9] exists to ensure consistent reads after updates to a master database. Before initiating a scale operation, the system ensures that the effect of the last scale operation has been realized. Figure 2 shows a flow diagram for bottleneck detection and resolution in our prototype system.

3 Experiments

In this section we describe the setup for an experimental evaluation of our prototype based on a testbed cloud using the RUBiS Web application and a synthetic workload generator.

3.1 Testbed Cloud

We built a small private heterogeneous compute cloud on five physical machines (Front-end, Node1, Node2, Node3, and Node4) using EUCALYPTUS. Front-end, Node1, and Node4 are Intel Pentium 4 machines with 2.84GHz, 2.66 GHz, and 2.66 GHz CPUs, respectively. Node2 is an Intel Celeron machine with a 2.4 GHz CPU. Node3 is an Intel Core 2 Duo machine with 2.6 GHz CPU. Front-end, Node2 and Node3 have 2 GB RAM while Node1 and Node4 have 1.5 GB RAM.

We used EUCALYPTUS to establish a cloud architecture comprised of one Cloud Controller (CLC), one Cluster Controller (CC), and four Node Controllers (NCs). We installed the CLC and CC on a front-end node attached to both our main LAN and the cloud's private network. We installed the NCs on four (Node1, Node2, Node3, and Node4) separate machines connected to the private network.

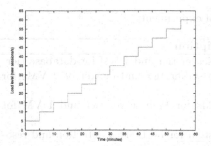

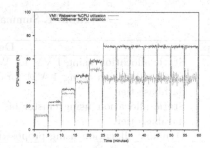

Fig. 3. Workload generation profile for all experiments

Fig. 4. CPU utilization of virtual machines used during Experiment 1

3.2 Workload Generation

We use `httperf` to generate synthetic workloads for RUBiS. We generate workloads for specific durations with a required number of user sessions per second. A user session emulates a visitor that browses categories and regions and also bids on items up for auction. Every five minutes, we increment the load level by 5, from load level 5 through load level 60. Each load level represents the number of user sessions per second; each user session makes 6 requests to static resources and 5 requests to dynamic resources including 5 pauses to simulate user think time. The dynamic resources consist of PHP pages that make read-only database queries. Figure 3 shows the workload levels we use for our experiments over time.

We performed four experiments based on this workload and RUBiS. Experiments 1, 2, and 3 profile the system's behavior using static allocation with different static resource allocations. Experiment 4 profiles the system's behavior under dynamic resource allocation using the proposed algorithm for bottleneck detection and resolution. We generate the same workload for each experiment except that Experiments 2 and 3 start at load level 25 instead of load level 5.

3.3 Experiment Details

In Experiment 1, we statically allocate one virtual machine to the Web server tier and one virtual machine to the database tier. In Experiment 2, we statically allocate 1 virtual machine for the Web server tier and a cluster of 2 virtual machines for the database tier. As discussed earlier, we modified RUBiS to perform load balancing across the database server instances; in this experiment, RUBiS performs load balancing across the static database server cluster. In Experiment 3, we statically allocate a cluster of 2 virtual machines for the Web server tier and 1 virtual machine for the database tier. In this experiment, Nginx performs load balancing of HTTP traffic across the static Web server cluster.

In Experiment 4, we use our proposed system to adapt to response time increases and rejection of requests by the Web server. Initially, we started two virtual machines on our testbed cloud. The Nginx-based Web server farm was initialized with one virtual machine hosting the Web server tier. Another single

Table 1. Summary of experiments

Exp.	Description
1	Static allocation using 1 VM for Web server tier and 1 VM for database tier.
2	Static allocation using 1 VM for Web server tier and cluster of 2 VMs for database tier.
3	Static allocation using cluster of 2 VMs for Web server tier and 1 VM for database tier.
4	Dynamic allocation using proposed system for bottleneck detection and resolution.

virtual machine was used to host the database tier. In this experiment, we tried to satisfy a SLA that enforces a one-second maximum average response time requirement for the RUBiS application regardless of load level using our proposed algorithm for bottleneck detection and resolution. The threshold for CPU saturation was set to 85% utilization. Table 1 summarizes the experiments.

4 Results

4.1 Experiment 1: Simple Static Allocation

This section describes the results we obtained in Experiment 1. Figure 4 shows the CPU utilization of the 2 virtual machines hosting the application tiers during Experiment 1. The downward spikes at the beginning of each load level occur because all user sessions are cleared between load level increments, and it takes some time for the system to return to a steady state. We do not observe any tier saturating its CPU during this experiment: after load level 25, the CPU utilization remains nearly constant, indicating that the CPU was not a bottleneck for this application with the given workload.

Figure 5(a) shows the throughput of the system during Experiment 1. After load level 25, we do not observe any growth in the system's throughput because one or both of the tiers have reached their saturation points. Although the load level increases with time, the system is unable to serve all requests, and it either rejects or queues the remaining requests.

Figure 5(b) shows the 95th percentile of average response time during Experiment 1. From load level 5 to load level 25, we observe a nearly constant response time, but after load level 25, the arrival rate exceeds the limits of the system's processing capability. One of the virtual machines hosting the application tiers becomes a bottleneck, then requests begin to spend more time in the queue and request processing time increases. From that point we observe a rapid growth in the response time. After load level 30, however, the queue also becomes saturated, and the system rejects most requests. Therefore, we do not observe further growth in the average response time. Clearly, the system only works efficiently from load level 5 to load level 25.

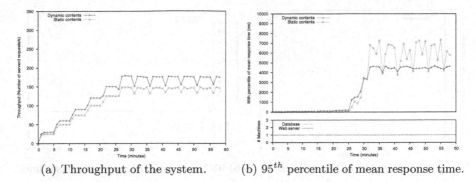

(a) Throughput of the system.   (b) 95th percentile of mean response time.

Fig. 5. Throughput and response time in Experiment 1

4.2 Experiment 2: Static Allocation Using Database Tier Replication and Load Balancing

We observed in Experiment 1 that after load level 25, the system's throughput and response time saturate. In Experiment 2, to test whether static allocation of an additional database server would resolve the bottleneck, we allocated two virtual machines to the database tier and one virtual machine to the Web server tier. We generated workload from load level 25 to load level 60. Figure 6(a) shows the throughput of the system during Experiment 2. After load level 30, we do not observe growth in the system throughput, because the system requires still more resources to satisfy the needs of the incoming workload.

Figure 6(b) shows the 95th percentile of the average response time during Experiment 2. From load level 25 to load level 30, we observe a nearly constant response time. We see that allocating more resources to the database tier helps the system to support an increase of 5 in the load level, and the system is able to satisfy response time requirements up to load level 30, but after load level 30, the arrival rate exceeds the limit of the system's processing capability and we observe a dramatic increase in system response time.

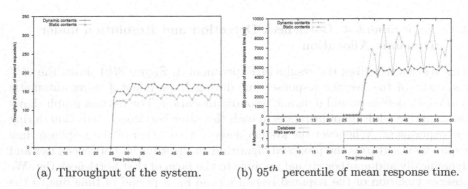

(a) Throughput of the system.   (b) 95th percentile of mean response time.

Fig. 6. Throughput and response time in Experiment 2

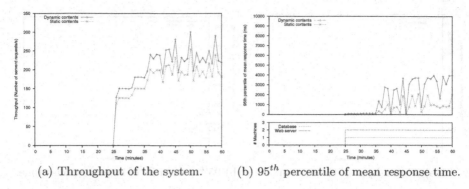

(a) Throughput of the system.   (b) 95th percentile of mean response time.

Fig. 7. Throughput and response time in Experiment 3

4.3   Experiment 3: Static Allocation Using Web Server Tier Replication and Load Balancing

In Experiment 3, to test whether static allocation of an additional Web server would resolve the bottleneck, we allocated two virtual machines to the Web server tier and one virtual machine to the database tier, and generated a workload from load level 25 to load level 60. Figure 7(a) shows the throughput of the system during Experiment 3. We do not observe growth in the system throughput after load level 35, because the system requires still more resources to satisfy the needs of the incoming requests.

Figure 7(b) shows the 95th percentile of average response times during Experiment 3. From load level 25 to load level 35, we observe a nearly constant response time, but after load level 35, the arrival rate exceeds the limit of the system's processing capacity and we observe a dramatic increase in the system response time.

Experiments 1, 2, and 3 show that it is difficult to obtain the best resource allocation for the system to satisfy response time requirements for an undefined load level. Clearly, we cannot provide a SLA guaranteeing a specific response time with an undefined load level for a multi-tier Web application using static resource allocation.

4.4   Experiment 4: Bottleneck Detection and Resolution under Dynamic Allocation

This section describes the results of Experiment 4. Figure 8(b) shows the 95th percentile of the average response time during Experiment 4 using automatic bottleneck detection and dynamic resource allocation. The bottom graph shows the adaptive addition of instances in each tier after bottleneck detection during the experiment. Whenever the system detects a violation of the response time requirements, it uses the proposed algorithm to identify the bottleneck tier and dynamically add another virtual machine to the farm of that bottleneck tier. We observe violation of the required response time for a period of time due to the latency of virtual machine boot-up and the time required to observe the effects

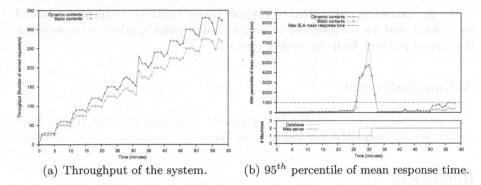

(a) Throughput of the system.　　　(b) 95th percentile of mean response time.

Fig. 8. Throughput and response time in Experiment 4

of previous scale operations. Figure 8(a) shows the system throughput during the experiment. We observe linear growth in the system throughput through the full range of load levels.

Figure 9 shows the CPU utilization of all virtual machines during the experiment. Initially, the system was configured with VM1 and VM2. After load level 25, VM3 is dynamically added to the system, and after load level 30, VM4 is dynamically added to the system. The differing steady-state levels of CPU utilization for the different VMs reflects the use of round-robin balancing and differing processor speeds for the physical nodes. We observe the same downward spike at the beginning of each load level as in the earlier experiments due to the time for the system to return to steady state after all user sessions are cleared.

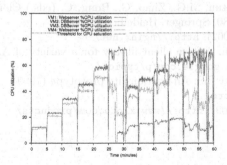

Fig. 9. CPU utilization of virtual machines during Experiment 4

5　Discussion and Conclusion

In this paper, we have described a prototype system that automatically identifies and resolves bottlenecks in a multi-tier application hosted on a EUCALYTPUS-based cloud. Experimental results show that automatic bottleneck detection and resolution can enable us to offer SLAs that define specific maximum response time requirement for multi-tier Web applications.

We are extending our system to support n-tier clustered applications hosted on a cloud, and we are planning to predict bottlenecks in advance to overcome the virtual machine boot-up latency problem.

Acknowledgments

This work was partly supported by a graduate fellowship from the Higher Education Commission (HEC) of Pakistan to WI.

References

1. Nurmi, D., Wolski, R., Grzegorczyk, C., Obertelli, G., Soman, S., Youseff, L., Zagorodnov, D.: The EUCALYPTUS Open-source Cloud-computing System. In: CCA 2008: Proceedings of the Cloud Computing and Its Applications Workshop, Chicago, IL, USA (2008)
2. Iqbal, W., Dailey, M., Carrera, D.: SLA-driven adaptive resource management for web applications on a heterogeneous compute cloud. In: Jaatun, M.G., Zhao, G., Rong, C. (eds.) CloudCom 2009. LNCS, vol. 5931, pp. 243–253. Springer, Heidelberg (2009)
3. Amazon Inc.: Amazon Web Services auto scaling (2009), http://aws.amazon.com/autoscaling/
4. Bodik, P., Griffith, R., Sutton, C., Fox, A., Jordan, M., Patterson, D.: Statistical machine learning makes automatic control practical for internet datacenters. In: HotCloud 2009: Proceedings of the Workshop on Hot Topics in Cloud Computing, San Diego, CA (2009)
5. Liu, H., Wee, S.: Web server farm in the cloud: Performance evaluation and dynamic architecture. In: Jaatun, M.G., Zhao, G., Rong, C. (eds.) CloudCom 2009. LNCS, vol. 5931, pp. 369–380. Springer, Heidelberg (2009)
6. Sysoev, I.: Nginx (2002), http://nginx.net/
7. Google Code: Typica: A Java client library for a variety of Amazon Web Services (2008), http://code.google.com/p/typica/
8. OW2 Consortium: RUBiS: An auction site prototype (1999), http://rubis.ow2.org/
9. xkoto: Gridscale (2009), http://www.xkoto.com/products/

An Effective Job Replication Technique Based on Reliability and Performance in Mobile Grids

Daeyong Jung[1], SungHo Chin[1], KwangSik Chung[2], Taeweon Suh[1],
HeonChang Yu[1], and JoonMin Gil[3],*

[1] Dept. of Computer Science and Education, Korea University, Seoul, Korea
{karat,wingtop,suhtw,yuhc}@korea.ac.kr
[2] Dept. of Computer Science, Korea National Open University, Seoul, Korea
kchung0825@knou.ac.kr
[3] School of Computer & Information Communications Engineering,
Catholic University of Daegu, Daegu, Korea
jmgil@cu.ac.kr

Abstract. Recently, many studies have attempted to utilize mobile nodes as resources in mobile grids. Due to their underlying restrictions such as intermittent communication disconnections, limited battery capacity, and so on, mobile nodes are less reliable than wired nodes for job processing. Therefore, it is imperative to find an enhanced job scheduling method to provide stable job processing for mobile grids. In this paper, we propose an efficient job scheduling method in mobile grids, which can determine the suitable number of replicas for a job based on resource (mobile node) information, node status, and access point information. In our job scheduling method, mobile nodes are divided into node groups, and the number of subjobs assigned to each node group is derived from the reliability and performance of the node group. Simulation results show that our scheduling algorithms can reduce the makespan of entire jobs in mobile grid environments compared with random-based job scheduling.

Keywords: Mobile Grid, Job Replication, Reliability, Failure Prevention.

1 Introduction

Grid computing is a distributed paradigm for processing large amounts of data and/or solving complex computational problems utilizing geographically distributed resources. It has been adopted in various fields such as meteorology, bio-technology, space science, and others [1]. Recently, the widespread popularity of mobile devices such as laptops, PDAs, and smart phones has led to the emergence of mobile grids. Due to this trend, those mobile devices have been utilized as grid resources [2,3]. However, several problems arise in such an environment. Due to the frequent disconnection and limited battery life of mobile

---

* Corresponding author.

R.-S. Chang et al. (Eds.): GPC 2010, LNCS 6104, pp. 47–58, 2010.
© Springer-Verlag Berlin Heidelberg 2010

devices, job failures which is most crucial problem in mobile grids, can frequently occur during job processing [4,5]. Job failure seriously lowers the performance of mobile grids.

Generally, the replication technique can be adopted to tolerate job failure in mobile grids. In this technique, a job is distributed to several nodes and processed concurrently [6]. Recently, several studies have adopted the job-replication concept to support more stable job execution in mobile grids. Even if these studies can provide stable job processing for mobile grid systems, the problem of redundant replicas is inevitable. This results in the waste of resources because the number of replicas for a job is statically determined without considering the reliability or performance of mobile nodes. Therefore, the job-replication based on a static number of replicas is not directly applicable to a mobile grid environment.

In this paper, we attempt to find a solution for efficient job processing in a mobile grid environment in which nodes have varying reliability and performance. To deal with the unpredictable environmental changes associated with the characteristics of these nodes, we propose a failure prevention scheme with the job-replication concept. In our scheme, we use a grouping method, classifying mobile nodes into node groups based on their reliability and performance. Based on the node groups, we present two kinds of job scheduling algorithms: one is reliability-based scheduling, and the other is reliability- and performance-based scheduling. In these two scheduling algorithms, a different number of replicas for a job are allocated to each node group. We derive the number of jobs to be allocated to each node group using group reliability and performance. Moreover, we conduct performance evaluations with simulations to demonstrate the effectiveness of our failure prevention scheme. Simulation results reveal that our scheduling algorithms show improvements in performance in terms of the makespan of entire jobs compared to a random-based scheduling algorithm.

The rest of this paper is organized as follows: Section 2 briefly describes related works on job scheduling in mobile grids. Section 3 presents our system architecture and its components. Section 4 presents our scheduling algorithms based on reliability and performance. Section 5 presents performance evaluations with simulations. Lastly, Section 6 concludes our paper.

2   Related Works

Mobile grid computing is emerging due to improvements in mobile network technology and mobile device capabilities. Because mobile devices such as PDAs, smart phones, and so on, are included in mobile grids as resources, the limitations of mobile devices directly affect the performance and reliability of mobile grid systems. A replication scheme is a popular solution to overcome these limitations. In the scheme, a job is replicated and dispatched to several nodes, and the replicated jobs are processed concurrently, improving the reliability of the job execution.

In [7], a threshold was determined for each mobile node to set how much of its resources can be allocated for job processing. Then, the remaining resources of the node were shared to execute jobs in other nodes, maximizing the usage rate of resources. The study only accounted for the available CPU and memory resources of mobile nodes in scheduling. Country to this study, we make a list about all kinds of resources (including CPU, memory, battery life, and so on) in the proxies so that these resources can be utilized when a job is allocated.

In [8], replicas were mapped to appropriate nodes using Bayesian networks. This study used static and dynamic parameters as mapping information. The static parameters included CPU type, frequency, storage capacity, and physical network transfer rate. The dynamic parameters included CPU usage rate, memory space, and bandwidth. Based on these parameters, this study determines whether jobs were replicated or migrated. However, it considered only current system attributes, whereas our study accounts for both current and past system attributes.

3   System Architecture

Figure 1 illustrates the mobile grid environment assumed in this paper. This environment consists of three parts: mobile grid networks, a traditional wired grid, and lots of mobile devices connected to a proxy. In each mobile device, the status manager monitors battery capacity and wireless signal strength between the mobile device and the access point (AP). The collected information is sent to the proxy server. Next, we focus on the proxy server, which plays an important role in our mobile grid architecture.

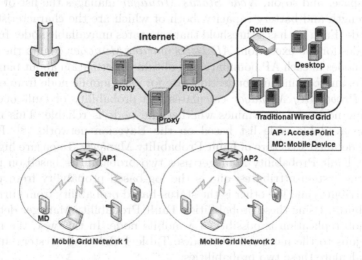

Fig. 1. The mobile grid environment

3.1 Proxy Server Structure

Figure 2 shows the proxy server structure, composed of Failure Prevention Scheduler, Task Distributor, the four managers, and Node Information Collector. In the proxy server, the four managers (Resource Information Manager, Node Status Manager, AP Information Manager, and Fault Probability Manager) are responsible for generating and maintaining a list of available nodes with the information collected from Node Information Collector. When a grid user requests a job execution, the Failure Prevention Scheduler allocates the requested job to the selected nodes from the given list. With the collected information, our scheduling scheme improves reliability and stability of job execution. *Node Information Collector* collects mobile node information and AP information, and provides the information to the four managers mentioned above.

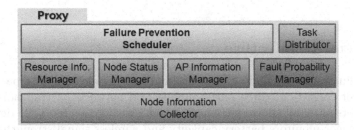

Fig. 2. The structure of Proxy Server

Resource Information Manager generate a list of CPU utilization, available memory space, and so on. *Node Status Manager* manages the list of wireless signal strength and battery capacity, both of which are the characteristics of a mobile node. Each list has a threshold that separates unavailable nodes from candidate nodes for job execution. *AP Information Manager* counts the number of mobile nodes in each AP boundary and obtains information about bandwidth, access rate, and continuous connection rate for each mobile node from each AP.

Fault Probability Manager calculates the probability of fault occurrence in a mobile node and determines whether the node is reliable. This manager makes the available node list based on the Bayesian networks [8]. Figure 3 shows the detailed structure of Fault Probability Manager. To ensure high node-reliability, Fault Probability Manager uses two probabilities based on previous and current system attributes; one is the log-based probability from previous system attributes and the other is the status-based probability from current system attributes. Using these probabilities, Fault Probability Manager determines whether job replication is possible in a mobile node. In this way, the manager allocates jobs to the more reliable nodes. Table 1 shows the system attributes used to calculate these two probabilities.

Failure Prevention Scheduler uses the information obtained from the four managers. The scheduler will be described in more detail in the next section.

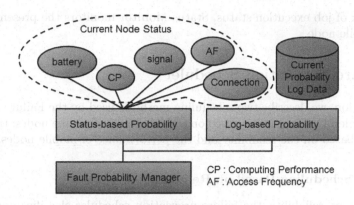

Fig. 3. Fault Probability Manager

Table 1. System Attributes

System Attribute	Property
Computing Performance (CP)	CPU usage rate, memory space
Battery	Battery capacity
Signal	Signal strength between node and AP
Frequency (AF)	Node access rate
Connection	Continuous connection rate

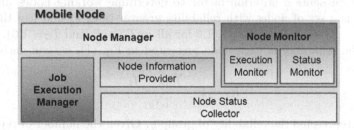

Fig. 4. The structure of a mobile node

Figure 4 shows the structure of a mobile node. In this figure, *Node Status Collector* collects the status information of a node, such as CPU utilization and memory space. *Node Information Provider* extracts resource information needed job execution using the status information collected by Node Status Collector and delivers the resource information to Node Manager. *Job Execution Manager* executes a requested job from a proxy and returns a job result to Node Manager, and then Node Manager delivers the result to the proxy. *Node Monitor* consists of Execution Monitor and Status Monitor. Execution Monitor keeps track of job execution status. Status Monitor monitors the present status of the mobile node.

4   Failure Prevention Scheduler

In this section, we describe two scheduling methods used by the Failure Prevention Scheduler. One method is based on the reliability of mobile nodes; the other method is based on the reliability and the performance of mobile nodes.

4.1   Job Scheduling Based on Reliability

Based on node reliability, the failure prevention scheduler classifies nodes into several groups and then replicates jobs to one of these groups. Let us consider reliability as the criterion to classify nodes. The reliability r_i of a node m_i is calculated by

$$r_i = 1 - f_i \tag{1}$$

where, f_i is the occurrence rate of a fault in a node m_i. It has been proven that nodes with reliability greater than 95% can feasibly deal with a fault in execution [9]. Therefore, we assume that only these nodes should participate in job execution. Let a set of these nodes be N and a number of groups be G. The node m_i is classified into one of G groups:

$$N = \{m_i | r_i \geq t, 1 \leq i \leq n\} \tag{2}$$

$$N_g = \{m_i | T_{g-1} \geq r_i \geq T_g, 1 \leq i \leq n\} \tag{3}$$

where, T represents a criterion factor to determine working nodes among all nodes. N_g is a set of nodes with reliability greater than T_g and less than T_{g-1} ($g = 1, 2, \cdots, G, 0 \leq T_{g-1} < T_g \leq 1.0$ for all g, $T_1 = T$, and $T_G = 1.0$).

Using the reliability of each node presented in Eq. (1), we can derive group reliability:

$$R_g = 1 - \frac{\sum_{i \in N_g} f_i}{|N_g|} \tag{4}$$

where, R_g represents the reliability of group g. Given the number of replicas for the last group G, C_G, we can derive the number of replicas for each group:

$$C_g^R = \frac{R_G}{R_g} \times C_G \tag{5}$$

Using Eqs. (4) and (5), the number of subjobs assigned to group g, J_g^R, is calculated by

$$J_g^R = \frac{1}{2} \times \left(\frac{R_g}{\sum_{i=1}^{G} R_i} + \frac{\frac{|N_g|}{C_g^R}}{\sum_{i=1}^{G} \frac{|N_i|}{C_i^R}} \right) \times J_{totel} \tag{6}$$

where, J_{total} represents the total number of subjobs.

4.2   Job Scheduling Based on Reliability and Performance

Job scheduling based on reliability and performance is similar to the job scheduling described in Section 4.1, except that replicas are distributed to groups considering both reliability and performance. Based on CPU utilization and available memory space, the performance of a mobile node m_i, p_i, is calculated by

$$p_i = \alpha \times (1 - CPU\_utilization) + \beta \times \frac{Availeible\_memory\_space}{Total\_memory\_space} \qquad (7)$$

where, α and β represent a weight parameter determining the importance of job execution ($\alpha + \beta = 1$). These parameters can be determined by the properties of the applications to be executed. Similar to the scheduling described in Section 4.1, this scheduling method uses only nodes with reliability greater than T (see Eq. (2)). These nodes are arranged in descending order by p_i. Thus, this job scheduling method simultaneously considers reliability and performance when a job is distributed to each group. Because mobile nodes are sorted by their performance, each group is assumed to have the same number of mobile nodes. Then, the average performance of group g, P_g, is calculated by

$$P_g = \frac{\sum_{i \in N_g} P_i}{|N_g|} \qquad (8)$$

where, N_g represents a set of nodes for group g. Given the number of replicas for the last group G, C_G, we can derive the number of replicas for each group as follows:

$$C_g^P = \frac{P_G}{P_g} \times C_G \qquad (9)$$

where, P_G and P_g represent the average performance of groups G and g, respectively ($g = 1, 2, \cdots, G$). In this equation, if all groups have similar performance, then the number of replicas assigned to each group is also similar. Otherwise, a different number of replicas is assigend to each group.

Using Eq. (9), the number of subjobs assigned to the group g, J_g^P, is calculated by

$$J_g^P = J_{total} \times C_g^P \qquad (10)$$

where, J_{total} represents total number of jobs. Equation (10) means that high performance groups have fewer jobs than low performance groups.

4.3   Scheduling Algorithm

Figure 5 describes the scheduling algorithm used for the failure prevention scheduler shown in Fig. 2. This algorithm is operated in cooperation with four managers in proxy server (Resource Information, Node Status, AP Information, and Fault Probability) and Node Information Collector.

Node Information Collector collects information from mobile nodes and AP (lines 5-14). Resource Information Manager collects and maintains the node information. Based on the information, the manager calculates p_i (lines 15-19). Node

```
 1: // MN : mobile node, AF : node access rate
 2: // Connect : continuous connection rate
 3: // AP : access point
 4: // Three managers : Resource Information, Node Status, AP Information
 5: EVENT Node Information Collector(){
 6: while information ≠ ∅ do
 7:    if (MN) then
 8:       Collect CPU, Memory, battery, and signal info;
 9:    end if
10:    if (AP) then
11:       Collect MN number, AF, and Connect info;
12:    end if
13: end while
14: }
15: EVENT Resource Information Manager (){
16:    Save CPU info and Memory info in MN;
17:    Compute p_i based on CPU info and Memory info;
18:    Order MNs by p_i;
19: }
20: EVENT Node Status Manager(){
21:    Save the wireless signal info and battery info in MN;
22: }
23: EVENT AP Information Manager(){
24:    Save the MN number, AF, and Connection info in AP;
25: }
26: EVENT Fault Probability Manager(){
27:    Compute current data through Bayesian network by three managers;
28:    New Log data = Current data + Old Log data;
29:    Save the New Log data;
30: }
31: EVENT Failure Prevention Scheduler(){
32: if scheduling based on reliability then
33:    Load data in Fault Probability Manager;
34:    Scheduling based on reliability calculated by Fault Probability Manager;
35: end if
36: if scheduling based on reliability and performance then
37:    Load data in Resource Information Manager;
38:    Load data in Fault Probability Manager;
39:    Scheduling based on reliability and performance calculated by Resource Infor-
       mation Manager and Fault Probability Manager;
40: end if
41: }
```

Fig. 5. Scheduling Algorithm

Status Manager collects the status of mobile nodes including wireless signal and battery life information (lines 20-22). AP Information Manager collects the number of mobile nodes, access rate, and connection information (lines 23-25). Fault

Probability Manager calculates the reliability of mobile nodes (lines 26-30). As shown in lines 31-41, Failure Prevention Scheduler determines job scheduling policy, which selects one of two scheduling schemes (reliability-based or reliability- and performance-based).

5 Performance Evaluation

In this section, we evaluate our scheduling algorithms and compare the performance of the algorithms with that of the random-based scheduling algorithm.

5.1 Simulation Environment

We conducted simulations with a Simgrid toolkit [10]. In the simulations, the node properties, such as job execution performance, network status, battery capacity, etc., were changed dynamically as jobs were executed. Table 2 shows the node properties used in our simulations.

Table 2. Node Properties

Attribute	Property
Job execution performance	- maintaining without any change of CPU and memory performances
Network status	- being changed as jobs are processed - checking whether the network is connected
Battery capacity	- being changed as jobs are processed - checking whether the power is on - consuming different capacity according to electrical power

In our scheduling methods, nodes are partitioned into nodes for job processing and replicas. In the scheduling method based on random mapping, nodes for a job execution are selected, and then the remaining nodes are randomly used for replicas.

Makespan is a commonly used metric to measure throughput in parallel systems. Generally, it is defined as the duration between the start time of the first job and the finish time of the last executed job [11]. For performance comparison, we use the performance improvement rate (PIR) which indicates the improvement in performance using the proposed algorithms over the baseline (algorithm based on random mapping). The PIR is defined as

$$PIR(\%) = \frac{makespan_{random} - makespan_{our}}{makespan_{random}} \times 100 \qquad (11)$$

where, $makespan_{random}$ and $makespan_{our}$ represent the makespan for random-based scheduling and for our scheduling, respectively.

5.2 Simulation Results

Before performing our simulations, we generated the reliability of the mobile nodes. Figure 6 shows the reliability distribution, in which the different numbers of nodes are sorted by reliability rank. Using this distribution, we evaluate our proposed scheduling algorithms with respect to the effect of the number of subjobs and the number of mobile nodes on the performance.

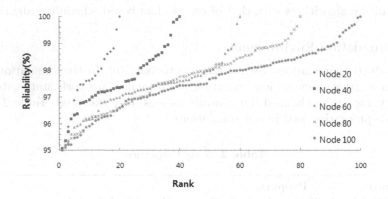

Fig. 6. Reliability distribution

Table 3 shows the simulation parameters used in our simulations. In the simulations, nodes with more than 95% reliability participated in job processing; i.e., T is set to 0.95. For simulation simplicity, we also assumed that the number of groups (G) was 2. So, the threshold value used to divide two groups (T_1) was set to 0.98. The number of replicas (C_G) used was three and five, respectively.

Table 3. Simulation parameters

Parameter descriptions	Values
Criterion to determine working nodes (T)	0.95
Number of groups (G)	2
Group threshold (T_1)	0.98
Number of replicas (C_G)	3, 5

Figure 7 shows the effect of our scheduling algorithms on PIR when three replicas were used for a job. Figure 7(a) indicates simulation results for a varying number of mobile nodes and a fixed number of subjobs. Figure 7(b) indicates simulation results for a fixed number of mobile nodes and a varying number of subjobs.

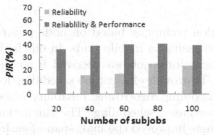

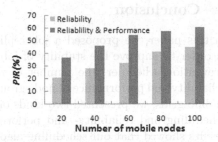

(a) PIR according to the number of sub-jobs

(b) PIR according to the number of mobile nodes

Fig. 7. The number of replicas is three

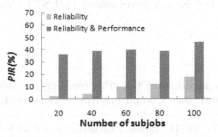

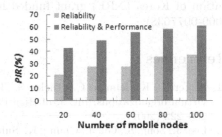

(a) PIR according to the number of sub-jobs

(b) PIR according to the number of mobile nodes

Fig. 8. The number of replicas is five

From this figure, we can see that our scheduling algorithms (the reliability-based scheduling and the reliability- and performance-based scheduling) improve performance by averages of 16% and 39%, respectively, over random-based scheduling. This performance improvement results from the consideration of node reliability and performance in the selection of node for job processing. As for the performance comparison of our scheduling algorithms, the reliability- and performance-based scheduling algorithm has higher performance than the reliability-based scheduling algorithm. This result is unsurprising, because the reliability- and performance-based scheduling algorithm considers both the reliability and the performance of nodes in the process of node selection.

Figure 8 shows the PIR when five replicas for a job were used in simulation. The results shown in Fig. 8 exhibit a trend similar to that in Fig. 7, except for the replicas used. In conclusion, we can see from the results of Figs. 7 and 8 that our job scheduling method based on reliability and performance is much better than other job scheduling algorithms, regardless of the number of replicas.

6 Conclusion

In this paper, we proposed a job replication technique based on node groups in order to improve the stability of job processing in mobile grids. In our fault prevention scheduler, the number of replicas for a job was derived from the reliability and performance of node groups. To provide efficient job scheduling for mobile grids, we presented two kinds of scheduling algorithms: reliability-based scheduling and reliability- and performance-based scheduling. The simulation results showed that our scheduling algorithms improved the makespan of entire jobs compared to the random-based scheduling algorithm. In the future, we plan to improve our scheduling algorithms by deriving optimal number of replicas for various mobile grid environments.

Acknowledgments. This work was supported by the National Research Foundation of Korea (NRF) grant funded by the Korea government (MEST) (No. 2009-0077638).

References

1. Foster, I., Kesselman, C., Tueke, S.: The anatomy of the grid: enabling scalable virtual organizations. Int. J. of High Performance Computing Applications 15(3), 200–222 (2001)
2. Lee, J., Song, S., Gil, J., Chung, K., Suh, T., Yu, H.: Balanced scheduling algorithm considering availability in mobile grid. In: Abdennadher, N., Petcu, D. (eds.) GPC 2009. LNCS, vol. 5529, pp. 211–222. Springer, Heidelberg (2009)
3. Litke, A., Halkos, D., Tserpes, K., Kyriazis, D., Varvarigou, T.: Fault tolerant and prioritized scheduling in OGSA-based mobile grids. Concurr. Comput.: Pract. Exper. 21(4), 533–556 (2009)
4. Forman, G., Zahorjan, J.: The challenges of mobile computing. IEEE Computer 27(4), 38–47 (1994)
5. Messig, M., Goscinski, A.: Autonomic system management in mobile grid environments, pp. 49–58. Australian Computer Society (2007)
6. Litke, A., Skoutas, D., Tserpes, K., Varvarigou, T.: Efficient task replication and management for adaptive fault tolerance in mobile grid environments. Future Generation Computer Systems 23(2), 163–178 (2007)
7. Gomes, A.T.A., Ziviani, A., Lima, L.S., Endler, M.: DICHOTOMY: A resource discovery and scheduling protocol for multihop ad hoc mobile grids. In: Proc. of 7th IEEE Int. Symp. on Cluster Computing and the Grid, pp. 719–724 (2007)
8. Yang, C., Huang, C., Hsiao, T.: A data grid file replication maintenance strategy using bayesian networks. In: Proc. of the 2008 Eighth Int. Conf. on Intelligent Systems Design and Applications, vol. 1, pp. 456–461 (2008)
9. Zhang, Y., Mandal, A., Koelbel, C., Cooper, K.: Combined fault tolerance and scheduling techniques for workflow applications on computational grids. In: Proc. of 9th IEEE Int. Symp. on Cluster Computing and the Grid, pp. 244–251 (2009)
10. Casanova, H.: Simgrid: A toolkit for the simulation of application scheduling. In: Proc. of 1st IEEE/ACM Int. Symp. on Cluster Computing and the Grid, pp. 430–437 (2001)
11. Sinnen, O.: Task scheduling for parallel systems. John Wiley, Chichester (2007)

A Matrix Scheduling Strategy with Multi-QoS Constraints in Computational Grid

Ding Ding, Siwei Luo, and Zhan Gao

Beijing Jiaotong University, Beijing 100044, China
dding@bjtu.edu.cn

Abstract. Focusing on the fact that the tasks involved in a grid environment may require quite different kinds of QoS and have various preferences on each QoS, a combination of metrics and policies is adopted to model QoS demands. Based on this taxonomy of QoS specifications, a Multiple Dimensional QoS constrained Matrix Scheduling Strategy(MDQS-MSS) is proposed in which three matrices are used to present the requirements of tasks, the capabilities of resources and the weight of QoS respectively. As a new approach in task scheduling with multi-QoS constraints, MDQS-MSS results in a reduction of time complexity compared with many traditional strategies. It is also proved via simulations that this matrix scheduling policy is much more efficient since it can not only satisfy the diverse requirements of QoS with different preference from the user perspectives, but also improve the resource utilization rate from the system perspectives.

1 Introduction

As an integrated computing and collaborative environment[1], the grid involves the interaction of many human players such as end-users and resources managers which usually have quite different goals, objectives and demand patterns. Thus, it is important for the grid to support scheduling strategy in accordance with multi-QoS policy[2].

In fact, since the QoS demands are always independent with each other, even conflict, multi-QoS constrained task scheduling is proven to be NP-hard and difficult to obtain the optimization[3]. At present, most of the solutions construct the final schemes by adopting heuristics based on different QoS models. In [4], QoS for network is integrated to make a better match among different level of QoS request/supply. [5] provides a flexible way of QoS based scheduling in which makespan and service ratio can be traded off by adjusting the preference factor in a local objective function. [6] defines another three QoS parameters, cost, deadline and reliability, with utility function for each dimension and uses a market model to maximize the global utility. [7,8] formulate the QoS based scheduling problem by using utility and penalty functions from both the user's perspective and the system's perspective. [9] develops a model with multi-QoS constraints and compares five scheduling heuristics based on that model. The multiobjective task scheduling problem with multi-QoS constraints is transformed to the

R.-S. Chang et al. (Eds.): GPC 2010, LNCS 6104, pp. 59–68, 2010.
© Springer-Verlag Berlin Heidelberg 2010

general multiobjective combinatorial problem in [10] and an evolutionary algorithm is put forward to solve it. All of the above heuristics consider the QoS based scheduling problem from different points of view besides makespan. However, some of them concentrate solely on different QoS demands and neglect the various preferences on each QoS, while some of them focus on the needs of the end-users and ignore the rule of fully utilizing the spare resource in grid.

In this paper, the QoS demands are defined from both metrics and policies and a multiple dimensional QoS constrained matrix scheduling strategy(MDQS-MSS) is proposed on top of this definition. MDQS-MSS provides a new approach in task scheduling in which matrix is used to present the requirements of tasks and the capabilities of machines; and to build the mapping between tasks and machines accordingly. Moreover, the algorithm formulates the QoS-based scheduling problem from two different perspectives, namely the user and the system perspectives, which is just in compliance with the rule of fully utilizing the spare resources in grid.

2   Grid Scheduling Model

The computational grid system considered in this study is assumed to be composed of k available data repositories, denoted by $S=\{s_1, s_2, \ldots, s_k\}$ and n heterogeneous machines, denoted by $M=\{m_1, m_2, \ldots, m_n\}$. Data repositories, with no data transfer between each other, can transmit data to any of the machine. But the cost of data transfer may vary a lot when a task is assigned to different machines.

In our model, task executing across different machines is out of consideration. The total set of tasks is composed of m meta-task $T=\{t_1, t_2, \ldots, t_m\}$ which is defined as a collection of independent tasks without data dependencies. For each task t_i, the following parameters are defined:

- ET_{ij}: the expected execution time of task t_i on machine m_j, which is defined as the amount of time taken by m_j to execute t_i given that m_j has no load when t_i is assigned.
- CT_{ij}: the expected completion time of task t_i on machine m_j, which is defined as the wall-clock time at which m_j completes t_i.
- $StartT_j$: the earliest available time of machine m_j.
- DI_i: the size of input for task t_i.
- DO_i: the size of output for task t_i.
- BW_{kj}: the bandwidth between data repository s_k and machine m_j.

Obviously, if the input of task t_i is already stored in data repository s_k and the output of task t_i will be transmitted to data repository s_l, CT_{ij} can be denoted as (1).

$$CT_{ij} = ET_{ij} + \frac{DI_i}{BW_{kj}} + \frac{DO_i}{BW_{lj}} + StartT_j \tag{1}$$

3   Problem Formulation

This paper is devoted to scheduling a collection of independent tasks with multi-QoS constraints onto a heterogeneous grid. By *heterogeneous* we mean that the resources may have not only various architectures and operating systems, but also quite different computational abilities and authorization mechanisms. Within such an environment, the scheduling algorithms must take into account the QoS desired by tasks and the ability of system resources to provide it.

3.1   QoS Modeling

In this paper, QoS is specified as a combination of metrics and policies. QoS metrics are used to specify performance parameters and have been considered for this study are *timeliness, reliability, security* and *data accuracy.*

- **Timeliness:** Timeliness defines a class of metrics that measure time related entities. Several timeliness parameters are provided for performing a given piece of work[11]. In this study, the deadline of a task is assumed to be one of the QoS requirements. Without loss of generality, the timeliness parameter of a machine is defined as the actual completion time of task running on it.
- **Reliability:** A long-time running task may experience failures during its execution, resulting in the wasting of system resources and poor overall performance. The reliability of a task is defined to be the probability that task can be completed successfully. The reliability of a machine is defined to be the failure rate in unit time.
- **Security:** Each user may require different levels of security for their task and data. The security of a task is defined to be the security level it needs and the security of a machine is defined to be the security level it can provide.
- **Data accuracy:** Due to the finite length of data representation, a task which involves floating-point arithmetic operations executing on a machine is always subject to *roundoff errors*. The data accuracy of a task is defined to be the level of data accuracy it needs and the data accuracy of a machine is defined to be the level of data accuracy it can provide.

QoS policies, including *hard, soft* and *best effort*, behave as the level of service. They do work on all above QoS metrics. Hard QoS indicates the most critical requirements and must be served during the task scheduling; otherwise the scheduling would be considered as invalid. Soft QoS is less critical but it would maximize the scheduling performance when it's served. Task scheduling would NOT be treated as invalid but less productive even if it could NOT be satisfied. Best effort QoS is unimportant or unnecessary. However, it would be more valuable when this kind of QoS is served.

3.2   Problem Definition

In our framework of QoS-based scheduling, it's necessary that all tasks submit the description of their multi-QoS requirements and all resources (machines here) provide the description of multi-QoS they can offer. Let d denote the number of QoS requirements. Let Q_i^j be either a finite or an infinite set of QoS choices for the jth QoS dimension of t_i and $q_i^j \in Q_i^j$ denote a QoS choices in the jth QoS dimension of t_i. Then, $Q_i = Q_i^1 \times Q_i^2 \times Q_i^3 \ldots \times Q_i^d$ defines a d dimensional space of the QoS choices of t_i and a point in this space is given by $q_i = (q_i^1, q_i^2, q_i^3, \ldots, q_i^d) \in Q_i$. In this study, d is fixed to four and timeliness, reliability, security and data accuracy would be one of the QoS dimensions according to the QoS model in 3.1.

Definition 1. *Task's Requirement Matrix*

$$TR_{m \times 4} = \begin{pmatrix} tr_{11} & tr_{12} & tr_{13} & tr_{14} \\ \vdots & & \ddots & \vdots \\ tr_{m1} & tr_{m2} & tr_{m3} & tr_{m4} \end{pmatrix} = \begin{pmatrix} TR_1 \\ TR_2 \\ \ldots \\ TR_m \end{pmatrix}$$

Definition 2. *Machine's Capability Matrix*

$$MC_{n \times 4} = \begin{pmatrix} mc_{11} & mc_{12} & mc_{13} & mc_{14} \\ \vdots & & \ddots & \vdots \\ mc_{n1} & mc_{n2} & mc_{n3} & mc_{n4} \end{pmatrix} = \begin{pmatrix} MC_1 \\ MC_2 \\ \ldots \\ MC_n \end{pmatrix}$$

Definition 3. *User's Preference Matrix*

$$UP_{m \times 4} = \begin{pmatrix} up_{11} & up_{12} & up_{13} & up_{14} \\ \vdots & & \ddots & \vdots \\ up_{m1} & up_{m2} & up_{m3} & up_{m4} \end{pmatrix} = \begin{pmatrix} UP_1 \\ UP_2 \\ \ldots \\ UP_m \end{pmatrix}$$

Task's requirement matrix and Machine's capability matrix describes the QoS requirements of each task and the capability of each machine on timeliness, reliability, security and data accuracy respectively. User's preference matrix indicates the degree of each user's preference on these four QoS dimensions. The last matrix is the basis of our task scheduling strategy.

4 QoS Driven Scheduling Algorithm

4.1 Multiple Dimensional QoS Constrained Matrix Scheduling Strategy

Details of MDQS-MSS are shown in Figure 1.

The overall scheduling is accomplished under the control of a for loop in which each task is processed in each round. In the 2nd step of the algorithm, a difference matrix, which is referred as $MC'_{n \times 4}$, is calculated to evaluate the gap between the requirements of current task and the capabilities of each machine. Since the negative of task's completion time is saved in task's requirement matrix and machine's capability matrix, the element of $MC'_{n \times 4}$ will be positive as long as

1. for $i:=1$ to m do

2. $MC'_{n \times 4} = \begin{pmatrix} MC_1 \\ MC_2 \\ ... \\ MC_n \end{pmatrix}_{n \times 4} - \begin{pmatrix} TR_i \\ TR_i \\ ... \\ TR_i \end{pmatrix}_{n \times 4}$

3.   for $j:=1$ to n do

4.   for $k:=1$ to 4 do

5.   if $up_{ik}=$'hard' and $mc'_{jk} < 0$ then $MC'_j=0$

6.   if $MC'=0$ then $T \leftarrow T\text{-}\{t_i\}$

7.   if there is only one none-zero row MC'_j in MC' then

8.   assign t_i to the machine m_j

9. $StartT_j = StartT_j + CT_{ij}$

10. $T \leftarrow T\text{-}\{t_i\}$

11.   endif

12.   if there are multiple none-zero rows in MC' then

13.   for $j:=1$ to n do

14.   if $MC'_j \neq 0$ then

15.   add the maximum value in its column to the absolute of each negative element

16. $Func(m_j) = \sum_{k=1}^{4} \frac{1}{mc'_{jk}} \times up_{ik}$

17.   endif

18. $Func_{max} = \max[Func(m_1), Func(m_2)...Func(m_n)]$

19.   assign t_i to the machine m_{max}

20. $StartT_{max} = StartT_{max} + CT_{imax}$

21. $T \leftarrow T\text{-}\{t_i\}$

22.   endif

23. endfor

Fig. 1. Multiple dimensional QoS constrained matrix scheduling strategy

the machine could meet the task's QoS demands. The possible negative elements are processed in step 3 to step 5. If any of negative elements is linked with hard QoS, which must be served according to the definition in section 3.1, the elements of the whole row in $MC'_{n \times 4}$ are forced to zero to indicate that this machine is NOT able to serve the QoS demands of current task.

From step 6 to step 22, the post-processed difference matrix $MC'_{n \times 4}$ is gone through case by case. In the worst case, $MC'_{n \times 4}$ is equal to 0, which indicates no available machine, and the task would be removed from the task set T directly in step 6; When there is only one none-zero row in $MC'_{n \times 4}$, the task is assigned to that unique machine in step 7 to step 11 to complete the task as far as possible. Then, the task will also be removed from the task set T and the start execution time in that machine is updated accordingly; When there are multiple none-zero rows in $MC'_{n \times 4}$, which indicate more than one machine could meet the QoS demands of current task, step 12 to step 22 are used to handle those cases by picking up the machine with "smallest" value in the difference matrix to improve scheduling performance. It is motivated by the fact that the "smaller" the value is, the closer the machine's capability and the task's demand is. This allocation mechanism could avoid the waste of resources by eliminating the occupation of a task with low QoS demands on the machine with high capabilities.

Specifically, the negative elements left in $MC'_{n \times 4}$ are processed in step 15. Although those negative elements are not hard QoS and not necessary to satisfy, they are un-served QoS demands after all. When there exists any machine that could meet those demands (positive element in difference matrix), priority should be given. In this case, the absolute of the negative element plus the maximum value in its column is calculated to make the post-processed value bigger than any existing positive value, ensuring that the original positive element is still with higher priority than the original negative element. This also works on the situation where there is more than one negative element, since the negative element with smaller absolute value will still be given more possibility to be selected. After that, the reciprocal of the post-processed element is calculated and multiplied by the corresponding element in user's preference matrix, which represents different preferences on each QoS of that task, i.e weight of QoS. Since the operation of reciprocal makes a smaller element bigger, and the different QoS in user's preference matrix is granted with different weight according to their level(In this paper, hard QoS, soft QoS and best-effort QoS are granted with a value of 1, 0.5 and 0.1 respectively), the above processing assures that the multiplied element for hard QoS produces much bigger gap than that for soft QoS, and similarly, the multiplied element for soft QoS produces much bigger gap than that for best-effort QoS. Finally, the following formula $Func(m_j) = \sum_{k=1}^{4} \frac{1}{mc'_{jk}} \times up_{ik}$ is used to calculate the utility of all the machines that could meet the QoS demands. And the machine with maximum utility will be picked up for the current task. Then, the task is removed from the task set T and the start execution time of allocated machine is updated accordingly.

4.2   Efficiency Analysis

In this matrix scheduling strategy, each task will be mapped to the machine with maximum utility via a for loop. And all of the four dimensional performance of each machine will be processed and compared in each iteration of the for loop. As a result, the number of tasks, the number of machines, as well as the number of QoS dimensions are all closely related to our strategy. Actually, the time complexity of MDQS-MSS is $O(4mn)$ which is less than the time complexity of most of the existing traditional algorithms($O(mmn)$) [12]. Moreover, MDQS-MSS is much simpler since it does not touch any other factors such as the number of iterations which is always used in GA.

5   Simulations

In our experimental testing, the total set of tasks is 1000 and the number of data repositories is fixed to 5. Each task randomly depends on a data repository to get input files and transmit output to a given data repository. Suppose that the size of each input and output file is known a-priori.

5.1 QoS Setting

Both the task and the machine are needed to be associated with four QoS dimensions, namely *timeliness*, *reliability*, *security* and *data accuracy*.

Let V_S denote the schedule length of the resulting task assignment, *rand* be a function which generates a uniformly distributed random number between 0 and 1, and V_D be a variable that controls the process of assigning deadlines to tasks. Then, the soft or hard deadline of task t_i is calculated as $D_i = (0.5 + V_D \times rand)V_S$. The soft or hard QoS requirement of task t_i in the reliability dimension is defined as $R_i = (0.5 + 0.5 \times rand)e^{-0.0001 V_S}$. Furthermore, each task is assigned a security level (poor, low, medium, or high) in random, poor in default and a data accuracy level (16, 32, 64, or 128) in random, 16 in default.

The completion time of task on machine can be calculated from (1) in which the expected execution time of task on machine is generated using the method proposed in [13], where *utask=umach=*100 and both *Vtask* and *Vmach* are taken to be 1.0 for high task and high machine heterogeneity. The failure rate of a machine is assumed to be uniformly distributed between 0.00005 and 0.0015 failures per unit time. Each machine is randomly associated with a security level (poor, low, medium, or high) and a data accuracy level(16, 32, 64, or 128).

For each QoS dimension of task, a service type is chosen as follows: A random number uniformly distributed between 0 and 1 is generated. If the number is less than $0.25V_Q$, the service type is set to hard. Otherwise, a second random number is generated. If this number is less than 0.5, the service type is set to soft. Otherwise, it is set to best-effort. Variable V_Q is used to control the process of choosing service types, where $1 \leq V_Q \leq 4$ (4 indicates highest probability of choosing the service type of a QoS dimension as hard).

5.2 Results

The simulations are carried out by fixing the value of V_Q to 2 to give a relatively uniform of three service type and then the performance of MDQS-MSS is compared with QoS-Min-min[4] and QoS-Sufferage[14]. The choosing of these two heuristics simply because they are also QoS-based strategies and outperformed others. For each scenario, all the results are the average value of 10 independent experiments.

Number of satisfied tasks. It can be seen from Figure 2, MDQS-MSS satisfies maximum number of tasks. It is benefited from the user's preference matrix since the tasks with hard QoS requirements are provided with the highest preference and will be satisfied first. For soft QoS and best-effort QoS, it will still produce some utility for its users even if they are not satisfied in defined range. QoS-Sufferage satisfied less number of tasks because tasks are scheduled based on the sufferage, which is independent of the service-type of the QoS dimensions. When

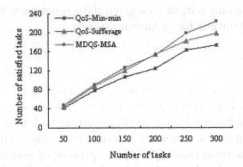

Fig. 2. Comparison on number of satisfied tasks

the machine which minimizes completion time for a task is assigned to a task
with higher sufferage value, the task has to wait for an entire cycle before it is
scheduled again. This may cause it to miss its deadline. QoS-Min-min performs
the worst for just concerning on the QoS requirements of data transfer.

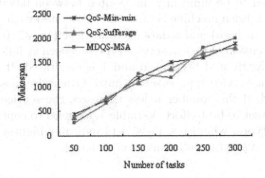

Fig. 3. Comparison on makespan

Makespan. As shown in Figure 3, none of the three heuristics perform a pure
liner increase in makespan with the number of tasks increased from 50 to 300.
The reason is that they all take other QoS demands into consideration as well as
completion time. Of these three heuristics, QoS-Sufferage provides the shortest
makespan since it tries to schedule tasks with more urgency in nature, while
QoS-Min-min and MDQS-MSS show a relatively longer makespan than QoS-
Sufferage. Specially, MDQS-MSS even produces a jumped makespan. That is
because all the hard QoS demands in all QoS dimensions of MDQS-MSS must
be satisfied without any exception and some of the machines in our highly heterogeneous simulated environment have too limited capability to be capable for
any task. Of course, the situation could be improved by the increment of machines. On the other hand, MDQS-MSS can also reduce the makespan in some

degree by choosing the machine with minimum completion time when more than one machines produce the same utility.

Resource utilization rate. Resource utilization rate, which is defined to be the ratio of the total load of used resource to the total load of available resource, is the most crucial indicator to measure the efficiency of task scheduling from the system point of view. Figure 4 shows that MDQS-MSS can provide more than 5% to 10% of resource utilization rate than both QoS-Min-Min and QoS-Sufferage. That is because MDQS-MSS can avoid assigning a higher performance resource to a lower QoS demand by picking up the appropriate resource with closest matching with QoS demands, but not the resource with best performance. The improvement of resource utilization rate is an important advantage of MDQS-MSS since it perfectly complied with the rule of fully utilizing the spare resources in grid.

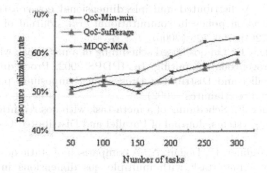

Fig. 4. Comparison on resource utilization rate

6   Conclusions

Task scheduling in grid environments is much more challenging because grid resources usually have rich diversity and the tasks involved in such environments usually have quite different QoS with various preferences. In this paper, a QoS model is made with the consideration of both grid resources and tasks, and a Multiple Dimensional QoS constrained Matrix Scheduling Strategy (MDQS-MSS) is proposed based on this model. MDQS-MSS provides a new approach in task scheduling with multi-QoS constraints in which three matrices are used to present the requirements of tasks, the capabilities of grid resources and the weight of QoS respectively. What is more important, this matrix scheduling algorithm can not only meet users' QoS requirements, but also utilize the system resources more efficiently. Simulation results confirm that MDQS-MSS is a simple policy with time complexity of $O(4mn)$ and can provide a better performance at number of satisfied tasks, makespan and resource utilization rate.

References

1. Foster, I., Kesselman, C.: The grid2: blueprint for a new computing infrastructure. Morgan Kaufmann Publishers, San Francisco (2004)
2. Kurowski, K., Nabrzyski, J., Pukacki, J.: User preference driven multiobjective resource management in grid environments. In: CCGRID 2001: Proceedings of the 1st IEEE/ACM International Symposium on Cluster Computing and the Grid, pp. 114–121. IEEE Computer Society, Los Alamitos (2001)
3. Maheswaran, M., Ali, S., Siegel, H.J., Hensgen, D., Freund, R.F.: Dynamic mapping of a class of independent tasks onto heterogeneous computing systems. Journal of Parallel and Distributed Computing 59(2), 107–131 (1999)
4. He, X.S., Sun, X.H., von Laszewski, G.: Qos guided min-min heuristic for grid task scheduling. The Journal of Computer Science and Technology 18(4), 442–451 (2003)
5. Ding, D., Luo, S.W., Gao, Z.: An object-adjustable heuristic scheduling strategy in grid environments. Journal of Computer Research and Development 44(9), 1572–1578 (2007)
6. Li, C.L., Li, L.Y.: A distributed multiple dimensional qos constrained resource scheduling optimization policy in computational grid. Journal of Computer and System Sciences 72(4), 706–726 (2006)
7. Dogan, A., Özgüner, F.: On qos-based scheduling of a meta-task with multiple qos demands in heterogeneous computing. In: IPDPS 2002: Proceedings of the 16th International Parallel and Distributed Processing Symposium, pp. 50–55. IEEE Computer Society, Los Alamitos (2002)
8. Dogan, A., Özgüner, F.: Scheduling of a meta-task with qos requirments in heterogeneous computing systems. Journal of Parallel and Distributed Computing 66(2), 181–196 (2006)
9. Golconda, K.S., Özgüner, F., Dogan, A.: A comparison of static qos-based scheduling heuristics for a meta-task with multiple qos dimensions in heterogeneous computing. In: IPDPS 2004: Proceedings of the 18th International Parallel and Distributed Processing Symposium. IEEE Computer Society Press, Los Alamitos (2004)
10. Zhang, W.Z., Hu, M.Z., Zhang, H.: A multiobjective evolutionary algorithm for grid job scheduling of multi-qos contraints. Journal of Computer Research and Development 43(11), 1855–1862 (2006)
11. Sabata, B., Chatterjee, S., et al.: Taxonomy for qos specifications. In: WORDS 1997: Proceedings of the 3rd International Workshop on Object-Oriented Real-Time Dependable Systems, pp. 97–107. IEEE Computer Society, Los Alamitos (1997)
12. Braun, T.D., Siegel, H.J., Beck, N., Bölöni, L.L., Maheswaran, M., Reuther, A.I., Robertson, J.P., Theys, M.D., Yao, B., Hensgen, D., Freund, R.F.: A comparison of eleven static heuristics for mapping a class of independent tasks onto heterogeneous distributed computing systems. Journal of Parallel and Distributed Computing 61(6), 810–837 (2001)
13. Ali, S., Siegel, H.J., Maheswaran, M., Ali, S., Hensgen, D.: Task execution time modeling for heterogeneous computing systems. In: HCW 2000: Proceedings of the 9th Heterogeneous Computing Workshop, Washington, DC, USA, pp. 185–199. IEEE Computer Society, Los Alamitos (2000)
14. Weng, C.L.: Study on economic-based resource management and scheduling strategy in the grid environment. PhD thesis, Shanghai Jiaotong University (2004)

The Mini-Grid Framework: Application Programming Support for Ad-Hoc, Peer-to-Peer Volunteer Grids

Jakob E. Bardram and Neelanarayanan Venkataraman

IT University of Copenhagen
Rued Langgaards Vej 7, DK-2300 Copenhagen S, Denmark
{bardram,nnve}@itu.dk

Abstract. Biological scientists work with bioinformatics algorithms that are either computational or data intensive in nature. Distributed platforms such as Grids and Peer-to-Peer (P2P) networks can be used for such algorithms. Classical Grid Computing platforms are available only to a restricted group of biologist, since they are expensive, and require skilled professionals for deployment and maintenance. Projects deployed using volunteer computing systems require a high visibility. The alternative, peer-to-peer platform is mainly used for sharing data. This paper presents the Mini-Grid Framework, a P2P infrastructure and programming framework for distribution of computational tasks like bioinformatics algorithm. The framework contributes with concepts and technologies for minimal configuration by non-technical end-users, a 'resource-push' auction approach for dynamic task distribution, and context modeling of tasks and resources in order to handle volatile execution environment. The efficiency of the infrastructure has been evaluated using experiments.

1 Introduction

The "Grid" refers to the vision of a hardware and software infrastructure providing dependable, consistent, fast, and inexpensive access to high-end computational capabilities [1]. Such a platform has great potential impact for many disciplines, such as bioinformatics. Generally, grid computing platforms can be classified into two main categories; classic high-end grids and volunteer computing grids [2]. Classical grids provide access to large-scale, intra-and-inter institutional high capacity resources such as clusters or multiprocessors [1, 3]. However, installing, configuring and customizing such solutions require high technical knowledge and dedicated hardware and software resources. For these reasons, the deployment and operational cost of such systems are substantial, which prevents its adoption and direct use by non-technical users, such as biological researchers.

Volunteer computing systems, on the other hand, allow formation of parallel computing networks by enabling ordinary Internet users to share their computer's idle processing power [4, 5]. Such systems require setting up a centralized control system responsible for managing the contributed clients, who in turn periodically request work from a central server. Volunteer computing is highly

R.-S. Chang et al. (Eds.): GPC 2010, LNCS 6104, pp. 69–80, 2010.

asymmetric; it is a 'master-slave' architecture in which volunteers supply computing resource but can not consume. Public outreach and incentive structures (like high-score competitions) play a significant role in attracting volunteers.

The current approaches to grid computing is, as such, very centralized both technically and in use. Only a relatively few dedicated scientists use the classic grids like Globus and in volunteering grids, setting up projects is rather centralized and require significant technical skills and effort. Our work builds on creating support for bioinformatics analysis in biology laboratories. In this setting we would like to support biologists to utilize available computational resources on an ad-hoc basis. The main challenges in this setting is to support users with no technical knowledge to perform all the tasks involved in grid computing, i.e. locating available resources, distributing tasks and data, monitor progress, intervene if necessary, and to recollect the results for further use. And we want to do this on the available resource infrastructure, like the desktop and laptop PCs in the lab. Compared to existing approaches to grid technology, this kind of scenarios put up requirements for supporting:

- Ease of deployment and management of the infrastructure.
- Dynamic peer-to-peer resource discovery.
- Encapsulating the context of the resources and users in resource modeling.
- Dynamic context-aware task distribution and scheduling.

This paper presents the Mini-Grid Framework, which is a programming API and runtime infrastructure enabling the formation of ad-hoc "mini-grids" in a local network environment. The main benefit of such an infrastructure is that it does not require any configuration or management overhead; a user submitting a job simply exploits the devices visible nearby at the moment. This infrastructure is an important step in the direction of allowing non-technical scientists – like biologists – to interactively use a grid in their daily work.

2   Related Work

Large-scale grids often build on the Globus Toolkit [3], deliver high-performance computational power to a restricted community with a specific goal, for example, TeraGrid[1]. However, installing, configuring, and customizing Globus middleware requires a highly skilled support team, such as the London e-Science Centre[2] or the Enabling Grids for E-science project[3]. Further, Globus based infrastructure requires third party resource brokers or meta-schedulers for task distribution and follows a hierarchical client-server model for scaling. Participating in grid projects involves time consuming networking and training processes.

Volunteer or Desktop Grids are designed to distribute computational tasks between desktop computers. Historically, the Condor project [4] pioneered using the idle time of organizational workstations to do parallel computing. Condor [6], based on a master-slave architecture, has a centralized scheduling model

---

[1] www.teragrid.org
[2] www.lesc.imperial.ac.uk
[3] www.eu-egee.org

and file-based configuration management. Condor discovers resources by advertisements [7] containing semi-structured data model – attribute/expression pairs which lack expressiveness – describing their capabilities.

The volunteer grids, e.g., the Berkeley Open Infrastructure for Network Computing (BOINC) [5, 8] is composed of a central scheduling server and a number of clients installed on the volunteers' machines. The client periodically contacts the server to report its availability and get workload. BOINC requires a fixed and static set of data servers deployed centrally that need to be maintained by each project team. Further, creating a volunteer computing application involves the process of obtaining and retaining volunteers, setting up high-profile initiatives like the the World Community Grid[4]. Other desktop grid technologies exists, like the Minimal Invasive Grid [9], and XtremWeb [10]. Commercial desktop grids, like Apple's Xgrid [11], uses similar centralized schedulers and controllers. All of these desktop grids are, however, using a client-server architecture consisting of a set of servers for project hosting, scheduling, and data management, and a set of clients which executes the workload.

Peer-to-Peer Grids distribute computation in a peer-to-peer fashion. For example, the OurGrid project uses a peer-to-peer topology between different laboratories [12]. Various protocols for supporting P2P service discovery (e.g. Gridnut [13] and GridSearch [14]) and P2P resource discovery [15] has been proposed. Organizing Condor pools in P2P network, requiring no central coordination, has been proposed in [16]. XtremWeb [17] envisages the use of peer-to-peer network for building volunteer computing platform.

Our framework having the ability to adapt their surroundings – context awareness, falls within the P2P Grid category, but has a different focus; instead of supporting inter-lab P2P grids, we are targeting *intra-lab* P2P grids – i.e. supporting grids amongst desktop computers inside a lab. Moreover, we target a very volatile and ad-hoc nature of grid resources, including laptops which frequently enters and leave a network. The terms "ad hoc" and "volatile" refers to the nature of virtual organizations that can be formed by the framework. We use a 'resource-push' approach for task distribution rather than complex resource discovery mechanism used in current P2P grids.

Although we adopt a market-oriented resource management system in our auctioning system, this is merely for allocating tasks to different resource based on their capabilities. Overall, our approach is oriented towards 'social computing' that enables equal sharing resource and collaboration. This is in contrast to the 'traditional' approach to market-oriented resource sharing in e.g. the Computational Clouds.

3   The Mini-Grid Framework

The Mini-Grid Framework is a runtime infrastructure and programming API for creating and running such mini-grids. This section provides an overview of our framework, including a description of its architecture, its auction based task

---

[4] www.worldcommunitygrid.org

distribution and resource discovery, its context modeling of resources and tasks, and its extension points for specializing its behavior.

3.1   Architecture

A conceptual illustration of the Mini-Grid Framework is shown in Fig. 1. The main components are *Resource Providers* donating computational power, *Resource Consumers* using computational power, and the *TaskBus* responsible for distributing tasks and control information. A device participating in the mini-grid can be a Resource Provider, or a Resource Consumer, or both.

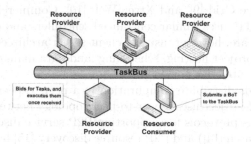

Fig. 1. A conceptual model of the Mini-Grid Architecture including the TaksBus and Resource Consumers and Resource Providers

As shown in Fig. 2, the Resource Consumer has three components; *Submitter*, *TaskBus*, and *Auctioneer*. Any Bag-of-Tasks (BoT) application interested in utilizing the infrastructure submits the tasks to the Submitter along with maximum life time of the task, called 'Time-To-Live' (TTL). TTL is a deadline fixed by the application within which it expects the results of the task. The business logic of a task is encapsulated in the execute method of the task. We assume that the application using the infrastructure does not know the execution time of a task in advance. The task include a *TaskContext* description detailing the requirements for the target software and hardware. The TaskBus is used to distribute tasks and results. Collection of bids in the auction process is delegated to an Auctioneer class that implements the auction strategy. The Auctioneer uses BidEvaluator to evaluated the submitted bids. The task distribution protocol is detailed in Section 3.2.

As shown in Fig. 3, the Resource Provider has five components; *Executor*, *TaskExecutor*, *Bidder*, *ResourceContext*, and the *TaskBus*. The Executor is responsible for managing the Resource Provider, to listen to task announcements, and using the Bidder to bid for tasks. The ResourceContext is responsible for checking if a task can be executed on this host and providing information for computing a Bid. The TaskExecutor is responsible for the execution of a task.

By extending the framework, the application developer can specify different types of bids suitable for his application. Bids can, for example, be calculated based on the speed of a host, or its level of security. The resource provider

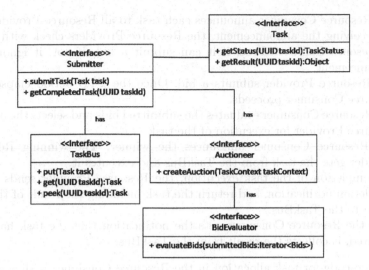

Fig. 2. Resource Consumer's Components

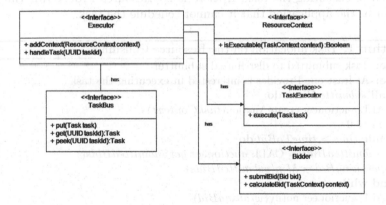

Fig. 3. Resource Provider's Components

computes the bid value by using the information provided by the ResourceContext. During the auction process, only resources that are currently participating in the mini-grid environment receive task requests and can submit bids. Thus it eliminates the need for a separate resource discovery mechanism.

3.2 Task Distribution Protocol

The Mini-Grid task distribution protocol is based on auctions. A constant named Time-to-Bid (TTB) specify the time that Resource Providers have to submit their bids. Task distribution involves 6+2 steps:

1. A BoT application generates tasks with a TaskContext description, and submits them to the Resource Consumer.

2. The Resource Consumer announces each task to all Resource Providers.
3. On receiving the announcement, the Resource Providers check with its local ResourceContext to see, if it can submit a bid. If not, it ignores the announcement.
4. The Resource Provider submits a bid. Once the TTB period elapses, the Resource Consumer proceeds.
5. The Resource Consumer evaluates the submitted bids and selects the optimal Resource Provider for execution of the task.
6. The Resource Consumer announces the winner. The winning Resource Provider gets the task from the TaskBus and executes it.
7. On completion of the task execution, the Resource Provider sends a task completion notification, and return the task including the result of the execution to the TaskBus.
8. Once the Resource Consumer gets the notification that the task has been executed, it collects the result from the TaskBus.

The pseudo-code for task allocation in the Resource Consumer is shown in algorithm 1. The algorithm proceeds if there is at least one Resource Provider interested in executing the task. If there is no Resource Provider, it times out and informs the application that it cannot schedule the task.

Algorithm 1. Task allocation on the Resource Consumer

Require: Task submitted to distributed submitter
Require: At least one Provider is interested in executing the task
1: **for all** $submittedTask$ **do**
2:    CALL auctioneer.createAuction($taskContext$)
3:    $time = 0$
4:    **while** $time > timeToBid$ **do**
5:      $submittedBids = $ CALL $auctioneer.getSubmittedBids()$
6:      $winningBid = Min(submittedBids)$
7:    **end while**
8:    CALL auctioneer.notify($winningBid$)
9: **end for**

In order to handle cases where an executing node (a Resource Provider) fails or go off-line, a simple failure handling mechanism has been implemented as part of the framework. Along with the task submission, the application specifies a wall-time before which the resource consumer expects the resource provider to complete the execution of the task. If the resource provider has not send a task completion notification before the wall-time elapses, the resource consumer assumes that resource provider has left the mini-grid environment. Then the resource provider re-auctions only the task for which it has not received the task completion notification. The application can specify the number of retires the resource provider can perform. In case the resource provider fails to receive task completion notification in all retries, then the application is notified. Delayed task completion notifications are ignored by the resource consumer. Thus the framework handles volatile nature of the mini-grid environment.

3.3 Context Modeling

The context model in the framework is a formal model of the characteristics of an entity. Context is based on the notion that entities have properties, and properties have values. Entities can be described by making statements that specify the properties of the entity and their values. For example, "Computer A has Intel Core 2 Extreme QX9650 processor" is a statement used to define the hardware context of Computer A. Such subject-predicate-object expressions describes the properties of the entity.

This approach provides expressiveness that permits semantic matching over the attribute/expression pairs used in Condor's ClassAds. For example, using attribute/expression mechanism a resource's operating system can be defined like "OS = value". When an application requires devices having operating system compatible to Unix, it has to issue a query requesting for disjunction of all Unix compatible operating system such as;

```
OS=Linux || OS=Solaris || OS=IRIX ||...
```

Defining such disjunctive set for abstract concepts may contain a number of elements making the traditional exact matching process more constrained. Instead, in our approach, Unix can be defined as a subclass of operating system and all variants of Unix operating systems can be defined as a type of Unix operating system. Using RDF, the above information can be represented as; "Unix is a operating system"; "Solaris is a type of Unix operating system"; etc. Then compatibility concept in domain knowledge can be defined as rules;

```
[compatibleOperatingSystem: ?p rdf:type ?q, ?q rdfs:subClassOf
operatingSystem -> ?p compatibleOS ?q]
```

Thus, the framework enables participation of resource providers in an auction based on semantic reasoning rather than simple attribute matching. Our approach is similar to the work done by John Broke et al. [18]. However, our approach is distributed compared to their centralized one.

In the framework, resources and tasks have context. Currently, we are using context modeling strictly for technical information about required hardware and software. However, the model is sufficiently generic to include other types of context information in the bidding and execution protocol. For example, it can model context like location of the device and define auction process for scheduling tasks on devices in a particular location.

3.4 Framework Extensions

The framework is highly extensible. For example, the default implementation of the BidEvaluator, schedules a task on the fastest resource possible. But by extending or overwriting this implementation, the application developer can define other goals such as scheduling the task on resource that has better networking capabilities, has a more stable configuration, or is trusted.

Similarly, the default auction strategy is a 'First Price Sealed Bid Auction' [19] in which bidders are not aware of each others' bid value and runs only a single round. When the bidders receive a bid request, they can determine the bid value based on their capability. However other types of auction can be used by extending the framework.

4   Implementation

The Mini-Grid Framework has been implemented in Java. It uses UDP multicasting for exchanging meta-information about tasks and bids among the participating devices, and uses TCP connections for exchanging tasks between submitters and executors. The TaskExecutor is based on a thread pool, and a simple sequential single-item auction (i.e., tasks are auctioned one at a time) has been implemented. Though bidding and clearing the auction is simple, it can miss the optimal allocation. However, combinatorial auctions where all tasks are auctioned and the bidding happens based on groups of tasks, can be implemented, but with increased complexity and communication overhead. By default the framework supports computation of the bid based on the current load of the resource. However, the framework supports definition of new types of bids suitable for the application being developed by extending the Bid interface.

Deployment of the mini-grid environment requires minimal configuration compared to existing approaches. The framework requires a multicast address for UDP communication and port numbers for TCP/UDP communication at the time of deployment. Further the framework requires proper configuration for enabling TCP/UDP communication at firewalls and other network equipments. These configuration requirements are similar to what is required for users to share their music collection via Apple iTunes.

The prototype has been integrated with the CLC Bio Workbench for bioinformatics research[5] and users of the workbench have the option of executing their bioinformatic algorithms (e.g., BLAST or Tree Alignment) in a mini-Grid environment. A pilot deployment for evaluating the framework is underway at the Danish iNano research centre[6].

5   Evaluation

In order to asses the effectiveness of the framework, we performed an empirical evaluation in which we compared its performance with a single machine. The performance is measured on two parameters:

Average waiting time – The average time elapsing from the arrival of the task at the Submitter to it starts execute at the Executor.

Average turn-around time – The average time elapsing from the arrival of the task at the Submitter to its completion at the Executor.

---

[5] www.clcbio.com
[6] www.inano.dk

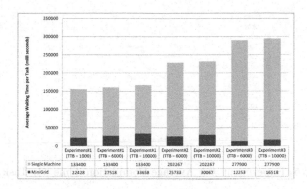

Fig. 4. Experiment #1– #3: Average Waiting Time per Task

For our study, the Mini-Grid ran on a set of 21 identical Intel Core Duo 2.33GHz desktop PCs with 2GB RAM, running MS Windows in a 100Mbs LAN. Each node could play both the role of resource provider and resource consumer, but for simplification one node was configured to act as a resource consumer, and the rest as resource providers with varying resource context. For each auction, the resource providers submitted different bids by using a random number generator. Tasks arrived at the Submitter in batch. For the experiment we have considered computational intensive tasks, i.e., the tasks keep the CPU busy for the period of their execution time and sequential single task auction for task distribution.

The main overhead in our approach is the time taken for auctioning the tasks. Hence in order to study the overhead in the our approach, we conducted three experiments that shows the impact of TTB on the average waiting time of a task. In these experiments, we varied the TTB and measured the average waiting time for a fixed number of tasks and nodes. The results of these experiments are shown in Fig. 5.

In experiment #1, 5 nodes participated and 10 tasks were submitted, and the TTB was 1,000, 6,000, and 10,000 milliseconds respectively. The experiments were repeated several times and average numbers are presented here for discussion. The results shows that the TTB influence the average waiting time by a proportional constant amount of time. We have considered different values for TTB, in order to study the behavior in different types of network. The result implies that the Mini-Grid application developer has to choose the TTB based on the type of network used for deployment. For example, in a wired local area network, a TTB value of 200 ms is sufficient.

Experiment #2 and #3 were conducted to compare the performance of the framework with single Intel Core Duo 2.33GHz desktop PCs having 2GB RAM. The second experiment was conducted with TTB = 6000 ms, using 10 nodes and 15 tasks, and 15 resources and 20 tasks, measuring the average waiting time for each task. We have computed the average waiting time for the same set of tasks when there is only one Executor, i.e. the case of a single machine. However, the single machine approach do not have the overhead of TTB. The result show that the mini-grid infrastructure outperforms a single machine.

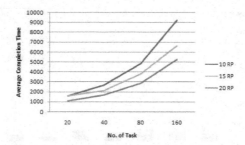

Fig. 5. Experiment #4: Average Completion Time per Task

Experiment #4 measured the average completion time by having fixed value for TTB (10000 ms) and task execution time (1000 sec.). We varied the number of resources participating in the Mini-Grid and the total number of tasks submitted. From the graph 5, we find that the average completion time changes only when the number of tasks is a multiple of number of resource providers. The average completion time decreases with increase in participation of resource providers.

Experiment #5 was conducted to measure the impact of concurrent task submission on the waiting time. The x-axis provides number of tasks submitted concurrently and the y-axis represents the average waiting time of each task as shown in Fig. 5. The waiting time is directly proportional to number tasks submitted concurrently. When the execution time of individual tasks are longer and small number of task are submitted concurrently, then this waiting time is insignificant. When large number of tasks with short execution time are submitted concurrently, this waiting time will affect the completion time of the task.

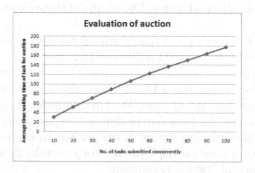

Fig. 6. Experiment #5: Impact of concurrent task submission during auctioning

6   Conclusion

In this paper we have presented the design, implementation and evaluation of the Mini-Grid Framework which includes an auction based scheduling algorithm for bag-of-tasks applications on ad-hoc Grids. In comparison to previous approaches published in the literature, our Framework eases deployment and management of the infrastructure, uses an auction-based task distribution protocol, and models execution context in a way which allow for semantic reasoning in the scheduling process. The framework is highly extendable and can be adapted to several types of applications.

The framework was evaluated by comparing the performance of our auction based task allocation to the task allocation in the single machine. The evaluation showed that a mini-grid will exploit available resources for parallel computing, thereby out-performing a single machine. The main overhead is associated with the time used for the auction process.

As an extensible framework, the Mini-Grid Framework has the fundamental building blocks for creating application that distribute bag-of-tasks in a medium size ad-hoc network of volunteer computers. Ongoing work is concerned with the design of context-aware scheduling and contingency management. Context-aware scheduling will enable scheduling that takes into account the physical setting of the involved nodes. Contingency management will help us run on more volatile and heterogeneous infrastructures.

Currently bioinformatics algorithms (e.g. BLAST) are being implemented as a part of the CLC Workbench to use the Mini-Grid infrastructure. This will enable us to leverage bioinformatics analysis in a biology lab using state-of-art user-friendly bioinformatic software and also to explore hardware accelerated bioinformatics algorithms running on the CLC Cube[7] and the CLC Cell[8].

References

[1] Foster, I., Kesselman, C.: Chapter 2: Computational Grids. In: The grid: blueprint for a new computing infrastructure, pp. 15–51. Morgan Kaufmann Publishers Inc, San Francisco (1999)
[2] Kurdi, H., Li, M., Al-Raweshidy, H.: A classification of emerging and traditional grid systems. IEEE Distributed Systems Online 9(3), 1–1 (2008)
[3] Foster, I.: Globus Toolkit version 4: Software for Service-Oriented Systems. Journal of Computer Science and Technology 21(4), 513–520 (2006)
[4] Litzkow, M., Livny, M., Mutka, M.: Condor - A Hunter of Idle Workstations. In: Proceedings of the 8th International Conference of Distributed Computing Systems, pp. 104–111. IEEE Press, Los Alamitos (1988)
[5] Anderson, D.P.: BOINC: a system for public-resource computing and storage. In: GC 2004: Proceedings of the Fifth IEEE/ACM International Workshop on Grid Computing, pp. 365–372. ACM Press, New York (2004)
[6] Thain, D., Tannenbaum, T., Livny, M.: Distributed computing in practice: the condor experience. Concurrency - Practice and Experience 17(2-4), 323–356 (2005)
[7] Raman, R., Livny, M., Solomon, M.: Matchmaking: distributed resource management for high throughput computing. In: Proceedings of The Seventh International Symposium on High Performance Distributed Computing, July 1998, pp. 140–146 (1998)

---

[7] www.clccube.com
[8] www.clccell.com

[8] Anderson, D.P., Christensen, C., Allen, B.: Grid resource management—designing a runtime system for volunteer computing. In: SC 2006: Proceedings of the, ACM/IEEE conference on Supercomputing, p. 126. ACM Press, New York (2006)

[9] Vinter, B.: The Architecture of the Minimum intrusion Grid, MiG. In: Broenink, J., Roebbers, H., Sunter, J., Welch, P., Wood, D. (eds.) Communicating Process Architectures. IOS Press, Amsterdam (2005)

[10] Fedak, G., Germain, C., Neri, V., Cappello, F.: XtremWeb: a generic global computing system. In: Proceedings of First IEEE/ACM International Symposium on Cluster Computing and the Grid, pp. 582–587. IEEE Press, Los Alamitos (2001)

[11] Kramer, D., MacInnis, M.: Utilization of a local grid of mac os based computers using xgrid. In: 13th IEEE International Symbosium on High Performance Distributed Computing, pp. 264–275 (2004)

[12] Cirne, W., Brasileiro, F., Andrade, N., Costa, L., Andrade, A., Novaes, R., Mowbray, M.: Labs of the World, Unite!!! Journal of Grid Computing 4(3), 225–246 (2006)

[13] Talia, D., Trunfio, P.: A P2P Grid Services-Based Protocol: Design and Evaluation. In: Danelutto, M., Vanneschi, M., Laforenza, D. (eds.) Euro-Par 2004. LNCS, vol. 3149, pp. 1022–1031. Springer, Heidelberg (2004)

[14] Koh, M., Song, J., Peng, L., See, S.: Service Registry Discovery using GridSearch P2P Framework. Proceeding of CCGrid 2, 11 (2006)

[15] Pham, T.V., Lau, L.M., Dew, P.M.: An Adaptive Approach to P2P Resource Discovery in Distributed Scientific Research Communities. Proceeding of CCGrid 2, 12 (2006)

[16] Butt, A.R., Zhang, R., Hu, Y.C.: A self-organizing flock of condors. J. Parallel Distrib. Comput. 66(1), 145–161 (2006)

[17] Fedak, G., Germain, C., Neri, V.: Xtremweb: A generic global computing system. In: Proceedings of the IEEE International Symposium on Cluster Computing and the Grid (CCGRID 2001), pp. 582–587 (2001)

[18] Brooke, J., Fellows, D., Garwood, K., Goble, C.: Semantic matching of grid resource descriptions. In: Proceedings of the European Across Grids Conference, pp. 240–249. Springer, Heidelberg (2004), http://www.Grid-interoperability.org/semres.pdf

[19] Klemperer, P.: 1. In: Auctions: Theory and Practice. Princeton University Press, Princeton (2004)

Human Movement Detection Algorithm Using 3-Axis Accelerometer Sensor Based on Low-Power Management Scheme for Mobile Health Care System*

Jaewan Shin[1], Dongkyoo Shin[1], Dongil Shin[1], Sungmin Her[2],
Soohan Kim[3], and Myungsoo Lee[3]

[1] Department of Computer Engineering, Sejong University, 98 Kunja-Dong, Kwangjin-Gu,
Seoul 143-747, Korea, Republic Of
shinnom@gce.sejong.ac.kr, {shindk,dshin}@sejong.ac.kr
[2] SevenCore Co., Ltd, Seocho-Dong, Seocho-Gu, Seoul 137-855, Korea, Republic Of
smher@sevencore.co.kr
[3] Samsung Eletronics Co., Ltd, Korea, Republic Of
ksoohan@samsung.com, myungsu.lee@samsung.com

Abstract. Phone and PDA mobile devices that recognize a user's movements and biometric information that can be utilized in a sensor system have been generating interest among users. This paper proposes a low-power management scheme that uses the baseband processor installed in a portable communications device to limit the electric power consumed by the device, along with a human movement detection algorithm that records and predicts the movement of the mobile user in a low-power mode. In addition, a mobile healthcare system is developed to use the proposed scheme and algorithm. This system uses 3-axis accelerometer sensors on an Android platform and calculates the amount of human movement from the sensor output. The user's uphill, downhill, flat area, climbing stairs, going down stairs, and jogging movements were measured with accuracies of 93.2%, 97.4%, 97.6%, 98.8%, 92.2%, and 90.8%, respectively.

Keywords: MEMS, Low-Power Management, Accelerometer Sensor, Movement Detection Algorithm.

1 Introduction

Due to the development of digital technology, PDAs, cameras, GPS units, mobile phones, and many other digital devices occupy a large portion of our lives. There were about 45 million mobile phone users in Korea in July 2009 [1]. These cellular phones provide various services and have been equipped with the ability to store a large amount of information. Accordingly, many companies inside and outside the country are doing research on ways to use the accelerometer sensors in the medical, logistics, and security systems fields. In addition, detecting biometric information and

---

* This research is supported by Ministry of Culture, Sports and Tourism(MCST) and Korea Creative Content Agency(KOCCA) in the Culture Technology(CT) Research & Development Program 2009.

R.-S. Chang et al. (Eds.): GPC 2010, LNCS 6104, pp. 81–90, 2010.

movement for health care is a growing trend. For example, phone features that apply the pedometer "MPTrain" and Nike "Sports Kit" measurements use a vertical accelerometer to determine a user's pace [2].

This paper discusses a built-in pedometer feature for low-power mobile devices that can accurately detect the number of steps using a proposed algorithm. The data obtained through the device can be sent to a server to build a health care system.

Chapter 2 describes the algorithm used to detect the steps taken. Chapter 3 shows how the necessary power is provided to implement the pedometer technology and discuses the health care system technology. Chapter 4 provides some experimental results using the proposed algorithm. Chapter 5 gives some conclusions and future research to meet the challenges.

We would like to draw your attention to the fact that it is not possible to modify a paper in any way, once it has been published. This applies to both the printed book and the online version of the publication. Every detail, including the order of the names of the authors, should be checked before the paper is sent to the Volume Editors.

2   Sensor and Human Movement Detection Algorithm

In order to perceive contextual information about a user's condition, we need a sensor, especially the accelerometer sensor. Two-axis and three-axis accelerometer sensors can be applied to objects. With a 3-axis accelerometer sensor, the acceleration can be measure in the x, y, and z-axis directions in three-dimensional space [3]. Based on the acceleration of gravity, the tilt angle of an object and its direction of movement can be detected. The gravitational accelerometer is based on the angle of inclination the Earth's gravity, where the orthogonal acceleration of gravity is 1G. Therefore, the acceleration of gravity is shown in Fig. 1. where the sin (tilted angle) can be represented by the relationship [4].

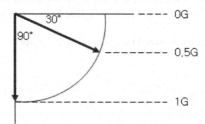

Fig. 1. G value derived from the angle

2.1   Human Movement Detection Algorithm

In this study, accelerometer data was collected by using a low-pass filter to enhance the high-frequency signals from the remaining low-frequency signals. Contiguous [High - Low - High] signals were used to find a peak signal, and the value of the differences and the gap are within the range specified as a threshold to recognize how much of the existing results were obtained with high accuracy. In addition to these threshold values, the user can adjust the fit to increase the reliability.

A person's gait is usually 2-3 times per second, the low - pass filter processing removed the unnecessary parts, and the associated gait data could be obtained. This filtered data is similar to the sin function graph. The direction of the ingredients, except for the size value (scalar), are satisfied for the following conditions and judged by one step.

- Within a certain interval [High Peak - Low Peak – High peak] their presence in the form of a peak point.
- The spacing between each peak in the above item should be within the specified range.
- Each peak value must be specified within the range of values.
- If the above conditions are satisfied, use the second highest peak value and then walk back to the first high peak value.
- In the last step, the second peak may not be high, so in this case, the first step uses the high peak and low peak values.

The above can be expressed in formulas as follows.

$$|r_{h1} - r_{h2}| \leq thd_1, \ r_{h1} - r_l \geq thd_2, \ r_{h2} - r_l \geq thd_3$$
$$thd_4 \leq r_{h1}, \ r_{h2} \leq thd_5, \ thd_6 \leq r_l \leq thd_7$$
$$thd_8 \leq l - h_1 \leq thd_9, \ thd_{10} \leq h_2 - l \leq thd_{11}$$

$$h_1 \equiv 1st \ High \ Peak \ Index(time)$$
$$h_2 \equiv 2nd \ High \ Peak \ Index(time)$$
$$l \equiv Low \ Peak \ Index(time)$$
$$r_{h1}, \ r_{h2} \equiv High \ Peak \ Value$$
$$r_l \equiv Low \ Peak \ value$$
$$thd_1 \sim thd_{11} \equiv Threshold \ Values.$$

(1)

To find the peak value of r is to find the inflection. The peak values for each time interval and the size of the difference is less than the specified range of discretion to ignore the noise or the previous peak value is compared with the merger.

Existing methods have a high peak value and it is common to judge the pace. The proposed approach considers the person's gait characteristics using continuous three peak values by using a low - pass filter. The accelerometer has the advantage of the filter.

2.2 Find Non-step Movements

The actual movement of people is given in the horizontal direction x, with y as the vertical direction.

First, the pace when detecting high peak and low peak accelerometer values at the point of the orientation angle is calculated to determine the specified range. This is represented by the following formula.

$$\theta = \cos^{-1} \frac{x_1 * x_2 + y_1 * y_2 + z_1 * z_2}{\sqrt{x_1^2 + y_1^2 + z_1^2}\sqrt{x_2^2 + y_2^2 + z_2^2}}$$

$$thd_{m1} \le \theta \le thd_{m2}$$

(2)

$$(x_1, y_1, z_1), (x_2, y_2, z_2) \equiv Acceleration\ vector\ at\ peaks.$$

The first high peak and low peak (x, y, z) vector sum of the second high peak and low peak (x, y, z) is found by calculating the vector sum of these vectors to calculate the angle to determine the specified range. Peaks with the same mass in the direction of the vector sum of the relative power and acceleration between peaks can tell which direction we are encountering. This is represented by a formula as follows.

$$\theta = \cos^{-1} \frac{x_{s1} * x_{s2} + y_{s1} * y_{s2} + z_{s1} * z_{s2}}{\sqrt{x_{s1}^2 + y_{s1}^2 + z_{s1}^2}\sqrt{x_{s2}^2 + y_{s2}^2 + z_{s2}^2}}$$

$$thd_{m3} \le \theta \le thd_{m4}$$

(3)

$$(x_{s1}, y_{s1}, z_{s1}) \equiv \sum_{i \to hl}^{l} v_i \quad (x_{s2}, y_{s2}, z_{s2}) \equiv \sum_{i \to l}^{k} v_i$$

$$v_i \equiv Acceleration\ vector\ at\ sampling\ time\ i.$$

2.3 Data Processing

(1) Accelerometer data generation step from the accelerometer. To create three-axis accelerometer data, 3-axis information can be collected from the accelerometer chip for the x, y, and z axes.

(2) The low-frequency data generation step (1) uses the noise generated by the accelerometer data step to remove high-frequency information. A low-pass filter is used. Thus, by removing the high-frequency information, the pace that depends on the movement occurring in the behavior of the low-frequency data and by other steps remains as the low-frequency data.

(3) The scalar transformation step uses the low-frequency data created in step 2 (x, y, z) to calculate the scalar value.

(4) The peak phase is derived from the generated data of high-frequency peak and low peak.

(5) The above is the difference between each peak within a specified range of values and each peak above the gap is within the specified range. The above steps will be treated as a high peak.

(6) The pace of the last step is immediately in the recognition stage, so there is no high peak. Also, at this stage after a single high peak and low peak in the angle and direction of the accelerometer, the single high peak and low peak vector sum that come immediately after the high peak and low peak in the degrees between the vector sum of one or two more within a specified range that meet the criteria will be treated as the pace.

(7) This is a recognition step for the continuous phase, given that the continuous pace of recovery is not certain if the pace does not improve, the pace of recovery to a certain constant in this series is recognized as a post-processing step.

(8) This is the results phase, where a step in the recognition phase or continuous phase recognition step information about the number of steps have been recognized as an application is sent to the user to display the steps.

3 Implementation of Low-Power Scheme on Mobile Equipment

3.1 Configuration of Hardware

This study used the basic hardware configuration shown in Fig. 2. The processor accelerometer of the EN terminal of the chip uses the On/Off, power, and accelerometer data only to get a connection.

Communication between the processor and the accelerometer sensor chip to implement the accelerometer sensor chip depends on the model of the SPI/I2C/ADC. For mobile devices to receive and handle data directly from the baseband processor, similar features can be used without a processor, handled outside of the MICOM (Micro Computer). In other words, the processor used in this research to reduce costs and save power does not require a separate MICOM.

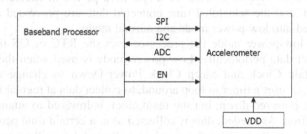

Fig. 2. Hardware Configuration

3.2 Configuration of Software

Typically in mobile devices, a CPU (e.g., ARM) low-power mode (Sleep mode) is supported. In this situation, the accelerometer chip reads the data periodically when possible. Thus, even if the processor is in low power mode, it continues to collect and store data. After a period of time it comes out of low-power mode and processes the gathered data all at once. Fig. 3. shows a flowchart of the overall software system.

In this study, the accelerometer of a real-time processing chip came with a sample basis, but in the low-power mode processing was difficult, because batch (Batch Process) is parallel. In other words, once there is a constant number of a sample of processed data, it is not treated until it is necessary to transmit the gathered data.

If there is no change in the extended gait, accelerometer sensors used to obtain data use a slow sampling-rate speed so that the entire system can reduce power consumption.

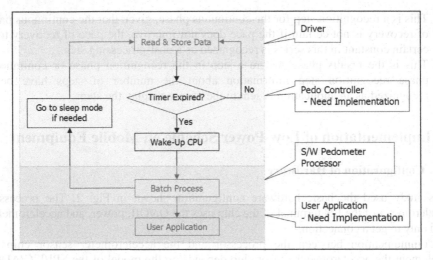

Fig. 3. Flowchart of the software system

3.3 Configuration of Modules

3.3.1 Pedo Controller Module

The Pedo Controller module is used for a specified period of accelerometer sensor data acquisition, and the scheduled time collected data are processed at once. This section is divided into low-power mode and normal mode.

First, in the low-power mode the processor uses the RTC or OS timer function simply to collect data periodically. Low-power mode is used when the processor is entering the Main Clock and Sleep Clock Power-Down to change the processor before the RTC, or uses a timer to loop around, to collect data at regular intervals. The processor is not powered-down, but the main clock is lowered to attain much lower power consumption. As needed, data is collected after a certain time period out of the low-power mode, and the reinstated main clock collected data will be processed in the meantime.

If not in low-power mode, Pedo controller creates a separate task (Pedo Task) for the pedometer. A Pedo Task Timer provided by the OS is used to collect data at regular intervals, including data collected from the low-power mode to count the number of steps. Next, the active Pedo Tasks during the processing of data are read one by one.

Fig. 4. shows the action commonly used in mobile phones. Qualcomm's CDMA baseband processor chip MSM shows the process of the action of moving from Sleep Mode and Idle Mode to Run Mode. Every 1.28 sec, the MSM processor wakes up (Wake-Up Interrupt). The MSM is in the Idle state and the Main Clock makes changes to TCXO. Pedo Task continues in operation for a while. The processes data will be stored in the meantime.

3.3.2 Software Pedometer Module

Data collected on the software pedometer module is used to detect the pace. This section operates independently of other parts.

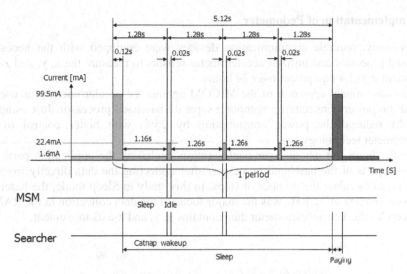

Fig. 4. Action phases of the MSM chip

The accelerometer data collected from real people reflect changes in the accelerometer and it is necessary to remove these elements. Therefore, data is collected on the person's pace and then filtered to the appropriate frequency bands for various settings to find the pace.

Fig. 5. shows the flow behavior of the pedometer software. The software flow shown is used to collect data from sensors to calculate the number of steps.

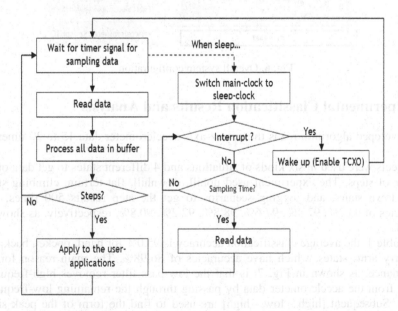

Fig. 5. Flowchart of the pedometer software operation

3.4 Implementation of Pedometer

In this study, portable communication devices were equipped with the necessary baseband processor and utilized accelerometer sensors to measure the x, y, and z-axis movement data for equipment over 24 hours.

The conventional approach of the MICOM against the accelerometer was used to control the power consumption without a separate baseband processor. Just using the MICOM reduced the power consumption by 25%, with better control of the accelerometer technology.

Fig. 6. shows the whole layer configuration, including the application parts and displayed parts of the baseband processor, after collecting the data directly from the hardware to calculate the number of steps. In this study in Sleep mode, the baseband processor running at 32 KHz was the major focus of the data collection in the RAM at the Sleep Mode. The accelerometer data contains x, y, and z-axis movement.

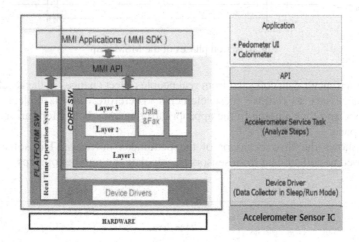

Fig. 6. Overall system configuration

4 Experimental Classification Results and Analysis

The developed algorithm reads the x, y, z-axis accelerometer data 15 to 20 times per second.

Subjects were used in six kinds of situations and 4 different states to get data on the number of steps. The experiment used uphill, downhill, flat terrain, climbing stairs, going down stairs, and jogging scenarios to get the step results 500 times, with accuracies of 93.2%, 97.4%, 97.6%, 98.8%, 92.2%, 90.8%, respectively, as shown in Table 1.

In Table 1, the average classification accuracy is 95.0% for hand, pocket, backpack, and carry arms states, which have accuracies of 86-98%. The main reason for this performance, as shown in Fig. 7, is that the low-pass filter removes high-frequency signals from the accelerometer data by passing through the remaining low-frequency signals. Subsequent [high - low - high] are used to find the form of the peak signal threshold within the range specified by the signal recognition only because of the pace.

Table 1. Result Categories for the proposed technology: S1, uphill road; S2, downhill road; S3, flat terrain; S4, climbing stairs; S5, going down stairs; S6, jogging

Result		Classification					
		S1	S2	S3	S4	S5	S6
original	S1	466	0	0	0	0	0
	S2	0	487	0	0	0	0
	S3	0	0	488	0	0	0
	S4	0	0	0	494	0	0
	S5	0	0	0	0	461	0
	S6	0	0	0	0	0	454

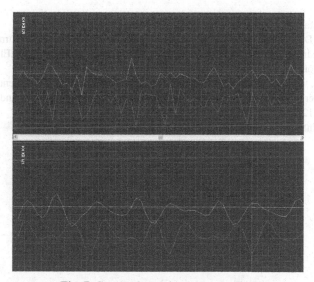

Fig. 7. Graph of applying low-pass filter

In addition, the baseband processor in sleep mode works most of the time and has the leverage of working with 32 KHz in sleep mode, data acquisition, Idle Mode, or Run Mode with the data already stored in the steps taken to task by performing calculations previously developed for mobile phones, compared with the pedometer average of 2.5 times the function developed as a mobile phone with a pedometer.

5   Conclusions

This paper showed how existing mobile handsets can be used without the use of MICOM equipped devices, which are essential to baseband processors. The accelerometer sensor was used to measure the movement of low-power technology, with the capability of working 24 hours on the pedometer-based Android platform, with features that have been developed for low-power cell phones. In addition, the data collected by the mobile phone was developed for real-time monitoring, can be sent to the server at regular intervals between the UI, and managed on a PC system.

An algorithm was developed to detect the steps taken using a low-pass filter to remove noise in the signal and recognize the critical range. In Idle Mode, the baseband processor for the collected data used a low-power technology pedometer function for 24 hours.

In a future study, algorithms to improve the accuracy using a compass sensor will be implemented using more than a three-axis accelerometer sensor to detect the exact number of steps and improve the algorithm. In addition, low-power sensors will be used to collect data, and this technique will be applied to the smart phone processors used in embedded systems.

References

1. Subscriber Statistics, Korean Communications Commission (July 2009)
2. Karantonis, D.M., Narayanan, M.R.: Implementation of a Real-Time Human Movement Classifier Using a Triaxial Accelerometer for Ambulatory Monitoring. IEEE Transactions on Information Techology in Biomedicine 10(1), 156–167 (2006)
3. Luinge, H.J., Veltink, P.H.: Inclination Measurement of Human Movement Using a 3-D Accelerometer with Autocalibration. IEEE Transactions on Neural Systems and Rehabilitation Engineering 12(1), 112–121 (2002)
4. Electronics Information Center, http://203.253.128.6:8088

A Genetic Context Interpreter for Context-Aware Systems in Pervasive Computing Environments

Been-Chian Chien and Shiang-Yi He

Department of Computer Science and Information Engineering
National University of Tainan, Tainan, Taiwan, R. O. C. 70005
bcchien@mail.nutn.edu.tw

Abstract. Developing context-aware applications in pervasive computing environments has attracted much attention from researchers in recent decade. Although dozens of context-aware computing paradigms were built these years, it is difficult for the present systems to extend the application domains and interoperate with other service systems due to the problem of heterogeneity among systems. In this paper, we propose and construct a generic context interpreter to overcome the dependence problem between context and hardware devices based on the proposed context-aware (CADBA) architecture. The idea of the context generic interpreter imports sensor data from sensor devices as an XML schema. Instead of interpretation widgets, interpretation scripts are produced by a context generator and a generic context interpreter is used to provide the semantic context for context-aware applications. A context editor is also designed by employing schema matching schemes for supporting intelligent context mapping between devices and context model.

Keywords: Context-aware computing, pervasive computing, generic context interpreter.

1 Introduction

Emergence of ubiquitous computing [17] and pervasive computing [11] brings the vision of integrating hardware, network systems, and information technologies to provide appropriate service for our lives in a vanishing way. With the rapid growth of wireless sensors and mobile devices, the research of pervasive computing is becoming important and popular in recent years. A context-aware system is a pervasive computing environment in which user's preference services can be detected by making use of context including location, time, date, nearby devices and other environmental activities to adapt the users' operations and behavior. All kinds of context-aware architectures have been designed and employed for a wide spectrum of applications [2]. Since the individual focus of each framework on its specific application domain, the current context-aware systems are heterogeneous in all aspects, such as hardware, mobile resources, operating systems, application software, and platforms. The serious heterogeneous characteristics of context-aware computing are especially important and become significant drawbacks while developing or integrating context-aware applications in pervasive computing environments.

R.-S. Chang et al. (Eds.): GPC 2010, LNCS 6104, pp. 91–100, 2010.

The concept of *context independence* was introduced in CADBA architecture [5]. Two types of context independence, *the physical context independence* and *the logical context independence*, are presented. The physical context independence is to prevent misinterpreting raw data from sensors with various specification standards; whereas the logical context independence is to allow context to be understood and applied by applications. As a result of context independence, cross-domain service applications will be able to be integrated into a unified context-aware system regardless of the heterogeneity in pervasive environment.

An OSGi-based service platform [7] based on Java VM is one of the practical solutions for accomplishing logical context independence. In this paper, a generic context interpreter is firstly proposed to overcome the physical context dependence problem between context and sensor devices in the framework of context-aware computing. The idea of the context generic interpreter imports sensor data from sensor devices as an XML schema. Instead of interpretation widgets, the context interpreter uses interpretation scripts being produced by a context generator and a generic context interpreter to provide semantic context for context-aware computing. An interface tool, the context editor, is designed by employing XML schema matching schemes for supporting intelligent context mapping between devices and context model.

2 Preliminaries

The term *context-aware* first appeared in 1994 mentioned by Schilit and Theimer [15]. Then, various context-aware computing architectures were proposed, for example, *Context Toolkit* [6], *Hydrogen* [10], *Gaia*, *SOCAM* [7], and the *CORTEX* system [4]. The above context-aware system architectures generally follow the framework presented in [2] which described a conceptual framework of a context-aware system containing *the sensors*, *the raw data*, *the preprocessing*, *the storage/management*, and *the application* layers. A context-aware system was utilized on its individual specific application domain of employment whatever the framework or architecture it used. Thus, the problem of heterogeneity issues was generally characterized not only on the physical devices but also on the logical context interoperability. To bridging the communication between heterogeneous devices, some researches on adapting and integrating systems sprout recently. A OSGi-based infrastructure [7] was proposed to adapt to changing context. In [3], Bartelt *et al.* proposed a system that integrates devices dynamically and enable interoperability between them. Nakazawa *et al.* [13] presented a framework for heterogeneity handling. Schmohl and Baumgarten [16] further derived a generalized context-aware architecture for pervasive computing environments to resolve the heterogeneity issues in both context-awareness and interoperability domains.

This work is based on another generalized context-aware architecture CADBA [5]. The architecture of CADBA is also structured by a five-layer framework consisting of the device layer, the interpretation layer, the context layer, the storage layer, and the application layer, as shown in Figure 1. The main modules and components for each layer are described as follows.

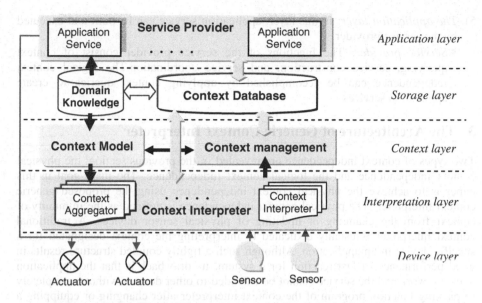

Fig. 1. The CADBA architecture for five-layer framework

1) *The device layer*: This layer contains the physical equipments and devices operated and used in the context-aware systems including sensors, identifiers, mobile devices, and actuators, etc.

2) *The interpretation layer*: The main components in this layer contain context interpreters and context aggregators.

   • *Context interpreter*: The context interpreter is used to interpret the structures of raw data from sensors and represent the information as low-level context called *sensor context*.

   • *Context aggregator*: The context aggregator then gathers the related low-level sensor context data to form a higher-level context. As soon as the context model is provided, context can be generated by context interpreters and aggregators.

3) *The context layer*: A context model and management are the main components.

   • *Context model*: The *context model* is essential and the CADBA uses ontology to represent the context model with OWL.

   • *Context management*: Context-aware computing implies the interconnection of people, devices, and environments. It makes possibility of sharing the users' context among each other in heterogeneous systems. The issues and challenges of context management include context configuration, device fault, context conflict, context inconsistency and security [9].

4) *The storage layer*: The storage layer stores not only the context data of the current status but also the historical context data in the context-aware system.

   • *Domain knowledge*: It contains the entire resources of the context-aware computing including places, persons, devices, and objects.

   • *Context database*: The context database is to provide the integration of current context and the storage of historical context data.

5) *The application layer*: In this layer, application service can be built and executed by the service provider.
   - *Service provider*: The functions of the service provider consist of context querying, service construction, and service coordination.The logical context independence can be accomplished by applying context queries to create application services.

3   The Architecture of Generic Context Interpreter

Two types of context independence are revealed in the previous section: the physical context independence and the logical context independence. The main goal in this paper is to achieve the physical context independence using the proposed generic context interpreter. The physical context independence is defined as the immunity of context from the changing or updating of physical sensor devices. A traditional context interpreter is usually dedicated to interpreting the context designated for a specific device in an application. Although such a tightly coupled structure results in good performance of fast reaction for a system, its drawback is that the application does not work and the service cannot be extended to other devices without completely re-packing function program of the context interpreter after changing or equipping a new sensor device. The physical context independence tries to maintain normal operations of the context-aware system regardless of changing, reconstructing, or replacing sensor devices anytime.

For designing a generic context interpreter, ontology with OWL representation is considered as the context model for the proposed architecture. The techniques of ontology fusion can be applied to integrate heterogeneous context models and the representation, OWL, is XML based scripts. It is formatted, unified, and standardized. While importing data from sensor devices, the XML format is also easy to convey the information extracted by data acquisition interface to the context interpreter. The context used in the CADBA architecture is divided into three levels *sensor context*, *event context*, and *scenario context* by means of XML context model.

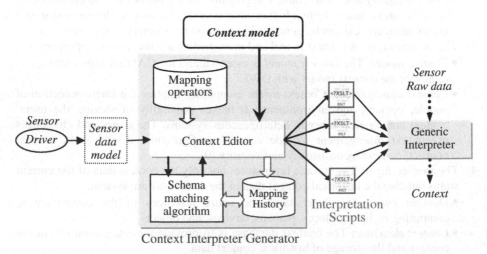

Fig. 2. The architecture of generic context interpreter

The architecture of the proposed generic context interpreter is shown in Figure 2. The main components are the context interpreter generator and the generic interpreter. The context interpreter generator further contains three functions: the mapping operators, the context editor and the schema matching algorithm. In this model, context interpreters generated by the interpreter generator are interpretation scripts instead of interpretation functions or programs. The interpretation script draws linking relationships and transforming methods between sensor data and the semantics in the context model. The generic interpreter then translates sensor raw data into context by the corresponding interpretation scripts while the context interpretation process being proceeded. We depict each component block as follows and the detailed design of function blocks will described in Section 4.

- **Sensor data model:** Sensor models can be provided by some techniques of connectivity standards, for example, UPnP and SOAP, which enable data transfer in XML-based procedure call. Each type of sensor delivers its sensor data by the predefined XML schema according to the hardware specification. Such a schema will be sent to the context editor for linking relationship rules with the context model.
- **Context model:** The context model is built for different application environment. For mapping context schema into sensor data schema, ontology with XML-based representation is used here.
- **Context interpreter generator:** Interpreter generator produces interpretation scripts which contain the mapping relationships between context schema and sensor data schema. The mapping interface tool is the context editor. The context editor supports a graphical user interface to assist users to link the relationship between context schema and sensor data schema. The mapping job can be finished manually or automatically by applying schema matching schemes.
- **Interpretation script:** The interpretation script uses XSL (eXtensible Stylesheet Language) to describe the schema mapping. The content of the script is the rules of transforming source data schema (sensor data) into target data schema (context).
- **Generic interpreter:** Since interpretation scripts are stated in XSL, the XSLT (XSL Transformation) Processor can be used to be the generic interpreter directly. The XSLT-Processor will read the sensor raw data with XML tag and interpret the context according to the corresponding interpretation script.

The interpretation flow consists two phrases: interpretation scripts generation and context interpretation. In the interpretation scripts generation phrase, mobile sensors prepared circumstances data schema in XML format and delivered them to the context interpreter generator. After sensor data schema was received by the context interpreter generator, the context editor is used to build the relationship between sensor data and sensor context according to the definitions in context model. An XSL script will be generated for interpreting the sensor context if the confirmation is done. Then, in the context interpretation phrase, the XSLT-Processor is used to translate original XML sensor raw data into XML sensor context defined in the context model.

After completing the definitions of sensor context, event context and scenario context can be aggregated from sensor context by the context editor as the same way.

4 Functional Design of Context Interpreter Generator

4.1 Mapping Operators

The function of mapping operators is to transfer the sensor raw data into semantic context. Four types of mapping operators are defined in the system. The operators are designed by XSL descriptions. These operators thus can be easily reused and modified to a new one.

Operator 1: *concat*

The concatenation operator is used to merge two separated data into one. For instance: date-time or firstname-lastname. The rule of concatenation operator in XSL is shown as the following.

```
<AllName>
        <xsl:value-of select="concat(concat(string(LastName), ' '), string(FirstName))"/>
</AllName>
```

Operator 2: *value-map*

This operator maps the raw data with a item value into the semantic context described in context model. It states that the item value is equal to the context in the system. For example, if "RFID-tag:0X8001" represents the context "Person: John". The definition of the operator in XSL description is shown as follows.

```
<xsl:template name="Value_map:Person">
        <xsl:param name="input" select="/.."/>
            <xsl:choose>
                    <xsl:when test="$input='0X8001'">
                            <xsl:value-of select="'John'"/>
                    </xsl:when>
            </xsl:choose>
</xsl:template>
```

Operator 3: *Value-Semantic*

The purpose of this operator is to process numerical values from senor raw data. For example, if temperature is lower than 16°C, the context "cold" will be interpreted and used in the system instead of the original numerical value. The XSL definition of the above context can be described as follows.

```
<xsl:template name="Value_Semanitc:Temperature">
        <xsl:param name="input_value" select="/.."/>
        <xsl:param name="lessThan" select="/.."/>
        <xsl:param name="Low_Semantic" select="/.."/>
        <xsl:choose>
                <xsl:when test="string(($input_value &lt; $lessThan)) != 'false'">
                        <xsl:value-of select="$Low_Semantic"/>
                </xsl:when>
        </xsl:choose>
</xsl:template>
```

Operator 4: *Conversion-Function*

This operation allows users to define formula for some specific requests. A practical example is the transform between degree centigrade and Fahrenheit scale. The transform formula is usually used to convert 20°C into 68°F.

```
<xsl:template name="Conversion:CelsiusToFahrenheit">
    <xsl:param name="CelsiusValue" select="/.."/>
    <xsl:value-of select="((($CelsiusValue * 9) div 5) + 32)"/>
</xsl:template>
```

4.2 Schema Matching Algorithms

The main function of schema matching algorithm is to assist users to retrieve related context from the historical mapping repository. Since the number of context is usually large in a context-aware application, the management of context is an important work. One of the issues is to find similar or even the same context mapping to develop context interpretation scripts. The advantage of using XML to represent context here is that XML schema matching method can be applied to search the sensor schema with high similarity. Making use of reusing the similar schema of context mapping, the new context mapping will be built quickly. A good XML schema matching algorithm can help users to construct intelligent context interpreter generator.

The XML schema and ontology matching problem is one of the research issues in data manipulation. There are many researches and discussion on such a topic. Two famous schema matching algorithm were applied in our work. The first is Cupid [12] proposed by Madhavan *et al.* The other is COMA++ [1] by Aumuller. We will discuss the effectiveness and efficiency of the two methods after applying to the context interpreter generator in Section 5.

4.3 The Context Editor

The context editor is designed for defining mapping operators, managing context mapping between sensor data schema and context model, and generating context interpretation scripts. A graphical user interface is provided to help users to finish the sensor binding efficiently and easily. The context mapping operation in a context editor is demonstrated as Figure 3. First, the editor reads the XML sensor data or

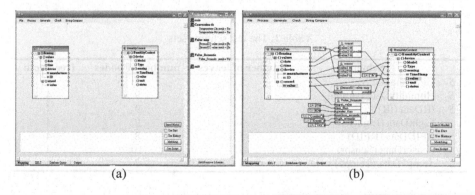

(a)   (b)

Fig. 3. The context editor

others context from the context model, and the corresponding context in the context-aware system are selected from the context model, as Figure 3(a) shows. The next step shown in Figure 4(b) is to arrange the interpreting operations. Some predefined transformation operators and user defined operators can be added into the system for transferring data values to meaningful context. At last, the finished context mapping is stored as XSL script to interpret the context in the context-aware system. Owing to the context interpreter is done by interpretation scripts, the context interpreter only builds a new context interpretation script instead of full-function program while mobile devices being updated or changed. The goal of the physical context independence is enforced.

5 System Construction and Evaluation

The generic context interpreter proposed in this paper used Mapforce API to develop user interface of context mapping in the context editor. The context editor provides both manual mapping and automatic mapping tools. The initial blank system needs build context mapping manually. Once more mapping datasets were accumulated in the mapping history, Users will be able to refer to the existing schema mapping cases and a similar sensor schema mapping was selected to modify as a new context mapping. The test schema sets include seven different sensor schemas listed in Table 1. The depths of schema structures are four levels. The number of leaves is between the range four and six. The number of nodes is in the range of seven to ten. We first ranked the similarity degree of each schema by experts as shown in Table 2. Then the schema matching algorithms, Cupid and COMA++, are tested on each schema. The matching results of similarity are evaluated and ranked, as shown in Table 3. To evaluate the performance of ranking, we refer to R_{norm} [8] values as the criterion of effectiveness.

The experimental results show that COMA++ is generally superior to Cupid in both effectiveness and efficiency. The R_{norm} values of COMA++ are better than Cupid for 5 schemas except S_5:RFID and S_6:Sensor. The reason is that the type of value(xs:decimal) in S_7:Temp matched the type of value(xs:string) in S_5 and S_6. This mistake causes the higher rank of S_7:Temp. It shows that COMA++ is relatively weak in the matching of types on leaves.

Table 1. The test schema sets

Schema	number of leaves	number of nodes	tree depth
S_1: GPSData (GPS)	5	9	4
S_2: HumidityData (Humid)	5	9	4
S_3: IRData (IR)	5	9	4
S_4: LightData (Light)	5	9	4
S_5: RFIDData (RFID)	5	8	4
S_6: SensorData (Sensor)	6	10	4
S_7: Temp2Data (Temp2)	4	7	4

Table 2. The ranking results of Experts for the test sets

Experts Rank	Schema						
	S_1 GPS	S_2 Humid	S_3 IR	S_4 Light	S_5 RFID	S_6 Sensor	S_7 Temp2
2	S_2 Humid	S_1 GPS	S_4 Light	S_2 Humid	S_1 GPS	S_1 GPS	S_4 Light
3	S_4 Light	S_4 Light	S_2 Humid	S_3 IR	S_2 Humid	S_2 Humid	S_1 GPS
4	S_3 IR	S_3 IR	S_1 GPS	S_1 GPS	S_4 Light	S_7 Temp2	S_2 Humid
5	S_6 Sensor	S_6 Sensor	S_7 Temp2	S_7 Temp2	S_3 IR	S_4 Light	S_3 IR
6	S_7 Temp2	S_7 Temp2	S_5 RFID	S_5 RFID	S_6 Sensor	S_3 IR	S_6 Sensor
7	S_5 RFID	S_5 RFID	S_6 Sensor	S_6 Sensor	S_7 Temp2	S_5 RFID	S_5 RFID

Table 3. The evaluation results of the of schema matching algorithms

Schema Rank	Cupid							COMA++						
	S_1	S_2	S_3	S_4	S_5	S_6	S_7	S_1	S_2	S_3	S_4	S_5	S_6	S_7
2	S_6	S_4	S_1	S_2	S_1	S_1	S_1	S_2	S_1	S_1	S_2	S_1	S_1	S_4
3	S_3	S_1	S_4	S_1	S_3	S_7	S_6	S_4	S_4	S_2	S_1	S_7	S_2	S_1
4	S_7	S_6	S_2	S_6	S_2	S_2	S_2	S_3	S_3	S_4	S_7	S_2	S_4	S_3
5	S_2	S_3	S_6	S_3	S_4	S_4	S_4	S_6	S_6	S_7	S_3	S_4	S_3	S_2
6	S_4	S_7	S_7	S_7	S_6	S_3	S_3	S_7	S_7	S_6	S_6	S_3	S_7	S_6
7	S_5	S_5	S_5	S_5	S_7	S_5	S_5	S_5	S_5	S_5	S_5	S_6	S_5	S_5
R_{norm}	0.667	0.905	0.801	0.801	0.905	0.952	0.762	1.000	1.000	0.857	0.857	0.81	0.905	0.952
Average	0.828							0.912						

6 Conclusion and Future Work

The main contribution of this paper is to propose a generic context interpreter to accomplish *physical context independence*. This work is based on the context-aware architecture, CADBA. Ontology based context model is used in this architecture. We design a generic context interpreter including context interpreter generator and a generic interpreter. A context interpretation script is proposed to replace function-based context interpreter. As we known, this is the originality of context provider or interpretation in context-aware computing. We also design a context editing tool for support the context mapping operation and devices maintenance. By introducing mapping operators and schema matching schemes, the generic context interpreter performs a more intelligent operating interface for users. The heterogeneity in pervasive context-aware computing will gain a graceful solution.

The problem of heterogeneity is a bottleneck while developing and extending context-aware systems in pervasive computing environment. The enforcement of context independence resolves dependency of devices and improves interoperability of applications. This work is intended as a starting point of future research on context generation. The problems of context management for context-aware computing will be paid more attention in the future.

Acknowledgments. This research was supported in part by the National Science Council of Taiwan, R.O.C. under contract NSC 98-2221-E-024-012.

References

1. Aumuller, D., Do, H., Massmann, S., Rahm, E.: Schema and Ontology Matching with COMA++. In: Proceedings of the 2005 ACM SIGMOD International Conference on Management of Data, pp. 906–908 (2005)
2. Baldauf, M., Dustdar, S., Rosenberg, F.: A Survey on Context-Aware Systems. International Journal of Ad Hoc and Ubiquitous Computing 2, 263–277 (2007)
3. Bartelt, C., Fischer, T., Niebuhr, D., Rausch, A., Seidl, F., Trapp, M.: Dynamic Integration of Heterogeneous Mobile Devices. In: Proceedings of the 2005 Workshop on Design and Evolution of Autonomic Application Software, pp. 1–7 (2005)
4. Biegel, G., Cahill, V.: A Framework for Developing Mobile, Context-Aware Applications. In: Proceedings of the 2nd IEEE Conference on Pervasive Computing and Communication, pp. 361–365 (2004)
5. Chien, B.C., Tsai, H.C., Hsueh, Y.K.: CADBA: A Context-aware Architecture based on Context Database for Mobile Computing. In: Proceedings of the International Workshop on Pervasive Media, in the Sixth International Conference on Ubiquitous Intelligence and Computing, Brisbane, Australia, pp. 367–372 (2009)
6. Dey, A.K., Abowd, G.D., Salber, D.: A Conceptual Framework and a Toolkit for Supporting the Rapid Prototyping of Context-Aware Applications. Human-Computer Interaction 16, 97–166 (2001)
7. Gu, T., Pung, H.K., Zhang, D.Q.: Toward an OSGi-Based Infrastructure for Context-Aware Applications. IEEE Pervasive Computing 3, 66–74 (2004)
8. Gudivada, V.N., Raghavan, V.V.: Design and Evaluation of Algorithms for Image Retrieval by Spatial Similarity. ACM Transactions on Information Systems 13, 115–144 (1995)
9. Hegering, H.G., Küpper, A., Linnhoff-Popien, C., Reiser, H.: Management challenges of context-aware services in ubiquitous environments. In: Brunner, M., Keller, A. (eds.) DSOM 2003. LNCS, vol. 2867, pp. 246–259. Springer, Heidelberg (2003)
10. Hofer, T., Schwinger, W., Pichler, M., Leonhartsberger, J., Altmann, G.: Context-Awareness on Mobile Devices–the Hydrogen Approach. In: Proceedings of the 36th Annual Hawaii International Conference on System Sciences, pp. 292–302 (2002)
11. Krill, P.: IBM Research Envisions Pervasive Computing. InfoWorld (2000)
12. Madhavan, J., Bernstein, P.A., Rahm, E.: Generic Schema Matching with Cupid. In: Proceedings of the 27th International Conference of Very Large Data Bases, pp. 49–58 (2001)
13. Nakazawa, J., Tokuda, H., Edwards, W.K., Ramachandran, U.: A Bridging Framework for Universal Interoperability in Pervasive Systems. In: Proceedings of the 26th IEEE International Conference on Distributed Computing Systems, pp. 3–3 (2006)
14. Roman, M., Hess, C., Cerqueira, R., Ranganathan, A., Campbell, R.H., Nahrstedt, K.: A Middle-Ware Infrastructure for Active Spaces. IEEE Pervasive Computing 1, 74–83 (2002)
15. Schilit, A., Theimer, M.: Disseminating Active Map Information to Mobile Hosts. IEEE Network 8, 22–32 (1994)
16. Schmohl, R., Baumgarten, U.: A Generalized Context-Aware Architecture in Heterogeneous Mobile Computing Environments. In: Proceedings of the 2008 The Fourth International Conference on Wireless and Mobile Communications, pp. 118–124 (2008)
17. Weiser, M.: The Computer for the 21st Century. Scientific American 265, 94–104 (1991)

Supporting Filename Partial Matches in Structured Peer-to-Peer Overlay

Guanling Lee, Jia-Sin Huang, and Yi-Chun Chen

Department of Computer Science and Information Engineering
National Dong Hwa University, Hualien, Taiwan, R.O.C
guanling@mail.ndhu.edu.tw, {fft16a,divien}@gmail.com

Abstract. In recent years, research issues associated with peer-to-peer (P2P) systems have been discussed widely. To resolve the file-availability problem and improve the workload, a method called the Distributed Hash Table (DHT) has been proposed. However, DHT-based systems in structured architectures cannot support efficient queries, such as a similarity query, range query, and partial-match query, due to the characteristics of the hash function. This study presents a novel scheme that supports filename partial-matches in structured P2P systems. The proposed approach supports complex queries and guarantees result quality. Experimental results demonstrate the effectiveness of the proposed approach.

Keywords: Peer-to-Peer overlay, DHT, Filename partial match.

1 Introduction

The P2P overlays can be classified as either unstructured or structured. Unstructured P2P overlays, such as Gnutella and Freenet, do not embed a logical and deterministic structure to organize peer nodes. These overlays need a particular message flooding type to search for specific items stored in overlays, resulting in poor efficiency. Several works [1] [2] are proposed to improve these drawbacks by changing search policy or overlay topology. They can ease the network cost effectively; however, file availability is still not solved.

Structured P2P systems, such as CAN [3] and Chord [5], utilize a Distributed Hash Table (DHT) to direct searches to specific node(s) holding the requested data. In DHT-based systems, each node manages a subspace partitioned in the key space, and maintains information about nodes connected as neighbors for use during query forwarding. Files are hashed into values, points in the key space, and published to nodes responsible for the keys. Based on this mechanism, DHT-based P2P systems reduce overhead load and maintain file availability. However, due to the hash characteristic, DHT-based systems can only support keyword searches.

This work discusses the problem of supporting filename partial match in structured P2P systems. Partial match of a filename search is widely used in Windows and UNIX systems as it is a useful and powerful user function. For example, a query "com*" can retrieve all files whose filename start with "com". "Computer.txt" and "commerce.txt" are examples of retrieved filenames.

R.-S. Chang et al. (Eds.): GPC 2010, LNCS 6104, pp. 101–108, 2010.
© Springer-Verlag Berlin Heidelberg 2010

In the proposed approach, the filename of published files are first translated to form the index sequences that can be mapped into a set of keys in a structured P2P system. During query processing, a query is transformed into one or several query phrase(s) and each query phrase is then mapped into a key in the P2P system structure. By using the key, a user can locate the node responsible for the key. There are some advantages in our work. First, all kinds of file types can be collected. Second, the recall of a query can be guaranteed.

The remainder of this paper is organized as follows. The problem definition is described in Section 2. Section 3 presents the proposed approach. Experimental results and analysis are discussed in Section 4. Section 5 summarizes this work.

2   Preliminaries

In the proposed approach, the filename of each published file is first partitioned into a set of d-length pieces (d-length indicates that this piece is d long) and each d-length piece is hashed into an index sequence $< v_0, v_1 ......, v_{d-1} >$, denoted as IS, with $0 \leq v_i \leq r-1$ and $0 \leq i \leq d-1$, where d means dimension in the mapping function and r is range in each dimension. How to translate a filename into a set of IS is discussed in Section 3. In the following, how to map an IS into a specific key in Chord is discussed.

Assume m is the size of a finger table, by Eq. (1), an IS can be mapped into a specific key in Chord. Similar mapping methods can be utilized to map an IS into a specific key in other structured P2P systems.

$$Loc(v_0, v_1 ......, v_{d-1}) = \sum_{j=0}^{d-1} (v_j) r^j \mod 2^m \tag{1}$$

For example, assume d = 2, r = 4 and m = 4. By Eq. 1, an IS <2, 3> is mapped into a specific key, 14 ($Loc(2,3) = (2 * 4^0 + 3 * 4^1) \mod 2^4 = 14$).

Furthermore, if r and d are chosen to satisfy the equation $r^d \mod 2^m = 0$, load balance can be achieved. The reason is discussed in Section 4.

3   File Publishing and Query Processing

3.1   File Publishing

For each published file, the sliding window partition method is applied to cut the filename into d-length pieces. Each piece is then put into a publish function, as in Eq. 2, and forms an IS. In Eq. 2, ISj denotes the index sequence formed by the d-length piece starting from the j-th character, p is the length of the published filename and h is a hash function such as "SHA-1" [4].

$$f(a_i) = \begin{cases} h[a_i] \bmod r, & \text{if } a_i \neq \text{'+'} \\ \text{random value from 0 to r-1,} & \text{if } a_i = \text{'+'} \end{cases}$$

$$IS_j = < f(a_j), f(a_{j+1}), ..., f(a_{j+d-1}) >, 0 \leq j \leq p-d \tag{2}$$

According to the above equation, each file can be represented as a collection of its corresponding ISj, $\{IS_0, IS_1, ..., IS_{p-d}\}$ and the collection is denoted as CIS. By Eq. 1, each IS in CIS is mapped into a specific key in Chord. Therefore, each file is mapped into (p-d+1) keys and placed in Chord.

For the case in which the filename length is shorter than d, (d-p) '+' is added to the end of the filename. After appending the filename, the filename length will be d. Hence, only one index is placed in chord. The reason for assigning a random value from 0 to (d-1) in Eq. 2 is to achieve load balance. That is, when the value is fixed, some peers will have additional workload. Due to the space limitation, the detail algorithm for file publish is omitted here.

3.2 Query Processing

In the proposed scheme, a section of the query string is selected to represent the query. This selected piece is input into Eq. 3 to form a query phrase (QP). Given a query S, QP is selected as follows. First, S is decomposed into several pieces according to '*'. If the query does not contain any '*', decomposition is unnecessary. By applying the sliding window partition method to all pieces, a set of QP candidates is retrieved. If the length of the QP candidate is shorter than d, "+" is added based on the position of '*' or at the end when the query does not contain '*', until its length is d. The QP candidate that contains the least number of '+' is chosen for input into Eq. 3, and QP is obtained. The '+' in the query means "just one character and regardless of which one it is, all characters in that position can be an answer." In Eq. 3, "−1" is used to deal with this situation. When the dimension value is "−1," the whole dimension must be searched. That is, QP will be extended into a set of QP, denoted as CQP, according to the range. Each QP in the CQP is mapped into a specific key in Chord using Eq. 1. According to the key, the peer responsible for the key in Chord is located.

$$m(s_i) = \begin{cases} h[s_i] \bmod r, & \text{if } s_i \neq \text{'+'} \\ \text{-1,} & \text{if } s_i = \text{'+'} \end{cases}$$

$$QP = < m(s_0), m(s_1), m(s_2), ..., m(s_{d-1}) > \tag{3}$$

Notably, because the filenames of published files may be shorter than d, if the leading character of the selected QP candidate is '+', the rotation process should be applied to find such a file. For example, when d=4, query string "*AB" is transformed into ++AB. For the case in which filename length is less than d, such as "AB" or "CAB", cannot be found in the search process. To deal with this situation, ++AB is rotated to form the set {++AB, +AB+, AB++} to find all possible files. Fig. 1 presents the algorithm in detail.

```
Algorithm   Search
Input :
        Q : query
        d : dimension
Procedure Query (Q,d)
1: Select the represented string S in Q
2: Translate S to QP according to equation 3
3: if (QP contains "-1")
4: {
5:    QP extends to CQP
6:    For each QP in CQP
7:    {
8:       Translate QP into a key according to equation 1
9:       Put the key into search_pool
10:   }
11:}
12:else
13:{
14:   Translate QP into a key according to equation 1
15:   Put the key into search_pool
16:}
17:For each key in the search_pool
18:   Search the peers responsible for the key
19:end
```

Fig. 1. Query processing

4 Experimental Results

4.1 Simulation Setup

All programs were written in Java and run on a PC with 3.0G Pentium 4 processor and 1G memory. The published filename is constituted by characters from A–Z and are generated synthetically.

During the simulation, the following metrics are discussed.

1. *Hop-count*, measured by the average number of nodes should be accessed when processing a query. In Chord, hop-count is bounded. In the worst case, the average hop-count is m, where m is the finger table size. However, in the proposed technique, when the selected QP contains '+', several subqueries are involved to retrieve query results. Therefore, how query types, number of dimensions and range affect hop-counts is discussed.

2. *Effectiveness* is measured by average precision and recall. Precision and recall are defined as follows.

$$Precision = \frac{number\ of\ relevant\ files}{number\ of\ relevant\ indices} \qquad (4)$$

$$Recall = \frac{number\ of\ retrieved\ files}{number\ of\ total\ relevant\ files} \qquad (5)$$

Table 1 shows the query types used in the simulation. And table 2 shows the default parameters of the simulation.

Table 1. Query types

Type	Description
One *	Query contains one star
S	Query wrapped by *
*S	Query start with a star
One +	Query contains one plus
Two +	Query contain two plus

Table 2. Default parameter setting

Parameter	Default setting
Number of published files per peer	10
Filename length	Random number from 5 to 25
Query length	Random number from 4 to 12
m (finger table size)	24
Dimension (d)	12
Range (r)	16

4.2 Hop-Count

During the simulation, the aggregation method is utilized to route the query. In the proposed algorithm, QP is extended to a set of QP when QP contains −1. To reduce network cost, the aggregation method is used. If the search path of several QPs is the same, we only need to traverse the path once. Figure 2 shows the effects of dimension. Regardless of query type, average hop-counts increase as dimension increases. This relationship exists because, during query processing, a query string is first partitioned into a set of pieces according to the position of '*.' As d increases, the piece length has increased likelihood to be shorter than d. As a result, '+' is added to the piece until its length is d. Therefore, QP is extended to a set of QP, which increases search cost.

Furthermore, the query containing one '*' will incur a large number of hop-counts; the reason is similar to that in the above discussion. That is, the query is partitioned into two small pieces that will have a little chance of being longer than d as d increases. Consequently, '+' will be added to the pieces and will increase search cost.

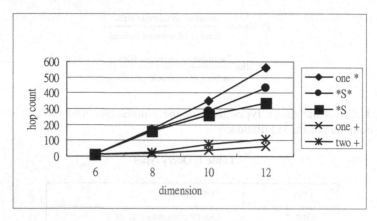

Fig. 2. Average hop-counts with different dimensions

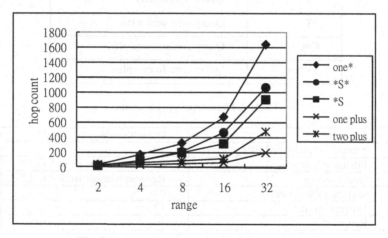

Fig. 3. Average hop-counts with different ranges

Fig. 3 shows the effects of range. Hop-counts increase as range increases. When QP contains '+', QP is extended to CQP according to the range. For example, if the range is 16, the CQP will contain 16 QPs when the original QP contains one '+,' and 16*16 QPs when the original QP contains two '+.' A large range results in a large search key pool. Therefore, hop-counts increase as range increases.

4.3 Effectiveness

Effectiveness is measured by average precision and recall. As discussed in Section 3.4, the recall of the proposed approach is 100%. Therefore, only precision is discussed in this section.

Fig. 4 shows the precision with different dimensions. The length of IS is d. A long IS improves discrimination in distinguishing between different files. Furthermore, when d is increasing, the number of indices yielded by each published file decreases. These two effects cause denominator of precision to decrease. Hence, precision increases as d increases.

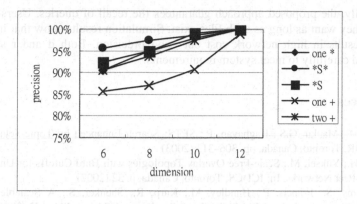

Fig. 4. Precision with different dimensions

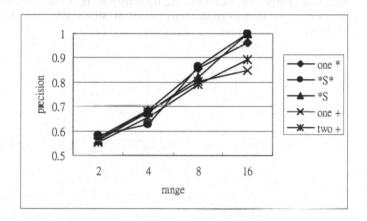

Fig. 5. Precision with different ranges when the dimension is 6

Fig. 5 shows the effect of range. In simulation, the default dimension is 6. Simulation results show that precision increases as range increases. The reason for this relationship is that collision probability of hashing a character into a value decreases as range increases. Consequently, precision increases.

5 Conclusion

This work presented a novel method that supports filename partial match in a P2P overlay. In the proposed approach, the filenames of published files are first translated to form index sequences that can be mapped into a set of keys in a structured P2P system. During query processing, a query is transformed into one or several query phrase(s), and each query phrase is mapped into a key in the structure P2P system. With this key, a user can find the node responsible for the key. Any structured P2P system employing the proposed approach can support filename partial matches.

Additionally, the proposed approach guarantees the recall of queries. Users can find any files they want as long as such files exist. Simulation results show that increasing d and r results in high network cost but good precision. Both d and r should be determined carefully to meet system requirements.

References

1. Bawa, M., Manku, G.S., Raghavan, P.: SETS: Search Enhanced by Topic-Segmentation. In: SIGIR, Toronto, Canada, pp. 306–313 (2003)
2. Guclu, H., Yuksel, M.: Scale-Free Overlay Topologies with Hard Cutoffs for Unstructured Peer-to-Peer Networks. In: ICDCS, Toronto, Canada, p. 32 (2007)
3. Ratnasamy, S., Francis, P., Handley, M., Karp, R., Shenker, S.: A Scalable Content-Addressable Network. In: ACM SIGCOMM, San Diego, USA, pp. 161–172 (2001)
4. http://www.w3.org/PICS/DSig/SHA1_1_0.html
5. Stoica, I., Morris, R., Karger, D., Kaashoek, M., Balakrishnan, H.: Chord: A scalable peer-to-peer lookup service for internet applications. In: ACM SIGCOMM, San Diego, USA, pp. 149–160 (2001)

EEG: A Way to Explore Learner's Affect in Pervasive Learning Systems

Jizheng Wan[1,2], Bin Hu[1,3,*], and Xiaowei Li[3]

[1] Department of Computing, Birmingham City University,
Birmingham B42 2SU, United Kingdom
[2] Corporate ICT, Birmingham City University, Birmingham B42 2SU, United Kingdom
[3] School of Information Science and Engineering, Lanzhou University, Lanzhou, China
{Bin.Hu,Jizheng.Wan}@bcu.ac.uk, lixwei@lzu.edu.cn

Abstract. Although scientists and researchers have achieved fruitful outcomes in exploring the ways of detecting and understanding learners affect in pervasive learning systems, it sounds still necessary to deepen the recognition of learners affect in learning procedure with innovative methodologies. Our research focused on using Electroencephalography (EEG) approach to explore learner's affect. We analysed the EEG data using different signal processing algorithms and a real time EEG feedback based prototype was implemented to evaluate our findings. The result of experiment was encouraging and further discussion was also included in this paper.

Keywords: Affective Learning, EEG, Pervasive Computing, FastICA, ApEn.

1 Introduction

In recent years, there has been an increased interest in studying brain activity during real-world experiences. In spite of the difficulty of precisely defining it, brain activity is an omnipresent and important factor in human life. People's moods heavily influence their ways of communicating and acting, as well as productivity [1], and also play a crucial role in learning process.

Affective learning has been described in different ways, which sometimes creates confusion on what issues are being considered. The most limited perspective focuses on looking at how emotion can support the learning process, while others take a more integrated approach in affect, cognition and learning, while yet others focus on affective education or affective development. Affective learning represents an internalization of positive attitudes toward course content, subject matter or the instructor [2]. Affective reactions include feelings of self-confidence, self-efficacy, attitudes, preferences, and dispositions which may be viewed as a specific type of learning outcome [3], and affective learning activities are directed at coping with these feelings that arise during learning, and that positively or negatively impact the learning process [4]. For example, fun and enjoyment are well known to be effective

---

* Correspondence author.

R.-S. Chang et al. (Eds.): GPC 2010, LNCS 6104, pp. 109–119, 2010.

in children's development, both supporting and deepening learning, as well as facilitating engagement and motivation [5].

However, Dirkx [6] suggests that the role of emotions is much more than a motivational concern, and that the active dimension provides the foundation on which rest the practical, conceptual and imaginative modes of learning. On the one hand, emotional experiences lend us the ability to better comprehend and regulate our activities, to understand our motivations, and how to fulfill our needs [7], on the other hand, emotion's role in stimulating thought should be taken into consideration. Therefore, affective learning requires the integration of cognitive, emotional and aesthetic dimensions, all of which are of interest in the learning process [8].

EEG signal is a measurement of currents that flow during synaptic excitations of the dendrites of many pyramidal neurons in the cerebral cortex [9]. When brain cells(neurons) are activated, the synaptic currents are produced within the dendrites. EEG signals are the signatures of neural activities. They are captured by multiple-electrode EEG machines either from inside the brain, over the cortex under the skull, or certain locations over the scalp, and can be recorded in different formats. The signals are normally presented in the time domain. A wide variety may be recorded, a proverbial zoo of dynamic signatures, each waveform dependent in its own way on time and frequency. EEG is often labeled according to apparent frequency range: delta(1-4Hz), theta(4-8Hz), alpha(8-13Hz), beta(13-20Hz), and gamma (roughly >20Hz) [9].

2   Relevant Research

A lot of prior research engaged in recognizing emotions with computers. For example, recognizing emotion from speech, facial expressions or a fusion of both methods. Measuring emotion from brain activity is a relatively new method, although some valuable conclusions have been published.

Early researchers found that the sensitivity of EEG changes in mental effort. For example, Hans Berger [10] and others [11] report a decrease in the amplitude of the alpha (8-13 Hz) rhythm during mental arithmetic tasks Other researchers have shown that higher memory loads cause increases in theta (4-8 Hz) and low-beta (13-15 Hz) power in the frontal midline regions of the scalp [12], gamma (>30 Hz) oscillations [13], as well as inter-electrode correlation, coherence, cross phase, and cross power [14]. David Grimes showed us an experiment about measuring working load with an EEG [15]. Prized et al. [16] built systems based on task load metric and their result shows that alpha decreases and theta increases with higher task load.

Bo Hong et al. [17] from Tsinghua University report that ApEn generally tends to increase during the process people pay attention to some stuff.

In the work of Delft university [1], participant's EEG signals was recorded and processed when they were viewing pictures selected from International Affective Picture System (IAPS) database. Their results show that EEG data contains enough information to recognize emotion.

R W Picard [18] of MIT proposed a solution using various sensors that can capture postural, facial, and skin-surface changes that carry affective information. They designed a system for automated recognition of a child's interest level in natural learning situations. Their research uses a combination of information from chair pressure patterns sensed by Tekscan pressure arrays and from upper facial features sensed by an IBM BlueEyes video camera. They achieved an accuracy of 76% on affect category recognition from chair pressure patterns, and 88% on nine basic postures that were identified as making up the affective behaviors.

Danny Oude Bos [19] conducted a research project to recognize emotion from brain signals measured with the BraInquiry EEG PET device. His work discussed the optimal placement of a limited number of electrodes for emotion recognition and the experimental phase, which finally was analyzed to see what results could be achieved.

2.1 Our Work

As we can see, most of these studies based on EEG signals processing aimed at recognizing common emotions. Our work focuses on affect in learning state and conducts a systematic analysis of relationship between EEG and affect. It is supposed to afford us a new way of understanding students' affect in learning process so as to trigger innovative thinking and enhance creativity in learning process.

Moreover, most existing studies obtain affective information through speech, motion, gesture, facial expression, etc. Designing affective learning experiments on learners while introducing limited disturbances on learners is one of the challenges.

New techniques need to be introduced to enrich the ways of understanding learners' affect better such as EEG approach.

3   System Architecture

Fig.1 shows the system architecture. Generally speaking, we use Nexus device to collect EEG signals from users during their learning process. These signals will received by their own mobile device through Bluetooth in real time. The mobile device will format these data and send back to our affective learning server where we use FastICA and ApEn algorithms to analyse these EEG signals. The feedback will send back to users' mobile device shortly.

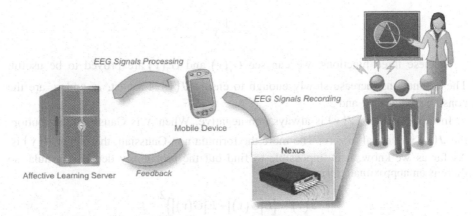

Fig. 1. System Architecture

4 EEG Signals Processing and Analysis

As we introduced in last section, signal processing and analysis is handled by the Affective Learning Server. As we can imagine, EEG signals indicate huge and complex information, which include the status of the whole body, physical and mental. Therefore, EEG signals refinement is quite a challenge work. Many algorithms have been proposed so far for processing EEG signals. Such as time-domain analysis, frequency-domain analysis, spatial-domain analysis and multi-way processing etc. In this particular case, we use FastICA and ApEn algorithms.

4.1 FastICA

FastICA based on negentropy is aimed at optimizing the algorithm via stochastic gradient algorithm to adjust the separate matrix W, and negentropy is used to estimate the non-Gaussian, its definition as follows [20]:

$$J(y) = Hg(y) - H(y)$$

$Hg(y)$ and $H(y)$ are the same Gaussian distribution covariance entropy of information. Because of the difficulties of calculation, we can use the following approximate formula:

$$J(y) = H_{gauss}(y) - H(y) \propto a\{E[G'(y)]\}^2 + b\{E[G(y)] - E[G(v)]\}^2$$

Whereas a, b are positive constant, $E(*)$ is the mathematical expectation, v is a standard Gaussian random variable. $G(*)$ is a non-quadratic form that usually choose these functions:

$$G_1(y) = \frac{1}{a_1} \log \cosh a_1 y$$

$$G_2(y) = -\frac{1}{a_2} \exp(-a_2 y^2 / 2)$$

$$G_3 = -\frac{1}{4} y^4$$

In these three functions, we can see $G_1(y)$ and $G_2(y)$ are proved to be useful. These functions increase slowly enough to ensure $J(y)$ is robust. a_1 and a_2 are the constants between 1 and 2.

In this condition, $J(y)$ is always non-negative. When y is Gaussian distribution, the $J(y)$ will equal to zero. The more the formula non-Gaussian, the bigger $J(y)$ is. As far as we know, it is impossible to find out the probability density formula, so there is an approximate formula:

$$J(y) \propto \{E[G(y)] - E[G(v)]\}^2$$

And then, we only need a optimizing algorithm to find W matrix, $Y = WX$, use this formula and maximize its negentropy.

The FastICA algorithm process shows below:

1. **Centralization of the EEG raw data**

   It's important to process the raw data, centralization also was called mean removal, which makes the signals' mean equal zero. In order to centralize the signal S, subtract it's mean $E[X]$, $X' = X - E[X]$, as a result, $E[X'] = E[X - E[X]] = E[X] - E[X] = 0$.

2. **Whitening matrix**

   Find a whitening matrix, and the output after the transform $X' = DX$, and the components of which are uncorrelated and the variance equals one. $E[XX^T] = I$, I is unit matrix

3. Select the number of components N which we need to estimate. Suppose the iteration $P < -1$

4. Choose an initial weighting vector W_0. W_0 is a random matrix between $[-1,1]$, it can be created by MATLAB.

5. Use this, $W_p = E\{ XG(W_p^T X) \} - E\{ G(W_p^T X) \}$, and then $W_p = W_p - \sum_{j=1}^{P-1} (W_p^T W_j) W_j$

6. $W_p = W_p / \|W_p\|$, this needs to judge if the iteration is constringency.

7. If W_p is not constringency, return to step 5.

8. $p = p + 1$, if $p < N$, return to step 4.

In fact, FastICA is usually fast and stable. However, from step 6 we can see that the marshalling sequence is uncertain. Using matched filter can solve this problem, and then the SNR (signal-to-noise) will be improved obviously by using the matched filter.

4.2 ApEn Algorithm

The ApEn algorithm process shows below [21] [22]:

1. Let the original data be $\langle X(n) \rangle = x(1), x(2),...,x(N)$, where N is the total number of data points. Form m-vectors $X(1), X(2),...,X(N-m+1)$ defined by:

$$X(i) = [x(i), x(i+1),...,x(i+m-1)], \qquad i = 1,2,...,N-m+1 \qquad (1)$$

2. Define the distance between $X(i)$ and $X(j)$, $d[X(i),X(j)]$, as the maximum absolute difference between their corresponding scalar elements, i.e.

$$d[X(i),X(j)] = \max_{k=1,2,...,m+1} (|x(i+k) - x(j+k)|) \qquad (2)$$

3. For a given $X(i)$, count the number of j ($j = 1,2,...,N-m+1$) for $j \neq i$ such that $d[X(i),X(j)] \leq r$, denoted ad $N_r^m(i)$. Then, for $i = 1,2,...,N-m+1$,

$$C_r^m(i) = N^m(i)/(N-m+1) \qquad (3)$$

The $C_r^m(i)$ values measure, within a tolerance r, the regularity (frequency) of patterns similar to one of the given window length m.

4. Compute the natural logarithm of each $C_r^m(i)$, and compute the average of it over i,

$$\phi^m(r) = \frac{1}{N-m+1} \sum_{i=1}^{N-m+1} \ln C_r^m(i) \tag{4}$$

Where $\phi^m(r)$ represents the average frequency of all the m-point patterns in the sequence, which is still close to each other.

5. Increase the dimension to $m+1$. Repeat step 1 to 4 and find $C_r^{m+1}(i)$ and $\phi^{m+1}(r)$

6. The approximate entropy is defined as:

$$ApEn(m,r) = \lim_{N \to \infty} [\phi^m(r) - \phi^{m+1}(r)] \tag{5}$$

In actual operation, the number of data point is limited when the data length is N and the result obtained through the above stops is the estimate of ApEn, which can be denoted as:

$$ApEn(m,r) = \phi^m(r) - \phi^{m+1}(r) \tag{6}$$

Obviously, the value of the estimate depends on m and r. The two parameters must be fixed before ApEn can be calculated. As suggested by Pincus [23], m can be taken as 2 and r can be taken as $(0.1 \; 0.25) \, SD_x$, where SD_x is the standard deviation of the original data sequence $\langle x(n) \rangle$. In our study we have used $m = 2$ and $r = 0.15$.

5 The Findings between EEG and Learning Affect

In our previous work, we built an affective learning web site which contains a variety of learning content, such as English, computer science, mathematics, etc. The learners were asked to visit the Web, as a learning process, whose EEG signal was recorded simultaneously. After partitioning the data sample into equal long slices in time domain, EEG signals were analyzed in three respects: amplitude analysis, frequency analysis and ApEn analysis.

5.1 Amplitude Analysis

Earlier experiments showed that participants were easier to pay attention when they learned simple, interesting materials, at the same time, changes in alpha wave amplitude were smaller, and amplitudes were also smaller on average. For example, Fig.2 shows comparison between amplitudes of two alpha wave segments of a user. Series 1 implies that the learner focuses on study. Series 2 denotes the opposite condition.

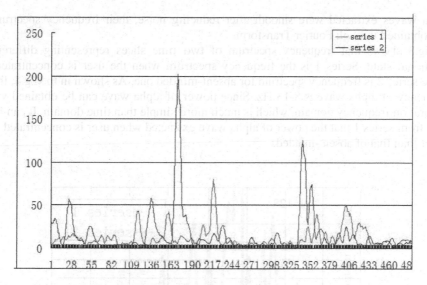

Fig. 2. Comparison between amplitudes of two alpha waves of a user in different mood

How to extract features to reflect the changes of mental states is very important.

In amplitude analysis, for every equivalent time slice we extract the following features: starting time, maximum amplitude, minimum amplitude and mean value of amplitude. Amplitude analysis result of a 60 seconds alpha wave is shown in Table 1. Over 60 Seconds of raw and computed data, starting at t =20 Sec is presented. 0.00% of the data was rejected (artifacts).

Table 1. Session overview statistics

Min	Max	Mean	Variance	StdDev
0.44	267.04	23.36	1077.65	32.83

Because of individual differences of EEG signals, there is no uniform standard to judge the meaning of signals. In our previous work, we proposed two solutions for the problem.

In recording alpha waves of a user in a certain period of time, generally two methods will be applied to assess his or her state of mind. One is to compare computed mean amplitude with common mean values when users are calm down and focused on study. If the computed mean amplitude is far more than common ones, then it may indicate that the user is somehow absent-minded. The other is to calculate the mean difference between the max and min amplitude and compare with the standard difference among all of the time-slices. Obviously, significant distinction between the two values implies loss of attention.

5.2 Frequency Analysis

There is not only amplitude but also frequency characteristics that should be taken into consideration. The same samples were used for frequency analysis. Since the alpha waves extracted were smooth after reducing noise, their frequency spectrum was obtained through Fourier Transform.

Fig.3 shows that frequency spectrum of two time slices representing different emotional state. Series 1 is the frequency spectrum when the user is concentrated, while series 2 is frequency spectrum for absent-minded one. As shown in the ⁻g.4, the frequency of alpha wave is 8-13 Hz. Since power of alpha wave can be obtained via integral on frequency domain, which is much more simple than time domain. It can be seen from series 1 that the power of alpha wave extracted when user is concentrated is lower than that of absent-minded.

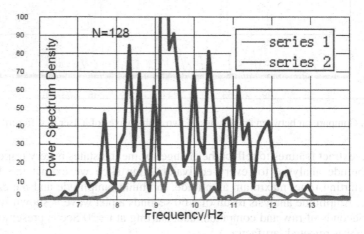

Fig. 3. Comparison of frequency spectrum of two alpha waves with the same person in different emotional state

5.3 ApEn Analysis

ApEn is a series of parameters and statistics recently introduced to quantify regularity in data without any priori knowledge of the system which generate them [24]. The first idea of ApEn was introduced by Steven M.Pincus in 1991 [23], and it is a useful and complex measure for biological time series data. ApEn is a statistical instrument initially designed to handle short and noisy time series data. Notably, it detects changes in underlying episodic behavior which is not reflected in peak occurrences or amplitudes [25]. The more complex the sequence data is, the more probably the new pattern appears and the larger the corresponding ApEn is. Please refer to section 4.2 for details.

In our prior work, we did some research of ApEn in the area of affective learning, and the experimental result showed that ApEn had a close relation to learners' attention. Fig.4 shows the comparison of ApEn of a same person in two different learning states. Series 1 implies that the learner was of inattention to the learning material. Series 2 denotes the opposite condition.

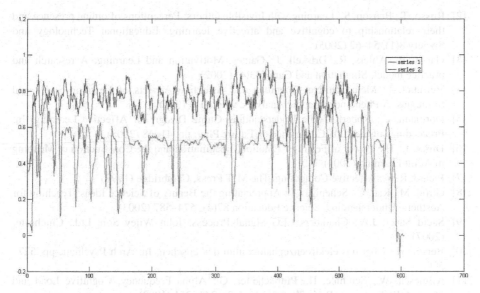

Fig. 4. Comparison of ApEn of a same person in two different learning states

These results give some proofs of the relation between EEG signal and affect in learning state. However this is not enough, because the number of features is too limited and we cannot obtain quantitative evaluation of these features. From this point of view, we propose the data mining based solution in order that more features could be taken into consideration and certain group of features that can describe affect better can be discovered and put into practice.

6   Conclusion and Discussion

In this paper we intend to find the relationship between the characteristics of the brain activity and the emotion changes in a learning process and apply it to practice. We analysed the EEG data using different signal processing algorithms and a real time EEG feedback based prototype was implemented to evaluate our findings.

In the first two sections, background information and related research have been presented. Then we introduced the system architecture and explained the algorithms we use to analyze EEG signal in detail. The outcomes have been shown in section 5 and these results can also contribute to assisting in understanding of learners' emotion in learning process.

References

[1] Horlings, R., Datcu, D., Rothkrantz, L.J.M.: Emotion Recognition using Brain Activity. In: Proceedings of the 9th International Conference on Computer Systems and Technologies and Workshop for PhD Students in Computing, pp. 11.1-1–11.1-6 (2008)

[2] Russo, T., Benson, S.: Learning with Invisible Others: Perceptions of online presence and their relationship to cognitive and affective learning. Educational Technology and Society 8(1), 54–62 (2005)

[3] Garris, R., Ahlers, R., Driskell, J.: Games, Motivation and Learning: A research and practice model. Simulation and Game 33(4) (2002)

[4] Vermunt, J.: Metacognitive, Cognitive and Affective Aspects of Learning Styles and Strategies: A Phenomenographic Analysis, vol. (31) (1996)

[5] Dormann, C.: Robert Biddle Understanding Game Design for Affective Learning. In: Proceedings of the 2008 Conference on Future Play, pp. 41–48 (2008)

[6] Dirkx, J.: The Power of Feelings: Emotion, Imagination and the Construction of Meaning in Adult Learning (2001)

[7] Picard, R.W.: Affective Computing. The MIT Press, Cambridge (1997)

[8] Girod, M., Rau, C., Schepige, A.: Appreciating the Beauty of Science Ideas: Teaching for Aesthetic Understanding. Science Education 87(4), 574–587 (2003)

[9] Saeid Sanei, J.A.: Chambers EEG Signal Process. John Wiley Son, Ltd., Chichester (2007)

[10] Berger, H.: Uber das elektroenzephalogramm des enschen. In: Arch Psychiatr, pp. 527–570

[11] Kilmesch, W., Schimke, H., Pfurtscheller, G.: Alpha Frequency, Cognitive Load and Memory Performance. Brain Topography 5(3), 241–251 (1993)

[12] Mecklinger, A., Kramer, A.F., Strayer, D.L.: Event Related Potentials and EEG Components in a Semantic Memory Search Task. Psychophysiology 29, 104–119 (1992)

[13] Howard, M.W., et al.: Gamma Oscillations Correlate with Working Memory Load in Humans. Cerebral Cortex 13, 1369–1374 (2007)

[14] Pleydell-Pearce, C.W., Whitecross, S.E., Dickson, B.T.: Multi-Variate Analysis of EEG: Predicting Cognition on the Basis of Frequency Decomposition, Inter-electrode Correlation, Coherence, Cross Phase and Cross Power. In: Hawaii International Conference on System Sciences, pp. 11–20 (2003)

[15] Grimes, D., Tan, D.S., Hudson, S.E., Henoy, P., Rao, R.P.N.: Feasibility and pragmatics of classifying working memory load with an electroencephalograph. In: Proceeding of the twenty-sixth annual SIGCHI conference on Human factors in computing systems, pp. 835–844 (2008)

[16] Prinzel, L.J., Pope, A.T., Freeman, F.G., Scerbo, M.W., Mikulka, P.J.: Empirical analysis of EEG and ERPs for psychophysiological adaptive task allocation, NASA, Technical Report TM-2001-211016 (2001)

[17] Hong, B., Tang, Q., Yang, F., Chen, T.: APEN and Cross-APEN: Property, Fast Algorithm and Preliminary Application to the Study of EEG and Congnition. Signal Processing 15(2), 100–108 (1999)

[18] Picard, R.W., Papert, S., Bender, W.: Affective Learning-A Manifesto. BT Technology Journal 22(4), 253–269 (2004)

[19] Bos, D.O.: EEG-Based Emotion Recognition (2006),
http://emi.uwi.utwente.nl/verslagen/capita-selecta/
CS-oudeBosDanny.PDF

[20] Eichele, T., Calhoun, V.D., Debener, S.: Mining EEG-fMRI using independent component analysis. International Journal of Psychophysiology (2009)

[21] Roberto, H., Mateo, A., Daniel, A.: Interpretation of Approximate Entropy: Analysis of Intracranial Pressure Approximate Entropy During Acute Intracranial Hypertension. IEEE Transactions on Biomedical Engineering 52, 1671–1680 (2005)

[22] Huang, L.Y., Wang, Y.M., Liu, J.P., Wang, J.: Approximate Entropy of EEG as a Measure of Cerebral Ischemic Injury. In: Proceedings of the 26th Annual International Conference of the IEEE EMBS, San Francisco, pp. 4537–4539 (2004)

[23] Pincus, S.M.: Approximate Entropy as a Measure of System Complexity. Proc. Natl. Acad. Sci. USA 88, 2297–2301 (1991)

[24] Pincus, S., Goldberger, A.: Physiological Time Series Analysis: What does Regularity Quantify? Heart. Circ. Physiol. 266, 1643–1656 (1994)

[25] Hornero, R., Abasolo, D.E., Jimeno, N., Espino, P.: Applying approximate entropy and central tendency measure to analyze time series generated by schizophrenic patients. In: 25th Annual International Conference of the IEEE EMBS, Cancun, pp. 2447–2450 (2003)

The Mission-Oriented Self-deploying Methods for Wireless Mobile Sensor Networks*

Shih-Chang Huang[**]

Department of Computer Science, National Formosa University,
YinLin, Taiwan, ROC
Fax: 886-5-6330456
schuang@nfu.edu.tw

Abstract. In the mission-oriented mobile sensor networks, the mobile sensor nodes actively organize and deploy themselves when an event arises in the target location. The mobile sensor nodes are instructed by the base station to build a communication path to the location of the event quickly. In this paper, two greedy methods are proposed to organize the mobile sensor nodes as the shortest communication path from the monitor node to the target location. To reduce the deploying time and save the energy consumed on moving, the sensor node with minimal moving distance is instructed to move. The proposed method can automatically organize the sensor nodes to build the communication path even the initially deployed network is disconnected. Simulation results show that the proposed methods can reduce the moving distance and shorten the deploying time.

Keywords: Greedy Algorithm, Self Organization, Mobile Sensor Networks, Mission-oriented.

1 Introduction

A sensor network is composed of many sensor nodes. These sensor nodes perform the environment monitoring, data collecting, and cooperate with others to return the collected data to the monitors. Many methods have been proposed for deploying the stationary sensor nodes factitiously to optimize the coverage area [1][2][3][4]. However, most applications of sensor nodes are for the uncertainty environment and the number of sensor nodes is too large to deploy factitiously. Thus, the sensor nodes are usually randomly spreading over the interesting area.

Basically, sensor nodes are stationary. After the sensor nodes are deployed by randomly spreading, the network connectivity cannot be guaranteed. If the sensor network is initially partitioned, the requirement of acute observation on the environment will be violated. Deploying more sensor nodes is the only way to solve the problem of multiple partitioned networks. From the aspects of the economic cost and the network

---

[*] This work was supported in part by the National Science Council, Taiwan, ROC, under grant NSC98-2218-E-150-001.
[**] Corresponding author.

R.-S. Chang et al. (Eds.): GPC 2010, LNCS 6104, pp. 120–129, 2010.
© Springer-Verlag Berlin Heidelberg 2010

management, deploying more sensor nodes is the worst solution. Thus, providing sensor nodes the mobile ability can help us to connect the sensor nodes even they are partitioned initially.

Almost all the proposed methods focus themselves on enlarging the coverage by changing the initial deploying position of the sensor nodes to cover a larger area. For example, in the cluster architecture, part of the deployed sensor nodes plays as the local central controllers to coordinate other sensor nodes to determine their locations [5][6][7]. The other algorithms use the repulsion concept or attraction concept such as the potential field to deploy the mobile sensor nodes [8]. Each sensor node keeps a feasible distance with other nodes and avoids staying too close or too far. The similar mechanism is the molecule density [9][10] [11].

After the deploying procedure terminates, sensor nodes in these approaches are still stationary. Once the event arises outside the deployed area, no mechanism is used to change the topology to cover the target location of the occurrence. This makes these deployed sensor nodes become functionless. Thus, the mission-oriented deploying method is considered.

In the mission-oriented deploying method, the sensor nodes are redeployed to build a link from the monitor to the target location when an event arises. As the event terminates, the deployed sensor nodes can be reused. The locomotion ability is necessary for mission-oriented deployment. The critical issue is how to build the link as quickly as possible.

A mission-oriented method is proposed in [12] to deploy sensor nodes. The object of this method is to deploy sensor nodes according to the changes of the environment by the using local information to reduce the communication overhead. Sensor nodes are moved according to the moving priority which tries to build a stable communication link. This method works if each node is aware of the positions of other sensor nodes. This assumption is hard to achieve if the events take place after sensor nodes are deployed. Claiming the event location for every sensor node will generate more communication overhead. Besides, it is impossible to claim the event location if the sensor nodes are initially partitioned.

Thus, in this paper, a mission-oriented deploying method is proposed to dynamically build a communication path from the monitor to the location of the occurrence. In order to report the event quickly, the proposed methods will greedily build the shortest communication path to the target location. The constructing time of this path is also minimized. When the initial network is partitioned, the proposed method can automatically reconstruct the path from the monitor to the target location.

The rest of this paper is organized as follows. The proposed models are given in section 2. In section 3, we give and discuss the simulation results. And the conclusions are in section 4.

2 Proposed Mission-Based Deploying Methods

Assume that each sensor node is aware of its position and has the locomotion ability. Each sensor node has different size of communication range. When a detecting command is issued, only the sink node knows the position of the target location. In the real case, the sink node can easily obtain the position of the target location via the satellite communication system. Due to the number of spread sensor nodes is limited, using the minimal number of sensor nodes to build the communication path from the monitor (in the following, we use sink node as the monitor) to the target location is necessary. By leaving more unused sensor nodes, multiple paths can be created concurrently when several detecting commands are issued at the same time.

2.1 The Greedy Self-deploying Algorithm

To build a communication path with the minimal number of sensor nodes, we have to find the shortest distance from the sink node to target location. The shortest path is the one that lines directly from the sink node to the target location. We denote this path as L. With the coordinates of the sink node and the target location, all positions on L can be obtained from the line equation (1).

$$\frac{x-x_s}{y-y_s} = \frac{x_t-x_s}{y_t-y_s} . \tag{1}$$

Where (x_s, y_s) and (x_t, y_t) are the coordinates of the sink node and the target location.

Next, some of the sensor nodes will be instructed to move to the position on L to build a physical communication path. Because a sensor node spends much time on physical movement, shortening the moving time of the sensor node is one major point on quickly building the communication path. Thus, the sensor node with the shortest moving distance is chosen to build the path.

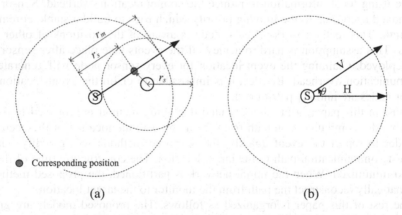

(a)   (b)

Fig. 1. Computing the distance and angle

The detail procedure is as following. Initially, all nodes except the sink node are marked as the *soldier* nodes which park at their locations waiting for instruction. When a command is issued, sink node acts as the first *marshal* node which instructs the soldier nodes to build the path toward the target location. The marshal node broadcasts a path construction request to the soldier nodes within its communication range. We denote those soldier nodes as a set Ω. This path construction request will contain the positions of the marshal node and the target location.

Each soldier node $S\{S \in \Omega\}$ computes its distance to the corresponding position on L. This corresponding position has a distance $d = \min(r_m, r_s)$ to the marshal node, where r_m and r_s are communication range of the marshal node and the soldier node S. Besides, the position is also closer to the target location than the position of marshal node. Fig. 1(a) shows the corresponding position. The polar coordinate system can help us to find the corresponding position of the soldier node S quickly. As the Fig. 1(b) shows, assume that the position of marshal node is (m_x, m_y), and the angle between L and the horizontal line is θ. The corresponding position in the polar coordinate system is (d, θ). Thus, the corresponding position of each S, (S_x, S_y), in Cartesian coordinate system can be easily gotten by (2).

$$\begin{cases} S_x = m_x + d \cos \theta \\ S_y = m_y + d \sin \theta \end{cases}. \tag{2}$$

By getting the (S_x, S_y) on the L, each S computes the distance from its current position (S_x^c, S_y^c) to the (S_x, S_y). The distance is $D_s = \sqrt{(S_x - S_x^c) + (S_y - S_y^c)}$. Each soldier node reports this distance to the marshal node. The soldier node with minimal D_s is chosen as the candidate who will be promoted as the next marshal node.

In (2), the angle θ can be obtained from the inner product of the unit vectors $\vec{V}$ and $\vec{H}$ shown as (3). The vector $\vec{V}$ starts from the position of marshal node toward the target location and the vector $\vec{H}$ is the vector of horizontal axis starting from the position of marshal node.

$$\theta = \cos^{-1}\left(\frac{\|\vec{V} \bullet \vec{H}\|}{\|\vec{V}\|\|\vec{H}\|}\right). \tag{3}$$

When the candidate reaches its corresponding position, it becomes a new marshal node and repeats the previous procedure. The previous marshal node becomes stationary and is marked as *senator*. This procedure stops until one marshal node covers the target location. A simple example illustrates the detail operation in Fig. 2.

Initially, the sensor nodes are deployed as the Fig. 2(a). The sink node S acts as the marshal node and broadcasts the path construction request to soldier nodes {A, B, C}, which are within its communication range. Among these three soldier nodes, B has the shortest distance to its corresponding position on L. B is instructed to be the candidate, shown as Fig. 2(b).

In Fig. 2(c), B steps into its corresponding position and becomes the marshal node. It starts to select the next candidate from {A, C, D}, which are within its communication range. Because the radii of these three nodes are shorter than B, they use their own radii to compute their corresponding positions on L. The soldier node D which has the shortest moving distance is selected to be the next marshal node.

In Fig. 2(d), D becomes the marshal node and only node E is in its communication range. Although the soldier node E has longer communication range than the marshal node D, the minimal range r_D is used. The procedures in the Fig. 2(d) and 2(e) are similar. The candidates in these two figures are E and F. In Fig. 2(f), because the

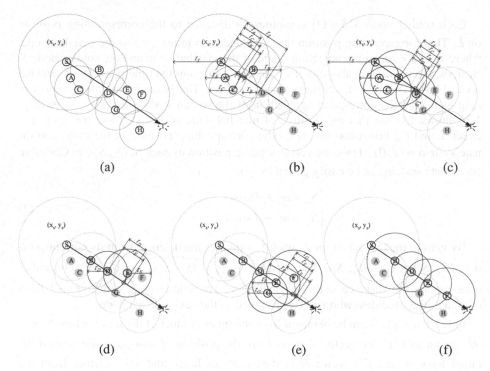

(a)   (b)   (c)

(d)   (e)   (f)

Fig. 2. The sensor nodes deploying example

marshal node F finds that the target location is under its radio coverage, the deploying procedure terminates.

2.2   Resignation on Disconnected Network

The example in Fig. 2 is a lucky case that every marshal node can find at least one soldier nodes within its communication range. However, in most cases, it is possible that the initially deployed network has been partitioned and marshal node cannot find any soldier node within its communication range. In this case, the marshal node, M_j, which cannot find any soldier node, will issue a *resignation* command back to its previous senator M_i. This senator M_i will be the marshal node again to pick a soldier node as the candidate from $\Omega_i \backslash \{M_j\}$. If no soldier node is found in Ω_i, the resignation command will be sent back to the previous senator again. When a soldier node is found, it follows the procedure in previous subsection to build the link. This procedure will continuously operate until a soldier node has been found or the sink node issues the resignation command. When the resignation command is issued by the sink node, it implies that network fails to the construct the path to target location.

2.3   Concurrent Moving

Initially, because the soldier nodes are not aware of the positions of the sink and the target location, the physical path of L must be built sequentially. However, in the network with multiple disconnected network partitions, when a resignation command is sent back to some previous senator, the deploying procedure is still restarted from this senator even some of the soldier nodes have already had the position of target location and the sink node.

Thus, an enhancement can be done by making those nodes which have ever been the marshal nodes but are closer to the target location than current marshal node move concurrently with the candidate to reduce the path constructing time. When current marshal node decides the candidate, the distance d is propagated to those nodes that have ever been the marshal node. After those nodes receive this distance, they will move toward the target location with distance d simultaneously with the candidate which is moving to its corresponding position on L.

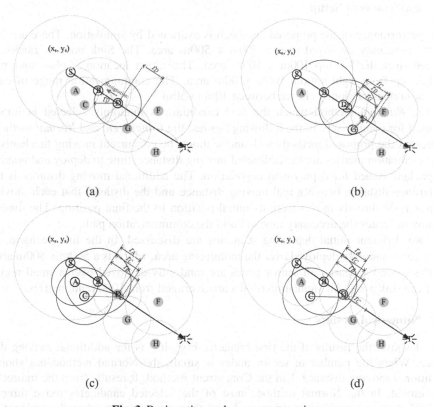

Fig. 3. Resignation and concurrent moving

Fig. 3 is a little example extended from the Fig. 2 which shows the resignation message during the path construction and the concurrent moving. Assume that the soldier node E does not exist. The deploying procedure in Fig. 2(d) will change to the one in Fig. 3(a) that marshal node D does not get any soldier node in its communication range. Thus, D issues a resignation command back to B. The marshal node B restarts to find a soldier node which has not ever been the marshal node yet to be the candidate. The soldier node C is selected shown as Fig. 3(b). Next, node C acts as the marshal node and restarts the deploying procedure, shown as the Fig. 3(c). Similarly, the deploying procedure terminates until the target location been covered.

If the concurrent moving is used, the marshal node B in Fig. 3(b) will announce the communication range of the candidate C, r_c, to node D. While the candidate C is moving to the corresponding position on L, node D can simultaneously move to the position on L toward the target location with distance r_c, shown as the Fig. 3(d).

3 Simulation Results

3.1 Environment Setup

The performance of the proposed approach is evaluated by simulation. There are 100 nodes randomly deployed over a 500m x 500m area. The Sink node is randomly placed over the left-top 100m x 100m area. The target location is also randomly picked up from right-bottom 100m x100m area. The communication range of each sensor node is randomly chosen between 40m to 50m.

The *Random* method which the next candidate is randomly selected is implemented for comparison. In the following figures, the *Concurrent* and *Normal* methods represent the proposed methods with and without the concurrent moving mechanism. The evaluation metrics are the additional moving distance, time to deploy and number of packets issued for deployment negotiation. The additional moving distance is the difference distance between real moving distance and the distance that each moving sensor node directly moves from its initial position to the final position. The time to deploy indicates the necessary time to build the communication path.

Two different initial deploying scenarios are discussed. In the first scenario, all nodes are randomly deployed over the monitoring area, which is a 500m x 500m area. In the second scenario, all sensor nodes are randomly deployed over a small region near the sink node. All simulation results are averaged from 1000 random tries.

3.2 Numerical Results

Fig. 4 shows the results of the first scenario. Fig. 4(a) is the additional moving distance. When the number of sensor nodes is small, the Normal method has shorter additional moving distance than the Concurrent method. It results from the indirectly movement. In the Normal method, most of the selected candidates move directly toward the corresponding position on L and then stop moving when the resignation commands are issued in the disconnected network. In the concurrent method, however, those sensor nodes that have ever been the marshal nodes will move indirectly to their final corresponding positions. As the number of sensor node increases, the probability to trigger the resignation message decreases. Thus, their difference diminishes. For the Random method, sensor nodes spend more additional moving distance, respectively.

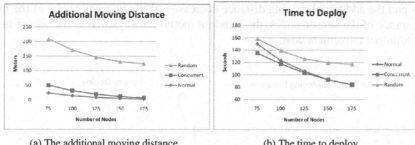

(a) The additional moving distance   (b) The time to deploy

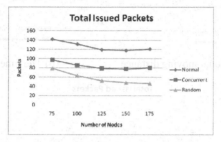

(c) The number of total issued packets

Fig. 4. The results of the first scenario

Fig. 4(b) shows the average time to build the communication path to target location. Assume that all sensor nodes have an average moving speed with 5 meters per second. The results show that the Concurrent method can slightly reduce the deploying time when the number of deployed sensor nodes is small. However, as the number of sensor node increases, more soldier nodes can be selected as the candidate. Thus, the advantage of the Concurrent method gradually diminishes. Without considering the distance of the sensor nodes to the corresponding positions on L, the Random method has the worst deploying time.

Fig. 4(c) shows the total number of issued packets when the sensor nodes are negotiating to construct the communication path to the target location. Skipping to collect the distances of all neighbor soldier nodes, the Random Method has the least number of issued packets. For the Concurrent Method, the sensor nodes can reduce several negotiation messages to the marshal nodes as a resignation command is issued. This makes it effectively reduce the number of issued packets than the Normal method. By collecting distances from all neighbor nodes to find the shortest moving distance, the Normal method has the worst results in this evaluation.

Fig. 5 is the results of the second scenario. The sensor nodes are initially deployed at the left-top areas with different size, 100x100, 150x150, 200x200, 250x250, and 300x300. The additional moving distance of the second scenario is shown in Fig. 5(a). In the second scenario, the differences additional moving distance of the Normal method and the Concurrent method become explicitly. The Normal method has the shortest additional moving distance. The reason is the same as Fig. 4. As the initial deploying area becomes large, the soldier nodes can be found near the current marshal nodes and the additional moving distance decreases. Without being aware of the moving distance of the sensor nodes, the Random method always makes the sensor nodes pay additional movement cost.

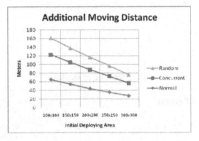

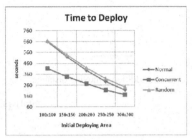

(a) The additional moving distance   (b) The time to deplay

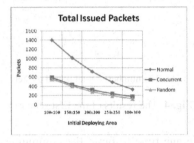

(c) The number of total issued packets

Fig. 5. The results of the second scenario

Fig. 5(b) shows the average time to construct the path to target location. The Concurrent method has the best results on this evaluation, respectively. For the Normal and the Random methods, the deploying time is very close. Because sensor nodes are initially deployed over a small region, the time for all the selected sensor nodes to reach the positions on L is almost the same. By applying the concurrent moving, the moving time of sensor nodes can be overlapped. The results also indicate that the Concurrent method is suitable to reduce the deploying time for the second scenario.

The Fig. 5(c) shows the total packets issued for building the communication path. Similar to Fig. 4(c), the Random method has the least number of issued packets and the Normal method has the worst results. A special point in this figure is that the number of issued packets in Concurrent method is only slightly higher than the Random method. As all nodes are initially deployed within a small region, the resignation command in the Random method will frequently deliver back to the senator node that is within the initial deploying region to find the next candidate. The negotiating packets will be similar to propagate the moving distance to the nodes which have ever been the marshal nodes in the Concurrent method. The additional issued packets for the Concurrent method are those to decide the next candidate. Therefore, its result is close to the Random method.

4 Conclusion

This paper proposes a self-deploying algorithm for the mission-oriented sensor networks. Sensor nodes will organize and deploy themselves once the monitor area has some events occur. In the proposed approach, sensor nodes can organize themselves even the initial deployed sensor network is partitioned. We apply a greedy method to quickly organize the mobile sensor nodes into a shortest communication path for relaying the reported information from the target location. A concurrent moving mechanism is also proposed to reduce the deploying time. Simulation results show that the concurrent moving can exhibit its advantages on reducing the deploying time and the number of issued packets for deploying.

References

1. Tsai, Y.R., Tsai, Y.J.: Sub-optimal Step-by-Step Node Deployment Algorithm for User Localization in Wireless Sensor Networks. In: Proc. of IEEE International Conference on Sensor Networks, Ubiquitous and Trustworthy Computing 2008, January 2008, pp. 114–121 (2008)
2. Yuan, Z.H., Wang, G.F.: Sensor Deployment Strategy for Collaborative Target Detection with Guaranteed Accuracy. In: Proc. of the 4th International Conference on Mobile Adhoc and Sensor Networks 2008, December 2008, pp. 68–71 (2008)
3. Popa, D.O., Stephanou, H.E., Helm, C., Sanderson, A.C.: Robotic deployment of sensor networks using potential fields. In: Proc. of. IEEE International Conference on Robotics and Automation 2004 (ICRA 2004), vol. 1, pp. 642–647 (2004)
4. Howard, A., Matari´c, M.J., Sukhatme, G.S.: An incremental self-deployment algorithm for mobile sensor networks. Autonomous Robots 13(2), 113–126 (2002)
5. Tan, K.H., Lewis, M.A.: Virtual Structures for High-Precision Cooperative Mobile Robotic Control. Autonomous Robots 4, 387–403 (1997)
6. Zou, Y., Krishnendu, C.: Sensor deployment and target localization based on virtual forces. In: Proc. of IEEE Twenty-Second Annual Joint Conference of the IEEE Computer and Communications Societies, April 2003, vol. 2, pp. 1293–1303 (2003)
7. Wu, X., Shu, L., Meng, M., Cho, J., Lee, S.: Coverage-Driven Self-Deployment for Cluster Based Mobile Sensor Networks. In: Proc. of The Sixth IEEE International Conference on Computer and Information Technology 2006, September 2006, pp. 226–226 (2006)
8. Lee, J., Dharne, A.D., Jayasuriya, S.: Potential Field Based Hierarchical Structure for Mobile Sensor Network Deployment. In: Proc. of American Control Conference 2007, July 2007, pp. 5946–59519 (2007)
9. Chang, R.S., Wang, S.H.: Self-Deployment by Density Control in Sensor Networks. IEEE Transactions on Vehicular Technology 57(3), 1745–1755 (2008)
10. Heo, N., Varshney, P.K.: An intelligent deployment and clustering algorithm for a distributed mobile sensor network. In: Proc. of IEEE International Conference on Systems, Man and Cybernetics 2003, October 2003, vol. 5, pp. 4576–4581 (2003)
11. Pac, M.R., Erkmen, A.M., Erkmen, I.: Scalable Self-Deployment of Mobile Sensor Networks: A Fluid Dynamics Approach. In: Proc. of IEEE/RSJ International Conference on Intelligent Robots and Systems 2006, October 2006, pp. 1446–1451 (2006)
12. Takahashi, J., Sekiyama, K., Fukuda, T.: Self-deployment algorithm for mobile sensor network based on connection priority criteria with obstacle avoidance. In: Proc. of IEEE International Conference on Robotics and Biomimetics (ROBIO 2007), December 2007, pp. 1434–1439 (2007)

Multi-Dimensional Resilient Statistical En-Route Filtering in Wireless Sensor Networks

Feng Yang[1,2], Xuehai Zhou[1,2], and Qiyuan Zhang[1]

[1] University of Science and Technology of China
230027 Hefei, China
[2] Suzhou Institute for Advanced Study, USTC,
215123 Suzhou, China
{yfus,johnkyo}@mail.ustc.edu.cn, xhzhou@ustc.edu.cn

Abstract. En-route filtering is an effective way to defeat false data injection attacks. Different from traditional one-dimensional en-route filtering mechanisms, we propose a multi-dimensional resilient statistical en-route filtering mechanism (MDSEF). In MDSEF, the overall key pool is divided into multiple sets and each set is composed of a number of groups where each group is composed of a number of keys. Each node could join one group in each set and obtain some keys from these groups. Since each node obtains keys from multiple groups, the covering performance and filtering effectiveness of the mechanism can be improved simultaneously. An axis-rotation method is proposed to associate the terrain with multiple sets and implement location-based key derivation. Moreover, a stepwise refinement distributed group joining method is proposed for nodes' group selection. Analysis and simulation results show that MDSEF could significantly improve the covering performance and filtering effectiveness without losing the resiliency against node compromise.

Keywords: Multi-dimensional en-route filtering, resiliency, security, wireless sensor networks.

1 Introduction

Wireless sensor networks (WSNs) have been applied widely in both civilian and military contexts. However, sensor nodes may be compromised and all the information stored in them may be obtained by adversaries. Adversaries can launch various attacks using these compromised nodes [1]. One important form of these attacks is false data injection [2]-[7]. Compromised nodes can inject a lot of forged packets to the network in order to exhaust network resources (e.g., energy, bandwidth, storage space).

In order to defeat false data injection attacks, a general framework is proposed in sensor networks. In this framework, each node stores a few symmetric keys shared with some other nodes for endorsing reports and filtering forged reports. Each symmetric key has an index. A legitimate report must carry T (T>1) distinct MACs(Message Authentication Codes) generated by sensing nodes using their symmetric keys. When a node receives a report, it checks whether there are T distinct

R.-S. Chang et al. (Eds.): GPC 2010, LNCS 6104, pp. 130–139, 2010.

MACs in the report. If the check fails, the report is dropped. Otherwise, if the node owns one key that is used to generate a MAC, it checks whether the carried MAC is equal to the MAC that it computes using the stored one. If the check fails, the report is also dropped. If the node doesn't have any of the keys or the MAC is correct, it forwards the report.

We refer to all previous statistical en-route filtering schemes as "one-dimensional schemes" because there are a number of groups and each node selects one group to join. Two nodes joining the same group share secret keys with a certain probability. Previous schemes concentrate on filtering effectiveness and resiliency. Filtering effectiveness means that how many hops that bogus reports are transmitted by before being filtered. Resiliency means that the scheme's performance degrades gracefully with the number of compromised nodes increasing. Besides, we take covering performance into consideration. Covering performance means whether a legitimate report could be generated when an event occurs randomly.

In traditional one-dimensional schemes, covering performance and filtering effectiveness cannot be improved simultaneously if the scheme is resilient. In this paper, we propose a multi-dimensional scheme (MDSEF). In MDSEF, there are M sets each of which is composed of $[T/M]$ groups. Each sensor node joins a group in each set. In other words, a node could join multiple groups. Analysis shows that covering performance and filtering effectiveness can be improved simultaneously in MDSEF. To improve the resiliency of the scheme, we propose a location-based key derivation scheme in which an axis-rotation method is used to associate the terrain with multiple sets. Meanwhile, a stepwise refinement group joining method is proposed.

The contributions of this paper are outlined as follows.

1. Sensor nodes in MDSEF could obtain keys from multiple groups from multiple sets. Therefore, covering performance and filtering effectiveness can be improved simultaneously.

2. To improve the resiliency of the scheme, we use the location-based key derivation. Meanwhile, in order to associate multiple sets with the terrain, we propose an axis-rotation method.

3. A stepwise refinement group joining method is proposed to help each sensor node select a group in each set, improving the covering performance of the scheme.

We have evaluated our design through simulations. The results show that MDSEF is efficient and resiliency.

The rest of the paper is organized as follows. In the next section, we review the background information. The proposed scheme and brief analysis are presented in section 3. Simulation results are provided in section 4. At last, we conclude the paper in section 5.

2   Background and Related Works

Based on the framework presented above, a number of schemes have been proposed [2]-[7]. We concentrate on statistical filtering schemes [5]-[7] in this paper. There are three main factors to evaluate statistical filtering schemes—covering performance, filtering effectiveness and resiliency. Covering performance means that whether a legitimate report could be generated when an event occurs in the terrain. Filtering effectiveness means that how many hops a forged report could be transmitted before being filtered. Resiliency means that how the scheme performs when the number of compromised nodes increases.

Three main statistical filtering schemes exist—SEF [5], LBRS [6] and GRSEF [7]. SEF [5] is the first statistical filtering scheme proposed to defeat false data injection attacks. There is an overall key pool in SEF, and every node has a small part of it. Any legitimate report carries T MACs generated with T keys in the key pool. By increasing the number of keys each node has, SEF obtains impressive covering performance and filtering effectiveness. However, SEF has a drawback that the whole scheme almost breaks down when attackers compromise 2T nodes. In order to solve the threshold problem, hao et al. proposed a location based resilient security solution (LBRS) [6]. In LBRS, the overall key pool is divided into L groups and the terrain is divided into cells. Each cell is associated with a key in each group. Each node selects a group to join in the bootstrapping phase randomly. Each node stores keys of cells within its sensing range (named sensing cells) and some randomly chosen remote cells (named verifiable cells). In order to improve filtering effectiveness and resiliency, LBRS used a location-guided key selection scheme. However, it relies on the static sink and geographical routing protocols. In order to improve the filtering effectiveness, GRSEF [7] divides the overall key pool into exact T groups. However, the covering performance degrades in GRSEF.

3   MDSEF: A Multi-Dimensional Statistical En-Route Filtering Scheme

3.1   System Model, Threat Model and the Motivation

We consider the situation that a geographic terrain is monitored by a large number of sensor nodes. The size and shape of the terrain can be approximately obtained before deployment. Once deployed, each node could get its location through techniques like in [14] and [15]. We assume that sensor nodes are static, however, the sink could move in all places. We assume that the sensing radius and transmission radius of sensor nodes are both static. The scheme doesn't rely on specific routing protocols.

We concentrate on false data injection attacks. A number of sensor nodes are compromised and attackers obtain all information stored in them. Compromised nodes inject a large number of bogus reports to the network. However, the sink is well-protected and cannot be compromised. The goal of the scheme is to improve covering performance and filtering effectiveness without losing resiliency against node compromise.

3.2   Scheme Overview

MDSEF follows the general en-route filtering framework in principle. A legitimate report should carry T MACs in which T is a predetermined parameter.

The overall operations are as follows. In traditional one-dimensional schemes, there are T or more groups and each node joins a group randomly. In MDSEF, there are M sets each of which is composed of $\lceil T/M \rceil$ groups. Each node joins a group in each set. And then, each node obtains keys according to its location and the groups it joins. In order to put the location-based key derivation into practice, we describe the axis-rotation method we use firstly.

There is a reference point (X_0, Y_0) in the terrain and a reference axis called axis 1. Axis i rotates θ_i degrees and we get axis i+1. Each axis corresponds to a set. As a result, there are M axes in the terrain. We assume that L_i indicates the length of the terrain's projection on axis i. The unit length of axis i is l_i, and axis i is divided into s_i segments where $s_i = L_i / l_i$. These segments are numbered 1, 2, 3... successively. Fig. 1. illustrates the situation that there are two axes in the terrain.

Based on the axis-rotation method, the overall operations are as follows.

(1) Pre-deployment phase
We divide the terrain into virtual cells. Therefore, each node is preloaded a reference point (X_0, Y_0), the direction the of reference axis and M-1 angles— $(\theta_1, ... \theta_i, ... \theta_{M-1})$ to implement the axis-location method. Meanwhile, each node is preload M master keys $K_1, K_2, ..., K_M$ and a secure one-way hash functions—$H_1()$ and $H_2()$, which are explained in the following subsections.

(2) Bootstrapping phase
Each node selects a group to join in each set during the bootstrapping phase using the stepwise refinement group joining method we propose.

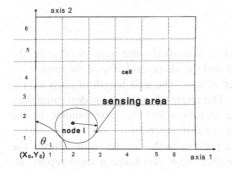

Fig. 1. A terrain associated with 2 sets

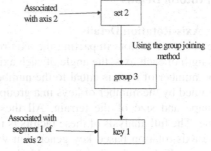

Fig. 2. Location-based key derivation

There are sensing segments and verifiable segments in MDSEF. As shown in Fig. 1, we consider axis 2 and we assume that node i joins group 1 in set 2. The sensing area covers segment 1 and segment 2 along axis 2. Therefore, node i picks up segment 1 and segment 2 as its sensing segments along axis 2. Node i obtains the secret key corresponding to segment 1 along axis 2—$H_1(K_2, 3, 1)$. Node i obtains the secret key corresponding to segment 2 using the same method. Node i randomly chooses remote segments along axis 2 as its verifiable segments. In Fig. 1, we assume that node i chooses segment 5. Node i obtains its verifiable segments' keys using the same method above. Each node repeats the process along every axis. Fig. 2 shows the location-based key derivation MDSEF.

All master keys and the hash function $H_1()$ are destroyed when the bootstrapping phase is finished.

(3) Generating and verifying reports

Upon an event, all detecting nodes organize themselves into local clusters and reach agreement on the event report including the event's location through techniques as in [8]. Each node then independently generates MACs using its keys bound to the event's segments along all axes, and it sends a list of tuples $\{\{1,S_1,MAC\},...\{i,S_i,MAC\},\{M,S_M,MAC\}\}$ to the cluster head. The i-th tuple corresponds to the i-th set, and S_i represents the group it joins in set i. The MAC is computed by $H_2(k,R)$ in which $H_2()$ is the preloaded hash function, k is the corresponding secret key, R is the initial report that all sensing nodes agree with.

When the cluster head collects T MACs from T distinct groups in M distinct sets, it sends out the report with the endorsement to the sink.

When an intermediate node receives a report, it first retrieves the event's location from the report, and then it can compute the event's segment number along each axis. Assuming that the node joins group I_j in set I and the event occurs on the k-th segment along axis I, the node checks whether it stores the key corresponding to k-th segment along axis I. If having such a key, it re-computes the MAC and compares to the carried one. If the verification fails, the report is dropped. Otherwise, the report is forwarded. When the sink receives the report, it performs final verification because it owns all keys of all groups along each axis.

3.3 Protocol Details

3.3.1 Axis-Rotation Details

There are some factors impacting the axis-rotation method—the number of axes, the unit length of each axis, the angle of each axis and the shape and size of the terrain.

The number of axes is equal to the number of sets. The unit length of each axis is determined by the number of keys in a group. The angle of each axis is determined by the shape and size of the terrain. All these factors affect the performance of the scheme. The full analysis of these factors is in our full paper [9].

The axis-rotation based key generation we present in the above section limits the degree to which captured nodes could abuse their keys. To forge a legal report, attackers must collect enough keys for a certain cell. However, the can only forge bogus reports occurring in a small portion of the terrain which makes locating and eliminating them easier.

3.3.2 Group Joining Method

In MDSEF, a legitimate report must carry T MACs from T groups. Each node joins a group in each set. Group joining is essentially a set k-cover problem [10]-[12]. Traditional set k-cover algorithms do not consider the situation that the program execution time is uncertain. Because the length of bootstrapping phase is varied, an absolutely random or determinate algorithm is not suitable. If the length is a little longer, an absolutely random algorithm can not give an approximately optimal answer. If the length is short, a determinate algorithm can not be finished. Therefore, we propose a stepwise refinement group joining method to solve this problem.

All nodes are preloaded a duration DT during which the group joining program is executed. After a node is deployed, it selects a group in each set using a random number generator. If DT is very short, each node selects groups randomly. If DT is a little longer, during the duration DT every sensor node carries out the following procedures to select groups it joins eventually.

CSMA/CA[13] is used in broadcasting to reduce collisions. If a certain node v needs to broadcast a message, it checks to be sure the channel is clear (no other node is transmitting at the time). If the channel is not clear, the node waits for a randomly chosen period of time, and then checks again to see if the channel is clear. If the channel is clear, then node v broadcasts a message $<v,L_v,\{G_1,G_2,...G_M\}>$, in which L_v represents the location of v and G_i represents the group it joins in set i. It is can be seen that all sensor nodes are equal because the random backoff method is used in CSMA/CA.

Any node, say node v, maintains a list composed of $<dist, \{G_1,G_2,...G_M\}>$ in which dist represents the minimum distance to nodes that join G_i in set i. If there are multiple nodes join the same groups in all sets, *dist* represents the distance to the nearest one from node v. Elements in the list are arranged in order of decreasing *dist*.

If node v receives a message $<u,L_u, \{G_1,G_2,...G_M\}>$ from node u, it computes and inserts the corresponding message $<dist,\{G_1,G_2,...G_M\}>$ to the list. The method that node v updates the tuple $<v, L_v , \{G_1,G_2,...G_M\}>$ is as follows. Without loss of generality, we consider the group node v joins in set *1*. We assume that set 1 is composed of 4 groups. If the list node v maintains is like $\{<5,\{4,...\}>, <1,\{3,...\}>\}$, it randomly joins group 1 or group 2 because its neighbors do not join these two groups. If the list node v maintains is $\{<15,\{4,...\}>, <10,\{3,...\}>, <5,\{2,...\}>, <1,\{1,...\}>\}$, node v joins group 4 because the neighbor joining this group is the farthest from it. Node v uses the same rule to select groups to join in other sets. When the updating phase is finished, node v broadcasts the message using CSMA/CA protocol.

In wireless sensor networks, a great number of efficient clustering methods have been proposed like WCA [16] and LEACH [17]. However, traditional clustering methods generally take into consideration the ideal degree, transmission power, mobility, and battery power of sensor nodes, etc. The proposed method takes covering performance into account which makes it different from traditional ones.

3.4 Analysis

Because the group joining method we propose is distributed and fair, uniform dividing can be approximately achieved. The property will be validated in section 4. Meanwhile, each node obtains keys from several groups; therefore, the coverage performance and filtering effectiveness of MDSEF are both better than one-dimensional schemes. However, MDSEF is still resilient against node compromise because the key-derivation scheme is substantially location-based.

The quantitative analysis is omitted here because of space constraint. Simulation results can be found in the next section.

4 Simulation Evaluation

In this section simulations are run to verify and complement our previous analysis. We examine the uniform property of the group joining method and evaluate the covering performance, filtering effectiveness and resiliency against node compromise of MDSEF respectively. We compare MDSEF with one-dimensional statistical en-route filtering schemes such as SEF, LBRS and GRSEF.

In our simulations, sensor nodes are spread over a 1Km×1Km field and the sink is at the center of field. The unit length of each axis is 25m. The Sensing range of each node is 25m, and the communication distance of each node is 50m. A legitimate packet should carry 8 MACs in our schemes. In our simulations, there are 2 sets and each set is composed of 4 groups in MDSEF. The duration for group joining is set one minute in MDSEF. The number of groups (called L) is set to 16 for SEF and LBRS. In LBRS, the beam width is set to 100m and the cell size is 25m and the meaning of these parameters is described in [6]. In GRSEF, parameters are set as in [7].

4.1 Uniform Property of the Group Joining Method

To verify the uniform property of the group joining method we propose, we examine the size of each group in each set. The number of sensor nodes is set to 500, 1000 and 2000 in turn. Table 1 shows the average size of each group in each set over 200 experiments. It can be seen that the average size of each group is approximate to N/G, where N means the number of sensor nodes and G means the number of groups in one set.

4.2 Covering Performance

We compare MDSEF with SEF, LBRS and GRSEF on the covering performance. The number of sensor nodes is set to 500, 1000 and 2000 in turn. To estimate the covering performance of each scheme, we apply 5000 times tests in turn. In each test, we randomly choose a position from the field and check if nodes within 25m have enough keys to mark the report recording the event occurring here.

Table 2 shows the coverage percentage of each scheme under different network size. We can see that the coverage percentage in MDSEF is apparently higher than all one-dimensional schemes. It is because that each sensor node stores keys from different sets in MDSEF and the stepwise refinement group joining method is used.

4.3 Filtering Effectiveness

We assume that attackers can generate N_c correct MACs. To compare MDSEF with SEF, LBRS and GRSEF on the filtering effectiveness, we let $N_c = 1,3,5$ respectively. We apply 10000 times random tests for each N_c. In each test, attackers randomly forge a report carrying N_c correct MACs. Each report is transmitted by h hops before being filtered. We examine the average of h for each scheme. Table 3 shows the results.

4.4 Resiliency against Node Compromise

We compare MDSEF with traditional schemes on resiliency. In our simulations, the number of randomly chosen compromised nodes gradually increases from 10 to 100. We apply 5000 times simulations for each number. We compute the percentage of compromised area in each simulation, and we get the percentage of total compromised area finally.

Fig. 3 shows the percentage of compromised area of each scheme. We can see that LBRS achieves better resiliency than other schemes because the beam model is adopted. However, LBRS requires the static sink and special routing protocols. The resiliency of GRSEF is a litter better than MDSEF because each node stores less secret keys in GRSEF. The resiliency of MDSEF is much better than SEF.

Table 2, Table 3 and Fig. 3 indicate that MDSEF is a resilient en-route filtering scheme with higher coverage percentage and filtering effectiveness.

Table 1. The average size of each group

N	SET 1				SET 2			
	G1	G2	G3	G4	G1	G2	G3	G4
500	122.7	128.5	125.3	123.5	123.6	122.8	127.1	126.5
1000	251.3	252.1	247.6	249.0	252.6	248.3	250.6	248.5
2000	501.1	498.1	502.7	498.1	499.3	502.3	501.1	497.3

Table 2. Coverage percentage of each scheme under different network size

	Coverage Percentage(%)		
N	MDSEF	SEF&LBRS	GRSEF
500	89.2	70.4	71.2
1000	97.4	90.1	91.3
2000	99.2	93.5	94.2

Table 3. The filtering effectiveness of each scheme

	Average of h			
N_c	MDSEF	SEF	LBRS	GRSEF
1	1.9	3.1	2.9	2.8
3	2.8	5.5	4.1	3.9
5	5.3	9.7	7.3	7.9

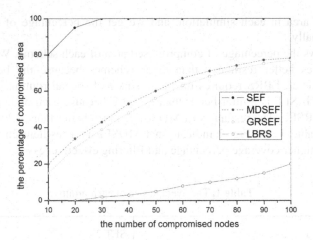

Fig. 3. Resiliency evaluation and comparison

5 Conclusion

In this paper, MDSEF is proposed to defeat false data injection attacks. MDSEF divides the key pool into multiple sets and each set is divided into multiple groups. Any sensor node obtains keys from a certain group in each set. That is, any sensor node stores keys from multiple groups. Therefore, the covering performance and filtering effectiveness can be improved simultaneously. An axis-rotation method is proposed to put multiple sets and location-aware key derivation into practice. The location-aware key derivation ensures the resiliency of the scheme. Moreover, a stepwise refinement group joining method is proposed to improve the covering performance of the scheme. Analysis and simulation results show that MDSEF significantly increases coverage percentage and filtering power without losing the resiliency against node compromise.

Acknowledgments. The authors would like to thank associate professor Songwu Lu in UCLA and Dr. Rui Wang in HKUST for their constructive advice. This work was supported in part by National Natural Science Foundation of China under grant 60873221.

References

1. Perrig, A., Stankovic, J., Wagner, D.: Security in wireless sensor networks. J. Comm. of ACM 47, 53–57 (2004)
2. Zhu, S., Jajodia, S., Ning, P.: An interleaved hop-by-hop authentication scheme for filtering of injected false data in sensor networks. In: 25th IEEE Symposium on Security and Privacy, pp. 259–271. IEEE Press, New York (2004)
3. Yu, Z., Guan, Y.: A dynamic scheme for en-route filtering false data. In: 3rd ACM International Conference on Embedded Networked Sensor Systems, pp. 294–295. ACM Press, New York (2005)

4. Ren, K., Lou, W., Zhang, Y.: LEDS: Providing location-aware end-to-end data security in wireless sensor networks. IEEE Tran. on Mob. Com. 7, 585–598 (2007)
5. Ye, F., Luo, H., Lu, S., Zhang, L.: Statistical en-route filtering of injected false data in sensor networks. IEEE JSAC 23, 839–850 (2005)
6. Yang, H., Ye, F., Yuan, Y., Lu, S., Arbaugh, W.: Toward resilient security in wireless sensor networks. In: 6th ACM International Symposium on Mobile Ad Hoc Networking and Computing, pp. 34–45. ACM Press, New York (2005)
7. Yu, L., Li, J.: Grouping-based resilient statistical en-route filtering for sensor networks. In: 28th IEEE International Conference on Computer Communications, pp. 1–12. IEEE Press, Los Alamitos (2009)
8. Ye, F., Lu, S., Zhang, L.: Gradient broadcast: A robust data delivery protocol for large scale sensor networks. ACM Wireless Networks 11, 285–298 (2005)
9. A fuller version of this paper, http://home.ustc.edu.cn/~yfus/MDSEF.pdf
10. Slijepcevic, S., Potkonjak, M.: Power efficient organization of wireless sensor networks. In: 37th IEEE International Conference on communications, pp. 472–476. IEEE Press, New York (2001)
11. Hastad, J.: Some optimal inapproximability results. JACM 48, 798–859 (2001)
12. Abrams, Z., Goel, A., Plotkin, S.A.: Set k-cover algorithms for energy efficient monitoring in wireless sensor networks. In: 3rd International Symposium on Information Processing in Sensor Networks, pp. 424–432. IEEE Press, New York (2004)
13. Editors of IEEE.: IEEE 802.11, Wireless LAN MAC and physical layer specifications (1997)
14. Albowicz, J., Chen, A., Zhang, L.: Recursive position estimation in sensor networks. In: 9th International Conference on Network Protocols, pp. 35–41. IEEE Press, New York (2001)
15. Cheng, X., Thaeler, A., Xue, G., Chen, D.: TPS: A time-based positioning scheme for outdoor wireless sensor networks. In: 23rd IEEE International Conference on Computer Communications, pp. 2685–2696. IEEE Press, New York (2004)
16. Chatterjee, M., Das, S.K., Turgut, D.: WCA: A Weighted Clustering Algorithm for Mobile Ad Hoc Networks. In: Cluster Computing. LNCS, vol. 5, pp. 193–204. Springer, Heidelberg (2002)
17. Heinzelman, W.R., Chandrakasan, A., Balakrishnan, H.: Energyefficient communication protocol for wireless micro sensor networks. In: 33rd Hawaii International Conference on System Sciences, pp. 1–10. IEEE Computer Society, Washington (2000)

Cross-Layer Based Rate Control for Lifetime Maximization in Wireless Sensor Networks

Xiaoyan Yin, Xingshe Zhou, Zhigang Li, and Shining Li

College of Computer, Northwestern Polytechnical University
Xi'an, China 710072
SCxiaoyanyin@gmail.com, zhouxs@nwpu.edu.cn,
{lzg.nwpu,dtlsn278}@yahoo.com.cn

Abstract. In wireless sensor networks (WSNs), lifetime maximization is a critical issue because of the restricted power supply. Therefore, the objective of lifetime maximization is to save energy for each sensor node. However, the application performance depends strongly on the amount of data gathered from each source node in the network. Higher data rates causes greater sensing and communication costs resulting in a reduction of the overall network lifetime. There is thus an inherent trade-off in maximizing the network lifetime and the application performance. In this paper, we take both application performance and lifetime maximization into account, use a cross layer optimization framework and propose a distributed rate control algorithm. Our numerical result shows that our scheme can maximize the network lifetime and guarantee the application performance.

Keywords: Wireless sensor networks, cross-layer, lifetime and rate control.

1 Introduction

Wireless sensor networks (WSNs) have a wide extent of applications in habitat monitoring, health care, object tracking, and battlefield surveillance, etc. Furthermore, future WSNs are expected to support application with high data rate requirements, for example, wireless multimedia sensor networks.

In WSNs, lifetime maximization is a critical issue because of the restricted power supply. Typically, sensor nodes are battery driven and, hence, have to operate on a limited energy budget. Furthermore, battery replacement is impossible in many sensor networks due to the inaccessible or hostile environments. Thus, energy is a scarce resource in wireless sensor networks and it is imperative that energy-efficient schemes be designed in order to prolong the operational lifetime of the network. The lifetime of a network is defined as the time until the death of the first node in [1]. We use a similar definition for network lifetime and consider the lifetime maximization problem in this paper.

On the other hand, the application performance depends strongly on the amount of data gathered from each source node in the network. Namely, more data from a video sensor could mean a better quality image while high-precision samples of a temperature field result in a more accurate characterization of the physical process. However, higher data rates causes greater sensing and communication costs resulting in a reduction of

R.-S. Chang et al. (Eds.): GPC 2010, LNCS 6104, pp. 140–149, 2010.

the overall network lifetime. In order to achieve high end-to-end throughput and long system duration, there is thus an inherent trade-off between the application performance and the network lifetime.

In order to achieve high end-to-end throughput in an energy efficient manner, rate control and power control need to be jointly designed and distributively implemented. Rate control (i.e., congestion control) mechanisms regulate the allowed source rates so that the total traffic load on any link does not exceed the available capacity. At the same time, the attainable data rates on wireless links depend on the interference levels, which in turn depend on the power control policy. Network resources can sometimes be allocated to change link capacities, therefore change the optimal solution to network utility maximization. For example, in WSNs, powers used for transmitting can be controlled to induce different Signal to Interference Ratios (SIR) on the links, and then changing the attainable capacity on each link.

Since the feasible rate region in WSNs depends on the power, the end-to-end rate optimization problem must be considered in a cross-layer framework, i.e., the rate control strategy must be implemented at both the transport layer and physical layer. In WSNs, every sensor node transmits the data to the sink consistently through a set of wireless links. If the aggregated traffic exceeds the link's capacity, a congestion occurs and the performance of the network is inevitably degraded. Hence, a congestion control algorithm is demanded by which the source nodes can adjust the transmission rates accordingly, from a congestion-avoidance standpoint. In addition, the operating power of each link, i.e., the power of the transmitter of the each link, needs to be regulated carefully as well. The excessive power causes dramatic interference to other links and thus deteriorates the overall performance of the wireless sensor network, in terms of overall achievable rate. More importantly, the unnecessary transmission will deplete the battery soon and the lifetime of the wireless sensor networks is severely devastated.

In this paper, we study a rate control scheme for life maximization in WSNs, from a cross layer optimization perspective. We conform to the network utility maximization (NUM) framework and incorporate the specific practical concern in resource-constrained WSNs. By utilizing the dual decomposition approach, we develop a joint power control and rate control algorithm in which each user adjusts its data rate based on feedback from the system and each node allocates transmission power to each link that emanates from it considering the demand on rate allocation and the channel condition of the link.

The rest of the paper is organized as follows. In Section 2, we briefly overview the related work. The cross layer optimization problem is formulated in Section 3. In Section 4, a distributed solution based on dual decomposition is established. A numerical example is provided in Section 5. Finally, we conclude this paper in Section 6.

2   Related Works

Recently, lifetime maximization in WSNs have focused on finding distributed routing algorithms and area coverage problem. Chang and Tassiulas [1] consider the problem of maximizing lifetime given a certain set of source-destination information rates that must be supported. Another important method for extending the network lifetime is to design a distributed and localized protocol that organizes the sensor nodes in sets for area coverage problem. In [2], Cardei et al. proposed an efficient heuristic MC-MIP with a mixed integer programming formulation. They schedule the sensor node activity such that every sensor alternates between sleep and active state, so as to prolong the network lifetime.

There are also several recent works ([3], [4], [5], [6], [7]) that address the question of cross-layer design in communication networks, especially in wireless networks. In [3], Xiao et al. formulate the problem of simultaneous routing and resource allocation in wireless networks and propose distributed algorithms via dual decomposition. In [4], Chiang proposes a distributed power control algorithm, that along with a TCP rate update mechanism, optimizes the end-to-end throughput in a wireless CDMA network. In [5], the network utility maximization (NUM) framework is applied to reverse-engineer the transport layer protocols. It turns out that the transport layer protocols are actually maximizing certain network utility functions implicitly. These results provide us a better understanding of the layered architecture of the network. In [6], the overall network is formulated as a complex optimization problem and each layer simultaneously optimizes a decomposed sub-problem and communicates with each other by explicitly or implicitly exchanging messages. In [7], Nama et al. proposed a similar framework to our work. However, we take energy consumption into account instead of introduce a lifetime-penalty function. In this paper, we emphasis on the resource-constrained networks where the limited network resources, such as network lifetime and the total bandwidth, are valuable and need to be addressed. In addition, the mutual interference between links is considered. The detailed problem formulation will be discussed in the next section.

3   System Model and Formulation

We consider a WSNs which consists of N sensor nodes and a sink. We use the multi-commodity flow to model the wireless sensor network, which represented by a directed graph $\mathcal{G}(\mathcal{V}, \mathcal{E})$, where $\mathcal{V}$ is the set of sensor nodes and $\mathcal{E}$ is the set of logical links. Each sensor node is associated with a utility function $U_n(x_n)$, which reflects the "utility" to the sensor node n when it generates data at rate x_n. We define $N(l)$ as the subset of sensor nodes that are traversing link l. Let $L_{OUT}(n)$ denote the set of outgoing links from node n, $L_{IN}(n)$ the set of incoming links to node n. Thus, in Fig.1,

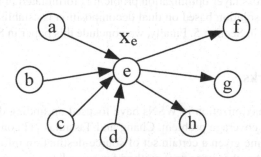

Fig. 1. Traffic analysis for node e

$L_{IN}(e) = \{l_{ae}, l_{be}, l_{ce}, l_{de}\}$ and $L_{OUT}(e) = \{l_{ef}, l_{eg}, l_{eh}\}$. We assume that the route utilized by the flow from node n is fixed and the set of links on this route is denoted as $l : l \in L(s)$. Sensor nodes are capable of varying their source rate and power level which allow the application performance to be tuned and also help avoid any congestion in the network. For a particular link $l \in L$, where L denotes the set of links in the wireless sensor networks, we present the set of nodes which utilize link l, as $n : n \in N(l)$.

3.1 Traffic Analysis for Sensor Nodes

In WSNs, apart from being sources of data, nodes also forward data for other nodes toward the sink. We assume data transmission is lossless and there is no compression of data at any node inside the network. Thus, according to the flow conservation constraint, we have

$$\sum_{j:(e,j)\in L_{OUT}(e)} r_{ej} - \sum_{i:(i,e)\in L_{IN}(e)} r_{ie} = x_e \qquad (1)$$

where r_{ij} can be interpreted as the average rate for non-negative flows over link (i,j) and x_e is the rate at which node e generates data. Specially, for a source node n which only generates data, we have

$$\sum_{j:(n,j)\in L_{OUT}(n)} r_{nj} = x_n \qquad (2)$$

And for a intermediate node n which only forwards traffic, we have

$$\sum_{i:(i,n)\in L_{IN}(n)} r_{in} = \sum_{j:(n,j)\in L_{OUT}(n)} r_{nj} \qquad (3)$$

3.2 Energy Consumption and Network Lifetime Maximization

In a typical WSNs, sensor nodes have much tighter energy constraints than the sinks and hence we will focus only on the energy consumed by sensor nodes. We characterize the energy consumption for each sensor node by the power used per bit for reliable transmission over link l (P_{tx}^l), for sensing (P_s), and for receiving (P_{rx}). The total average power consumed by node n is given by

$$P_n^{avg} = \sum_{i:(i,n)\in L_{in}(n)} r_{in}P_{rx} + \sum_{j:(n,j)\in L_{out}(n)} r_{nj}P_{tx}^l + x_n P_s \qquad (4)$$

According to [8], most of energy consumption is used for transmitting and receiving, and energy used for sensing can be omitted. As shown in [8], energy used for transmitting is larger than energy used for receiving a bit. Therefore, we can treat transmitting and receiving similarly in terms of energy consumption, Eq.4 is rewritten accordingly as follows:

$$P_n^{avg} \approx (\sum_{i:(i,n)\in L_{IN}(n)} r_{in} + \sum_{j:(n,j)\in L_{OUT}(n)} r_{nj})P_{tx}^l \qquad (5)$$

If $E_n > 0$ denotes this initial energy of node n, then the lifetime of the node is given by $t_n = E_n/P_n^{avg}$. The network lifetime denoted by t_{nwk}, is defined as the time until the death of the first node, i.e., $t_{nwk} = \min t_n$, where $n \in N$. Therefore, the problem of maximizing the network lifetime can then be stated as $\max t_{nwk}$, where $t_{nwk} \geq 0$.

Obviously, allocation of zero source rates throughout the network will result in the longest network lifetime, and nevertheless the worst application performance. Therefore, we should take both network lifetime and application performance into account. A cross-layer design problem that results in an optimal allocation of source rates to guarantee a desired application performance while also prolonging the lifetime of the network is studied in the next subsection.

3.3   Formulation for Rate Control with Lifetime Maximization

We use NUM-based cross-layer design approach here. For each sensor node n, a certain value of data rate x_n at which node n generates data results in a utility value. We use $U_n(x_n)$ to represent the utility function of sensor node n. Therefore, a natural objective function to characterize the application performance is the summation of the utility function of all sensor nodes. By incorporating the network lifetime maximization at the same time, we formulate the cross layer optimization problem, Q1, as follows:

$$Q1 : max\{\sum_n U_n(x_n) + t_{nwk}\} \tag{6}$$

Keeping that in mind, maximization of the network lifetime means minimization of the power consumption. Therefore, Eq. (6) can be rewritten as following:

$$Q1 : max\{\sum_n U_n(x_n) - P_n^{avg}\} \tag{7}$$

where, $P_n^{avg} \leq E_n/t$, where $\forall n \in N$ and t denotes a lower bound for the node lifetime. Reasonably, we have

$$Q1 : \quad \max \sum_n U_n(x_n)$$
$$- \sum_l \left(\sum_{i:(i,n)\in L_{IN}(n)} r_{in} + \sum_{j:(n,j)\in L_{OUT}(n)} r_{nj} \right) P_{tx}^l$$

We assume that each link has a unity bandwidth and a Shannon capacity c_l, which is approximated as $\log_2(\gamma_l)$, i.e., $c_l = \log_2(\gamma_l), \forall l$, as assumed in [4], where γ_l is the SINR value of link l. In order to avoid congestion at link l, we have the following constraints as

$$\sum_{n:n\in N(l)} x_n \leq c_l \; \forall l \tag{8}$$

In addition, the SINR value, γ_l, of each link l can be expressed as

$$\gamma_l = \frac{P_{tx}^l G_{l,l}}{\sum_{k\neq l} P_{tx}^k G_{k,l} + N_l} \tag{9}$$

where P_{tx}^i is the power of link i used for transmission and $G_{m,n}$ is the channel gain between link m and link n. The white Gaussian noise is denoted by N_l, for link l. Therefore, the achievable rate on a wireless link is global function of all the interfering powers.

Finally, we formulate the cross-layer based rate control with lifetime maximization problem as follows:

$$Q1: \quad \max \sum_n U_n(x_n)$$
$$- \sum_l (\sum_{i:(i,n)\in L_{IN}(n)} r_{in} + \sum_{j:(n,j)\in L_{OUT}(n)} r_{nj})P_{tx}^l$$

s.t.

$$\sum_{n:n\in N(l)} x_n \le c_l \ \forall l \tag{10}$$

$$c_l = \log_2(\gamma_l) \ \forall l \tag{11}$$

$$\gamma_l = \frac{P_{tx}^l G_{l,l}}{\sum_{k\neq l} P_{tx}^k G_{k,l} + N_l} \tag{12}$$

Note that in **Q1**, the first summation is the total utility of the network and the second one is the power consumption used for transmitting and receiving. Therefore, the objective function in **Q1** take both application performance and lifetime maximization into consideration. The transport layer and physical layer parameters are coupled in constrain Eq. (10), it states that the traffic load on each link must be less than or equal to the average data rate that is offered by that link.

4 Cross-Layer Optimization via Dual Decomposition

4.1 Dual Decomposition

In our work, we adopt the log-utility functions to achieve the proportional fairness among different flows, as shown in [9], i.e.,

$$U_n(x_n) = \log x_n \tag{13}$$

To solve Q1, we utilize the dual decomposition approach to decouple the coupling constraint Eq. (10). We first obtain the Lagrangian of Q1. Let x, p, λ be the vector of source rates, link powers and link congestion prices, respectively, we have

$$L(\mathbf{x}, \mathbf{p}, \lambda)$$
$$= \sum_n U_n(x_n) - \sum_l (\sum_{i:(i,n)\in L_{IN}(n)} r_{in} + \sum_{j:(n,j)\in L_{OUT}(n)} r_{nj})P_{tx}^l$$
$$- \sum_l \lambda_l (\sum_{n:n\in N(l)} x_n - c_l)$$
$$= \sum_n \{U_n(x_n) - (\sum_{l:l\in L(n)} \lambda_l)x_n\}$$
$$+ \sum_l \{\lambda_l c_l - (\sum_{i:(i,n)\in L_{IN}(n)} r_{in} + \sum_{j:(n,j)\in L_{OUT}(n)} r_{nj})P_{tx}^l\}$$

Define

$$v(\lambda) = \sup_{\mathbf{x}, \mathbf{P}} L(\mathbf{x}, \mathbf{P}, \lambda) \qquad (14)$$

where sup denotes the supremum. Then, the dual problem corresponding to the primal problem is given by

$$\textbf{Dual Q2} : \min v(\lambda) \qquad (15)$$

The basic idea is that instead of solving the coupled original problem **Q1**, we alternatively pursue the optimum solution of the dual problem **Q2**. Indeed, it is trivial to find an inner point of the constraints in **Q1**. Therefore, the Slater condition is satisfied and the strong duality property holds, as shown in [10].

The dual function $v(\lambda)$ can be decomposed into the following two subproblems which are evaluated separately in the transport layer $\{x_n\}$ and physical layer $\{P_{tx}^l\}$. We define two corresponding optimization sub-problems as

$$\textbf{Q3} : \max \sum_n \{U_n(x_n) - (\sum_{l:l\in L(n)} \lambda_l)x_n\}$$

and

$$\textbf{Q4} : \max \sum_l \{\lambda_l c_l - (\sum_{i:(i,n)\in L_{IN}(n)} r_{in}$$

$$+ \sum_{j:(n,j)\in L_{OUT}(n)} r_{nj})P_{tx}^l\}$$

In **Q3**, λ is the congestion price charged by the links. Specifically, $\sum_{l:l\in L(n)} \lambda_l$ is the aggregated congestion price charged by the particular routing path. The rate control algorithm is implemented in such a way that both the net utility of each sensor node and the lifetime of the network are maximized, given the congestion prices. Due to the concavity of Eq. (13), **Q3** is a convex optimization problem. Meanwhile, **Q4** is also a convex optimization problem because of the concavity of $\sum_l \lambda_l c_l$ with respect to the power vector, which is verified in [4], and the linearity of $(\sum_{i:(i,n)\in L_{IN}(n)} r_{in} + \sum_{j:(n,j)\in L_{OUT}(n)} r_{nj})P_{tx}^l$. Thus, both **Q3** and **Q4** can be solved by using a sub-gradient projection algorithm. We have

$$\frac{\partial Q3}{\partial x_n} = \sum_n \{\frac{1}{x_n} - \sum_{l:l\in L(n)} \lambda_l\}$$

Given the announced congestion prices, each independent source node adjusts the data rate in order to maximize **Q3**, we obtain the optimum value of rate as

$$x_n(t+1) = [\frac{1}{\sum_{l:l\in L(n)} \lambda_l(t)}]^+ \qquad (16)$$

where $[x]^+$ means $\max(0, x)$.

$$\frac{\partial Q4}{\partial P_{tx}^l} = \frac{\lambda_l}{\ln 2 P_{tx}^l} - \left(\sum_{i:(i,n)\in L_{IN}(n)} r_{in} + \sum_{j:(n,j)\in L_{OUT}(n)} r_{nj} \right)$$
$$- \sum_{j:j\neq l} m_j G_{l,j}$$

where $m_j = \frac{\lambda_j \gamma_j}{\ln 2 P_{tx}^j G_{j,j}}$ is the message calculated by link j. To summarize, the updating rule for each link's power is

$$P_{tx}^l(t+1) = [P_{tx}^l(t) + \beta(t)\{\frac{\lambda_l(t)}{\ln 2 P_{tx}^l(t)} - \sum_{j:j\neq l} m_j G_{j,j}$$
$$-\left(\sum_{i:(i,n)\in L_{IN}(n)} r_{in} + \sum_{j:(n,j)\in L_{OUT}(n)} r_{nj} \right)\}]^+ \tag{17}$$

where $0 \leq \beta(t) \leq 1$ is the step size in the gradient descent process. The updating rule for the message m_l is

$$m_l(t+1) = \frac{\lambda_l(t)\gamma_l(t)}{\ln 2 P_{tx}^l(t) G_{l,l}} \tag{18}$$

Given the optimum value $x^* = [x_1^*, ..., x_N^*]$ and $P_{tx}^* = [P_{tx}^{1*}, ..., P_{tx}^{L*}]$, where $|L|$ is the number of link in the network, Eq. (14) can be rewritten as

$$v(\lambda) = \sup_{x,P} L(x, P, \lambda) = \sum_n \{U_n(x_n^*) - (\sum_{l:l\in L(n)} \lambda_l)x_n^*\}$$
$$+ \sum_l \{\lambda_l c_l^* - (\sum_{i:(i,n)\in L_{IN}(n)} r_{in} + \sum_{j:(j,n)\in L_{OUT}(n)} r_{nj})P_{tx}^{l*}\}$$

Accordingly, each link will calculate new congestion prices which optimize the dual problem **Q2**. Keeping that in mind, **Q2** is always a convex optimization. To obtain the dual global optimum solution, denoted by $\lambda^* = [\lambda_1^*, ..., \lambda_L^*]$. Taking the derivative of above equation with respect to λ, we have

$$\frac{\partial v}{\partial \lambda_l} = c_l^* - \sum_{n:n\in N(l)} x_n^*$$

Therefore, the updating rules for the congestion prices of each link are provided by

$$\lambda_l(t+1) = [\lambda_l(t) - \beta(t)\{c_l^*(t) - \sum_{n:n\in N(l)} x_n^*(t)\}]^+ \tag{19}$$

Recall that λ_l is the link congestion price charged by link l. The updating dynamics actually incorporate the supply and demand rule in economics. For instance, $\sum_{n:n\in N(l)} x_n^*(t)$ is the overall data rate through link l, i.e., the bandwidth demand, whereas $c_l^*(t)$ is the supply that link l can provide at time t. If the demand exceeds the supply, link l will increase the price an vice versa.

4.2 Distributed Implementation of Rate Control Algorithm

In this subsection, we systematically describe the proposed distributed rate control for lifetime maximization from an engineering implementation perspective.

 – **For each sensor node** n:
    Updates the data rate as shown in Eq. (16).
 – **For each link** l:
    Updates the power as shown in Eq. (17).
    Updates the message as shown in Eq. (18) and broadcasts it.
    Adjusts the link congestion price, λ_l, as shown in Eq. (19).

5   Numerical Example

We consider an illustrative WSNs shown in Fig.2. We assume that the original energy
for each sensor node is 10000 units, and energy consumption for receiving and for transmitting is 13 unti/packet and 15 unit/packet, respectively. Three flows are originated by
node 1, 2 and 3, respectively, which consistently deliver the generated traffic to the sink.
In Fig.2, we denote a, b, and c, which are random numbers between 0 and 1, and generated by the function rand(), as the probabilities that the corresponding flows pick the
available pathes.

As shown in Fig.2, each source node has two acyclic paths to reach the sink. For
example, for node 1, it can go either $1 \rightarrow 4 \rightarrow S$ or $1 \rightarrow 5 \rightarrow S$ towards the sink. The
congestion price function follows Eq. (19). The traffic is randomly generated at each

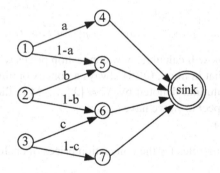

Fig. 2. Logical topology for a numerical example

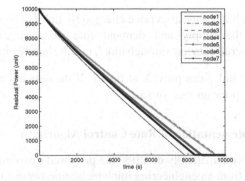

Fig. 3. Energy expenditure per node over time

source node with Gaussian distribution. The mean is 5 and the variance is 1. On the other hand, the actual achievable data rate is a function of the transmission power. We use the same stepsize for the sub-gradient approach in Eqs. (16), (17) and (18), which is inversely proportional to the number of iterations.

Fig.3 depicts the evolution of energy consumption for 7 sensor nodes. From Fig.3, it is apparent that our scheme is indeed a optimal solution for lifetime maximization. We can observe that the decline gradient for 7 nodes are similar. This imply that all the sensor nodes will die almost at the same time.

6 Conclusion

In this paper, we propose a cross-layer based rate control scheme for lifetime maximization in WSNs. The cross-layer optimization problem decomposes vertically into two separate problems. We solve these two problems using dual decomposition and then provide a distributed rate control algorithm. Finally, Our numerical example verifies that our scheme can both maximize the lifetime and guarantee the application performance in WSNs.

Acknowledgments. This work was supported in part by the National Natural Science Foundation of China under grant No.60736017 and by the National Key Technology R&D Program of China under grant No.2007BAD79B02, No.2007BAD79B03.

References

1. Chang, J., Tassiulas, L.: Maximum lifetime routing in wireless sensor networks. IEEE Transaction on Networking 12(4), 609–619 (2004)
2. Cardei, M., Du, D.: Improving wireless sensor network lifetime through power aware organization. ACM Wireless Networks 11(3), 333–340 (2005)
3. Xiao, L., Johnasson, M., Boyd, S.: Simultaneous routing and resource allocation via dual decompostion. IEEE Transaction on Communications 52(7), 1136–1144 (2004)
4. Chiang, M.: To layer or not to layer: Balancing transport and physical layers in wireless multihop networks. In: Proc. of IEEE INFOCOM 2004, Hong Kong (March 2004)
5. Low, S., Lapsley, D.: Optimization flow contorl-i: Basic algorithm and convergence. IEEE/ACM Transactions on Networking 7(6), 861–874 (1999)
6. Chiang, M., Low, S., Calderbank, A., Doyle, J.: Layering as optimization decomposition: Questions and answers. In: Proc. of IEEE Milcom 2006, Washington, DC, USA (October 2006)
7. Nama, H., Chiang, M., Mandayam, N.: Utility-lifetime trade-off in self-regulating wireless sensor networks: A cross-layer design approach. In: Proc. of IEEE ICC 2006, Istanbul, Turkey (June 2006)
8. Estrin, D.: Tutorial wireless sensor networks part iv: Sensor network protocols. In: Proc. of ACM MobiCom 2002, Atlanta, Georgia, USA (September 2002)
9. Kelly, F., Maulloo, A., Tan, D.: Rate control for communication networks: Shadow prices, proportional fairness ans stability. The Journal of the operational Research Society 49(3), 237–252 (1998)
10. Boyd, S., Vandenberghe, L.: Convex Optimization. Cambridge University Press, Cambridge (2003)

A 2D Barcode Validation System for Mobile Commerce

David Kuo, Daniel Wong, Jerry Gao, and Lee Chang

San Jose State University
davidkuo75@gmail.com, earthconfed@gmail.com,
gaojerry@email.sjsu.edu, lee.chang@sjsu.edu

Abstract. The widely deployment of wireless networks and mobile technologies and the significant increase in the number of mobile device users have created a very strong demand for emerging mobile commerce applications and services. Barcode-based identification and validation solutions have been considered as an important part of electronic commerce systems, particularly in electronic supply chain systems. This paper reports a mobile-based 2D barcode validation system as a part of mobile commerce systems. This barcode-based validation solution is developed based on the Data Matrix 2D-Barcode standard to support barcode-based validation in mobile commerce systems on mobile devices. Furthermore, the paper also demonstrates its application by building a mobile movie ticketing system.

Keywords: mobile commerce, barcode-based application, barcode validation, electronic commerce, mobile device-based application.

1 Introduction

The widely deployment of wireless networks and mobile technologies and the significant increase in the number of mobile device users have created a very strong demand for emerging mobile commerce applications and services. According to [1], 2D barcodes can be used to support pre-sale, buy-and-sell, and post-sale activities for mobile commerce transactions. For example, 2D barcodes can be used as advertisements, coupons, or promotional materials that can be captured and decoded by the user with mobile devices. Moreover, 2D barcodes enable mobile devices to become a point-of-sale device that reads the barcode and facilitates payment transactions. After a payment transaction, 2D barcodes can be used by customers as a receipt or proof of purchase to gain access to the purchased goods and services with their mobile phones. Until recently, people are gradually realized the importance of 2D barcode and its great application value in M-Commerce because of the followings [1].

- 2D barcodes provide a new effective input channel for mobile customers carrying mobile devices with inbuilt cameras.
- 2D barcode is becoming a popular approach to present semantic mobile data with standard formats.
- 2D barcodes support a new interactive and efficient approach between mobile customers and wireless application systems.

R.-S. Chang et al. (Eds.): GPC 2010, LNCS 6104, pp. 150–161, 2010.
© Springer-Verlag Berlin Heidelberg 2010

However, although there are many benefits of using 2D barcodes, they are not widely utilized in the United States especially in mobile commerce. This paper reports the research, architecture, design, security, and issues of implementing a mobile-based 2D barcode validation system to encourage readers to adopt 2D barcodes into mobile commerce systems. This barcode-based validation solution is developed based on the Data Matrix 2D-Barcode standard to support barcode-based validation in mobile commerce systems on mobile devices. Furthermore, the paper also demonstrates its application by building a mobile movie ticketing system.

This paper is structured as follows. The next section covers the basics of 2D barcodes and related supporting technologies. Section 3 reviews the related work in mobile commerce and applications. Section 4 and 5 present a 2D barcode based validation system, including the system architecture, functional components, and used technologies as well as its 2D barcode-based framework. Section 6 reports its application in a movie ticketing prototype system in mobile commerce. Finally, the conclusion remarks are given in Section 7.

2 Understanding 2D Barcodes and Supporting Technologies

Although there are a number of widely used 2D barcodes today, different barcodes and standards are used in different countries and industry segments. Figure 1 shows the samples of three popular types of 2D barcodes. Quick Response (QR) code is mostly used in Japan. It can encode not only binary and text data, but also Japanese characters. Japanese companies use them to encode product information. Data Matrix 2D barcodes are popularly used in United States [3]. It is printed on parcel labels on product packages to track the shipment and identify a product in a supply chain. Both QR code and Data Matrix have been standardized by International Standard Organization (ISO). Other 2D barcodes include ColorCode, VS Code, Visual Code, Shot Code, etc [2].

a) QR Code   b) PDF417   c) Data Matrix

Fig. 1. 2D Barcode Samples   **Fig. 2.** Metrologic Elite MS7580 Genesis area-imaging scanner

Data Matrix Standard. As described in [4], "Data Matrix is a two-dimensional matrix symbology, which is made up of square modules arranged within a perimeter finder pattern." According to its standard specification (the ISO/IEC 16022 specification), a Data Matrix symbol is composed of three parts: the encoded data, four borders, and the quite zone. Each part contains either white or black solid squares called modules. A black module represents one, and a white module represents zero or vice versa depends on the configuration. To facilitate the scanning devices to locate the symbols, a Data Matrix symbol contains an L shape solid modules to define the orientation, boarder, and size of the shape. The other two sides are represented by broken modules alternating between white and black. The whole symbol is surrounded with white modules marked as the quite zone. A Data Matrix symbol uses Reed-Solomon ECC level 200 for error detection and correction. The two types of Error Checking Correction (ECC) are ECC 000–140 and ECC 200. The maximum data that a Data Matrix code can encode is 2,335 alphanumeric characters or 1,556 bytes. Because of its advantages and compact size, the Data Matrix barcode is one of the 2D barcodes that is often used with mobile devices. Using 2D barcodes (like Data Matrix), we need to understand of its standard, encoding and decoding processes, and its error detection and correction rules.

Encoding and Decoding Processes. According to the ISO Data Matrix specification [4], an encoding process for creating a Data Matrix symbol consists of the following steps.

1. Evaluate the given data stream to determine the best encoding scheme and convert the data into codewords.
2. Generate the error checking and correction codewords.
3. Place codewords in the symbol.

A decoding process is needed to enable hardware devices and software programs to locate and decode Data Matrix barcodes (or symbols). This process includes the following steps.

1. Find the candidate areas that might contain the L-shape finder.
2. Find the finder in these candidate areas.
3. Find the two lines that are outside but closest to the finder.
4. Find the two opposite sides of the finder with alternating black and white modules.
5. Find the line that passes through alternating black and white modules for each side.
6. For each side, find the number of data modules.
7. Find the centerline that passes through the alternating modules for each side.
8. Use the centerline to find all the data modules from left to right and bottom to top until reaching to the borders.

Error Correction and Codeword Generation. The ECC 200 symbols use Reed-Solomon for error checking. The Reed-Solomon code is given by the equation R-S(n, k) = $(2^m - 1, 2^m - 1 - 2t)$, where k is the number of codewords of actual encoded data, n is the total number of codewords, m is the number of bits in a codeword, and t is the number of error codewords that can be corrected. 8 is a popular value for m since it's the number of bits in a byte. The number of checking codewords is calculated as 2t = n − k. The checking codewords are the reminder of the data codewords divided by the generator polynomials. If encoded data is damaged or distorted, the checking codewords can be used to restore the data (URL: www.informit.com/).

2D Barcode Scanners. As the article in [5] points out, choosing the right 2D barcode scanner can be challenging when developing a mobile 2D barcode application. Not all types of barcode scanners are able to read 2D barcodes from the screen of mobile devices. For example, laser barcode scanners cannot read barcodes from LCD screens. Most retailers today do not have the right equipment to read barcodes from mobile devices.

Due to the popularity and advantages of using 2D barcodes with mobile devices, more barcode scanners are built with the imaging technology. These scanners are often called imagers. A 2D barcode imager works similar to a digital camera. It is equipped with an imaging sensor. It reads a barcode by first capturing its image and then decodes its data. This feature allows the imagers to decode barcodes from self-illuminating displays. Moreover, most imagers support both 1D and 2D barcodes, making them suitable for mixed barcode environments. The scanner interface has also been evolved in the past few years. The latest 2D barcode scanners support keyboard simulation and the UBS interface [6]. This allows the scanner to simulate the key-board through the USB interface, entering the decoded data as if it was entered by the keyboard. Figure 2 shows a 2D barcode scanner that is able to scan LCD displays. A 2D barcode imager normally needs to be attached to a PC or a laptop for it to work with the barcode application. However, in many cases, mobile barcode imagers are needed. Hence, another type of 2D barcode scanner is built into a PDA. The barcode reader and the client application can be combined into one device. The PDA 2D bar-code scanner increases the mobility for the barcode inspectors, but the cost is much higher.

3 Related Work in Mobile Commerce

Barcodes have been widely used for identifying products and delivering information. The invention of 2D barcodes has significantly increased the security and data capac-ity for a barcode. As mobile devices are built with more sophisticated functions sell-ing at more affordable prices, there are new mobile applications with 2D barcodes. Most cell phones today are built in with a camera. One type of 2D barcode applica-tions is to use camera-enabled cell phones as barcode readers to decode the barcode content. This allows users to collect more information just by a click of a button. The other type of usage is to use the mobile device as a carrier of 2D barcodes, which are validated directly from the mobile device at the point of use. For such applications, a comprehensive 2D barcode processing, delivering, and validation system is needed. This is very useful in mobile-commerce where digital tickets, coupons, and invoices can be delivered to mobile devices as 2D barcodes. They can be used anytime and anywhere for mobile commerce applications.

According to [1], there are different types of 2D barcode mobile applications.

- As discussed in [2][13], in Japan, 2D barcodes can be seen on websites, street signs, product packages, stores, magazines, and ads. Most camera-enabled cell phones in Japan are built with a barcode reader. A survey shows that in year 2006, 82.6% of the respondents had used their barcode readers on their cell phones with QR codes [2]. This allows users to collect information without tedious data entry. This type of application can also be used in zoos or museums for users to collect detailed information on an animal or a historical art piece [7].

- 2D barcodes can be utilized in pre-sale, buy-and-sale, and post-sale activities, where purchase information, invoices, and promotional materials such as coupons and advertisements can be encoded into 2D barcodes and delivered to customers' cell phones through emails or MMS.
- 2D barcodes can also be used for wireless payments [12]. Payment transaction information (such as credit card data) can be encoded into 2D barcodes and used at retail stores, taxi, payment terminals, and even mobile internet payment. However, using 2D barcodes for payments has security issues that need to be addressed. Since 2D barcodes are just electronic image files, they can be easily transferred and copied. Therefore, 2D barcode payment systems need to be carefully designed and rigorously tested to ensure a secure environment for using these barcodes.

The rest of this section reviews some 2D barcode-based application systems and validation solutions for mobile commerce.

Airline 2D Barcode Boarding Passes. As described in [8], airlines are using mobile 2D barcode validation systems to replace paper-based boarding passes in order to speed up the boarding time. During the check-in process, the airline staff sends the boarding information as a 2D barcode to the passenger's cell phone through the Multimedia Messaging Service (MMS). When the passenger passes the security checkpoints or boards on a plane, the security staff scans the barcode to reveal the passenger's boarding information and identity for ID validation against his/her passport. The International Air Transport Association (IATA) has approved to use 2D barcodes as boarding passes [10]. By 2010, every airline will implement a mobile 2D barcode boarding pass solution. Today, both Air Canada and Northwest Airlines have already implemented this technology [9][10].

Sports Game Ticketing Services. Another type of mobile barcode validation systems can be seen in concert and game ticketing services. When combined with mobile payment services, the whole transaction from purchasing to receiving the ticket can be done using a mobile phone. Mobiqa, a mobile barcode solution provider, partnered with PayPal to provide a mobile payment and ticket delivering service for rugby games (URL: www.mobiqa.com/live/files/RugbyLeaguecasestudy.pdf). The system allows users to purchase tickets using the PayPal Mobile service. Once the transaction is complete, the ticket information is encoded into a barcode, and then sent to the user's mobile device. When the user arrives at the venue, the staff scans the barcode from the user's mobile device using a scanner. The scanner validates the barcode with the system to support ticket validation.

2D Barcode Medical Prescription System. Application examples are also found in pharmaceutical science. The Taiwan government developed a 2D barcode prescription system (2DBPS) for its National Health Insurance (NHI) [11]. With this system, doctors' medical prescriptions are encoded as 2D barcodes and given to patients. When patients arrive at a pharmacy, the pharmacist only needs to scan the barcode to validate the prescription with the back-end server. This system has several advantages. Firstly, it reduces human errors occurred in manual data entry. Drugs can be dispensed more accurately. Secondly, it saves time for doctors, patients, and pharmacists by reducing manual labors such as writing prescription and entering prescription data. Lastly, it increases patient's privacy because medical prescription data are presented as 2D barcode.

4 An Overview of a 2D Barcode-Based Validation Solution

To support the product delivery (or pick-up) and merchandise check-out in mobile commerce applications, we need a 2D barcode-based validation solution to integrate with electronic payment systems (or mobile POS-based terminals). To use 2D barcodes, the users just need to bring their mobile devices to a point-of-use terminal. The merchant staff uses a 2D barcode scanner along with the mobile client to read the barcode off the screen of a mobile device. Each barcode is validated against the server through the Internet, and then the user identity and purchasing record are verified. If the result is fine, the merchant will accept the user's barcode as the invoice. This section describes the system infrastructure and related components.

System Infrastructure and Architecture. The 2D Barcode Validation System consists of three portions, the server, the client, and the end user. They are connected by three types of networks as shown in Figure 3.

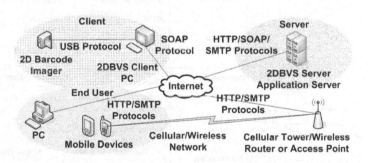

Fig. 3. System Infrastructure

The 2D Barcode Validation System includes a server, a mobile client, a USB 2D barcode imager, and a backend database server. As shown in Figure 4, the 2D Barcode Validation System has its 4-tier architecture to increase the independency between different layers and reduce their change impacts.

- *The user interface layer* has a point-of-use GUI client and a web client running in the Web browser of a PC or mobile device.
- *The communication layer* provides communication protocols including HTTP and SOAP.
- *The service layer* provides the application functional services. These services include 2D barcode framework, security framework, validation service, and account management.
- *The database layer* consists of entity models, database access libraries, and a relational database management system.

Server Components. The server consists of the 2D barcode web application running on a J2EE application server. The web application contains the mobile/web store, 2D barcode framework, validation web services, and data access services. As shown in Figure 5, the server includes the following service components.

- 2D barcode web store – it provides an interface for users to purchase 2D barcodes.
- Validation Service - it allows the client to validate barcodes.
- User Service – it manages user accounts and authentications.
- Order and Payment Services – they manage orders and payment processes.
- Event Service - it manages event and ticket records.
- Encryption Service – it abstracts the security framework and the encryption logic.
- 2D Barcode Service – this contains the encoding and decoding algorithms. It works in conjunction with Device Configuration Manager to produce the best image for each different type of mobile devices. Based on different mobile device profiles, the barcode service encodes different sizes of images to best display for the mobile device. This ensures interoperability for the 2D barcode imager to accurately read the 2D barcode from different mobile device screens.

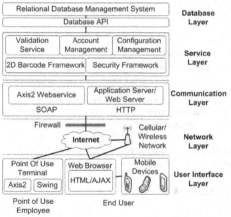

Fig. 4. System Architecture

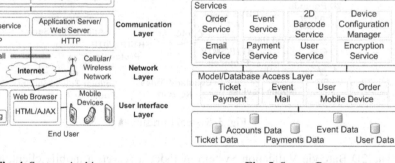

Fig. 5. Server Components

Client Components. The client system consists of a GUI application and a 2D barcode imager that allows barcode inspectors to validate and display the content of the issued 2D barcodes. It is installed in the merchant stores where 2D barcodes need to be validated. It consists of the components shown in Figure 6. Each component of the client system is described in details as follows.

- Client GUI – This GUI interface supports client users to interact with the system.
- 2D Barcode Validation Handler – It is responsible for validating 2D barcodes with the server.
- Secure Session Establisher – It is responsible to establish a secure session between the client and the server.

- Security Framework Client – This is the security framework on the client system. It contains the libraries and interfaces for encrypting and decrypting data and generating certificates to establish secure sessions.
- Web Service Client – It's the client web service interface that communicates with the web services provided by the server.
- 2D Barcode Imager – This refers to the 2D barcode scanner hardware, which can be used to scan 2D barcodes from mobile devices and feed them to the system.

Security Components. In the security encryption framework, all purchasing information (such as invoices or tickets) is encoded into a 2D barcode using two different security solutions. The details are reported in [13].

- An asymmetric encryption (Rivest, Shamir, and Adleman) is used to ensure that all the barcodes are generated by the server application. Another asymmetric encryption (Elliptic Curve Cryptography) is used to provide a secure channel between the server and the client.
- A symmetric encryption (Advanced Encryption Standard) is used for validating the actual barcode owner by encrypting the barcode information using a passphrase provided by the owner. The security framework mainly uses the security components from the previous Secure Mobile Payment System developed by the SJSU graduate students [12]. As shown in Figure 7, it was modified to support the underlying encryption and decryption. The framework contains various cryptography utilities for ECC, RSA, and symmetric cryptographies. Table 1 summarizes the security methods used in the proposed system.

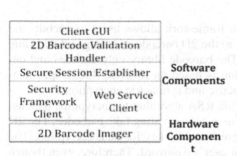

Fig. 6. Client Components   **Fig. 7.** Security Components

Table 1. Security Methods

Security Target	Password Based	Symmetric (AES)	Asymmetric (RSA)	Asymmetric (ECC)	Barcode Based
Client User/Consumer	x				
Client System		x	x	x	
Server System		x	x	x	
Secured Session				x	
Insensitive Data			x		x
Sensitive Data		x			x

Used Technologies. Several technologies are used in developing the system. They are summarized below.

- *Client Technologies* – We used Java and **Java Swing API** and **NetBeans GUI framework** to create client GUI components. A Metrologic Elite MS7580 Genesis area-imaging scanner (at $366.47) is used with the PS2 keyboard wedge interface. As shown in (URL: www.totalbarcode.com), this scanner supports both 1D and 2D barcodes. In addition, the scanner supports USB and RS232 interfaces and uses the imaging technology to read barcodes from LCD screens. We have successfully tested this scanner with different LCD displays.
- *Server Technologies* – The server is developed based on the Java EE platform. The **Bouncy Castle Crypto API** is used to implement cryptographic algorithms to encrypt and decrypt the barcode data. Moreover, the **Axis2 framework** is used to implement the validation web services. **JSON** (JavaScript Object Notation) is used throughout the system for passing the data.
- *Middle-tier Technologies* – The system uses a J2ME 2D barcode encoding and decoding algorithm provided by **www.drhu.org**, and it's ported to the J2SE environment to support barcode encoding for movie tickets in our demo system. The other used technologies are **JavaMail API, Servlet, JSP, Struts 2, Ext JS 2.0, Spring Framework, Apache Velocity, Tiles**, and **Quartz**. The **Apache Tomcat** application server is used to support Internet communications with clients.
- *Data-tier Technologies* – The **MySQL** relational database management system (RDBMS) is used as the back-end database. **Java Persistence API** and **Hibernate** are used to support the communications with the database.

5   The 2D Barcode Solution

2D Barcode Framework. The 2D barcode framework allows users to encode and decode information. It consists of two parts: a) the 2D barcode encoding and decoding library, and b) and the encryption library. The barcode library only encodes and decodes Data Matrix barcodes and its algorithm is based on ISO/IEC 16022 specification. The encryption library provides asymmetric and symmetric encryptions.

The asymmetric encryption method uses the RSA algorithm to encrypt the data using the server's private key to prevent malicious users creating fake barcodes. The 2D barcode validation client system has the server's public key for data decryption. The server's public key is encrypted by the client user's password. Therefore, even though a malicious user compromises the client system, without knowing the client user's password, no one can decrypt the data. This method is more suitable for insensitive data and the point-of-use terminals that need a faster validation process since it does not require the user to enter a passphrase. The symmetric encryption uses AES algorithm. It allows the user to encrypt data using a passphrase before it is encoded into a barcode. Therefore, this method is more suitable for sensitive data.

The 2D barcode framework provides the following function features:

- Encode and decode 2D Data Matrix barcode images.
- Convert an image object into a byte array and vise versa.
- Provide symmetric and asymmetric encryption and decryption.
- Exposed through web services to allow remote clients to utilize its functionality.

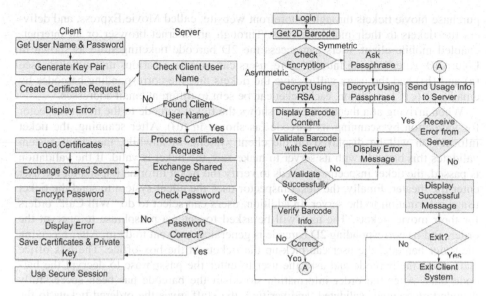

Fig. 8. Secure Session Setup Process   **Fig. 9.** Client Barcode Validation Process

2D Barcode Validation. The 2D barcode validation process consists of two steps: 1) establish a secure session 2) and validate the barcode through the secure session. The process of establishing a secure session is represented in Figure 8. To set up a secure session with the server, the client first generates an ECC key pair and sends a certificate request to the server. The server responses back with the CA certificate, and then it exchanges its shared secret with the client. After the secure session is established, the client can use it to encrypt the client user's username and password and send them to the server to complete the login process. If the login information is successfully authenticated, the client encrypts and saves the certificates and the private key and the secure session is ready. Otherwise, the client discards these security data and asks the client user to enter the password again.

To validate a barcode, as described in Figure 9, the client system first gets the decoded data from the GUI and decrypts the barcode content. After the decryption, the client system displays the decrypted data on the screen and sends it to the server for validation using the established secure session. Then, the server searches for the barcode usage database to see if the given barcode is a validate one. If the validation result is fine, then a successful response will be returned. Otherwise, the server sends a descriptive error message back to the client. The barcode inspector can proceed to verify the barcode information such as the user's name and the product information. If everything is correct, the client system sends the barcode usage record to the server to prevent further uses.

6 A 2D Barcode Validation Application – Mobile Movie Tickets

To demonstrate the usage of this system, a 2D barcode ticketing prototype system is implemented. Based on the 2D barcode-ticketing scenario, the system allows users to purchase movie tickets through a storefront website, called Movie Express, and delivers the tickets to their mobile devices. Through an internet browser or an internet-enabled mobile client, users can access the 2D barcode ticketing store as shown in Figure 10. After logging into the store, users can purchase various movie tickets (see (a) and (b)) and the users will receive the tickets and the corresponding barcodes by email (see (c)). In addition, each ticket can be sent to different email addresses.

When arriving at a theater, the user shows the ticket barcode to the ticket inspector for validation by scanning its barcode (as shown in (d)). After scanning, the ticket information will be displayed on the client system. Meanwhile, the client system validates this barcode with its server to make sure the ticket is valid. If the validation is passed, the ticket inspector proceeds to verify the ticket information and let the user enter the theater. Finally, the ticket inspector uses the client system to send the ticket usage information to the server. In addition, users can select to do "Will Call" orders for their movie tickets. The user will be asked to enter a passphrase to encrypt the order, and its corresponding 2D barcode is generated and sent to them. After receiving the order barcode, the user can pick-up the tickets at the box office. The box office staff scans the barcode and asks the user to enter the passphrase to decrypt the barcode data. After the order information stored in the barcode has been successfully decoded, decrypted, validated, and verified, the staff gives the ordered tickets to the user to complete the process.

| a) Home page | b) Showtime details | c) Received movie ticket | d) Scanning the barcode on Android G1 |

Fig. 10. Movie Ticket Purchase and Barcode Delivery

7 Conclusion

Using 2D barcodes with mobile devices has many benefits. It provides mobility, security, and convenience. Although there are numerous mobile 2D barcode technologies in the market, there are no academic research reports or papers discussing about 2D barcode-based validation solutions and systems. This paper introduces a 2D barcode validation system for mobile commerce applications. It provides a secure way to encode ticket and order information into 2D barcodes, which can be easily transported through email or MMS.

Mobile commerce is becoming a lucrative market for merchants, banks, and service businesses. 2D barcodes have become the de-facto standard for carrying information in mobile commerce. The proposed validation solution provides a secure way to process and validate 2D barcodes for mobile commerce. It works effectively while we apply it in the movie ticketing prototype. Similarly, it also can be used for e-validation in other situations, such as retail-oriented check-out, product delivery and pick-up, station-based payment, terminal-based, and coupon check-up. For the future research direction, we are working on an integrated mobile commerce solution based on 2D barcodes from advertising and payment to validation.

References

1. Gao, J., Prakash, L., Jagatesan, R.: Understanding 2D-BarCodes Technology and Applications in M-Commerce – Design and Implementation of A 2D Barcode Processing Solution. In: The Proceedings of COMPSAC 2007, vol. 2, pp. 49–56 (2007)
2. Kato, H., Tan, K.T.: Pervasive 2D Barcodes for Camera Phone Applications. IEEE Pervasive Computing 6(4), 76–85 (2007)
3. The 2D data matrix barcode. Computing & Control Engineering Journal 16(6), 39- (2006)
4. Information technology – International symbology specification – Data matrix, ISO/IEC 16022:2000(E) (2000)
5. Honeywell, Mobile Ticketing Choosing the Right Technology Platform is Critical to your Program Success, Mobile Ticketing Technology – Airport International
6. Automation, 2D Barcode Imagers and Readers, 2D Barcode Imagers and Readers at IDAutomation
7. O'Hara, K., Kindberg, T., Glancy, M., Baptista, L., Sukumaran, B., Kahana, G., Rowbotham, J.: Social Practice in Location-based Collecting. In: Proceedings of the SIGCHI Conference on Human Factors in Computing Systems, San Jose, CA, pp. 1225–1234 (2007)
8. Bouchard, T., Hemon, M., Gagnon, F., Gravel, V., Munger, O.: Mobile Telephones Used as Boarding Passes: Enabling Technologies and Experimental Results. In: The Proceedings of Forth International Conference on Autonomic and Autonomous Systems (ICAS 2008), pp. 255–259 (2008)
9. IATA, IATA Standard Paves Way for Global Mobile Phone Check-in, http://www.iata.org/pressroom/pr/2007-11-10-01.htm
10. Air Canada, Mobile Check-in, aircanada.com – Travel Info – Mobile Services, http://www.aircanada.com/en/travelinfo/traveller/mobile/mci.html
11. Wang, W.L., Lin, C.H.: A Study of Two-dimensional Barcode Prescription System for Pharmacists' Activities of NHI Contracted Pharmacy. Yakugaku Zasshi 128, 123–127
12. Gao, J., Kulkarni, V., Ranavat, H., Chang, L., Hsing, M.: A 2D Barcode-Based Mobile Payment System. In: The 3rd International Conference on Multimedia and Ubiquitous Engineering (MUE 2009), June 2009, pp. 320–329 (2009)
13. Vandenhouten, R., Seiz, M.: Identification and tracking goods with the mobile phone. In: The Proceedings of International Symposium on Logistics and Industrial Informatic (LINDI 2007), Wildau, pp. 25–29 (2007)

A Petri-Net Based Context Representation in Smart Car Environment

Jie Sun, Yongping Zhang, and Kejia He

School of Electronic and Information Engineering,
Ningbo University of Technology
{sunjie,ypz}@nbut.cn, start_learn@163.com

Abstract. Driving is a complex process influenced by a wide range of factors, especially complex interactions between the driver, the vehicle and the environment. This paper aims at the representation of complex situations in smart car domain. Unlike existing context-aware systems which isolate one context situation from another, such as road congestion and car deceleration, this paper proposes a context model which considers the driver, vehicle and environment as a whole. The paper tries to discover the inherent relationship between the situations in the smart car environment, and proposes a context model to support the representation of situations and their correlation. The detailed example scenarios are given to illustrate our idea.

Keywords: context modeling, petri-net, smart car, ubiquitous computing.

1 Introduction

The smart car is becoming a promising application domain of ubiquitous computing, which aims at assisting the driver with easier driving, less workload and less chance of getting injured [1]. For this purpose, a smart car must collect and analyze the relevant information about the driving task, i.e., context. Driving is a complex process influenced by a wide range of factors: traffic, vehicle speed, distraction, fatigue, errors, and even capabilities and experience of the driver. How to represent the complexity is the basis for a car to be smart.

Lots of smart cars have been developed in the past decade. However, the knowledge representation in the smart car area is not paid enough attention. Most commonly used approach is getting low level context from sensors, which is applicable in direct service development, but is not sufficient for representation of complex knowledge in the changeable and complex driving environment. New representation approach is required to describe the intricate and complex interactions between the driver, the car and the environment.

The remainder of the paper is organized as follows. A general introduction of a smart car is given in Section 2. Section 3 proposes a novel representation approach for definition and classification of information in a smart car environment. We give the model of the smart car to illustrate how our approach works in Section 4. The performance evaluation is shown in Section 5. Section 6 introduces the related work of context representation approaches in smart car. The conclusions are given in Section 7.

R.-S. Chang et al. (Eds.): GPC 2010, LNCS 6104, pp. 162–173, 2010.
© Springer-Verlag Berlin Heidelberg 2010

2 Smart Car

A smart car is a comprehensive integration of many different sensors, control modules, actuators, and so on [2]. A smart car can monitor the driving environment, assess the possible risks, and take appropriate actions to avoid or reduce the risk. A general architecture of a smart car is shown in Figure 1.

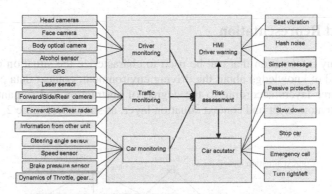

Fig. 1. The general architecture of a smart car

The information, i.e., context, needing to be collected for a smart car includes:

1) **Traffic situation:** A variety of scanning technologies are used to recognize the distance between the car and other road users. Active environments sensing in- and out-car will be a general capability in near future [3]. Lidar-, radar- or vision-based approaches can be used to provide the positioning information. The radar and lidar sensors provide information about the relative position and relative velocity of an object. Multiple cameras are able to eliminate blind spots, recognize obstacles, and record the surroundings. Besides the sensing technology described above, the car can get traffic information from Internet or nearby cars.

2) **Driver situation:** Drivers represent the highest safety risk. Almost 95% of the accidents are due to human factors and in almost three-quarters of the cases human behaviour is solely to blame [4]. Smart cars present promising potentials to assist drivers in improving their situational awareness and reducing errors. With cameras monitoring the driver's gaze and activity, smart cars attempt to keep the driver's attention on the road ahead. Physiological sensors can detect whether the driver is in good condition.

3) **Car situation:** The dynamics of a car can be read from the engine, the throttle and the brake. These data will be transferred by controller area networks (CAN) in order to analyze whether the car functions normally.

Assessment module determines the risk of driving task according to the situation of traffic, driver and car. Different levels of risk will lead to different responses, including notifying the driver through HMI (Human Machine Interface) and taking emergency actions by car actuators. HMI warns the driver of the potential risks in non-emergent situations. For an example, a fatigue driver would be awakened by an acoustic alarm or vibrating seat. Visual indications should be applied in a cautious way, since complex graph or long text sentence will seriously impair the driver's attention and possibly cause harm. The actuators will execute specified control on the car without the driver's commands. The smart car will adopt active measures such as stopping the car in case that the driver is unable to act properly, or applying passive protection to reduce possible harm in abrupt accidents, for example, popping up airbags.

3 Context Representation

Context is any information that can be used to characterize the situation of an entity [5]. As a kind of knowledge about the driving environment, context data can be separated into three layers according to the degree of abstraction and semantics: sensor layer, context atom layer and context situation layer, as shown in Figure 2.

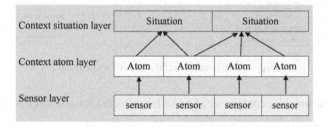

Fig. 2. The three-layer of context data

3.1 Context Atoms

Sensor layer is the source of context data. Context atoms are retrieved from sensors, serving as an abstraction between the physical world and semantic world. For each type of context atom, a descriptive name must be assigned for applications to use the context. The name comes from the ontology library and is domain-specific. In smart car, we use three classes of ontology to provide agreed understanding of contexts, as shown in Figure 3:

- **Ontology for environment contexts:** Environmental contexts are related to physical environments. The ontology of physical environments in the smart car includes the description of weather status, the road surface status, the traffic information, the road signs, the signal lamp and the network status.
- **Ontology for car contexts:** The ontology of the smart car includes three parts: the power system, the security system and the comfort system. The power system concerns the engine status, the accelerograph, the power (gasoline) etc.. The security system includes factors impacting the safety of the car and the driver, such as the status of the air bag, the safe belt, the ABS, the reverse-aids, the navigation system, the electronic lock, etc.. The comfort system is about entertainment, the air condition, and windows.

- **Ontology for driver contexts:** The driver contexts detect the user's physiological status, including heart beating, blood pressure, density of carbon dioxide, diameter of pupils etc. From the information we want to deduce the healthy status and mental status of the driver to determine whether he is sick or is able to continue driving. We implement the ontology using protégé, as shown in Figure 4.

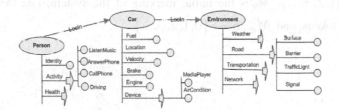

Fig. 3. Ontology for context atoms

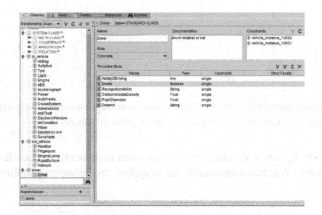

Fig. 4. Smart Car Ontology implemented with protégé

3.2 Context Situation

Context atoms layer provides the elementary conceptual data pieces and use ontology to provide the definition of attributes and classes. However, it is unable to represent complex knowledge, such as the potential danger of two-car collision. Thus a situation layer is built on the top of atom layer. The main purpose of situation layer is to fuse individual context atoms into meaningful context situations. A context situation represents the current state of a specific entity.

We choose Petri net [6] to represent context situation for its excellent performance in modeling concurrent computation and distributed system. Each place of the Petri net corresponds to a context situation, and each transition of the Petri net is extended to represent the correlation between context situations. We can formalize the definition of context situations into: A context situation model is a quintuple:

$$SN = (S,T,F,W,M_0) \tag{1}$$

Where S is the finite set of places to define context situations and $S = \{s_1, s_2, ..., s_m\}$. T is the finite set of transitions between context situations and $T = \{t_1, t_2, ..., t_n\}$. F is a function that defines the correlation by directed arcs form transitions to places, and $F \subseteq (S \times T) \cup (T \times S)$. W is the weight of each transition and $W \rightarrow \{1, 2, 3, ...\}$. M_0 is the initial marking of the system, i.e., the initial assignment of tokens, and $M_0 : S \rightarrow \{0, 1, 2, 3, ...\}$.

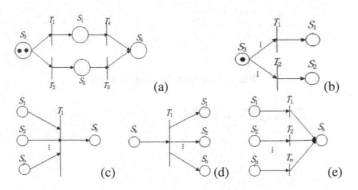

Fig. 5. The different correlations of two context situations represented using petri net: (a) Concurrency situations; (b) Conflict situations; (c) - (e): Causal situations

A transition indicates a situation change and can represent the correlation between context situations. We can summarize the correlations between situations into three classes:

(1) Concurrency: Context situation S_1 and S_2 are independent of each other, as shown in Figure 5 (a). They can take place in the same time and be responded at any sequence without influence. S_3 contain two tokens, which is indicated in black dot in the figure. The number of black dot represents the number of tokens. We mention all the transition weight is 1, so the transition T_1 and T_2 can be enabled and fired at the same time. Consequently, the model has the same probability to reach context situation S_1 and S_2, and the reach order does not matter.

(2) Conflict: If context situation S_1 and S_2 take place in the same time and they will compete for the user's attention or the resource, we call the two contexts are concurrent contexts.

Figure 5 (b) shows that S_3 contain only one token, so the transition T_1 and T_2 must compete for the token to be enabled and fired. Consequently, there is only one context situation for the model to reach. If transition T_1 is enabled and fires, the token of S_3 is consumed and thus transition T_2 is dead. The reverse is also true. So we use conflict correlation to represent the either-or condition.

(3) Causality: Context situation S_2 is derived from S_1, we call this relationship is causality. If context S_2 derives from S_1, then there is a path from context S_1 to S_2. We call context S_1 the parent of context S_2. We call the nodes that have not any input edges as leaves, which represent context atoms coming from sensors. So the reasoning process will generate a graph, where each of the intermediate nodes represents an intermediate sub-target of reasoning and a sub-graph represents a local reasoning process for the corresponding intermediate sub-target.

As shown in Figure 5 (c)- (e), the causality is represented as:

(c): IF S1 and S2,...,and Sn THEN Sk (CF=ui)

Where $p_k = \min(p_1 * u_i, p_2 * u_i, ..., p_n * u_i)$.

(d): IF Sk THEN S1 and S2,...,and Sn (CF=ui)

Where $p_1 = p_2 = ... = p_n = p_k * u_i$.

(e): IF S1 or S2,...,or Sn THEN Sk (CF=ui)

Where $p_k = \max(p_1 * u_i, p_2 * u_i, ..., p_n * u_i)$.

In which, p_i is the confidence of context situation S_i and CF is the confidence of the inference rule.

4   An Application Scenario: The Smart Car

Petri net is a powerful tool for the description and analysis of concurrence and synchronization in parallel systems. Using the approach described in Section 3, we can represent the smart car environment as shown in Figure 6. Part of the definitions of the situations and transitions are listed in Table 1.

The first step in building the context model is to specify the situations demanding the smart car to recognize and react to. For a specified application environment, the situations are definite and can be defined beforehand. The variables that can not be pointed out beforehand are changes of the situations.

The model describes the scenarios from the driver enters the smart car to the driver arrives at the destination, including:

Scenario 1: The smart car sets our
The initial situation is that the driver enters the smart car. From the initial situation, we have five concurrent output arcs which represent five sequential scenarios independent of each other. So we assign the token of the initial situation to be 5.

The five concurrent scenarios are: 1) the weather detection inside the car, including temperature, humidity and the quality of the air; 2) the new device detection, such as the personal digital assistant (PDA), iPhone and MP4 player; 3) Network detection, such as the wi-fi and Bluetooth. 4) Speech detection, to determine whether the user in the car is speaking. If the user is speaking, the detection will determine whether the speech is vocal command. If it is, the voice command will be executed; 5) drive the car.

The scenarios 1 to 4 are circular, ready to detect the new changes in the smart car.

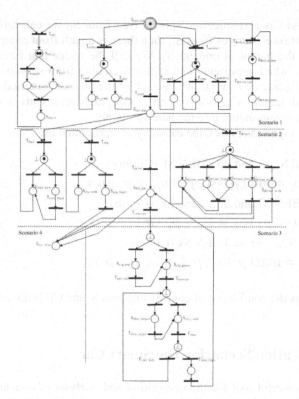

Fig. 6. Petri net model of the smart car, where each node is a context situation, and each directed edge indicates the transition between different situations. Symbol ⊥ in the node represents the conflict relationship.

Table 1. Part of the description of situations and transitions in the Petri net model of smart car

Identity	Type	Detail
$S_{initial}$	situation	The initial situation of the smart car
S_{car_run}	situation	The smart car is ready to operate
S_{dri_cst}	situation	The car drives at a constant speed
S_{sig_red}	situation	The traffic light is red
S_{sig_green}	situation	The traffic light is green
S_{dist_danger}	situation	The distance between cars is dangerous
S_{dist_safe}	situation	The distance between cars is safe
S_{turn_left}	situation	The smart car is ready to turn left
S_{turn_right}	situation	The smart car is ready to turn right
S_{car_stop}	situation	The smart car is stopped
T_{start}	transition	The smart car begins to operate
T_{drive}	transition	The smart car begins to drive
$T_{intersec}$	transition	The smart car enters a intersection
$T_{barrier}$	transition	There is a barrier in front of the car
T_{lane}	transition	the car needs to change the lane
T_{dist_adjust}	transition	The car adjusts its speed

Situations 1 to 3 are circular to detect the new changes in the smart car.

Scenario 2: Driving environment inside the car

During the driving, there are four concurrent arcs which represent four scenarios independent of each other: 1) fuel supply detection: to estimate whether the residual fuel is enough to drive to the destination. There are two statuses: "normal" means the residual fuel is more than a threshold amount and "insufficient" means the residual fuel is less than a threshold amount. The smart car can only in one of the two statuses at any given instance, so the two statuses are conflict. We model the statuses to be of conflict correlation. 2) Engine detection: to determine whether the engine functions normally. There are two statuses: "normal" means the engine functions well and "fault" means the engine is in trouble. The two statuses are exclusive options, so we model the statuses to be of conflict correlation. If the engine is in status of "fault", the smart car will execute operation of "StopCar". 3) Driver detection: to estimate whether the driver is competent for the driving. The driver situation includes "normal" and four abnormal statuses: "Drowsy", "Abstracted", "Drunk" and "Sick". In the first two situations, the smart car will awake the driver by harsh noise. In the latter two scenarios, the smart car has to slow down and park on the roadside. 4) The driving behavior: detail is described in next scenario.

Scenario 3: The driving behavior

Driving behavior represents the process of driving and adapting speed according to the traffic and road situation. We take information that will impact the driving task into account, such as traffic light, the distance between cars, and the lane.

Driving scenario is specified into: 1) the car drives at a constant speed; 2) when the car arrives at an intersection or T-junction, it recognizes the traffic light. If the light is red, the car must evaluate the distance from the car ahead and from the stop line. If the distance is less than 1 meter the smart car will slow down. If the distance is less than 0.5m, the car will stop. Thus the smart car will always maintain safe distance from the car ahead. 3) If the traffic light is green or the traffic light turns green from red, the smart car must determine the direction and the lane. If the car needs to turn left, there will be two lane-changing. The first lane change occurs when the car turns left and leaves the left lane, and the second occurs when the car drives into the right lane. Afterwards, the smart car continues to drive at a constant speed.

Scenario 4: The smart car arrives at the destination

After the smart car arrives at the destination, it will turn down the engine and check all the digital devices in the car. The anti-theft system will work.

5 Analysis and Performance Evaluation

The main phase of the analysis of the model is the study of its reachability graph and transient analysis.

The reachability graph of a Petri net is a graph representation of its possible firing sequences, including a node for each reachable system state and an arc for each possible transition from one situation to another. It suffers from the state space explosion problem. In our experiment, the modules are independent of each other, so we can construct the reachability graph separately without lose of legality. The graphs are shown in Figure 7.

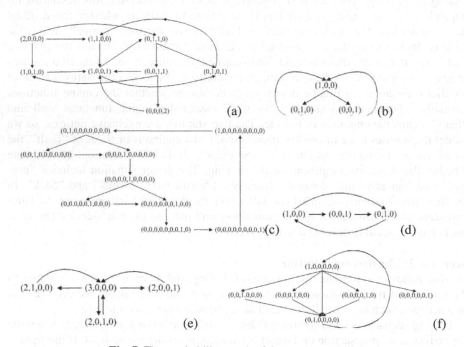

Fig. 7. The reachability graph of the smart car model

From Figure 7, the liveness of the Petri net model can be analyzed. Smart car is a special application domain with the definition of conflict correlation, so some transition cannot be fired in particular condition. According to the liveness definition, each of the transitions is L1-liveness for it can be fired at least once in some firing sequence, so the Petri net model of the smart car is L1-liveness [6].

A transient analysis shows the behavior of the model from a starting point in time to a predefined time. We use the time consumption for the processing sequence of context sensing, processing, situation clustering, and service invoking to assess efficiency of context recognition. The response time equation is denoted as:

$$T = T_s + T_{wap} + T_{recg} + T_{parse} + T_{net} \tag{2}$$

where T_s is the delay time for conveying the data from the sensor to the context infrastructure, T_{wap} is the delay time for context atom management, including mapping sensor data into semantic atoms and publishing them to those subscribing the context, T_{recg} is the delay time to match the current context atoms into a situation pattern, T_{parse} is the delay time to parse the situation profile to find out the appropriate service of the situation, and T_{net} is the delay time for conveying the service message to a certain actuator.

Table 2. Response time in the smart car (Unit: Second)

Person	T_s	T_{wap}	T_{recg}	T_{parse}	T_{net}	Total
One	0.1	0.2	0.8	0.08	0.2	1.4
Two	0.1	0.4	0.8	0.09	0.2	1.6

Table 2 shows the response time performance of two people in the smart car environment. The delay appears close in each session, so the averages are listed for evaluation. The data rate of the sensor network using ZigBee is 250 kbit/s in the 2.4 GHz band, with a 14-byte format including the head and the data. The data rate of CAN bus is 1Mbps, with an 8- byte format including the message identity in the first byte and the priority and length in the second byte. So the communication delay from the sensor network to the context infrastructure and the delay from the context infrastructure to the actuator are less than 1ms and can be neglected.

Context representation and recognition is a computationally intensive task. However, it is still feasible for non-time-critical applications, so the efficiency (with delay of nearly 1.5 second) is acceptable. For time-critical applications such as collision avoidance systems and navigating systems, we need to improve the sensing technology and the analysis method of situation recognition.

6   Related Work

The early cognition of context comes from Schilit [7] and Dey [5], which mostly defines location, time and identity. Strang [8] gives a survey of the current approaches to modeling context.

Ontologies are powerful tool to specify concepts and interrelationships, providing a uniform way for specifying the model's concepts, relations, and properties. Hence ontology-based context model is commonly applied by different context-aware projects.

CoOL (Context Ontology Language) [9] includes two subsets: CoOL Core and CoOL Integration. CoOL Core uses aspect, scale and context information to define concepts. Each aspect aggregates one or more scales, and each scale aggregates one or more context information. CoOL Integration is a collection of schema and protocol extensions.

CONON (the Context Ontology) [10] defines 14 core classes to model Person, Location, Activity and Computational Entities. It provides an upper context ontology that captures general concepts about basic context, and also provides extensibility for adding domain-specific ontology in a hierarchical manner.

SOUPA (Standard Ontology for Ubiquitous and Pervasive Applications) [11] consists of two distinctive but related set of ontologies: SOUPA Core and SOUPA Extension. The SOUPA Core ontologies define generic vocabularies that are universal for building pervasive computing applications. The SOUPA Extension ontologies define additional vocabularies for supporting specific types of applications and provide examples for defining new ontology extensions.

As for interrelationship among contexts, Karen [12] argues that context information is highly interrelated when discussing the characteristics of context information.

Recently more and more research attention is paid on smart car. Intelligent transportation systems and Advanced Driver Assistant System have made rapid progresses over the past two decades in both transportation infrastructures and vehicles themselves [13]. The Europe Union has sponsored many projects of the smart car. Many projects use state vectors to model and represent the information collected from the driving environment.

The AIDE (Adaptive Integrated Driver-vehicle InterfacE) [14] project uses DVE state vector obtained from the Driver-vehicle-environment monitor to model context. Christopher [15] presents a modular state-vector-based modeling. The exhaust system model includes an input file and output file. The input file describes the engine exhaust conditions over time to model different engine/vehicle combinations under different drive cycles. The system converts the information from the input data file into the state vector. After the process ends, the program creates an output file. The output data can be used to validate and tune the model to the actual components in production or under development.

ADAS (Advanced Driver Assistance Systems) project [16] defines the environment, vehicle, and driver states as driver's gazing region, time to lane crossing, and time to collision. These states are estimated by enhanced detection and tracking methods from in- and out-of-vehicle vision systems.

Reference [17] defines three major states from in- and out-of-vehicle vision systems: 1) Traffic environment state, estimated from the position and relative velocity of the front vehicle; 2) Vehicle state, estimated from the lane position and lateral offset; 3) Driver state, including Driver's gazing region estimated from the driver's gazing direction.

7 Conclusion and Future Work

This paper presents a context representation approach in smart car, consisting of context atoms that define the basic concept and attributes of each entity and context situations that represent complex knowledge. Context situation tries to discover the inherent relationship between different elements in the smart car environment.

This paper attempts to represent complex scenarios in smart car using Petri-net. We describe the theory and then apply the theory in the smart car domain. After building the context model, we analyze it and make a performance evaluation.

Our future work includes applying more sophisticated sensing technologies to detect the physiological and psychological status of the driver to enhance the smart car prototype. Knowledge-based inference approaches will be developed and asserted into the risk assessment module for more reliable decision-making. More considerations and efforts will be made for driver intention prediction.

References

1. Moite, S.: How smart can a car be. In: Proceedings of the Intelligent Vehicles 1992 Symposium, pp. 277–279 (1992)
2. FeiYue, W.: Driving into the Future with ITS. IEEE Intelligent Systems 21(3), 94–95 (2006)

3. Tang, S., FeiYue, W., Qinghai, M.: ITSC 05: Current Issues and Research Trends. IEEE Intelligent Systems 21(2), 96–102 (2006)
4. Rau, P.S.: A heavy vehicle drowsy driver detection and warning system: scientific issues and technical challenges. In: Proceeding of 16th International Technical Conference on the Enhanced Safety of Vehicles (ESV 1998), Canada (1998)
5. Dey, A.K., Salber, D., Abowd, G.D.: A Conceptual Framework and a Toolkit for Supporting the Rapid Prototyping of Context-Aware Applications. Human-Computer Interaction (HCI) Journal 16(2), 97–166 (2001)
6. Murata, T.: Petri nets: Properties, analysis and applications. Proc. IEEE 77(4), 541–580 (1989)
7. Schilit, B.N., Theimer, M.: Disseminating active map information to mobile hosts. IEEE Network 8(5), 22–32 (1994)
8. Strang, T., LinnhoffPopien, C.: A Context Modeling Survey. In: Workshop on Advanced Context Modelling, Reasoning and Management as part of UbiComp 2004, The Sixth International Conference on Ubiquitous Computing (2004)
9. Strang, T., Linnho-Popien, C., Frank, K.: CoOL: A Context Ontology Language to enable Contextual Interoperability. In: Stefani, J.-B., Demeure, I., Hagimont, D. (eds.) DAIS 2003. LNCS, vol. 2893, pp. 236–247. Springer, Heidelberg (2003)
10. Xiaohang, W., Daqing, Z., Gu, T., Kengpung, H.: Ontology based context modeling and reasoning using OWL. In: Proceedings of the Second IEEE Annual Conference on Pervasive Computing and Communications Workshops, pp. 18–22 (2004)
11. Chen, H., Perich, F., Finin, T., Joshi, A.: SOUPA: standard ontology for ubiquitous and pervasive applications. In: The First Annual International Conference on Mobile and Ubiquitous Systems: Networking and Services, pp. 258–267 (2004)
12. Henricksen, K., Indulska, J., Rakotonirainy, A.: Modeling context information in pervasive computing system. In: Mattern, F., Naghshineh, M. (eds.) PERVASIVE 2002. LNCS, vol. 2414, pp. 167–180. Springer, Heidelberg (2006)
13. Feiyue, W., Daniel, Z., Liuqing, Y.: Smart Cars on Smart Roads, An IEEE Intelligent Transportation Systems Society Update. IEEE Pervasive Computing 5(4), 68–69 (2006)
14. Broström, R., Engström, J., Agnvall, A., Markkula, G.: Towards the next generation intelligent driver information system (IDIS): the VOLVO car interaction manager concept (2006), http://www.cedes.se/handouts/070301%20RB.pdf
15. Graff, C., de Weck, O.: A Modular State-Vector Based Modeling Architecture for Diesel Exhaust System Design, Analysis and Optimization. In: 11th AIAA/ISSMO Multidisciplinary Analysis and Optimization Conference, Portsmouth, pp. 6–8 (2006)
16. Küçükay, F., Bergholz, J.: Driver Assistant Systems. In: International Conference on Automotive Technologies, Turkey (2004)
17. Kim, S.Y., Choi, H.C., Won, W.J., Oh, S.Y.: Driving environment assessment using fusion of in- and our-of-vehicle vision systems. International Journal of Automotive Technology 10(1), 103–113 (2009)

A New Distributed and Hierarchical Mechanism for Service Discovery in Grid Environment

Leyli Mohamad Khanli[1] and Saeed Ebadi[2]

[1] Assistance professor, Computer science, Tabriz University, Iran
[2] Islamic Azad University – Tabriz Branch, Iran
L-Khanli@tabrizu.ac.ir, Sa_Ebadi@Yahoo.com

Abstract. In grid environment, resources and services distributed with dynamic and heterogeneous characteristics. Efficient service discovery is one challenging issue in grid environment. In this paper, we propose a new distributed and hierarchical mechanism for service discovery in grid environment. This approach has five layers that in previous works presented in four layers. Root layer added as coverage for service index of under layers. For improvement fault tolerant in proposed approach, after find requested service, action of service discovery not stopped and continue that find several instance of requested service. These services will be sent to cache of institution layer that, other services will be replaced immediately if necessary. Also for speed up service discovery, Nodes in one level which are the same parent send query to each other directly. Performance evaluation shows that our approach achieves a good efficiency, stability and consistency.

Keywords: Service discovery, Grid Computing.

1 Introduction

Grid computing is emerging as a novel approach of employing distributed computational and storage resources to solve large-scale problems in science, engineering, and commerce. Grid computing on a large scale requires scalable and efficient resource and services registration and lookup. Traditional approaches maintain a centralized server or a set of hierarchically organized servers to index resource information. For example, Globus[1] uses an LDAP-based directory service named MDS [Fitzgerald et al, 1997] for resource registration and lookup. However, the centralized servers can become a registration bottleneck in a highly dynamic environment where many resources join, leave, and change characteristics any time. Thus, it does not scale well to a large number of grid nodes across autonomous organizations. Also, centralized approaches have the inherent drawback of a single point of failure. Hierarchical approaches provide better capability and failure tolerance by introducing a set of hierarchically organized servers and partitioning resource information on different servers, similar to the DNS.

In this paper, we propose a new distributed and hierarchical mechanism for service discovery in grid environment. This approach has five layers that are respectively client and service layer, institution layer, organization layer, domain layer, and root

R.-S. Chang et al. (Eds.): GPC 2010, LNCS 6104, pp. 174–182, 2010.

layer. For improvement fault tolerant in proposed approach, after find requested service, action of service discovery not stopped and continue that find several instance of requested service. Proposed mechanism for service discovery in grid environment will describe in section 3.

2 Related Works

Much work is relevant to our study. In grids, service discovery is usually managed with centralized or hierarchical mechanism. For example, Condor matchmaker and UDDI use a centralized mechanism to manage their resources[1].

For resource management in distributed environments, large scale and dynamic mode, hierarchical management is used. Chord [2], Pastry [3], Tapastery [4], DST [5], GNSD [6] and DST-based [7] approaches use hierarchical mechanism for service discovery. Chord [2], Pastry [3] and Tapastery [4] approaches has build search-efficient indexing structures that provide good scalability and search performance. However they are all structured, to update the routing table of all nodes when a node joins or leaves are more complicated.

GNSD[6] approach use tree architecture for management and services discovery. Main idea of GNSD is that the nodes that are one level and have same parent, exchange their services list. Namely a node in a level, maintains your list of own and sibling services. This architecture is shown in Fig.1 [6].

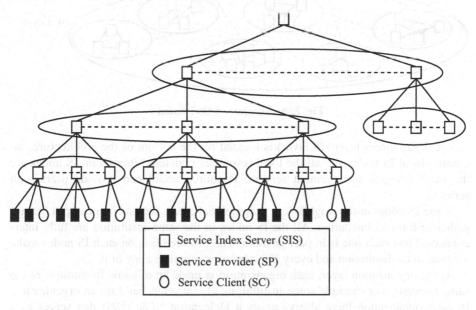

Service Index Server (SIS)

Service Provider (SP)

Service Client (SC)

Fig. 1. Architecture of GNSD

GNSD reduce request distance and because that service discovery done quick. But disadvantage of this method is consistency of nodes service index. When a service to leave or added to grid environment. It must update nodes services index, In addition to a parent node also sibling nodes must update services and resources indexes and this work consume much time, and regarding to the dynamic environment of grid, the service indexes was incompatible.

DST-based [7] approach provide an architecture based on distributed spanning tree. The architecture has four layers: Local Resources layer (IS layer), Institution layer, Organization layer and Domain layer. This architecture is shown in Fig.2 [7]. In this figure, the first and second layers are shown in one layer.

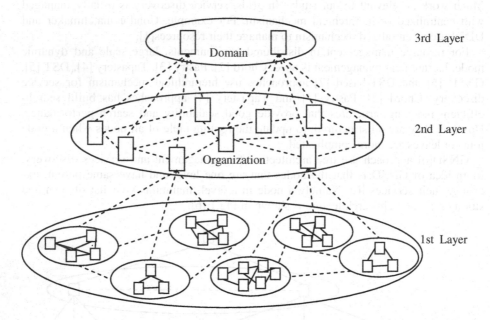

Fig. 2. Architecture of DST-based

Local Resources layer (IS layer) is located on the bottom of the architecture, including local IS nodes and all the local resources registered into them. IS nodes are the local resource management servers. Resource nodes can provide users with services.

Some IS nodes in the neighboring geographical areas, such as in a campus, get together to form an institution. All the IS nodes in the same Institution are fully interconnected and each one is in peer position. The resource lists on each IS nodes make a whole in the Institution and every IS node has a complete copy of it.

At the organization layer, each organization is made up of some Institutions of the same interests. For example some institutions of education build up an organization. In each organization there always exists a Delegation Node (DN) that serves as a clustering node, gathering the information of the resources to form a Resource Index.

In this approach, each organization has 14 Institutions at most and every Institution has a global unique hexadecimal ID from 0000H to FFFFH. The first three bits of its ID point to the ID of the organization which contains the Institution. The first two bits means the Domain's ID. The structure of ID is shown in Fig. 3 [7].

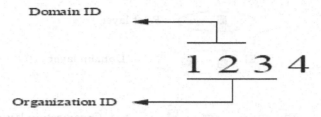

Fig. 3. Structure of institution ID in DST-based

A transfer request from one domain to another domain is most important weakness of four-layer architecture of DST-based approach. In this way, when the request reaches to domain layer (e.g. domain 23) and requested service does not exist in any organizations of that domain, regarding to four-layer architecture that domain is last level; it is actually impossible request sending to another domain (e.g. domain 14). Because of this reason we propose fifth layer (root layer) add to this architecture.

3 Proposed Mechanism

Proposed mechanism has five layers that in previous works [7] presented in four layers. Root layer added as coverage for service index of under layers. For improvement fault tolerant in proposed approach, after find requested service, action of service discovery not stopped and continue that find several instance of requested service. These services will be sent to cache of institution layer that other services will be replaced immediately if necessary. Also for speed up service discovery, nodes in one level which are the same parent send query to each other directly.

3.1 Distributed and Hierarchical Architecture

We use hierarchical and distributed architecture in proposed mechanism for service discovery in grid environment. This architecture has five layers that were presupposing the four-layer DST-based [7] architecture and adding a fifth layer to this architecture has been proposed. In DST-based approach, transfer request from one domain to another domain is most important weakness of four-layer. In this way, when the request reaches to domain layer and requested service does not exist in any organizations of that domain, regarding to four-layer architecture that domain is last level; it is actually impossible request sending to another domain. Because of this reason we propose fifth layer (root layer) add to this architecture.

These layers are respectively client and service layer, institution layer, organization layer, domain layer, and root layer. This architecture is shown in Fig. 4.

Client and service Layer that placed in lowest level includes local service providers (SP) and local service consumers (SC). When service providers join to grid, must be recorded within this layer. Information about type of resource and services that provides and other resources and services features must be registered.

Upper layers are responsible for maintenance services indexes. Also when a client want to join to grid and use from services and resources, must be registered within this layer.

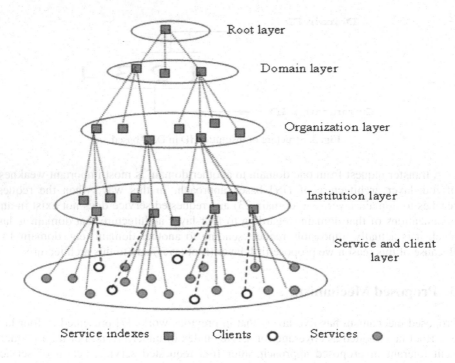

Fig. 4. Distributed spanning tree architecture

3.1.1 Root layer

In the root layer too, each node consists of several domain layer nodes. A node always selected as a delegation node (DN) between nodes of each root layer that provide the services such as nodes clustering and collect service information for make a service index for the entire organization.

When a client node issues a request, it understands through the node DN that whether the required service exists in this root node and thus the query path will be determined. DN node was selecting among all nodes in an root according to different policies such as the node capability and their work load.

3.2 Layers Coding Mechanism

Each institution in hierarchical architecture has a unique hexadecimal ID of the range 0000H to FFFFH. First three bits of an institution ID, is organization ID that includes Institution. First two bits, is domain ID range and the first bit determines the ID of the root that is shown in Fig. 5.

Being the hexadecimal ID, the maximum numbers of each organization is including 15 institutions. For instance, organization no. 235H includes 15 institutions from No. 2351H to No. 235FH. Number 1230H assigned to the Institution that including the organization DN. The requests from outside first come to such Institutions to check whether there are the required services in their organizations.

Fig. 5. Structure of institution ID

3.3 Service Discovery Process

Service discovery process performed in several steps. When a user sends a service discovery request to his institution node, institution node first check whether the required services are registered on itself. Institution node perform this action with search in itself services indexes.

If the required services are found, the institution node will return the services information to the user, otherwise go on to next step. It will first ask the DN of its Organization whether there are required services in the other institution of the same Organization, If the service not exists here too, Sends request to DN of next upper layers hierarchically that discover required services.

3.4 Efficiency Improvement

In this paper have been used two ideas for to improve service discovery performance. These ideas in addition to improve performance, has better fault tolerance.

3.4.1 Multiple Service Discover

In the proposed approach, the user request for service discovery, moving from lowest level towards higher levels that found required service. In this mechanism, after the required service was discovered, and service delivered to the SC node, Search operation will not stop and the system search to discover other instance of this service.

This action is done to improve fault tolerance and speed up service replacing time with another, when the service is faced with problem or service provider to leave the grid. After discover other instance of required service providers, addresses of these services are sent to the cache of Institution that service requester is its member. If the service was corrupted for any cause, other services that already been discovered and cached, will be replaced immediately.

Use of multiple alternative services consumes more memory rather than use of one. But we use multiple alternative services because that, firstly until alternative services will needed, these might leave the grid environment and cause that search operation is performed again and increase response time to request. Secondly this is less important disadvantage, regarding to recent advances in the field of memory production and produce high space memories.

3.4.2 Directly Communication

For reduce traffic in higher layers and reduce request route and also strength hierarchical structure when facing to fault, in proposed mechanism, all nodes in a one level

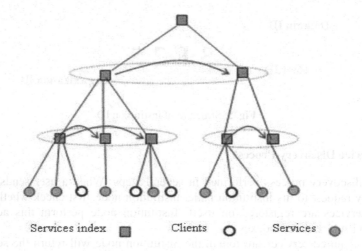

Fig. 6. Send request directly

which are same parent, send request to another directly. In service discovery time, if service was not found in own node indexes list, nodes send request directly to another. How done work shown in Fig. 6.

This causes that reduce traffic of high level layers nodes that has more management responsibility and decrease request rout for a step. Also, if the parent node there is a problem, nodes can connect together will increase system stability. In GNSD [6] approach, sibling nodes always maintain together index of services. In this case speed of service discovery is higher, but disadvantage of this approach is consistency discussion of services index of nodes.

4 Performance Evaluation

Basic features of proposed mechanism for Grid service discovery based on hierarchical and distributed architecture are efficiency, stability and consistency. Each of which they are described in next subsections.

4.1 Efficiency

Considering that in proposed approach, all nodes in a level which has the same parent, send request together directly in service discovery time if the service not existed in own service indexes, caused to reduce a step service discovery path and service discovery done more quickly. It can also cause to be decrease traffic in high level layer that has more responsibility for managing the nodes.

4.2 Stability

Stability is important features of the Grid system and has better performance when faced with fault. In the proposed approach, as mentioned, after the desired service was discovered and delivered to the requester, search operation will not stop the system search to discover other instance of this service. This action be done to improve fault tolerance and speed up service replacing time with another, When the service is faced with problem or service provider to leave the grid.

If any cause system unable to provides service, another service that already been discovered and has been cached immediately replaced. Also considering that the proposed approach, sibling nodes always keeping each other services indexes, If there is a problem in the parent node, nodes can directly be connected with each other and increase system stability.

4.3 Consistency

In GNSD [6] approach, sibling nodes always maintain together index of services. In this case speed of service discovery is higher, but disadvantage of this approach is consistency discussion of services index of nodes. When a service to leave or added to grid environment. It must update nodes services index, In addition to a parent node also sibling nodes must update services and resources indexes and this work consume much time. And regarding to the dynamic environment of grid, the service indexes was incompatible.

However, in our proposed approach for service discovery in grid environment, sibling nodes not maintain indexes of together services and resources and only if needed, send requests to each other nodes directly that this has more consistency with the list of service indexes nodes.

5 Conclusion

In Grid environment that resources and services are in large scale and distributed, service discovery is very importance. In this paper, a hierarchical mechanism based on distributed spanning tree for service discovery in Grid environment was presented. This architecture has five. These layers are respectively client and service layer, institution layer, organization layer, domain layer, and root layer. Lowest level includes local service providers and local service consumers. Upper layers are responsible for maintenance services indexes.

In proposed mechanism, after the required service was discovered, and service delivered to the user, search operation will not stop and the system search to discover other instance of this service. This action is done to improve fault tolerance and speed up service replacing time with another, when the service is faced with problem or service provider to leave the grid. Also for reduce traffic in higher layers and reduce request route and also strength hierarchical structure when facing to fault, in proposed mechanism, all nodes in a one level which are same parent, send request to another directly. Performance evaluation was showed that our approach achieves a good efficiency, stability and consistency.

References

1. Globus Toolkit, http://www.globus.org/tookit
2. Stoica, I., Morris, R., Karger, D., Kaashoek, M.F., Balakrishnan, H.: Chord: A Scalable Peer-to-Peer lookup Service for Internet Applications. In: ACM SIGCOMM (2001)

3. Rowstron, A., Druschel, P.: Pastry: Scalable, Distributed Object Location and Routing for Large-Scale Peer-to-Peer Systems. In: Proceedings of the IFIP/ACM International Conference on Distributed Systems Platforms (2001)
4. Zhao, B.Y., Kubiatowicz, J.D., Joseph, A.D.: Tapestry: An Infrastructure for Fault-tolerant Wide-area Location and Routing. Technical Report, UCB/CSD-01-114 (2000)
5. Dahan, S., Nicod, J., Philippe, L.: The Distributed Spanning Tree: A Scalable Interconnection Topology for Efficient and Equitable Traversal. In: International Symposium on Cluster Computing and the Grid. IEEE, Los Alamitos (2005)
6. Tao, Y., Jin, H., Shi, X.: GNSD: A Novel Service Discovery Mechanism for Grid Environment. In: Proceedings of the International Conference on Next Generation Web Services Practices. IEEE, Los Alamitos (2006)
7. Hua, X., Cao, Y., Huang, H.: The Distributed Spanning-Tree Based Service Discovery in Grid Environment. In: Proceedings of the Fifth International Conference on Machine Learning and Cybernetics, Dalian (2006)

DSOA: A Service Oriented Architecture for Ubiquitous Applications

Fabricio Nogueira Buzeto, Carlos Botelho de Paula Filho,
Carla Denise Castanho, and Ricardo Pezzuol Jacobi

Departamento de Ciências da Computação , Instituto de Ciências Exatas
Universidade de Brasília (UnB)
Campus Universitário Darcy Ribeiro - Asa Norte - ICC Centro - Caixa postal 4466
70.910-900 - Brasília - DF, Brazil
fabricio@intacto.com.br, carlosbpf@intacto.com.br,
carlacastanho@cic.unb.br, rjacobi@cic.unb.br
http://www.cic.unb.br

Abstract. Ubiquitous environments are composed by a wide variety of
devices, each one with different characteristics like communication protocol, programming and hardware platforms. These devices range from
powerful equipments, like PCs, to limited ones, like cell phones, sensors
and actuators. The services provided by an ubiquitous environment rely
on the interaction among devices. In order to support the development of
applications in this context, the heterogeneity of communication protocols must be abstracted and the functionalities dynamically provided by
devices should be easily available to application developers. This paper
proposes a Device Service Oriented Architecture (DSOA) as an abstraction layer to help organizing devices and its resources in a ubiquitous
environment, while hiding details about communication protocols from
developers. Based on DSOA, a lightweight middleware (uOS) and a high
level protocol (uP) were developed. A use case is presented to illustrate
the application of these concepts.

1 Introduction

Computing powered devices became part of our daily lives. Cell phones, fur-
nitures, home appliances and even clothes are endowed with processing power
and communication capabilities, establishing the basis for the creation of smart
spaces [17]. These spaces are not only characterized by the presence of such
equipments but also by the intelligence they carry to coordinate actions in order
to aid users in their tasks. According to *ubicomp* principles, this assistance must
be delivered requiring minimum user attention [11].

In order to take these actions the applications must be aware of which resources and devices are available in the environment. They must also communicate with each other sharing information gathered about the environment.
Besides, the mobility of devices and users in the smart space must be taken
into account. All these factors should be considered when developing ubiquitous
applications [5].

R.-S. Chang et al. (Eds.): GPC 2010, LNCS 6104, pp. 183–192, 2010.

In order to abstract and simplify the complexity of the environment, it is common place the adoption of middlewares that facilitate the implementation of smart spaces. There are some important characteristics that must be addressed by middlewares for *ubicomp*.

- *Limited devices* are part of the smart space, so its limitations like CPU, memory, bandwidth and battery life must be considered. Such issues can be seen in middlewares like the MundoCore [7].
- *Interaction details* on how applications and resources interact must be addressed. Not only synchronous but asynchronous communication must be taken into consideration, like done by the MoCA middleware [15]. Communication can be taken not only in small messages, but also be handled in stream-like communication as considered by the MediaBroker project [9].
- *Platform heterogeneity* among devices. The hardware and software must be considered in order to allow the integration of as many as possible devices to the smart space. This type of concern is presented in projects like the Mundo-Core [7] and WSAMI [14] which provides solutions to multiple programming platforms.

The utilization of SOA [6] helps modeling applications and resources in the smart space, abstracting lower details of the environment. Approaches in this field can be seen in works like WSAMI [14] which utilizes a SOAP [16] solution, and Home SOA [3] which presents an OSGi-SOA [1] solution.

In this work it will be presented the *DSOA* (Device Service Oriented Architecture, section 2) as a natural way to model a smart space and present its strategies to handle the characteristics presented before. Along with that the *uP* (Ubiquitous Protocol, section 3) is presented as a lightweight multiplatform communication interface to access the resources of the smart space and it also presented the middleware *uOS* (Ubiquitous OS, section 4) for building applications in such context. In section 5 we present a use case for validating the proposed model and in section 6 the obtained results are presented. Some final considerations about this research are discussed in section 7.

2   The DSOA Architecture

The great variety of devices and interactions among them in an intelligent environment are the basis for implementing the ubicomp. This interaction occurs by means of applications and resources available in the smart space. Applications need to be aware of the functionalities provided by the devices. This type of dynamics must be orchestrated by a common interface of communication.

The concepts of SOA [6] are well suited for this kind of scenario, but they do not address all the characteristics of an ubicomp environment properly. For instance, SOA does not specify how communication must occur, without distinguishing between synchronous and asynchronous interactions. DSOA (Device Service Oriented Architecture) extends the concepts of SOA adding new features derived from ubiquitous computing requirements. The following subsections present the key concepts of the DSOA and the communication strategies in the smart space.

2.1 Basic Concepts

The smart space: *The smart space is a neither empty nor unitary set of devices provided with computing power and interconnected by a communication network in a collaborative way.*

It defines the environmental scope addressed by *DSOA* from which we can highlight three points. (i) A smart space cannot be defined as a single device. (ii) All devices must have a way to communicate with each other. This can be done with any type of technology or set of them. Being capable of exchanging information is the basis for devices to interact and coordinate actions. (iii) Devices collaborate in order to provide services to the user in a transparent way, which is one of the main purposes of ubicomp.

Devices: *A device is a computing equipment with communication capabilities, which must host applications or make resources available in the smart space.*

Resources: *"A resource is a group of functionalities logically related. These functionalities must be accessible in the environment through pre-defined interfaces."*

The concept of resource allows applications to be aware of a set of functionalities (services) in a more cohesive way. Some functionalities present dependencies or correlation with each other. Consider an air-conditioner as a resource. It can provide the functionality for setting the desired temperature and another for setting the fan speed. These are two different functionalities, but both are associated to the same resource.

Resources can be either physical (like screen, keyboard, speaker, etc.) or logical (like user positioning, converters, etc.). Logical resources can provide new functionalities by accessing other resources. In SOA this is known as "composition". Imagine a camera resource that provides video stream functionality in raw format. A video conversion resource can provide a compression functionality of the same stream in a different format, like H.264/AVC.

A resource must be available to the smart space applications through a known public interface. In the *DSOA* a resource is uniquely identified by a *name* (or *identifier*) and the *set of services* it provides.

Services: *A service is the implementation of a functionality made available in the smart space through a resource with a known public interface.*

The service is responsible for providing the execution of functionalities of the resource. A service is only relevant if it's capable of producing an effect that can be verified by other entities in the smart space. This effect can be an exchange of information between the resource and the application, or a change in the state of the environment (perceived by another application or user).

The interface of a service is defined by the *resource* the service is part of. A *name* (or *identifier*) is responsible for uniquely identifying the service in a resource. The *parameters* that specify the information required for the execution of the service are also part of its interface.

The Environment: Figure 1 exemplifies the organization of a *DSOA* environment according to the previews definitions. The smart space is composed by devices responsible for providing computing power to the environment. These devices host applications and resources that are used to bring intelligence to the environment. Resources, on the other hand, have their functionalities represented as services.

An application[1] accesses the services in the smart space through the resource's interface. For example, an

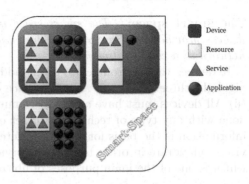

Fig. 1. Sample *DSOA* smart space environment and its entities

application needs to access all available cameras in the environment. This is done querying the smart space for available resources with the corresponding identifier. Knowing all cameras available, the application verifies which ones are compatible with the expected interface. From this list, the application can choose the one that fits best.

Roles: *DSOA* defines three roles for devices during communication:

- A device acts as a *consumer* if it has a resource or application accessing services in the smart space.
- A device plays the role of a *provider* when it enables the access to a service through its defined interface. In addition, it is the provider responsibility to supply the information about its resources and services.
- The entity that keeps track of information about the resources and services available in the smart space is the *register*. This can be done by monitoring devices and their available resources, or by providing means for each device to do that spontaneously.

A single device can act in any combination of these roles at any time, but any device must fit in at least one of these roles in order to be considered part of the smart space.

2.2 Communication Strategies

DSOA defines two groups of strategies to deal with the interaction details stated in section 1.

---

[1] Regarding interaction, resources act as applications since they are allowed to access other resources.

Data Transport: Concerning the way a service provider and a consumer can exchange data, *DSOA* presents two strategies.

- *Discrete messages* are defined as the ones which carry information with known size. They are characterized by mutual knowledge of the beginning and the end of data in the communication. This strategy is used for small scale and discrete information, like requests for actions or queries.
- *Continuum data* are characterized by an information flow with no previous knowledge of its ending. The common usage of this type of communication is in data streams transmissions, like audio/video, or large scale data transfers.

To handle each strategy *DSOA* defines two types of logical "channels" in the communication networks available in the smart space. Discrete messages are transmitted through a single *control channel* for each device. Continuum data must be transported through specific *data channels* for each continuum interaction. This way each interaction has control of its own data flow.

Device Interaction: In a *DSOA* smart space each service can be accessed in two different ways:

- A *synchronous* interaction occurs when a consumer starts its service request and a provider responds in a request-response manner. Common uses of this type of interaction strategy can be found in command requests (like lowering the air-conditioner temperature) or in a simple information query (like asking for the current room temperature).
- Some interactions don't start immediately after the client request. This type of interaction is defined as *asynchronous* and has the following steps. (i) A client asks a provider to be informed about the occurrence of an event. (ii) The provider receives the request and waits for the event to happen. (iii) In an arbitrary moment (which may never happen) the provider notifies the client of the occurrence of the event. This type of interaction is commonly used to identify changes on the environment like user actions or temperature changes.

3   uP

uP (ubiquitous protocol) consists of a set of protocols created for interfacing communications in a *DSOA* compliant smart space. The uP messages are in JSON [2] format. JSON was chosen mainly because of its characteristics of portability in a variety of computing and programming platforms. The use of UTF8 [18] encoding and a message format specification tackle the platform heterogeneity issue mentioned in section 1.

JSON has a structured format of representing data which facilitates message handling and future expansion of any predefined message. Since such characteristics are also found in XML [13] format, which is commonly used, comparative tests were performed[2]. The results have shown that JSON messages tend to generate smaller messages and demand less processor power. Figure 2(a) shows that

---

[2] Test were performed in a Gateway P-172X FX 2.40 GHz Intel Core 2 Duo T8300 2x2 GB DDR II SDRAM 667 MHz 3MB L2 Cache, Windows Vista.

XML messages tend raise more rapidly than JSON as the number of fields increases. It's worth mentioning that the size of a message determines the amount of memory and bandwidth that a device must have. In figure 2(b) can be observed that JSON messages take less than 1.2 ms to be decoded, while the XML messages show an exponential growth. This impacts in the amount of processing power needed and therefore in the battery life. Limited devices are part of the ubicomp environment (section 1), making JSON a suitable choice for this task.

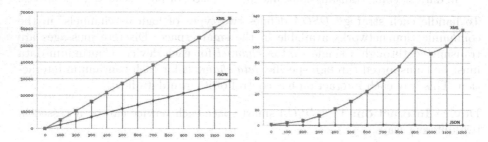

(a) Number of fields versus message size represented in JSON and XML

(b) Number of fields versus time to deal with a message in JSON and XML

uP specifies the representation of the basic concepts of *DSOA*, as devices, resources and services. These representations determine how information will be exchanged between devices. The service representation includes the information needed to accomplish DSOA strategies. Resources are represented as drivers which are responsible for implementing its interface.

The protocols in *uP* are responsible for defining how services must be addressed (*base protocols*) and how basic information about devices and the smart space can be queried (*complementary protocols*).

The *base protocols* are the SCP (Service Call Protocol) and the EVP (Event protocol), which are respectvely responsible for handling synchronous and asynchronous services. Using three simple message formats (Service Call, Service Response and Notify), these protocols are able to handle both discrete messages and continuous data.

The *complementary protocols* are built on top of the base protocols and act as services on a device. They are available through two resource drivers. The Device Driver is responsible for sharing information about the device itself. Its services provide interfaces for (i) listing the available drivers in the device, (ii) exchanging device meta information, (iii) removing device information and (iv) establishing a security context. The Register Driver is responsible for providing the information about device's neighborhood and provides services for (i) sharing information about known devices and their drivers, and also (ii) publishing and (iii) unpublishing drivers and devices.

4   uOS

In order to assist the construction and coordination of applications and resources in a *DSOA* smart space, a middleware named *uOS* (ubiquitous OS) was developed. The current version of this middleware is available in JSE and JME platforms. Figure 2 shows an overview of the *uOS*.

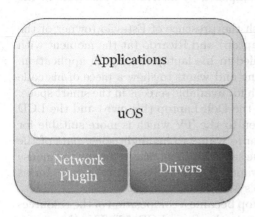

The *uOS* utilizes a layered architecture for abstracting the lower level details of the environment. The lower layer of the middleware is the *network layer*, responsible for managing the *network plugins*. Each plugin encapsulates the implementation details for a communication technology. It's also responsibility of the plugin to provide mechanisms for device discovering in the smart space. This mechanism is called *radar* and helps continuously monitor the set of devices present in the smart space. The current implementation of the *uOS* provides plugins for Bluetooth, TCP, UDP and RTP technologies.

Fig. 2. Overview of responsibilities according to the *uOS* middleware

The message layer is responsible for translating the data from and to the network layer using *uP* protocol message formats.

The adaptability layer manages the lifecycle of applications and drivers in the device. *uOS* handles all service calls and events sent to the drivers. It also provides an interface for applications and resource drivers to access the smart space functionalities like resource discovery, service call and event management.

uOS provides full implementations of the Device Driver and Register Driver specified in the *uP* protocol, making available the services for sharing information among devices. The Device Driver provides an implementation [4] of a simple authentication protocol for limited devices, which establishes a security context for communication.

5   Use Case – The Hydra Application

To exemplify the application of the *DSOA* architecture and the *uOS/uP* operation a case of study is proposed. It was constructed as follows.

First of all, the chosen smart space is a meeting room. In this place we have available a Dell Laptop, a MacBook, a Sony Ericson w580i cell phone and a Sony LCD 52" TV connected to a PC. These devices were modeled as follows:

- The Dell Laptop and Mac Book make available in the smart space their keyboard, mouse, webcam and video output (screen) as resources.

- The Sony Ericson w580i cell phone provides keyboard and mouse resources to the smart space.
- The PC provides a video output (screen) resource for the Sony LCD 52" TV.

The Hydra application enables a computer to redirect its common I/O peripherals, like keyboard and mouse, to resources available in the smart space. This way, a single machine can be seen as composed by distributed resources in the smart space.

For example, we have a meeting with the presence of Estevão (owner of the MacBook), Lucas (Owner of the Dell laptop) and Ricardo (at the moment with his w580i cell phone). Lucas has installed in his laptop the Hydra application. He is responsible for starting the meeting and wants to show a piece of his code to the others. Using Hydra, Lucas search for available screens in the smart space. It finds three available, the Mac Book, the Dell Laptop (his own) and the LCD TV. Lucas chooses to redirect his screen to the TV which is more suitable for visualization. During the meeting, Ricardo wants to highlight some part of the code during the discussion. Following the same process Lucas redirects the mouse to Ricardo's cell phone. Later Estevão wants to make a change in the code. Lucas then redirects the keyboard to Estevão's Mac Book.

At the end of the meeting, Lucas' laptop became a composition of the resources it access in the smart space. Its screen is the Sony LCD 52" TV, the mouse the Sony Ericson w580i cell phone and the keyboard the Mac Book. All this integrated through the Hydra application running in the Dell Laptop.

6   Results

The analysis of the Hydra use case highlights some key features of *DSOA* architecture. The way resources were defined and their services made available in the meeting room are strongly related to what the devices were capable of sharing between each other. This model of resources is not influenced by the applications built on top of the smart space. Other applications could use the same resources for different purposes. This is related to the fact that the *DSOA* has a more natural way[3] of representing the smart space among applications in contrast to other propositions like the MPACC[12].

In Hydra all drivers and applications can be implemented using the API provided by the middleware. The middleware is responsible for handling the device and resource discovery process along with delegating service calls to the respective drivers.

Considering application footprint, WSAMI is available in a 3.9 MB package and MundoCore in a 42 KB package. The *uOS* implementation is available in 85 KB for JME and 1,256 KB for JSE. The difference between the size of JME and JSE distribution due to the use of different libraries and APIs. The small size of the distribution allows the *uOS* to be used in devices with memory limitations.

---

[3] This refers to the fact that *DSOA* resource representation are closer to the real resource in the smart space.

The average time consumed by MundoCore during transactions is 2.67 ms [8] (when using java and XML). No performance evaluation was found with the WSAMI middleware, but SOAP [10] tests show that best performance for java is 4.7 ms. In [3] is presented a SOA solution built upon the OSGi middleware which achieves an average of 8.3 s. In performance tests[4] the uOS presents an average load of 1.72 ms. This shows that the uOS and uP drains little processing power from the hardware. This not only increase the range of devices able to run uOS applications but also make it less energy consuming.

7 Conclusion

$DSOA$, uOS and uP are part of a larger project called UbiquitOS which aims to the development of ubiquitous applications. This project range from the definition of smart space organizations to application development involving artificial intelligence, user profile analysis, and alternative user interfaces, among others.

We presented the $DSOA$ architecture and how it assists modeling an ubiquitous environment using a more natural approach. Besides, we described the $DSOA$ strategies to deal with common interactions issues in a smart space. The use of uP and uOS for building applications in this scenario was presented and compared to other solutions. The results show a consistency of the implemented solution in accordance to the established requisites of a ubiquitous environment.

References

1. The OSGi Alliance. Osgi service platform core specification (June 2009)
2. Crockford, D.: The application/json media type for javascript object notation (json). Technical report, Network Working Group, JSON.org (2006)
3. Bottaro, A., et al.: Home soa: facing protocol heterogeneity in pervasive applications. In: ICPS 2008: Proceedings of the 5th international conference on Pervasive services, pp. 73–80. ACM, New York (2008)
4. Ribeiro, B., et al.: Autenticação mútua entre dispositivos no middleware uos. In: SBSEG (2009)
5. Costa, C.A., et al.: Toward a general software infrastructure for ubiquitous computing. IEEE Pervasive Computing 7(1), 64–73 (2008)
6. MacKenzie, C.M., et al.: Reference Model for Service Oriented Architecture 1.0. OASIS (2006)
7. Aitenbichler, E., et al.: MundoCore: A Light-weight Infrastructure for Pervasive Computing. Pervasive and Mobile Computing (2007)
8. Schmitt, J., et al.: An extensible framework for context-aware communication management using heterogeneous sensor networks. Technical Report TR-KOM-2008-08, KOM - TU-Darmstadt (November 2008)
9. Modahl, M., et al.: Mediabroker: An architecture for pervasive computing. Georgia Institute of Technology (2004)

---

[4] Test were performed in a Dell Vostro 1500, Intel(R) Core(TM)2 Duo CPU T7500 @ 2.20GHz 2x2 GB DD2 333MHz, Windows Vista.

10. Head, M.R., et al.: A benchmark suite for soap-based communication in grid web services. In: SC 2005: Proceedings of the 2005 ACM/IEEE conference on Super-computing, Washington, DC, USA. p. 19. IEEE Computer Society, Los Alamitos (2005)
11. Weiser, M., et al.: Designing calm technology. Technical report, Xerox PARC (1995)
12. Roman et al. A model for ubiquitous applications. Technical report, University of Illinois at Urbana-Champaign, Champaign, IL, USA (2001)
13. Bray, T., et al.: Extensible markup language (xml) 1.1 (second edition). Technical report, W3C (2006)
14. Issarny, V., et al.: Wsami: A middleware infrastructure for ambient intelligence based on web services. Technical report, ARLES Research Page (2005)
15. Sacramento, V., et al.: Moca: A middleware for developing collaborative applications for mobile users. IEEE Distributed Systems Online 5(10) (2004)
16. W3C. Soap specification. Technical report, W3C (2000), http://www.w3.org/TR/soap/
17. Weiser, M.: The world is not a desktop. ACM Interactions (1993)
18. Yergeau, F.: Utf-8, a transformation format of iso 10646. Technical report, Alis Technologies (2003)

Monitoring Service Using Markov Chain Model in Mobile Grid Environment*

JiSu Park[1], KwangSik Chung[2], EunYoung Lee[3], YoungSik Jeong[4], and HeonChang Yu[1,**]

[1] Dept. of Computer Science Education, Korea University
{bluejisu,yuhc}@korea.ac.kr
[2] Dept. of Computer Science, Korea National Open University
kchung0825@knou.ac.kr
[3] Dept. of Computer Science, Dongduk Women's University
elee@dongduk.ac.kr
[4] Dept. of Computer Engineering, Wonkwang University
ysjeong@wku.ac.kr

Abstract. Recently mobile devices become considered as grid resources as the technology of mobile devices and wireless communication network improves. But mobile devices have several problems such as instability of wireless communication, intermittent connection, limitation of power supply, and low communication bandwidth. These problems make it difficult to use mobile grid computing resources for stable job processing effectively. For stable resource participation of mobile devices, a monitoring scheme that collects and analyzes dynamic information of mobile devices, such as CPU, memory, storage, network and location, is required. But, if the time interval of monitoring is very short, overhead of collecting information increases. The scheme, however, cannot keep correct state information in dynamic environments if the interval is very long. This paper proposes a monitoring service scheme that adjusts the time interval of monitoring according to the state information predicted by Markov Chain model.

Keywords: Mobile Grid, Markov Chain Model, Monitoring, Monitoring time interval.

1 Introduction

Grid computing has been studied primarily in wired communication networks. As wireless communication networks are gradually developed, and as capacity and performance of mobile devices become better current researches on mobile grid computing considers a mobile device as one of grid computing resources [1][2]. But mobile devices have a few of problems, such as instability of wireless communication, intermittent connection, limitation of power supply, low communication bandwidth

* This research was supported by a Korea University Grant (2010).
** Corresponding Author.

R.-S. Chang et al. (Eds.): GPC 2010, LNCS 6104, pp. 193–203, 2010.

and dynamic environment. These problems make it difficult to use mobile devices as one of grid computing resource. One of solutions is a monitoring scheme that analyzes dynamic information of mobile devices for ensuring stable participation as a grid computing resource.

In order to solve the above problems, previous researches relied on scheduling techniques or fault tolerance techniques. Resource scheduling and fault tolerance techniques calculate state information through monitoring resource information. But, if resources information is not provided correctly and timely, the incorrect information would cause an accuracy problem at reliability calculation. Therefore, a monitoring scheme that can collect and analyze dynamic information for ensuring the stable participation of resources is required. Monitoring scheme needs to be changed dynamically in real time to monitor correct state information and to reflect characteristics of mobile resources that change dynamically. But, if the time interval of monitoring is very short the overhead of collecting information increases. The scheme, however, cannot keep correct state information in dynamic environments if the interval is very long.

This paper proposes a monitoring service scheme that adjust the time interval of monitoring according to the state information predicted by Markov Chain model. In mobile grid, the values of CPU, memory, storage, battery, network bandwidth utilization, and Location are changed frequently, and we use Markov Chain model to predict next state values. Monitoring time intervals are calculated by using job processing time and predicted state value.

2   Related Works

The monitoring services used in grid usually adopt the pull model, the push model or the hybrid model [3]. In the pull model, a message is sent to a client in order to request resource information, but in the push model, resource information is sent to a server according to policy decided by a client. In the pull model, because resource information of clients is required whenever resource information is needed, the monitoring overhead gets less. But this model has long response time and is not used in dynamic environments because requests are sent to clients regardless of their states. In the push model, because a system administrator determines the monitoring time intervals, this interval is static. But, if the time interval of monitoring is very short, the overhead of collecting information increases. The scheme, however, cannot keep correct state information in dynamic environments if the interval is very long. Therefore, this paper proposes a monitoring service that can change the monitoring time interval in dynamic environments.

One of the previous researches tried to determine the monitoring time interval and apply it through the observation of dynamic state of resource information [4]. It is based on the push model and has much less monitoring overhead than other models that monitor in real time. But this scheme is restricted to only CPU among resources high performance environment, so it is difficult to use this scheme in mobile grid environment where resources change more rapidly.

MDS4[5] was developed as a part of Globus project and used resource monitoring for selecting grid resource. MDS4 used standard interfaces to approach to data, such as, publication, discovery, subscription, and notification of data. And it used standard web services, such as WS-Resource Properties, WS-Base Notification, and WS-Service Group. Higher level services such as index services, trigger s services, information providers and WebMDS, are included in MDS4 components. Because MDS4 is based on the pull model, it is difficult to be deployed in dynamic environment.

GMA[6] consists of directory services, producers, and consumers. The directory service supports publishing and discovering producers, consumers, and events. Producers can make monitoring data and pass information to consumers. Consumers can access and use monitoring information. GMA provides a basic composition method of monitoring system, but does not define the details for implementation. The missing details result in the lack of compatibility among the monitoring applications which are implemented based on the specification.

3   Mobile Grid System Architecture

Mobile grid environment has a system structure that consists of an existing wired grid and a wireless grid. However, due to problems such as heterogeneity between mobile devices, low network bandwidth, and highly intermittent connection, it is difficult to integrate mobile devices directly with grid environments. To mediate between mobile devices and wired grids, a proxy is used. The roles of the proxy are as follows: supplementing insufficient performance of mobile devices, connecting mobile devices with wired grids, and managing mobile devices.

The proposed mobile grid architecture is shown in Fig. 1. The function of each component is as follows.

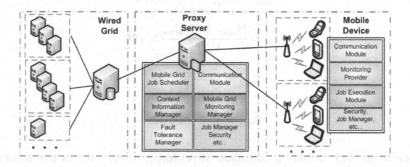

Fig. 1. Mobile Grid Architecture

The proxy server consists of Mobile Grid Job Scheduler, Fault Tolerance Manager, Communication Module, Context Information Manager, Job Manager, and Mobile Grid Monitoring Manager: Context Information Manager collects context information of mobile devices, and Mobile Grid Job Scheduler allocates a job to resources according to contexts. Mobile Grid Monitoring Manager decides monitoring time interval with collected information. The server has components for basic grid functionalities, which are Job Manager, Fault Tolerance Manager, and Communication Module.

The mobile device consists of Communication Module, Monitoring Provider to collect mobile device's information and to send the information to a proxy, Job Manager to manage jobs from a proxy, and Job Execution Module to run the job and send processing result to a proxy.

4   Monitoring Time Interval Algorithm Using Markov Chain Model

Markov Chain Model (MCM) is a useful scheme to analyze the changes or development of a particular system and predicts probabilistically the changes from a particular state to the next state [7].

The state information of mobile resources is changed according to utilization of system (CPU, memory, battery, storage, and network bandwidth) and location. We propose an algorithm which uses MCM to predict the next state and calculates a monitoring time interval according to the predicted states.

4.1   Monitoring Information

Resources to be monitored in mobile grid are CPU, memory, storage, battery, network bandwidth, and location. The information collected from mobile devices is used to calculate the utilization of grid resources respectively. The utilization of each resource, such as CPU, memory, storage, and battery, is written in C_{util}, M_{util}, S_{util}, and B_{util}.

$$C_{util} = \frac{C_{user} + C_{sys}}{C_{total}} \times 100$$

$$M_{util} = \frac{M_{user} + M_{cache}}{M_{total}} \times 100$$

$$S_{util} = \frac{S_{cur}}{S_{total}} \times 100$$

$$B_{util} = \frac{B_{cur}}{B_{total}} \times 100$$

The subscript 'util' denotes a utilization of resource, 'user' denotes a utilization of user, 'sys' denotes a utilization of system, 'cache' denotes a cache memory, 'cur' denotes a current utilization and 'total' denotes a maximum available utilization.

Network bandwidth means a remaining bandwidth subtracting current network traffic usage from maximum available bandwidth and it changes according to the network traffic usage during a fixed interval. Therefore, the utilization of the Network bandwidth (N_{util}) is calculated as follows.

$$N_{util} = \frac{(N_{total} - N_{bw})}{N_{total}} \times 100$$

$$N_{bw} = |\frac{1}{T} \int_t^{T+t} (C - \lambda(t))dt|$$

N_{bw} is an available bandwidth at time t, C is a capacity of maximum available bandwidth, and λ is a network traffic.

Location information uses GPS information and the distance is calculated by subtracting the value of current location from the value of AP (Access Point) location. That is, it uses a distance between the center of AP area and the current location.

$$L_{per} = \frac{L_{cen} - L_{cur}}{L_{lim}} \times 100$$

$$L_{cur} = \sqrt{(D_{lat})^2 + (D_{long})^2 + (D_{sp})^2}$$

L_{per} is the rate about distance between the center of AP area and the current location, L_{lim} is the communication coverage of distance of AP, Lcen is the center of AP of current area, Dlat, Dlong, and Dsp are GPS's latitude, longitude, and speed information, and Lcur is the current location of resource.

4.2 Markov Chain Modeling

Markov Chain model uses the change of state information over time and calculates state transition probabilities from the current state to the next state. In mobile grid, states are defined as follows S_{st}(Stable State) stands for an operation-available state. U_{st} (Unstable State) stands for an operation-available-but-discontinued state, and D_{st}(Disable State) stands for an operation-unavailable state due to faults or network disconnection.

MCM is modeled as the following matrix table P (Fig. 2). In matrix table state $S_{st}I$ means the state S_{st} at time I. Therefore, the occurrence probability of each state at time I can be written as $P_{S_{st}I}$, $P_{U_{st}I}$, $P_{D_{st}I}$ respectively.

	$S_{st}J$	$U_{st}J$	$D_{st}J$
$S_{st}I$	$P_{S_{st}IS_{st}J}$	$P_{S_{st}IU_{st}J}$	$P_{S_{st}ID_{st}J}$
P = $U_{st}I$	$P_{U_{st}IS_{st}J}$	$P_{U_{st}IU_{st}J}$	$P_{US_{st}ID_{st}J}$
$D_{st}I$	$P_{D_{st}IS_{st}J}$	$P_{D_{st}IU_{st}J}$	$P_{D_{st}ID_{st}J}$

Fig. 2. Matrix Table P

$P_{S_{st}IS_{st}J}$ means the probability that S_{st} at time I transits to S_{st} at time J. Therefore, the state transition probability from time J to time I can be calculated as following.

$$P_J = P_I \times P_{I-1}$$

The probability of the previous state is needed to predict the next state. Previous data is used to calculate the probability of the previous state. Previous state information is also used to calculate an initial state probability. An initial state probability is calculated as follows.

$$\Pi = \{\pi_1, \pi_2, \dots, \pi_m\}$$

π_i is an initial state probability of a state i (if $\pi_1 = P_{S_{st}}$, then $P_{S_{st}}$ is an initial state probability of S_{st}) and m is the number of states for $1 \le i \le m$ and $\sum_{i=1}^m \Pi = 1$.

4.3 Monitoring Time Interval

The more jobs are processed, the more monitoring information is used. Likewise, the fewer jobs are processed, the less information is used. Because the monitoring information changes according to resource utilization, the monitoring time interval has to be related with a job processing time. At the same time, the monitoring time interval is also related with each state because the range of resource utilization differs in states.

If the monitoring time interval is short at S_{st}, unnecessary information is accumulated and overhead occurs due to information collection. But, if the monitoring time interval is long, it is difficult to analyze the necessary state for resource usage or sudden faults. Therefore, if a value predicted by MCM is S_{st}, the monitoring time interval is calculated by job processing time and S_{st}'s usage limitation rate. At S_{st}, the monitoring time interval is called as I_{SJTI} (Stable Job Processing Time Interval).

$$I_{SJTI} = J_{pt} \times (1 - R_{sul}),$$

where J_{pt} is job processing time and R_{sul} is S_{st}'s usage limitation rate.

In an unstable state U_{st}, no one knows how resource information will change, nor which state will be the next state. The next state would be a disable state U_{st}. Therefore, the monitoring time interval of U_{st} must be shorter than that of S_{st}. At D_{st}, the monitoring time interval is called as I_{UJTI} (Unstable Job Processing Time Interval), and it is calculated by a job processing time and the usage limitation rate U_{st}'s and D_{st}'s.

$$I_{UJTI} = J_{pt} \times (1 - R_{uul}) \times R_{dul},$$

where R_{uul} is U_{st}'s usage limitation rate and R_{dul} is D_{st}'s usage limitation rate.

In the case of battery information, it is changed continuously even if no job is processed. That means that when calculating a monitoring time interval, the information that is changed regardless of processing jobs must be also taken into consideration. This interval is called as I_{STI} (Static Time Interval), and it can be set by a system administrator.

4.4 Monitoring Time Interval Algorithm

The monitoring time interval is calculated through the following phases: collecting the information of previous state, setting an initial state probability, calculating

Markov transition matrix, predicting the next state, and estimating accuracy. In the first phase, the information of previous state is collected during a fixed period (for example, an hour or a day etc.). In this paper, the monitoring time interval can be decided according to usage patterns of mobile devices [8][9]. In [8], usage patterns of mobile devices on a day are similar to that of the same day every week. Therefore, the information of previous state is collected from the data of the same day a week ago.

```
// Parameter Definition
int Sₛₜ, Uₛₜ, Dₛₜ; // Usage Limitation Value of Stable,
Unstable, Disable State

int scount, ucount, dcount; //Number of States

int jobProcessTime; // Job Process Time

int stateEstimation; // Predicted Information of Next
State

int nextInforValue; // Information of Next State

int accuracy, inaccuracy; // Estimated Accuracy(or
Inaccuracy)

float[] stateTMatrix; // Probability of Transition
State

int[] prevStateInformation; // Information of
Previous State

float[] prevStateProb; // Probability of Previous
State

float[] prevInitProbV; // Initial State Probability
// Information Collection of Previous State
void collectStateInformation(int[]
prevStateInformation) {
for(int i=1, i<=prevStateInformation.length, i++) {
    if (prevStateInformation[i] == Sₛₜ) scount++;
    else if (prevStateInformation[i] == Uₛₜ) ucount++;
    else
       dcount++;
} }
```

In the second and third phase, an initial state probability is set out of the collected state information. The state transition probability is also calculated and the next state is predicted out of the calculated probability.

```
// Calculation of Initial State Probability
float[] prevStateValue() {
```
$$\pi_1 = \frac{scount}{scount+ucount+dcount} \times 100;$$
$$\pi_2 = \frac{ucount}{scount+ucount+dcount} \times 100;$$
$$\pi_3 = \frac{dcount}{scount+ucount+dcount} \times 100;$$
```
    return Π = {π₁,π₂,π₃} ; }
```
return $\Pi = \{\pi_1, \pi_2, \pi_3\}$; }
```
// Calculation of Markov Transition Matrix
float calculateTransitionProbability(float[]
stateTMatrix, float[] prevInitProbV) {
```
return $P_J = \sum_{n=1}^{m} P_I \times P_{I-1}$; }

The fourth phase is for calculating a monitoring time interval.

```
// Decision of Interval Time
int intervalTime(int stateEstimation) {
    if (stateEstimation > U_st)
```
return $I_{SJTI} = J_{pt} \times (1 - R_{sul})$;
```
    else if (stateEstimation > D_st)
```
return $I_{UJTI} = J_{pt} \times (1 - R_{uul}) \times R_{dul}$
```
    return  I_STI; }
```

At the last phase, accuracy is calculated to estimate whether or not the prediction is correct.

```
// Calculation of Accuracy Value
void accuracyCal(int stateEstimation, int nextInforValue){
    if (stateEstimation == nextInforValue)
        accuracy++;
    else inaccuracy++;    }
//Calculation of Accuracy Rate
int accuracyRate() {
```
return $\frac{accuracy}{accuracy+inaccuracy} \times 100;$ }

5 Simulation

In this paper, we implement a monitoring module for simulation of calculating monitoring time intervals in Java. Functions that are not supported in Java are implemented by using JNI, SIGAR[10] and RXTX[11]. The monitoring module collects CPU, memory, storage, battery, network bandwidth and location(GPS) information. The configuration of mobile device for information collection is as follows; CPU: Intel Duo P8600 2.4Ghz, Memory: 4GB, Storage: 120GB, LAN: 54Mbps, GPS: BluetoothGPS.

Fig. 3 presents the monitoring information collected by the mobile device using the monitoring module. But, the graphs show that the collected information except for CPU remained unaffected. This is because the resource performance of the mobile device is higher than the required performance for job processing. With the data in Fig. 3, it is difficult to demonstrate the efficiency of monitoring time intervals calculated with MCM. Therefore, this paper shows the simulation result based on CPU information with many changes. Simulation phases are composed of: the first phase where a monitoring time interval is calculated, the second phase where a predicted state of CPU is compared with the next monitoring state, and then, the last phase where the accuracy for the prediction is evaluated.

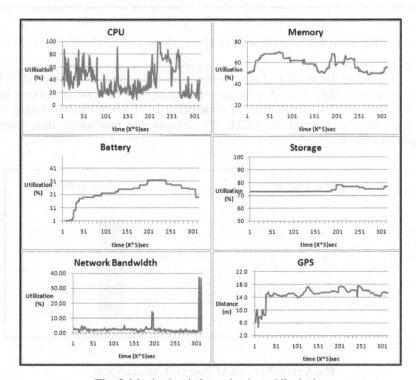

Fig. 3. Monitoring information in mobile device

Fig. 4 (a) presents monitoring time intervals by rate. The higher the rate is, the shorter the monitoring time interval is. Job processing time is set to 300 seconds to calculate monitoring time interval. Also, S_{st}'s, U_{st}'s, and D_{st}'s values are set as following values using CPU utilization(C_{util})[12].

$$S_{st} : \quad 0\% \leq C_{util} \leq 70\%$$
$$U_{st} : 70\% < C_{util} \leq 90\%$$
$$D_{st} : 90\% < C_{util}$$

Monitoring time interval rate (MI_{rate}) is $\dfrac{MI}{J_{pt}} \times 100$.

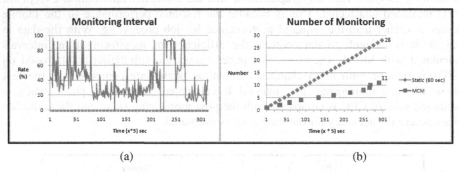

(a)   (b)

Fig. 4. (a) Monitoring time interval Rate ; (b) Number of Monitoring

Fig. 4 (b) shows the number of monitoring against monitoring time interval. When a static monitoring time interval is 60 seconds, the number of static monitoring is 28 for 1,500 seconds. But, the number of monitoring is 11 when the monitoring time interval is calculated based on MCM. This means that monitoring time interval changes dynamically.

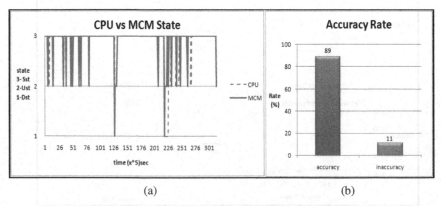

(a)   (b)

Fig. 5. (a) CPU vs MCM State ; (b) Accuracy Rate

Fig. 5 (a) shows the difference between the predicted state of CPU based on MCM and the next state. Fig. 5 (b) shows that the accuracy of predicted state is 89%.

6   Conclusion and Future Works

A mobile grid using mobile devices as resources must do a stable job scheduling by collecting dynamically changing information. So we have to adjust the monitoring time interval dynamically according to state information.

This paper proposed an algorithm that adjusts the monitoring time interval by using MCM that calculates state transition probabilities of mobile resource. The proposed algorithm uses MCM to predict the next state and determine the monitoring time interval. The algorithm does not collect unnecessary information, and thus reduces the overhead of information collection. The algorithm is also suitable for dynamic mobile grid environment.

For the future work, we will study a job management and fault tolerant algorithm using the proposed monitoring service in this paper.

References

1. Foster, I.: The Anatomy of the Grid: Enabling Scalable Virtual Organizations. In: CCGRID 2001 (2001)
2. Foster, I.: What is the Grid? A Three Point Checklist (2002),
   http://www-fp.mcs.anl.gov/~foster (visit 2009.6.15)
3. R-GMA: Relational Grid Monitoring Architecture (December 2003),
   http://rgma.org/ (visit 2009.08.20)
4. Huhl, E.N.: An Optimal and Dynamic Monitoring time interval for Grid Resource Environments. In: ICCS 2004 (2004)
5. MDS, http://www.globus.org/toolkit/mds/ (visit 2009.08.25)
6. GMA White Paper, http://www-didc.lbl.gov/GGFPERF/GMA-WG/ (visit 2009. 08.26)
7. Whittaker, J.A., Thomason, M.G.: A Markov chain model for statistical software testing. IEEE Transactions (1994)
8. Song, S.J., Yu, H.C.: The Scheduling method considering the Using Pattern of the Mobile device in Mobile Grid. Journal of Korea Association of Computer Education (2008)
9. Lee, J.H., Sung, J.S., Joon, M.G., Chung, K.S., Suh, T., Yu, H.C.: Balanced Scheduling Algorithm Considering Availability in Mobile Grid. In: Abdennadher, N., Petcu, D. (eds.) GPC 2009, Geneva. LNCS, vol. 5529, pp. 211–222. Springer, Heidelberg (2009)
10. SIGAR, http://www.hyperic.com/ (visit 2009.11.20)
11. RXTX, http://rxtx.qbang.org/ (visit 2009.11.23)
12. http://www-903.ibm.com/kr/event/download/
    20080612_360_notes/s360.pdf (visit 2009.11. 25)

Modeling Grid Workflow by Coloured Grid Service Net

Hong Feng Lai

Department of Business Management,
National United University
1, LeinDa road, Miaoli city, 360, Taiwan
walden.lai@msa.hinet.net

Abstract. With the increasing transactions in distributed and heterogeneous computing environment, the requirement for integrating and managing large-scale resource and service is crucial. To allocate resource and service is a challenge to grid systems. This paper proposed a coloured grid service net (CGSN) method that integrates agent-based workflow and coloured Petri net. First, we introduce a workflow specification module to express the service sending/receiving, state changing, process execution, and resource sharing. We then apply CGSN to model a grid system that involves message transferring forward and backward between agents. After being validated by simulation of CPN Tools, the soundness of CGSN model can be verified by state space analysis under the support of CPN Tools, e.g. the reachability graph, liveness and fairness property. The results indicate that using the CGSN to model grid systems is feasible.

Keywords: grid service, multi-agent systems, coloured grid service net, grid workflow.

1 Introduction

To date, with the increasing transactions in distributed and heterogeneous computing environment, the requirement for integrating and managing large-scale resource and service across organizational boundaries is crucial [1]. Web service is a basic component of web-based application. Grid service is a special web service that possesses the autonomic configuration and management properties such as the self-organizing and self-healing [2]. Grid workflow is an important grid service, which is designed to promote the efficiency of grid task, and to automate business process by transferring necessary messages to the executors of business processes based on business rules.

In a grid system, service deployment may involve the coordination and distribution of services among diverse resources [3]. The design and use of protocols to aid the allocation resources and services is still of great interest to the designers of internet-based environment [4]. A grid could be taken as a number of interacting agents [5]. To express interaction between agents, three types of techniques and tools to rule interaction have been proposed: protocol oriented, statechart-based [5], and Petri net [6] based approaches. The examples of protocol oriented approaches include: simple

R.-S. Chang et al. (Eds.): GPC 2010, LNCS 6104, pp. 204–213, 2010.
© Springer-Verlag Berlin Heidelberg 2010

object access protocol (SOAP), contract net protocol [7], interaction protocol [8], and message sequence chart [9].

Using statecharts to model the interaction of grid service, the elementary and composite services are expressed in statechart that is translated into XML documents for subsequent processing [1, 5, 10].

Applying Petri net to express the behavior and interaction between resource and service in grid system, the objects corresponding to place set, and the transaction between objects corresponding to transition set. Some examples include: workflow[3], Documentary Petri net [11], Coloured Petri net [12], Task net [13], Gridflow net [14], and colored workflow net [15]. Most of above work aim at extending their modeling capability, e.g. Documentary Petri net extends Petri net with sending documentary messages. Gridflow, Task net and colored workflow extend Petri net-based workflow system with multi-set modeling capability.

Most of past work paid little attention to resource factors except colored workflow net [15]. There are three reasons why we focus on resource issues. First, since resources are scarce and precious, they should be scheduled, dispatched, and monitored effectively. Secondly, the upcoming virtual society will be strongly based on computer-supported cooperative work and networked virtual environment. Thirdly, to coordinate the distributed resource is important for the grid systems.

To resolve the issue involves in resource sharing, coordination and conflict avoidance for grid systems, the purpose of this paper is to propose a new modeling method coloured grid service net (CGSN). CGSN combines resource dimension, instance and process view [3], which can express the resource utilization in workflow system. Our approach will initially establish a generic module, and then construct more complicated model based on the generic module.

The prerequisite for developing a grid system is to keep the requirement specifications simple and easy to validate and verify. CGSN is a systematic method based on the functional decomposition that conforms to the rule of "divide and conquer". In this paper, the CGSN was applied to model a grid system. Additionally, the soundness of CGSN model can be verified by state space analysis under the support of CPN Tools. The rest of this paper consists of the following sections. Section 2 gives the background and methodology. Section 3 describes how to model a grid system using CGSN. The results of simulation and state space analysis are presented in Section 4. Section 5 illustrates the related work. Concluding remarks are given in Section 6.

2 Methodology

2.1 Petri Net and Coloured Petri Net

Petri nets could display dynamic behavior with place nodes (circles), transition nodes (bars) and arcs connecting transitions with places. Petri net is frequently used tool for modeling parallel or concurrent systems. By mathematical view, the state of a Petri nets can be expressed as algebraic equations, M vector, and other mathematical models representing the behavior of systems. The approaches of PN analysis include three types: matrix analysis, reachability analysis, and reduction or decomposition [6]. Reachability analysis enumerates all reachable marking.

Definition 1. Petri net (PN).

A Petri net (PN) is defined as a 4-tuple, PN=(P, T, A, M_0), where P is a finite set of places; T is a finite set of transitions; A $\subseteq$ T × P $\cup$ P × T is the acres set; M_0 describes initial marking.

Coloured Petri Nets (CPNs) provide compact descriptions of concurrent systems by including abstract data types within the basic Petri net framework. Place types are defined in a set of declarations. A marking of a place defines a collection of data values, known as multi sets.

Definition 2. Coloured Petri Net (CPN) [12].

A CPN is defined as 9-tuple, CPN = (Σ, P, T, A, N, C, G, E, IN):

(1) Σ is a finite colour set;

(2) (P, T, A) means basic Petri Net. P is the places set, T is the transitions set, A $\subseteq$ T × P $\cup$ P × T is the acres set;

(3) N is a node function: A $\rightarrow$ P × T $\cup$ T × P;

(4) C is a colour function: P$\rightarrow \Sigma$;

(5) E is an arc function: A $\rightarrow$ expression, such that $\forall a \in$ A:[Type(E(a)) = C(p(a))$_{MS} \wedge$ Type(Var(E(a))) $\subseteq \Sigma$] where p(a) denote the place of N(a);

(6) G is a guard function: T$\rightarrow$ expression, such that $\forall t \in$ T:[Type(G(t)) = Boolean $\wedge$ Type(Var(G(t))) $\subseteq \Sigma$];

(7) IN is an initialization function: P $\rightarrow$ expression, such that $\forall p \in$ P:[type(IN(p)) = C(p)$_{MS} \wedge$ Var(IN(p)) = Φ];   where Type(v) denotes the type of a variable, C(p)$_{MS}$ denotes the multi-set over a colour set C(p), Var(E) denotes the set of variables in E.

2.2 Coloured Grid Service Net

Coloured grid service net (CGSN) extends the CPN and workflow with resource dimension [3]. Each CGSN denotes the internal process, interface message and resource utilization of participant agent.

Definition 3. (Coloured grid service net, CGSN).

A Coloured grid service net is defined as 3-tuple, CGSN = (CPN, RM, SM)

(1) RM and SM are subsets of P, where RM is a set of receiving message places, and SM is a set of sending message places, i.e. RM, SM $\subseteq$ P: | RM | >= 1, | SM | >= 1, and $\forall r \in$ RM, ˙r = Φ; $\forall s \in$ SM, s˙ = Φ.

(2) $\forall x \in$ P $\cup$ T $\vee$ x $\in$ RM $\vee$ x $\in$ SM, x is on the path from r $\in$ RM to s $\in$ SM.

Basic component of CGSN for an agent is depicted in Fig. 1. The agent receives and sends messages using message_i (RM) and message_k (SM). These two places are the interface between the agent and other agents (involoved agents). The transition receive selects the appropriate messages from message_i using the side condition agent, thus ensuring that only a message for the agent reaches the place msg_un_processs (Agent * Messages). A process can only be invoked by a message in the place msg_un_process (conflict choice, decision).

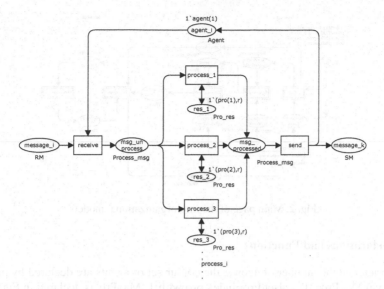

Fig. 1. Basic component of CGSN

The CGSN realizes an encapsulation of the agent's state and behavior. A process executes its appropriate function using the resource Pro_res (type of Pro*Res). A resource place is a control signal for preventing the conflicts between processes. After executing process_i, a responding message is put into the place msg_processed (type of Agent*Messages) that is sent to message_k by the transition send. Therefore, the specific state and behavior of an agent is realized through the token values of coloured set and the firing of transitions.

3 Apply CGSN to Interorganizational Example

3.1 Interorganizational Example

In this paper, we give a workflow example that involves three types of participant agents: 100 clients, 10 processers, 10 sub_processers, and 3 types of control agents: scheduler, dispatcher, and monitor as shown in Fig. 2. The control agents are exploited to schedule, dispatch, and monitor the process of grid service.

The clients send service request to client agent. The client agent then transfers this service request to scheduler agent. The scheduler agent receives the service request and decide its sequence according to the schedule rules and send the results to dispatcher agent. The dispatcher agent decide which one processer to execute the service request. To execute the client service request, the processer agent transfer sub_service request to sub_processer agents. The client is then informed that the service request has been accepted by monitor agent. Moreover, the monitor agent tracks the progress status of service and work, and responds these messages to dispatcher, scheduler, and client agent.

After sub_service having been completed, these results are reassembled and delivered to the client. After delivery message being sent, the client responses and send acknowledge to processer. As the processer agents receives the acknowledge, then response notification is sent to client agent.

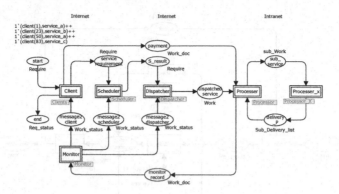

Fig. 2. Main page of the interorganizational model

3.2 Declarations and Functions

To parameterize the number of agents, the colour set of agents are declared by parameter, e.g. val MaxPro=10, colset Pro=index pro with 1..MaxPro as declared in Fig. 3.

```
▼Declarations
  ▼Standard declarations
    ▼val MaxPro=10;
    ▼colset Pro=index pro with 1..MaxPro;
    ▼var p:Pro;
    ▼val MaxSub=10;
    ▼colset Sub=index sub with 1..MaxSub;
    ▼val MaxClient=100;
    ▼colset ClientSet= index client with 1..MaxClient;
    ▼var c:ClientSet;
    ▼colset Schedulerset= with s1;
    ▼colset Dispatcherset= with d1;
    ▼colset Monitorset= with m1;
    ▼var s:Sub;
    ▼colset Service_item = with service_a|service_b|service_c;
    ▼val di_ex=1`client(1)++1`client(10)++1`client(18)++1`client(83);
    ▼colset Require=product ClientSet*Service_item;
    ▼colset Work= product  ClientSet*Pro* Service_item ;
    ▼colset Status= with announcing|waiting|recieved_not|recieved_del|
        recieved_inv|recieved_order|sent_order|notified|sent_del|sent_inv|
        processing|sent_PO|recieved_P|recieved_payment|paid|pay_not|done;
    ▼var st:Status;
    ▼colset Sit_status =product Service_item * Status;
    ▼colset Req_status= product Require* Status;
    ▼colset Work_status = product Work* Status;
    ▼var sit:Service_item;
    ▼colset Sub_service_item = with sub_service_1|sub_service_2|
        sub_service_3|sub_service_4;
    ▼var pod_it: Sub_service_item;
    ▼colset sub_Work= product  Pro*Sub*Sub_service_item ;
    ▼var pod:sub_Work;
    ▼colset Sub_Status= with recieved|produced|checked|on_hand|nOK;
    ▼var ps:Sub_Status;
    ▼colset sub_Work_status = product sub_Work*Sub_Status;
    ▼colset Resource = with R;
    ▼colset S_resource= product Schedulerset*Resource;
    ▶colset D_resource
    ▼colset M_resource= product Monitorset*Resource;
    ▼colset Agent=with A;
    ▼colset Sub_resource = product Sub *Resource;
    ▼colset Pro_resource = product Pro*Resource;
    ▼colset Cus_resource= product Agent * Resource;
    ▼colset Document = string;
    ▼var doc:Document;
    ▼colset Work_doc= product Work*Document;
```

Fig. 3. Declarations of interorganizational model

Sub_processer 1 produces part products of type_a and type_c, Sub_processer 2 produces part products of type_b and type_c. Sub_processer 3 produces part products of type_c and type_a. These assigning and dispatching rules are defined in "funWorkflow.sml" as expressed in Fig. 4.

```
(* The following function is to assign services to corresponding processors *)
fun dispatch (sit:Service_item) =
case sit of
    service_a =>pro(1)
  | service_b =>pro(2)
  | service_c => pro(3);

(* The following function is to dispatch service_items to corresponding sub_service *)
fun assign (p:Pro, sit:Service_item) =
case sit of
    service_a =>1`(p, sub(1),sub_service_1)++1`(p, sub(2),sub_service_2)
  | service_b =>1`(p, sub(2),sub_service_2)++1`(p, sub(3),sub_service_3)
  | service_c => 1`(p, sub(3),sub_service_3)++1`(p, sub(1),sub_service_1);
```

Fig. 4. Assigning and dispatching functions

3.3   CGSN of Agents

Fig. 5-6 indicates the corresponding service flows: Client workflow and Processer workflow. Each of the local workflows is described by a CGSN. However, the input and output places of the subnets which correspond to the processer and the sub_processer have been omitted.

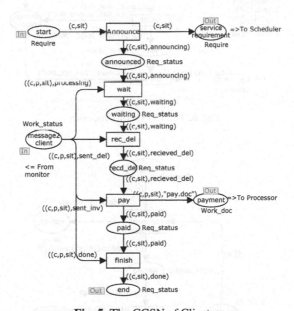

Fig. 5. The CGSN of Client

The subnets of Fig. 6 which corresponds to a processor workflow is a CGSN (see Definition 3) where p-order is a receiving place and delivery is a sending place. The function of dispatcher is to receive the task sequence from scheduler, and assign service to processor.

The CGSN of dispatcher is displayed in Fig. 7, where color set work_staus records various status of work such as "announcing, waiting, recieved_not, recieved_del, recieved_inv, recieved_task, sent_task, notified, sent_del, sent_inv, processing, sent_PO, recieved_P, paid, recieved_payment, pay_not, done".

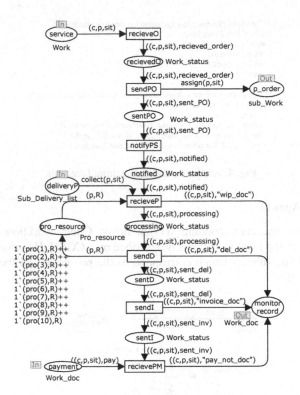

Fig. 6. The CGSN of Processer

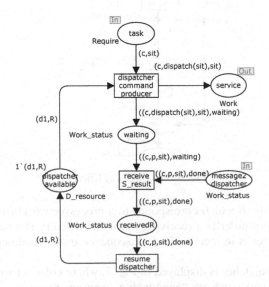

Fig. 7. The CGSN of dispatcher

4 Simulation Result and State Space Analysis

Using CPN Tools, the simulation result displays that the CGSN model seems to terminate in the desired state. Furthermore, after executing state space analysis by CPN Tools, the result includes: reachability graph, state space, SCC graph, fairness properties and liveness properties.

After entering the SS and computing strongly connected component, reachability graph can be drawn, and the report of state space analysis can be expressed as Table 1.

Table 1. Report of state space analysis

Properties:	Client*Pro*Sub: 3*3*3	: 100*10*10
State Space: Nodes	1152	37,120
State Space: Arcs	2800	127,744
State Space: Secs	0	130
State Space: Status	Full	Full
Scc Graph: Nodes	1152	37,120
Scc Graph: Arcs	2800	127,744
Scc Graph: Secs	1	8
Home Marking	[1152]	[37120]
Dead Markings	[1152]	[37120]
Dead Transition Instances	None	None
Fairness Properties	No infinite occurrence	No infinite occurrence

The status of state space being full guarantees that for a directed graph, there is a node for each reachable marking and an arc for each occurring binding element. The home properties: home marking denotes a marking which could be reached from any other reachable marking. For Client*Pro*Sub: 100*10*10, the home marking denotes "1`((client(1), service_a), done)++ 1`((client(23), service_b), done) ++ 1`((client(50), service_a), done) ++ 1` ((client(83), service_c), done)".

A dead marking denotes that there is no binding element being enabled. For Client*Pro*Sub: 100*10*10, node [37120] is both a home marking and a dead marking, that is always possible to terminate the workflow with the correct result.

A dead transition means that there are no reachable markings to make the transition enabled. Therefore, no dead transition guarantees that each transition can fire at least once, i.e. all the specified actions are executable [12]. In Table 1 the modeled system indicates that all transitions can be fired.

5 Related Work

To model the state change in grid systems, in [5, 10] states are specified with calls to web services, and transitions are expressed by events, conditions, and variable assignment operations. In [10] they divide the web service architecture into service builder, service deployer, and the service discovery engine. The service deployer generates the routing tables of every state of a composite service, which is similar to the control agents scheduler and dispatcher in our approach. However, using statecharts approach, as the number of states increases (e.g. 37120 in Table 1), it is obviously hard to name and record the state in statecharts.

The complexity of interactions between agents will also emerge from protocol-based approaches. For example, interaction protocol (IP) diagram indicates interactions between agents and roles along a timeline. Agents are assigned to roles. A role is a specification of the action that an object should fill. Messages between agent roles are shown as arrows signifying an asynchronous communication. The message sequence chart (MSC) are a graphical language for expressing communications between entities [9]. The exchanged messages and the ordering of events of a system could be visualized by a message sequence chart. In Fig. 10, there are five kinds of messages: service_request, notifications, deliveries, invoices and payments.

As the number of agents increases, using IP or MSC for message interaction is quite complicated. For example, as order of Client*Pro*Sub equals 100*10*10, it is hard to draw and distinguish the complicated messages. However, using CGSN approach, as order of Client*Pro*Sub increases; the message interaction between agents maintain the same as the main page in Fig. 2.

Using Petri net to model grid system, resource and service are expressed by place, and the transitions of event, condition, and process are denoted by transition. In [16] they apply basic Petri net to model the real-time Grid transaction. The modeling capability is limited since time and multi-set declaration is absent. In [17] they propose Petri net based grid workflow verification and optimization toolkit (PGWFT) to model and verify the grid workflow via the formal properties of Petri net.

The extended Petri net such as Documentary Petri net [11], Gridflow [14], Coloured Petri net [12], Task net [13], and colored workflow net [15] have proposed to model grid workflow. The token number of receiving and sending palaces in the token number of input and output places are limited to be one. CGSN are not limited to model multi-resource in real world. To model the carrying messages of resources or service, in [11] they propose documentary Petri net to express document messages in workflow system. The CGSN with product declaration in Fig. 3, documentary messages can be carried by color token. Moreover, most of Petri net based workflow system paid little attention to resource factors, while the CGSN aims at resource sharing and deadlock free issues.

6   Conclusions

Since grid systems contain heterogeneous service components and resources, to interact and behave under a consistent way is serious. Our approach is to establish a model that could define and express the interactions and interoperability between agents from diverse domains. This paper proposed a method CGSN that integrates the process, case, and resource viewpoints based on coloured Petri net and agent-based concepts. We introduce a specification module of a grid service net (definition 3) that expresses the message transferring, state changing, process execution, and resource sharing.

An example of a grid system is modeled by the CGSN, which involves message transferring forward and backward between participant agents: client, processers, and sub_processers. The grid service is deployed by control agents: schedulers, dispatchers, and monitors to sequence, allocate, and track the status of grid service. The overall behavior of the grid system could be validated by simulated by CPN Tools and state space analysis. The CGSN approach for interorganizational service flow demonstrates its feasibility.

As the number of involved agent increases, the overall structure keeps consistent by the CGSN approach. Moreover, it will be interesting to investigate the properties of the state space. In other words, how the behavior of grid systems affected by the parameters of MaxClient, MaxPro and MaxSub deserves further exploring.

References

1. Boström, P., Waldén, M.: Development of Fault Tolerant Grid Applications Using Distributed B. Integrated Formal Methods, 167-186 (2005)
2. Bassiliades, N., Anagnostopoulos, D., Vlahavas, I.: Web Service Composition Using a Deductive XML Rule Language. Distributed and Parallel Databases 17, 135–178 (2005)
3. van der Aalst, W.M.P.: Process-oriented architectures for electronic commerce and interorganizational workflow. Information Systems 24, 639–671 (1999)
4. Bacarin, E., van der Aalst, W.M.P., Madeira, E., Medeiros, C.B.: Towards Modeling and Simulating a Multi-party Negotiation Protocol with Colored Petri Nets. In: Jensen, K. (ed.) Eighth Workshop and Tutorial on Practical Use of Coloured Petri Nets and the CPN Tools (CPN 2007), Aarhus, Denmark. DAIMI, vol. 584, pp. 29–48 (2007)
5. Gao, L., Ding, Y.: A Flexible Communication Scheme to Support Grid Service Emergence. In: Gervasi, O., Gavrilova, M.L., Kumar, V., Laganá, A., Lee, H.P., Mun, Y., Taniar, D., Tan, C.J.K. (eds.) ICCSA 2005. LNCS, vol. 3482, pp. 69–78. Springer, Heidelberg (2005)
6. Murata, T.: Petri nets: Properties, analysis and applications. Proceedings of the IEEE 77, 541–580 (1989)
7. Smith, R.G.: The Contract Net Protocol: High-Level Communication and Control in a Distributed Problem Solver. Transactions on Computers C-29, 1104–1113 (1980)
8. Bauer, B., Muller, J.P., Odell, J.: Agent UML: A formalism for specifying multiagent interaction. In: Cuabcarubu, P., Wooldridge, M. (eds.) AOSE 2001. LNCS, vol. 2222, pp. 91–103. Springer, Heidelberg (2002)
9. Mauw, S., Reniers, M.A.: An algebraic semantics of basic message sequence charts. The Computer Journal 37, 269–277 (1994)
10. Benatallah, B., Dumas, M., Maamar, Z.: Definition and execution of composite web services: The SELFSERV project. Bulletin of IEEE TC on Data Engineering 25, 47–52 (2002)
11. Lee, R.M.: INTERPROCS: a Java-based prototyping environment for distributed electronic trade procedures. In: Thirty-First Hawaii International Conference on System Sciences, vol. 4, pp. 202–209 (1998)
12. Jensen, K., Kristensen, L., Wells, L.: Coloured Petri Nets and CPN Tools for modelling and validation of concurrent systems. International Journal on Software Tools for Technology Transfer (STTT) 9, 213–254 (2007)
13. Choi, I., Park, C., Lee, C.: Task net: Transactional workflow model based on colored Petri net. European Journal of Operational Research 136, 383–402 (2002)
14. Bo, C., Liu, Q., Yang, G.: Distributed Gridflow Model and Implementation. In: Jin, H., Reed, D., Jiang, W. (eds.) NPC 2005. LNCS, vol. 3779, pp. 84–87. Springer, Heidelberg (2005)
15. van der Aalst, W.M.P., Bakker, P.J.M., Moleman, A.J., Lassen, K.B., Jørgensen, J.B.: From Requirements via Colored Workflow Nets to an Implementation in Several Workflow Systems. In: Jensen, K. (ed.) Eighth Workshop and Tutorial on Practical Use of Coloured Petri Nets and the CPN Tools (CPN 2007), Aarhus, Denmark. DAIMI, vol. 584, pp. 187–206 (2007)
16. Tang, F., Li, M., Huang, J.Z.: Real-time transaction processing for autonomic Grid applications. Engineering Applications of Artificial Intelligence 17, 799–807 (2004)
17. Cao, H., Jin, H., Wu, S., Tao, Y.: PGWFT: A Petri Net Based Grid Workflow Verification and Optimization Toolkit. In: Wu, S., Yang, L.T., Xu, T.L. (eds.) GPC 2008. LNCS, vol. 5036, pp. 48–58. Springer, Heidelberg (2008)

A Lower Bound on Greedy Embedding in Euclidean Plane

Lei Cao[1], Andrew Strelzoff[2], and Jonathan Z. Sun[2]

[1] Department of Electrical Engineering, University of Mississippi
University, MS 38677, USA
lcao@olemiss.edu
[2] School of Computing, University of Southern Mississippi
Hattiesburg, MS 39406, USA
{andrew.strelzoff,jonathan.sun}@usm.edu

Abstract. Greedy embedding is the key of geometric greedy routing in p2p networks. It embeds a graph (the topological structure of the p2p network) in a metric space such that between any source-destination pair, there is a distance decreasing path for message delivery. It is known that any graph can be greedily embedded in the hyperbolic plane with using $O(\log n)$ bits for each node's coordinates [7]. Interestingly, on greedy embedding in the Euclidean plane, existing embedding algorithms result in coordinates with $\Omega(n)$ bits. It was recently proved that $\Omega(n)$ is a lower bound of the coordinates' bit length if one uses Cartesian or polar coordinate system and preserves the planar embedding of a planar graph when greedily embedding it in the Euclidean plan [2]. In this paper we strengthen this result by further proving that $\Omega(n)$ is still a lower bound even if the graph is allowed to take free embedding in the plane.

1 Introduction

1.1 Motivation

Geometric routing, also referred to as *geographic routing*, is a well studied approach to ad hoc p2p routing. The idea is to embed the network topology (a graph) into a metric space by assigning virtual coordinates to the vertices, so that routing decisions to relay a message from a source vertex to a destination vertex are made locally at each vertex on the routing path, based on the virtual geometric information. *Greedy routing* is a natural abstraction of this model, where each node decides where to forward the message using only the virtual coordinates of its neighbors (adjacent vertices). The key step of geometric greedy routing is *greedy embedding*, that is, to embed a graph into a metric space so that greedy routing decisions guarantee message delivery. We will give a formal definition in Section 1.2. Greedy routing seems to be impressively convenient and efficient compared to many traditional routing schemes, because each node (vertex) now only needs to maintain the locations of itself and its neighbors instead of the link status of the entire network. However, this impression is contingent to a hidden assumption that the coordinates of the embedded vertices

R.-S. Chang et al. (Eds.): GPC 2010, LNCS 6104, pp. 214–223, 2010.

are succinctly represented in bytes or bits. Conventionally, the bit length of a coordinate is determined by byte and can be taken as $O(\log n)$ in computational complexity, where n is the size (amount of vertices) of the input graph. However, this can not be taken for granted in many greedy embedding algorithms.

It is well known that the Euclidean space of constant dimensionality is not able to provide greedy embedding for all graphs. Nevertheless, due to its elegancy in theory and convenience in practise, many research efforts have been directed on the greedy embedding of certain classes of graphs in the Euclidean plane. (See Section 1.3.) The issue of coordinates' bit length was largely overlooked in previous work, as many previous embedding algorithms recursively draw (embed) the graph into a smaller and smaller (or bigger and bigger) area as a fractal, resulting in $\Omega(n)$ (sometimes even $\Omega(n \log n)$) bits for some vertices' coordinates. This drawback indeed makes the greedy embedding ill-suited for the motivating application of geometric greedy routing. Because with such bit length, it is no longer more efficient to maintain, to update, and to calculate the coordinates of a few (say $O(\log n)$) neighbors than to do these for an entire network that uses $O(\log n)$-bit coordinates.

Therefore, we naturally have this question: are these $\Omega(n)$-bit coordinates inevitable in the greedy embedding of some graphs in the Euclidean plane, or are they just due to shortcomings of the existing embedding algorithms and can be somehow overcome? Noticing the recent result of Eppstein and Goodrich [7] that any graph can be greedily embedded in hyperbolic plane using $O(\log n)$ bit coordinates, the answer to this question could be a critical indicator regarding the future of using the Euclidean plane for geometric greedy routing.

1.2 Terminologies

Graphs studied in this paper are connected simple undirected graphs. *Embedding* a graph into a metric space is to associate to each vertex a point location in the metric space. A path $(v_0, v_1, \ldots, v_t)$ in the embedded graph from v_0 to v_t is a *distance decreasing path* iff each step along the path moves closer to the destination v_t, i.e., $d(v_i, v_t) \geq d(v_j, v_t)$ for any $i \leq j$, where $d(x, y)$ is the distance between x and y defined by the metric space. The embedding of a graph into the metric space is *greedy embedding* iff for any two vertices $v_i \neq v_j$, there is a distance decreasing path from v_i to v_j in the embedded graph.

Greedy routing is straightforward in greedy embedding. If each node v_i routes the package to one of its adjacent nodes v_{i+1} that is closer to the destination v_t, i.e., with $d(v_{i+1}, v_t) \leq d(v_i, v_t)$, then the package is guaranteed to arrive v_t following a distance decreasing path. Since by definition of greedy embedding, any node v_i that is not adjacent to the destination v_t must have an adjacent neighbor v_{i+1} that is closer to v_t, greedy routing in greedy embedding guarantees message delivery between any source and destination.

We use *coordinate complexity* for the bit length of coordinates. Denote by $\mathcal{P}$ a metric space, G_n a graph with n vertices, and $Embed_{\mathcal{P}}(G_n)$ a greedy embedding of G_n in $\mathcal{P}$. The coordinate complexity of $Embed_{\mathcal{P}}(G_n)$, denoted by

$C(Embed_\mathcal{P}(G_n))$, is the maximum number of bits that are needed to represent the coordinates of a vertex in $\mathcal{P}(G_n)$. Furthermore, the coordinate complexity of greedily embedding G_n in $\mathcal{P}$, denoted by $C(\mathcal{P}, G_n)$, is the minimum $C(Embed_\mathcal{P}(G_n))$ taken from all possible $Embed_\mathcal{P}(G_n)$. That is, a) if $C(Embed_\mathcal{P}(G_n)) = f(n)$, then there exists a vertex in G_n whose coordinates in $Embed_\mathcal{P}(G_n)$ take $f(n)$ bits; b) if $C(\mathcal{P}, G_n) = f(n)$, then $C(Embed_\mathcal{P}(G_n)) = \Omega(f(n))$ for any greedy embedding of G_n in $\mathcal{P}$. In practice, $O(\log n)$, $O(poly(\log n))$, or $\Omega(n)$ coordinate complexity leads to ideally efficient, efficient, or inefficient greedy routing, respectively. We call greedy embedding with $O(poly(\log n))$ coordinate complexity the *succinct greedy embedding*. (See [7,2,9].)

1.3 Related Work

The earliest study on geometric routing, which are similar to but different than the geometric greedy routing in this paper in various ways, include the Geocast of Navas and Imielinski [17], the geographic distance routing (GEDIR) algorithm of Lin and Stojmenovic [14], the directional routing (DIR), a.k.a., compass routing algorithm of Basagni et al. [1], Ko and Vaidya [11], and Kranakis et al. [12], just to name a few. Among these, the DIR / compass routing is a close relative to the geometric greedy routing we address in this paper, in which the network is embedded in Euclidean plane and each node forwards message to an edge with the closest slope to that of the line segment connecting the source and the destination.

Regarding to greedy embedding as defined in this paper, Papadimitriou and Ratajczak [18] conjectured that every 3-connected planar graph has greedy embedding in Euclidean plane. Dhandapani [5] proved a special case on triangulations, and Leighton and Moitra [13] recently proved the whole conjecture. Many previous results, such as in [3,4,6], are covered by this conjecture. Some other results on embedding planar graphs into Euclidean plane can be found in [8]. In contrast with the intricacy of greedy embedding in Euclidean space, Kleinberg [10] provided a polynomial-time algorithm for greedily embedding any network topology (planar or not) in hyperbolic plane.

Regarding to coordinate complexity and succinctness, Maymounkov [15] obtained a greedy embedding scheme in 3D hyperbolic space with coordinate complexity $O(\log^2 n)$; Eppstein and Goodrich [7] provided a method of greedy embedding in 2D hyperbolic plane with coordinate complexity $O(\log n)$; Muhammad [16] gave a hybrid greedy / face routing algorithm for planar graphs with coordinate complexity $O(\log n)$; and Goodrich and Strash [9] recently provided an involved coordinate system (actually a non-trivial compression / coding of coordinates) for greedy embedding of 3-connected planar graphs in the Euclidean plane that uses only $O(\log n)$ bits per coordinate. As a negative result, Cao, Strelzoff, and Sun [2] proved that $\Omega(n)$ is a lower bound of coordinate complexity for greedy embedding in the Euclidean plane, given the constraints that Cartesian or polar coordinate system is used and the graph is a planar graph with a fixed planar embedding that needs to be preserved in the greedy embedding.

1.4 Our Result

On the one hand, the lower bound in [2] is weak in term of the constraint with fixed planar embedding. Note that most algorithms of greedy embedding in the Euclidean plane [18,5,13,8,3,4,6] don't preserve a fixed planar embedding. Indeed, a greedy embedding doesn't have to be a planar embedding, and a graph that can be greedily embedded in the Euclidean plane doesn't have to be a planar graph. On the other hand, the coordinate compression in [9] is quite involved and unlikely to be easily implemented in a practical protocol. Note that Cartesian and polar are the two coordinate systems people are most familiar with in the Euclidean space, and a motivation of using Euclidean plane for greedy embedding is for simple location and distance calculation with Cartesian or polar coordinates. Therefore, it remains an interesting problem to find out the best coordinate complexity in Euclidean plane greedy embedding that is not contingent to fixed planar embedding but uses Cartesian or polar coordinates without compression. In this paper, we prove that $\Omega(n)$ is still a lower bound for this case. Our main result is as follows.

Theorem 1. *Using Cartesian or polar coordinates, the coordinate complexity of greedily embedding a graph in the Euclidean space is $\Omega(n)$. That is, there exists graph G_n such that $C(\mathcal{P}, G_n) = \Omega(n)$, where $\mathcal{P}$ is the Euclidean plane with Cartesian or polar coordinates.*

2 Preliminaries

As warm-up, we first give intuitive explanations why greedy embedding could result in coordinates of high precision that takes more than $\log n$ bits, how to approach to the proof of the lower bound, and what is the major difficulty that makes the problem non-trivial.

2.1 Angular Resolution Rules

Obviously, a distance decreasing path in Euclidean space cannot form very sharp angles. For example, if an embedded graph G contains a path of three vertices (v_1, v_2, v_3) that forms an angle $\leq 60°$ at v_2 in the embedding, and v_1 and v_3 are not adjacent in G, then the moves along (v_1, v_2, v_3) and (v_3, v_2, v_1) can not be both distance-decreasing moves. Thus, if (v_1, v_2, v_3) is the only path between v_1 and v_3 then the angle $\leq 60°$ at v_2 disqualifies the embedding to be a greedy embedding. This simple phenomenon is the inherent reason that some graphs don't have greedy embedding in Euclidean space, and some that can be greedily embedded in Euclidean space must use coordinates of exponentially high precision. For trivial examples, a star with one center vertex and 7 peripheral vertices cannot be greedily embedded in the Euclidean plane; and furthermore, for any Euclidean space of constant dimensionality, there is a star of constant size depending on the dimensionality that can not be greedily embedded. It is for the same reason that any greedily embedded graph in the Euclidean plane must maintain enough angular resolution in all non-triangulated faces. In order to satisfy such ubiquitous local constraints we call the *angular resolution rules*, greedy embedding algorithms often have to draw (embed) a branch of the graph recursively into a smaller and smaller (or bigger and bigger) area, like a fractal. It is during this recursive embedding process that more and more digits of precision are needed to represent the coordinates of the latterly embedded vertices.

2.2   Idea of the Lower Bound

Our idea of proving a lower bound for coordinate complexity is by counter example, i.e., a greedily embedable graph that enforces the above described recursive embedding process. Specifically, we design a recursively defined sequence of graphs G_n, where $n = 1, 2, \ldots$, is the number of vertices in G_n, such that a) G_n can be greedily embedded in the Euclidean plane; and b) for any greedy embedding of G_n in the Euclidean plane, if d_{max} and d_{min} are the max. and min. Euclidean distances between two vertices, then $\frac{d_{max}}{d_{min}}$ is an exponential function of n. Intuitively, this is to enforce that the growing branches of G_n (while n increases) be embedded into an exponentially large or exponentially small area in the plane, so that linear bits of coordinate precision becomes inevitable.

2.3   Difficulty with Diversity of Embedding

The major difficulty of this lower bound problem is that there are unknown amount of different ways to embed a graph in the plane. Some greedy embedding algorithms result in exponential areas; but it doesn't mean all other greedy embedding methods have to, too. Note that enumerating all possible planar embeddings doesn't help with the problem, because a graph that can be greedily embedded in the plane is not necessarily a planar graph; neither is a greedy embedding of a planar graph necessarily a planar embedding.

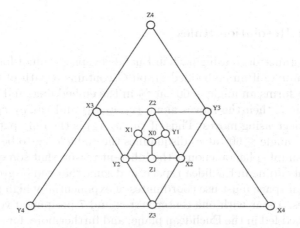

Fig. 1. A recursive graph that spans into exponential size area

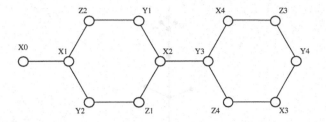

Fig. 2. An alternative way of greedily embedding the graph in Fig 1 that fits in linear size area. Here not all edges in Fig. 1 are showed. However, the edges presented already form a greedy embedding, and adding the rest edges in Fig. 1 won't destroy it.

At the end of this section, we use the following example to demonstrate how different two greedy embeddings of a same graph could be, which makes the lower bound not contingent to fixed embedding a much harder problem than the one solved in [2]. See Fig. 1 and Fig. 2.

3 The Lower Bound Resilient to Embedding

The recursive graph G_n we design for the lower bound is a tree with two roots u and v and one growing branch that generates a triple x_i, y_i, z_i at each knot and ends at a tip t, as showed in Fig 3. (From here we abuse the symbol C_n in Section 1.2 by letting G_n have n levels and $3(n+2)$ vertices.) We first explain that the embedding in Fig 3 is a greedy embedding in the Euclidean plane and it grows into an exponentially smaller area that takes $\Omega(n)$ bits of precision to represent the coordinates of the tip vertex t (as well as the vertices x_i, y_i, z_i approaching t). Then we argue that any greedy embedding of this G_n in the Euclidean plane can not deviate from the embedding in Fig 3 very much, and indeed any deviation could only result in faster shrink of the branch of t so that the $\Omega(n)$-bit lower bound remains.

3.1 Embedding G_n in the Plane

We now explain the embedding in Fig 3 in details. The four vertices y_0, u, v, z_0 are embedded to have unit distance from x_0 and to form three $60°$ angles, making y_0, x_0, z_0 a horizontal line. The stem $(x_0, x_1, \ldots, x_n, t)$ forms a vertical line. Each pair of leaves y_i, z_i are embedded symmetrically, with decreasing lengths

$$d(x_{i+1}, y_{i+1}) = d(x_{i+1}, z_{i+1}) \le d(x_i, y_i) = d(x_i, z_i) \tag{1}$$

and decreasing angles

$$\begin{aligned} \angle y_{i+1} x_{i+1} x_{i+2} &= \angle z_{i+1} x_{i+1} x_{i+2} \\ &\le \angle y_i x_i x_{i+1} = \angle z_i x_i x_{i+1}. \end{aligned} \tag{2}$$

Now we zoom into one knot on the stem, as showed in Fig 4, to see the numeric details. Let $\alpha = \frac{\pi}{6n} = \frac{30°}{n}$. When i increases, we proceed the embedding so

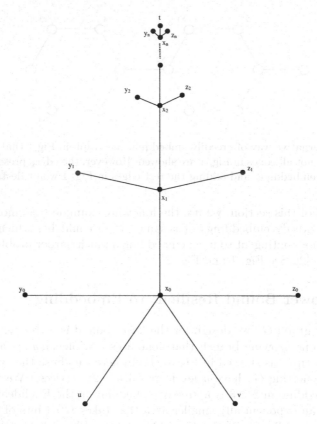

Fig. 3. Greedy embedding that grows to a tip

that the pair of leaves (x_i, y_i) and (x_i, z_i) gradually fold more and more upward, where the equal angles (x_i, y_i) and (x_i, z_i) form with the horizontal line are $i\alpha$. Based on this folding angle, we next describe how to determine the positions to embed $x_{i+1}, y_{i+1}, z_{i+1}$ after x_i, y_i, z_i are embedded.

Let m_i and m_i' be the midpoints of (x_i, y_i) and (x_i, z_i), and L_i and L_i' be the perpendicular bisectors of (x_i, y_i) and (x_i, z_i). Draw two lines L_{i+1} and L_{i+1}' that pass m_i and m_i' and form angles of α with L_i and L_i'. Let (x_{i+1}, y_{i+1}) be perpendicular to L_{i+1} and let it intersect with the vertical stem S (drawn as an infinite vertical line passing x_0), L_{i+1}, and L_i at points x_{i+1}, m_{i+1}, and y_{i+1}, respectively. The positions of x_{i+1}, m_{i+1}, and y_{i+1} are then determined by moving the line $x_{i+1}, m_{i+1}, y_{i+1})$ upward along L_{i+1} while keeping it perpendicular to L_{i+1}, and stopping at the moment when $d(y_{i+1}, m_{i+1}) = d(x_{i+1}, m_{i+1})$, i.e., when L_{i+1} becomes the perpendicular bisector of (x_{i+1}, y_{i+1}). The position of z_{i+1} is determined similarly, symmetric to the position of y_{i+1}.

By pre-setting $\alpha = \frac{\pi}{6n} = \frac{30°}{n}$ based on n, the above embedding process can be proceeded at all levels $i = 1, 2, \ldots, n$. Finally, (y_n, x_n) and (z_n, x_n) will form $60°$ angles with the perpendicular stem S, and we finish the embedding process by

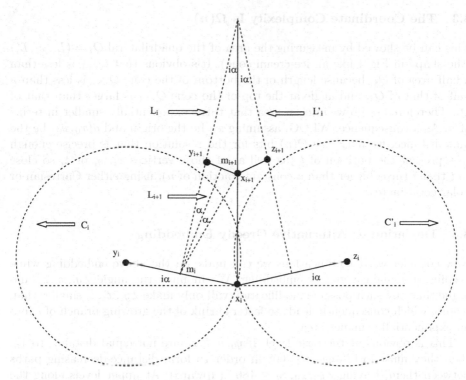

Fig. 4. Flexibility

putting t at the intersection of L_n and L'_n, which makes $d(y_n, x_n) = d(z_n, x_n) = d(t, x_n)$. (See Fig 4.)

3.2   The Embedding Is Greedy

We sketch an argument in the following that the above procedure yields a greedy embedding in the Euclidean plane.

1. Let C_i and C'_i be two circles centered at y_i and z_i and with radius $d(y_i, x_i) = d(z_i, x_i)$. It's not hard to verify that all the vertices above x_i on the growing branch are embedded in the area enclosed by L_i and L'_i (a cone) and excluded by C_i and C'_i. (We provide detailed argument in the full paper. Here the fact is illustrated in Fig 4.) This guarantees that (x_{i+1}, x_i, y_i) is a bidirectional distance-decreasing path.
2. The face that L_{i+1} is the perpendicular bisector of (x_{i+1}, y_{i+1}) guarantees that $(y_{i+1}, x_{i+1}, x_i, y_i)$ is a bidirectional distance-decreasing path.
3. An inductive argument (again details are in the full paper) can then be made to show that a path from y_i to y_j, for any $i \neq j$, is a distance-decreasing path. Based on this, it's easy to see that the paths between any y_i and z_j, plus all other possible paths in G_n, are also distance-decreasing paths. Therefore the entire graph is greedily embedded.

3.3   The Coordinate Complexity Is $\Omega(n)$

This can be showed by measuring the area of the quadrilateral $Q_i = (L_i, x_i, L'_i)$ (the shape in Fig 4 like an ice-cream cone). It's obvious that Q_{i+1} is less than a half area of Q_i, because length of the bottom of the cone Q_{i+1} is less than a half of that of Q_i, and angle at the top of the cone Q_{i+1} is larger than that of Q_i. Therefore G_n grows into an area that turns exponentially smaller in terms of n. As a consequence, WLOG, assuming x_0 be the origin and $d(x_0, y_0)$ be the unit distance, we must use $\Omega(n)$ bits for the resolution that is precise enough to represent the position of t (as well as of those vertices x_i, y_i or z_i so close to t that i turns bigger than a constant fraction of n), using either Cartesian or polar coordinates.

3.4   Deviation or Alternative Greedy Embedding

Now consider what modifications we can make on the above embedding while keeping it remain a greedy embedding. We monitor the angle $\angle y_i, x_i, z_i$ and argue that any such possible modification will only make $\angle y_i, x_i, z_i$ smaller than before, which consequently leads to faster shrink of the growing branch of t into an exponentially smaller area.

This is obvious at the base level. If y_0, u, v, z_0 are not equal distance to x_0, then they must form angles $\geq 60°$ in order to form distance-decreasing paths between them, leaving $\angle y_0, x_0, z_0 \leq 180°$ (upward). At upper levels along the growing branch, there are the following three cases of modifications one can make:

1. y_{i+1} and z_{i+1} don't have to be on L_i and L'_i; they can be placed inside the cone formed by L_i and L'_i and/or at a higher position;
2. G_n doesn't have to be symmetric; the stem $S = (x_0, x_1, \ldots, x_n, t)$ can be a polyline with bends;
3. x_{i+1} doesn't have to be in between of y_i and z_i; the two leaves y_i and z_i can be on the same side and the stem folds down instead of growing upward.

For case 1, it only causes the cone formed by L_i and L'_i in Fig 4 to shrink faster. For case 2, one still needs to satisfy the constraints of the circles and perpendicular bisectors in Section 3.2 (see Fig 4) in order to keep a greedy embedding, therefore result in a skewed cone at each level i which bounds the area for embedding the vertices upper than x_i. The only difference is that the new cone consists of two (left and right) unequal triangles. And it's easy to argue that the smaller triangle shrinks at least by half of the area at the next level. For case 3, the two leaves y_i and z_i are on the same side of the stem. Since they have to span a $\geq 60°$ angle, the stem has to fold down to the other side and leave even less area for embedding the rest of the branch.

This concludes the proof that any greedy embedding of the graph G_n in Fig 3 in the Euclidean plane must have coordinate complexity of $\Omega(n)$, if Cartesian or polar coordinates are used.

References

1. Basagni, S., Chlamtac, I., Syrotiuk, V., Woodward, B.: A distance routing effect algorithm for mobility (dream). In: MobiCom 1998: Proceedings of the 4th ACM/IEEE int. conf. on Mobile computing and networking, pp. 76–84 (1998)
2. Cao, L., Strelzoff, A., Sun, J.Z.: On succinctness of geometric greedy routing in euclidean plane. In: Proc. The 10th International Symposium on Pervasive Systems, Algorithms and Networks (December 2009)
3. Chen, M.B., Gotsman, C., Gortler, S.J.: Routing with guaranteed delivery on virtual coordinate. In: Proc. Canadian Conf. on Comp. Geom. (2006)
4. Chen, M.B., Gotsman, C., Wormser, C.: Distributed computation of virtual coordinates. In: SCG 2007: Proceedings of the twenty-third annual symposium on Computational geometry, pp. 210–219 (2007)
5. Dhandapani, R.: Greedy drawings of triangulations. In: SODA 2008: Proceedings of the 9th annual ACM-SIAM symposium on Discrete algorithms, pp. 102–111 (2008)
6. Dillencourt, M.B., Smith, W.D.: Graph-theoretical conditions for inscribability and delaunay realizability. Discrete Mathematics 161, 63–77 (1996)
7. Eppstein, D., Goodrich, M.T.: Succinct greedy graph drawing in the hyperbolic plane. In: Tollis, I.G., Patrignani, M. (eds.) GD 2008. LNCS, vol. 5417, pp. 14–25. Springer, Heidelberg (2009)
8. Frey, H., Stojmenovic, I.: On delivery guarantees of face and combined greedy-face routing in ad hoc and sensor networks. In: MobiCom 2006: Proceedings of the 12th annual international conference on Mobile computing and networking, pp. 390–401 (2006)
9. Goodrich, M.T., Strash, D.: Succinct greedy geometric routing in the euclidean plane. In: Dong, Y., Du, D.-Z., Ibarra, O. (eds.) ISAAC 2009. LNCS, vol. 5878. Springer, Heidelberg (2009)
10. Kleinberg, R.: Geographic routing using hyperbolic space. In: INFOCOM 2007: 26th IEEE International Conference on Computer Communications, pp. 1902–1909 (2007)
11. Ko, Y.B., Vaidya, N.: Geocasting in mobile ad hoc networks: Location-based multicast algorithms. In: Proc. 2nd IEEE Workshop on Mobile Computing Systems and Applications (WMCSA), pp. 101–110 (1999)
12. Kranakis, E., Singh, H., Urrutia, J.: Compass routing on geometric networks. In: Proc. 11 th Canadian Conference on Computational Geometry, pp. 51–54 (1999)
13. Leighton, T., Moitra, A.: Some results on greedy embeddings in metric spaces. In: FOCS 2008: 49th Annual IEEE Symposium on Foundations of Computer Science, pp. 337–346 (2008)
14. Lin, X., Stojmenovic, I.: Geographic distance routing in ad hoc wireless networks. Tech. rep., University of Ottawa (December 1998)
15. Maymounkov, P.: Greedy embeddings, trees, and euclidean vs. lobachevsky geometry. Tech. rep., M.I.T (2006) (manuscript), http://pdos.csail.mit.edu/petar/papers/maymounkov-greedy-prelim.pdf
16. Muhammad, R.: A distributed geometric routing algorithm for ad hoc wireless networks. In: Proceedings of the International Conference on Information Technology (ITNG 2007), pp. 961–963 (2007)
17. Navas, J.C., Imielinski, T.: Geocast – geographic addressing and routing. In: MobiCom 1997: Proceedings of the 3rd annual ACM/IEEE international conference on Mobile computing and networking, pp. 66–76 (1997)
18. Papadimitriou, C.H., Ratajczak, D.: On a conjecture related to geometric routing. Theor. Comput. Sci. 344(1), 3–14 (2005)

Performance of Parallel Bit-Reversal with Cilk and UPC for Fast Fourier Transform

Tien-Hsiung Weng, Sheng-Wei Huang, Wei-Duen Liau, and Kuan-Ching Li

Department of Computer Science and Information Engineering
Providence University
Shalu, Taichung 43301, Taiwan
{thweng,kuancli}@pu.edu.tw

Abstract. Bit-reversal is widely known being an important program, as essential part of Fast Fourier Transform. If not carefully and well designed, it may easily take large portion of FFT application's total execution time. In this paper, we present a parallel implementation of Bit-reversal for FFT using Cilk and UPC. Based on our previous work of creating parallel Bit-reversal using OpenMP in SPMD style from an unparallelized and sequential algorithm, we could note that keeping the existing parallelism by reorganizing the same program using Cilk and UPC libraries is possible yet achieving good performance. Experimental results were obtained by executing these parallel codes on two multi-core SMP platforms, and they show to be very promising.

Keywords: Shared-memory parallel programming, OpenMP, Cilk, UPC, Bit-reversal, FFT.

1 Introduction

On present day multi-core systems have been widely used and concurrency will become mainstream. However, most recent applications are still mostly written in sequential one. The process of developing sequential applications has been time consuming and the reality is that it is even harder and more challanging for developing a parallel one. In order to fully utilize these systems, parallel applications should be designed and developed either from the existing sequential codes or from scratch if there is not exist a sequential one. Fortunately, programming shared memory parallel codes is easier than programming message passing codes. There are a number of popular shared memory parallel programming models/languages we can choose from, and they are listed as OpenMP, Cilk, UPC, Itanium, ITBB, among others. In this paper, we present an implementation of parallel bit-reversal to perform input data permutation in FFT using Cilk and UPC.

The Fast Fourier Transform (FFT) is one of the most important algorithms used in many fields of science and engineering, especially in acoustic and signal processing and computational fluid dynamics for solving PDEs. The FFT [2] uses a divide and conquer strategy to evaluate a polynomial of degree n at the n complex nth roots of unity. FFT is easier to parallelize and many parallel FFT algorithms on shared

R.-S. Chang et al. (Eds.): GPC 2010, LNCS 6104, pp. 224–233, 2010.

memory machines have been studied and developed. The FFT program is composed of two main parts. First, data reordering in the Fast Fourier Transform by permuting the element of data array using Bit-reversing of the array index. This first stage involves finding the DFT of the individual values, and it simply passes the values along. Next, each of remaining stages the computation of a polynomial of degree n at the n complex nth roots of unity is used to compute a new value depending on the values of the previous stage; this process, we named as butterfly operation.

Our goal in this work is to realize a Cilk and UPC implementation of the Bit-reversal for FFT from our previous work. Our previous work is to implement an OpenMP SPMD style Bit-reversal code from un-parallelizable sequential code [14]. A Bit-reversal is an operation for an exchange data between A[i] and A[bit-reversal[i]], where the value of i is from 0 to n-1 and value of n is usually 2 to the power of b. Then bit-reverse[i] = j, the value of j is obtained from reversing b bits from value of i. When the Bit-reversal is not properly designed, it can take a substantial fraction of total execution time to perform the FFT [4].

UPC[17,18,19] is an extension of ISO C 99. It is designed as a parallel programming language that utilizes SPMD model of parallelism within a global address space that provides a uniform programming model for both shared and distributed memory hardware. Cilk[17,18,19] is a multithreaded parallel programming language extention to standard C, consisting of cilk, spawn, and sync, inlet, abort keywords, which are easier to use for the users as well as enabling users to parallelize the application written in recursive programs.

We first discuss works related to this research in section 2. Later in section 3 we discuss the important design of our algorithm and comparing with the original sequential algorithm. Then, we present the results of our evaluation on the parallel version of Bit-reversal running on two multi-core CPU SMP computing platforms. Discussion on experimental results of parallel programs is performed in section 5, and finally, we give our conclusions and future work in section 6.

2   Related Work

The data reordering in FFT program using Bit-reversing of array index has been widely studied [3,4,6,8,9,10,12]. Most of the algorithms proposed are mainly for uniprocessor systems[4,6,8,9]. The optimal Bit-reversal using vector permutations have been proposed by Lokhmotov [6]; their experiments have been running on single processor, though they claimed that their algorithm can be parallelized as well. Takahashi [13] implemented an OpenMP parallel FFT on IA-64 processors, where their code is a recursive FFT algorithm written in Fortran 90, though their bit-reversal algorithm is not presented. An algebraic framework for FFT permutation algorithm using SISAL, a functional language, an performance measurement was performed on a Cray C-90 and SUN Sparc5 machines [3,10]. Bit-reversal program must be carefully designed since it may take about 10~30% of the overall FFT computational time [6]. Moreover, it also can produce significant cache misses when its input data size is very large. This is due to the exchange between two data elements of an array that located in the distance far apart during the permutation of the data element using

Bit-reversal of the array index. And, some of Bit-reverse sequential algorithms are non-trivial to be parallelized.

Our work is based on the sequential Bit-reversal algorithm proposed by Rodriguez [8], in which they designed an improved Bit-reversal algorithm for FFT. Even though their sequential algorithm appeared to be the best, it is not parallelizable without re-writing completely its algorithm into a parallel one.

In the previous work, we proposed OpenMP implementation of Bit-reversal for the FFT using the so-called SPMD (Single Program Multiple Data) style of OpenMP, in which we achieved the reduction on the number of cache misses and data locality that is the main concern in the design of our code. The SPMD style of OpenMP code is distinct from ordinary OpenMP code. In most ordinary OpenMP program, shared arrays are declared and parallel for directives are used to distribute work among threads via explicit loop scheduling. In the SPMD style, systematic array privatiza-tions by creating private instances of sub-arrays gives opportunities to spread compu-tation among threads in the manner that ensures data locality. An in-depth study about SPMD style of OpenMP also can be found in [5]. Programs written in SPMD style of OpenMP has been shown to provide scalable performance that is superior to a straightforward parallelization of loop for ccNUMA systems [1,11]. It is feasible to rewrite this SPMD style OpenMP code into Cilk and UPC parallel code, as we will discuss it in section 4.

3 Sequential Code

Our work is based on an un-parallelizable sequential code proposed by Rodriguez [8]. In this section, we first give an overview of this program, and then we will discuss how we transform into a parallel one in next section.

In their original algorithm, computation of the bit-reversal of index for data reor-dering calculates only the required bit-reversal of indices, which also eliminates the number of unnecessary bit-reversal and swaps. The bit-reversal is computed as bi-

$$treverse = \sum_{k=0}^{p-1} b_{p-1-k} 2^k$$; this corresponds to the sequential pseudo-code as shown in Fig. 1

where p is the total number of bits, b is the binary value, and k is k-th position of the binary from the most significant digits. It uses only array A to store its input data and final results. When the algorithm uses only array A, the data reordering must perform the exchange between elements of A. Even though the swapping is only a simple exchange between the two elements of an array, it actually involves three assignment statements or copies actions. For instances, the $swap(A[i],A[bitreverse(i)])$ produces the copy $A[i]$ to $Temp$, then $A[bitreverse(i)]$ to $A[i]$, and then $Temp$ to $A[i]$. The merit of this algorithm is that it does not really convert the binary representation from the decimal and vice versa.

In this original sequential code as shown in Fig. 1, it computes the index upper bound for the variable last = (N- 1- N2) where N2 is $\sqrt{N}$ when number of bits is even and is $\sqrt{2N}$ when number of bits is odd. This eliminates the unnecessary computation of bit-reversal, which reduces number of swaps. In term of the number of moves, it is actually takes 3*(N-N2)/2 moves, which is 1.5*(N-N2).

```
0  Bit-reverse(N,p) {
        1        NV2 = N >>1;
2       last = (N-1)-(1<<((p+1)>>1));
3       j=0;
4       for(i=1;i<=last; i++) {
5           for(k=NV2; k<=j; k>>=1) j -=k;
6           j += k;
7           if (i < j) Swap(A[i],A[j]);
8       } // end of for
9  }   // end of Bit-reverse
```

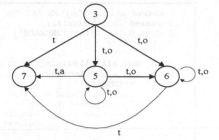

Fig. 1. An Improve Bit-reversal function by Rodriguez   **Fig. 2.** Data dependence graph of Fig1

In Fig. 1, the program code is not parallelizable due to presence of true and output data dependences between loop iterations of statements $j = j - k$, $j = j + k$, and if $(i<j)$. Its data dependence graph is shown in Fig. 2; there are true, anti and output dependences between the statements labeled on each edge as t, a and o respectively. For instance, there are true dependence between statements 3 and 7; true and output dependences between statements 5 and 6, 3 and 5, as well as 3 and 6; the loop on node 6 means there is true and output dependence between statement 6 itself on different iteration of the for loop. As the result, the value of variable j is accumulated for the entire nested for loop, this means that the computation for value of j is depend on the previous value of j. Hence, in order to parallelize this code, modification of this code is mandatory.

4 Parallel Version of Bit-Reversal

We implemented our parallel code as presented in this paper by modifying from the one developed by Rodriguez. The original program designed by Rodriguez was not parallelizable because there are present true data dependences, as discussed in the previous section.

In order to write a Bit-reversal parallel code using the SPMD style from the existing un-parallelizable sequential code, we first remove the true data dependence between iteration of variable j, by the pre-computation of the accumulated value of j for each starting chunk of iteration that is stored in array offset[i] where i is for thread i to total number of threads, which later it will be used by thread i during parallel execution. This pre-computation of offset is performed serially. The segment of code for calculation of offset[i] value is pre-computed for thread i and is shown on line 6-17 of Fig. 3. During the parallel execution of each threads, master thread or thread 0 will access the accumulated starting value of j from offset[0], thread 1 will access the accumulated starting value of j from offset[1], thread 2 will access accumulated starting value of j from offset[2], and so on. At the first glimpse on this observation, it seems more pre-computation for accumulated value of j to be done, in reality, it actually only compute t number of elements for array offset, where t is the maximum number of threads.

```
0  shared struct COMPLEX *A, *M, *bit_ptr;
1  shared int chunksize;
2  shared int offset[THREADS];
3  int main() {
   ....
4    A =upc_all_alloc(num_th, size/num_th*sizeof(struct COMPLEX));
5    M =upc_all_alloc(num_th, size/num_th*sizeof(struct COMPLEX));
6    if (MYTHREAD==0) {
7        for(i=0; i<num_th; i++) {
8            if (i==0) j=0;
9            else {  k = num_th/2;
10                 while(k<=j) {
11                     j = j-k; k = k /2;
12                 } // end while
13                 j = j + k; offset[i] = j;
14             } // end else
15        } // end for
16        chunksize = size / num_th;
17   } // end if
18   upc_barrier;
19   upc_forall(j=0; j<THREADS; j++) {
20       bit_ptr = &M[chunksize*MYTHREAD];
21       for(i=0;i<chunksize; i++) {
22           if (i==0) num=0;
23           else {  k = size / 2;
24                   while(k<=num) {
25                       num = num - k; k = k /2;
26                   } // end while
27                   num = num +k;
28               } // end else
29               bit_ptr=A[num+offset[MYTHREAD]];
30           bit_pr++;
31       } // end for
```

Fig. 3. UPC version of Bit-reversal

The pre-computation of array offset is inspired by the idea and the characteristic of divide and conquer as we perceive from other viewpoint. To clarify the idea behind this, we use the following simple example. Lets N be the input size of array A, t be the number of threads, then the number of bits b can be computed as log2N, the chunk size is computed as N / t; In this example, we use N equal to 16. In Fig 4, the top level represents the original values of an Array A. At each next level, it is further divided into two equal chunk size recursively: chunk one is obtained from chosen the even index that we called it even index chunk and the other is obtained from the odd index as odd index chunk. At the end, the Bit-reversal permutation of the input data is completed, in this example, A[0]=A[0], A[1]=A[8], A[2]=A[4], A[3]=A[12], ..., A[14]=A[7], A[15]=A[15] shown at level 5 or the last level. The first shaded element of each chunk at each level is obtained from its parent's first two elements except the one at level 1. As we observed, the first element of even index chunk is obtained from its parent first element and the odd index chunk first element is obtained from its parent second element. We call this first element of each chunk the offset that we stored in the array offset. At level 2, we can have two element of array offset, that is, offset[0] is 0 and offset[1] is 1. At this level, it has two chunks that suitable for distribution of works into two threads. Further, at level 3, we can obtain offset[0:3] is {0, 2, 1, 3} where it has four chunks and is suitable for four threads. Similarly, level 4 is appropriate for work-sharing into eight threads and its offset[0:7] ={0, 4, 2, 6, 1, 5, 3, 7}. Even though the pre-computation of offset is from the idea of divide and conquer, this code is implemented iteratively instead of recursive code.

In our scheme, depending on the number of threads t, we allocate t elements for array offset as described above. In the pre-computation of offset shown in Fig. 3 of line 6-17, when number of threads t = 2, we got offset[0:1] is {0,1}; after the pre-computation of offset, there is a upc_barrier statement, which uses to ensure that all threads must reach that point before they can proceed further. Next, the main computation of parallel Bit-reversal is performed by upc_forall statement of the code in line 19-31 of Fig. 3. In UPC version of bit-reversal we proposed, the variables A, M, chunksize, offset are declared as shared, all others are declared as private. The declaration of shared struct COMPLEX *bit_ptr at line 0 of Fig. 3 is a private pointer to shared, which gives each thread an independent pointer, stored in its private space but pointing into the shared space. Therefore, shared in this context qualifies the pointed to variable, and it creates only private pointers to it. This declaration is therefore allowed since the pointers themselves are not shared.

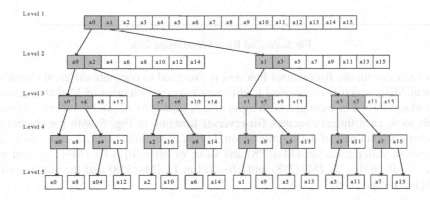

Fig. 4. Bit-reversal by divide and conquer

The Bit-reversal using SPMD style OpenMP has been implemented and the detail can be found in [15]. Fig. 5 is the parallel code of Bit-reversal using Cilk that is very similar to OpenMP SPMD style implementation. In front of each procedure, the cilk keyword is used. It first computes chunk size by dividing the input size by the number of threads. The boundaries of each data to be processed is pre-computed in array address[i] for thread i. Next, depending on nthreads (the number of threads), at line 6-9 the spawn keyword is used. Each thread will invoke the Bit-reversal function with five parameters as shown at line 8 of Fig. 5. The first parameter is the first location of array A, the second is address or location of the M that mapped from M+address, the third is n as the size of input, then chunk size, and finally, the fifth is the offset that have computed earlier.

Parallelism is created for spawn keyword precedes the invocation of procedure Bit-reversal. Each spawn thread will work on the same Bit-reversal sub-program, but it computes on the different part of data. This code is simple and easy to write. The sync statement is a local barrier is required before the final result of computation of bit-reversal is used further.

```
1 cilk FFT(*A,*M,*address,*offset,n,nthreads) {
2       int chunksize;
3       struct COMPLEX *ptr;
4       chunksize = n/nthreads;
5       /* Compute Offset */
6       for(i=0;i<nthreads;i++) {
7         ptr = &(M[ chunksize * i]);
8         spawn  Bit_reverse(A,ptr, n,chunksize,offset[i]);
9       sync; }
10 ...//other computation such as butterfly operation
11 }
12 cilk Bit_reverse(*A,*M,n,chunksize,offset) {
13      for(i=0;i<chunksize;i++) {
14           if(i==0) j=0;
15           else { k=n/2;
16               while(k<=j) {
17                   j=j-k; k=k/2;
18                   }//end while
19                   j=j+k;
20           }//end else
21           ptr=A[j+offset];
22           ptr++;
23      }  // end for
24 }
```

Fig 5. Parallel Bit-reversal using Cilk

In each thread, the Bit-reversal function is executed to compute different chunk of element M[i], which is correspond to different part data element of M that is passed from M+address. For example, with input size N equals to 32, and number of threads equals to 4, each thread executes Bit-reversal function in Fig. 5 with parameters to perform different part of data computation. In this case, thread 0, 1, 2, and 3 will call Bit-reverse with parameters (M+(0*8) and value of offset[0] is 0), (M+(1*8) and the value of offset[1] is 2), (M+(2*8) and offset[2] is 1), (M+(3*8) and the value of offset[3] is 3) respectively.

5 Experiments

Experimental results based on data reordering by Bit-reversal are performed on two Linux/Cent OS high end SMP computing platforms. The former one is on a 4 dual-core CPUs 2.6GHz Intel Xeon64 / Dell 6850 platform with 4 GB of main memory, 16KB L1 cache, 1MB L2 cache, and 4 MB L3 cache, while the latter one is a 4 dual-core CPUs 2.8 GHz AMD-Opteron^{TM} 8200 / Dell 6950 with 8GB of main memory, 64KB L1 cache, 1MB L2 cache.

We have implemented three parallel versions of Bit-reversal code, by instrumenting or modifying serial C with shared memory libraries, namely UPC, OpenMP and Cilk. The advantage of our early implementation in SPMD style OpenMP is that it is feasible to convert into one another. We compile the parallel version of our UPC program shown in Fig. 3 using upcc with –pthread and –T flag. The UPC program is compiled using upcc with -pthreads –O2 –T nthreads flags, and it executes gcc version 3.4.6. The Cilk version as shown in Fig. 5 is compiled with cilklocal and gcc version 3.4.6.

In order to explain the shortcoming about the performance of our design algorithm on a uniprocessor machine, we also wrote a version of sequential algorithm, compiled with gcc with -O2 flag, and then execute with different size of input data to compare with the original sequential code designed by Rodriguez. The experimental result on the two platforms is shown in Fig. 6 and 7. Our version of sequential code is labeled with Wen, while original sequential version by Rodriguez is labeled with Rod. Both are executed with input data size of 224 up to 227. The results show that the performance of our sequential code is around 50% percent slower than the original sequential code as the input size grows larger. In the original program, Rod, there are approximately only N/2 number of swap; even though each swap involves 3 copies or moves, so with total of 1.5N number of copies or moves, but only one cache miss on each swap will occurred, so the total of misses is N/2 times. Our sequential code involves only N copies or moves, but each move will cause cache miss, hence there will be approximately the total of N cache misses.

Fig. 10 and 13 shows the performance of three parallel versions of Bit-reversal of which namely OpenMP, Cilk, and UPC on Dell 6850 and Dell 6950 platforms. Our experiment is performed base on our SPMD style of OpenMP parallel code with different input sizes starting from 226 and 227. The performance results of our parallel SPMD style of OpenMP, Cilk, and UPC code shows scalable as the number of processors increases. But, with number of threads less equal to 8, the overhead of UPC code is significant, this probably due to more memory requirements of the UPC code. With number of thread equals to one, the large number of cache misses overhead occurred, this lead to longer execution time, which is twice as much as the number of size increases. This overhead is amortized by the increasing number of threads. With increased number of threads, the total number of cache misses is reduced to as the number of chunk size. For instance, with n equals to 226, with one thread, the number of cache miss will be 226 times, and with 16 threads, the cache misses will reduce to 226/16 times.

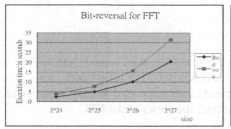

Fig. 6. Sequential code on Dell6850   Fig. 7. Sequential code on Dell6950

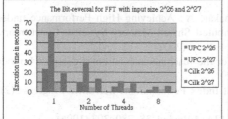
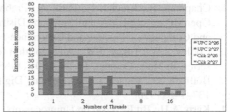

Fig. 8. The result on Dell6850   Fig. 9. Data size 2^{26} on Dell6950

Fig. 8 and Fig. 9 show the performance of three parallel versions of Bit-reversal and data size is 226 and 227 on Dell 6950, which is composed by faster processors and more memory available when compared with the Dell 6850 platform. The experiment is performed based on our SPMD style of OpenMP, UPC, and Cilk. The UPC code is getting better performance when it is executed on 8 threads, but still the overhead is significant when number of threads is less equal to two. The performance result describes three parallel versions code shows scalable as the number of processors increases. With number of thread equals to one, the large number of cache misses overhead occurred, this lead to longer execution time, which is twice as much as the number of size increases. This overhead is amortized by the increasing number of threads. With increased number of threads, the total number of cache misses is reduced to as the number of chunk size.

6 Conclusions and Future Work

We have developed a practical SPMD style Bit-Reversal of OpenMP, UPC, and Cilk for parallel FFT program from the existing un-parallelizable sequential code. It is a practical, easy to develop and maintain, as well as required only less programming effort. In our algorithm, it utilities to increase number of threads to reduce the cache miss. However, our experimental results are promising in this respect despite more memory spaces are used. There may be more improvements are possible in the future.

We will continue research for the implementation parallel FFT program base on our Bit-reversal algorithm, either iterative or parallel recursive one using Intel task queuing construct of OpenMP. We will also implement this algorithm using hybrid model like MPI with OpenMP in distribute system, and then compared them with other implementations.

Acknowledgement

This paper is based upon work supported by National Science Council (NSC), Taiwan under grants NSC96-2221-E-126-004-MY3 and NSC98-2218-E-007-005-. Any opinions, findings, and conclusions or recommendations expressed in this material are those of the authors and do not necessarily reflect the views of the NSC.

References

1. Chapman, B., Bregier, F., Patil, A., Prabhakar, A.: Achieving High Performance under OpenMP on ccNUMA and Software Distributed Shared Memory Systems. Concurrency and Computation Practice and Experience 14, 1–17 (2002)
2. Cooley, J.W., Tukey, J.W.: An algorithm for the machine calculation of complex Fourier series. In Math. Comput. 19, 297–301 (1965)
3. Bollman, D., Seguel, J., Feo, J.: Fast Digit-Index Permutations. Scientific Progress 5(2), 137–146 (1996)
4. Karp, A.H.: Bit Reversal on Uniprocessors. SIAM Review 38, 289–307 (1996)

5. Liu, Z., Chapman, B., Wen, Y., Huang, L., Weng, T., Hernandez, O.: Analyses for the Translation of OpenMP Codes into SPMD Style with Array Privatization. In: Voss, M.J. (ed.) WOMPAT 2003. LNCS, vol. 2716, pp. 244–259. Springer, Heidelberg (2003)
6. Lokhmotov, A., Mycroft, A.: Optimal bit-reversal using vector permutations. In: Proceedings of ACM Symposium on the 19th Parallel Algorithms and Architectures, pp. 198–199 (2007)
7. OpenMP Architecture Review Board. Fortran 2.0 and C/C++ 2.0 Specifications, http://www.openmp.org
8. Rodriguez, J.J.: An improved Bit-reversal algorithm for the fast Fourier transform. In: Proceedings of International Conference on Acoustics, Speech, and Signal Processing, vol. 3, pp. 1407–1410 (1988)
9. Rubio, M., Gómez, P., Drouiche, K.: A new superfast bit reversal algorithm. International Journal of Adaptive Control and Signal Processing 16(10), 703–707 (2002)
10. Seguel, J., Bollman, D., Feo, J.: A Framework for the Design and Implementation of FFT Permutation Algorithms. IEEE Transactions on Parallel and Distributed Systems 11(7), 625–635 (2000)
11. Wallcraft, A.J.: SPMD OpenMP vs. MPI for Ocean Models. In: Proceedings of First European Workshops on OpenMP (EWOMP 1999), Lund, Sweden (1999)
12. Zhang, Z., Zhang, X.: Fast Bit-Reversals on Uniprocessors and Shared-Memory Multiprocessors. SIAM Journal on Scientific Computing 22(6), 2113–2134 (2000)
13. Takahashi, D., Sato, M., Boku, T.: An OpenMP Implementation of Parallel FFT and Its Performance on IA-64 Processors. In: Voss, M.J. (ed.) WOMPAT 2003. LNCS, vol. 2716, pp. 99–108. Springer, Heidelberg (2003)
14. Weng, T.-H., Huang, S.-W., Perng, R.-K., Hsu, C.-H., Li, K. C.: A Practical OpenMP Implementation of Bit-reversal for Fast Fourier Transform. In: Proceeding of the 4th International Conference on Scalable Information Systems (ICST 2009), Hong Kong, June 10-11 (2009)
15. Berkeley UPC Documentation, http://upc.lbl.gov/docs/
16. El-Ghazawi, T., Smith, L.: UPC: Unified Parallel C. In: Proceedings of the 2006 ACM. IEEE conference on Supercomputing (2006)
17. Frigo, M., Leiserson, C.E., Randall, K.H.: The Implementation of the Cilk-5 Multithreaded Language. In: ACM SIGPLAN 1998 Conference on Programming Language Design and Implementation, pp. 212–223 (1998)
18. The MIT Cilk Project, http://supertech.csail.mit.edu/cilk/
19. Frigo, M.: Multithreaded programming in Cilk. In: Proceddings of the 2007 international workshop on parallel symbolic computation (2007)
20. Leiserson, C.E.: The Cilk++ concurrency platform. In: Annual ACM IEEE Design Automation Conference archive, Proceedings of the 46th Annual Design Automation Conference, pp. 522–527 (2009)

Variable-Sized Map and Locality-Aware Reduce on Public-Resource Grids

Po-Cheng Chen[1,*], Yen-Liang Su[1,*], Jyh-Biau Chang[2], and Ce-Kuen Shieh[1]

[1] Institute of Computer and Communication Engineering,
Department of Electrical Engineering, National Cheng Kung University, Taiwan
[2] Department of Digital Applications, Leader University, Taiwan

Abstract. This paper presents a grid-enabled MapReduce framework called "Ussop". Ussop provides its users with a set of C-language based MapReduce APIs and an efficient runtime system for exploiting the computing resources available on public-resource grids. Considering the volatility nature of the grid environment, Ussop introduces two novel task scheduling algorithms, namely: Variable-Sized Map Scheduling (VSMS) and Locality-Aware Reduce Scheduling (LARS). VSMS dynamically adjusts the size of the map tasks according to the computing power of grid nodes. Moreover, LARS minimizes the data transfer cost of exchanging the intermediate data over a wide-area network. The experimental results indicate that both VSMS and LARS achieved superior performance than the conventional scheduling algorithms.

Keywords: MapReduce, Public Resource Grids, Load Balance, Heterogeneity, Non-dedication.

1 Introduction

MapReduce [1], popularized by Google, is an emerging programming model for large-scale data-parallel applications such as web indexing, data mining, and scientific simulation [2]. Recently, there has been a dramatic proliferation of research concerned with various MapReduce framework design and implementation. For example, Apache Hadoop [3] is an open source implementation of MapReduce. Besides, Phoenix [4] implemented the MapReduce model for the shared memory architecture, i.e. multi-core and multiprocessor systems. Moreover, Mars [5] implemented MapReduce on the graphic processors and Rafique, et al. implemented MapReduce for the Cell B.E. architecture [6]. While substantial studies have been performed on providing MapReduce frameworks for dedicated data center environment [1, 3], virtual machine clusters [7-8] or even inside a single machine [4-5], relatively little literature has been published on leveraging MapReduce model on public-resource grids [9].

On the industry front, companies such as Google and its competitors may have adequate budgets for constructing large-scale data centers to provide sufficient computing and storage resource. On the other hand, non-profit organizations could

---

[*] These authors contributed equally to this project and should be considered co-first authors.

R.-S. Chang et al. (Eds.): GPC 2010, LNCS 6104, pp. 234–243, 2010.
© Springer-Verlag Berlin Heidelberg 2010

not afford to build their own large scale data centers without any financial support. Fortunately, public-resource grids, which federate donated computational power and storage to run as a cooperative system for harvesting the idle CPU cycles and unexploited disk space, may be a feasible platform for running MapReduce applications of non-profit computing projects. However, running the MapReduce model in the grid environment differs markedly from running it in the data center environment in at least two aspects.

Firstly, the grid environment has the volatility feature. Unlike data centers, which commonly consist of homogeneous and dedicated nodes, public-resource grids usually consist of heterogeneous and non-dedicated nodes. Grid nodes are probably supercomputers, single or multi-processor/multi-core PCs; the computing capability of each of them is normally different from others. Moreover, each grid node is shared between its owner and multiple grid users; and thus when a MapReduce application is run on a grid, the owner's and other grid users' job compete concurrently against the MapReduce application for the grid node resources. Such circumstances make a difficulty of the MapReduce job scheduling. According to the MapReduce programming model, all map tasks have to be finished before reduce tasks get started; Still most of conventional map task scheduling algorithms [1, 3, 8] assign equal-sized map tasks to each of map workers. Apparently, a map task of the MapReduce application running on the grid node with the poorest capability, i.e. straggler [1, 8], will introduce a bottleneck effect degrading the performance of the entire MapReduce application. Therefore, a requirement exists for a grid-aware map task scheduling algorithm capable of dynamically balancing the workload distribution between volatile grid nodes.

Secondly, the nodes in a data center are connected to each other over a local area network (LAN), while the nodes in a public-resource grid are often distributed over a wide area network (WAN). When a reduce worker requests associated intermediate key/value pairs produced by map workers, the cost of inter-site communication in the grid environment is obviously higher than the cost of intra-site communication in the data center environment. In this situation, the unsteadily available bandwidth of a WAN causes another difficulty of the MapReduce job scheduling. However, most of available reduce task scheduling algorithms [1, 3, 8] assumes that all data transfers are intra-site communication. To address this problem, it is desirable to develop a grid-aware reduce task scheduling algorithm to minimize inter-site communication over a WAN.

According to the above discussions, this paper presents a grid-enabled MapReduce framework called "Ussop". Ussop provides its users with a set of C-language based MapReduce APIs and an efficient runtime system for exploiting the dynamic and non-dedicated resources available on public-resource grids. Ussop hides the complexity of job parallelization, task distribution, and data partition from the users. It uses the variable-sized map scheduling (VSMS) algorithm during the map phase. VSMS algorithm achieves load balance by dynamically adjusting the size of a map task and assigning larger-sized map tasks to the grid nodes with higher capability. Moreover, it uses the locality-aware reduce scheduling (LARS) algorithm during the reduce phase. LARS minimizes the cost of data transfer by assigning a reduce task to an appropriate grid node in accordance with the data locality information. Thus, Ussop can alleviate the straggler problem [1, 8] caused by various availabilities of grid nodes, and enhance the performance of a MapReduce job.

The remainder of this paper is organized as follows: Section 2 briefly reviews the major MapReduce frameworks presented in the literature. Section 3 discusses the design and implementation of Ussop, while Section 4 evaluates its performance under exhaustive experiments. Finally, Section 5 presents some concluding remarks and indicates the intended direction of future research.

2 Related Work

Several notable MapReduce frameworks have been proposed in the literature [1, 3-7, 10]. They are briefly compared with Ussop in this section.

Cloudlet [7] implemented MapReduce on virtual machine clusters to gain the benefits of the virtualization technique such as better performance in management and security issues. However, running a MapReduce application on such environment suffers from poor performance due to the heavy overhead of I/O virtualization. Specifically, virtual machines hosted by the same physical node have to compete for the limited network bandwidth against each other. To address this problem, Cloudlet divided the reduce phase of original MapReduce programming model into the local and the global reduces phases. The local reduce phase executes the sort and reduce functions within the same physical node, thereby minimizing the network bandwidth competition. On the other hand, the reduce workers running in a grid are distributed over more diverse network environment than that in a virtual machine cluster, consequently Ussop adopts the LARS algorithms to minimize inter-site communication over a WAN.

The conventional speculative execution mechanisms [1, 3, 8] only consider running a MapReduce application in a data center environment, which consists of homogeneous nodes. Such algorithms may misjudge any node with poorer resource availability as a straggler. Accordingly, Zaharia, et al has clearly indicated that the speculative execution strategy of Hadoop may be not robust enough for the environment more volatile than a data center environment [8]. To enhance the original speculative execution strategy, they proposed the Longest-Approximate-Time-to-End (LATE) algorithm. The LATE algorithm defines both a cap on the number of speculative tasks and a slow task threshold to prevent unnecessary speculative execution. In contrast, Ussop adopts the VSMS algorithms to reduce the adverse performance impact due to the straggler problem by dynamically balancing the workload distribution between volatile grid nodes.

MapReduce.Net [10] is somewhat similar to Ussop. MapReduce.Net harvests the idle resource in an enterprise grid environment, and uses these resources to execute MapReduce applications. Due to the volatility feature of grid nodes, both MapReduce.Net and Ussop dynamically assign reduce tasks to appropriate nodes by using a locality-aware scheduling algorithm rather than a static scheduling algorithm [1, 3, 8] to assign tasks. However, the task size in MapReduce.Net is equal-sized and the task size in Ussop is variable in accord with the computing power of workers.

Moreover, in the literature [6], the dynamic work unit scaling (DWUS) algorithm is also similar to the VSMS algorithm of Ussop. This literature [6] was targeted for supporting MapReduce on a cluster consisting of well-provisioned blades and computing accelerators with limited memory and I/O capacity. Therefore, when an application starts, a binary search method was used by DWUS for achieving the highest service rate. The binary search method is only executed in a period of time. Then, the final workload size determined is used for the rest of the application execution. However, the task size in Ussop is dynamic because of the volatility nature of the grid environment.

3   Ussop: System Design and Implementation

Many MapReduce frameworks have been designed for various platforms; however, Ussop is designed for a public-resource grid environment. Figure 1 illustrates the general system overview of Ussop. Once a MapReduce application is submitted to the Ussop portal, the Ussop portal chooses several grid nodes to run the application. One of these gird nodes is chosen to be the master of the application and the rest are chosen to be workers. Each idle worker then requests a map or a reduce task from the master.

When a worker is assigned a map task, firstly it has to read the corresponding input data. Existing MapReduce frameworks such as Google's implementation and Hadoop run MapReduce applications inside a dedicated data center. They assume that the replicas of the input data have been distributed across nodes in the data center in advanced. On the contrary, the grid nodes exploited by Ussop are chosen on-demand; thus the input data cannot be stored in these grid nodes in advance. Consequently, the map worker has to read the input data from the user's node that submits the MapReduce job or from the remote replica servers.

The grid nodes exploited by Ussop are usually from several geographically-distributed sites. Moreover, they are normally heterogeneous and non-dedicated. Obviously, the homogeneity assumptions of conventional designs do not hold in Ussop anymore. Thus, Ussop introduces new scheduling algorithms, i.e. VSMS for the map tasks assignment and LARS for the reduce tasks assignment. The remainder of this section describes the concept of VSMS and LARS and the implementation of Ussop in detail.

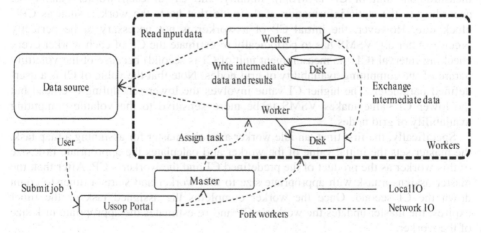

Fig. 1. System overview of Ussop

3.1   Variable-Sized Map Scheduling (VSMS)

Conventional MapReduce frameworks assume that workers can perform tasks at the roughly same rate. Thus, the master of such frameworks assigns equal-sized map tasks to idle workers. Moreover, such frameworks also assume that any detectably slow node is a straggler of a faulty node [1, 3, 8]. Consequently, they speculatively re-execute the tasks that are supposed to be stragglers.

However, these assumptions can be broken in Ussop due to the heterogeneity and the non-dedication natures of a public-resource grid environment. Specifically, a node with lower computing capability and a node with higher computing capability can never perform the equivalent workload at the same rate. Furthermore, the computing capability of a grid node is naturally volatile due to the resource contention between the node owner's workload and grid users' workload. In other words, during the execution, a task may be performed at the different rate even though it is executed by the same worker all the time. Additionally, the conventional speculative execution algorithms are not robust enough for the Ussop system model. The reason is that not only such algorithms may misjudge any node with poorer resource availability as a straggler but also the transfer cost of the input data in Ussop is much higher than that in a data center environment.

Obviously, Ussop has to balance the workload between all workers by dynamically adjusting the size of a task in accordance with the computing capability of the worker who is responsible for executing the task. Having done so, Ussop can also avoid misjudging a grid node with poorer resource availability as a faulty node. Ussop uses the variable-sized map scheduling algorithm (VSMS) to decide the appropriate task size of each worker. The principle of VSMS is that the master should assign coarser-grained tasks to the workers with more powerful computing availability.

Like most existing scheduling algorithms for map tasks assignment, VSMS also presumes that the processed progress of a map task is proportional to how much input data has been processed. Therefore, VSMS defines the computing power (CP) of a worker as how much input data can be processed by the worker per second (the measurement unit of CP is MB/s). Initially, the CP of each worker can be set according to the static information of the node that hosts the worker, such as CPU clock rate. However, the initial CP of a worker is not necessary to be perfectly precise. After all, VSMS has to periodically re-estimate the CP of each worker every checking interval (CI, the measurement unit of CI is second) because of the volatility nature of the computing availability of grid nodes. Note that the value of CI is a user-defined parameter. The higher CI value involves the lower scheduling overhead but the lower CI value makes VSMS to be more sensitive to the volatile computing availability of grid nodes.

Specifically, the first time, an idle worker asks the master for assigning a map task, the master sets the initial value of the worker and calculates the appropriate task size of this worker as the product of the predefined CI and the worker's CP. After that, the master assigns a task with appropriate size to this worker and starts a timer to count down the CI second. Once the worker completes the assigned task or the timer expires, the master updates the worker's CP and re-estimates the appropriate task size of the worker.

3.2   Locality Aware Reduce Scheduling (LARS)

Once a map task is completed, it generates several intermediate key/value pairs. Each node periodically uses the same hash function for partitioning these intermediate key/value pairs into several local regions. Then, through gathering the regions with the same hash value from all nodes into a reduce task, the intermediate key/value pairs with the same intermediate key must be in the same reduce task. Conventional MapReduce frameworks do not put much effort to schedule reduce tasks. They uses a static reduce task scheduling algorithm [1, 3, 8], which assigns each reduce task to a worker in advance before all map tasks getting started. According to such a scheduling algorithm, a MapReduce framework can pipeline the input data transfer for reduce tasks with map tasks execution, consequently reducing the turnaround time of a MapReduce job.

Unfortunately, such a static scheduling algorithm is not suitable for Ussop because of the volatility nature of the computing availability of grid nodes. In other words, a pre-decided grid node might not be available anymore in the reduce phase. On the contrary, Ussop uses a just-in-time scheduling algorithm called locality-aware reduce scheduling (LARS). LARS defers the input data transfer until the reduce task is assigned to the corresponding node. LARS is a local optimization solution for minimizing the data transfer cost. Once any worker in a node is idle, the master knows that which non-assigned task processes the largest local region. (Note that each node sends the size of each local region to the master after the map phase is done.) Subsequently, the master assigns the reduce task which processes the largest local region to the idle worker. By using LARS, therefore, each node can avoid transferring large local regions that the node owns to other nodes.

3.3   Implementation

The Ussop framework was implemented by making the use of Teamster-G [11], a page-based, grid-enabled software DSM system. Teamster-G integrates several grid nodes to form a virtual multi-processor computer for executing multi-threaded parallel applications. Teamster-G makes the main memories of these distributed nodes look like a single shared memory with a unique address space, namely a virtual global memory image (GMI) [11]. Therefore, the issues about data consistency management between distributed nodes did not bother the development of the Ussop framework. Note that Teamster-G also provides the resource reconfiguration function [12], thus Ussop can be easily extended to support task migration in the future. Overall, Teamster-G facilitates developing the Ussop MapReduce framework for the grid environment.

4   Performance Evaluation and Analysis

To explore the practicality and benefit of Ussop, the performance of the VSMS algorithm was compared with the performance of two equal-sized map scheduling algorithms; One of them was the reproduction of Hadoop's native scheduling algorithm (RHS) [3, 8] and the other was RHS without the speculation mechanism (RHSN). Moreover, the performance of the LARS algorithm was also compared with a static reduce scheduling (SRS) algorithm, which assigns reduce tasks to workers in the round-robin manner. Note that three different levels of the task size, 4MB and 16MB, were adopted by both RHS and RHSN, considering that the task size may affect the scheduling performance.

All experiments were performed on the emulated grid consisted of two Sites (*Site A* and *Site B*). There were four nodes in *Site A* and two nodes in *Site B*. Each node in *Site A* ran Linux 2.6 on two 2.4GHz AMD Opteron Dual Core processors with 4GB RAM. Moreover, each node in *Site B* ran Linux 2.6 on a four-way SMP, 500MHz Pentium III Xeon with 512MB RAM. According to this hardware configuration, the experimental parameters of the VSMS algorithm were defined as follows: the CI was 10 seconds and the initial CP of nodes in *Site A* was 2MB/s and in *Site B* was 1MB/S. Moreover, the number of the parallel task workers created by each algorithm is equal to the total number of CPU cores of all computing nodes.

The PC router was used for emulating the wide-area link latency and bandwidth. The PC router ran a network emulation package, namely NIST Net v2.0.12b. The emulated round-trip time (RTT) and the emulated bandwidth between nodes in *Site A* and nodes in *Site B* were 40 ms and 12 Mbps, respectively. The values of both the emulated RTT and bandwidth were based on the measured RTT and the measured bandwidth between two sites, one was located within the National Cheng Kung University in Taiwan, and the other was located within the Chinese University of Hong Kong in Hong Kong.

The benchmark application used in all experiments was "word count". Word count is a typical example of MapReduce applications. It counts the frequency of each word in the input data. The input data used in all experiments consisted of two copies of Linux 2.6 source code; the size of the input data was 606MB. To simplify the complexity of the performance evaluation, the input data was replicated and stored in each node before starting all experiments.

4.1   Experiments on Map Task Scheduling Algorithms

Figure 2a show the results derived from executing the benchmark application, word count, on the emulated public-resource grid by using different map scheduling algorithms, namely VSMS, RHS, and RHSN. It illustrates the normalized performance associated with various scheduling algorithms against that of RHSN-16 (RHSN with 16MB task size). The emulated grid was a heterogeneous environment in this experiment; however, there was no owner's or other grid users' job competing against the benchmark application for the computing capability.

Figure 2a reveals that VSMS achieved the best performance than other map scheduling algorithm. With respect to using the identical task size in RHS and RHSN, figure 2a also displays that RHS, enabling speculative execution, achieved superior performance than RHSN, disabling speculative execution. These results were expected since the speculative execution can effectively alleviate the adverse effect caused by load imbalance. However, the prevention is always better than cure; VSMS prevents load imbalance by dynamically adjusting the size of a map task, and therefore needs not waste any computing power for task re-execution.

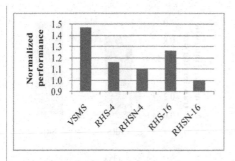
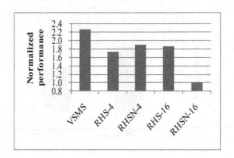

(a) Map scheduling algorithms perform in a heterogeneous environment

(b) Map scheduling algorithms perform in a non-dedicated environment

Fig. 2. The performance of various map scheduling algorithms

Figure 2b also show the results derived from executing the benchmark application on the emulated public-resource grid by using different map scheduling algorithm. However, this time the emulated grid was not only a heterogeneous environment but also a non-dedicated environment. Specifically, three artificial workloads for emulating owner's job were periodically injected into two nodes in *site A* and one node in *site B*. The artificial workload was a parallel application searching for Mersenne numbers; it created four threads to do the searching. These artificial workloads concurrently competed against the benchmark application for the computing capability during the experiment.

Figure 2b reveals that VSMS still achieved the best performance than other map scheduling algorithms in this experiment. Compared to the results derived from the last experiment, there was greater performance gap between VSMS and RHSN-16 in this experiment. This finding suggests that the importance of dynamically adjusting the size of a map task is noticeable especially when the MapReduce applications are running on a non-dedicated environment.

Moreover, it is important to note that RHSN-4, disabling speculative execution, was more efficient than RHS-4, enabling speculative execution, and even slightly better than RHS-16, also enabling speculative execution and having less scheduling overhead. This result could be explained by a flawed assumption of the RHS algorithm. Specifically, RHS has a fixed threshold for selecting tasks to re-execute; beyond this threshold all tasks that are "equally slow" and have an equal chance to be re-executed. However, this fixed threshold may cause excessively many tasks to be re-executed. Unfortunately, these speculative tasks cannot but compete concurrently against the normal tasks for the limited computing resources, and thus causing a vicious cycle of brining more speculative tasks and finally degrading the overall performance.

4.2   Experiments on Reduce Task Scheduling Algorithms

Figure 3 shows the results derived from executing the benchmark application, word count, on the emulated public-resource grid by using the identical map scheduling algorithm, VSMS, with two different reduce scheduling algorithms, namely LARS

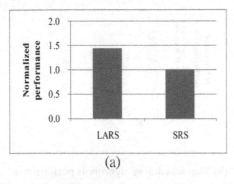
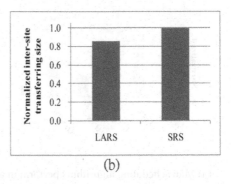

(a)   (b)

Fig. 3. Reduce scheduling algorithms perform in a WAN environment

and SRS. Figure 3a illustrates the normalized performance associated with various scheduling algorithms against that of SRS. The result displays that LARS was 1.45 times faster than SRS. To quantify the adversely affect due to the high latency and limited bandwidth network condition, the amount of the inter-site data transfers was also calculated in this experiment. Figure 3b also indicates that LARS efficiently shrunk the amount of the inter-site data transfers was shrunk to 0.86 times of that in the case of SRS. Although LARS does not directly take minimizing the inter-site data transfers into account, it avoids transferring large regions out; thus, it somewhat decreases the inter-site data transfers.

5   Conclusion

This study has presented a MapReduce framework designated as Ussop to enable running MapReduce application on public-resource grids. Considering the volatility nature of grid nodes and the unsteadily available bandwidth of a WAN, Ussop introduces VSMS and LARS algorithms to alleviate the potential performance penalty due to these features of public-resource grids. VSMS assign an idle worker a map task according to the knowledge about dynamic computing power of the worker. Moreover, LARS takes the distribution of intermediate data requested by reduce tasks into account when assign an idle worker a reduce task. Experimental results indicate that both VSMS and LARS achieved superior overall performance than conventional scheduling algorithms especially when the MapReduce applications are running on a non-dedicated and heterogeneous environment.

In a future study, the performance of Ussop will be further enhanced via the addition of more efficient mechanisms. For example, although the current version of VSMS works well in practice, the situation described below has to point out. When a grid node owner's workload is in the over-loaded state, all of the CPU cycles are dedicated to the owner's workload and none are available for allocation to a map task. To account for this situation, the current version of VSMS cannot but still re-execute the map task on the other worker as conventional scheduling algorithms do. However, more sophisticated solutions that could be resource reconfiguration [12] or task migration will be adopted in the next version of Ussop. In addition, the current version of LARS is only a local optimization solution. Perhaps the reduce task scheduling could be mapped into a maximum bipartite matching problem for searching a global optimization solution of the reduce task scheduling.

References

1. Dean, J., Ghemawat, S.: MapReduce: Simplified data processing on large clusters. In: 6th USENIX Symposium on Operating Systems Design and Implementation. USENIX (2004)
2. Applications and organizations using Hadoop, http://wiki.apache.org/hadoop/PoweredBy
3. Apache Hadoop, http://hadoop.apache.org/
4. Ranger, C., Raghuraman, R., Penmetsa, A., Bradski, G., Kozyrakis, C.: Evaluating MapReduce for Multi-core and Multiprocessor Systems. In: IEEE 13th International Symposium on High Performance Computer Architecture, pp. 13–24 (2007)
5. He, B., Fang, W., Luo, Q., Govindaraju, N.K., Wang, T.: Mars: a MapReduce framework on graphics processors. In: 17th International Conference on Parallel Architectures and Compilation Techniques, pp. 260–269. ACM, Toronto (2008)
6. Rafique, M.M., Rose, B., Butt, A.R., Nikolopoulos, D.S.: Supporting MapReduce on large-scale asymmetric multi-core clusters. ACM SIGOPS Operating Systems Review 43, 25–34 (2009)
7. Ibrahim, S., Jin, H., Cheng, B., Cao, H., Wu, S., Qi, L.: CLOUDLET: towards mapreduce implementation on virtual machines. In: 18th ACM International Symposium on High Performance Distributed Computing, pp. 65–66. ACM, Garching (2009)
8. Zaharia, M., Konwinski, A., Joseph, A., Katz, R., Stoica, I.: Improving mapreduce performance in heterogeneous environments. In: 8th USENIX Symposium on Operating Systems Design and Implementation. USENIX (2008)
9. Merzky, A., Stamou, K., Jha, S.: Application Level Interoperability between Clouds and Grids. In: Workshops at the Grid and Pervasive Computing Conference, pp. 143–150. IEEE Computer Society, Los Alamitos (2009)
10. Jin, C., Buyya, R.: MapReduce Programming Model for .NET-Based Cloud Computing. In: Sips, H., Epema, D., Lin, H.-X. (eds.) Euro-Par 2009 Parallel Processing. LNCS, vol. 5704, pp. 417–428. Springer, Heidelberg (2009)
11. Liang, T.Y., Wu, C.Y., Chang, J.B., Shieh, C.K.: Teamster-G: a grid-enabled software DSM system. In: IEEE International Symposium on Cluster Computing and the Grid, vol. 2 (2005)
12. Chen, P., Chang, J., Liang, T., Shieh, C.: A progressive multi-layer resource reconfiguration framework for time-shared grid systems. Future Generation Computer Systems 25, 662–673 (2009)

Actor Garbage Collection Using Vertex-Preserving Actor-to-Object Graph Transformations

Wei-Jen Wang[1], Carlos Varela[2], Fu-Hau Hsu[1,*], and Cheng-Hsien Tang[1]

[1] Department of Computer Science and Information Engineering
National Central University, Taiwan
[2] Department of Computer Science
Rensselaer Polytechnic Institute, USA

Abstract. Large-scale distributed computing applications require concurrent programming models that support modular and compositional software development. The actor model supports the development of independent software components with its asynchronous message-passing communication and state encapsulation properties. Automatic actor garbage collection is necessary for high-level actor-oriented programming, but identifying live actors is not as intuitive and easy as identifying live passive objects in a reference graph. However, a transformation method can turn an actor reference graph into a passive object reference graph, which enables the use of passive object garbage collection algorithms and simplifies the problem of actor garbage collection. In this paper, we formally define *potential communication* by introducing two binary relations - the *may-talk-to* and the *may-transitively-talk-to* relations, which are then used to define the set of *live actors*. We also devise two vertex-preserving transformation methods to transform an actor reference graph into a passive object reference graph. We provide correctness proofs for the proposed algorithms. The experimental results also show that the proposed algorithms are efficient.

Keywords: Garbage collection, actors, active objects, program transformation.

1 Introduction

Parallel and distributed computing applications are working on increasingly larger data sets and require more parallelism to better exploit new hardware such as multi-core architectures and graphical processing units. These applications demand concurrent programming models that support modular and compositional software development. The actor model of computation [1,2,3] can be used to reason about and to build such massively parallel and distributed computing systems. The fundamental computing unit of actor systems is a reactive

---

* Corresponding author.

R.-S. Chang et al. (Eds.): GPC 2010, LNCS 6104, pp. 244–255, 2010.
© Springer-Verlag Berlin Heidelberg 2010

entity called the *actor*, which encapsulates a thread of control along with its internal state. Communication of actors is through asynchronous message passing, in which message sending is non-blocking and message reception is unordered (non-FIFO).

High-level actor-oriented programming languages [4] support dynamic actor creation and actor reference passing, such as SALSA [3], Scala [5], E [6] and Erlang [7]. Introducing automatic actor garbage collection [8, 9, 10] to actor-oriented programming languages simplifies the problem of dynamic lifetime management of actors because the computing resources occupied by actor garbage can be reclaimed without manual intervention. Automatic actor garbage collection can reduce programmers' efforts on their sometimes error-prone manual lifetime management of actors, and can also let them focus on developing application functionality. Therefore automatic actor garbage collection is necessary for high-level actor-oriented programming.

1.1 Actor Garbage Problem

The widely used definition of live actors is described in [8]. Conceptually, the set of live actors consists of the set of root actors and the set of actors which can potentially communicate with the root set of actors. The set of actor garbage is then defined as the complement set of live actors. However, the term "potentially communicate with" is too abstract to make an operational definition. [10] proposes a more operational definition of actor garbage.

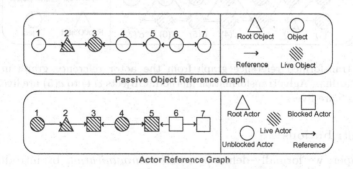

Fig. 1. Objects 2 and 3 are live, while Actors 1 to 5 are live

Both the passive object garbage collection problem and the actor garbage collection problem can be expressed as directed graph problems, consisting of directed edges (references) and vertices (objects or actors). The major difference resides in the state of each vertex — a non-root object has only one state; a non-root actor can either be *unblocked* or *blocked* and its state changes dynamically. An actor is unblocked if it is processing a message or has messages in its message box; it is blocked otherwise. Consider the example in Figure 1. It illustrates that a passive object reference graph and an actor reference graph can have different set of live objects/actors even given the same set of vertices and references. The upper half of Figure 1 shows a passive object reference graph, where Objects 2 and 3 are live. The lower half of Figure 1 shows a similar actor reference graph, where Actors 1 to 5 are live. Actor 1 is live because it can send a message to the set of root actors. Actors 3 to 5 are live because Actor 2 and Actor 4 can send their references to Actor 3 and Actor 5, and change them to the unblocked state respectively. As a result, Actors 3 to 5 can become unblocked and can transitively send messages to the root set of actors.

1.2   Transformation Technique

An actor garbage collection algorithm is not as intuitive as a passive object collection algorithm [11, 12] because it has more restrictions. However, Vardhan and Agha [9] have pointed out that an actor reference graph can be transformed into a passive object reference graph, which enables the use of passive object garbage collection algorithms. The problem of the transformed reference graph is that it produces at least three times as many references and about twice as many vertices as the original actor reference graph. Figure 2 shows an object reference graph which is transformed from the actor reference graph in Figure 1 using the Vardhan-Agha transformation method. The transformed reference graph consists of 14 vertices and 21 edges.

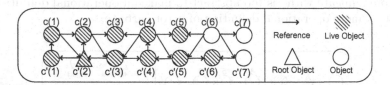

Fig. 2. A transformed reference graph from the actor reference graph in Figure 1 using the Vardhan-Agha transformation method. Objects $c(1)$ to $c(5)$ are live, implying Actors 1 to 5 are live.

1.3   Contributions

In this paper, we formally define *potential communication* by introducing two binary relations — the *may-talk-to* and the *may-transitively-talk-to* relations, which are then used to define the set of live actors. We devise two vertex-preserving transformation methods, each of which can transform an actor reference graph into a passive object reference graph. Compared to the Vardhan-Agha transformation method, both of our methods only require adding new edges for transformation. The experimental results also show that our algorithms are more efficient than the Vardhan-Agha transformation method.

1.4   Outline of This Paper

The rest of the paper is organized as follows: Section 2 briefly introduced related actor garbage collection work. Section 3 defines garbage. Section 4 provides two novel vertex-preserving transformation methods, and proves that actor garbage collection is equivalent to passive object garbage collection. Section 5 explains how we implement the proposed algorithms, and compare them to the Vardhan-Agha algorithm. Section 6 presents conclusions.

2 Related Work

At the beginning stage of the actor model (the 1970s and the early 1980s), state encapsulation is not a requisite. Processes (or processors) which use asynchronous messages for communication are usually considered as actors, even though processes can have references to remote objects. Halstead's algorithm [13] deals with garbage collection on a set of connected processors, each of which is viewed as a root and maintains references to objects. Based on the same assumption of memory sharing and Baker's garbage collection algorithm [14], Lieberman and Hewitt [15] proposed a concurrent generational garbage collection algorithm which spends proportionately less effort reclaiming objects with longer lifetimes, and makes different storage for objects according to their age.

In the middle 1980s, Agha emphasized the importance of state encapsulation in the actor model [1] because it is an essential feature for modular software development. As a result, the change of the actor model leads to the need of new actor marking strategies because traditional passive object garbage collection strategies cannot be directly reused. Kafura et al. [8, 16, 17] proposed the Push-Pull algorithm and the Is-Black algorithm. Dickman proposed the *partition merging* algorithm [18] which treats all unblocked actors as potential roots, divides actors into several large partitions, and then verifies each partition from the root actors using an Euler cycle traversal algorithm. Vardhan and Agha proposed a problem transformation technique to do actor garbage collection which is described in Section 1 and [9].

3 Definition of Garbage

In this section, we formally define the passive object garbage collection problem using the *transitive reachability* relation $\rightsquigarrow$. We then propose a new model to define the actor garbage collection problem using the *may-talk-to* $\leftrightsquigarrow$ and the may-transitively-talk-to $\leftrightsquigarrow^*$ relations. The definitions will be used in Section 4 to prove equivalence of actor garbage collection and passive object garbage collection.

3.1 Garbage in Passive Object Systems

The essential concept of passive object garbage is based on the idea of the possibility of object manipulation. *Root* objects are objects that can be directly accessed by the thread of control. *Live* objects are those transitively reachable from the root objects by following references, while *garbage* objects are those who are not live. The problem of passive object garbage collection can be represented as a graph problem. To concisely describe the problem, we introduce *transitive reachability* $\leadsto$. The transitive reachability relation is *reflective* ($a \leadsto a$) and *transitive* (($a \leadsto b$) $\wedge$ ($b \leadsto c$) $\Rightarrow$ ($a \leadsto c$)). Then we use it to define the passive object garbage collection problem.

Definition 1. *Transitive reachability*[1].
Object (or actor) o_q *is transitively reachable from* o_p, *denoted by*

$$o_p \leadsto o_q,$$

if and only if $o_p = o_q \vee (\exists o_u : \overline{o_p o_u} \wedge o_u \leadsto o_q)$.
Otherwise, we say $o_p \not\leadsto o_q$.

Definition 2. *Live passive objects.*
Given a passive object reference graph $G = \langle V, E \rangle$, *where* V *represents objects and* E *represents references, let* R *represent roots such that* $R \subseteq V$: *The problem of passive object garbage collection is to find the set of live objects,* $Live_{object}(G, R)$, *where*

$$Live_{object}(G, R) \equiv \{o_{live} \mid \exists o_{root} : (o_{root} \in R \wedge o_{live} \in V \wedge o_{root} \leadsto o_{live})\}$$

3.2   Garbage in Actor Systems

The definition of actor garbage is defined as having the ability to communicate with any of the *root actors*, where root actors are I/O services or public services such as web services and databases. We assume that *every actor/object has a reference to itself*, which is not necessarily true in the actor model [2]. The widely used definition of live actors proposed by Kafura et al. [8] is based on the possibility of message reception from or message delivery to the root actors — a *live* actor is one which can either receive messages from the root actors or send messages to the root actors. The original definition of live actors is denotational because it uses the concept of "potential" communication which must be considered along with possible state transitions from the present system configuration (system state). To make it more operational, the state of an actor (unblocked or blocked) and the referential relationship of actors must be used instead, as follows:

Definition 3. *Potential communication from* a_p *to* a_q.
Let the current system configuration be S. *Potential communication from Actor* a_p *to Actor* a_q *(or message reception of* a_q *from* a_p) *is defined as:*

$$\exists S_{future} : (a_p \text{ is unblocked} \wedge a_p \leadsto a_q \text{ at } S_{future}) \wedge (S \rightarrow^* S_{future}).$$

---

[1] $\overline{ab}$ is defined as a reference (or a directed edge) from a to b.
[2] The assumption that every actor/object has a reference to itself is used in most programming languages.

Definition 3 says that there exists potential communication from Actor a_p to Actor a_q if and only if both a_p will become unblocked and $a_p \leadsto a_q$ will become true at a future system configuration. In other words, the unblocked actor a_p can send a message to a_q along the path from a_p to a_q at a future system configuration. In other words, the unblocked actor a_p can send a message to a_q along the path from a_p to a_q at a future system configuration.

Now, consider two actors, a_p and a_q. If they are both transitively reachable from an unblocked actor or a root actor, namely a_{mid}, message delivery from Actor a_p to Actor a_q (or from a_q to a_p) is possible. The reason is that there exists a sequence of state transitions such that a_{mid} transitively makes a_p unblocked and transitively creates a directional path to a_q. As a result, $a_p \leadsto a_q$ is possible. The relationship of a_p and a_q can be expressed by the *may-talk-to* relation, defined as $\longleftrightarrow$ (Definition 4). It is also possible that a message can be delivered from a_p to another new actor a_r if $(a_p \longleftrightarrow a_q \wedge a_q \longleftrightarrow a_r)$ because the unblocked actors can create a path to connect a_p and a_r. The generalized idea of the *may-transitively-talk-to* relation, $\longleftrightarrow^*$, is shown in Definition 5 to represent potential communication.

Definition 4. *May-talk-to $\longleftrightarrow$.*
Given an actor reference graph $G = \langle V, E \rangle$ and $\{a_p, a_q\} \subseteq V$, where V represents actors and E represents references, let R represent roots and U represent unblocked actors such that $R, U \subseteq V$, then:

$$a_p \longleftrightarrow a_q \iff \exists a_u : a_u \in (U \cup R) \wedge a_u \leadsto a_p \wedge a_u \leadsto a_q.$$

We call $\longleftrightarrow$ the may-talk-to relation.

Definition 5. *May-transitively-talk-to $\longleftrightarrow^*$.*
Following Definition 4,

$$a_p \longleftrightarrow^* a_q \iff a_p \longleftrightarrow a_q \vee \exists a_{mid} : (a_p \longleftrightarrow a_{mid} \wedge a_{mid} \longleftrightarrow^* a_q).$$

We call $\longleftrightarrow^*$ the may-transitively-talk-to relation.

Notice that the $\longleftrightarrow$ and $\longleftrightarrow^*$ relations are constrained by the set of unblocked actors and root actors of the current system configuration. By using the $\longleftrightarrow^*$ relation, the definition of the set of live actors can be concisely rewritten:

Definition 6. *Live actors.*
Given an actor reference graph $G = \langle V, E \rangle$, where V represents actors and E represents references, let R represent roots and U represent unblocked actors such that $R, U \subseteq V$. The problem of actor garbage collection is to find the set of live actors $Live_{actor}(G, R, U)$, where

$$Live_{actor}(G, R, U) \equiv \{a_{live} \mid \exists a_{root} : (a_{root} \in R \wedge a_{live} \in V \wedge a_{root} \longleftrightarrow^* a_{live})\}$$

4   Equivalence of Actor Garbage Collection and Passive Object Garbage Collection

This section presents two novel transformation methods that demonstrate the equivalence of object and actor garbage collection.

4.1 Transformation from Passive Object Garbage Collection to Actor Garbage Collection

Transformation from passive object garbage collection to actor garbage collection is easier because the passive object garbage collection problem is a sub-problem of actor garbage collection. Let the passive object reference graph be $G = \langle V, E \rangle$ and the set of roots be R. Let the transformed actor reference graph be $G' = \langle V', E' \rangle$, the set of roots be R', and U' be the set of unblocked actors. The problem of passive object garbage collection can be transformed into the problem of actor garbage collection by assigning $V' = V$, $E' = E$, $R' = R$ and $U' = \emptyset$. Then for any two objects o_r and o_q, we get $(o_r \leadsto o_q \wedge o_r \in R) \Longleftrightarrow (o_r \leadsto o_r \wedge o_r \leadsto o_q \wedge o_r \in R) \Longleftrightarrow (o_r \leadsto^* o_q \wedge o_r \in R)$. Therefore the set $Live_{object}(G, R) = Live_{actor}(G', R', U')$.

4.2 Transformation from Actor Garbage Collection to Passive Object Garbage Collection

Now, consider the backward transformation. Let the actor reference graph be $G = \langle V, E \rangle$, R be the roots and U be the unblocked actors. If there exist $G' = \langle V', E' \rangle$ and R' such that $Live_{actor}(G, R, U) = Live_{object}(G', R')$, we say the actor garbage collection problem can be transformed into the passive object garbage collection problem.

Transformation by Direct Back-Pointers to Unblocked Actors. The direct back-pointer transformation method can transform actor garbage collection into passive object garbage collection by making $E' = E \cup \{\overline{a_q a_u} \mid a_u \in (U \cup R) \wedge a_u \leadsto a_q\}$. Figure 3 shows what the actor reference graph in Figure 1 transforms into. Notice that we use the term *back-pointers* to describe the newly added references and to avoid ambiguity with the term *references*. Theorem 1 shows that the direct back-pointer transformation method is correct.

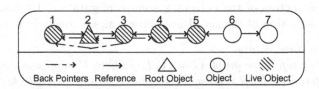

Fig. 3. An example of transformation by direct back-pointers to unblocked actors

Theorem 1. *Direct back-pointer transformation.*
Let the actor reference graph be $G = \langle V, E \rangle$, R be the set of roots, and U be the set of unblocked actors. Let $E' = E \cup \{\overline{a_q a_u} \mid a_u \in (U \cup R) \wedge a_u \leadsto a_q\}$, and $G' = \langle V, E' \rangle$ and $R' = R$.

$$Live_{actor}(G, R, U) = Live_{object}(G', R')$$

Proof. Let $Live_{actor}(G, R, U) = \{a_{live} \mid \exists a_{root} : (a_{root} \in R \wedge a_{live} \in V \wedge a_{root} \leadsto^* a_{live})\}$, and $Live_{object}(G', R') = \{o_{live} \mid \exists o_{root} : (o_{root} \in R' \wedge o_{live} \in V \wedge o_{root} \leadsto o_{live})\}$.

Now, consider the first case, $Live_{actor}(G, R, U) \subseteq Live_{object}(G', R')$. Let a_r and a_l be actors and $a_r \in R \wedge a_l \in V$. Then in G:

$a_r \leadsto^* a_l \implies$

$\exists a_{mid,1}, a_{mid,2}, ..., a_{mid,n} : a_r \leadsto a_{mid,1} \leadsto a_{mid,2} \leadsto ... \leadsto a_{mid,n} \leadsto a_l \implies$

$\exists a_{mid,1}, a_{mid,2}, ..., a_{mid,n}, a_{u,1}, a_{u,2}, ..., a_{u,n+1} : \{a_{u,1}, a_{u,2}, ..., a_{u,n}\} \subseteq (U \cup R) \wedge$
$(a_{u,1} \leadsto a_r \wedge a_{u,1} \leadsto a_{mid,1}) \wedge (a_{u,2} \leadsto a_{mid,1} \wedge a_{u,2} \leadsto a_{mid,2}) \wedge ... \wedge ((a_{u,n+1} \leadsto a_{mid,n} \wedge a_{u,n+1} \leadsto a_l))$.

The above statement is true in G' because $E \subseteq E'$. Since $\forall a_x, a_y : a_x \in (U \cup R) \wedge a_y \in V \wedge a_x \leadsto a_y \implies a_y \leadsto a_x$ in G', we know $\exists a_{mid,1}, a_{mid,2}, ..., a_{mid,n}, a_{u,1}, a_{u,2}, ..., a_{u,n+1} : \{a_{u,1}, a_{u,2}, ..., a_{u,n}\} \subseteq (U \cup R) \wedge$
$a_r \leadsto a_{u,1} \leadsto a_{mid,1} \leadsto a_{u,2} \leadsto a_{mid,2} ... \leadsto a_{mid,n} \leadsto a_{u,n+1} \leadsto a_l$.
Therefore $Live_{actor}(G, R, U) \subseteq Live_{object}(G', R')$.

Now, consider the other case that
$Live_{object}(G', R') \subseteq Live_{actor}(G, R, U)$.

For any a_r and a_l, $a_r \in R' \wedge a_l \in V' \wedge a_r \leadsto a_l$ in G',
let $\{\overline{a_{x,1}a_{u,1}}, \overline{a_{x,2}a_{u,2}}, ..., \overline{a_{x,n}a_{u,n}}\} \subseteq (E' - E)$ and be part of $a_r \leadsto a_l$ in G', such that
$(a_r \leadsto a_{x,1} \wedge \overline{a_{x,1}a_{u,1}} \in (E' - E)) \wedge (a_{u,1} \leadsto a_{x,2} \wedge \overline{a_{x,2}a_{u,2}} \in (E' - E)) \wedge ... (a_{u,n-1} \leadsto a_{x,n} \wedge \overline{a_{x,n}a_{u,n}} \in (E' - E)) \wedge a_{u,n} \leadsto a_l$.
Since a reference $\overline{a_q a_p}$ in $(E' - E)$ implies that $a_p \in (U \cup R) \wedge a_q \in V \wedge a_p \leadsto a_q$, we get $a_r \leadsto a_r \wedge (a_r \leadsto a_{x,1} \wedge a_{u,1} \leadsto a_{x,1}) \wedge (a_{u,1} \leadsto a_{x,2} \wedge a_{u,2} \leadsto a_{x,2}) \wedge ... \wedge (a_{u,n-1} \leadsto a_{x,n} \wedge a_{u,n} \leadsto a_{x,n}) \wedge a_{u,n} \leadsto a_l \implies$
$a_r \leadsto a_{x,1} \wedge a_{x,1} \leadsto a_{x,2} \wedge ... \wedge a_{x,n-1} \leadsto a_{x,n} \wedge a_{x,n} \leadsto a_l \implies$
$a_r \leadsto^* a_l$.
Therefore $Live_{object}(G', R') \subseteq Live_{actor}(G, R, U)$.

Transformation by Indirect Back-Pointers to Unblocked Actors. The indirect back-pointer transformation method transforms actor garbage collection into passive object garbage collection by making the reference set $E' = E \cup \{\overline{a_q a_p} \mid a_u \in (U \cup R) \wedge \overline{a_p a_q} \in E \wedge a_u \leadsto a_p\}$. Figure 4 shows what the actor reference graph in Figure 1 transforms into. Notice that $\overline{a_q a_p} \in E'$ implies that $\overline{a_p a_q} \in E$. Therefore the total number of back-pointers must be no bigger than the total number of edges in the actor reference graph G. Theorem 2 shows that the indirect back-pointer transformation method is correct. Since the correctness

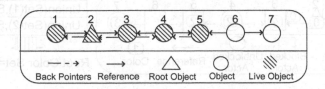

Fig. 4. An example of transformation using indirect back-pointers to unblocked actors

proof for the indirect back-pointer transformation method is very similar to the proof for the direct back-pointer transformation method, we will leave it to the readers.

Theorem 2. *Indirect back-pointer transformation.*
Let the actor reference graph be $G = \langle V, E \rangle$, R *be the set of roots, and* U *be the set of unblocked actors. Let* $E' = E \cup \{\overline{a_q a_p} \mid \exists a_u : a_u \in (U \cup R) \wedge \overline{a_p a_q} \in E \wedge a_u \rightsquigarrow a_p\}$, *and* $G' = \langle V, E' \rangle$ *and* $R' = R$.

$$Live_{actor}(G, R, U) = Live_{object}(G', R')$$

5   Implementation and Experimental Results

Theorem 1 or Theorem 2 can directly turn into an actor garbage collection algorithm by simply adding new back-pointers in the actor reference graph. Theorem 2 is a better choice to model the back-pointer algorithm because it generates fewer back-pointers.

Based on Theorem 1, we also propose the *N-color algorithm*. The idea comes from the strategy of turning "a back-pointer to an unblocked/root actor" into a special color, that is, two actors could have the same color if both of them have back-pointers to the same unblocked/root actor. A root color is defined as Color 0. To avoid multiple colors in an actor, only one color is allowed in each actor. Once different colors conflict in an actor, we combine the colors by using disjoint set operations [19]. Since any color conflict implies the two representative unblocked/root actors have the relation of $\rightsquigarrow^*$, we can conclude that actors marked by any color in a disjoint set containing a root color are live. Actors marked by the same colors may talk to each other because they are directly reachable from the same unblocked actor. Color conflict implies the may-transitively-talk-to relationship. Therefore, combining conflict colors is equivalent to grouping the set of actors that may transitively talk to each other. If a root color is included in this set, every actor in the set may transitively talk to the root. Take Figure 5 for example. Actors marked by Colors 0, 1, or 2 are live. Unmarked actors and actors with Color 3 are garbage. Color 0 can be viewed as a back-pointer to the root; Color 1 represents a back-pointer to unblocked Actor 1; Color 2 represents a back-pointer to unblocked Actor 4; Color 3 represents a back-pointer to unblocked Actor 7.

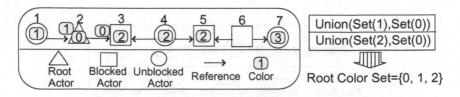

Fig. 5. An example for the N-color algorithm

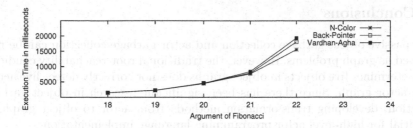

Fig. 6. Performance evaluation using a SALSA Fibonacci number program

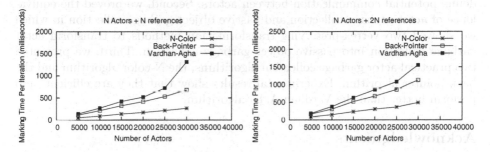

Fig. 7. Execution time of marking N actors

Let N be the number of actors, E the number of references in the system, and M be the number of unblocked actors. The time complexity of the back-pointer algorithm is $O(N + E)$, and its extra space complexity is $O(N + E)$. The time complexity of the algorithm is $O(N + E \lg^* M)$, and its extra space complexity is $O(M + N)$ where $O(M)$ is for the disjoint set operations and $O(N)$ is for marking.

We implement the N-color algorithm, the back-pointer algorithm, and the Vardhan-Agha transformation method on SALSA 2.0 [20]. SALSA is implemented by Java and all SALSA programs are compiled into Java source code. Figure 6 shows the total execution time of executing a SALSA Fibonacci program with different algorithms. In the experiment, the actor garbage collector is triggered every one second to do a complete scan of garbage and to reclaim all garbage and each scan may involve tens of thousands of actors and messages. The result shows that the N-color algorithm is less intrusive than the back-pointer algorithm, which is less intrusive than the Vardhan-Agha algorithm. We also measure the average execution time of marking N live actors using our algorithms and the Vardhan-Agha algorithm, as shown in Figure 7. The left side is the result of marking N actors and N references, and the right side shows the result of marking N actors and 2N references. All the results suggest that the N-Color algorithm is the best among them, and the back-pointer algorithm is the second. The result can attribute to: (1) the N-Color algorithm demands less expensive memory operations, and (2) the function $lg^* M$ grows extremely slow, and therefore $O(N + E \lg^* M)$ is very close to $O(N + E)$ in practice.

6   Conclusions

Both passive object garbage collection and actor garbage collection can be represented as graph problems. However, the traditional root-reachability condition that determines live objects in object graphs does not correctly detect live actors in an actor graph. Since there has been significant research in object garbage collection, developing transformation methods from actor to object graphs is benefitial for high-level actor programming language implementation.

This paper has made some contributions. First, we introduced the *may-talk-to* (⤳) and the *may-transitively-talk-to* (⤳*) relations to explain and formally define potential communication between actors. Second, we proved the equivalence of actor garbage collection and passive object garbage collection in which we showed two vertex-preserving transformation methods to transform actor garbage collection into passive object garbage collection. Third, we presented two practical actor garbage collection algorithms, the N-color algorithm and the back-pointer algorithm. Experimental results show that they are efficient, and perform better than the Vardhan-Agha algorithm.

Acknowledgments

The authors would like to thank Yousaf Shah and Ping Wang of Rensselaer Polytechnic Institute, USA, for their comments and suggestions. This work was supported in part by the Taiwan National Science Council under Grant NSC-98-2221-E-008-080.

References

1. Agha, G.: Actors: A Model of Concurrent Computation in Distributed Systems. MIT Press, Cambridge (1986)
2. Hewitt, C.: Viewing control structures as patterns of passing messages. Journal of Artificial Intelligence 8(3), 323–364 (1977)
3. Varela, C.A., Agha, G.: Programming dynamically reconfigurable open systems with SALSA. In: ACM SIGPLAN Notices. OOPSLA 2001 ACM Conference on Object-Oriented Systems, Languages and Applications, December 2001, vol. 36(12), pp. 20–34 (2001)
4. Karmani, R.K., Shali, A., Agha, G.: Actor frameworks for the jvm platform: a comparative analysis. In: PPPJ 2009: Proceedings of the 7th International Conference on Principles and Practice of Programming in Java, pp. 11–20. ACM, New York (2009)
5. Moors, A., Piessens, F., Odersky, M.: Generics of a higher kind. In: OOPSLA 2008, pp. 423–438. ACM, New York (2008)
6. ERights. org: The E Programming Language (2009), http://ERights.org/
7. Armstrong, J., Virding, R., Wikström, C., Williams, M.: Concurrent Programming in Erlang, 2nd edn. Prentice-Hall, Englewood Cliffs (1996)
8. Kafura, D., Washabaugh, D., Nelson, J.: Garbage collection of actors. In: OOPSLA 1990 ACM Conference on Object-Oriented Systems, Languages and Applications, October 1990, pp. 126–134. ACM Press, New York (1990)

9. Vardhan, A., Agha, G.: Using passive object garbage collection algorithms for garbage collection of active objects. In: ISMM 2002. ACM SIGPLAN Notices, Berlin, June 2002, pp. 106–113. ACM Press, New York (2002)
10. Wang, W., Varela, C.A.: Distributed garbage collection for mobile actor systems: The pseudo root approach. In: Chung, Y.-C., Moreira, J.E. (eds.) GPC 2006. LNCS, vol. 3947, pp. 360–372. Springer, Heidelberg (2006)
11. Jones, R.E.: Garbage Collection: Algorithms for Automatic Dynamic Memory Management. In: Lins, R. (ed.) Distributed Garbage Collection, July 1996. Wiley, Chichester (1996)
12. Abdullahi, S.E., Ringwood, A.: Garbage collecting the internet: A survey of distributed garbage collection. ACM Computing Surveys 30(3), 330–373 (1998)
13. Halstead, R.H.: Reference Tree Networks: Virtual Machine and Implementation. PhD thesis, MIT Laboratory for Computer Science, Technical report MIT/LCS/TR–222 (July 1979)
14. Baker, H.G.: List processing in real-time on a serial computer. Communications of the ACM 21(4), 280–294 (1978)
15. Lieberman, H., Hewitt, C.: A real-time garbage collector based on the lifetimes of objects. Commun. ACM 26(6), 419–429 (1983)
16. Washabaugh, D.: Real-time garbage collection of actors in a distributed system. Master's thesis, Virginia Tech, Blacksburg, VA (February 1990)
17. Nelson, J.: Automatic, incremental, on-the-fly garbage collection of actors. Master's thesis, Virginia Tech, Blacksburg, VA (February 1989)
18. Dickman, P.: Incremental, distributed orphan detection and actor garbage collection using graph partitioning and Euler cycles. In: Babaoğlu, Ö., Marzullo, K. (eds.) WDAG 1996. LNCS, vol. 1151, pp. 141–158. Springer, Heidelberg (1996)
19. Cormen, T.H., Leiserson, C.E., Rivest, R.L., Stein, C.: 21. In: Introduction to Algorithms, 2nd edn., pp. 498–522. MIT Press/McGraw-Hill (2001)
20. Worldwide Computing Laboratory: The SALSA Programming Language (2009), http://wcl.cs.rpi.edu/salsa/

Scalable Grid Resource Allocation for Scientific Workflows Using Hybrid Metaheuristics

Georg Buss, Kevin Lee, and Daniel Veit

Dieter Schwarz Chair of Business Administration, E-Business and E-Government
University of Mannheim, Schloss
Mannheim, Germany
{buss,lee,veit}@bwl.uni-mannheim.de

Abstract. Grid infrastructure is a valuable tool for scientific users, but it is characterized by a high level of complexity which makes it difficult for them to quantify their requirements and allocate resources. In this paper, we show that resource trading is a viable and scalable approach for scientific users to consume resources. We propose the use of Grid resource bundles to specify supply and demand combined with a hybrid metaheuristic method to determine the allocation of resources in a market-based approach. We evaluate this through the application domain of scientific workflow execution on the Grid.

1 Introduction

Many applications in science involve complex, large-scale and computationally intensive tasks which require a vast amount of computational resources provided in a globally distributed way. Computational Grids [1] allow resources from geographically distributed providers to be utilized by a single user to perform a single computational task. There is however a disconnect between the highly technical skills often necessary to utilize Grid resources and a scientists focus on their research domain. This is potentially limiting the use of Grids by scientific users. The two main challenges to solve this problem are i) improvements to high-level tools and task description languages [2], and ii) market structures to enable providers and users the ability to dynamically trade resources based on the principle of utility maximization [3].

A substantial amount of research has been undertaken in the area of high-level support for scientific usage of Grid resources, but there is of yet little practical support for market based resource allocation for end users. Current approaches to exchange Grid resources generally involve complex contractual relationships between institutions with grid resources; because of this there is no open market for trading grid resources between providers and users. This also makes it difficult for users to seek out and get, based on their valuation, access to specific resources for short term usage. More recently Cloud Computing has emerged [4], allowing rapid access to resources, but with very static pricing structures.

A promising solution to this problem of dynamic resource markets for Grids is the use of bundles to describe the resources offered or needed. These resources (such as processors, RAM or storage) are characterized by attributes (such as speed or size) and

R.-S. Chang et al. (Eds.): GPC 2010, LNCS 6104, pp. 256–267, 2010.

complex scheduling requirements (such as uptime and required time spans) as well as a valuation or reservation price. Viewing Grid resource as complex 'bundles' allows their availability and requirement to be described and traded in an open market. Taking such an approach, the matching of providers and consumers of resources can take place in a open market using combinatorial exchange mechanisms [5].

The trading of Grid resources via an exchange mechanism requires a centralized institution. Users submit bundles of required resources which are matched with provider bundles of available resources. Previous approaches formulated this problem as a generalization of the $\mathcal{NP}$-complete combinatorial allocation problem [6] which is found to be inapproximable within given bounds[7]. In this paper we propose the use of hybrid-metaheuristics as a scalable approach to solve the winner determination problem in Grid resource trading to allow scientists to access resources though a marketplace.

The remainder of this paper is structured as follows. Section 2 introduces scientific workflow execution in the Grid to motivation our approach. In Section 3 we introduce a formal description of the problem of trading grid-based resources. Section 4 describes a solution to the defined problem using a hybrid-metaheuristics approach. Section 5 evaluates the proposed solution. Finally, Section 6 concludes and discusses future work.

2 Workflow Execution on the Grid

Complex scientific applications are typically modeled as a workflow [2] which describes the tasks to be performed, their dependencies as well as the data and computations required to be completed. To enable as wide a range of scientists as possible to utilize the powerful resources of global Grids, application workflows can be described in a high level logical or abstract way, without references to concrete resources. This allows scientists to concentrate on efficiently describing the application rather than how it is executed. Workflow engines such as Taverna[8], Triana[9] and Pegasus[2] convert abstract workflows to an executable workflow which can then be executed on the Grid.

To convert an abstract workflow to one that is executable, the workflow has to be refined by mapping it to actual grid-based computational and storage resources. The workflow engine performs a number of steps to produce a concrete workflow including finding the actual input files, optimizing the workflow structure, finding resources and generating grid submission configurations. For example, the Pegasus workflow engine [2] queries the Globus Monitoring and Discovery Service (MDS) [10] to determine the number, availability, characteristics of Grid resources.

As yet, workflow engines do not commonly make decisions to schedule resources based on the economic impact of those decisions, even though the resources in question are of great value and in great demand. In this paper we introduce a scalable trading mechanism which can be used to enhance the mapping process of workflow engines, such as the Pegasus Site-Selection [2] stage. Rather than attempting to minimize execution time [11], we propose a market-based site-selection mechanism that determines an allocation based on the valuation for resources.

In our approach, we assume that idle resources are announced to a grid monitoring service. These resources can then be offered to resource consumers as reserved instances through a trading mechanism. Resources are offered or requested as bundles consisting of a number of parameters [5]. A resource offer or request is structured by the amount of required RAM, disk space and grid worker nodes. Requested hard disc space can be aggregated from various resources sellers, however, RAM and worker nodes have to be provided by a single seller. To allow the trading of resources, we assume that the Grid monitoring service runs the exchange mechanism collecting resource supply and demand requests. Requests timeout after a given time frame for a predefined amount of periods allowing reserved resources instance to be cleared.

3   Grid Resource Trading

To describe the problem of Grid resource trading we take the multi-attribute combinatorial exchange mechanism described in [5]. The set $G = \{g_1, \ldots, g_{|G|}\}$ specifies the computational resources available in the exchange mechanisms where G denotes all the goods to be traded in a trading market and a g_k is a specific resource. A bundle S_i denotes a subset of all the resources in G. Therefore the set $S = \{S_1, \ldots, S_{|S|}\}$ of bundles covers all the possible subsets of G. A computational resource g_k itself is defined by a set of cardinal quality attributes $A_k = \{a_1, \ldots, a_{|A_k|}\}$.

The exchange mechanism which is for the workflow scenario run by the grid monitoring service allows both the sellers and buyers of resources to place blind orders. Buyer orders specify what resources are required, and seller orders specify what resources are available. Potential buyers n out of the set $N = \{n_1, \ldots, n_{|N|}\}$ of buyers are allowed to submit an order of multiple bundle bids $B_n = \{B_{n,1}(S_1) \oplus \ldots \oplus B_{n,u}(S_i)\}$. The respective bundle bids are XOR concatenated.

$$
\begin{aligned}
B_{n,f}(S_i) = \{ & \langle v_n(S_i), s_n(S_i), e_n(S_i), l_n(S_i), \\
& q_n(S_i, g_1, a_{g_1,1}), \ldots, q_n(S_i, g_G, a_{g_G, A_j}), \\
& \gamma_n(S_i, g_1), \ldots, \gamma_n(S_i, g_G), \\
& \varphi_n(S_i, g_1, g_2), \ldots, \varphi_n(S_i, g_G, g_{G-1}) \rangle \}
\end{aligned}
$$

The valuation $v_n(S_i)$ is the amount the buyer is willing to pay for the bundle S_i per time slot. The number of slots the resources are required for is given by $s_n(S_i)$. A buyer bid defines a period of time slots within which the required slots have to be allocated. The period is given by $e_n(S_i)$ for the earliest possible time slot and $l_n(S_i)$ for the latest possible time slot. The minimum quality of the resources g_k contained in a bundle bid S_i is specified for each resource attribute a_{g_k, A_j} by $q_n(S_i, g_k, a_{g_k, A_j})$. In addition bundle bids may contain two types of fulfillment constraints. A coupling constraint $\gamma_n(S_i, g_1)$ specifies the maximum number of sellers allowed to allocate a required resource g_k. The co-allocation $\varphi_n(S_i, g_k, g_j)$ constraint requires a pair of resources g_k, g_j to be allocated from the same single seller.

Following the requirements for workflows (Section 2) the set of resources for the application domain is given as $G = \{\text{RAM, disk space, worker nodes}\}$. Each of these resources is described by a single attribute: $A_{RAM} = \{\text{Megabyte}\}, A_{HD-Space} = \{\text{Megabyte}\}, A_{Nodes} = \{\text{Number of nodes}\}$. For the scenario envisioned buyers request a certain quality of bundle S_1. The bundle S_1 is defined as $S_1 = \{\text{RAM, HD-Space, Nodes}\}$; it contains all the types of resources specified. There is no splitting constraint present as the HD-Space can be aggregated from the whole set of seller bids. The assumption that RAM and the number of nodes have to be allocated from the same seller is modeled buy the coupling constraint $\varphi_n(S_1, g_{RAM}, g_{Nodes})$. A buyer submits a request for a single bundle S_1 which matches her needs exactly.

Potential sellers m out of the set of $M = \{m_1, \ldots, m_{|M|}\}$ may submit an order of multiple bundle bids $B_m = \{B_{m,1}(S_i) \vee \ldots \vee B_{m,u}(S_i)\}$. The bundle bids are OR concatenated. Any number of seller orders may be part of the final allocation. A single seller bundle bid is of the form:

$$B_{m,f}(S_i) = \{\langle r_m(S_i), e_m(S_i), l_m(S_i),$$
$$q_m(S_i, g_1, a_{g_1,1}), \ldots, q_m(S_i, g_G, a_{g_G, A_j}), \rangle\}$$

The reservation price $r_m(S_i)$ specifies the minimum price a seller is willing to sell the specified bundle of resources per time slot. It is assumed that a seller bid is valid for the range of time slots given by $e_m(S_i)$ and $l_m(S_i)$. The quality of the resource services g_k is given by $q_m(S_i, g_k, a_{g_k, A_j})$. For the purpose of modeling the domain of workflows, sellers are able to submit offers in terms of two types of bundles. This is the bundle S_1 which was introduced above. The second bundle S_2 models an offer of HD-Space only ($S_2 = \{HD\text{-}Space\}$). A seller is free to submit an offer for both or one of the bundles either. This description includes free disposal (buyers do not care about taking extra units, sellers do not care about keeping units of winning bids) except when resources are coupled.

Given a collection of buyer and seller bundle orders the multi-attribute winner determination problem is to identify a set of winning bids out of the total set of bids. An optimal set of winning buyer and seller bids determines an allocation that maximizes the overall surplus while meeting time, capacity, coupling and co-allocation constraints. An allocation is described by the variables $x_{n,t}(S_i) \in \{0,1\}$ and $y_{n,m,t}(S_i) \in [0,1]$. The binary variable $x_{n,t} = 1$ if buyer n is allocated bundle S_i in time slot t. The real valued variable $y_{m,n,t}$ denotes the percentage of bundle S_i allocated from seller m to buyer n in time slot t. The surplus of an allocation is given by:

$$(x,y) \in arg\ max \left(\sum_{n \in N} \sum_{S_i \in S} \sum_{t \in T} v_n(S_i) x_{n,t} - \sum_{m \in M} \sum_{n \in N} \sum_{S_i \in S} \sum_{t \in T} r_m(S_i) y_{m,n,t} \right.$$
$$\left. |(x,y)\ is\ a\ feasible\ allocation \right)$$

4   Heuristic Solutions to the Grid Resource Trading Problem

Solving the problem with a standard solver optimally becomes computationally intractable for small problems of realistic size [5]. To tackle the problem we propose the use of local search based [12] hybrid metaheuristics. We focus on integrative hybrid metaheuristics that incorporate an exact algorithm into a metaheuristic to solve subproblems to optimality [13]. Section 4.1 details the problem representation as well as the operators which define the neighborhood structure and Section 4.2 presents solutions based on hybrid metaheuristics.

4.1   Problem Representation

A problem instance is represented as depicted in figure 1. The buyer orders are split up into the single bundle bids $B_{n,f}(S_i)$. The single buyer bundle bids are stored in an ordered set B_b. For each buyer bid $B_{n,f}(S_i)$ a list of possible time slots t is kept. For each of these time slots the available seller bundle bids $B_{m,f}(S_i)$ are stored in the set $B_{s,t}(S_i)$. The overall idea is to reduce the $|n| : |m|$ allocation problem to be scheduled into a given number of time slots to several $1 : |m|$ allocation problems to be solved for a single time slot t. The $1 : |m|$ allocation problem for a given buyer bundle bid $B_{n,f}(S_i)$ and a given time slot t can be formalized as follows:

$$y \in arg\ max \left(v_n(S_i) - \sum_{m \in M} \sum_{S_i \in S} r_m(S_i) y_{m,n} \mid y\ is\ a\ feasible\ allocation \right)$$

In case of no coupling or collocation constraints the problem becomes a linear, continuous, optimization problem. This type of problem can be solved efficiently by a linear programming solver. If coupling or co-allocation constraints are present the problem is of combinatorial nature with complexity reduced significantly compared to the original $|n| : |m|$ allocation problem.

The problem representation is evaluated by passing through the sequence of buyer bundle bids starting with the first bundle bid. The time slots the buyer bid is valid for $(e_n(S_i), l_n(S_i))$ are checked in the given order. A check of a time slot requires solving the, possibly constrained, $1 : |m|$ allocation problem. As soon as the amount of computational resources requested is available for a sufficient number of time slots the buyer bid is included into the allocation and the construction process is continued with the next buyer bid. A check of a time slot is valid only if there is a valid solution to the $1 : |m|$ allocation problem. Therefore no infeasible solution can be encoded by the problem representation. In case the buyer is already part of the allocation with another bid (XOR constraint) the evaluation of the specific bid is skipped and the process is continued with the next bid in the sequence. The evaluation process is summarized in algorithm 1. To solve the $1 : |m|$ problem we use the optimization engine lpsolve. Solving the problem to optimality covers the search of a large number of solutions.

Local search based metaheuristics start from an initial point in the search space and aim to iteratively improve on the current solution [12]. Solutions of higher quality are identified by the evaluation of the solutions within the neighborhood of the current solution. We introduce two operators, $\mathcal{N}_1(B_b)$ and $\mathcal{N}_2(T(B_{n,f}(S_i)))$, spanning the neighborhood structures. Both functions are applied to an ordered set and are defined as a transposition. A transposition is a function that swaps two elements of an ordered set. The neighborhood structure is given by any solution that can be reached by a single transposition on the elements of the respective sets.

The function $\mathcal{N}_1(B_b)$ operates on the set of buyer bids B_b. Swapping two bids at the positions (i, j) coincides to a repositioning in the evaluation procedure. In case of scarce resources an allocation for a bid in a leading position becomes more likely, and to sellers with lower reservation prices. The function $\mathcal{N}_2(T(B_{n,f}(S_i)))$ operates on the set of slots available for a given buyer bid. It swaps for each buyer bid two of the slots which changes the order these are passed in the evaluation procedure and therefore the allocation. Both operators are illustrated in figure 1.

Algorithm 1. Evaluate

$s \leftarrow 0$ \\allocation surplus
B_b \\ordered set of buyer bids
$T(B_{n,f}(S_i))$ \\ordered set of slots for a given buyer bid
$B_{s,t}(S_i)$ \\seller bids available in time slot t for the bundle S_i
$B_{alloc} \leftarrow \emptyset$ \\buyers that are part of the allocation (XOR - Constraint)
\\iterate over all buyer bids
while hasNext(B_b) **do**
   $B_{n,f}(S_i) \leftarrow$ next(B_b)
   \\test if the buyer n is part of the allocation already
   if $n \in B_{alloc}$ **then**
      continue with the next iteration
   end if
   $s' \leftarrow 0$
   $slots \leftarrow s_n(S_i)$
   \\iterate over the slots
   while hasNext($T(B_{n,f}(S_i))$) **do**
      $B_{s,t}(S_i) \leftarrow$ next($T(B_{n,f}(S_i))$)
      $s'' \leftarrow$ solve($B_{n,f}(S_i), B_{s,t}(S_i)$) \\solve the $1 : |m|$ allocation problem for time slot t
      if $isFeasilbe(s'')$ **then**
         $s' \leftarrow s' + s''$ \\add the surplus to surplus of the allocation
         $slots \leftarrow slots - 1$ \\save that the slot was successfully allocated
      end if
      \\test if the allocation for $B_{n,f}(S_i)$ is completed
      if $slots == 0$ **then**
         $s \leftarrow s + s'$ \\add surplus to overall surplus
         $B_{alloc} \cup n$ \\save that buyer n was successful with a bid
         continue with the next buyer bid
      end if
   end while
end while

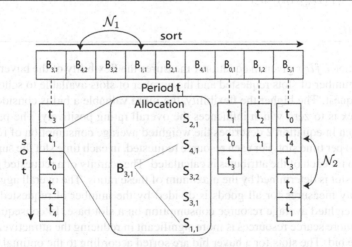

Fig. 1. Problem Representation

4.2 Metaheuristic Based Solution

Local search based methods require an initial solution to improve on, a suitable representation of the problem to be solved and a neighborhood structure to traverse the solution space. The initial solution is provided by a greedy type algorithm we proposed in [14]. The basic steps are illustrated in algorithm 2. The procedure starts with an empty allocation. In the initialization phase the buyer bundle bids and the respective time slots are ordered. The buyer bids are sorted in descending order according to the attractiveness for the inclusion into the allocation (cf. figure 1). The attractiveness of a bundle bid is calculated from the valuation of a bid adjusted by the weighted average consumption of resources (wac) and the flexibility ($flex$) in a time scheduling sense: $\frac{v_n(S_i)s_n(S_i)}{flex*wac}$.

$$flex = \frac{s_n(S_i)}{l_n(S_i) - e_n(S_i)} \tag{1}$$

$$wac(S_i) = \frac{\sum_{S_i \ni g_k} \sum_{e_n(S_i)}^{l_n(S_i)} \max_{a_{g_k,j} \in A_j} \frac{q_n(S_i,g_k,a_{g_k,j})}{\sum_{B_{s,t}(S_i) \ni S_j} q_m(S_j,g_k,a_{g_k,j})}}{l_n(S_i) - e_n(S_i)} \tag{2}$$

Algorithm 2. Greedy Implementation

$s \leftarrow 0$ \\surplus
B_b \\set of buyer bids
$T(B_{n,f}(S_i))$ \\set of slots for a given buyer bid
$p_1 \leftarrow \frac{v_n(S_i)s_n(S_i)}{flex*wac}$ \\sorting criterion buyer bid
$p_2 \leftarrow surplus$ \\sorting criterion seller bid

$sort(B_b, p_1)$
for all $B_{n,f}(S_i) \in B$ **do**
    $sortSlots(T(B_{n,f}(S_i)), p_2)$
end for
$s \leftarrow eval(B)$

The parameter $flex$ given in equation 1 measures the flexibility of the buyer bid as a ratio of the number of slots requested and the number of slots available to schedule the resources request. The higher the flexibility, the more valuable a bid is considered and the closer flex is to zero which influences the overall rating positively. The parameter $wac(S_i)$ given in equation 2 describes the weighted average consumption of resources of a buyer bid per time slot. For each resource requested, in each time slot the supply and demand ratio for each of the attributes is calculated. The scarcity of a requested good for a given time slot is determined by the maximum of these ratios. The overall aggregation of the scarcity measures for all goods is divided by the number of requested slots to obtain the weighted average resource consumption on a slot base. In consequence the demand for more scarce resources is more significant in reducing the attractiveness of a buyer bundle bid. The slots for a buyer bid are sorted according to the optimal solution (calculated using lpsolve [15]) of the $1 : |m|$ allocation problem.

A simulated annealing (SA) version based on the original proposal [16] with an adapted cooling schedule was chosen for guiding the improvement on a starting solution. SA is an intensely studied metaheuristic which has provided good results for a various number of combinatorial problems [17]. A standard SA implementation takes four parameters. This is the initial temperature value of the system T_s, a stopping criterion given by a final temperature value T_e, a parameter p specifying the number of steps at each temperature level and a temperature reduction function [18].

Algorithm 3. Simulated Annealing Implementation

$B_b \leftarrow GenerateInitialSolution()$
$T_s \leftarrow surplus(getFirstElement(B_b))$ \\initial Temperature
$T_e \leftarrow 0.1 T_s$
$t_{max} = 180\ seconds$
$k \leftarrow 3$ \\number of iterations at N_2 level
$p \leftarrow 1$ \\number of steps at each temperature level
while time limit not met **do**
    $B_b' \leftarrow randomNeighbor(\mathcal{N}_1(B_b))$
    if $(eval(B_b) < eval(B_b'))$ **then**
        $B_b \leftarrow B_b'$
    else
        if $random[0,1) < P(B_b', T)$ **then**
            $B_b \leftarrow B_b'$
        else
            $T \leftarrow UpdateTemperature(T, p)$
            continue with the next iteration of the main loop
        end if
    end if
    for k iterations **do**
        $B_b' \leftarrow randomNeighbor(\mathcal{N}_2(B_b))$
        if $(eval(B_b) < eval(B_b'))$ **then**
            $B_b \leftarrow B_b'$
            continue with next iteration of the main loop
        end if
    end for
    $T \leftarrow UpdateTemperature(T, p)$
end while

The temperature reduction function is generally given by $T_{t+1} = \alpha T_t$ where $T_0 = T_s$. However, we are interested in a comparison of solution methods based on wall clock time: t_{max}. Therefore temperature is reduced in dependence of time instead of a static parameter: $T(t) = T_s(\frac{T_e}{T_s})^{\frac{t}{t_{max}}}$ [19]. The function ensures that $T(0) = T_s$ and $T(t_{max}) = T_e$. Between these points the temperature is set according to $T(t)$. SA always accepts movements to superior solutions. However its key feature is its mechanism to escape local optima by accepting with a certain probability a solution worse compared to the current solution. The probability for accepting a solution that causes a decrease of $|\Delta|$ in the objective function is given by the acceptance function $P(\Delta) = \exp(\frac{-|\Delta|}{T})$ [20]. This acceptance function implies first that a small decrease of the objective function is more likely to be accepted than a large decrease. Second in the beginning of the search when T is high most down-hill moves are accepted.

Algorithm 3 shows how SA is applied to the problem. The initial solution is generated based on the greedy approach presented. T_s is set such that a decrease in the objective function value by the surplus of the first accepted bid is accepted with a probability of 80 percent [21]. The surplus of the first accepted bid is used to approximate the maximum change in the objective function by the exchange of two bids. This coincides to omitting the bid from the evaluation. T_e is set to ten percent of the value of T_s. While the time limit is not met a random neighbor B_b' according to $\mathcal{N}_1(B_b')$ is chosen. B_b' is accepted either if it improves the solution quality or if it is accepted according to $P(\Delta)$. The search proceeds with the next neighbor $\mathcal{N}_1(B_b)$ otherwise. For each iteration the temperature is reduced. In case B_b' is accepted a refinement phase based on local search is started. The factor k determines how often an improvement according to the neighborhood $\mathcal{N}_2$ is tested. The first time the solution is improved the process is continued with the next iteration of the main loop.

5   Experimental Evaluation

This section evaluates the metaheuristic approach to grid resource trading using the approach introduced in Section 4. Two sets of Experiments are performed (setup as described in Section 5.1). We first asses the quality of the SA approach based on a comparison to the allocation computed by the commonly available standard solver lpsolve [15]. We then provide the results of the initial greedy heuristic and a first improvement local search algorithm equal to the SA approach but without the probabilistic element to escape local optima. Results are presented in Section 5.2.

5.1   Experiment Description

To study the heuristic methods under simulation we produce random variants from a real world data set. This allows us to keep the macro-structure of characteristic bids for the workflow domain fixed while varying the numbers of bids. The data is obtained from the execution of a 0.2 degree montage workflow [2] of Messier M17 on Grid resources. We assume that a buyer wants to allocate the resources required for a complete execution of such a workflow. This translates to specifying a bid for the bundle S_1 which satisfies the requirements at each point in time. Based on this the attributes of a buyer bid are set as follows: $A_{RAM} = \{86.4\}$, $A_{HD-Space} = \{171\}$, $A_{Nodes} = \{9\}$; a single execution of a workflow is assumed to take 5 whole time slots while a range of 10 time slots is open for trade. As valuations are not available from the data sets these are generated as the sum of a fixed amount of 1000 units and a variable, from uniform distribution drawn between 0 and 100 units. For seller bids on the bundle S_1 (S_2) the attributes are defined as: $A_{RAM} = \{168\}$, $A_{HD-Space} = \{300\}$, $A_{Nodes} = \{20\}$ ($A_{HD-Space} = \{100\}$). The reservation prices are determined by a fixed part 1500 (100) and a variable, from a uniform distribution drawn, value of up to 150 (10).

Two sets of experiments are performed (A and B) that differ in the distribution of buyer bids. For experiment A the requests are normally distributed with a mean value of three and variance of one. This models a peak in demand for resources between time slot three and time slot eight. For experiment B the requests for resources are uniformly distributed over the time slots. For each type of experiments ten bidding scenarios differing in the number of buyer and seller bids were created. The scenarios comprise 20,40,60,80,100,120,140,160,180 and 200 bundle bids. For each scenario the number of bids is equally distributed between seller and buyer bids. Half of the sellers offer bundle S_1 and half of the sellers offer bundle S_2. For each of the ten bidding scenarios ten instances were generated. The time to solve the allocation problem was set to the reasonable time of three minutes.

5.2 Experiment Results and Analysis

To asses the quality of the approach described in Section 4.2 we first performed a comparison between the lpsolve solver and our approach, over different time requirements. We tested the scalability of lpsolve for very small scale bidding scenarios of type B experiments. Table 1 summarizes the results indicating whether the optimal solution was found (Opt), an intermediary solution was provided (Inter.) or the solver did not return any solution (KO). The results show that for very simple problems lpsolve returns an optimal solution for both 3 and 60 minutes. For slightly more complicated problems lpsolve returns intermeadiate results only, and no optimal solution. For complex problems lpsolve fails to produce any results. As lpsolve fails to produce results with relatively complex experiments, the following experiments evaluate the SA approach with the greedy approach detailed in Section 4.2 and a basic local search.

Table 2 summarizes the results of experiments A and B. The comparison of the heuristic methods is based on the percentage deviation to the best surplus found [22]. The deviation column shows the average percentage deviation of the ten simulation runs performed for the bidding scenario. The corresponding Best/10 column indicates the number of times the heuristic reported the best result. The last row of the table shows the average error for all bidding scenarios for a single heuristic method.

Table 1. Results using lpsolve for small scale scenarios

Time	Scenario			
	2/2	4/4	6/6	10/10
3 min. (Opt/Inter./KO)	3/0/0	0/3/0	0/1/2	0/0/3
60 min. (Opt/Inter./KO)	3/0/0	0/3/0	0/1/2	0/0/3

For both experiments SA shows on average the best performance. SA does not always find the allocation with the maximum surplus but is always closer to the best solution than local search. Both local search and SA improve significantly on the greedy starting solution. With increasing number of bids the factor of improvement decreases; this is because the time for the evaluation is kept constant while the size of the scenario and neighborhood of an allocation to be searched is increased significantly.

The variation between the results of experiment A and B can be explained by the structural differences of the underlying scenarios. The uniform distribution of time slot requirements for experiment B results in less competition for the offered resources

Table 2. Experimental Results and Analysis

Scenario	Experiment A					Experiment B				
	Sim. Annealing		Local Search		Greedy	Sim. Annealing		Local Search		Greedy
	Dev.	Best/10	Dev.	Best/10	Dev.	Dev.	Best/10	Dev.	Best/10	Dev.
10/10	0.00	10/10	4.83	0/10	35.14	0.00	10/10	5.11	0/10	26.02
20/20	0.17	9/10	2.64	1/10	32.13	1.37	5/10	1.83	5/10	27.06
30/30	0.02	8/10	2.25	2/10	27.26	0.30	8/10	1.88	2/10	25.30
40/40	0.55	6/10	1.14	4/10	28.48	0.81	7/10	1.85	3/10	23.32
50/50	0.51	7/10	2.45	3/10	22.74	0.87	8/10	3.05	2/10	19.37
60/60	0.24	7/10	2.97	3/10	21.29	1.63	5/10	2.40	5/10	16.87
70/70	0.00	10/10	7.29	0/10	21.69	2.17	5/10	1.44	5/10	15.51
80/80	0.35	8/10	7.10	2/10	17.02	0.53	8/10	2.62	2/10	14.21
90/90	0.00	10/10	5.80	0/10	12.16	0.13	7/10	1.68	3/10	10.17
100/100	0.17	7/10	4.37	3/10	8.05	0.61	8/10	5.81	2/10	9.14
Average	0.20	82/100	4.08	18/100	22.60	0.84	71/100	2.77	29/100	18.70

compared to the peak in demand modeled for the scenarios in experiment A. From a scheduling perspective there are few options to check in experiment B. The greedy approach in both experiments shows that the deviation to the best solution is bigger for the scenarios of experiment A. The same holds for the comparison of the local search procedures. The scenarios in experiment B require a less extensive search for a promising basic solution to improve on but fine tuning of the initial solution which is the domain of local search. This becomes evident by the smaller average deviation of the results of the local search procedure in comparison to the SA approach. Furthermore the best solution is identified for 71 percent of the simulation runs of experiment B by the SA approach in comparison to 82 percent of the simulation runs of experiment A. In summary, standard solvers like lpsolve provide allocations for very small scale scenarios only and heuristic solutions provide a scalable alternative producing good results for the problem of resource allocation. The simulated annealing-based approach presented here can be used to improve significantly on greedy results.

6 Conclusions

This paper has presented a hybrid metaheurstic approach to the trading of grid resources for the execution of scientific workflows. It has described a trading approach for grid resources and detailed metaheuristics to efficiently trade resources. These metaheuristics have been evaluated through the execution of scientific workflows. We showed that for the scientific workflow domain heuristic solutions provide a scalable alternative compared to standard solvers like lpsolve. Future work will involve the scaling up of the approach to more resource providers and consumers, and increasing the number and types of scientific workflows. Expanded work will involve the evaluation of different and more complex workflow types, as well as other types of applications.

References

1. Foster, I.: The grid: A new infrastructure for 21st century science. Physics Today 55(2), 42–47 (2002)
2. Deelman, E., et al.: Pegasus: A framework for mapping complex scientific workflows onto distributed systems. Scientific Programming 13(3), 219–237 (2005)

3. Broberg, J., Venugopal, S., Buyya, R.: Market-oriented grids and utility computing: The state-of-the-art and future directions. Journal of Grid Computing 6(3), 255–276 (2008)
4. Buyya, R., Yeo, C.S., Venugopal, S., Broberg, J., Brandic, I.: Cloud computing and emerging it platforms: Vision, hype, and reality for delivering computing as the 5th utility. Future Gener. Comput. Syst. 25(6), 599–616 (2009)
5. Schnizler, B., Neumann, D., Veit, D., Weinhardt, C.: Trading grid services - a multi-attribute combinatorial approach. European Journal of Operational Research 187(3), 943–961 (2008)
6. Rothkopf, M.H., Pekeč, A., Harstad, R.M.: Computationally manageable combinational auctions. Management Science 44(8), 1131–1147 (1998)
7. Sandholm, T.: Algorithm for optimal winner determination in combinatorial auctions. Artificial Intelligence 135(1-2), 1–54 (2002)
8. Oinn, T., et al.: Taverna: lessons in creating a workflow environment for the life sciences: Research articles. Concurr. Comput.: Pract. Exper. 18(10), 1067–1100 (2006)
9. Taylor, I., Shields, M., Wang, I., Harrison, A.: Visual grid workflow in triana. Journal of Grid Computing 3(3), 153–169 (2005)
10. Fitzgerald, S.: Grid information services for distributed resource sharing. In: Proc. 10th IEEE Intl. Symposium on High Performance Distributed Computing (2001)
11. Lee, K., Paton, N.W., Sakellariou, R., Fernandes, A.A.A.: Utility driven adaptive workflow execution. In: CCGrid (2009)
12. Blum, C., Roli, A.: Metaheuristics in combinatorial optimization: Overview and conceptual comparison. ACM Computing Surveys 35(3), 268–308 (2003)
13. Puchinger, J., Raidl, G.R.: Combining metaheuristics and exact algorithms in combinatorial optimization: A survey and classification. In: Artificial Intelligence and Knowledge Engineering Applications: A Bioinspired Approach, pp. 41–53. Springer, Berlin (2005)
14. Buss, G., Lee, K., Veit, D.: Scalable grid resource trading with greedy heuristics. To appear in Fourth International Workshop on P2P, Parallel, Grid and Internet Computing (3PGIC-2010) (February 2010)
15. Lpsolve 5.5.0.14, a mixed integer linear programming (milp) solver, http://lpsolve.sourceforge.net/
16. Kirkpatrick, S., Gelatt Jr., C.D., Vecchi, M.P.: Optimization by simulated annealing. Science 220(4598), 671–680 (1983)
17. Suman, B., Kumar, P.: A survey of simulated annealing as a tool for single and multiobjective optimization. Journal of the Operational Research Society 57(10), 1143–1160 (2006)
18. Aarts, E.H.L., Korst, J.H.M., van Laarhoven, P.J.M.: Simulated annealing. In: Aarts, E.H.L., Lenstra, J.K. (eds.) Local Search in Combinatorial Optimization, pp. 91–120. John Wiley & Sons, Chichester (1997)
19. Petersen, H.L., Madsen, O.B.G.: The double travelling salesman problem with multiple stacks - formulation and heuristic solution approaches. European Journal of Operational Research 198(1), 139–147 (2009)
20. Metropolis, N., Rosenbluth, A., Rosenbluth, M., Teller, A., Teller, E.: Equation of state calculations by fast computing machines. Journal of Chemical Physics 21, 1087–1092 (1953)
21. Kouvelis, P., Kim, M.W.: Unidirectional loop network layout problem in automated manufacturing systems. Oper. Res. 40(3), 533–550 (1992)
22. Rardin, R.L., Uzsoy, R.: Experimental evaluation of heuristic optimization algorithms: A tutorial. Journal of Heuristics 7(3), 261–304 (2001)

Pareto Front Based Realistic Soft Real-Time Task Scheduling with Multi-objective Genetic Algorithm in Unstructured Heterogeneous Distributed System

Nafiseh Sedaghat[1], Hamid Tabatabaee-Yazdi[2,*], and Mohammad-R Akbarzadeh-T[3]

[1] Department of Artificial Intelligence, Islamic Azad University, Mashhad Branch, Iran
[2] Department of Computer Engineering, Islamic Azad University, Qouchan Branch, Iran
Hamid.tabatabaee@gmail.com
[3] Department of Electerical Engineering, Ferdowsi University, Mashhad, Iran

Abstract. Task scheduling is an essential aspect of parallel processing system. This problem assumes fully connected processors and ignores contention on the communication links. However, as arbitrary processor network (APN), communication contention has a strong influence on the execution time of a parallel application. In this paper, we propose multi-objective genetic algorithm to solve task scheduling problem with time constraints in unstructured heterogeneous processors to find the scheduling with minimum makespan and total tardiness. To optimize objectives, we use Pareto front based technique, vector based method. In this problem, just like tasks, we schedule messages on suitable links during the minimization of the makespan and total tardiness. To find a path for transferring a message between processors we use classic routing algorithm. We compare our method with BSA method that is a well known algorithm. Experimental results show our method is better than BSA and yield better makespan and total tardiness.

Keywords: DAG, Distributed system, Edge scheduling, Genetic algorithm, Heterogeneous system, Link contention, Multi-objective Optimization, Precedence constraint, Real time system, Routing, Soft real time, Task scheduling.

1 Introduction

Distributed heterogeneous system has become widely used for scientific and commercial applications such as high-definition television, medical imaging, etc.. These systems require a mixture of general-purpose machines, programmable digital machines, and application specific integrated circuits [1]. A distributed heterogeneous system involves multiple heterogeneous modules connected by arbitrary architecture and interacting with one another to solve a problem. More and more evidence shows that scheduling parallel task is a key factor in obtaining high performance in such a system. The common objective of scheduling is to map tasks onto machines and order

---

* Corresponding Author.

R.-S. Chang et al. (Eds.): GPC 2010, LNCS 6104, pp. 268–279, 2010.
© Springer-Verlag Berlin Heidelberg 2010

their execution so that task precedence requirements are satisfied and there is a minimum schedule length (makespan) [1]. In majority scheduling algorithms, processors are assumed to be fully-connected, and no attention is paid to link contention or routing strategies used for communication [2]. Actually, most heterogeneous systems cannot meet this condition and their processors are linked by an arbitrary processor network (APN) [1]. Macey and Zomaya [1] showed that the consideration of link contention is significant for producing accurate and efficient schedules.

We are interested in APN algorithms that both schedule tasks and messages on arbitrary networks consisting of heterogeneous processors and communication links. Scheduling tasks while considering link contention for a heterogeneous system is a relatively less explored research topic and very few algorithms for this problem have been designed [2]; also real time systems is not explored until now. Real-time systems are characterized by computational activities with timing constraints and classified into two categories: hard real-time system and soft real-time system. The goal of the scheduling algorithms in hard real-time system is to meet all tasks' deadlines, in other words, to keep the feasibility of scheduling through admission control. On the other hand, in the soft real time system in which usefulness of results produced by a task decreases over time after the deadline expires without causing any damage to the controlled environment [3].

All of research in this topic is concerned with the minimization of a single criterion-the makespan in non real time system. However, in practice, many industries such as aircraft, electronics, semiconductors manufacturing, etc., have tradeoffs in their scheduling problems where multiple objectives need to be considered in order to optimize the overall performance of the system. Obviously, the multi-objective scheduling problems are more complex than the scheduling problems with one criterion, and it is hard to find a compromise solution because the objectives are often inconsistent, conflicting or even contradictory [4].

In this paper, we propose genetic algorithm for soft real time scheduling and mapping precedence-constrained tasks with time constraints to an arbitrary network of heterogeneous processors. We consider link contention and just like tasks, messages are also scheduled and mapped to suitable links during the minimization of the finish time of tasks and total tardiness. For finding a path for transferring a message between processors we use a classic routing algorithm. In classic routing we select a path based on speed of links. To evaluate our method, we generate random DAGs with different sparsity based on Bernoulli distribution and compare our method with BSA method that is a well known algorithm in this problem.

The rest of the paper is organized as follows: Section 2 presents definition of task scheduling problem in classic and contention awareness model. In Section 3, we review some related work and in Section 4 we present our method. In Section 5, the simulation experimental results are presented and analyzed. This paper concludes with Section 6 and in this section, we discuss about future works.

2 Task Scheduling

In task scheduling, the program to be scheduled is represented by a directed acyclic graph $G = (V, E, w, c)$. The nodes in V represent the tasks and the edges in E

represent the communications between the tasks. An edge $e_{ij} \in E$ from node n_i to n_j, $n_i, n_j \in V$, represents the communication from node n_i to node n_j. The positive weight $w(n)$ associated with node $n \in V$ represents its computation cost and the non-negative weight $c(e_{ij})$ associated with edge $e_{ij} \in E$ represents its communication cost [5]. All instructions or operations of one task are executed in sequential order; there is no parallelism within a task. The set $\{n_x \in V : e_{xi} \in E\}$ of all direct predecessors of n_i is denoted by $pred(n_i)$ and the set $\{n_x \in V : e_{ix} \in E\}$ of all direct successors of n_i, is denoted by $succ(n_i)$[6].

A schedule of a DAG is the association of a start time and a processor with every node of the DAG. $t_s(n, P)$ denotes the start time and $w(n, P)$ the execution time of node $n \in V$ on processor $p \in P$. Thus, the node's finish time is given by $t_f(n, P) = t_s(n, P) + w(n, P)$. The processor to which n is allocated is denoted by $proc(n)$. For such a schedule to be feasible, the following two conditions must be fulfilled for all nodes in G [6]:

1. In each time only one task can be executed on a processor.
2. Every tasks must be received all of required information from other tasks before its execution.

2.1   Classic Scheduling [6]

Most scheduling algorithms employ a strongly idealized model of the target parallel system [3, 7-9]. This model, which shall be referred to as the classic model, $M_{classic} = (P, w)$, consists of a finite set of dedicated processors $\mathbf{P}$ connected by a fully connected communication network and local communication has zero costs and also communication can be performed concurrently. Based on this model, the earliest start time of node only depends on the finish time of the node's predecessors and the communication time between them.

Definition 1 (Earliest Start Time). *The earliest start time of $n_j \in V$, $n_i \prec n_j$ is given by*

$$t_s^e(n_j) = \max_{\forall n_i \in V, n_i \prec n_j} \left\{ t_f(n_i) + \begin{cases} 0 & if \ proc(n_i) = proc(n_j) \\ c(e_{ij}) & otherwise \end{cases} \right\} \quad (1)$$

Based on this system model, the edge finish time only depends on the finish time of the origin node and the communication time.

Definition 2 (Edge Finish Time). *The edge finish time of $e_{ij} \in E$ is given by*

$$t_f(e_{ij}) = t_f(n_i) + \begin{cases} 0 & if \ proc(n_i) = proc(n_j) \\ c(e_{ij}) & otherwise \end{cases} \quad (2)$$

Thus, communication can overlap with the computation of other nodes, an unlimited number of communications can be performed at the same time, and communication has the same cost $c(e_{ij})$, regardless of the origin and the destination processor, unless the communication is local [6].

2.2 Contention Aware Scheduling [6]

The classic scheduling model does not consider any kind of contention for communication resources. To make task scheduling contention aware, and thereby more realistic, the communication network is modeled by a graph, where processors are represented by vertices and the edges reflect the communication links. The awareness for contention is achieved by edge scheduling, i.e., the scheduling of the edges of the DAG onto the links of the network graph, in a very similar manner to how the nodes are scheduled on the processors.

Here, it suffices to define the topology network graph to be $TG = (\mathbf{P}, \mathbf{L})$, where $\mathbf{P}$ is a set of vertices representing the processors and $\mathbf{L}$ is a set of edges representing the communication links. Fig. 3 shows an example of these systems; in this figure, weight of vertices indicates to processing speed of processor and weight of edges indicates to speed of communication links.

The notions of concurrent communication and a fully connected network found in the classic model are substituted by the notion of scheduling the edges $\mathbf{E}$ on the communication links $\mathbf{L}$. Corresponding to the scheduling of the nodes, $t_s(e, L)$ and $t_f(e, L)$ denote the start and finish time of edge $e \in \mathbf{E}$ on link $L \in \mathbf{L}$, respectively.

When a communication, represented by the edge e, is performed between two distinct processors P_{src} and P_{dst}, the routing algorithm of TG returns a route from P_{src} to P_{dst}: $R =< L_1, L_2, ..., L_l >$, $L_i \in \mathbf{L}$ for $i = 1, 2, ..., l$. The edge e is scheduled on each link of the route. This only affects the scheduling of the nodes with an altered definition of the edge finish time (Definition 3).

Definition 3 (Edge Finish Time—Contention Model). *Let $G = (V, E, w, c)$ be a DAG and $M_{TG} = ((\mathbf{P}, \mathbf{L}), w)$ a parallel system. Let $R =< L_1, L_2, ..., L_l >$ be the route for the communication of $e_{ij} \in E$, $n_i, n_j \in V$, if $proc(n_i) \neq proc(n_j)$. The finish time of e_{ij} is*

$$t_f(e_{ij}) = \begin{cases} t_f(n_i) & if\ proc(n_i) = proc(n_j) \\ t_f(e_{ij}, L_l) & otherwise \end{cases} \tag{3}$$

Thus, the edge finish time $t_f(e_{ij})$ is now the finish time of e_{ij} on the last link of the route, L_l, unless the communication is local.

3 Related Work

There are only a few scheduling algorithms that consider arbitrary topology for processors network and contention on network links. These algorithms do not consider time constraints for tasks and discuss about non-real-time systems. This group of algorithms is called the APN (arbitrary processor network) scheduling algorithms [10]. Two well-known scheduling algorithms for APNs are Dynamic-Level Scheduling (DLS) algorithm and the Bubble Scheduling and Allocation (BSA) algorithm [11].

The DLS Algorithm [11] is a list scheduling heuristic that assigns the node priorities by using an attribute called *dynamic level* (DL). The dynamic level of a task T_i on a processor P_j is equal to

$$DL(T_i, P_j) = blevel^S(T_i) - EST(T_i, P_j) \tag{4}$$

This reflects how well task T_i and processor P_j are matched. The *blevel* value of a task T_i, is the length of the longest path from T_i to the exit task including all computation and communication costs on the path. The DLS algorithm uses static *blevel* value, $blevel^S$, which is computed by considering only the computation costs. At each scheduling step, the algorithm selects (ready node, available processor) pair that maximizes the value of the dynamic level. The computation costs of tasks are set with the median values. A new term, $\Delta(T_i, P_j)$, is added to previous equation for heterogeneous processors, which is equal to the difference between the median execution time of task T_i and its execution time on processor P_j. The DLS algorithm requires a message routing method that is supplied by the user; and no specific routing algorithm is presented in their paper. BSA algorithm [2] has two phases. In the first phase, the tasks are all scheduled to a single processor–effectively the parallel program is serialized. Then, each task is considered in turn for possible migration to the neighbor processors. The objective of this process is to improve the finish time of tasks because a task migrates only if it cans "bubble up". If a task is selected for migration, the communication messages from its predecessors are scheduled to the communication link between the new processor and the original processor. After all the tasks in the original processor are considered, the first phase of scheduling is completed. In the second phase, the same process is repeated on one of the neighbor processor. Thus, a task migrated from the original processor to a neighbor processor may have an opportunity to migrate again to a processor one more hop away from the original processor. This incremental scheduling by migration process is repeated for all the processors in a breadth-first fashion.

4   The Proposed Algorithm

In this paper, we consider the soft real time scheduling precedence-constrained tasks to an arbitrary network of heterogeneous processors with considering link contentions. Therefore, scheduling algorithms for such systems must schedule the tasks as well as the communication traffic by treating both the processors and communication links as equally important resources. We use genetic algorithm for finding best scheduling in this environment that has minimum finish time of tasks and total tardiness. In the evaluation function, tasks and messages both are scheduled on processors and links, respectively. For mapping messages on links, we use classic routing algorithm to determine the best path between source and destination processors. In the following, we present structure of multi-objective genetic algorithm and routing algorithm.

4.1   Multi-objective Genetic Algorithm

- *Encoding*

Each individual in the population represents a possible schedule. Fig. 1 shows the encoding used. Each character is a mapping between a task and processor. Each character contains the unique identification number of a task, with S being used to delimit different processor queues, where P_i is processor i [12].

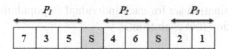

Fig. 1. An individual in GA

- *Decoding*

The fitness function of the task-scheduling problem is to determine the assignment of tasks of a given application to processors so that its schedule length and its total tardiness are minimized. For computing schedule length and total tardiness, we schedule precedence-constrained tasks (DAG's nodes) and messages (DAG's edges) on processors and links, respectively. While the start time of a node is constrained by the data ready time of its incoming edges, the start time of an edge is restricted by the finish time of its origin node. The scheduling of an edge differs further from that of a node, in that an edge might be scheduled on more than one link. A communication between two nodes, which are scheduled on two different but not adjacent processors, utilizes communication route of intermediate links between the two processors. The edge representing this communication must be scheduled on each of the involved links. To determine involved links we use classic routing algorithm that is explained in the next subsections. We use insertion policy for scheduling nodes and edges and calculate makespan and total tardiness for each individual. Makespan is calculated from this formulation:

$$makespan = \max_{n_j \in V} C(n_j) \tag{5}$$

where $C(n_j)$ is completion time of task j.

Also total tardiness is calculated from this formulation:

$$total\ tardiness = \sum_{n_j \in V} \max \{0, (C(n_j) - D(n_j))\} \tag{6}$$

where $C(n_j)$ is completion time of task j, and $D(n_j)$ is deadline of task j .

- *Evaluation Function*

In each generation we need to compare individuals and sort them based on their fitness. For performing it, we use a multi-objective method, vector based to determine quality of each chromosome. In this method for each solution one has to determine how many solutions dominate it and the set of solutions to which it dominates. The domination between two solutions is defined as [13].

All points which are not dominated by any other point are called the non-dominated points of class one, or simply non-dominated points. Usually the non-dominated points together make up a front in the objective space and are often visualized to represent a non-domination front. The points lying on the non-domination front, by definition, do not get dominated by any other point in the objective space, hence they are Pareto-optimal points (together they constitute the Pareto-optimal front), and the corresponding variable vectors are called Pareto optimal solutions [13].

We calculate non-domination set for each individual in population and sort population based on non-domination into each front.

- *Evolution Strategy*

We use tournament selection in proposed method. After the selection process is completed, we use the cycle crossover method [14] to promote exploration as used in [15]. For mutation, we randomly swap elements of a randomly chosen individual in the population. In each generation, the population with the current population and current offspring is sorted again based on non-domination and only the best N individuals are selected, where N is the population size. The initial population is generated randomly. MoGA will evolve the population until one or more stopping conditions are met. The best individual is selected after each generation and if it does not improve for 30 generations, GA stops evolving. The maximum number of generations is set at 200 because the quality of the schedules returned with more than that number does not justify the increased computation cost.

4.2 Routing Algorithm

To transfer a message from a task to another task, scheduled on different processors, we must determine a path between P_{Src} and P_{Dst}, based on network topology graph and busy time of links for preventing contention. We propose all links are full duplex and we use store-and-forward (SAF) [11] switching for message transfer. In this paper we assume that the time of preparing a sending message on source processor and receiving a message on destination processor is zero. Also, we assume that the time of store-and-forward process on each intermediate processor is zero.

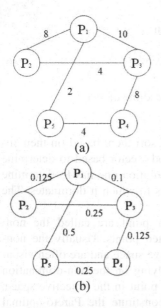

(a)

(b)

Source & destination	Shortest Path	Path length
P_1 & P_2	$P_1 P_2$	0.125
P_1 & P_3	$P_1 P_3$	0.1
P_1 & P_4	$P_1 P_3 P_4$	0.225
P_1 & P_5	$P_1 P_3 P_4 P_5$	0.475
P_2 & P_3	$P_2 P_1 P_3$	0.225
P_2 & P_4	$P_2 P_1 P_3 P_4$	0.35
P_2 & P_5	$P_2 P_1 P_3 P_4 P_5$	0.6
P_3 & P_4	$P_3 P_4$	0.125
P_3 & P_5	$P_3 P_4 P_5$	0.375
P_4 & P_5	$P_4 P_5$	0.25

(c)

Fig. 2. a) An example of processor topology with speed of links; b) Time distances between processors; c) Shortest paths between processors and their lengths

To find best route for transferring message from P_{Src} to P_{Dst} we use Floyd algorithm [16]. First, based on speed of links, we calculate the time distances between processors and then we implement Floyd algorithm and choose shortest path between P_{Src} and P_{Dst}. This algorithm is simple and its results are good.

Fig. 2 shows an example of routing algorithm. Fig. 2 (a) shows network topology that weights of edges show speed of links between processors. Fig. 2 (b) shows network topology that weight of edges shows time distances between processors that is calculated by:

$$TD(Src, Dest) = \frac{1}{c(e_{Src,Dest})} \tag{7}$$

Where $c(e_{Src,Dest})$ is the weight of link between Src and $Dest$ processor. Fig. 2 (c) shows shortest path and its cost (time distance) network that is found by Floyd algorithm. Due to we use full duplex links,

$$TD(Src, Dest) = TD(Dest, Src) \tag{8}$$

and

$$Path(Src, Dest) = Path(Dest, Src) \tag{9}$$

5 Experimental Results

In this section, we describe the performance of our algorithm on random examples including task graphs (DAGs) generated using the P-Method [17].

The P-Method of generating a random DAG is based on the probabilistic construction of an adjacency matrix of a task graph. For each element, when the Bernoulli trial is a success, then the element is assigned a value of one; for a failure the element is given a value of zero. The parameter p can be considered to be the sparsity of the task graph. With this method, a probability parameter of $p = 1$ creates a totally sequential task graph, and $p = 0$ creates an inherently parallel one.

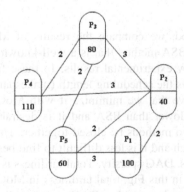

Fig. 3. Unstructured heterogeneous distributed system

The P-method was used to generate 5 DAGs based on parameter p ($p =$ $0.1, 0.2, 0.3, 0.4, 0.5$). The number of tasks in each task graph was 40. The weight of each node (computation cost of each task) and edge (communication cost between tasks) in task graph was chosen randomly based on normal distribution. For generating deadline of tasks we use this formulation:

$$D_i = t^e_{s\,i} + \max_{p \in P} c_i + \alpha \tag{10}$$

Where D_i is deadline of task i; $t^e_{s\,i}$ is an earliest start time of ith task which is calculated by (3); next term is maximum computation cost of task i on processors and α is a constant that shows laxity time; in this paper we set $\alpha = 10$.

We schedule these task graphs with 5 unstructured heterogeneous distributed processors. Fig. 3 shows its topology. The weights associated with each processor show processing speed of processor and weights associated with each link show transferring rate of each link. For computing the execution time each task on each processor, it is enough to divide computation cost of task to processing speed of processor.

Characteristics of MoGA are: population size: 40, crossover probability: 0.8, mutation probability: 0.2.

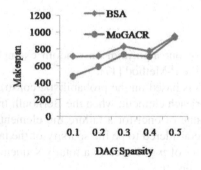

Fig. 4. Makespan	Fig. 5. Total Tardiness

To evaluate our method, we compare the results of MoGA scheduling classic routing (MoGACR) with BSA method that is a well-known link contention scheduling method. Figs 4-7 show experimental results. In these figures, horizontal axis is DAG sparsity. Fig. 4 shows the scheduling length (makespan) vs. DAG sparsity. Makespan is the first objective that we minimize it with MoGA. As shown in Fig. 4, MoGACR has makespan lower than BSA and it is desirable. When the sparsity is increased, makespan of two methods be closed together. This is because the sequentiality of a task graph is high and it is less difficult to find best found schedules. Fig. 5 shows the total tardiness vs. DAG sparsity. Total tardiness is the second objective that we minimize it; as shown in this Fig. total tardiness in MoGACR in $sparsity = 0.1$ is less than BSA method and in another DAGs total tardiness is equal to zero that show all of time constraints have been satisfied.

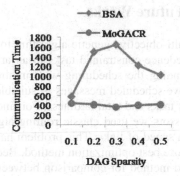

Fig. 6. Total communication time

Fig. 6 shows the total communication time in scheduling. Communication time is the duration time of sending messages on links and it is desirable to minimize it by choosing best route between processors. As shown in this figure, BSA has most total communication time and wastes most time for communicating. MoGACR has lower communication time than BSA due to in MoGACR we transfer messages via shortest path that is determined by Floyd algorithm.

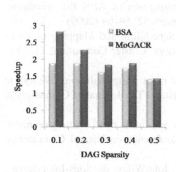

Fig. 7. Speedup

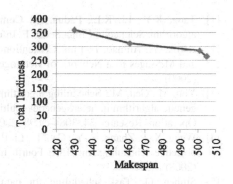

Fig. 8. Pareto solution

The speedup is defined as the ratio of sequential time $seq(G) = \sum_{n \in V} w(n)$ (local communication has zero costs) to the makespan of the produced scheduling; therefore we want to increase this ratio. As shown in Fig. 7, BSA has lower speedup than that of MoGACR. When the sparsity is increased, speedup is decreased. This is because the sequentiality of a task graph is high and best solution trends to sequential execution. Fig. 8 shows the Pareto solution of makespan vs. total tardiness. We expect to this curve is close to center. It means we expect to have zero total tardiness and also minimum makespan.

6 Conclusions and Future Works

In this paper, we used multi-objective genetic algorithm to solve the problem of soft real-time scheduling precedence-constrained tasks to an arbitrary network of heterogeneous processors for finding the scheduling with minimum finish time and total tardiness. Just like tasks, we scheduled messages to suitable links during the minimization of the finish time of tasks and total tardiness. For finding a path for transferring a message between processors we used classic routing algorithm. In classic routing we selected path based on speed of links. This problem has a large search space and because of it we must choose best optimization method. Because of having two objectives we used vector-based method for comparison between chromosomes. With this method we yielded better scheduling. In order to evaluate our method, we generated random DAGs with different sparsity based on Bernoulli distribution. We compared results of our method with that of BSA method. Experimental results showed our method (MoGACR) finds scheduling with lower makespan and total tardiness than BSA in all DAGs with different sparsity. This means our method has capability of facing with different types of DAGs with different sparsities.

In the future we plan to consider link contention awareness problem in dynamic environment and by it move to more realistic scheduling problem.

References

[1] Tang, X.Y., Li, K.L., Padua, D.: Communication contention in APN list scheduling algorithm. Science in China Series F: Information Sciences 52, 59–69 (2009)

[2] Kwok, Y., Ahmad, I.: Link Contention-Constrained Scheduling and Mapping of Tasks and Messages to a Network of Heterogeneous Processors. Cluster Computing, 113–124 (2000)

[3] Yoo, M., Gen, M.: Scheduling algorithm for real-time tasks using multiobjective hybrid genetic algorithm in heterogeneous multiprocessors system. The Journal of Computers & Operations Research 34, 3084–3098 (2007)

[4] Wang, X.-J., Zhang, C.-Y., Gao, L., Li, P.-G.: A survey and future trend of study on multi-objective scheduling. In: IEEE Fourth International Conference on Natural Computation (2008)

[5] Sinnen, O.: Task scheduling for parallel systems. JohnWiley & Sons-Interscience, Hoboken (2007)

[6] Sinnen, O., Sousa, L.A., Sandnes, F.E.: Toward a realistic task scheduling model. IEEE Trans. Parallel and Distributed Systems 17, 263–275 (2006)

[7] Cheng, S.-C., Shiau, D.-F., Huang, Y.-M., Lin, Y.-T.: Dynamic hard-real-time scheduling using genetic algorithm for multiprocessor task with resource and timing constraints. Expert Systems with Applications 36, 852–860 (2009)

[8] Yoo, M.: Real-time task scheduling by multiobjective genetic algorithm. Systems & Software 82, 619–628 (2009)

[9] Shin, K., Cha, M., Jang, M., Jung, J., Yoon, W., Choi, S.: Task scheduling algorithm using minimized duplications in homogeneous systems. Parallel and Distributed Computing 68, 1146–1156 (2008)

[10] Kwok, Y.K., Ahmad, I.: Benchmarking and comparison of the task graph scheduling algorithms. Parallel and Distributed Computing 59, 381–422 (1999)

[11] Alkaya, A.F., Topcuoglu, H.R.: A task scheduling algorithm for arbitrarily-connected processors with awareness of link contention. Cluster Computing 9, 417–431 (2006)

[12] Page, A.J., Naughton, T.J.: Dynamic task scheduling using genetic algorithms for heterogeneous distributed computing. In: Proceedings of the 19th IEEE International Parallel and Distributed Processing Symposium, IPDPS 2005 (2005)

[13] Guliashki, V., Toshev, H., Korsemov, C.: Survey of Evolutionary Algorithms Used in Multiobjective Optimization. Bulgarian Academy of Sciences (2009)

[14] Oliver, I.M., Smith, D.J., Holland, J.: A study of permutation crossover operators on the traveling salesman problem. In: Second International Conference on Genetic Algorithms on Genetic algorithms and their application, pp. 224–230. Lawrence Erlbaum Associates, inc., Mahwah (1987)

[15] Zomaya, A.Y., Teh, Y.-H.: Observations on Using Genetic Algorithms for Dynamic Load-Balancing. IEEE Trans. Parallel and Distributed Systems 12, 899–911 (2001)

[16] Cormen, T.H., Leiserson, C.E., Rivest, R.L., Stein, C.: Introduction to Algorithms, 2nd edn. The MIT Press, Cambridge (2001)

[17] Al-Sharaeh, S., Wells, B.E.: A Comparison of Heuristics for List Schedules using The Box-method and P-method for Random Digraph Generation. In: Proceedings of the 28th Southeastern Symposium on System Theory, pp. 467–471 (1996)

Job Scheduling Techniques for Distributed Systems with Temporal Constraints

Ping-Yi Lin[1] and Pangfeng Liu[1,2]

[1] Department of Computer Science and Information Engineering
National Taiwan University
[2] Graduate Institute of Networking and Multimedia, National Taiwan University
pangfeng@csie.ntu.edu.tw

Abstract. Advance reservation of resources imporves quality-of-service by assuring the availability of resources at a future time. However, it tends to fragment the available resources time and may lead to poor system utilization. This paper proposes new job scheduling techniques to address this temporal fragmentation problem. The goal is to schedule jobs with dependency to processors whose available times are fragmented into non-continuous time slots. We propose a greedy algorithm to find the optimal schedule for jobs with single chain dependency. We also propose a dynamic programming algorithm to find the optimal schedule for jobs with multiple-chain dependency. In order to reduce scheduling time, we also propose three efficient heuristic algorithms. Experimental results indicate that these heuristics are scalable and can find near optimal solutions.

1 Introduction

Advance reservation of resources improves quality-of-service by assuring the availability of resources at a future time. However, it tends to fragment the available resources time and may lead to poor system utilization. Jobs that are too long for the current available time slots will have to wait for a longer time slot later, therefore the system utilization may suffer and the total execution time may prolong. As a result we should take special consideration while scheduling jobs for systems that support advance reservation policy.

One should also consider autonomous site policy while scheduling jobs for grid systems. A grid system usually consists of autonomous sites, and each of them may have its own *management policy*. One important principle of grid system is *not* to interfere with local site policy. For example, a site may determine that it will only provide CPU time at night and reserve CPU during office hours for local users. The global grid scheduling must respect this local policy in order to maintain an integrated image of grid service.

Advance reservation and grid site local policy will fragment available time of grid services, and this causes *temporal constraints*. This paper focuses on this temporal constraint, by which we mean the available time of resource is *not* continuous in time domain. Rather, there are time slots that we cannot utilize

R.-S. Chang et al. (Eds.): GPC 2010, LNCS 6104, pp. 280–289, 2010.

due to advance reservation or local policy. As a result our scheduling algorithm must consider temporal constraint and develop new algorithm without assuming that the resource is available at all time.

This paper focuses on jobs with linear dependency. In other words, a group of jobs is scheduled to run and the i-th job cannot start until the $i - 1$-th job finishes. This linear dependency follows the logical consequence of the computation. For example, a computation phase cannot start until the preprocessing finishes, or the data cannot be rendered visually until all the objects are given the correct locations. The scheduling problem for linear dependency jobs is hard even without temporal constraints on processors – it is shown to be NP-complete by the work of Du et al. [7].

We propose new scheduling techniques for linear-dependent jobs under resource temporal constraint. First, we propose a greedy algorithm to find the optimal schedule for jobs with a *single* chain dependency. Next, we propose a dynamic programming algorithm to find the optimal schedule for jobs with multiple-chain dependency. In order to reduce scheduling time, we also propose three efficient heuristic algorithms. Experimental results indicate that these heuristics are scalable and find near optimal schedules.

The rest of the paper is organized as follows. Section 2 reviews related works on scheduling problems under other job dependency constraints, and works under temporal constraints on processor clusters. Section 3 describes our system model in details. Section 4 and Section 5 describes our dynamic programming algorithm and heuristic algorithms for the scheduling problem. Section 6 reports our experimental results. Section 7 gives concluding remarks and discusses possible future works.

2   Related Works

Scheduling job for execution on parallel and distributed systems has been studied for years and proven to be a very difficult problem. General scheduling problems on multi-processor system have been shown to be NP-complete [14]. Even if there are only two processors with identical computing capacity and no data dependency between jobs, the problem remains NP-complete [8]. Du et. al. [7] proves that even for two processors with the same capacity, the scheduling problem remains NP-hard. Many heuristic algorithms have been proposed to achieve better performance for scheduling independent tasks in heterogeneous distributed systems. Braun et. al. [2] compares the results of eleven different heuristic algorithms for this problem under identical system assumption.

Resource management policy is very important in meeting QoS requirement of users and achieving better performance when scheduling jobs on a parallel and distributed system. For example, *advance reservation* of resources is a mechanism that has been studied in [1,9,12,13]. Previous works [10,15] also give theoretical proofs that advance reservations indeed improves the performance predictability. However advance reservation does not scale well in these previous works. Castillo et al. [4,5] propose computational geometry based scheduling algorithm to solve the scalability problem. Singh et al. [11] also propose a multi-objective genetic algorithm formulation for selecting the set of resources that optimizes the application performance while minimizing the resource costs.

Most works mentioned above focus on scheduling of *independent* jobs. However, workflow applications have become popular in recent years. A workflow application can be represented as a directed acyclic graph (DAG), where the nodes represent individual jobs and the edges represent job dependencies. The challenge of scheduling workflow applications is discussed in [6], and several heuristics have been proposed and summarized in [16]. There are also results considering special cases of workflow applications. For example, Kubiak [3] provides the NP-hard proof of tree-like precedence constraints on jobs with two servers having different capacity, and proposes an approximation algorithm for the scheduling problem.

In this paper, we consider scheduling jobs with *multiple* linear dependency in a Grid system with time constraint on the resources. We consider both the temporal constraints on servers and the linear dependency among jobs, and propose a dynamic programming technique to find the optimal schedule. To further reduce scheduling time, we also propose three efficient heuristic algorithms that find near optimal schedules.

3   Problem Description

A Grid system G is defined as follow. G has m processors $p_1, \ldots, p_m$ with homogeneous processing capabilities. The available time of processors is fragmented, and we use *available* periods to denote time periods during which a processor can run jobs. We use I to denote the set of available periods, and each element $I_{i,j}$ in I indicates the j-th available periods on processor p_i. Each $I_{i,j}$ is a two-parameter tuple $(s_{i,j}, e_{i,j})$, where $s_{i,j}$ is the *starting time* of the available period, and $e_{i,j}$ is the *ending time* of the available period.

The system has n *job chains* $H_1, \ldots, H_n$. A job chain $H_i = \{J_{i,1}, \ldots, J_{i,h_i}\}$ is a chain of jobs that follows linear dependency, where h_i is the number of jobs in job chain H_i, and $J_{i,k}$ is the k-th job within job chain H_i. The linear dependency mandates that $J_{i,j}$ cannot start until $J_{i,j-1}$ finishes. We also use $t_{i,j}$ to denote the execution time of job $J_{i,j}$. The system does not allow preemption; therefore, once a job starts on a processor, its execution will not be interrupted.

3.1   Schedule

A scheduler assigns jobs to processors without violating *temporal constraints* on processors and *linear dependency* on jobs. That is, we can only run a job during the available periods of a processor and we can only do so after we have finished its predecessor in the job chain. The scheduler must determine a *schedule S* that maps jobs to processors in their available time. The goal is to determine a schedule that minimizes the total makespan, i.e., the time for the last job to finish.

When there is only one job chain H_1, we can use a simple greedy algorithm to obtain the optimal schedule. Next, we consider more general job dependency workflow such as tree. We prove that, if the job dependency forms a tree and the processors have temporal constraints, the scheduling problem is NP-complete (Theorem 1).

Theorem 1. *The scheduling problem for jobs with tree dependency and processors with temporal constraint is NP-complete.*

Proof. We prove the NP-completeness of the scheduling problem by reducing the 2-partition problem to this scheduling problem. A problem instance I from the 2-partition problem has k numbers $n_1, \ldots, n_k$, and we would like to know whether it is possible to partition the numbers into two groups of equal sum. That is, each group has a sum $\frac{\sum_{i=1}^{k} n_i}{2} = B$.

Given a problem instance of 2-partition, we construct an instance of our scheduling problem as follows. We construct a skewed binary tree of $2k$ nodes. This tree consists of main "chain" of k jobs, each with execution time 1. These jobs will be denoted as *light* jobs. From each of the light job we grow a *heavy* job of execution time mn_i, where $m > k$.

We would like to schedule these jobs into two processors – server 1 and server 2. Server 2 has two available time – $(0, k)$ and $(mB, 2mB)$, and server 1 has only one available time $(mB, 2mB)$. Recall that $B = \frac{\sum_{i=1}^{k} n_i}{2}$, which is half of the sum of n_i in the 2-partition problem instance I. We would like to know whether the jobs can finish before time $2mB$, and we will refer to this problem instance as I'.

It is easy to see that if there is a solution for the 2-partition problem instance I, then there is a solution for our scheduling problem instance I'. All the light jobs on the main chain will be assigned to server 2. The available time $(0, k)$ is sufficient because there are k light jobs and each of them has execution time 1. The heavy jobs that grow out of the main chain will be assigned to either server 1 or 2, according to the solution from the 2-partition problem instance I. Since the solution of I partitions the numbers into two groups, each having a sum B, the heavy jobs will fit into the two available time slots.

Now we need to show that if there is a solution for I' then there is a solution for I. We first observe that no heavy job can fit into the first available time interval $(0, k)$ since $m > k$, so the first interval has all the light jobs. That also means all the heavy jobs must go into the two $(mB, 2mB)$ available time intervals. We also observe that there will be no precedence constraints among heavy jobs, since all the light jobs finish before time $mB > k$. Therefore, we can consider heavy jobs as independent. Also, since the sum of the lengths of the two intervals is exactly the total heavy job execution time, they must be precisely packed into these two intervals. Consequently, we can use the mapping from heavy jobs to processors as a solution to I. The theorem follows.

The other frequently occuring workflow patterns include multiple linear chains and serial-parallel graph. In the rest of the paper, we will focus on these two workflow patterns. It has been shown that when there are multiple job chains, the scheduling problem is NP-complete [7]. We propose a dynamic programming algorithm to find the optimal schedule. To reduce scheduling time, we also propose three efficient heuristic algorihtms to find near optimal solutions. We also show that the dynamic programming can be generalized to schedule jobs to heterogeneous processors. It can also be generalized to handle serial-parallel graph types of dependency.

4   Scheduling with Dynamic Programming

The dynamic programming schedules jobs in phases. In each phase, the algorithm chooses one job and adds it into the "partial" schedule of this phase. For ease of explanation, we use the *current schedule* to denote the partial schedule at current scheduling step.

We define *ready time* for a job chain, and *ready time sequence* for a set of job chains. The ready time of a job chain H_1, denoted by R_{H_1}, is the completion time of the last job being processed in a job chain. The ready time sequence of the set of job chains is the sequence of ready time of all job chains in that set, and is denoted as $R_H = (R_{H_1}, \ldots, R_{H_n})$. Note that the ready time and ready time sequence are defined over the current schedule, and will change after a new job is added into the current schedule in every phase.

We define *last completion time* of a processor and *last completion time sequence* for all processors. The last completion time of a processors p is the completion time of the last job assigned to p, and is denoted as L_p. Similarly, we can define *last completion time sequence* as the sequence of the last completion time of all processors, which is denoted as $L_G = (L_{p_1}, \ldots, L_{p_m})$. Note that if we assign job $J_{i,j}$ to processor p_k in the current phase, both the ready time of job chain H_i and the last completion time of processor p_k will be updated to the completion time of job $J_{i,j}$. Finally we define the *finished job* vector for job chains. Let $U = (u_1, \ldots, u_n)$ be a finished job vector such that u_i is the numbers of *finished* jobs in job chain H_i.

Let L_G be a last completion time sequence for a grid system G and R_H be a ready time sequence for a job chain set H, and U be a finished job vector. We define $E(L_G, R_H, U)$ to be the *minimum* makespan for a last completion time sequence L_G and ready time sequence R_H, and a finished job vector U. By definition the optimal makespan of a given job chain set H for a processor set G is $E((0, \ldots, 0), (0, \ldots, 0), (0, \ldots, 0))$.

We now describe how to update a last completion time sequence L_G and a ready time sequence R_H when we schedule a new job $J_{i,j}$ to processor p_k. First we note that only L_{p_k} in L_G and R_{H_i} in R_H need to be updated, i.e., the completion time corresponding to processor p_k in L_G and the ready time corresponding to job $J_{i,j}$ in job chain H_i. The new value for both L_{p_k} and R_{H_i} is the completion time of $J_{i,j}$, which can be determined by assigning $J_{i,j}$ to the *first* available time slot period, i.e. minimum l, such that the time slot $I_{k,l}$ on p_k satisfies the condition that $e_{k,l} - t_{i,j} \geq \max(s_{k,l}, L_{p_k}, R_{H_i})$. Recall that

$e_{k,l}$ and $s_{k,l}$ are the starting and ending time of time slot $I_{k,l}$. Formally we use $x(L_{p_k}, R_{H_i}, J_{i,j})$ to denote this minimum index l for time slots on processor k.

$$x(L_{p_k}, R_{H_i}, J_{i,j}) = \min\{l | e_{k,l} - t_{i,j} \geq \max(s_{k,l}, L_{p_k}, R_{H_i})\} \quad (1)$$

After assigning a job of a job chain to a time slot of a processor we need to update the last completion time of that processor and the ready time of that job chain. Formally after assigning job $J_{i,j}$ to time slot $I_{k,l}$ on processor p_k we update the last completion time L_{p_k} for p_k and the ready time R_{H_i} for job chain H_i. For ease of notation we use l^* to denote the time slot index $x(L_{p_k}, R_{H_i}, J_{i,j})$ from Equation 1. Then the starting time of $J_{i,j}$ will be $\max(s_{k,l^*}, L_{p_k}, R_{H_i})$, and the processing time $t_{i,j}$, the completion time of $J_{i,j}$ will be $\max(s_{k,l^*}, L_{p_k}, R_{H_i}) + t_{i,j}$. Therefore, we update both L_{p_k} and R_{H_i} to $\max(s_{k,l^*}, L_{p_k}, R_{H_i}) + t_{i,j}$.

We now use a function $T(L_G, R_H, J_{i,j}, p_k) = (L'_G, R'_H)$ to describe the new last completion time and the new ready time after we assign $J_{i,j}$ to a processor p_k based on the old last completion time sequence L_G and the old ready time sequence R_H. That is, L_G and R_H are the last completion time sequence and the ready time sequence before the scheduling, and L'_G and R'_H are ones after the scheduling respectively. L'_G and R'_H can be computed as follows.

$$l^* = \min\{l | e_{k,l} - t_{i,j} \geq \max(s_{k,l}, L_{p_k}, R_{H_i})\} \quad (2)$$

$$L'_{p_v} = \begin{cases} L_{p_v}, & \text{if } v \neq k \\ \max(s_{k,l^*}, L_{p_k}, R_{H_i}) + t_{i,j}, & \text{if } v = k \end{cases} \quad (3)$$

$$R'_{H_v} = \begin{cases} R_{H_v}, & \text{if } v \neq i \\ \max(s_{k,l^*}, L_{p_k}, R_{H_i}) + t_{i,j}, & \text{if } v = i \end{cases} \quad (4)$$

Now we describe how to update the finished job vector U after assigning a new job to a time slot. Note that in each round, we can only choose the first remaining job in each chain to execute because of the linear dependency, i.e., jobs $J_{1,u_1+1}, \ldots, J_{n,u_n+1}$. Therefore, we define an increase-by-1 function $Q(U, e) = (u'_1, \ldots, u'_n)$ as follows.

$$Q(U, e) = (u'_1, \ldots, u'_n) \quad (5)$$

$$u'_i = u_i, \quad \text{if } i \neq e \quad (6)$$

$$u'_i = u_i + 1, \quad \text{if } i = e \quad (7)$$

Next, the recursive formula for the optimal makespan function $E(L_G, R_H, U)$ can be defined as in Equation 8. We consider the first remaining job of all job chains and all processors p_k in G, assign the job to the processor, and choose one that results in minimum makespan.

$$E(L_G, R_H, U) = \min_{p_k \in G} \min_i E(T(L_G, R_H, J_{i,j}, p_k), Q(U, j)), \quad \text{s.t. } j = u_i + 1 < h_i$$
$$(8)$$

The terminal condition for $E(L_G, R_H, H)$ is when all jobs are scheduled. Formally we have $u_i = h_i, 1 \leq i \leq n$, which means the number of finished jobs is equal to the number of jobs in a job chain. In these cases the makespan is the maximum ready time within the ready time sequence R_H. Note that this maximum ready time is also equal to the maximum last completion time within the last completion time sequence L_G.

$$E(L_G, R_H, (h_1, \ldots, h_n)) = \max_{i \leq n} R_{H_i} = \max_{k \leq m} L_{p_k} \tag{9}$$

5   Scheduling with Heuristic Algorithms

Although dynamic programming can find the optimal solution, its time complexity is high. To reduce scheduling time, we propose two classes of heuristic algorithms: (1) *chain ordering heuristic* and (2) *longest job first heuristic*.

5.1   The Chain Ordering Heuristic

The chain ordering heuristic is a greedy heuristic that schedules one job chain at a time according to a particular order. The order is determined by the measuring function of scheduling. In this paper we consider two measuring functions – *average execution time* and *makespan*.

Average Execution Time. We use *average execution time* (denoted by a_i) of job chains to determine the scheduling order among job chains. The average execution time of a job chain is the average execution time of jobs within this job chain, i.e., $a_i = \frac{\sum_{j=1}^{h_i} t_{i,j}}{h_i}$. We sort the average execution time a_i in *descending* order, and schedule one job chain onto processors in each iteration using the earliest completion time first algorithm describing in Section 3.

We think scheduling job chains in descending average execution time might reduce the makespan for the following reasons. If we assign jobs with smaller average execution time first, we tend to delay the execution of some long jobs. Those long jobs can easily become the bottleneck of their job chains. If we schedule long jobs first we might have more options to place them, and it is more likely to find suitable and earlier time slots for them, hence reducing the makespan.

Expected Makespan. We can use *expected makespan* of job chains to decide the scheduling order among them. The expected makespan of a job chain is the makespan that we assume that the system only has the current job chain to schedule, and all processors are available. The optimal makespan can be calculated using the greedy method we described for one job chain case in Section 3.1. After we determine the job chain order we then schedule job chains by *increasing* makespan order.

5.2   Longest Job First Heuristic

The two heuristics described earlier are easy to implement, but do not perform well in some special cases. For example, if a job chain H_1 has a long job $J_{1,j}$

and many short jobs, and another job chain H_2 has jobs that have nearly the same execution time, and the average execution time a_1 is smaller than a_2. The average execution time heuristic in Section 5.1 will schedule H_2 first. However, the long job $J_{1,j}$ will be the bottleneck of its chain, and this may cause average execution time heuristic not perform well under this situation.

To handle such special cases we propose *longest job first heuristic* that schedules one job at a time, instead of one job chain at a time. In every iteration we choose the job with the longest processing time from the next jobs of all job chains, and assign it to the processor with earliest completion time. By choosing one job at a time, we make decision based on each job, rather than on job chains. The intuition is that we might handle special cases well because we are not required to schedule the entire chain.

6   Experiments

The setting of the number of jobs chains and processors in our experiment is as follows. We consider two cases of job chains and processors. In the first case we have 2 processors and 3 job chains, and in the second case we have 3 processors and 2 job chains. In the first case job chains compete the available time slots more often than in the second case.

Other parameters in our experiments are described as follows. In the first case the number of jobs per job chain is from 1 to 5. In the second case, the number of jobs per job chain is from 3 to 8. The length of available time slots and the gaps between two time slots are randomly chosen in the range of 1 to 50. Therefore the processors are available about half of time. The execution time of job is randomly chosen in the range of 1 to 40. We run the experiment for 100 times for each parameter set, and calculate the average results.

We now compare the performance of different heuristics, using the optimal solution from the dynamic programming as a base. We use *relative makespan* as the measurement of performance. The relative makespan from a heuristic is the makespan divided by the optimal makespan from the dynamic programming. The relative makespans are shown in Figure 1.

In Figure 1 we compare the relative makespan from three heuristics when we have 2 processors and 3 job chains. The heuristics are chain-ordering using average execution (*order-avg*), chain-ordering using expected makespan (*order-mk*), and longest job first (*LJF*) described in Section 5.1, Section 5.1, and Section 5.2. First we find that the relative makespans of all heuristics are no more than 1.25 for any number of jobs per chain. Second, we find that longest job first heuristic outperforms the other two heuristics. That is because the longest job first heuristic considers one job at a time job so that the scheduling is more flexible in choosing jobs.

In Figure 1 we compare the relative makespan from the three heuristics when we have 3 processors and 2 job chains. Job chains now do not need to compete for the available periods as often as in the previous case, therefore we observe that all three relative makespan are now reduced to be less than 1.2. We also find

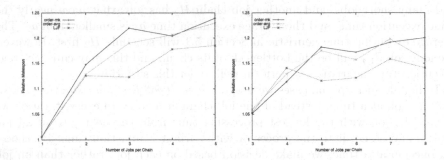

Fig. 1. Relative makespan for 2 servers and 3 chains (on the left), and 3 servers and 2 chains (on the right)

that the relative makespans of the three heuristics now become closer to each other. Nevertheless the longest job first heuristic still has the best performance.

7   Conclusion

This paper proposes novel techniques for scheduling jobs with dependency constraint to processors whose available time are fragmented into time slots. We discuss two job dependency patterns – tree and chains. We show that it is NP-complete to schedule jobs with a tree dependency pattern. For linear chains, we propose a dynamic programming algorithm to find the optimal schedule. We also show that the dynamic programming can be generalized to schedule jobs to heterogeneous processors and to schedule multiple job chains as well as jobs with serial-parallel graph types of dependency. Furthermore, in order to reduce the scheduling time, we also propose three heuristic algorithms. Experimental results indicate that these heuristics produce near optimal schedules.

We are investigating a more precise analysis on the hardness of the scheduling jobs with linear dependency, since at this moment we do not have a NP-complete proof, or a polynomial time algorithm. We also plan to generalize our linear dependency dynamic programming to a broader class of workflow patterns.

References

1. Al-ali, R.J., Amin, K., Laszewski, G., Rana, O.F., Walker, D.W., Hategan, M., Zaluzec, N.: Analysis and provision of qos for distributed grid applications. Journal of Grid Computing 2(2), 163–182 (2004)
2. Braun, T., Siegel, H., Beck, N., Boloni, L., Maheswaran, M., Reuther, A., Robertson, J., Theys, M., Yao, B., Hensgen, D., Freund, R.: A comparison of eleven static heuristics for mapping a class of independent tasks onto heterogeneous distributed computing systems. Journal of Parallel and Distributed Computing 61(6), 810–837 (2001)
3. Brucker, P.: Scheduling Algorithms. Springer, Heidelberg (2007)

4. Castillo, C., Rouskas, G., Harfoush, K.: On the design of online scheduling algorithms for advance reservations and qos in grids. In: Proceedings of IEEE International on Parallel and Distributed Processing Symposium, IPDPS 2007, pp. 1–10 (2007)
5. Castillo, C., Rouskas, G., Harfoush, K.: Efficient resource management using advance reservations for heterogeneous grids. In: Proceedings of IEEE International Symposium on Parallel and Distributed Processing, IPDPS 2008, pp. 1–12 (2008)
6. Dail, H., Sievert, O., Berman, F., Casanova, H., Yarkhan, A., Vadhiyar, S., Dongarra, J., Liu, C., Yang, L., Angulo, D., Foster, I.: Scheduling in the grid application development software project (2003)
7. Du, J., Leung, J.Y.T., Young, G.H.: Scheduling chain-structured tasks to minimize makespan and mean flow time. Information and Computation 92(2), 219–236 (1991)
8. Garey, M., Johnson, D.: Computers and Intractability: A Guide to the Theory of NP-Completeness. WH Freeman and Co., New York (1979)
9. Krauter, K., Buyya, R., Maheswaran, M.: A taxonomy and survey of grid resource management systems. Software Practice and Experience 32, 135–164 (2002)
10. Mcgough, A.S., Afzal, A., Darlington, J., Furmento, N., Mayer, A., Young, L.: Making the grid predictable through reservations and performance modelling. The Computer Journal 48(3), 358–368 (2005)
11. Singh, G., Kesselman, C., Deelman, E.: A provisioning model and its comparison with best-effort for performance-cost optimization in grids. In: HPDC 2007: Proceedings of the 16th international symposium on High performance distributed computing, pp. 117–126. ACM, New York (2007)
12. Smith, W., Foster, I., Taylor, V.: Scheduling with advanced reservations. In: Proceedings of IPDPS 2000, pp. 127–132 (2000)
13. Sulistio, A., Buyya, R.: A grid simulation infrastructure supporting advance reservation (2004)
14. Ullman, J.D.: Np-complete scheduling problems. Journal of Computer and System Sciences 10(3), 384–393 (1975)
15. Wieczorek, M., Siddiqui, M., Villazon, A., Prodan, R., Fahringer, T.: Applying advance reservation to increase predictability of workflow execution on the grid. In: Proceedings of Second IEEE International Conference on e-Science and Grid Computing, e-Science 2006, p. 82 (2006)
16. Yu, J., Buyya, R., Ramamohanarao, K.: Workflow scheduling algorithms for grid computing. Studies in Computational Intelligence. Springer, Heidelberg (2008)

Replica-Aware Job Scheduling in Distributed Systems

Wei-Cheng Liao[1] and Jan-Jan Wu[2,3]

[1] Department of Computer Science and Information Engineering
National Taiwan University
[2] Institute of Information Science, Academia Sinica
[3] Research Center for Information Technology Innovation, Academia Sinica
wuj@iis.sinica.edu.tw

Abstract. This paper proposes an effective replica-aware scheduling algorithm for independent jobs in Grid and distributed systems. The proposed algorithm considers not only the execution time of jobs but also the location and transfer time of data and data replica that these jobs require. We propose a cost model to estimate the starting time and earliest completion time of a job and its associated data (original or replicated). Based on the estimated time, the scheduling algorithm finds a proper execution sequence for the jobs and the data with the goal to minimize the makespan of the jobs. Our experiment results demonstrate that the proposed algorithm is scalable and outperforms a random job selection strategy. We also show that the proposed algorithm performs well compared to a conservative theoretical lower bound, with performance within 15% of the lower bound on average and within 40% in the worst case.

1 Introduction

There are many grid applications that solve various problems in different research areas, and almost all of them require input data to find the final solutions. The computation cannot proceed without the required data. Furthermore, Grid systems are often built across the wide area network. Thus, the communication latencies between sites are usually high. High communication latencies have significant impact on the efficiency of data transfer. To improve the efficiency of data transfer, replication is a widely used technique.

In this paper, we study the task scheduling problem in heterogeneous distributed systems that provide data replication. General scheduling problems on multi-processor system has been shown to be NP-complete [1]. Even if there are only two processors with identical computing capacity and jobs do not share data, the problem remains NP-complete because it is a special case of the 2-Partition problem [2].

Most applications deployed in grid systems require input data [3,4], and these applications may submit a large number of tasks into the grid continuously. Since independent jobs may share common data files, many heuristic algorithms

R.-S. Chang et al. (Eds.): GPC 2010, LNCS 6104, pp. 290–299, 2010.
© Springer-Verlag Berlin Heidelberg 2010

have been proposed to address the issues of data or file sharing. Casanova, et. al. proposed heuristic algorithms to take advantage of file sharing in order to achieve better performance [5,6]. These works achieve good performance via file sharing, but the performance gain may be further improved by the use of replication. We believe that an integrated strategy that consider scheduling and replication simultaneously will provide a good opportunity for improving system performance.

There have been works that integrate scheduling and replication in order to improve system performance [7,8,9,10]. Ranganathan and Foster combined scheduling and replication strategy by using a two-stage scheduling that combines an external scheduler and a dataset scheduler. However they only address the issue of single file dependency [7]. Chakrabarti, et. al. extend the data sharing model to deal with multiple data requirement [8]. Tang, et. al. proposed both centralized and distributed heuristic algorithms for dynamic replication, and combine them with job scheduling algorithm to solve on-line scheduling problem [9]. Desprez and Vernois propose a linear programming technique for shared data scheduling [10]. The integrated strategies mentioned above require explicit replication services to monitoring the replication status of the system periodically so as to re-replicate data items whenever necessary in order to avoid communication contention on a single node. In addition, these works do not utilize the existing replicas that have been generated from previous execution of tasks.

In this paper, we propose an effective replica-aware scheduling algorithm for executing independent jobs in Grid and distributed systems. The proposed algorithm considers not only the execution time of jobs but also the location and transfer time of data and data replica that these jobs require. We propose a cost model to estimate the starting time and earliest completion time of a job and its associated data (original or replicated). Based on the estimated time, the scheduling algorithm finds a proper execution sequence for the jobs and the data with the goal to minimize the makespan of the jobs. Our experiment results demonstrate that the proposed algorithm is scalable and outperforms a random job selection strategy. We also show that the proposed algorithm performs well compared to a conservative theoretical lower bound, with performance within 15% of the lower bound on average and within 40% in the worst case.

The rest of the paper is organized as follows. In Section 2, we describe our system model. Section 3 describes our scheduling algorithm. Section 4 reports our experiment results. Finally, Section 5 gives some concluding remarks and discuss possible future work.

2 System Model

We now describe our Grid system model for the replica-aware shared-data scheduling problem. The Grid system consists of computing nodes, and each node has direct links to all the other nodes in the system. That is, the link connection within a Grid system is a complete graph $G = (V, E)$, where a node $v \in V$ is a computing node and an edge $e = (u, v) \in E$ is a link between node u and node v. The system is heterogeneous so that both the computing capabilities of nodes and the latencies of communication links may be different. We denote the computing capability of a node v as $|v|$, and the latency of link (u, v) as $|(u, v)|$.

2.1   Computation

Initially a set of independent jobs are submitted into the system. Our system model assumes that a computing node executes jobs one at a time and the execution is non-preemptive. Formally we use J_v to denote the *job execution sequence* of node v, which initially has all the jobs assigned to node v for execution. Node v will execute the first job in J_v, then remove it from J_v when the execution finishes. That is, a job j must wait for the other jobs that are in front of it in J_v to finish before it can start. Let $|j|$ denote the amount of computation of job j. Recall that $|v|$ is the computation power of node v, so the time for node v to execute job j can be defined as $\frac{|j|}{|v|}$.

In addition to waiting for other jobs assigned to the same node, a job must also wait for the data in order to proceed. Let D_j denote the data required by job j, then D_j must be available for node v before v can start executing j. Therefore, we define that a job j is *ready* at node v if all data in D_j are available at v and j is now at the *head* of execution sequence J_v. After the execution, j will be removed from J_v so that the next job in J_v can become ready. In the following we will describe the communication mechanism that node v acquires all the data it needs, i.e., the set D_j for all job j in the execution sequence J_v.

2.2   Communication

We adopt the full-duplex one-port communication model in [11]. In the full-duplex one-port model, each node can simultaneously send/receive one data item to/from one of its neighbors. Note that the sending and receiving are independent so a node can send and receive messages at the same time. We further assume that the communication is non-preemptive, i.e., a computing node cannot send another data item before the current sending operation finishes. Similarly, a node cannot receive a new data item before the current message has been completely received.

We assume that each computing node v will send data according to a *sending sequence* S_v. If a node v wants to send data d to destination node u, v can start sending only if the following are true: (1) Data item d is at the *head* of the sending sequence S_v, (2) Node v has d, i.e. it already has received d from other nodes, and (3) The destination node u of data d is not receiving data items from other sources.

Note that since we adopt the full-duplex one-port model, if the destination u is receiving data item from other nodes, v must wait until the transfer completes. The communication time for v to send data d to u by link (u, v) is defined as $|d| \times |(u, v)|$. Furthermore, we assume that all data items are originally stored in a *data warehouse*, which is a special node that provides all the data needed by jobs. We also assume that the data warehouse does not provide computation service. The size of each data item may be different, so we denote the size of data item d by $|d|$.

The system replicates data to increase the data access efficiency. The "passive" replication mechanism works as follows. A node v becomes a replica server of data d when v completes receiving a data d from other nodes. The reason is that, if node v is executing or has executed a job that requires data d, then d is already available at node v. Once node v has d, it becomes a replica server for data item d so that other nodes can request data item d from v. This "recycling" of data that were already brought into a node due to prior job execution incurs no extra communication overhead, and can certainly increase data access efficiency since the data could be obtained in neighboring nodes.

2.3   The Scheduling Problem

For every computing node v, a schedule Ψ is a collection of an execution sequence of (J_v) and a data sending sequence (S_v). Formally, we define Ψ as (J, S) where J is the set of job execution sequences of all nodes, i.e., $J = \{J_v | v \in V\}$, and $S = \{S_v | v \in V\}$ is the set of sending sequences of all nodes.

The sending sequences of data warehouse and computing nodes determine how data are propagated among nodes. A computing node will receive whatever data that is sent to it at the earliest time, and starts receiving the next data only when it completes receiving the current data. Therefore, once the sending sequences of all nodes are determined, the time for a data to arrive at a node is also determined.

After we determine the arrival time of all data at node v, we can determine the *ready time* and the *completion time* of all jobs in J_v. Recall that a job j is ready at node v if all data in D_j are available at v and j is at the head of execution queue J_v. Therefore, we can determine the ready time for the first job j in J_v since we know the arrival time of all data in D_j. Recall that $|v|$ denotes the computation power of node v, so the time for node v to execute the first job j in J_v can be defined as $\frac{|j|}{|v|}$. The completion time is therefore the sum of ready time and the execution time of j, and we can determine the ready time and the completion time from the first to the last job in J_v. The completion time of the last job in J_v is the *complete time* of node v. The maximum completion time of all nodes is the *total completion time*.

We consider the following problem in this paper. Given a Grid system $G = (V, E)$, a set of jobs J and a set of data D, find a schedule $\Psi = (J, S)$ that minimizes the total completion time, where $J = \{J_v | v \in V\}$ and $S = \{S_v | v \in V\}$ are the sets of execution and sending sequences of nodes in V respectively.

3   Replica-Aware Scheduling Algorithm

Our scheduling algorithm is based on a greedy heuristic. The proposed greedy heuristic assigns jobs to computing nodes iteratively until all jobs are assigned.

Each iteration of the heuristic algorithm contains two phases. The first phase is the *selection* phase and the second phase is the *assignment* phase. In the selection phase the heuristic algorithm evaluates each remaining job, and selects the job that can finish at the earliest time to run for this iteration. The evaluation uses a Earliest-Completion-First heuristic to collect data for the current job in order to estimate the completion time, so that it can determines a data sending sequence for each computing node. Finally, the algorithm assigns the chosen job j to a computing node that can complete j at the earliest possible time.

At the assignment phase, the algorithm incrementally updates the schedule according to the assignment made for this iteration. Formally we use Ψ_k to denote the schedule at the end of the k-th iteration, and the algorithm will update Ψ_k into Ψ_{k+1} during the k-th iteration. Initially all job execution and data sending sequences in Ψ_0 are empty sequences, which indicates that no job execution or data sending have been scheduled. Then in every iteration the heuristic algorithm will schedule a job and concatenate it to the execution sequence where the job is schedule to run, and schedule the associated data transfers and concatenate them in the data sending sequences of the data senders. Eventually, the assignment phase results in a final schedule that contains all the jobs and data.

3.1   Evaluation of Completion Time of Jobs

In this section we describe how to evaluate remaining jobs in order to determine the next job to execute, and how to update the sending and receiving sequences after a job is assigned at each iteration. In the rest of this section we assume that we are now at the k-th iteration unless specified otherwise.

As mentioned in Section 2.3, we can use a given schedule to estimate the job completion time and data arrival time on each node. As a result we use $C_j(j,v)$ to denote the completion time of job j on node v, and $C_r(d,v)$ for the arrival time of data item d on node v, and $C_s(d,v,u)$ for the time node v completes sending d to node u. Note that we can determine these values when given the job execution and data sending sequence in Ψ_{k-1}.

For ease of presentation, we use j_v to denote the last job on node v, r_v as the last receiving data item, and s_v as the last sending data item on node v. Also note that these are all *current* values so that once a new job or data is scheduled, they will refer to the most up-to-date "last" job or data. Other notations that will be used in our algorithm are listed in Table 1.

Estimated Finish Time. In the selection phase the heuristic algorithm evaluates each job according to its minimum *estimated finish time*. The estimated finish time of job j at node v is defined as its *estimated ready time* at node v plus the execution time $\frac{|j|}{|v|}$. The minimum estimated finish time of a job j is the minimum among all estimated finish times of j at every computing nodes in the grid system.

Estimated ready time of a job j. We now define the *estimated ready time* of a job j on a node v. Recall that job j is ready at node v, as mentioned in Section 2,

Table 1. Additional notations used in describing the heuristic algorithm

Notation	Description
D_v	data items stored in the local storage of node v
D_j^v	data items required by j and already at v
$\overline{D}_j^v$	data items required by j but not at v
Ψ_k	schedule at k-th iteration
j_v	the last job in the execution sequence of node v
r_v	the last data item that node v received
s_v	the last data item that node v sent
$C_j(j, v)$	completion time of job j on node v
$C_r(d, v)$	arrival time of data d on node v
$C_s(d, v, u)$	completion time for v to send d to u
t_d^v	estimated data available time at node v
t_j^v	estimated completion time of j at node v

when all jobs before j in the execution sequence of node v have completed, and all data items needed by j (denoted by D_j) are available at node v.

There are two conditions a job j has to wait in order to become ready at node v – the jobs before j completes execution and the data set D_j is available at v. Recall that j_v is the current *last* job at node v, and its completion time is $C_j(j_v, v)$. If we could estimate when data items in D_j will be available at v, then we can estimate when j can start. Formally we use *estimated available time* of D_j at v to denote the earliest time all data in D_j will be available at v. It is obvious that the estimated ready time of a job j at node v is the maximum of $C_j(j_v, v)$ and the estimated available time of D_j. We now formally define the estimated available time for a data set D_j.

Estimated available time of data set D_j. We first observe that some data in D_j could have already been brought into node v, so we do not need to retrieve them, therefore in order to estimate the available times we only focus on the data that are in D_j but not current at node v. For ease of notation we partition D_j into two subsets – those that are already at v is denoted by D_j^v and those that are not is denoted by $\overline{D}_j^v$.

There are two cases to considered. First if $\overline{D}_j^v$ is an empty set then all data in D_j are already at node v. Recall that $C_r(d, v)$ is the arrival time of data item d on node v. The estimated available time of D_j at node v is the maximum $C_r(d, v)$ for all data d in D_j in this case. The second case is that when $\overline{D}_j^v$ is not empty, i.e., there are some data items that are in D_j but not in D_v. Now we need to decide an order to receive these data in $\overline{D}_j^v$ so that the data set $\overline{D}_j^v$ can be brought into v at the earliest time. This will reduce the data waiting time should we decide to assign job j to node v.

We use a Earliest-Available-Time-First heuristic to determine the order for v to receive data in $\overline{D}_j^v$. Let t_d^v denote the earliest time of $d \in \overline{D}_j^v$ at node v. For each data item $d \in \overline{D}_j^i$, we estimate the earliest time of d to be transferred into v, and choose the data d that has the minimum t_d^v to be received next.

$$t_d^v = \min_{u \in V}\{\max\{C_r(r_v, v), C_s(s_u, u, x)\} + |d| \times |(u, v)|\}. \tag{1}$$

Note that in Equation 1 we consider all possible source u that could send data d to v. The transfer from u to v could not begin until the sender u finishes sending its current last data s_u to the destination x of s_u, or the receiver v finishes receiving its current last data r_v. The transfer completes when both parties are ready, plus the transfer time of data d along the link (u, v).

Using the Earliest-Available-Time-First heuristic, we choose the data item d that has the minimum available time t_d^v and add d into the receiving sequence of v and the sending sequence of u. We repeat this selection until all data item in $\overline{D}_j^v$ are received. The data available time of data set D_j is the arrival time of the last data items in D_j arrives at node v.

Note that for every d and u we choose, we need to add d to the sending sequence of u and receiving sequence of v. This will affect the last receiving data r_v of v and last sending data s_u, so that the later choices of data to receive from $\overline{D}_j^v$ will take into consideration that the transfer of d from u to v has already been scheduled.

3.2   Job Assignment

After evaluating all estimated finish times of remaining jobs, the heuristic algorithm chooses the job and node combination that has the earliest estimated finish time. After selecting job and computing node we need to update the schedule Ψ since we have assigned a job j to a computing node v. We first append j to the job execution sequence J_v, and update the receiving sequence of v and the corresponding sending sequences of nodes that send D_j to v.

4   Experimental Results

In this section we conduct experiments to evaluate the performance of the proposed scheduling algorithm. We derive a conservative theoretical lower bound as the basis for comparison. We also implement a random job selection heuristic for the purpose of comparisons with our algorithm.

4.1   Environment Settings

The parameters in our experiments are as follows. There are 32 computing nodes, 128 data items and 512 jobs in the system. We use the notion of *reference node* and *reference link* to represent a relative performance metrics for nodes and links in our experiments. A reference node is the node with computing capacity to execute *one* unit job in *one* unit of time. Similarly, a *reference link* is the link with latency to transmit *one* unit data item in *one* unit of time. The computing

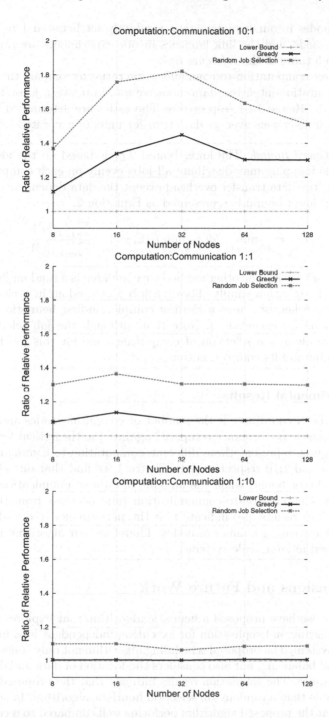

Fig. 1. The relative performance of the heuristic algorithms to the theoretical lower bound. The number of nodes is from 8 to 128.

capacity of nodes in our experiments is randomly set between 1 to 5 times of the *reference node*, and the link latencies in our experiments are randomly set between 1 to 5 times of the *reference link*.

We use three computation-to-communication ratios to compare the characteristics of computation-intensive, data-intensive and in-between jobs. The ratio is set to 10 : 1, 1 : 10 and 1 : 1 respectively. The ratios are determined by average computation units versus average data transfer units of generated jobs.

Theoretical Lower Bound. The lower bound T_{L1} is based on the idea that an ideal schedule mapping may distribute all jobs evenly on each computing node and minimize the data transfer overhead except the data dependency set of the first job. This lower bound is represented as Equation 2.

$$T_{L1} = \min_{d \in \cup_{j \in J} D_j} |d| \times \min_{u,v \in V} (|(u, v)|) + \frac{\sum_{j \in J} (|j|)}{\sum_{v \in V} (|v|)} \tag{2}$$

Random Job Selection. The other method we compared is a random job selection heuristic. This algorithm simply chooses a job j at random in each scheduling phase. Then the heuristic uses a Earliest-completion-first heuristic to select a computing node for executing j. Note that although the job selection to be executed is random, the selection of computing node for this job is carefully selected to minimize its completion time.

4.2   Experimental Results

In Figure 1 the X coordinate is the number of computing nodes and Y coordinate is the relative performance compared against the theoretical lower bound. The three figures represent three different computation-to-communication ratios, 10:1, 1:1 and 1:10 respectively. In Figure 1 we find that our algorithm is closer to the lower bound when the amount of data communication increases, i.e., when the computation-to-communication ratio decrease from 10:1, to 1:1, and to 1:10. The results also indicate that the performance of our algorithm is scalable with increasing number of nodes. Therefore, our algorithm is expected to perform well in large scale systems.

5   Conclusions and Future Work

In this paper, we have proposed a heuristic algorithm that explores the advantage of file sharing and replication for executing independent jobs in a Grid or distributed system. The proposed scheduling algorithm not only considers execution time load balancing, but also considers the location of data and data replica these jobs require. The simulation results indicate that the proposed algorithm is more scalable than a random job selection heuristic algorithm. In addition, we also show that the proposed algorithm performs well compared to a conservative theoretical lower bound, with performance within 15% of the lower bound on average and within 40% in the worst case.

While the simulation indicates efficient schedules, the overhead of the scheduler is not taken into account in this work. We believe that the scheduler itself is also very important to the overall system performance, therefore we would like to find a more efficient heuristic while maintaining the same level of scheduling quality as our current heuristic. It means we need to optimize the data allocation heuristic part, which is the most time-consuming part of our algorithm.

We also consider the possibility of integrating our heuristic into real grid systems. In our previous work, we develop a Grid file system [12], which can request a data from multiple sources and simultaneously receiving fragments of that data. We would like to extend our system model and algorithms to accommodate such "multi-source" data collection.

References

1. Ullman, J.D.: NP-complete scheduling problems. Journal of Computer and System Sciences 10(3), 384–393 (1975)
2. Garey, M., Johnson, D.: Computers and Intractability: A Guide to the Theory of NP-Completeness. WH Freeman and Co., New York (1979)
3. Casanova, H., Obertelli, G., Berman, F., Wolski, R.: The apples parameter sweep template: user-level middleware for the grid. In: Proceedings of the ACM/IEEE conference on Supercomputing, pp. 75–76 (2000)
4. Altschul, S., Gish, W., Miller, W., Myers, E., Lipman, D.: Basic local alignment search tool. Journal of Molecular Biology 215(3), 403–410 (1990)
5. Casanova, H., Legrand, A., Zagorodnov, D., Berman, F.: Using simulation to evaluate scheduling heuristics for a class of applications in grid environments. Technical Report RR-1999-46, LIP, ENS (2000)
6. Casanova, H., Legrand, A., Zagorodnov, D., Berman, F.: Heuristics for scheduling parameter sweep applications in grid environments. In: Proceedings of Heterogeneous Computing Workshop, pp. 349–363 (2000)
7. Ranganathan, K., Foster, I.: Simulation studies of computation and data scheduling algorithms for data grids. Journal of Grid Computing 1(10), 53–62 (2003)
8. Chakrabarti, A., Dheepak, R., Sengupta, S.: Integration of scheduling and replication in data grids. In: Bougé, L., Prasanna, V.K. (eds.) HiPC 2004. LNCS, vol. 3296, pp. 375–385. Springer, Heidelberg (2004)
9. Tang, M., Lee, B., Tang, X., Yeo, C.: Combining data replication algorithms and job scheduling heuristics in the data grid. In: Cunha, J.C., Medeiros, P.D. (eds.) Euro-Par 2005. LNCS, vol. 3648, pp. 381–390. Springer, Heidelberg (2005)
10. Desprez, F., Vernois, A.: Simultaneous scheduling of replication and computation for data-intensive applications on the grid. Journal of Grid Computing 4(1), 19–31 (2006)
11. Beaumont, O., Legrand, A., Marchal, L., Robert, Y.: Pipelining broadcasts on heterogeneous platforms. IEEE Transactions on Parallel and Distributed Systems 16(4), 300–313 (2005)
12. Chen, C., Hsu, C., Wu, J., Liu, P.: GFS: A distributed file system with multi-source data access and replication for grid computing. In: The 5th Workshop on Grid Technologies and Applications (2008)

Online Scheduling of Workflow Applications in Grid Environment

Chih-Chiang Hsu[1], Kuo-Chan Huang[2], and Feng-Jian Wang[1]

[1] Department of Computer Science
National Chiao Tung University
1001, University Road, Hsinchu, Taiwan
chanurnk@gmail.com, fjwang@cs.nctu.edu.tw
[2] Department of Computer and Information Science
National Taichung University
140, Min-Shen Road, Taichung, Taiwan
kchuang@mail.ntcu.edu.tw

Abstract. Scheduling workflow applications in grid environments is a great challenge, because it is an NP-complete problem. Many heuristic methods have been presented in the literature and most of them deal with a single workflow application at a time. In recent years, there are several heuristic methods proposed to deal with concurrent workflows or online workflows, but they do not work with workflows composed of data-parallel tasks. In this paper, we present an online scheduling approach for multiple mixed-parallel workflows in grid environments. The proposed approach was evaluated with a series of simulation experiments and the results show that the proposed approach delivers good performance and outperforms other methods under various workloads.

Keywords: workflow, grid, mixed-parallel, online scheduling.

1 Introduction

Grid environments are an important platform for running high-performance and distributed applications. Many large-scale scientific applications are usually constructed as workflows due to large amounts of interrelated computation and communication, e.g., Montage [12] and EMAN [11]. A Grid environment is composed of widespread resources from different administrative domains. Miguel et al. [1] indicates that a Grid environment usually has the characteristics: heterogeneity, large scale and geographical distribution. Task scheduling in Grid is a NP-complete problem [2] [10], therefore many heuristic methods have been proposed. The workflow scheduling problem in Grid environments is a great challenge. In the past years, there are many static heuristic methods proposed [3] [4] [5] [6] [7] [8] [9] [14] [18]. They are designed to schedule only one single workflow at a time.

In this paper, we present a new approach called Online Workflow Management (*OWM*) for scheduling multiple online mixed-parallel workflows. There are four

R.-S. Chang et al. (Eds.): GPC 2010, LNCS 6104, pp. 300–310, 2010.
© Springer-Verlag Berlin Heidelberg 2010

processes in *OWM*: Critical Path Workflow Scheduling (CPWS), Task Scheduling, Multi-Processor Task Rearrangement and Adaptive Allocation (AA). CPWS process submits tasks into the waiting queue. Task scheduling and AA processes prioritize the tasks in the queue and assign the task with highest priority to processors for execution respectively. In data-parallel task scheduling, there may be some scheduling holes which are formed when the free processors are not enough for the first task in the queue. The multi-processor task rearrangement process works for dealing with scheduling holes to improve utilization. Many approaches can be adopted in this process, including first fit, easy backfilling [16], and conservative backfilling [16].

To evaluate the proposed OWM, we developed a simulator using discrete-event based techniques for experiments. Task-waiting queue and event queue keep the tasks and events for processing. The grid environment is assumed to consist of several dispersed clusters, each containing a specific amount of processors. A workflow is represented by direct acyclic graph (DAG). A series of simulation experiments were conducted and the results show that *OWM* has better performance than *RANK_HYBD* [17] and *Fairness_Dynamic* based on the Fairness (F2) [19] in handling online workflows. For workflows composed of data-parallel tasks, the experimental results show that *OWM(FCFS)* performs almost equally to *OWM(conservative)*, and outperforms *OWM(easy)* and *OWM(first fit)*.

The remainder of this paper is organized as follows. Section 2 discusses related work. Section 3 presents the *OWM* approach. Section 4 presents the experiments and discusses the results. Section 5 concludes the paper.

2 Related Work

In the past years, most works dealing with workflow scheduling [3] [4] [5] [6] [7] [8] [9] [14] [18] were restricted to single workflow application. Zhao et al. [19] envisaged a scenario that need to schedule multiple workflow applications at the same time. They proposed two approaches: composition approach and fairness approach.

(1) The composition approach merges multiple workflows into a single workflow first. Then, list scheduling heuristic methods, such as HEFT [7] and HHS [18], can be used to schedule the merged workflow.

(2) The main idea of fairness approach is that when a task completes, it will re-calculate the slowdown value of each workflow against other workflows and make a decision on which workflow should be considered next.

The composition and the fairness approaches are static algorithms and not feasible to deal with online workflow applications, *i.e.* multiple workflows come at different times. RANK_HYBD [17] is designed to deal with online workflow applications submitted by different users at different times. The task scheduling approach of RANK_HYBD sorts the tasks in *waiting queue* using the following rules repeatedly.

(1) If tasks in *waiting queue* come from multiple workflows, the tasks are sorted in ascending order of their rank value ($rank_u$) where $rank_u$ is described in HEFT [7];

(2) If all tasks belong to the same workflow, the tasks are sorted in descending order of their rank value ($rank_u$).

However, the number of processors to be used by each task is limited to a single processor. It is not feasible to deal with workflows composed of data-parallel tasks. T. N'takpe' et al. proposed a scheduling approach for mixed parallel applications on Heterogeneous platforms [13]. Mixed parallelism is a combination of task parallelism and data parallelism where the former indicates that an application has more than one task that can execute concurrently and the latter means a task can run using more than one resource simultaneously.

The scheduling approach in [13] is only suitable for a single workflow. T. N'takpe' et al. further developed an approach to deal with concurrent mixed parallel applications [15]. Concurrent scheduling for mixed parallel applications contains two steps: constrained resource allocation and concurrent mapping. The former aims at finding an optimal allocation for each task. The number of processors is determined in this step. The latter prioritizes tasks of workflows. However, the approach in [15] is restricted to concurrent workflows submitted at the same time. It is infeasible to deal with online workflows submitted at different times. The OWM proposed in this paper is designed to deal with multiple online mixed-parallel workflows that previous methods cannot handle well.

3   Online Workflow Management in Grid Environments

This section presents the Online Workflow Management (OWM) approach proposed in this paper for multiple online mixed-parallel workflow applications. Figure 1 shows the structure of *OWM*. In *OWM*, there are four processes: *Critical Path Workflow Scheduling* (*CPWS*), Task Scheduling, multi-processor task rearrangement and *Adaptive Allocation* (*AA*), and three data structures: online workflows, a grid environment and a waiting queue. The processes are represented by solid boxes, and the data structures are represented by dotted boxes.

When workflows come into the system or tasks complete successfully, *CPWS*, takes the critical path in workflows into account, and submits the tasks of online workflows into the waiting queue. The task scheduling process in *OWM* adopts the RANK_HYBD method in [17]. In RANK_HYBD, the task execution order is sorted based on the length of tasks' critical path. If all tasks in the waiting queue belong to the same workflow, they are sorted in the descending order. Otherwise, the tasks in different workflows are sorted in the ascending order. In parallel task scheduling, there may be some scheduling holes which are formed when the free processors are not enough for the first task in the queue. The multi-processor task rearrangement process in *OWM* works for minimizing holes to improve utilization Several techniques might be used in the process including first fit, easy backfilling [16], and conservative backfilling [16] approaches. When there are free processors in the grid environment, *AA* takes the first task (the highest priority task) in the waiting queue, and selects the required processors to execute the task.

A task in a workflow has four states: *finished, submitted, ready* and *unready*. A *finished* task means the task has completed its execution successfully. A *submitted* task means the task is in the waiting queue. A task is *ready* when all necessary predecessor(s) of the task have finished, otherwise, the task is *unready*. When a new workflow arrives, *CPWS* is adopted to calculate rank$_u$ of each task in the workflow

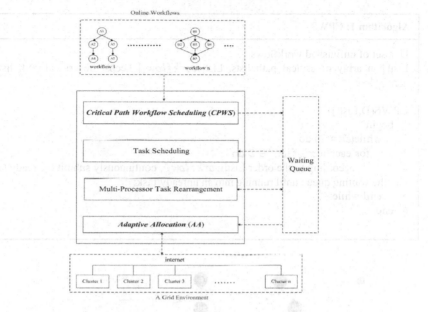

Fig. 1. Online Workflow Management (OWM)

and sort the tasks in descending order of rank$_u$ into a list. The list is named the critical path list. Here, rank$_u$ is the upward rank of a task [7] which measures the length of critical path from a task t$_i$ to the exit task. The definition of rank$_u$ is as below

$$rank_u(t_i) = \overline{w_i} + \max_{t_j \in succ(t_i)}(\overline{c_{i,j}} + rank_u(t_j))$$ (1)

where $succ(t_i)$ is the set of immediate successors of task t_i, $\overline{c_{i,j}}$ is the average communication cost of edge (i, j), and $\overline{w_i}$ is the average computation cost of task t_i. The computation of a rank starts from the exit task and traverses up along the task graph recursively. Thus, the rank is called upward rank, and the upward rank of the exit task t_{exit} is

$$rank_u(t_{exit}) = \overline{w_{exit}}$$ (2)

The system maintains an array List[] and List[$workflow_i$] points to the critical path list of $workflow_i$. According to the order in each critical path list, *CPWS* continuously submits the ready tasks in the list into the waiting queue until running into an unready task. The details of *CPWS* are described in Algorithm 1.

Figure 2 shows an example of *CPWS*. The critical path list of each workflow is sorted in descending order of rank$_u$. The critical path list for workflow A is A1→A2→A3→A5→A4 and the critical path list for workflow B is B1→B3→B4→B5→B2. A1, A2, B1 and B3 have finished. A3, A4, B2 and B4 are ready. A5 and B5 are unready. According to the order in the critical path lists, *CPWS* submits tasks A3 and B4.

Algorithm 1: CPWS

D: a set of unfinished workflows
List[]:an array of critical path lists. List[$workflow_i$] keeps the critical path list of $workflow_i$

CPWS(D,List[])
1 **begin**
2   **while**($D \neq \emptyset$) **do**
3   **for** each $workflow_i \in D$ **do**
4   according to the order List[$workflow_i$], continuously submit the ready tasks into the waiting queue until running into an unready task;
5   **end while**
6 **end**

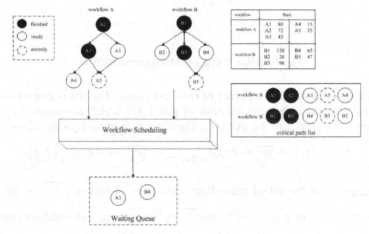

Fig. 2. An example of *CPWS*

The following presents the Adaptive Allocation (AA) process. To better describe the process, we define the following quantities:

- The **Estimated Computation Time ECT(t, p)** is defined as the estimated execution time of task t on processor group p.
- The **Estimated File Communication Time EFCT(t, p)** is defined as the estimated communication time required by task t on processor group p to receive all necessary files before execution.
- The **Estimated Available Time EAT(t, p)** is defined as the earliest time when processor group p has a large enough time slot to execute task t.
- The **Estimated Finish Time EFT(t, p)** is defined as the estimated time when task t completes on processor group p:

$$EFT(t,p) = EAT(t,p) + ECT(t,p) + EFCT(t,p) \qquad (3)$$

The main idea of *AA* is described below:

(1)   When the number of clusters that can immediately execute the first task is 1, said Ci, AA first finds the cluster, said Cj, with the earliest estimated available time among other clusters. If the estimated finish time of the first task on Cj is earlier than that on Ci, the task will be kept in the waiting queue. Otherwise, AA allocates the task to Ci for immediate execution.

Algorithm 2: AA

T: a set of tasks in the waiting queue
R: a set of free processors
C: a set of clusters

$AA(T,R,C)$
01 begin
02 while($T \neq \emptyset$ and $R \neq \emptyset$) do
03   select $t_i \in T$, where t_i with the highest priority task;
04   If workflows are composed of data-parallel tasks
05   *Multi-Processor Task Rearrangement;

06   If *allocateNumberOfClusters*(R, t_i) = 0
07   task t_i keeps waiting in the waiting queue;
08   else if *allocateNumberOfClusters*(R, t_i) = 1
09   the free processor group $p_x \in C_x$ and calculate $EFT(t_i, p_x)$;
10   find the processor group $p_y \in C_y$ with the earliest estimated available time among other clusters, where $C_x \neq C_y$;
11   If $EFT(t_i, p_x) \leq EFT(t_i, p_y)$
12   Assign task t_i to the processor(s) p_x;
13        $T = T - \{t_i\}$;
14        $R = R - \{p_x\}$;
15   else
16   task t_i keeps waiting in the waiting queue;
17   else   // *allocateNumberOfClusters*(R, t_i)> 1
18   for each processor group $p_k \in R$ do
19   calculate $EFT(t_i, p_k)$;   // $EAT(t_i,p_k)$ = current time
20   Assign task t_i to the processor group p_k that has earliest estimated finish time, $EFT(t_i, p_k)$;
21        $T = T - \{t_i\}$;
22        $R = R - \{p_k\}$;
23 end while
24 end
25 int *allocateNumberOfClusters*(R, t_i){
26   numberOfCluster=0;
27   for each cluster C_i do
28   If free processors in $C_i \geq$ processors that t_i requires
29   numberOfClusters++;
30   return numberOfClusters;
31 }

(2)   When the number of clusters that can accommodate the highest priority task is larger than 1, AA allocates the highest priority task to the cluster that has the earliest estimated finish time.

The details of *AA* are described in Algorithm 2. When there are free processors and the waiting queue contains at least one task, AA selects the first tasks and follows the above allocation rules. In parallel task scheduling, if the number of free processors is not enough for a task, the idle processors become a scheduling hole. To overcome this problem, we perform multi-processor task rearrangement to minimize the scheduling hole as shown in lines 4 to 5. The techniques which can be applied in multi-processor task rearrangement include first fit, easy backfilling [16] and conservative backfilling [16]. The first fit approach allocates the first waiting task that can fit into the scheduling hole. The conservative backfilling approach moves tasks forward only if they do not delay previous tasks in the queue. The easy backfilling approach is more aggressive and allows tasks to skip ahead provided they do not delay the job at the head   of   the   queue   [16].   Lines   25   to   31   show   a   function (*allocateNumberOfClusters*(R, t_i)). It returns the number of clusters that can accommodate the first task. If the function returns 1, the steps in lines 8 to 16 work for rule 1 described previously. If the function returns a number larger than 1, the steps in lines 17 to 22 work for rule 2.

4   Experimental Results

This section presents the simulation experiments used to evaluate the proposed OWM approach and discuss the experimental results. The performance metrics used in our experiments are described below:

- **makespan**: the time between submission and completion of a workflow, including execution time and waiting time.
- **Schedule Length Ratio** (SLR): makespan usually varies widely among workflows with different sizes and other properties. To measure the scheduling efficiency objectively, we can use another performance metric derived from makespan, which calculates the ratio of a workflow's makespan over the best possible schedule length in a given environment. The performance is called Schedule Length Ratio (SLR) and defined by $SLR = \dfrac{makespan}{CPL}$ where CPL represents the Critical Path Length of a workflow. SLR is not sensitive to the size of a workflow.
- **win** (%): used for the comparison of different algorithms. For a workflow, one of the algorithms has the shortest makespan. The win value of an algorithm means the percentage of the workflows that have the shortest makespan when applying this algorithm. From users' perspective, the higher win value leads to the higher satisfaction.

In the following experiments, we compare OWM with two other approaches: *RANK_HYBD* and *Fairness_Dynamic*. To better clarify the differences between these three approaches, we partition the complete scheduling process into three

(a) RANK_HYBD   (b) Fairness_Dynamic   (c) OWM

Fig. 3. The difference between RANK_HYBD, Fairness_Dynamic and OWM

components, workflow scheduling, task scheduling and allocation approaches. Figure 3 describes these three approaches according to the three components. *RANK_HYBD* [17] is shown in figure 3(a). The Fairness approach (F2) in [19] is a static algorithm and can not deal with online workflows. In the following experiments, we modify the Fairness (F2) approach to handle online workflows by replacing the original workflow scheduling and allocation approaches in this approach with *SWS* and *SA* respectively. We call this new approach as *Fairness_Dynamic* in figure 3(b). Here, *SWS* stands for *Simple Workflow Scheduling*, which simply submits each ready task into the waiting queue, and *SA* represents *Simple Allocation*, which selects the highest priority task and allocates it to the free processor group that has the earliest estimated finish time.

To experiment with different workload characteristics, we use the following parameters to generate different types of workflows. A workflow is represented as a Directed Acyclic Graph (DAG).

- Node={20, 40, 60, 80, 100}
- Shape={0.5, 1.0, 2.0}
- OutDegree={1, 2, 3, 4, 5}
- CCR={0.1, 0.5, 1.0, 1.5, 2.0}
- BRange={0.1, 0.25, 0.5, 0.75, 1.0}
- WDAG=100~1000

The values of these parameters are randomly selected from the corresponding sets given above for each DAG. The arrival interval value between DAGs is set based on Poisson distribution. Each experiment involves 20 runs, and each run has 100 unique DAGs in a grid environment that contains 3 clusters each containing 30~50 processors respectively.

In the experiment, we also take other factors into account: the distribution of tasks' computation cost (*Wi_DisType*) and the computation intensity of a workflow represented by CCR (*computationIntensity*). The average computation cost of each task is randomly generated from a probability distribution within the range $[1, 2 \times WDAG]$. We experimented with both a uniform distribution and an exponential distribution for tasks' computation cost. CCR is randomly selected from the set {0.1, 0.5, 1.0, 1.5, 2.0}. For computation-intensive workflows, CCR is randomly selected form the set {0.1, 0.5}, and for communication-intensive workflows, CCR is randomly selected from the set {1.5, 2.0}.

Figures 4, 5 and 6 show the results of different mean arrival intervals according to different performance metrics: average makespan, average SLR and win (%) respectively. It can be easily seen that when the system is more crowded, i.e., smaller arrival interval in the figures, *OWM* outperforms the other two algorithms significantly. When all DAGs are submitted at the same time, i.e., the zero arrival interval in the figures, *OWM* outperforms *Fainess_Dynamic* by 26% and 49%, and outperforms *RANK_HYBD* by 13% and 20% for average makespan and average SLR respectively, as shown in figures 4 and 5. *Fairness_Dynamic* has pool performance for average SLR, because it achieves fairness by the cost of enlarging the makespan of the workflows with shorter critical path length. *OWM* wins in terms of makespan in 94.55% of workflows as shown in figure 6. From users' perspective, it means 94.55% users may prefer *OWM*. When workflows arrive at an interval about 400 time units, these three algorithms perform almost equivalently for average makespan, average SLR and win (%) because one workflow almost come in after another one finishes. In real environments, most high-performance centers are overloaded, therefore *OWM* can outperform others in such environments.

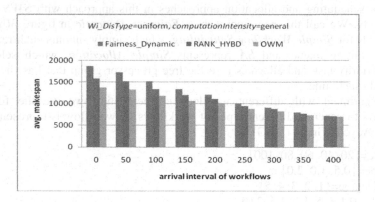

Fig. 4. Results of different mean arrival intervals for average makespan

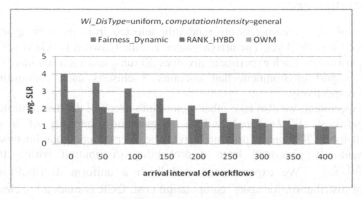

Fig. 5. Results of different mean arrival intervals for average SLR

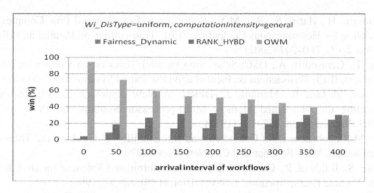

Fig. 6. Results of different mean arrival intervals for win (%)

5 Conclusion

Most workflow scheduling algorithms are restricted to handle only one single workflow. There are few researches for scheduling online workflows. In the paper, we propose an online workflow management (*OWM*) approach for scheduling multiple online mixed-parallel workflows in a grid environment. Our experiments show that *OWM* outperforms *RANK_HYBD* and *Fairness_Dynamic* for average makesapn, average SLR and win (%) under different experimental workloads.

Moreover, *RANK_HYBD* and *Fairness_Dynamic* do not work with mixed-parallel workflows composed of data-parallel tasks. There are few studies focused on mixed-parallel workflow scheduling. Our OWM takes this issue into account. OWM incorporates well-known approaches, *e.g.* first fit, easy backfilling and conservative backfilling, to deal with the allocation issue for workflows composed of data-parallel tasks.

References

1. Miguel, L.B., Yannis, A.D., Eduardo, G.S.: Grid Characteristics and uses: a Grid Definition. In: Fernández Rivera, F., Bubak, M., Gómez Tato, A., Doallo, R. (eds.) Across Grids 2003. LNCS, vol. 2970, pp. 291–298. Springer, Heidelberg (2004)
2. Ullman, J.D.: NP-Complete Scheduling Problems. J. Computer and Systems Sciences 10, 384–393 (1975)
3. Wu, M., Gajski, D.: Hypertool: A Programming Aid for Message Passing Systems. IEEE Transactions on Parallel and Distributed Systems 1, 330–343 (1990)
4. Kwok, Y., Ahmad, I.: Dynamic Critical-Path Scheduling: An Effective Technique for Allocation Task Graphs to Multi-processors. IEEE Transactions on Parallel and Distributed Systems 7(5), 506–521 (1996)
5. Sih, G.C., Lee, E.A.: A Compile-Time Scheduling Heuristic for Interconnection-Constrained Heterogeneous Processor Architectures. IEEE Transactions on Parallel and Distributed Systems 4(2), 175–186 (1993)
6. EI-Rewini, H., Lewis, T.G.: Scheduling Parallel Program Tasks onto Arbitrary Target Machines. J. Parallel and Distributed Computing 9, 138–153 (1990)

7. Topcuoglu, H., Hariri, S., Wu, M.Y.: Performance-Effective and Low-Complexity Task Scheduling for Heterogeneous Computing. IEEE Transactions on Parallel and Distributed Systems 2(13), 260–247 (2002)
8. Yang, T., Gerasoulis, A.: DSC: Scheduling Parallel Tasks on an Unbounded Number of Processors. IEEE Transactions on Parallel and Distributed Systems 5(9), 951–967 (1994)
9. Park, G., Shirazi, B., Marquis, J.: DFRN: A New Approach for Duplication Based Scheduling for Distributed Memory Multi-processor Systems. In: Proc. Int'l. Conf. Parallel Processing, pp. 157–166 (1997)
10. Gary, M.R., Johnson, D.S.: Computers and Intractability: A Guide to the Theory of NP-Completeness. W.H. Freeman and Co., New York (1979)
11. Ludtke, S., Baldwin, P., Chiu, W.: EMAN: Semiautomated Software for High Resolution Single-Particle Reconstructions. J. Struct. Biol. (128), 82–97 (1999)
12. Singh, G., Deelman, E., Berriman, G.B., et al.: Montage: a Grid Enabled Image Mosaic Service for the National Virtual Observatory. In: Astronomical Data Analysis Software and Systems (ADASS), vol. (13) (2003)
13. N'takpe', T., Suter, F.: A Comparison of Scheduling Approaches for Mixed-Parallel Applications on Heterogeneous Platforms. In: 6th International Symposium on Parallel and Distributed Computing (IS-PDC), Hagenberg, Austria, July 2007, pp. 250–257 (2007)
14. Mandal, A., Kennedy, K., Koelbel, C., Marin, G., Mellor-Crummey, J., Liu, B., Johnsson, L.: Scheduling Strategies for Mapping Application workflows on to the Grid. In: 14thIEEE Symposium on High Performance Distributed Computing (HPDC 14), pp. 125–134 (2005)
15. N'takpe', T., Suter, F.: Concurrent Scheduling of Parallel Task Graphs on Multi-Clusters Using Constrained Resource Allocations. Rapport de recherché n° 6774 (December 2008)
16. Mu'alem, A.W., Feitelson, D.G.: Utilization, Predictability, Workloads,and User Runtime Estimates in Scheduling the IBM SP2 with Backfilling. IEEE Transactions onParalleland Distributed Systems 12(6) (June 2001)
17. Yu, Z., Shi, W.: A Planner-Guided Scheduling Strategy for Multiple Workflow Applications. In: On Parallel Processing Workshops, ICPP-W 2008, September 8-12 (2008)
18. Sakellariou, R., Zhao, H.: A hybrid heuristic for DAG scheduling on heterogeneous systems. In: 18th International Parallel and Distributed Processing Symposium (IPDPS 2004), p. 111. IEEE Computer Society, Los Alamitos (2004)
19. Zhao, H., Sakellarious, R.: Scheduling Multiple DAGs onto Heterogeneous Systems. In: Proceedings ofthe 15th Heterogeneous Computing Workshop (HCW), Rhodes Island, Greece (2006)

Securing Interoperable Grid Services in ARC Grid Middleware

Weizhong Qiang[1,2], Aleksandr Konstantinov[2,3], Mattias Ellert[4], and Hai Jin[1]

[1] Huazhong University of Science and Technology, School of Computer Science and Technology, 1037 Luoyu Road, Wuhan, China
[2] University of Oslo, Department of Physics, P.O. Box 1048, Blindern, 0316 Oslo, Norway
[3] Vilnius University, Institute of Material Science and Applied Research, Sauletekio al. 9, Vilnius 2040, Lithuania
[4] Uppsala University, Department of Nuclear and Particle Physics, Box 535, 75121 Uppsala, Sweden
wzqiang@hust.edu.cn

Abstract. Grid middleware provides a way to integrate computational and storage resouces for supporting large-scale applications that span across multiple domains. Implicitly, Grid middlware eliminates the interoperability obstacle between different resources. However, with the emerging of a bunch of Grid middlewares, to provide interoperability between Grid middlewares themselves is an important challenge in production Grid infrasturtures. Web Service technologies (specifically, Simple Object Access Protocol) have been adopted in most of the Grid middlewares as the XML messaging protocol for the interoperability in the application layer. For other layers, standard protocols are also adopted for interoperability, e.g., HTTP is utilized as service transport protocol. On the other hand, security is a key issue that needs to be taken into account on each layer, for instance, WS-Security (Web Service Security) is considered as an augment on SOAP protocol for applying security to Web Services; GSI (Globus Security Infrastructure) is considered as an protocol for applying security to transport layer. We present the design consideration and implementation about how to provide flexible support for security protocols in the Advanced Resource Connector(ARC) Grid middleware, and this way clients or/and services developed in ARC middleware can easily interoperate with service/client developed in other middlewares, such as gLite and Globus Toolkit. Also, a flexible authorization framework is presented that can secure the Grid services with configurable authorization modules, as well as a variety of authorization policies.

1 Introduction

Grid middleware [1] provides a way to integrate computational and storage resouces for supporting large-scale applications that span across multiple domains. Implicitly, Grid middlware eliminates the interoperability obstacle between different resources. However, we have all seen the fact that different Grid middlewares

R.-S. Chang et al. (Eds.): GPC 2010, LNCS 6104, pp. 311–320, 2010.
© Springer-Verlag Berlin Heidelberg 2010

have been developed, and deployed in different production Grid infrastructures, therefore, to provide interoperability between Grid middlewares themselves is an important challenge in production Grid infrasturtures.

Web Service technologies (specifically, Simple Object Access Protocol) have been adopted in most of the Grid middlewares as the XML messaging protocol for the interoperability in the application layer. For other layers, standard protocols are also adopted for interoperability, e.g., HTTP is utilized as service transport protocol.

Moreover, security is a key issue that needs to be taken into account on each layer, for instance, WS-Security (Web Service Security) is considered as an augment on SOAP protocol for applying security to Web Services; GSI (Globus Security Infrastructure) [2] is considered as an protocol for applying security to transport layer.

More specifically, GSI is leveraged by the Globus Toolkit [3] and gLite middlewares [4] to provide mutual authentication, confidential communication and single sign-on on. The GSI implementes the Generic Security Services Application Program Interface (GSS-API) [5] with some extensions [6]. GSS-API is an IETF standard for programs to access security services, which can address the problem of many similar but incompatible security services. The GSS-API implementation in GSI utilizes the OpenSSL library as security service. The extensions [6] are specific for e.g. credential export/import, delegation at any time, credential extensions handling, etc. Although the implementation of GSS-API in GSI uses the similar concept as that in Secure Sockets Layer(SSL) or Transport Layer Security(TLS) for its mutual authentication and confidential communication, it is not compatible with any version of SSL or TLS. Therefore, from the perspective of ARC middleware, in order to achieve fully interoperability with those middlwares that utilizes the GSI implementation of GSS-API, such as gLite and Globus Toolkit, this kind of specific GSS-API implementation should be adopted by ARC middlware, or similar implementation should be re-implemented in ARC middleware. On the other hand, another benefit that we should utilize in ARC middleware is the credential delegation mechanism, a key building block for single sign-on, which is natively provided by GSS-API specification, and sophistically enhanced by the GSI implementation.

On the application layer, the Web Services provide a standard interface for application description (via WSDL specification) and interaction (via SOAP specification). The Service-Oriented Architecture [7] has been adpoted by most of the Grid middlewares, such as Globus Toolkit [3], gLite [4], and ARC [8]. Globus Toolkit (more specifically, the Java WS Core of Globus Toolkit version 4) utilizes the Java version of Apache Axis [9]. gSOAP [10](a solution for implementation of C/C++ Web Services) is utilized by some Grid middlewares for the Web Service functionality. From the perspective of ARC, a novel solution for the implementation of Web Service is developed for the implementation of Web Service with different programming languages, such as C/C++, Java and Python.

The ARC middleware provide a modular architecture which is easy to add new functionalities or replace old functionalities with old ones, for instance, it is modular enough to easily support different communication protocols.

In this paper, we present the design consideration and implementation about how to provide flexible support for security protocols in the Advanced Resource Connector(ARC) Grid middleware, and this way clients or/and services developed in ARC middleware can easily interoperate with service/client developed in other middlewares, such as gLite [4] and Globus Toolkit [3]. We also present the flexible authorization framework that can secure the Grid services with configurable authorization modules, as well as a variety of authorization policies.

The remainder of this paper is organized as follows. Section 2 presents the ARC Grid middleware, where Section 3 describes the secure protocols in ARC middleware and the flexible authorization framework. We present related work in Section 4 and give our conclusions in Section 5.

2   The ARC Grid Middleware

ARC(Advanced Resource Connector) [8] is an open source Grid middleware solution released under Apache license. It is developed and maintained by NorduGrid Collaboration. Currently, the ARC middleware has been deployed and used in production environment, and been one of the widely deployed Grid middlewares in the world.

Initially, ARC middleware aimes at developing self-organized, fault-tolerant, non-intrusive, easy-manageable Grid middleware, specifically, it provides Grid services for job submission and management, resource characterization, resource aggregation and discovery, basic data management, integration of grid security solution, etc. To meet the the trend of adopting Service-Oriented Architecture, this middleware has been developed in the context of KnowARC project [11], an EU-funded development project for providing a Web Service oriented Grid middleware which will provide higher levels of resource and user abstraction through well-defined Web Service interface, to achieve fully interoperability with other service-oriented Grid middlwares.

ARC middleware includes a lightweight Web Service container called Hosting Environment Daemon (HED) which provides a plug-in based modular architecture for adding/replacing functionalities (e.g., a bunch of plug-ins have been implemented to support TCP, TLS/SSL, HTTP and SOAP protocols respectively), as well as a hosting environment for chaining and executing those functionalities together with the Web Services on the application layer.

As the key part of the implementation of ARC middleware, there is a lightweight Web Service container called Hosting Environment Daemon (HED) which provides a hosting for various services at application level, as well as a bunch of modules to support flexible, interoperatible, and efficient communication mechanism for building SOAP based Web Services.

Since the whole design of the HED is built around the idea of flexibility and modularity, the developer can easily concentrate Web Service implementation on the application layer, or he can work on the middleware level to implement another communication protocol or authentication mechanism; and the deployer can easily deploy and re-use the different modules for different kinds of requirements.

3   Securing Interoperable Grid Services in ARC Grid Middleware

Figure 1 illustrates the architecture of the HED. A few components called Message Chain Component(MCC) are implemented to support different protocols. For instance, as shown in the example message flow, HTTP MCC will process stream from TLS MCC to parse HTTP message and pass its body to SOAP MCC, and also process SOAP response from SOAP MCC to generate HTTP message and then pass this message to TLS MCC.

Service administrator can re-configure the MCCs according to the interoperability requirements with the peer end. As an example, the configuration marked with dashed lines is compatible to WSE(Web Services Enhancement for .NET)

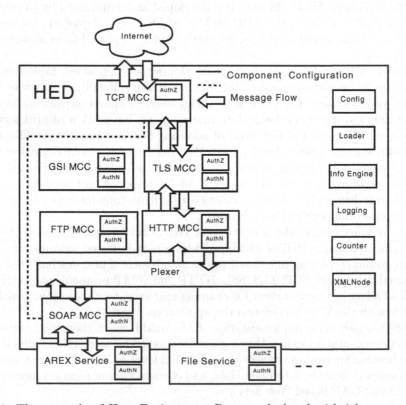

Fig. 1. The example of Host Environment Daemon deployed with job management service(A-REX) and file service

SOAP message mechanism (c.f. WSEs *SoapSender* and *SoapReceiver*) [12]. Another example configuration could be SOAP over HTTPG (HTTP over GSI) which is needed to interoperate with services like Storage Resource Manager (SRM)[13] service. This shows the flexibility of HED in terms of protocols support.

Currently some protocols have been supported, including TCP, TLS, GSI, HTTP, SOAP. New protocols can be supported if needed by implementing the MCC interface.

HED contains a framework for implementing and enforcing authentication and authorization. Each MCC or Service has a common interface for implementing various authentication and authorization functionality. Each functionality can be implemented as a pluggable and configurable component (plug-in) called *SecHandler* which is C++ class and provides method for processing message that travels through MCC or Service. Each MCC or Service is usually configured with two queues of *SecHandler* – one for incoming message and one for outgoing message respectively. All *SecHandler* components attached to the queue are executed sequentially. If any of them fails, message processing fails as well. In Figure 1, the *AuthZ* and *AuthN* sub-modules inside MCCs and Services are examples of *SecHandler*.

As explained above, HED is supposed to act as a Web/Grid Service container, but on the client side, from implementation perspective, there is similar architecture implemented for processing messages from different protocols and handling security functionality, also there is a specific application programming interface (API) for developers to easily write Web Service client code.

3.1 Support of TLS Protocol

The TLS (and its predecessor, SSL) is supported for mutual authentication between client and server. In detail, the processing of TLS/SSL is implemented inside TLS MCC by utilizing the OpenSSL library [13]. In addition to normal X.509 certificate, the proxy certificate (with RFC 3820 format) can also be provided by the client side and consumed by the server side, therefore, the "single sign-on" feature of GSI is also provided in TLS MCC due to the support of proxy certificate. OpenSSL library has already support the consumption of proxy certificate since version 0.9.7g, so the TLS MCC can inherently utilize this functionality.

Another feature of GSI is the credential delegation, which allows a user to act on another user's behalf. In GSI, the delegating of a credential is supported in the implementation of GSS-API. While in the impelemention of TLS MCC, the delegating of a credential is achieved through the application level, which means the implementation of Grid service and client is supposed to take care of the credential delegation, by invoking a delegation library which acts as the wrapper of the delegation protocol.

Since the solution of VOMS (Virtual Organization Management Service) [14] has been adopted by Grid middlewares such as gLite for the purpose of attribute-based authorization, the proxy with VOMS attribute extention should be parsed by the code of ARC. On the other hand, TLS MCC takes charge of the parsing of distinguished name(DN) of peer certificate, therefore it should also be TLS MCC to parse the voms attributes of peer certificate. Instead of using the VOMS API library for verifying and parsing VOMS attribute certificate (AC) hosted in the extension part of proxy certificate, we develope a new library for this purpose, therefore the dependency on VOMS API library is not required. The syntax of VOMS attribute that is parsed is as follows: */VO= "vo name"/Group= "group name"/Role= "role name"*.

Besides the mutual authentication provided by TLS/SSL, server-side TLS/SSL is the other option, in which only the server side is required to provide X.509 certificate which will be verified by the client side, while the client side is not required to provide X.509 certificate. The server-side TLS/SSL is commonly used in the cases where client side is supposed to provide credentials such as username/password instead of X.509 certificate. Service administrators can easily switch on server-side TLS/SSL by changing the configurarion of TLS MCC.

A new independent client utility for generating proxy certificate is developed (called *arcproxy*), which covers almost all of the functionality of the existing proxy generation utilities, including grid-proxy-init, voms-proxy-init, myproxy-init. The reason why this client utility is developed in ARC middleware is that we would depend on the packages from other Grid middleware as less as possible, while still provide the functionalities as much as possbile.

3.2 Support of GSI Protocol

In order to provide the interoperability with other Grid middlewares that requires Globus GSI communication, the GSI MCC is implemented which can be deployed as the replacement of TLS MCC.

The implementation of GSI MCC is based on the Globus implementation of GSS-API. In detail, four main functions of GSS-API are invoked: *gss_init_sec_context*, *gss_accept_sec_context*, *gss_unwrap*, *gss_wrap*.

Owing to the features provided by GSS-API, such as mutual authentication, credential delegation, the GSI MCC can inherently provides those features as well.

The VOMS attribute certificate (AC) is parsed in GSI MCC, after the success of the construction of security context (the function *gss_accept_sec_context* returns positive result).

The GSI MCC can be flexibly configured on demand. If a client needs to contact some SRM service [15] (that requires SOAP on HTTPG), then SOAP MCC, HTTP MCC, GSI MCC, and TCP MCC can be chained together, and the implementation of this client (configured on top of SOAP MCC) is only supposed to process the application level protocol of SRM client, not supposed to process anything related to lower layer protocols. If a client needs to contact the myproxy server, then GSI MCC and TCP MCC can be chained together, and the implementation of this client is only supposed to process the application layer protocol of myproxy client. These two use cases have been exemplified in the SRM client utility (to be used to contact SRM service), and the proxy client utility (to be used to contact MyProxy service) of ARC middleware.

3.3   Authorization Based on Information from Security Protocols

Each MCC or service is supposed to respectively parse some information when it processes the message payload. For instance, the TCP MCC parses IP address and port used by peer side; the TLS MCC (and GSI MCC) parses the distinguished name related to the X509 certificate utilized by the client, and the VOMS attributes (precisely the FQANs, Fully Qualified Attribute Names). All of the information that has been parsed from the incoming message payload will be composed into some format, for example, it can be composed into the XACML request format according to the XACML context schema [16].

There is a flexible authorization framework implemented in ARC middleware. Each MCC or service can independently contains one or a few authorization modules(see Figure 1). For instance, the TCP MCC can carry out the authorization based on the peer side's IP address and port, the TLS MCC can carry out the authorization on the basis of the distinguished name related to the X509 certificate, or the VOMS attributes, and the service can carry out the authorization based on the service specific attributes, such as the SOAP actions. From another angle, we can see that coarse grain and fine grain authorization can easily be achieved in this authorization framework. The chained MCCs are actually functioning as the service container. The coarse grain authorization (or container-based authorization) can be achived by MCCs since those MCCs can only process those attributes that are commonly shared by services, while fine grain authorization (or service-based authorization) can be respectively achieved by those services that are hosted inside this container.

On the other hand, different authorization modules can respectively process different types of access control policies. A few types of policies have already been supported in our middleware, such as XACML policy, gridmap-like policy, ARC policy(a simplified version of XACML policy), GACL(Grid Access Control Language) policy, etc. Different authorization modules take care of the parsing of different types of policy, as well as the composing of different types of authorization request accordingly. Also other developers can develop their own authorization modules for processing their own policy with some specific format, by implementing the common interface of authorization module.

The elements of some complicated policy, such as the XACML policy, can actually be reduced as *name:value* pairs. We see that the granularity of authorization is also related to the *name* of each element of policy. Some of the *name* can only be assigned with a *value* which is specific to one entity (such as the distinguished name of an entity), while some of the *name* can be assigned with a *value* which can be shared by many entities (such as the VOMS attribute). Therefore, if all of the *name* in an authorization policy is not able to be assigned to any *value* that is specific for one entity, then this policy is a coarse grain policy. Therefore the granularity of authorization can be controlled by specifying the policy. One scenario of the usage of coarse grain policy is that the authorization policies of many Grid services that are related to the same Virtual Organization can be defined just once on some centralized server corresponding to VOMS server, and these policies can be either downloaded to the Grid services and then evaluated locally, or evaluated remotely on this centralized server (and then the evaluation result will be downloaded to the Grid services). The advantage of this scenario is the scalability.

A new XACML policy evaluation engine is developed in ARC using C/C++. The evaluation engine can be either invoked by authorization module that is hosted by MCC or service, or invoked by an independent authorization service. These two kinds of invocation of evaluation engine corresponds to the local policy evaluation and remote policy evaluation. For the remote policy evaluation, *"SOAP Profile of XACML-SAML"* [18] is used to carry the policy evaluation request and the policy evaluation response. The interoperability with other authorization service is also considered. Argus service(gLite authorization service) [17] is an authorization service that supports policies based on XACML. Since *"SOAP Profile of XACML-SAML"* [18] is used in Argus service, the policy evaluation client is possbile to interoperate with this external authorization service.

4   Related Work

The Globus Toolkit C WS Core [19] is a C implementation of Grid middleware, which the same as our ARC Grid middleware also support the developement of Grid services secured by GSI. However, there is no flexible authorization framework provided by Globus Toolkit C WS Core, and the Grid services deployed in C WS Core can only use the "self" authorization scheme. Also it is not possible for a Grid service to retrieve the distinguished name of the peer side, not to mention the VOMS attributes and any other attribute.

The GSI plug-in for gSOAP [20] is an open source solution to develop secure, GSI-enabled Web Services suitable for grid environments. This plug-in provides ways to retrieve the distinguished name of the peer side, and also the VOMS attributes. But it does not provide a flexible framework to support different types of authorization policies. Also it does not provide any evaluation engine that support standard policy, such as XACML. Another difference is that GSI plug-in for gSOAP provides an interface which exposes the GSI library invocation to service/client developers, whereas the ARC middleware provides a completely transparent interface where the developers only need to take care of the application itself.

The gLite authorization service [17] provides external an authorization service which is specific for providing central grid-wide banning list. The authorization framework of our work is more flexible, since the authorization engine can be sitting locally or remotely, and various types of policies can be supported.

5   Conclusion

We described the design and implementation of how to secure Grid services in ARC Grid middleware. We have introduced the modular design of ARC Grid middleware, and the support of two protocols that secure communication on the transport layer: TLS/SSL and GSI. The support of the two protocols can achieve complete interoperability with other Grid middlwares such as the Globus Toolkit and gLite. We have also introduced the flexible authorization framework that can provide both coarse grain authorization and fine grain authorization, on the base of the attributes parsed on different protocol layers. Also we have reported the interoperability with the gLite authorization service. We the solution proposed and implemented in ARC middleware is a competive approach for securing interoperable Grid services. Our future work will be focused on completing the work of supporting message-level security, to achieve the interoperability on the message level for ARC middleware.

Acknowledgments

This work decribed in this paper was supported by the European Union in the 6th Framework Program through the KnowARC project (Grant IST 032691).

References

1. Berman, F., Fox, G., Hey, T.: Grid Computing: Making the Global Infrastructure a Reality. John Wiley & Sons, Chichester (2003)
2. Foster, I., Kesselman, C., Tsudik, G., Tuecke, S.: A Security Architecture for Computational Grids. In: Proceedings of ACM Conference on Computers and Security, pp. 83–91. ACM, New York (1998)
3. Foster, I., Kesselman, C.: Globus: A Metacomputing Infrastructure Toolkit. Intl. J. Supercomputer Applications 11(2), 115–128 (1997)
4. gLite: Lightweight Middleware for Grid Computing, http://glite.web.cern.ch/glite/
5. Linn, J.: Generic Security Service Application Program Interface, Version 2. INTERNET RFC 2078 (1997)
6. GSS-API Extensions, http://www.ggf.org/documents/GFD.24.pdf
7. Marks, E., Bell, M.: Service Oriented Architecture: A Planning and Implementation Guide for Business and Technology. John Wiley & Sons, Chichester (2006)
8. Design document of new version ARC, https://www.knowarc.eu/documents/Knowarc_D1.1-1_07.pdf
9. Apache Axis web site, http://ws.apache.org/axis
10. van Engelen, R., Gallivan, K.: The gSOAP Toolkit for Web Services and Peer-To-Peer Computing Networks. In: Proceedings of the 2nd IEEE International Symposium on Cluster Computing and the Grid (CCGrid 2002), Berlin, Germany, May 21-24, pp. 128–135. IEEE, Los Alamitos (2002)
11. KnowARC project web site, https://www.knowarc.eu/
12. Web Services Enhancements 2.0 Service Pack 2, http://msdn.microsoft.com/en-us/library/
13. OpenSSL: The Open Source toolkit for SSL/TLS, http://www.openssl.org/
14. Alfieri, R., Cecchini, R., Ciaschini, V., dell Agnello, L., Frohner, R., Lrentey, K., Spataro, F.: From gridmap-file to VOMS: managing authorization in a Grid environment. Future Generation Comp. Syst. 21(4), 549–558 (2005)
15. Shoshani, A., et al.: Storage Resource Managers: Recent International Experience on Requirements and Multiple Co-Operating Implementations. In: 24th IEEE Conference on Mass Storage Systems and Technologies (MSST 2007), San Diego, California, USA, September 2007. IEEE Computer Society, Los Alamitos (2007)

16. XACML specifications, http://www.oasis-open.org/specs/#xacmlv2.0
17. gLite authorization framework,
    https://twiki.cern.ch/twiki/bin/view/EGEE/AuthorizationFramework
18. SOAP Profile of XACML-SAML,
    http://www.switch.ch/grid/support/documents/xacmlsaml.pdf
19. Globus C WS Core web site, http://dev.globus.org/wiki/C_WS_Core
20. Cafaro, M., Lezzi, D., Fiore, S., Aloisio, G., van Engelen, R.: The GSI plug-in for
    gSOAP: building cross-grid interoperable secure grid services. In: Wyrzykowski, R.,
    Dongarra, J., Karczewski, K., Wasniewski, J. (eds.) PPAM 2007. LNCS, vol. 4967,
    pp. 894–901. Springer, Heidelberg (2008)

A New Game Theoretical Resource Allocation Algorithm for Cloud Computing

Fei Teng and Frédéric Magoulès

Applied Mathematics and Systems Laboratory
Ecole Centrale Paris
92295 Chatenay-Malabry Cedex, France
`fei.teng@ecp.fr`

Abstract. Cloud computing and other computing paradigms share the similar visions which aim to implement parallel computations on large distributed resources. However, this cloud computing is more involved in purchasing and consuming manners between providers and users than others. So how to allocate resources reasonably to cater requirements from both sides attracts wide attentions. Based on game theory, we introduce a new Bayesian Nash Equilibrium Allocation algorithm to solve resource management problem in cloud computing. This algorithm fully considers several criteria such as the heterogeneous distribution of resources, rational exchange behaviors of cloud users, incomplete common information and dynamic successive allocation. Compared to former researches, experimental results presented in this paper show that even though rivals' information is uncertain, cloud users can receive Nash equilibrium allocation solutions by gambling stage by stage. Furthermore, the resource price evaluated by the algorithm will converge to the optimal price at the end of the gambling sequence.

Keywords: cloud computing, resource allocation, game theory, Nash equilibrium.

1 Introduction

From 2007, the term cloud computing becomes one of the most buzz words in IT industry, which implies computing is not only operated on local computers, but on centralized facilities by third-party compute and storage utilities. It refers to both the applications delivered as services over the Internet and system hardware and software in datacenter as service provider [1]. Recently, heaps of industry projects have been started including Amazon Elastic Compute Cloud, IBM Blue Cloud, and Microsoft Windows Azure. Meanwhile, HP, Intel and Yahoo have announced the creation of a global, multi-data center, open source cloud computing testbed for industry, research and education. The father of grid computing, I. Foster, explains the ambiguous cloud in such a way "A large-scale of distributed computing paradigm that is driven by economies of scale, in which a pool of abstracted virtualized, dynamically-scalable, managed computing power, storage, platforms, and services are delivered on demand to external customers over the Internet"[2]. From this definition, we can conclude several key points which differ cloud from other distributed computing paradigms, such as hardware virtualization, dynamic provision, web service negotiation and economies of scale[3]. These new

R.-S. Chang et al. (Eds.): GPC 2010, LNCS 6104, pp. 321–330, 2010.

characters inspire researchers and engineers to reconsider the resource allocation algorithms on the cloud system.

In cloud computing, resource allocation refers to allocate CPUs and other network resources among various cloud consumers. Global users and resources hold their own supply and demand strategies, so market mechanism turns out to be appropriate to manage resource in such complex distributed environments[4]. Popcorn[5] utilizes virtual currency for users submitting tasks to a centralized server, while Walras [6] achieves a convergent distributed implementation of equilibrium theory, in which customers bid according to their own price functions to match supply and demand. Besides, the Cloudbus [7] provides a service brokering infrastructure and a core middleware for deploying applications in the datacenter to realize the vision of global cloud computing marketplace.

The mentioned frameworks above can support conceptual environments for grid or cloud resource allocation, but the shortcomings come from lacking of overall equilibrium utility and optimization from the point of view of consumers. Therefore we introduce game theory to solve resource allocation problem in cloud environment. The resource allocation strategies based on Nash equilibrium are inclined to analyze how these selfish and rational users make decisions. For individual, the best choice depends on others behaviors [8]. Khan and Ahmad [9] are committed to simple game theoretic allocation scheme comparison with different design rationales: noncooperative, semicooperative and cooperative. R.T. Maheswaran and J. Bredin [10] develop decentralized negotiation strategies which, with appropriate relaxation, converge to Nash equilibrium. B. An [11] presents a proportional resource allocation mechanism for multi-agent system and gives game theoretical analysis. A. Galstyan [12] studies a minimalist decentralized algorithm for resource allocation in grid environment focusing on scattered distribution and robust performance.

However, when an auction is proceeding in a real market environment, one bidder does not know how much others would like to pay for the computing resource. We therefore seek to accomplish a new allocation algorithm named Bayesian Nash Equilibrium Allocation (BNEA) in cloud system to address the above challenge. Meanwhile we will combine new important features of cloud computing. For example, large-scale users participate in the auction separately with imperfect information, and the selfish but rational users dynamically bid for their sequential tasks. This algorithm not only allows users to adjust next bids automatically, but also makes bidding price converge to Nash equilibrium to realize Pareto efficient situations in the end.

The rest of the paper is organized as follows. Section 2 we derive mathematical theoretical results in the bid-proportion auction model without complete information. In section 3, a new BNEA algorithm is given, which is applicably designed for multiuser and multi-task cloud environment. Section 4 illustrates cloud computing simulation framework and experimental scenario, while experimental results are provided and analyzed. Conclusion will be offered in the last section.

2   Game Theoretical Resource Management

In cloud computing, it is rare that computational resources are allocated totally to a single user. What we expect is that resources will be shared in the cloud datacenter.

In the text, we will focus discussion on bid proportion auction model where resources are allocated to users in proportion to their bids, which is better fit for the large-scale sharing resources problem.

2.1 Bayesian Nash Equilibrium

The bid-proportion auction model assumes K types of resources $C = [C_1, C_2, \ldots, C_K]$ in computational cloud market, each resource offers a specific service corresponding to a specific job type. There are N users competing for K resources to finish their jobs. Each job is composed by a set of sequent subtasks q_k^i, which stands for the task size in job sequence. i_th user bids for k_th task at price b_k^i. Total bids for k_th task is $\Theta_k = \sum_{i=1}^{N} b_k^i$, while $\theta_k^{-i} = \sum_{j \neq i}^{N} b_k^j$ is given as the sum of other bids except i_th user's b_k^i.

For i_th user, it is given finite budget E^i, and time and cost taken to complete k_th task are defined by

$$t_k^i = \frac{q_k^i \Theta_k}{C_k b_k^i} = \frac{q_k^i \cdot (b_k^i + \theta_k^{-i})}{C_k b_k^i}$$

$$e_k^i = \frac{q_k^i \Theta_k}{C_k} = \frac{q_k^i \cdot (b_k^i + \theta_k^{-i})}{c_k} \tag{1}$$

Smart customers in cloud market always wish to pay less for better service, so free market aggravates competitions among different users. Game theory can offer the density of the whole system, which is an equilibrium solution among all participants. Now we clarify the optimization object that cloud customers want complete their tasks as fast as possible with finite budgets. Particularly for i_th user, it can't exceed given E^i when it attempts to minimize the total time taken to finish all tasks.

$$\min \sum_{k=1}^{K} t_k^i \quad s.t. \quad \sum_{k=1}^{K} e_k^i \leq E^i \tag{2}$$

The Hamilton equation is built by introducing the Lagrangian

$$\mathcal{L} = \sum_{k=1}^{K} t_k^i + \lambda^i (\sum_{k=1}^{K} e_k^i - E^i) \tag{3}$$

Taking partial derivative with respect to b_k^i, the fist-derivative condition is set to zero.

$$\frac{\partial \mathcal{L}}{\partial b_k^i} = \frac{-q_k^i \theta_k^{-i}}{C_k (b_k^i)^2} + \frac{\lambda^i q_k^i}{C_k} = 0 \tag{4}$$

We then have $\lambda^i = \frac{\theta_k^{-i}}{(b_k^i)^2}$, so the relationship between any two bids is expressed as $b_k^i = b_j^i \sqrt{\frac{\theta_k^{-i}}{\theta_j^{-i}}}$. Taking partial derivative with respect to λ^i and substituting of b_k^i by b_1^i using the relationship between two bids, we obtain

$$\frac{\partial \mathcal{L}}{\partial \lambda^i} = \frac{q_1^i}{C_1}(b_1^i + \theta_1^{-i}) + \sum_{k \neq 1}^{K} \frac{q_k^i}{C_k}(\sqrt{\frac{\theta_k^{-i}}{\theta_1^{-i}}} b_1^i + \theta_k^{-i}) - E^i = 0 \tag{5}$$

Degenerating the above equation, i_th user will bid for its k_th task

$$b_k^i = \frac{E^i - \sum_{j=1}^{k-1} \frac{q_j^i}{C_j} \theta_j^{-i} - \frac{q_k^i}{C_k} \theta_k^{-i} - \sum_{j=k+1}^{K} \frac{q_j^i}{C_j} \hat{\theta}_j^{-i}}{\sum_{j=1}^{k-1} \frac{q_j^i}{C_j} \sqrt{\frac{\theta_j^{-i}}{\theta_k^{-i}}} + \frac{q_k^i}{C_k} + \sum_{j=k+1}^{K} \frac{q_j^i}{C_j} \sqrt{\frac{\hat{\theta}_j^{-i}}{\theta_k^{-i}}}} \tag{6}$$

b_k^i is a function $f_k^i(\theta_1^{-i}, \cdots, \Theta_k, \hat{\theta}_{k+1}^{-i}, \cdots, \hat{\theta}_K^{-i})$ containing K parameters. We suppose that every user holds its own bidding function B^i, which decides the user's bid price. Bid b_k^i is considered as a sample for B^i. Here we take $p(B^i) \sim N(\mu^i, \sigma^2)$ distributed normally for instance, with mean μ^i and variance σ^2. For these N independent users $B^1 \cdots B^N$, according to the normal distribution properties, their liner combination is also normally distributed.

$$p(\Theta) \sim N(\mu_{all}, \sigma_{all}^2)$$
$$\mu_{all} = \sum_{i=1}^{N} \mu^i \tag{7}$$
$$\sigma_{all}^2 = N\sigma^2$$

Under imperfect information scenario, each user knows well its own bidding function, that is to say μ^i is known, while has no idea about others distribution parameters $\mu^j, \forall j \neq i$. μ_{all} is estimated as $\hat{\mu_{all}} = \frac{1}{k} \sum_{j=1}^{k} \Theta_j$. Furthermore, Θ_k is one of Θ sample distributing normally $N(\hat{\mu}, \tau^2)$ where μ is unknown and τ^2 is known. In probability theory, Bayes theorem explains how the probability of a hypothesis given observed evidence depends on its inverse, so the posteriori distribution can be calculated from the priori $p(\Theta)$ and the likelihood function $p(\Theta_k \mid \Theta)$

$$p(\Theta|\Theta_k) = \frac{p(\Theta_k|\Theta)\,p(\Theta)}{\int p(\Theta_k|\Theta)\,p(\Theta)\,d\Theta} \tag{8}$$

Especially, the normal distribution is conjugate to itself, so we have $p(\Theta|\Theta_k) \sim N(\hat{\mu}_k, \hat{\sigma}_k^2)$. The posteriori hyperparameters are achieved by Bayesian learning mechanism.

$$\hat{\mu}_k = \frac{\frac{\hat{\mu_{all}}}{\sigma_{all}^2} + \frac{\sum_{j=1}^{k} \Theta_j}{\tau^2}}{\frac{1}{\sigma_{all}^2} + \frac{k}{\tau^2}} \qquad k \in 1, \cdots, K \tag{9}$$

With the maximum likelihood prediction value of resource price, all unknown variables are estimated as follows

$$\hat{\theta}_j^{-i} = \hat{\mu}_j - \mu^i \qquad j \in k+1, \cdots, K \tag{10}$$

After substituting $\theta_k^{-i} = \Theta_k - b_k^i$ and introducing the following three parameters

$$\alpha_k^i = E^i - \sum_{j=1}^{k-1} \frac{q_j^i}{C_j} \theta_j^{-i} - \sum_{j=k+1}^{K} \frac{q_j^i}{C_j} \hat{\theta}_j^{-i}$$
$$\beta_k^i = \frac{q_k^i}{C_k} \tag{11}$$
$$\gamma_k^i = \sum_{j=1}^{k-1} \frac{q_j^i}{C_j} \sqrt{\theta_j^{-i}} + \sum_{j=k+1}^{K} \frac{q_j^i}{C_j} \sqrt{\hat{\theta}_j^{-i}}$$

We obtain the explicit function $f_k^i(\Theta_k, \alpha_k^i, \beta_k^i, \gamma_k^i)$ of b_k^i

$$b_k^i = f_k^i(\Theta_k, \alpha_k^i, \beta_k^i, \gamma_k^i) = \frac{(\alpha_k^i - \beta_k^i \Theta_k)^2}{2(\gamma_k^i)^2} \left(-1 + \sqrt{1 + \frac{4(\gamma_k^i)^2 \Theta_k}{(\alpha_k^i - \beta_k^i \Theta_k)^2}} \right) \qquad (12)$$

$$\Theta_k \in (0, \frac{\alpha_k^i}{\beta_k^i})$$

According to equation (12), $\frac{\alpha_k^i}{\beta_k^i}$ stands for the remaining budget of the current task. If the total bid Θ_k exceed the range, the user will quit auction and bid zero.

2.2 Numerial Analysis

In this section, we will analyze bidding strategies from mathematical expressions, putting emphasis on the influences from budget, the number of competitors and balance of inter-sequence tasks.

Figure 1 firstly illustrates that the number of participated users has a huge impact on bid price. With more and more users joining in the competition, the curve is softened, while the participated bid range shrinks. For example, when there are two users in the system, the i-th user bid is approximately close to the total resource utilization, however, when eight users try to access datacenter, each user gets very limited resource.

From equation (12), we can conclude that any bid is not only decided by the participated users, but also by the whole tasks sequence. If future task load turns to heavier, the current bid will decrease. The second sub figure displays a user under heavy stress of others bids. It gives smaller bid than before when budget and auction participants are unchanged, because it has to save more money for future tasks. The third sub figure implies how the best response fluctuates as the user becomes wealthier. Growing budget allows user to submit a larger positive bid, that is to say, it will have more rights to make decisions. This result is well fit to market reality, which means a company's financial capability will decide its market share.

In addition, observing the above three figures, we clarify external factors (number of users, sum of other bids) affect bid function more strongly than internal factors (budget, task size), because the change rates are steep in the former two pictures.

Returning to the choice of equilibrium strategy for all users, Figure 2 supplies us the equilibrium solutions for dynamic bid system. The slope one means sum of all bids. Obviously, in order to achieve optimum utilization, the bids sum on k-th task should

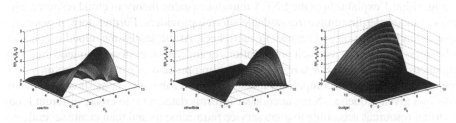

Fig. 1. Bid tendency fluctuated by number of rivals, future bids and budget

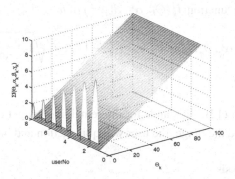

Fig. 2. Equilibrium floated by number of users

equal Θ_k. So the intersection of Θ_k and $\sum f(\Theta_k)$ represents the only stable solution among the set of possible bids. From Figure 2, we find how the final resource price fluctuates by different number of users. The increasing amount of competitors uplifts resource price and makes resource be scarcer, so the resource price is soaring. Once the price is too high to exceed users' ability, customers could not shoulder and will quit the competitive bidding. The resource price will consequently decrease more quickly, and equilibrium point will be archived earlier than before.

3   Resource Allocation in Cloud Computing

Combining unique features of cloud-based infrastructures and co-hosted virtualized services on datacenter, we propose a new Bayesian Nash equilibrium Allocation (BNEA) algorithm in cloud computing system.

The participants are generally classified to three categories: user, auctioneer and datacenter. Users who are self-interested and rational bid in terms of their own demand and price functions in the market. Auctioneer is the mid-person who takes charge of receiving the datacenter register information and collection of users' task queues. Meanwhile, it will try to cater users' needs and make the system achieve the maximum utilization. Datacenters integrate distributed hardware, database, storage devices, application software and operating system to build a resource pool and virtualizes applicable computing resources according to users' requirements.

Algorithm 1 explains how the BNEA introduces game theory in cloud resource allocation. Datacenter first initialize available service providers. Furthermore, it generates a provision information and register in auctioneer. At the same time, cloud users, such as business companies, research organizations or individual customers, queue their task sequences in auctioneer. For simplifying gambling process in game, here we only consider that all cloud users compete for the same type of job which consists of same set of tasks in a given sequence. Next, auctioneer informs datacenter to create different kinds of virtual resources according to users service requirements and then create several successive auctions. In every auction stage, auctioneer should build contact between users and resource. From auction's aspect, it firstly initializes the sum of bids, which stands

---

Algorithm 1. Bayesian Nash Equilibrium Allocation

Require: $N \geq 2$
1: datacenter registers in auctioneer
2: cloud users submit tasks to auctioneer
3: auctioneer informs datacenter to virtualize K kinds of resources according to task types
4: auctioneer creates K auctions
5: **for all** auction k **do**
6:     initialize resource scarcity $\Theta_k = 0$
7:     initialize bidding upper bound $upBound_k = \infty$
8:     **repeat**
9:         bid for task k with the price b_k^i
10:     **until** all cloud users finish bidding
11:     auction k receive sum of bids $\sum_{i=1}^{N} b_k^i$
12:     **for all** cloud user i **do**
13:         $\{b_1^i, \cdots, b_{k-1}^i\} \leftarrow b_k^i$
14:         estimate $\hat{\mu_{all}^i} = \frac{1}{k-1} \sum_{i=1}^{k-1} \Theta_{k-1}$
15:         Bayesian learn and estimate $\{\hat{\mu_{k+1}}, \cdots, \hat{\mu_K}\}$
16:         calculate $\{\theta_1^{-i}, \cdots, \theta_{k-1}^{-i}\}, \forall \theta_k^{-i} = \Theta_k - b_k^i$
17:         estimate $\{\hat{\theta_{k+1}^{-i}}, \cdots, \hat{\theta_K^{-i}}\}, \forall \hat{\theta_k^{-i}} = \hat{\mu_k} - \mu^i$
18:         calculate coefficient set $\{\alpha_k^i, \beta_k^i, \gamma_k^i\}$
19:         build new bid function $f_k^i(\Theta_k, \alpha_k^i, \beta_k^i, \gamma_k^i)$, and send it to auction k
20:         update $upBound_k = \min(\frac{\alpha_k^i}{\beta_k^i})$
21:     **end for**
22:     receive all the bidding functions $\{f_k^1, \cdots, f_k^i, \cdots, f_k^N\}$
23:     search for $\Theta_k = \sum_{i=1}^{N} f_k^i, \Theta_k \in \{0, upBound_k\}$
24:     update $\{\Theta_1, \cdots, \Theta_{k-1}\} \leftarrow \Theta_k$
25:     **for all** cloud user i **do**
26:         auction k send resource in $\frac{b_k^i}{\Theta_k}$ proportion to cloud user i
27:     **end for**
28: **end for**

---

for the resource scarcity. Besides, if the bound for the reasonable bid is too narrow, some poor users will quit the gambling. After all the users finish bidding, the auction collects them and calculates the sum as the resource initial price. As a game participant, cloud user only knows its price function, as well as the common knowledge of incurred bid sums. According to mathematics analysis in last section, the difficulty exists how cloud user estimates the bid sums for future auctions under the incomplete information condition. We use Bayesian learn mechanism to dynamically update price functions. Next, holding all users' price functions, auction could search the Nash equilibrium allocation scheme by bisection method in the assigned bound. Finally, auction allocates resource in balanced proportion which satisfies no one can benefit by changing its bid unilaterally.

4 Cloud Simulation Result

Building cloud experiment testbed on real infrastructure is so expensive and time consuming that it is impossible to evaluate the performance of various usage and resource scenarios in a repeatable and controllable manner [13]. We therefore utilize a generalized simulation framework, Cloudsim [7], to emulate the cloud-based infrastructures and application service. It extends from another popular grid simulator Gridsim [14], which is widely used in research of economy driven resource management policies on large scale distributed computing systems.

To model the resource datacenter, variation of CPU processors, storages, bandwidths, operation systems, virtualization standards and machine locations are considered when we initialize the heterogeneous computing resources configuration. To model cloud consumers, application tasks are created, including all information related to task execution management details such as tasks processing requirements, expressed in MIPS, disk I/O operations and the size of input files.

We choose eight users competing for the similar job. Each job is composed of 80 subtasks that will be processed sequentially. All these users bid according to their economic capabilities and priorities under constrained budgets. The priority can be signified by bidding mean price which distribute uniformly from 10 $/s to 45 $/s. The bidding functions follow normal distributions, variance parameters of which are taken 0.01, 0.1 and 1.0 respectively. All the users have no idea about others economic situations, but will keep on estimating them from prior behaviors.

All these eight bidder's behaviors under indulgent budgets are examined firstly. The solid lines represent the situations where common knowledge are well known for all the competitors. That is to say, each user holds other bids in hand, so it can adjust its behavior exactly.

Figure 3 points out that the rich bidders would like to improve their current payment to get a larger allocation to execute their jobs as fast as possible. Competition leads equilibrium price rising, higher than the anticipated cost. That is why the equilibrium price is higher than the mean price in the beginning. However, with available money for current task decreasing consumers turn to be less aggressive. Finally, all bid prices will converge to their original mean bids and equilibrium is achieved in the whole system.

When the common knowledge is incomplete, users experientially estimate others bidding functions using those previous equilibrium prices. If the bidding fluctuate slightly with variance equals 0.01, the BNEA algorithm has little difference in resource allocations from the perfect model proposed by Bredin[15]. If users bid unstably, accurate forecasting turns to be more difficult because of bidding fluctuation. Simulation results show that resource allocation converges gradually to the optimal equilibrium allocation as long as the reliefs are trained repeatedly in the sequential games.

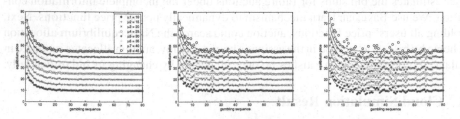

Fig. 3. Bid prediction with variance = 0.01/0.1/1 under indulgent budget

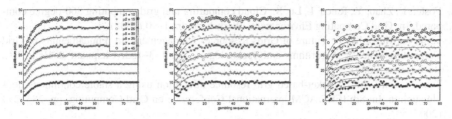

Fig. 4. Bid prediction with variance = 0.01/0.1/1 under austere budget

When consumers' funds are insufficient, they suffer the limitation of austere budgets. One consequence is that all the bidders show more cautions at first, because they have to save enough money to complete remaining tasks. Along with better understanding about its rivals, each user eyes for the whole chess-board. Finally, the equilibrium responses will reach the original mean price. Figure 4 reveals that the equilibrium prices fluctuate in the gambling games. Compared to Figure 3, if users are poor, bid prices escalate progressively till converges are achieved. Instability will bring similar influence on estimation accuracy under austere budget condition.

5 Conclusion

This research investigates game theoretical scheme for cloud resource allocation. We analyze the bid proportion model proposed by Bredin[15], and evolve the model from perfect information to a stricter condition that concerns the lack of common knowledge among large-scale distributed cloud users. By introducing Bayesian learning mechanism, we derive that Nash equilibrium solution exists among all the possibilities prices, which means no one can get a better benefit without damaging others.

In addition, we propose a general algorithm which is well suited to cloud computing scenario. Furthermore, the performance of the proposed approach is evaluated by Cloudsim experimentation. Simulation results show that BNEA algorithm is effective and easily implemented. By sequent gambling stage by stage, cloud users can learn quickly from prior allocation results, and resource price converges to the optimal equilibrium price. The conclusion demonstrates that the BNEA algorithm could satisfy heterogeneous demands of cloud consumers and is a potential feasible method for optimal resource allocation in cloud computing.

In this proportion model resource price is fixed totally by bidders, so we should reconsider that resource supplier participates in price setting. Besides, generalization of price prediction mechanisms and response delay problems are some issues to be addressed in the future.

References

1. Armbrust, M., Fox, A., Griffith, R.: Above the clouds: A berkeley view of cloud computing. Technical Report UCB/EECS-2009-28, EECS Department, University of California, Berkeley (2009)

2. Foster, I., Zhao, Y., Raicu, I., Lu, S.: Cloud computing and grid computing 360-degree compared. In: Grid Computing Environments Workshop, pp. 1–10 (2008)
3. Teng, F., Magoulès, F.: Future of Grids Resources Management. In: Fundamentals of Grid Computing: Theory, Algorithms and Technologies, pp. 133–153. Chapman & Hall/CRC, Boca Raton (2009)
4. Tan, Z., Gurd, J.R.: Market-based grid resource allocation using a stable continuous double auction. In: 8th IEEE/ACM International Conference on Grid Computing, pp. 283–290 (2007)
5. Regev, O., Nisan, N.: The popcorn market – an online market for computational resources. In: Proceedings of 1st International Conference on Information and Computation Economies, pp. 148–157. ACM Press, New York (1998)
6. Qin, C., Shapley, L., Shimomura, K.: The walras core of an economy and its limit theorem. Journal of Mathematical Economics 42(2), 180–197 (2006)
7. Buyya, R., Ranjan, R., Calheiros, R.N.: Modeling and simulation of scalable cloud computing environments and the cloudsim toolkit: challenges and opportunities. In: Proceedings of the 7th High Performance Computing and Simulation Conference, Leipzig, Germany, IEEE Press, Los Alamitos (2009)
8. Li, Z.j., Cheng, C.t., Huang, F.x.: Utility-driven solution for optimal resource allocation in computational grid. Computer Languages, Systems and Structures 35(4), 406–421 (2009)
9. Khan, S., Ahmad, I.: Non-cooperative, semi-cooperative, and cooperative games-based grid resource allocation. In: Parallel and Distributed Processing Symposium, vol. 0, p. 101 (2006)
10. Maheswaran, R.T., Basar, T.: Nash equilibrium and decentralized negotiation in auctioning divisible resources. Group Decision and Negotiation 13(2003) (2003)
11. An, B., Miao, C., Shen, Z.: Market based resource allocation with incomplete information. In: Proceedings of the 20th International Joint Conference on Artifical Intelligence, pp. 1193–1198. Morgan Kaufmann Publishers Inc., San Francisco (2007)
12. Galstyan, A., Kolar, S., Lerman, K.: Resource allocation games with changing resource capacities. In: Proceedings of the International Conference on Autonomous Agents and Multi-Agent Systems, pp. 145–152. ACM Press, New York (2002)
13. Gustedt, J., Jeannot, E., Quinson, M.: Experimental validation in large-scale systems: a survey of methodologies. Parallel Processing Letters 19, 399–418 (2009)
14. Sulistio, A., Cibej, U., Venugopal, S., Robic, B., Buyya, R.: A toolkit for modelling and simulating data grids: an extension to gridsim. Concurrency and Computation: Practice & Experience 20(13), 1591–1609 (2008)
15. Bredin, J., Kotz, D., Rus, D., Maheswaran, R.T., Imer, Ç., Basar, T.: Computational markets to regulate mobile-agent systems. Autonomous Agents and Multi-Agent Systems 6(3), 235–263 (2003)

CPRS: A Cloud-Based Program Recommendation System for Digital TV Platforms

Lai Chin-Feng[1], Chang Jui-Hung[1], Hu Chia-Cheng[2],
Huang Yueh-Min[1], and Chao Han-Chieh[3]

[1] Department of Engineering Science, National Chung Kung University Tainan, Taiwan
cinfon@gmail.com
{changrh,huang}@mail.ncku.edu.tw
[2] Department of Information Management, Naval Academy, Kaohsiung, Taiwan
cchu@cna.edu.tw
[3] College of Electrical Engineering and Computer Science,
National Ilan University, Ilan, Taiwan
hcc@mail.niu.edu.tw

Abstract. Traditional electronic program guides (EPGs) cannot be used to find popular TV programs. A personalized digital video broadcasting – terrestrial (DVB-T) digital TV program recommendation system is ideal for providing TV program suggestions based on statistics results obtained from analyzing large-scale data. The frequency and duration of the programs that users have watched are collected and weighted by data mining techniques. A large dataset produces results that best represent a viewer's preferences of TV programs in a specific area. To process such a massive amount viewer preference data, the bottleneck of scalability and computing power must be removed. In this paper, an architecture for a TV program recommendation system based on cloud computing and a map-reduce framework, the map-reduce version of k-means and the k-nearest neighbor (kNN) algorithm, is introduced and applied. The proposed architecture provides a scalable and powerful backend to support the demand of large-scale data processing for a program recommendation system.

Keywords: map-reduce, electronic program guide (EPG), k-nearest neighbor (kNN), k-means.

1 Introduction

An electronic program guide (EPG), which consists of a digital set-top box (STB) [1], is a digital guide for scheduling broadcast television or radio programs with functions that allow a user to navigate, select, and discover content by criteria such as time, title, channel, and genre [2].

Several methods for retrieving and filtering information from a TV program dataset have been proposed to allow a user to select a program based on topics of interest [3].Besides that, many recommendation systems for EPGs have been proposed for recommending TV programs according to user habits [4]. However, the popularity of a TV program is also a key factor in whether a user selects to watch it, and the above recommendation systems cannot measure the popularity of a TV program.

R.-S. Chang et al. (Eds.): GPC 2010, LNCS 6104, pp. 331–340, 2010.
© Springer-Verlag Berlin Heidelberg 2010

This work proposes a cloud-based program recommendation system (CPRS) for digital TV platforms. In CPRS, the time-consuming problem of grouping a large number of users into clusters is alleviated by using a map-reduce programming framework and a cloud computing technique.

In this paper, k-means and k nearest neighbor (kNN) are used to group users into clusters and to add a new user into a grouped cluster, respectively. Each program is assigned a weight, which is the sum of time periods that users have watched it. The weight of the program is used to indicate its popularity. Then, the k-means method is used to group users into clusters based on the weights. The kNN method is used to add a new user into a grouped cluster. Popular programs in the predicted cluster and in similar clusters are recommended to the user.

The viewership of TV programs is massive. A large dataset produces results that best represent a viewer's preferences of TV programs. However, large datasets require a lot of computation power. Cloud computing techniques can be used to analyze these datasets due to their computation power and scalable structure.

The rest of this paper is organized as follows. Section 2 describes related technologies and background. In Section 3, the architecture of CPRS is described. Section 4 describes the system implementation and experiment results. Finally, the contributions of this paper are summarized in Section 5.

2 Related Work

Due to the increasing number of TV programs, choosing suitable programs has become a challenge. In academic field, many methods have been applied to recommendation systems [5] for TV programs, such as fuzzy logic.

2.1 Cloud Computing

In recent years, cloud computing has become popular in both industry and academia. The core part of cloud computing is map-reduce, which was first proposed by Dean et al. [6], makes clustering and parallel computing on a large set of machines easy and affordable.

Many researchers have proposed novel ideas for using clouding computing to solve problems[7, 8].Researchers have also applied cloud computing to build applications or solve existing problems. Schaffer et al. described how NCSU's (North Carolina State University) virtual computing lab (VCL) applied cloud computing to achieve a cost-effective resource distribution of computation power [9, 10]. Mika discussed the use of semantic web content structure in the cloud [11,12] by using Yahoo! Pig to process RDF data in the cloud; the performance and working process were discussed in detail. Al-Zoube presented a cloud-computing-based solution for e-learning environments [13].

2.2 K-means and K Nearest Neighbors (kNN)

K-means is an unsupervised learning algorithm. It can be used to classify or group objects or data into a number of k groups based on their attribute. The k-means algorithm has been widely applied to solve many data mining and information retrieval problems, such as market segmentation [14], recommendation systems [15], and dimension reduction [16].

Given a positive integer k as a number of means, a set of means $C = \{c_1, c_2, ..., c_m\}$ where m = k, a set of objects or data $X = \{x_1, x_2, ..., x_n\}$ have n points to be classified into k groups. K-means clusters n points into k groups as follows. First, the k means in C are initialized randomly or by some heuristic. In the second step, each point in $x_i \in X$ is assigned to the nearest mean in $c_j \in C$, where $1 \leq i \leq n$ and $1 \leq j \leq m$:

$$\sum_{i=1}^{n} \min_{1 \leq j \leq k}(x_i - c_j)^2$$

After all points in X are grouped to a mean point, the centroids of each group are calculated as new means in the third step. The second and third steps are repeated until convergence is achieved.

kNN [17] is a supervised learning method which classifies objects based on training data. It is generally used to solve classification problems like text categorization [18], and web page classification [19]. Recently, kNN has been applied to solve complex problems such as image de-noising [20], protein function annotation and prediction.

3 Proposed System Architecture

The proposed CPRS structure, which is designed to be implemented in a cloud-based environment, is divided into two parts. As shown in Fig .1, digital television client (DTC), which is used by each client to receive the TV program. After DTC is used to view the programs, CRSS records the information of programs selected by DTC. After a period of time, the user history is evaluated for recent viewing trends. Then, the recommendation data of CRSS is updated with evaluation results.

The second part is the criteria of CRSS by exploiting the map-reduce programming framework, the servers are connected as the clusters. Since the television program description is limited, a content-based recommendation mechanism cannot recommend all programs to users. After the user preferences have been recorded for a period of time, users with similar interests in programs are grouped. Hence, popular programs

Fig. 1. Proposed system architecture

in the cluster and in similar clusters can be recommended to users. For example, in Fig.1, CRSS forms DTV Client1, Client2, and Client3, and Client4 into a group (cluster). The key to clustering is the selection of neighbors. Good neighbors are users that have long viewing durations. Therefore, for new users, the system only recommends programs; it does not add them to clusters. When the viewing duration of the user grows, the system assigns him/her to a proper cluster.

3.1 Cloud-Based Rating Sharing Servers (CRSS) Architectural Components

The cloud-based rating sharing servers include 4 modules: DVB-SI, User Behavior Profile, Cluster of User Profiles, and Recommendation. The electronic program guide (EPG) is fetched from the DVB-T signal. User Behavior Profile stores all user related information including age and number of program views. In Cluster of User Profiles, the system calculates and organizes the number of views and viewing durations of programs for the user; clustering is performed using the user age and program genre preferences. DVB-SI is not the focus of this paper. User Behavior Profile, Cluster of User Profiles, and Recommendation are discussed in the next section.

3.1.1 User Behavior Profile
The user's program viewing history and the information obtained from EPG are saved as a User Behavior Profile. The profile includes the channel, viewing date, time, program title, frequency, and viewing duration. The Recommendation module obtains the user's preferences from the User Behavior Profile, and combines them with the description of television programs from the EPG and popular programs recommended by CRSS to identify the preferred program types of a user at a specified time. After users have watched programs for a period of time, their user profiles are sent to CRSS for user clustering.

Here is the output information:

11->Living Channel-> 2008-12-24 05:30:00-> 00:30-> The Legend And The Hero ->1:37

3.1.2 Cluster of User Profiles
Fig. 3 shows the Cloud-based Rating Sharing Servers used for collecting and clustering user behavior profiles. The clustering part of CRSS is implemented using a map-reduce model. The cluster process includes following steps:

a) **Data collection**
Each user selected programs from 2008/12/23 to 2008/12/30, and input his or her age and location. Assume that there are U user profiles and j programs in user profile i, $u_i = \{(pg_1, f_1, p_1), (pg_2, f_2, p_2), ..., (pg_j, f_j, p_j)\}$, where pg_j is the program j, f_j is the frequency the user i has watched pg_j, and p_j is the duration the user i has watched pg_j.

b) **Preprocessing**
Programs are ignored in a user's profile under two conditions:

1. A program is watched once and the viewing duration is less than 2/3 of the total program length.
2. A program is watched more than once and the viewing duration is less than the total program length multiplied by the number of times the user has watched the program.

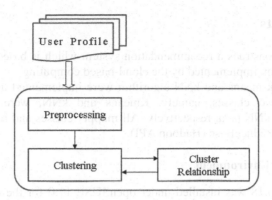

Fig. 3. Flowchart of CRSS

These two conditions showed the history of users watching programs; the conditions can define the effectiveness of the program. When a program is watched for only a short duration, it is classified as uninteresting. A boundary is set to classify uninteresting programs.

Each channel, age and location of the user, viewing date, time, program title, viewing frequency of a program, and viewing duration of a program is converted into a vector in order to be clustered and classified by the system. In the proposed system, the weight of a program in the user's profile is the viewing duration. Therefore, u_i is converted into vector i, $v_i = \{p_1, p_2, ...,p_J\}$.

c) Clustering

U vectors are used to perform k-means to cluster users' profiles into k groups. The viewing duration of a program in each cluster is summed to indicate the popularity of the program in the cluster. Assume that there are L programs in cluster r, $cl_r = \{(pg_1, cp_1), (pg_2, cp_2), ..., (pg_j, cp_j)\}$, where pg_j is the program j and $cp_j = \sum_{p_j \text{ in } cl_r} P_j$. In the proposed system, program j with the first three largest cp_j (i.e., the popular program) in a cluster is recommended to users in the cluster.

d) Cluster relationship

The relationship among clusters is defined by the durations of programs in clusters. k clusters are converted into k vectors, $clv_r = \{cp_1, cp_2, ..., cp_L\}$. k vectors are used to perform k-means to group clusters of users' profiles. A group thus has similar clusters.

3.1.3 User Recommendation

When a user is watching programs, the User Recommendation module connects to CRSS and retrieves clusters of user profiles that contain popular programs. The system uses kNN to predict his or her cluster, cl_r, according to viewing habits (user profile), then automatically recommends the popular programs in cl_r to the user. If a user who has no history is watching programs, the system recommends popular programs in each cluster.

4   Experiments

The experiment construes a recommendation system which is based on the K-means and kNN algorithm, implemented by the cloud-based computing.

The proposed k-means and kNN algorithm were implemented using Java and the Hadoop API. Two classes, namely, Kmeans and kNN, were implemented as Kmeans.java and kNN.java, respectively. All mapper classes and reducer classes are extend from MapReduceBase (Hadoop API).

4.1   Experiment Environment

Apache Hadoop 0.18 was installed under openSUSE 11.0 for the experiments. One machine ran as the name node in the cloud. 10,000 user profiles (approximately 40 megabytes) were generated for the experiment. The operating system for cloud computing was Linux in VMWARE (hadoop installed). The operating system for the standard computer was Windows XP. The amount of RAM and the CPU were the same for both systems.

Due to limited resources, only two computers were tested in the cloud computing setting. Experiments with more computers will be conducted in the future.

4.2   K-means Implementation

For k-means, map and reduce must be performed iteratively, so it must be ensured that the output of map-reduce in each loop can be reused.

The row format of input is:

[id] [age] [area_name] [program_name] [viewing_frequency] [total_viewing_time]

Some of the experiment input data are listed in Table 1.

Table 1. Records of user viewing habits

Id	Age	Area name	Program name	Viewing_ frequency	Total_viewing _time
1	10	Taichung City	Mobile TV_Follow Me!	9	193
1	10	Taichung City	Hakka Channel Special Program me	5	97
2	9	Taichung City	Misc.Channel_Speak English with Channel Gong-Shi	6	84

a) Preparation phase

Since a user, identified by id, can have multiple entry, the input data must be grouped to ensure that there is only one id per row. Subclasses prepareMap and prepreReduce under the Kmeans class are thus implemented. In the map function of prepareMap, tokens are extracted from each row, and <key, value> is collected as <id, [age, program_name, viewing_frequency, total_viewing_time]>.

In the reduce process implemented in the reduce function of prepreReduce, information is collected by id.

organizeMap and organizeReduce classes are implemented to rearrange the output from prepareMap and prepareReduce classes, respectively. In the map function of organizeMap, each field is extracted and collected as:

<id, [age | program_name1, viewing_frequency1, total_viewing_time1: program_name2, viewing_frequency2, total_viewing_time2:...] >

b) K-means Map/Reduce Phase

In the map phase, subclass KmeansMap is implemented to handle the map function. KmeansMap accesses the initial random central points by implementing function "configure", which is available from the "mapper" interface. In the configure function, KmeansMap accesses the jobConf object and obtains the values of central points sent to jobConf before the map reduce job starts.

The map function takes the input from the preparation phase, and finds the closest central point of each point. For this experiment, age was used to calculate distance.

The age of each entry was extracted and used to calculate the distance from 3 central points. The id of the nearest central point, which is the cluster id, and the distance to that central point are collected in the <key, value> set as:

<id, [age | cluster id , distance, central point | program_name1, viewing_frequency1, total_viewing_time1: program_name2, viewing_frequency2, total_viewing_time2:..] >

The reduce phase of k-means simply collects the results from the map phase, implemented in the KmeansReduce subclass.

Some of experiment output data from the map/reduce phase are shown in Table 2.

Table 2. Records of user viewing habits by age group

998   19l0,3.0,16.0lHakka Channel Signal Test,1,81:Misc. Channel_Hikaru no Go,1,25:Hakka Channel Hakka Exclusive,2,12

c) Centroid Refesh Phase

After the map and reduce phase of k-means, every entry is associated with a cluster id. The next step is to calculate the centroid of each cluster and to refresh the central point for the next clustering loop. KmeansCentroidMap and KmeansCentroidReduce subclasses were implemented to perform this job.

The map function of the KmeansCentroidMap class uses output from the previous k-means map/reduce phase. Only age, id, and cluster information are collected. Cluster id is used as the key to collect data: <key, value> is collected as <cluster id, [age1, id1| age2,id2|...]>.

Some of experiment output data from cancroids refresh Map/Reduce are listed in Table 3.

Table 3. Result of clustering by age group

0	55,431l38,371l29,429l26,498l58,374l37,428l38,376l...
1	15,999l21,517l16,529l17,533l16,538l22,539l20,541l...
2	67,418l81,419l69,387l83,386l98,384l69,381l78,378l...

The output from centroid refresh Map/Reduce is then read and new central points are calculated using the means age information related to each cluster.

d) Output Phase

The k-means map phase, the k-means reduce phase, and the centroid refresh phase are repeated until the differences between new central points and the previous central points are all less than 0.5. When the new central points meet this requirement, the program enters the output phase. The only job of the output phase is to copy the input of the last k-means map/reduce phase to the output folder.

4.3 kNN Implementation

The output of section 4.2.2 is the training data of the kNN algorithm. A class called kNN is implemented to handle this algorithm.

a) Preparation Phase

The new point (user's age) can be directly input from the command line or read from a file. When the program starts, it saves the new point to the jobConf object so that any map function run under related jobConf objects can access the new point through the configure function provided by the mapper interface of the Hadoop API.

b) kNN Map/Reduce Phase

In the kNN algorithm, when a new point is to be clustered based on training data, the distance from the new point to all training points is first calculated to obtain the nearest n neighbours. Subclasses kNNMap and kNNReduce are implemented to handle this task. In the map function of kNNMap, age and cluster id are extracted, and the distance from the new point to age in each entry is calculated. <key, value> is collected as < distance, [cluster id, age]>.

The reduction is handled by the kNNReduce subclass, which passes the results of the map phase"to the output.

c) Nearest Neighbor Phase

The output of the kNN map/reduce phase is a list of neighbors ordered by distance. The task of the nearest neighbor phase is to obtain the top 3 nearest entries from the output of the kNN map/reduce phase. The most frequently appearing cluster id is set as the cluster id of the new point.

4.4 Program Recommendation Implementation

The final phase of the system is to recommend programs to the new user based on the cluster. After the kNN phase, the cluster id of the new user is known. kNNResMap and kNNResReduce subclasses are implemented in the kNN class to handle this task.

a) Preparation Phase

The cluster id is sent to jobConf so that the upcoming map function can access it.

b) Recommendation –Map/Reduce Phase

The output of the k-means map/reduce phase is used as the input. program_name and total_viewing_time are collected. Since more than one total_viewing_time can be associated with a program name, the total_viewing_time of all users is used. The data is collected as < key, value> in:

<program_name,   [total_viewing_time1,   total_viewing_time2, total_viewing_time3...]>

The reduce phase passes the results to the output, sorted by program_name.

c) **Output Phase**

The program_name and total_viewing_time of the dataset in the previous phase are collected. In this phase, the average viewing time of each program is calculated and a program list sorted by the average viewing time is produced for recommendation. Subclasses kNNResMap and kNNResReduce are implemented to handle this task. In the map function of kNNResMap, all total viewing times of a program are extracted, and average_viewing _time is calculated as the mean of all total_viewing_time to a program_name. Output <key,value> is collected as <average_viewing_time, program_name>.

In the reduce function, the results are collected and sorted by average_viewing_time.

5 Conclusion

The CPRS architecture was proposed and implemented to improve existing television channel recommendation systems. The system provides users with smart recommendation functions. The back-end of the recommendation server is designed to use the power of cloud-computing, which can be extended to clusters of computers to process large numbers of user records in a short period of time. In the future, the content of EPG will be utilized to recommend better programs for users. Popular programs that are frequently selected by users will be analyzed, and related statistics will be provided to producers or providers of TV programs.

The proposed system was implemented using a cloud computing framework, which uses the map-reduce programming model. The map-reduce versions of k-means and kNN, the two core algorithms in the proposed system, were introduced. The proposed method can be extended to suit various recommendation systems. For example, location-based information can also be used as a dimension of clustering.

To ensure accurate and suitable program recommendation results, the amount of data and computation time need to be considered. More user profiles and longer histories of a set of users should improve the recommendation results. With the power of cloud-computing, it is possible to recommend programs using a very large dataset.

References

1. Johan, P., Michiel, V.S., Jun, W., Marcel, J.T.R., Henk, S.: P2P-based PVR Recommendation using Friends, Taste Buddies and Superpeers. In: Proceedings of Beyond Personalization 2005, San Diego, pp. 66–71 (2005)
2. Xu, J.A., Araki, K.: A Personalized Recommendation System for Electronic Program Guide, pp. 1146–1149 (2005)
3. ETSI EN 300 468 V1.7.1, Digital Video Broadcasting (DVB); Specification for Service Information (SI) in DVB System (2005)
4. Zhiwen, Y., Xingshe, Z.: TV3P: an adaptive assistant for personalized TV. IEEE Transactions on Consumer Electronics 50, 393–399 (2004)

5. Velusamy, S., Gopal, L., Bhatnagar, S., Varadarajan, S.: An efficient ad recommendation system for TV programs. In: Multimedia Systems (2008)
6. Dean, J., Ghemawat, S.: MapReduce: Simplified Data Processing on Large Clusters. In: OSDI (2004) (to appear)
7. McKinley, P.K., Samimi, F.A., Shapiro, J.K., Tang, C.: Service Clouds: a distributed infrastructure for constructing autonomic communication services. In: Proceeding of 2nd IEEE International Symposium on Dependable, Autonomic and Secure Computing (2006)
8. Cohen, J.: Graph Twiddling in a MapReduce World. Computing in Science and Engineering 11(4), 29–41 (2009), doi:10.1109/MCSE.2009.120
9. Grossman, R.L.: The Case for Cloud Computing. IT Professional 11(2), 23–27 (2009)
10. Schaffer, H.E., Averitt, S.F., Hoit, M.I., Peeler, A., Sills, E.D., Vouk, M.A.: NCSU's Virtual Computing Lab: A Cloud Computing Solution. Computer 42(7), 94–97 (2009)
11. Mika, P., Tummarello, G.: Web Semantics in the Clouds. IEEE Intelligent Systems 23(5), 82–87 (2008)
12. Yang, H.-c., Dasdan, A., Hsiao, R.-L., Parker, D.S.: Map-reduce-merge: simplified relational data processing on large clusters. In: SIGMOD 2007: Proceedings of the 2007 ACM SIGMOD international conference on Management of data (2007)
13. Al-Zoube, M.: E-Learning on the Cloud. International Arab Journal of e-Technology 1(2) (June 2009)
14. Kuo, R.J., Ho, L.M., Hu, C.M.: Integration of self-organizing feature map and K-means algorithm for market segmentation. Computers and Operations Research 29, 1475–1493 (2002)
15. Kim, K.J., Ahn, H.: A recommender system using GA K-means clustering in an online shopping market. International Journal of Expert Systems with Applications 34, 1200–1209 (2008)
16. Nhat, V.D.M., Lee, S.: k-means discriminant maps for data visualization and classification. In: Proceedings of the 2008 ACM symposium on Applied computing, pp. 1187–1191 (2008)
17. Alpaydin, E.: Introduction to Machine Learning. MIT Press, Cambridge (2004)
18. Li, B., Lu, Q., Yu, S.W.: An adaptive k-nearest neighbor text categorization strategy. ACM Transactions on Asian Language Information Processing 3, 215–226 (2004)
19. Kwon, O.W., Lee, J.H.: Web page classification based on k-nearest neighbor approach. In: Proceedings of the fifth international workshop on Information retrieval with Asian languages, pp. 9–15 (2000)
20. Qi, Y.I., Atallah, M.J.: Efficient Privacy-Preserving k-Nearest Neighbor Search. In: Proceedings of the 2008 The 28th International Conference on Distributed Computing Systems, pp. 311–319 (2008)

Monitoring and Status Representation of Devices in Wireless Grids

Mahantesh N. Birje[1] and Sunilkumar S. Manvi[2]

[1] Basaveshwar Engineering College, Bagalkot-587102, India
[2] REVA Institute of Technology and Management, Bangalore-560064, India
{mnbirje,agentsun2002}@yahoo.com

Abstract. Grid Computing is a concept, a network, a work in progress, part hype and part reality, and it is increasingly capturing the attention of the computing community. The advancements in wireless technologies and increased number of wireless device users supported the evolution of wireless grids. Grid information server (GIS) has to maintain the most up-to-date resource status information of all devices, so that, application can be scheduled to devices that meet its resource requirements.

Each wireless device is resource constrained, and its resource status keeps on varying dynamically depending upon number of applications it is executing, amount of data it is communicating, battery level, and mobility. In order to keep up-to-date resource status, a continuous monitoring is needed. The increase in number of status delivery of such monitored observations will consume lot much of bandwidth, making the database size of grid information server to grow continuously over a period of time.

To solve this problem, we consider moderate number of communications of status updates that balances both bandwidth consumption and resource status accuracy. Also, we propose three methods to represent these update messages so that bandwidth requirement and latency of communication with GIS is reduced. Normal representation, Variable bit length representation, and Relative difference representation methods are proposed and analyzed. Relative difference method is analyzed in best case as well as in worst case, and is found to be more efficient compared to other two methods in terms of memory requirements.

Keywords: Wireless grid, resource status, resource monitoring window, relative difference.

1 Introduction

Grid is a pool of resources distributed over a wide area of network. Wireless grid computing is evolving because of the fast developments in wireless technology and grid computing technology. Wireless grids extend the capability of grid computing to wireless devices. These devices include resources like processors, memory, bandwidth, code repositories, softwares, etc. Generally wireless devices are characterized by reduced CPU performance, small secondary storage, heightened battery consumption sensitivity, and unreliable low-bandwidth

R.-S. Chang et al. (Eds.): GPC 2010, LNCS 6104, pp. 341–352, 2010.
© Springer-Verlag Berlin Heidelberg 2010

communication. The reason for increased scope, popularity, and usage of mobile wireless devices is their small size, low cost, easy handling, and mobility.

In general, wireless grids are characterized as follows:

- No centralized control
- Consists of small, low powered devices
- Includes heterogeneous resources, applications and interfaces
- New types of resources like cameras, GPS trackers and sensors can be shared among grid devices
- Dynamic and unstable users / resources
- Geographically dispersed resources, with different management policies
- Different security requirement and policies

While the grid is the best way to achieve large-scale resource sharing in a heterogeneous environment, the mobile community has to face many challenges to enter this application domain. The integration of mobile devices is extremely challenging because of many deficiencies that wireless communication and mobile devices have. Wireless networks are of low bandwidth and reliability, while mobile devices have much less resources available than desktop computers. A number of unique challenges must be overcome when building a grid application for these devices such as resource status monitoring, resource status communication, resource discovery, resource allocation, power consumption, energy-efcient medium access, mobility, etc.

Monitoring is the act of collecting information concerning the characteristics and status of resources of interest. More the number of observations more is the accuracy of resource status information, but it adds more load on monitoring process, and more bandwidth consumption (communication cost). Also every monitored (observed) status need not be communicated to update the status, because, two or more successive observation status may be almost similar. Otherwise, it consumes bandwidth and memory unnecessarily.

The locally monitored resource status of a device has to be communicated to grid information server. This can be done in two ways: 1) By pulling the information from each device continuously or periodically or as and when required according to specific needs. 2) By pushing the information to the server either continuously or periodically or when updation occurs. Each option has its own advantages and disadvantages interms of response time, bandwidth requirement, status information accuracy, and others. For real-time critical applications option 1) may not be suitable, because, by the time the server gets response about very recent status, application may start suffering from delay. So option 2) is preferred in such situations. But the resource constraint factor of wireless device may not support continuous pushing of information. Also periodical pushes may suffer from loss of accuracy of status depending upon the period considered: more the period lesser the accuracy will be, and lesser the period more the number of pushes will be, consuming more memory and bandwidth. So, we have designed a strategy that considers only moderate number of observations, and three different methods to represent these observations: Normal representation, Variable bit length representation, and Relative difference representation. Relative difference method effectively reduces bandwidth and memory consumption, and also improves the accuracy. As concerned to our knowledge, this is a new approach for monitoring, updation, and communication of local resources of a device.

Rest of the paper is organized as follows: section 2 presents related works. Section 3 discusses the proposed work. Simulation and results are presented in section 4 and 5 respectively, followed by conclusions in section 6.

2   Related Works

Computational grids are emerging as a new computing paradigm for solving grand challenge applications in science, engineering and economics, and can be defined as large-scale high-performance distributed computing environments that provide access to high-end computational resources [1, 2]. Wireless devices extended to access these resources can form wireless computational grid. But it presents the challenge of integrating these wireless mobile devices with computational grids [3]. To solve computationally expensive tasks papers [4, 5] have proposed an approach to the design of wireless grid architecture that enables mobile devices within a wireless cell to form computational grid. The work given in [6] proposed an extension to the architecture of [4, 5]. It proposed a multi-cell wireless computational grid, which is based on location area concept in GSM cellular networks, and is capable of greater device mobility tolerance.

The paper [7] presents an abstract model and a comprehensive taxonomy for describing resource management architectures. The taxonomy is used to identify approaches followed in the implementation of existing resource management systems for grids. In the paper [8] a Grid Resource Information Monitoring (GRIM) prototype is introduced. To support the constantly changing resource states in the GRIM prototype, the push-based data delivery protocol named Grid Resource Information Retrieving is provided.

In the work [9] a taxonomy of grid monitoring systems is proposed, which is basically based on a given systems scope, scalability, generality and flexibility. Monitoring and Discovery System (MDS) [10] is well-known monitoring software in Globus toolkits. The information sources are registered to index servers in MDS [11]. The users can query directory servers to obtain detailed descriptions about resources. MDS consists of three basic services, which are the Information Provider, the Grid Resource Information Service , and the Grid Index Information Service. In [12], a three-tier architecture that contains coherence protocols based on the pull model to serve the up-to-date information is proposed. In order to minimize the number of late updates, consistent strategies are developed according to the polling rate, such as the Regular Polling strategy, Adaptive Polling strategy, and Slacker Polling strategy in [13].

Minimizing communication overhead in widely distributed environments is the main challenge to be addressed. To monitor grid infrastructure and to maintain system-wide invariants and detect abnormal events with minimal communication overhead, paper [14] presents threshold based distributed triggering mechanism. The work given in [15, 16] solved the problem of detecting threshold violations with specied accuracy while minimizing communication overhead, as well as providing the exibility for users to trade off communication overhead with detection accuracy.

3   Proposed Work

This paper extends our previous work presented in [17], and describes three ways of representing device resource status. We monitor the status of resources like processor, primary memory, bandwidth, signal, battery, and secondary memory of a device. These resources are assigned different relative frequencies (depending on their importance or critical need) and accordingly monitored to generate resource monitoring window [17]. This window is transmitted to Grid Information Server. This section discusses about environment considered, and resource monitoring window representation methods along with algorithms.

3.1   Environment

Figure 1 shows the environment considered for proposed scheme. It consists of wireless devices that monitor their local resource status, and a Grid Information Server (GIS), which maintains the most recent status of each device resources in its resource repository (RR).

- **Wireless Device:** It consists of resources like processor, primary memory, secondary memory, bandwidth, operating system(s), software applications, etc. The resource state changes dynamically depending on number of jobs allocated/running, device mobility, signal strength, and battery power.
- **Grid Information Server:** GIS consists of a database called Resource Repository (RR). All wireless device's resource status will be stored in its RR. Each device in an environment can get information of any other device from GIS and then it can interact with it . GIS also provides device information to the schedulers that allocate jobs to particular devices.

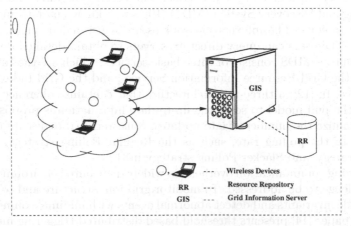

Fig. 1. System Environment

3.2   Resource Monitoring Window

The resources we would like to monitor include processor, primary memory, bandwidth, signal, battery power, and secondary memory. Each resource is associated with an identifier as shown in figure 2a). Each resource is observed with some relative frequency assigned to it, according to its critical importance. It assumes, relative_frequency $(1) = 6$, relative_frequency $(2, 3) = 3$, and relative_frequency $(4, 5, 6) = 1$. Hence these resources can be categorized into three subsets [17] as follows: $S = \{S1, S2, S3\}$, where $S1 = \{1\}$, $S2 = \{2, 3\}$, $S3 = \{4, 5, 6\}$. The resources are monitored according to these relative frequencies in interleaved manner as shown in figure 2b. This monitored resource set constitutes a window called Resource Monitoring Window (RMW), constituting of fifteen status values of resources. This RMW is transmitted to GIS to provide changed status of resources.

Questions arise like: how many number of RMWs (updates) are to be generated in a given interval of time ?, can we represent these RMWs in an efficient way so that memory required is reduced ?, can we communicate these RMWs so that bandwidth consumption is reduced?. Next paragraph describes the solution of first question. Solutions for latter two questions are discussed in next subsection.

In a given time interval T, assume that at least $Umin$ number of RMWs are needed to maintain the minimal accuracy, and $Umax$ is the maximum number of RMWs needed to maintain the maximum degree of accuracy. For $Umin$ number of RMWs, let $Bmin$ be the bandwidth needed and $Amin$ be the accuracy achieved. For $Umax$ number of RMWs, let $Bmax$ be the bandwidth needed and $Amax$ be the accuracy achieved. More the number of RMWs transmitted to GIS more is the accuracy achieved; but, it consumes more bandwidth and memory of resource constrained wireless devices; and vice - versa. There is a trade-off between accuracy of resource status achieved and consumption of bandwidth and memory. To balance this tradeoff we calculate the intersection point of two curves: bandwidth consumption and accuracy achieved. This intersection point, $Umod$, gives the moderate number of RMWs to be considered in a given interval T. So, it transmits $Umod$ number of RMWs during T.

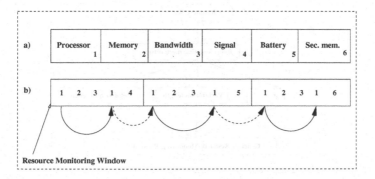

Fig. 2. Interleaving of resources: a) Resource set b) Resource monitoring window

3.3   Status Representation Methods

Figure 3 shows a flowchart of resource status representation methods. It includes three methods: 1) Normal representation, 2) Variable bit length representation, and 3) Relative difference representation. An RMW generated by each method is different and is explained below:

Normal representation: It is a general method to represent RMW. Each resource status value is represented by a word of some fixed number of bits. Generally word can take 16, 32, or 64 bits. Let us consider 16 bit word (2 bytes). Since RMW consists of fifteen status values, size of RMW is 30 bytes. It is represented as RMW_N.

Variable bit length representation: It is a method to reduce the size of RMW. Each status will be represented by some number of bits (lesser than or equal to 16 bits) depending upon its value. If status value is V at any given instance, then $\lceil log_2 V \rceil$ represents the number of bits used to represent that value. So each status value may take different number of bits. Lesser the value of resource status, lesser the no. of bits it needs, and vice versa. In this method the size of RMW is represented as RMW_V, and its size is given by

$$\sum_{i=1}^{15} \lceil log_2 V_i \rceil$$

Relative difference representation: It is an enhancement over variable bit representation method. It needs some bits R $(R \le \lceil log_2 V \rceil)$ to represent the difference in status values of successive observations of same resource. Here, first value needs $\lceil log_2 V \rceil$ bits, second value needs less than it since it represents the difference value (*Change*) with respect to first, third value represents the difference with respect to second, and so on. Hence next successive values need

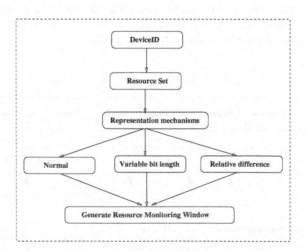

Fig. 3. Flowchart of the status representation mechanism

$\lceil log_2 Change \rceil$ number of bits. If there is no difference (i.e. difference value is 0) then it needs only one bit. In this method the size of RMW is represented as RMW_R.

3.4   Illustration

We illustrate the working mechanism of the above three representation methods of RMW. The RMW consists of totally fifteen status values (six values of processor, three of memory, three of bandwidth, and one each of signal, battery and secondary memory). Each resource status value is represented by 2 bytes in normal method, $\lceil log_2 V \rceil$ bits are used by variable bit method (V is status value in percentage), and R bits are used by relative difference method (R $\leq$ $\lceil log_2 V \rceil$). So R can take value in range of < 1, 7 >.

The Processor load is considered for discussion. Six processor load observations are made in a RMW (marked as 1, 2, 3, 4, 5, 6 in figure 4). Figure 4 shows the number of bits used by each method for these six successive processor load values. Normal method needs 16 bits for each observed value. Variable bit needs $\lceil log_2 V \rceil$ bits to represent the processor load value. In relative difference method, first observation of a resource needs as many bits as needed by variable bit method (i. e. $\lceil log_2 V \rceil$), but in its successive observations, difference with respect to its previous value is considered, which needs lesser bits (R $\leq$ $\lceil log_2 V \rceil$).

We observe that relative difference representation method needs lesser number of bits than variable bit representation method, which in turn needs lesser number of bits compared to normal method.

Sl. No.	Processor load	Change	Normal	Variable bit	Relative difference
1	10	----	16	4	4
2	14	4	16	4	3
3	14	0	16	4	1
4	20	6	16	5	3
5	16	-4	16	4	3
6	16	0	16	4	1

Fig. 4. Example of three methods for representing processor load (Resource 1)

Algorithms. This part presents algorithms of variable bit length representation and relative difference representation methods. An algorithm for variable bit length representation method is as follows:

Algorithm: **VariableBitLength(RMW_N)**
Input : RMW_N
Output : RMW_V such that Size(RMW_V) < Size(RMW_N)

Assumptions: Each resource value in RMW_N is assumed to be of same size (2 bytes)

Nomenclature: RMW_N, RMW_V - are resource monitoring windows represented by normal and variable bit length methods respectively. $RMW_N[\mathrm{i}]$ - resource status value at i^{th} position of RMW_N; $1 \leq \mathrm{i} \leq 15$.

RMW_V = NULL
Size(RMW_V) = 0

//To calculate RMW_V and Size(RMW_V)
For each resource status in RMW_N do
   nob = $\lceil \log_2(RMW_N[i]) \rceil$
   RMW_V [i] = 'nob' bit status value
   Size(RMW_V) = Size(RMW_V) + nob
EndFor
Return RMW_V, Size(RMW_V)
EndAlgorithm

An algorithm for relative difference representation method is as follows: Algorithm: **RelativeDifference(RMW_N)**
Input : RMW_N
Output : RMW_R such that Size(RMW_R) < Size(RMW_V) < Size(RMW_N)
Assumptions: Each resource value in RMW_N is assumed to be of same size (2 bytes)
Nomenclature: RMW_N, RMW_R - are resource monitoring windows represented by normal and relative difference methods respectively. $RMW_N[\mathrm{i}]$ - resource status value at i^{th} position of RMW_N. For any $\mathrm{i} \leq 0$, $RMW_R[\mathrm{i}]$ = Null.

//To calculate RMW_R and Size(RMW_R)
For i = 1 to 15 in steps of 5 do
   $RMW_R[\mathrm{i}]$ = RMW_N [i] - RMW_N [i-2]
   Size($RMW_R[\mathrm{i}]$) = $\lceil log_2(RMW_R[i]) \rceil$

   $RMW_R[\mathrm{i}+1]$ = RMW_N [i+1] - RMW_N [i-4]
   Size($RMW_R[\mathrm{i}+1]$) = $\lceil log_2(RMW_R[i+1]) \rceil$

   $RMW_R[\mathrm{i}+2]$ = RMW_N [i+2] - RMW_N [i-3]
   Size($RMW_R[\mathrm{i}+2]$) = $\lceil log_2(RMW_R[i+2]) \rceil$

   $RMW_R[\mathrm{i}+3]$ = RMW_N [i+3] - RMW_N [i]
   Size($RMW_R[\mathrm{i}+3]$) = $\lceil log_2(RMW_R[i+3]) \rceil$

   $RMW_R[\mathrm{i}+4]$ = RMW_N [i+4]
   Size($RMW_R[\mathrm{i}+4]$) = $\lceil log_2(RMW_R[i+4]) \rceil$
EndFor
Return RMW_R, Size(RMW_R)
EndAlgorithm

4   Simulation Procedure

The cellular network based mobile wireless grid model is considered for simulation. g number of wireless grids are considered. The grid is represented as a square, with its side length l, and simulation area $l * l$ sq meters. The environment includes a GIS server that maintains the details of devices resource status in its repository, RR. The grid consists of n number of mobile wireless devices. Each device consists of m number of resources to be monitored: D = { $r_1, r_2, r_3, r_4, ... r_m$ }. Each resource is assigned a relative frequency according to which it is observed. Resources are grouped into i subsets, where each resource of a subset has same relative frequency. Each resource in set is monitored according to its relative frequency. $Umod$ number of interleaved RMWs are generated.

RMW_N represents the resource monitoring window generated by normal representation, and its size is 240 bits. RMW_V represents the window generated by variable bit length and each resource status size is $\lceil log_2 V \rceil$, where V is status value. RMW_R is the window generated by relative difference method. Here, change in successive status values of a particular resource is found. It needs R bits (R $\leq \lceil log_2 V \rceil$) to represent this change.

Simulation is done assuming following values: g= 1, l=100 meters, n= 10 nodes, m = 6, i.e. D = { $r_1, r_2, r_3, r_4, r_5, r_6$ }. The variables $r_1, r_2, r_3, r_4, r_5, and\ r_6$ represent dynamically changing values of processor, primary memory, bandwidth, signal, battery, and secondary memory respectively. These values are generated randomly. i = 3, rel-freq (S1) = 6, rel-freq (S2) = 3, rel-freq (S3) = 1. Umin = 5, Umax = 20. Each resource needs 16 bits to represent its value, Size(RMW_N) = 15 * 16 = 240 bits.

The **simulation algorithm** is as follows:

– Generate a mobile wireless grid using the specified parameters.
– Generate the current resource status vector of the device in grid
– Apply the Interleaved resource monitoring scheme to generate resource monitoring window, RMW. Generate Umod number of RMWs in a given interval of monitoring.
– This RMW represents the window generated by normal representation method, and is referred as RMW_N.
– Apply variable bit length method over RMW_N and genereate RMW_V
– Apply relative difference method over RMW_N and genereate RMW_R
– Compute the performance parameters.

To evaluate the proposed methods following performance metrics are computed.

– *Memory requirement:*
  It is the number of bits used by RMW to hold fifteen status values of different resources.
– *Bandwidth requirement:* It is the bandwidth required to communicate RMWs with GIS.

– *Reduction Rate (RR):* It is defined as the ratio of number of bits used by general method to the number of bits used by improved method. The reduction rate (of a memory or bandwidth) is calculated as follows:

$$RR = \frac{Number\ of\ bits\ needed\ by\ Normal(or Variable)\ method}{Number\ of\ bits\ needed\ by\ Variable(or Relative)\ method}$$

5   Results

This section presents some of the observations made during simulation. Figure 5 shows the memory requirement of processor status values for six observations. It shows the number of bits required to store six values of single resource (processor) for each RMW generated by three different methods. The normal method needs 16 bits for each status value, variable bit length method needs $\lceil log_2 V \rceil$ (V is processor load value at particular observation slot), and relative difference needs lesser bits than variable bit length method. It is observed that *relative difference method reduces memory drastically if resource status does not change frequently.*

Figure 6 shows memory requirement of a RMW with respect to each method. It clearly presents that relative difference method needs very less number of bits compared to other two methods for every RMW. Figure 7 shows the memory size reduction rate of particular method compared to another. It is seen that relative difference method achieves more reduction in size than other two methods.

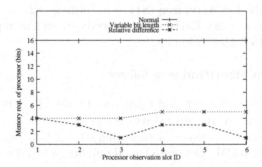

Fig. 5. Memory requirements of six observations of processor load in a RMW

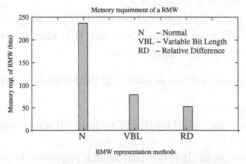

Fig. 6. Memory requirement of a RMW

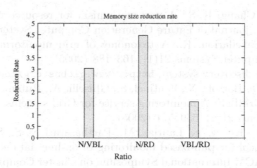

Fig. 7. Memory size reduction rate of three methods

6   Conclusion

Resource monitoring window consists of status of observed resources of a device. To maintain up-to-date status information more number of observations are transmitted from wireless device to grid information server. But communicating more number of observations consumes more bandwidth, and memory. It is needed to maintain the accuracy level and possibly minimise the bandwidth and memory requirements.

This paper considers moderate number of transmissions to balance bandwidth and accuracy. Mainly it focuses on reducing the size of resource monitoring window. Three methods are proposed to achieve this: Normal, Variable bit length, and Relative difference. It is observed from the results that Relative difference method is more efficient in terms of memory requirement, bandwidth requirement, and communication latency than other two methods.

References

1. Foster, I., Kesselman, C.: The Grid: Blueprint for a New Computing Infrastructure. Elsevier publishers, Amsterdam (2009)
2. Foster, I., Kesselman, C.: The Globus Project: a Status Report. In: Proc. of IPPS/SPDP 1998, Workshop on Heterogeneous Computing, pp. 4–18 (1998)
3. Phan, T., Huang, L., Dulan, C.: Challenge: Integrating Mobile Wireless Devices into the Computational Grid. In: Proc. of the 8th International Conference on Mobile Computing and Networking, Atlanta, GA (2002)
4. Kurkovsky, S., Bhagyavati, Ray, A.: A Collaborative Problem-Solving Framework for Mobile Devices. In: ACMSE 2004, Huntsville, Alabama, USA, April 2-3 (2004)
5. Kurkovsky, S., Bhagyavati: Modeling a Computational Grid of Mobile Devices as a Multi-Agent System. In: Proc. of 2003 International Conference on Artificial Intelligence, Las Vegas, NV (2003)
6. Mudali, P., Adigun, M.O., Emuoyibofarhe, J.O.: Minimizing the Negative Effects of Device Mobility in Cell-based Ad-hoc Wireless Computational Grids. In: SATNAC, Stellenbosch, South Africa, vol. 1, p. 10 (2006)
7. Krauter, K., Buyya, R., Maheswaran, M.: A taxonomy and survey of grid resource management systems for distributed computing. Intl. journal of Software Practice and Experience, John Wiley 32, 135–164 (2002)

8. Chung, W.-C., Chang, R.-S.: A new mechanism for resource monitoring in Grid computing. Intl. journal of Future Generation Computer Systems 25, 1–7 (2009)
9. Zanikolas, S., Sakellariou, R.: A taxonomy of grid monitoring systems. Future Generation Computer Systems 21(1), 163–188 (2005)
10. Monitoring and discovery system, http://www.globus.org/toolkit/mds/
11. Andreozzi, S., De Bortoli, N., Fantinel, S., Ghiselli, A., Rubini, G.L., Tortone, G., Vistoli, M.C.: GridICE: A monitoring service for Grid systems. Future Generation Computer Systems 21(4), 559–571 (2005)
12. Sundaresanz, R., Kurcy, T., Lauriaz, M., Parthasarathyz, S., Saltz, J.: A slacker coherence protocol for pull-based monitoring of on-line data sources. In: Proc. of the 3rd IEEE/ACM International Symposium on Cluster Computing and the Grid, pp. 250–254 (2003)
13. Sundaresanz, R., Kurcy, T., Lauriaz, M., Parthasarathyz, S., Saltz, J.: Adaptive polling of grid resource monitors using a slacker coherence model. In: Proc. of the 12th IEEE International Symposium on High Performance Distributed Computing, pp. 260–269 (2003)
14. Huang, L., Garofalakis, M., Hellerstein, J., Joseph, A., Taft, N.: Toward Sophisticated Detection With Distributed Triggers. In: SIGCOMM 2006 Workshops, Pisa, Italy, September 11-15 (2006)
15. Huang, L., Garofalakis, M., Joseph, A., Taft, N.: Communication-efficient tracking of distributed triggers. Technical report (2006)
16. Keralapura, R., Cormode, G., Ramamirtham, J.: Communication-efficient distributed monitoring of thresholded counts. In: ACM SIGMOD (2006)
17. Manvi, S.S., Birje, M.N.: Device Resource Status Monitoring System in Wireless Grids. In: ACEEE Intl. conference on Advances in Computing, Control, and Telecommunication Technologies (ACT 2009), Trivandrum, Kerala, India, December 28-29 (2009)

Diagnosis from Bayesian Networks with Fuzzy Parameters – A Case in Supply Chains

Han-Ying Kao[1,*], Chia-Hui Huang[2], Chu-Ling Hsu[3], and Chiao-Ling Huang[1]

[1] Institute of Networking and Multimedia Technology, National Dong Hwa University
No.1 Sec.2 Da Hsueh Road, Shoufeng, Hualien 97401, Taiwan, R.O.C.
teresak@mail.ndhu.edu.tw, s121690@hotmail.com
[2] Department of Information Management, Kainan University
No.1 Kainan Road, Luzhu Shiang, Taoyuan 33857, Taiwan, R.O.C.
leohuang@mail.knu.edu.tw
[3] National Dong Hwa University Library
No.1 Sec.2 Da Hsueh Road, Shoufeng, Hualien 97401, Taiwan, R.O.C.
bhat_celine@hotmail.com

Abstract. Bayesian networks have been widely used as knowledge models in business, engineering, biomedicine, and so on. When a network is learned with incomplete knowledge, the numerical model based on probability theory needs to be extended. This study presents a robust approach for diagnosis from Bayesian networks with fuzzy parameters. A simulation algorithm is designed to answer the queries from the models. The formulation of piecewise linear possibility distribution functions maintain the scalability in exact approaches.

Keywords: Bayesian networks, fuzzy parameters, diagnosis, piecewise linear membership functions, simulation.

1 Introduction

Bayesian networks [3,8,17] are directed acyclic graphs (DAG) in which the nodes represent the variables, the arcs represent the direct causal influences between the linked variables, and the influences are quantified by conditional probabilities. Such networks are widely used as knowledge models in situations under uncertainty [8]. Since expert systems require both predictive and diagnostic information, two types of reasoning are common in Bayesian networks, deduction and abduction. Deduction, or prediction, is a logical process based on a hypothesis for deducing evidence in situations involving uncertainty. Oppositely, abduction, or diagnosis, is a logical process that hypothetically explains experimental observations [17].

Several methods have been developed for solving abductive or diagnostic reasoning problems in Bayesian networks. Precise methods exploit the independence structure contained in the network to efficiently propagate uncertainty [3,17]. Stochastic simulation methods provide an alternative approach

---

* Corresponding author.

R.-S. Chang et al. (Eds.): GPC 2010, LNCS 6104, pp. 353–362, 2010.
© Springer-Verlag Berlin Heidelberg 2010

suitable for highly connected networks, in which exact algorithms can be inefficient [3,17]. Two other approaches have been proposed for symbolic inference in Bayesian networks, the symbolic probabilistic inference algorithm (SPI) and symbolic calculations based on minor modifications of standard numerical propagation algorithms [3,19].

1.1 Uncertainties in Bayesian Networks

Most previous studies on Bayesian networks used probability distributions associated with random variables as the numerical models. Before modeling the Bayesian network, we first identify the source of uncertainty in reasoning systems. The sources of uncertainty can be classified as (a) stochastic properties of the system, which manifest with random behaviors of the variables; (b) incomplete knowledge, which makes personal or subjective judgments inevitable; (c) semantic vagueness in system features, such as *high* manufacturing capability, *good* stock control performance, *high* customer satisfaction, and so on. Taking difference sources of uncertainties into account, probabilistic approach may be insufficient to the context of reasoning. Therefore, this study intends to integrate the concept of possibility [2,5,15,23] and proposes fuzzy parameters in Bayesian networks.

Let F be a fuzzy subset of a universe of discourse U which is characterized by its membership function μ_F. Let X be a variable taking values in U, and let F act as a fuzzy restriction, $R(X)$, that is

$$R(X) = F. \tag{1}$$

associated with a possibility distribution, Π_X, with X postulated to be equal to $R(X)$, i.e.

$$\Pi_X = R(X). \tag{2}$$

Correspondingly, the possibility distribution function associated with X is denoted by π_X and is defined to be numerically equal to the membership function of F, that is

$$\pi_X = \mu_F. \tag{3}$$

Thus, $\pi_X(u)$, the possibility that $X = u$, is postulated to be equal to $\pi_F(u)$.

If we replace X in (1)–(3) with the probability P, then P is defined as a fuzzy probability whose value is expressed with a possibility distribution. The details of the expression will be given in next section.

As for the graphical decision model with possibility approach, Yamada [21] addressed uncertain reasoning with multiple causes and conditional possibilities on a causal network model, which focuses on the causal effect in two layered networks. Rodríguez-Muñiz et al. [18] explored the statistical rules for modeling fuzzy random variables and utilities in influence diagrams mainly based on the value-preserving transformations. Later, López-Díaz and Rodríguez-Muñiz [13] analyzed how to evaluate influence diagrams with multiple value nodes in terms of fuzzy random variables by dynamic programming. Both emphasize on evaluation and ignore diagnostic reasoning.

At the same time, studies on fuzzy probabilities and parameters as an alternative approach in fuzzy logic framework are developed. Zadeh [24,25] constructed the generalized theory of uncertainty (GTU) and include fuzzy probability as one building block of the fuzzy logic. Li and Kao [11] used fuzzy parameters to formulate the soft constraints in learning average causal effects from imperfect experiments. Later the multiple-objective nonlinear programming models are developed to solve constrained diagnostic reasoning and decision problems [9,12]. Shipley and Johnson [20] proposed a fuzzy sets-based selection of employee to meet the projects' goals for the preferred cognitive style. They design an algorithm based on belief in the fuzzy probability of a cognitive style fitting a defined goal. Abdelaziz and Marish [1] introduced a multistage stochastic program with triangular fuzzy probability distributions. In the study, the α-cut method is used as the defuzzification technique for the minimax approach to decompose the stochastic program.

1.2 Supply Chain Management

Supply chain management is widely recognized as a key to business success, particularly for multinational industries and global markets. Some studies have examined causal effects in supply chains, including the dynamics of buyer-supplier relationships [6,7,16,22], the strategic role of buying firms in structuring supplier-supplier relationships and supply chain effectiveness [4], the relationship between just in-time purchasing techniques and supply chain performance [10], and so on. Notably, Naim et al. [14] designed a methodology for diagnosing European automotive supply chains, which generated the cause-and-effect diagram of the two-echelon supply chain. Considering the nature of uncertainties, we introduce fuzzy parameters in the numerical model.

In the rest of this paper, section 2 first addresses the problem and the model. Section 3 designs the simulation algorithm for diagnosis from the Bayesian network with fuzzy parameters. Finally, section 4 presents the case study and section 5 gives the concluding remarks.

2   Problem and Model

Consider a Bayesian network in Fig. 1. Let $\mathbf{X}$ stands for the set of nodes. For all nodes, we use the uppercase letters to represent the variables and lowercase letters for their values. Without loss of generality, all nodes are assumed to have two possible states, *low* and *high*. For convenience of illustration, let $+x$ stands for $X = 1$ and $\neg x$ stands for $X = 0$. Usually, the relationships among the nodes are expressed with probability distributions. However, incomplete knowledge and subjective judgments may cause the probability parameters hard to estimate and imprecise. Hence this study uses fuzzy probability distributions to model the uncertainty. Let the probability distributions for Fig. 1 be given in Table 1.

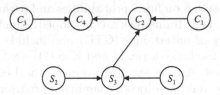

Fig. 1. An example of Bayesian network

Table 1. The distributions for the nodes in Fig. 1

$P(+c_1) = \tilde{p}_1$	
$P(+c_2 \mid +c_1, +s_3) = \tilde{p}_2$	$P(+c_2 \mid \neg c_1, +s_3) = \tilde{p}_3$
$P(+c_2 \mid +c_1, \neg s_3) = \tilde{p}_4$	$P(+c_2 \mid \neg c_1, \neg s_3) = \tilde{p}_5$
$P(+c_3) = \tilde{p}_6$	
$P(+c_4 \mid +c_2, +c_3) = \tilde{p}_7$	$P(+c_4 \mid \neg c_2, +c_3) = \tilde{p}_8$
$P(+c_4 \mid +c_2, \neg c_3) = \tilde{p}_9$	$P(+c_4 \mid \neg c_2, \neg c_3) = \tilde{p}_{10}$
$P(+s_1) = \tilde{p}_{11}$	
$P(+s_2) = \tilde{p}_{12}$	
$P(+s_3 \mid +s_1, +s_2) = \tilde{p}_{13}$	$P(+s_3 \mid \neg s_1, +s_2) = \tilde{p}_{14}$
$P(+s_3 \mid +s_1, \neg s_2) = \tilde{p}_{15}$	$P(+s_3 \mid \neg s_1, \neg s_2) = \tilde{p}_{16}$

We express the fuzzy parameter $\tilde{p}_i$, $(\underline{p}_i, p_i^*, \overline{p}_i)$ with the triangular possibility distribution function (Fig. 2) as below [9,12]

$$
\pi(p_i) = \begin{cases} \pi(\underline{p}_i) + s_1(p_i - \underline{p}_i) + \dfrac{s_2 - s_1}{2}(|p_i - p_i^*| + p_i - p_i^*), \underline{p}_i \leq p_i \leq \overline{p}_i, \\ 0, \text{elsewhere.} \end{cases} \quad (4)
$$

where $s_1 = \frac{1}{p_i^* - \underline{p}_i}$, $s_2 = \frac{1}{\overline{p}_i - p_i^*}$.

The piecewise linear function in (4) can be formulated as follow

$$
\begin{aligned}
\pi(p_i) &= z_1 \pi(\underline{p}_i) + z_2 \pi(p_i^*) + z_3 \pi(\overline{p}_i), \\
z_1 &\leq y_1, z_2 \leq y_1 + y_2, z_3 \leq y_2, \\
p_i &= z_1 \underline{p}_i + z_2 p_i^* + z_3 \overline{p}_i, \\
y_1 &+ y_2 = 1, y_i \in \{0, 1\}, i = 1, 2, \\
z_1 &+ z_2 + z_3 = 1, z_j \geq 0, j = 1, 2, 3.
\end{aligned} \quad (5)
$$

The formulation of possibility distribution functions maintains the scalability in exact propagation methods.

Given the evidence, we need to compute the posterior distributions of every proposition in the system, where the evidence set $E = \{+c_2, \neg c_4, +s_3\}$ is known. Therefore, the problem can be expressed specifically as finding $P(c_1 \mid +c_2, \neg c_4, +s_3)$, $P(c_3 \mid +c_2, \neg c_4, +s_3)$, $P(s_1 \mid +c_2, \neg c_4, +s_3)$, and $P(s_2 \mid +c_2, \neg c_4, +s_3)$.

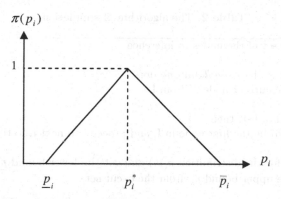

Fig. 2. The triangular possibility distribution of a fuzzy probability

Based on the network structure and the chain rule [8,17], the joint distribution of Fig. 1 is

$$P(x) = P(s_1)P(s_2)P(s_3|s_1,s_2)P(c_1)P(c_3)P(c_2|c_1,s_3)P(c_4|c_2,c_3). \qquad (6)$$

Notably, this study uses crisp random variables (nodes) with probability distributions whose parameters are fuzzy numbers, and expanded the probability distributions into possibility probability distributions. The axioms for the probability theory still hold in this approach [1,9,11,12,20,24,25]. Thus the fuzzy probabilities in the sample space sums to 1; that is $\sum_x P(x) = 1$. This has been regarded as a feasible link between probability and possibility theory [24,25].

3 Diagnostics with Simulation

The problem in section 2 is a typical diagnostic query in supply chains. This study develops a simulation algorithm to answer the query.

For the binary node X, we denote by W_X the state of all variables except X, then the value of X will be chosen by a ratio of $P(+x|W_X)$ to $P(\neg x|W_X)$. The distribution of X conditioned on the values W_X of all other variables in the system, $P(x|W_X)$, can be calculate by purely local computations [17]. Hence, the distributions of $P(x|W_X)$ are expressed in (7)–(10).

$$P(c_1|W_{c_1}) = \beta P(c_1)P(c_2|c_1,s_3), \qquad (7)$$
$$P(c_3|W_{c_3}) = \beta P(c_3)P(c_4|c_2,c_3), \qquad (8)$$
$$P(s_1|W_{s_1}) = \beta P(s_1)P(s_3|s_1,s_2), \qquad (9)$$
$$P(s_2|W_{s_2}) = \beta P(s_2)P(s_3|s_1,s_2), \qquad (10)$$

where β is the normalizing constant. Note that $P(x|W_X)$ is determined by inspecting only neighboring variables belonging to X's Markov blanket. The algorithm of simulation is listed in Table 2.

Table 2. The algorithm of simulation

Set L ← the set of the nodes to inference.

For *iteration* ← 1 to *simulation_no* do:
  Choose the current node X from L.

  If X is end of list, then
    Set X to be the first node in L and proceed to next iteration.

  Set α-cut for the distribution $\pi_{(p_i)}$ and get the lower bound $\underline{p}_i^\alpha$
    and the upper bound $\overline{p}_i^\alpha$ from the α-cut set.

  Compute $\dfrac{P(X=1|W_X)}{P(X=0|W_X)}$ as defined in (7)–(10) with the lower bounds
    and the upper bounds of the α-cut set for $\pi_{(p_i)}$. Get x from a random
    number generator favoring 1 by the ratio $\dfrac{P(X=1|W_X)}{P(X=0|W_X)}$.

  If $x = 1$, then count(x) ← count(x) + 1.
  End. /* of for */

For each x in L do:
  /* The belief or posterior probability function */
  Compute $BEL(x) = $ count(x) / *simulation_no*.
  End. /* of for each */

End. /* of Algorithm */

---

4   Case Study in Supply Chain Management

Consider a two-echelon supply chain in Fig. 1. There are two sets of variables: customer and supplier. The stock control quality of the customer (C_1) and the supplier's schedule alterations (S_3) influence the component supply for the customer (C_2). The component supply for the customer (C_2) and the accuracy of Bill of Materials (B.O.M.) in the customer (C_3) influence the schedule adherence of the customer (C_4). At the same time, the scheduling flexibility (S_1) and the finished goods safety stock of the supplier (S_3) together affect the supplier's schedule alterations (S_3). A typical query from the Bayesian network is demonstrated as follow.

The supplier encounters frequent schedule alterations ($S_3 = 1$); the customer has low schedule adherence ($C_4 = 0$) but has satisfactory component supply ($C_2 = 1$). What are possible causes of the poor schedule adherence? How likely do they account for the inefficiency?

The solution is simulated with 10000 iterations for the target precision. We set the α-level at 0.1, 0.2, ..., 0.9 and 1.0 to obtain the results in Table 3.

Table 3. The simulation results

α	$P(c_1\|+c_2,\neg c_4,+s_3)$ By $\underline{p}_i^\alpha$	By $\overline{p}_i^\alpha$	$P(c_3\|+c_2,\neg c_4,+s_3)$ By $\underline{p}_i^\alpha$	By $\overline{p}_i^\alpha$	$P(s_1\|+c_2,\neg c_4,+s_3)$ By $\underline{p}_i^\alpha$	By $\overline{p}_i^\alpha$	$P(s_2\|+c_2,\neg c_4,+s_3)$ By $\underline{p}_i^\alpha$	By $\overline{p}_i^\alpha$
0.0	0.7562	0.7745	0.7626	0.9260	0.2808	0.4631	0.4214	0.7447
0.1	0.7203	0.8136	0.7664	0.9323	0.2842	0.4407	0.4335	0.7314
0.2	0.7351	0.7846	0.7412	0.9155	0.3084	0.4299	0.4137	0.7231
0.3	0.7478	0.7754	0.7944	0.9008	0.3098	0.4284	0.4585	0.7089
0.4	0.7411	0.7764	0.7768	0.9183	0.3029	0.4141	0.4861	0.6778
0.5	0.7496	0.7665	0.7939	0.8926	0.3248	0.3831	0.5067	0.6884
0.6	0.7210	0.7849	0.7959	0.8868	0.3411	0.3952	0.4771	0.6373
0.7	0.7222	0.7763	0.8067	0.8792	0.3269	0.3919	0.5160	0.6263
0.8	0.7434	0.7520	0.8168	0.8799	0.3307	0.3831	0.5521	0.5927
0.9	0.7484	0.7523	0.8337	0.8499	0.3545	0.3612	0.5537	0.6060
1.0	0.7489	0.7489	0.8036	0.8036	0.3594	0.3594	0.5715	0.5715

Based on Fig. 3–6, the simulated distributions of the posterior probabilities are roughly triangular, except $P(c_1\|+c_2,\neg c_4,+s_3)$. So we approximate the fuzzy posterior probabilities as follow. $P(c_3\|+c_2,\neg c_4,+s_3)=(0.7626, 0.8036, 0.9260)$, $P(s_1\|+c_2,\neg c_4,+s_3)=(0.2808, 0.3594, 0.4631)$, $P(s_2\|+c_2,\neg c_4,+s_3)=(0.4214, 0.5715, 0.7447)$.

If we exclude the outcomes of $P(c_1\|+c_2,\neg c_4,+s_3)$ at $\alpha=0$, its distribution can be approximated as triangular $(0.7203, 0.7489, 0.8136)$. The results imply that the probabilities for good stock control $P(c_1\|+c_2,\neg c_4,+s_3)$ and B.O.M. accuracy $P(c_3\|+c_2,\neg c_4,+s_3)$ in the customer level are relatively high. However, the probabilities for high scheduling flexibility $P(s_1\|+c_2,\neg c_4,+s_3)$ and plentiful finished goods safety stock $P(s_2\|+c_2,\neg c_4,+s_3)$ of the suppler are relatively low and moderate, respectively. Therefore to improve the supply chain performance, the status of S_1 and S_2 should be inspected and fixed.

In comparison with other exact inference algorithms, take global computation with linear or nonlinear programming for example [9,11,12]. The proposed simulation with α-cut is feasible and efficient, especially when the network grows large-scaled. Besides, it provides sensitivity analysis information under

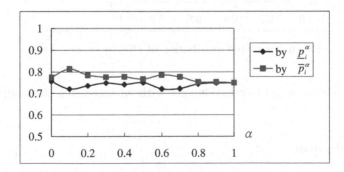

Fig. 3. Simulated distribution of $P(c_1\|+c_2,\neg c_4,+s_3)$

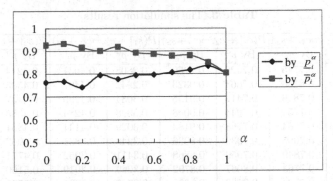

Fig. 4. Simulated distribution of $P(c_3| + c_2, \neg c_4, +s_3)$

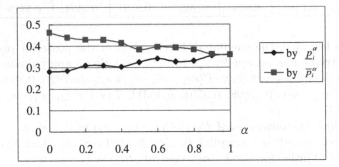

Fig. 5. Simulated distribution of $P(s_1| + c_2, \neg c_4, +s_3)$

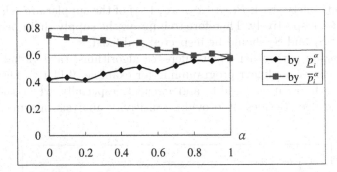

Fig. 6. Simulated distribution of $P(s_2| + c_2, \neg c_4, +s_3)$

different scenarios as the α-value changes without increasing the computational complexity.

5 Conclusion

This study presents a robust method of bridging qualitative and quantitative methods for supply chain diagnostics, namely Bayesian networks with the hybrid possibility-probability approach. Considering different sources of uncertainty, this paper uses possibility-probability distributions as the numerical models for the Bayesian network, where the fuzzy parameters are described with a set of possibility distributions. In real-world systems, the possibility-probability distributions can be maintained with updated knowledge. The outputs include qualitative results which are more akin to the senses of humans, and the quantitative results clarify the likelihood of the causal features. This study intends to contribute to the bridge of qualitative and quantitative reasoning in supply chain systems.

Acknowledgement

The authors appreciate the anonymous referees for their careful reading and the fruitful comments for the manuscript. Also special thanks to the National Science Council, Taiwan, R.O.C., for financially supporting this research under grant No. NSC 97-2410-H-259-065-, 98-2410-H-259-006- (H.Y. Kao) and NSC 98-2410-H-424-004- (C.H. Huang).

References

1. Abdelaziz, F.B., Masri, H.: Multistage stochastic programming with fuzzy probability distribution. Fuzzy Sets and Systems 160, 3239–3249 (2009)
2. Bouchon, B.: Fuzzy inferences and conditional possibility distributions. Fuzzy Sets and Systems 23, 33–41 (1987)
3. Castillo, E., Gutoerre, J.M., Hadi, A.S.: Expert systems and probabilistic network models. Springer, New York (1997)
4. Choi, T.Y., Wu, Z., Ellram, L., Koka, B.R.: Supplier-supplier relationships and their implications for buyer-supplier relationships. IEEE Transactions on Engineering Management 49, 119–130 (2002)
5. Coletti, G., Scozzafava, R.: Conditional probability, fuzzy sets, and possibility: a unifying view. Fuzzy Sets and Systems 144, 227–249 (2004)
6. Heide, J.B., John, G.: Alliances in industrial purchasing: The determinants of joint action in buyer-supplier relationships. Journal of Marketing Research 27, 24–36 (1990)
7. Holm, D.B., Eriksson, K., Johanson, J.: Creating value through mutual commitment to business network relationships. Strategic Management Journal 20, 467–486 (1999)
8. Jensen, F.V.: Bayesian networks and decision graphs. Springer, New York (2001)
9. Kao, H.Y., Li, H.L.: A diagnostic reasoning and optimal treatment model for bacterial infections with fuzzy information. Computer Methods and Programs in Biomedicine 77, 23–37 (2005)
10. Kaynak, H.: The relationship between just-in-time purchasing techniques and firm performance. IEEE Transactions on Engineering Management 49, 205–217 (2002)
11. Li, H.L., Kao, H.Y.: Causal reasoning from imperfect experiments and fuzzy information. International Journal of Fuzzy Systems 6, 44–51 (2004)
12. Li, H.L., Kao, H.Y.: Constrained abductive reasoning with fuzzy parameters in Bayesian networks. Computers and Operations Research 32, 87–105 (2005)

13. López-Díaz, M., Rodríguez-Muñiz, L.J.: Influence diagrams with super value nodes involving imprecise information. European Journal of Operational Research 179, 203–219 (2007)
14. Naim, M.M., Childerhouse, P., Disney, S.M., Towill, D.R.: A supply chain diagnostic methodology: determining the vector of change. Computers and Industrial Engineering 43, 135–157 (2002)
15. Nguyen, H.T.: On conditional possibility distributions. Fuzzy Sets and Systems 1, 299–309 (1978)
16. Olsen, R.F., Ellram, L.M.: A portfolio approach to supplier relationships. Industrial Marketing Management 26, 101–113 (1997)
17. Pearl, J.: Probabilistic reasoning in intelligent systems: networks of plausible inference. Morgan Kaufmann Publishers, Inc., San Francisco (1988)
18. Rodríguez-Muñiz, L.J., López-Díaz, M., Ángeles Gil, M.: Solving influence diagrams with fuzzy chance and value nodes. European Journal of Operational Research 167, 444–460 (2005)
19. Shacher, R.D., D'Ambrosio, B., DelFabero, B.: Symbolic probabilistic inference in belief networks. In: Proceedings of 8th National Conference on Artificial Intelligence, pp. 126–131 (1990)
20. Shipley, M.F., Johnson, M.: A fuzzy approach for selecting project membership to achieve cognitive style goals. European Journal of Operational Research 192, 918–928 (2009)
21. Yamada, K.: Diagnosis under compound effects and multiple causes by means of the conditional causal possibility approach. Fuzzy Sets and Systems 145, 183–212 (2004)
22. Youssef, M.A.: Agile manufacturing: A necessary condition competing in global markets. Industrial Engineering 24, 18–20 (1992)
23. Zadeh, L.A.: Fuzzy sets as a basis for a theory of possibility. Fuzzy Sets and Systems 1, 3–28 (1978)
24. Zadeh, L.A.: Generalized theory of uncertainty (GTU)–principal concepts and ideas. Computational Statistics & Data Analysis 51, 15–46 (2007)
25. Zadeh, L.A.: Is there a need for fuzzy logic? Information Sciences 178, 2751–2779 (2008)

Packaging and Generating Mechanism of Image Processing Services on Heterogeneous Grid Platforms

Ran Zheng, Jian Lan, Qin Zhang, and Hai Jin

Services Computing Technology and System Lab
Cluster and Grid Computing Lab
School of Computer Science and Technology
Huazhong University of Science and Technology, Wuhan, 430074, China
hjin@hust.edu.cn

Abstract. It is a difficult issue to support interactive image processing software in grid environment, which requires special mapping methods over grid architecture. Interactive service packaging, mapping of interactive interface mechanism are reviewed in heterogeneous grid architecture. *Grid Service Automated Packaging and Generating System* (GS-APGS) for image processing software is designed to provide grid service packaging and generating tools to create friendly human-machine interfaces. It includes interactive operation-message mapping in packaging, service-message mapping feedback control in grid service generation, and preservation and restoration of continuous interactive state in overall mapping. Experiments show that GA-APGS can reduce more than 50% time on service packaging and deployment than terminal command-line mode.

1 Introduction

Various images, produced by cameras, x-ray devices, electron microscopes, radar and etc., are useful widely in many fields such as entertainment, medical treatment, business, industrial, military, and academic. But these images can not be used directly, which must be done various analysis and transformation to extract or obtain useful information. Abundant image processing tools and software can not be setup on normal personal PCs because of their high-performance computing requirements, which need to be installed and used on limited high-performance workstations or servers. Grid computing is a better solution to share these helpful tools for the public. The new problem is how to deploy so many applications to heterogeneous grid nodes (such as Globus Toolkit [1], UNICORE [2], CGSP [3] [4] and GOS [5]) with their unchangeable interactivities conveniently and speedily.

This paper elaborates to design *Grid Service Automated Packaging and Generating System* (GS-APGS) of image processing software, which can get the targets of interactive mapping between operations and messages, feedback control mapping between messages and services, and preservation and restoration of continuous interactive states. The rest of this paper is organized as follows: Section 2

R.-S. Chang et al. (Eds.): GPC 2010, LNCS 6104, pp. 363–372, 2010.

discusses the related works. GS-APGS and the service operations are introduced in Section 3. Schema mapping mechanisms of GS-APGS are described in Section 4. Experiments and results are presented in Section 5. Finally, the conclusion is given out in Section 6.

2   Related Works

Interactivity means that probable interactive actions with users will happen during the execution. It is urgent to provide a mechanism to continue supporting the feature when executed in grid environment.

Many grid researchers pay more attention to the grid integration and service representation, but pay little attention on solving interactive-intensive requirements associated. Appea [6] enables grid application developers enmesh interactivity in applications. As an application development platform, Appea provides API to construct grid applications without worrying about technical details. But application scenario developer must be responsible for expressing the scenarios, and the users must be proficient in the use of application development notation and Eclipse-based developer GUI. The grid-enabled *Volumetric Image Visualization Environment* (VIVE) [7] is an interactive analysis tool for 3D medical images, facilitating diagnosis, surgical planning, and etc. It improves understanding of complex anatomies by providing an interactive 3D environment with simple web-based user interface. The lightweight Java/VRML client enables user interaction and 3D rendering within web browser. User can interact with visualization server in grid. The grid provides computing and storage resources, as well as access methods required for volumetric data processing.

Although Appea and VIVE realize web interactive mode and transform shallow interactive software, the user-oriented interactive interfaces are obviously simple, and there are lots of limitations on software programming languages. They are not suitable for packaging and generating common interactive image processing grid services.

3   GA-APGS Platform and Service Operations

3.1   Platform Structure

Grid Service Automated Packaging and Generating System (GS-APGS) aims at providing the support for various grid integration, including different computer hardware environment, different applications or tools, even different grid middleware. Some issues, such as the diversity, strong interactivity, software configuration of platform dependence and data dependence, should be considered in GS-APGS. The pivotal technologies to solve them involve environment loading, interactive operation encapsulation, interactivity-message/message-service mapping, and the integration of heterogeneous grid servers and platforms.

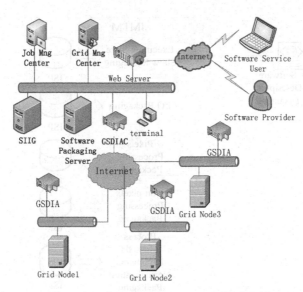

Fig. 1. Topological Structure of GS-APGS

Grid service agent is adopted to shield the differences of service packaging and deploying mechanisms in different heterogeneous grid platforms. Fig.1. shows the topological structure of GS-APGS. *Grid Service Deploying and Invoking Agents* (GSDIA) are configured before distributed heterogeneous grid nodes as unify accessing interfaces to shield the different detail grid operations. Center Server acts as a manager of grid nodes and a bridge for grid users with the components of software packaging server, service invoking interface generator, grid management center, job management center, *Grid Service Deploying and Invoking Agent Center* (GSDIAC) and web server, which are responsible for software packaging, service generation and overall management, and grid platform portal.

3.2   Software Service Packaging, Deploying and Invoking

Interactive Message Transforming Middleware (IMTM) is the front-end interactive message mapping entity, in which *Interactive Scenario Pool* (ISP) is used for packaging procedures. Software description document is built when submitting, and then is transferred into IMTM, where software service entity is packaged step by step with the assistance of ISP, shown in Fig.2.

Software operation interfaces are customized by GS-APGS interactive templates, which are the integration of front-end interactivities. Serialized messages are generated and gained from interactive interfaces, which must be continually corresponding with both front portal operations and software service in backend grid nodes. Interactive interfaces are utilized for interactive software to monitor various service operations such as upload and download, text manipulation, parameters submission, 3D visualization, result demonstrability, error report.

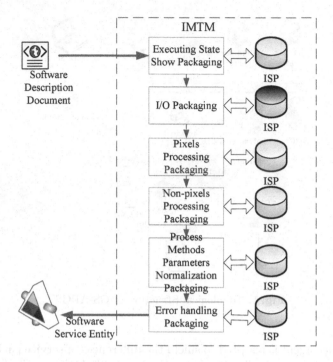

Fig. 2. Software Packaging Procedure

On heterogeneous grid platforms, GSDIA acts as a pivotal server in GS-APGS structure, through which software services are provided and used as grid services. GSDIAC is responsible for distributing service entities on each node. Service entities are unified to deploy on distributed grid nodes by GSDIA.

The friendly human-machine interface is automatically generated by *Service Invoking Interface Generator* (SIIG) with better user experience, which realizes client-service interactive reconstruction with four functions possessed in SIIG: interactive operations simulation, front-end information simplification, scenario recovery, and image/text results presentation.

4   Interactive Mapping Approach

In this section, an interactive mapping approach among operation, message and service is described. The approach is comprised of interactive operation-message mapping in packaging, service-message mapping with feedback controller in generating, and preservation and restoration of continuous interactivity in mapping.

4.1   Interactive Mapping between Operation and Message

It is an inevitable fact that grid services are separated from grid portal or client when execution because of single software architecture. How to reconstruct the interaction before the separation between front-end and backend machine is the main issue to package interactive software to software grid services.

Software Object (SO) is the representation of distributed application components. In order to describe the relationship of distributed application components, distributed component interfaces must be provided with functionality, performance, and its status. SO is also defined via software service interfaces, service request and interactive message protocol. Considering coupled with external communication and other connected components, *Software Interfaces* (SI) is defined as $SI =< SresI, SreqI, SstatI, CFI >$.

- *SresI* (Software Service Responding Interface): a set of packaged services and interactive interface protocols.
- *SreqI* (Software Service Requesting Interface): a set of software service requests.
- *SstatI* (Software Runtime State Interface): a set of scheduling states and attributes of local function in each service package.
- *CFI* (Software Configuration Interface): a set of complex non-functional interfaces, such as timing, synchronization, including resource control interfaces, performance configuration interface and synthesis interface.

Interactive messages are the backbone between grid server and web client user. Messages between web client and grid servers are divided into two kinds of messages: operation messages in front-end client and feedback messages in backend server. Traditionally, each procedure is defined as two steps: serialization and de-serialization. The processing is as follows:

1. User's operation is defined as A in (1).

$$A = \{Action_1, Action_2, Action_3, ...\} \tag{1}$$

2. A will be processed then as a specific operative action message, which is defined as M in (2).

$$M = \{Msg_1, Msg_2, Msg_3, ...\} \tag{2}$$

3. Service interfaces receive the message M, process, calculate, and return feedback messages through service-message mapping mechanism, the feedback messages is defined as M' in (3).

$$M' = \{Msg'_1, Msg'_2, Msg'_3, ...\} \tag{3}$$

4. Messages M' is transmitted to front-end web, which catches the messages, and de-serializes them as a feedback server action, defining as A' in (4).

$$A' = \{Action'_1, Action'_2, Action'_3, ...\} \tag{4}$$

Template-based improvements on traditional transformation of human-machine operation messages are made in GS-APGS. Fig.3 shows the new transformation method of human-machine operation messages.

For each order $< A, M >$, procedure f ensures $M = f(A)$. Due to the great generality among interactive operations, the improvement is described as follows:

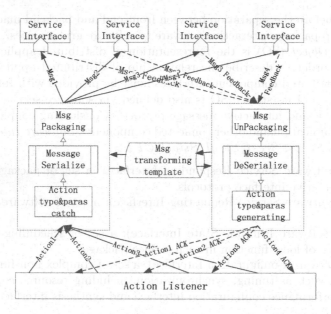

Fig. 3. Interactive Operation-Message Mapping with Message Transforming Template

1. Through the processing g (such as the interested region of the normalized processing), versatile action A is defined as B in (5).

$$B = g(A) \tag{5}$$

2. Universal B can be prescribed as (6), and added into transforming templates. In each step of analyzing and processing action type and parameters, A can be transformed into B (additional certain fixed parameters $p(A)$).

$$B = \{B_1, B_2, B_3, ...\} \tag{6}$$

3. The serializability templates for messages are ordered pair $< B, C >$ lists, by which B can be matched, and the return result is C, as in (7).

$$C = \{C_1, C_2, C_3, ...\} \tag{7}$$

4. The last step of message packaging procedure h combines $p(A)$ with the output C, and the last message M will be returned as (8).

$$M = h(C, p(A)) \tag{8}$$

4.2 Service-Message Mapping with Feedback Control

A mapping table is needed in the procedure of operation message-service mapping. The mapping table is consisted of key words and the corresponding elements. To be more specific, it consists of interactive message types and the corresponding interactive processing interfaces. For a given interactive message, its corresponding interactive processing interface can be found from the table quickly. Because the processing objects of grid service object is various images; the main load depends on the response time of grid node, I/O transmission of large-scale pictures over Internet and etc. Feedback control [8] are leaded in five decisive factor: CPU utilization $L(C)$, I/O transmission $L(I)$, network latency quantity $L(N)$, response time of grid $L(R)$, the number of processes executing $L(P)$. It obtains the relative weight of load value $L(Gi)$ through these several factors, as shown in (9).

$$L(G_i) = (c_1, c_2, c_3, c_4, c_5) \begin{pmatrix} L(C_i) \\ L(I_i) \\ L(N_i) \\ L(R_i) \\ L(P_i) \end{pmatrix}, \sum c = 1, i = 1, 2, 3, \ldots \quad (9)$$

Five impact factors weight parameter c_i. The initial value of c_i is determined by node log registered. The different response time will strongly impact the influence of the results.

When grid node finishes the task J_j, feedback control for handling J_j will be started, namely grid node G_i, to update $L(C_i)$ with grid agent service access.

In the new coming task J_{j+1} according to the overall updated by feedback controller, the load and processing capacity are reappraised, shown in (10).

$$L'(G_i) = k_i * (c_1, c_2, c_3, c_4, c_5) \begin{pmatrix} L'(C_i) \\ L'(I_i) \\ L'(N_i) \\ L'(R_i) \\ L'(P_i) \end{pmatrix}, \sum c = 1, i = 1, 2, 3, \ldots \quad (10)$$

k_i means the weight of grid node's hardware processing capacity.

Then the most suitable grid node (minimum of $L'(G_i)$) will be scheduled.

In message-service mapping model, GS-APGS receives user's interactive operations, and then finds out each interface which can process the message according to the message type. After this step, GS-APGS records these grid nodes' evaluation value, selects the node with the smallest value to participate in *Service Primitive* (SP) generation and service execution.

4.3 Preservation and Restoration of Continuous Interactive Mapping States

While software services are in use, GS-APGS needs to maintain the sustainability and interactivity, and each interactive operation request and service response should be consistent to every grid node. Based on the mechanism, GS-APGS maintains the continuous process through service session [9], and realizes the preservation and restoration of continuously interactive states.

Because grid computing nodes are widely distributed over Internet, grid nodes may be overweight, or make mistakes of software services. If there are no services to maintain sustainable mechanism, reliable response is unreachable.

Due to the continuously front-end interactive message, every interactive action-message request and software service response will not always be in the same node. If there is no consideration of continuous states, there will be only an interaction between users and grid nodes. Therefore, GS-APGS creates a software service session of front end to establish the state sustainability, shown in Fig.4.

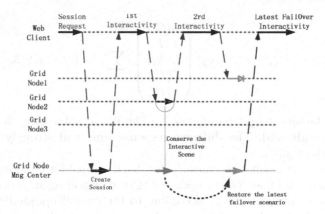

Fig. 4. Preservation and Restoration of Continuous Interactive States with Service Session

5   Experiments and Results

A demo system of GS-APGS is built with central server and 4 grid nodes. Central server is configured with Intel(R) Xeon(TM) 2.40GHz*2 CPU and 1GB RAM. Distributed grid computing nodes are deployed with two different grid platforms CGSP and GOS. The detail configurations are shown in Table 1. The interactive software-ImageJ [10] is packaged and generated as software service.

When a grid node is used as terminal command-line mode (not using GS-APGS), the whole execution can be divided into 5 parts: web portal, interactive command, transmission, grid response and file share. The compared execution time is shown in Fig.5, from which we can find that the elapsed time of web portal is nearly equal with grid response time, and grid response time has a great influence on its whole time.

Same experiments in GS-APGS are done with great changes. The duration in GS-APGS is 28,874ms, 42ms, 30ms and 9ms, compared with the elapsed time by terminal command-line in each grid node, as shown in Fig.6. Obviously, after packaging and generating in the first grid node, the packaging and generating time will be apparently reduced.

The result shows that users can utilize GS-APGS to package software, deploy procreant grid services and generate user interfaces automatically. It can save more than 50% time in the procedure of service packaging and deployment.

Table 1. Grid Node Environments

Grid Node	Hardware	Software
node10.CGSP	Pentium III 1GHz, 512MB RAM, 40GB Disk	Red Hat Enterprise Linux 5, Java SDK J2SE 1.5.0, ANT 1.6.5, CGSP2.1 container2.1.0
BlueGrid.CGSP	Intel Xeon 2.40GHz*2, 1GB RAM, 64GB Disk	Red Hat Enterprise Linux 5, Java SDK J2SE 1.5.0, ANT 1.6.5, CGSP2.1 container2.1.0
node10.GOS	Pentium III 1GHz, 512MB RAM, 40GB Disk	Red Hat Linux 9.0, Java SDK J2SE 1.5.0, MySQL4.0.20, GOS 3.1.0, jakarta tomcat 5.0.28, Java SDK J2SE 1.5.0
BlueGrid.GOS	Intel Xeon 2.40GHz*2, 1GB RAM, 64GB Disk	Red Hat Enterprise Linux 5, GOS 3.1.0, jakarta tomcat 5.0.28, Java SDK J2SE 1.5.0, MySQL 5.0.22

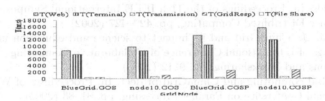

Fig. 5. Software Service Invoking Time Test

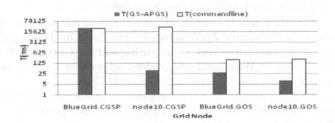

Fig. 6. GS-APGS Packaging and Generating Time Test

6 Conclusions

Although grid application development platforms make little attention on interactive requirements associated with user requirements, we study the interactive software service mechanism with GS-APGS.

In this paper, a brief overview of GS-APGS topological structure is given, and interactive operation-message-service mapping approaches are proposed, which include interactive operation-message mapping in packaging, service-message mapping feedback control in grid service generation, and preservation and restoration of continuous interactive state in overall mapping. In the approach, GS-APGS can deal with failover task and reduce service generating times. It can save more than 50% time on service packaging and deployment than terminal command-line mode. Further research will focus on the expansibility and reliability of GS-APGS.

Acknowledgment

This work is supported by National High Technology Research and Development Program of China (863 Program) under grant No.2006AA01A115, National Natural Science Foundation of China (No.60803006).

References

1. Mache, J., Apon, A.: Teaching Grid Computing: Topics, Exercises, and Experiences. IEEE Transactions on Education 50, 3–9 (2007)
2. Michael, R., Philipp, W.: UNICORE-Globus interoperability: getting the best of both worlds. In: Proceedings of the 11th IEEE International Symposium on High Performance Distributed Computing, pp. 422–427 (2002)
3. Hai, J., Li, Q.: ChinaGrid and its impact to science and education in China. In: Proceedings of International Conference of Collaborative Computing: Networking, Applications and Worksharing, pp. 9–12 (2005)
4. Hai, J.: Grid computing and ChinaGrid project. In: Proceedings of Workshops of International Conference on Parallel Processing, pp. 81–83 (2005)
5. Zhiwei, X., Huaming, L., Bingchen, L., et al.: Two approaches to collaborative computing. In: Proceedings of the 8th International Conference on Computer Supported Cooperative Work in Design, pp. 1–10 (2004)
6. Nowakowski, P., Harezlak, D., Bubak, M., et al.: A New Approach to Development and Execution of Interactive Applications on the Grid. In: Proceedings of IEEE International Symposium on Cluster Computing and the Grid, pp. 681–686 (2008)
7. Branko, M., Zoran, J.: Web-based grid-enabled interaction with 3D medical data. Future Generation Computer Systems 22, 385–392 (2006)
8. Mihai, S., Dan, I., Sanda, M.: Performance analysis of a distributed question/answering system. IEEE Trans. on Parallel and Distributed Systems 13, 579–596 (2002)
9. De, T., Vanhastel, F., Vlaeminck, S., et al.: Design and implementation of a generic software architecture for the management of next-generation residential services. In: Proceedings of IFIP/IEEE Eighth International Symposium on Integrated Network Management, pp. 605–618 (2003)
10. Sage, D., Neumann, F., Hediger, F., et al.: Automatic tracking of individual fluorescence particles: application to the study of chromosome dynamics. IEEE Transactions on Image Processing 14, 1372–1383 (2005)

AvPM: An Avatar-Based Personal Messenger for Low Bandwidth Networks

Yu-En Wu and Cheng-Chin Chiang

Department of Computer Science & Information Engineering,
National Dong Hwa University, Shoufeng, Hualien, Taiwan
ccchiang@mail.ndhu.edu.tw

Abstract. This paper presents the novel design of an avatar-based personal messenger called the AvPM. Differing a lot from the common messengers like Microsoft MSN and Yahoo Messenger, the proposed AvPM allows the receiving site to synthesize on the fly a virtual avatar having the synchronized voices, facial expressions and head poses of the speaker at the speaking site. More importantly, the visual data transmitted by the AvPM is not a large volume of compressed video of the speaker's appearance, but a small amount of synthesizing parameters for rendering the synchronized avatar's appearance. This novel feature makes the AvPM very suitable for personal audio-visual communication over low-bandwidth networks. The experimental results show that the AvPM outperforms the MSN and H.264 in terms of the required network bandwidth and the rendered audio-visual quality.

1 Introduction

In recent years, the stabilized and popularized network infrastructure has created a paradigm shift in the life model of everyone. Nowadays, many people do their routine work remotely over interconnected networks to save both time and money. Among the many daily personal activities taken place on the networks, personal communication would be the most important and frequent one. From the text-based emails in earlier years to the video conferences in the present day, we have witnessed that the integration of multimedia and network technologies has made an epoch-making transition on the modality of personal communication. The new networked multimedia modality of personal communication has fascinated many people, particularly the younger population, and has explored a highly potential market on telecommunication. Many audio-visual messengers such as Microsoft MSN, Yahoo Messengers, Google Talk, Skype and so on are all successful products emerged from this new trend of networked multimedia. However, due to the space-consuming nature of multimedia data, higher-quality multimedia communication demands higher bandwidths and better reliability from networks. Some researchers have developed various compression techniques for multimedia data and rate-control protocols for multimedia transmission.

In this paper, we present our work in developing a novel avatar-based personal messenger, called the AvPM, for networked personal chatting. Users can

R.-S. Chang et al. (Eds.): GPC 2010, LNCS 6104, pp. 373–384, 2010.

undertake audio-visual chatting through this messenger. A big salient feature of the proposed messenger is its capability of instantly creating virtual avatars at the receiving site. In addition, the appearances, including the facial expressions and head poses, as well as the voices of the avatars are synchronized with those of the speakers at the speaking site. The speaker can choose his or her favored avatar for visual output at the receiving site. This interesting messenger appeals more to users than the common personal messengers. More importantly, since the visual output of the avatar is instantly synthesized at the receiving site, the proposed messenger demands a much lower network bandwidth to transmit the synthesizing parameters than do the common personal messengers.

The design of the proposed AvPM comprises mainly two parts. The first part concerns how to transfer the speaker's facial appearance captured from a camera to that of the synthesized avatar. This transfer involves the processes to automatically track the speaker's face on video frames and to synthesize the facial expressions on the avatar's face. The second part deals with how to transmit the synthesizing parameters and the voice data and how to synchronize the voice and visual data during the playback at the receiving site. For the tasks of the first part, we employ the active appearance model (AAM) [2] which is a powerful parametric representation of the shapes and textures of visual objects. It is the AAM that facilitates both the tracking and the representation of the speaker's face in the proposed personal messenger. The AAM uses only a very small amount of parameters to represent the appearance of a human face and thus demands only a very low bandwidth from the networks. For the tasks of the second part, we design a simple buffering mechanism for streaming and synchronizing the audio-visual data.

Fig. 1 shows the block diagram of the architecture of the proposed AvPM. At the speaking site, the voice recording module operates continuously to acquire the voices of the speaker from a microphone. Meanwhile, a video capturing module is responsible for capturing the video of the speaker. On each captured video frame, the AAM tracking module tracks and extracts the speaker's face. The tracking result of the AAM gives the synthesizing parameters for composing the face of a specific avatar at the receiving site. These synthesizing parameters are packed and then transmitted to the receiving site through Internet. At the receiving site, the received packets are buffered by a buffering module. The buffered visual packets are used by an avatar synthesizing module to synthesize the appearance of a specified avatar. The synthesized avatar facial appearance is then synchronized with the received voices by a audio-visual synchronizing module. Finally, the synchronized visual data and voice data are played by the playback module at the receiving site.

2   Related Work

For commonly-used personal messengers, the delivered visual data is the compressed video of the speaker. There have been many advanced techniques for compressing the video, even though the video is compressed, the size of transmitted

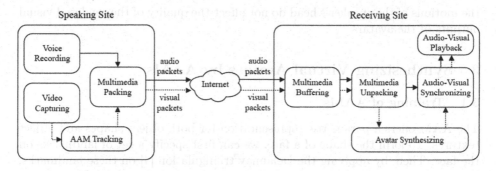

Fig. 1. The system architecture of the proposed AvPM

data is still large. Therefore, the network bandwidth plays a critical role in promoting the applications of audio-visual personal messengers. To further reduce the requirement of the network bandwidth for the audio-visual personal messengers, some researchers proposed two alternative ways. One is to virtually synthesize an animated avatar at the receiving site [6]. No lip syncing is required for the synthesized virtual avatar. This approach aims only at transmitting good-quality voices to the receiving site. The photo-realistic and vivid rendering of the avatar's appearance is not the emphasized goal for this approach. Nevertheless, this approach is not appealing to those people who care about both the visual and hearing contacts. The other alternative is to extract the speaker's face texture and then mapped the texture to a 2D or 3D model of an avatar [10,7]. This approach is more attractive than the first one because the facial expressions of the speaker are visible to the receiving site. However, although the face texture is usually smaller than a video frame in size, the image data needing to be transferred may still be large.

For transmitting multimedia over networks, there have been some well-known video compression standards, such as the MPEG-4 and the H.264 [9,8]. These standards allow the multimedia to be transmitted at different quality depending on the available network bandwidth. Generally speaking, the transmission of good-quality multimedia is acquired from higher network bandwidth. For low-bandwidth networks, the achieved quality of multimedia is very limited. According to the principles underlying these compression standards, the compression ratio fluctuates sensitively with the speaker's head motions. For large head motions, the required bandwidth gets large because the larger error residuals induced by motion compensation must be encoded with more bits. If only a low bandwidth is available, then the data must be encoded with fewer bits. As a result, the quality of the reconstructed video would be degraded.

The AvPM proposed in this paper has some superior features over the existing work. Firstly, the AvPM emphasizes the efficacy of communication via both the audio data and the visual data. Secondly, the synthesized avatars have vivid and photo-realistic appearances synchronized with the speakers. Thirdly, the network bandwidth required by the AvPM is very low even though no multimedia compression is employed. Fourthly, as no motion-based compression is needed, the motions of the speaker's head do not affect the quality of the rendered visual outputs of the avatars.

3 Synthesizing Virtual Avatars by AAMs

3.1 Training of AAMs

The AAM offers a parametric representation for both object shapes and object textures. To form the shape of a face, we can first specify a set of landmarks on the face. Then, by applying the Delaunay triangulation [4] on these landmarks, we can obtain a polygonal mesh, which covers the whole face, as the face shape. Therefore, we can use the vector $\mathbf{s} = [x_1, y_1, \ldots, x_i, y_i, \ldots, x_L, y_L]$, where (x_i, y_i) is the coordinate of the ith landmark and L is the number of landmarks, to serve as a straightforward representation of the face shape. To reduce the dimension of the shape vector $\mathbf{s}$, the principal component analysis (PCA) [4] is performed to derive a more compact representing subspace which can be spanned by a set of basis vectors called eigenshapes. Similarly, a texture vector can be obtained by arranging the 2D pixel values of a face image into a 1D vector. Also by the PCA, the original texture space can be reduced to a compact subspace spanned by a set of eigentextures. It should be noted that all landmarks must be located either automatically or manually on each face image before the PCA. With the located landmarks, the Procrustes analysis [3] is then performed to normalize the faces to have comparable positions, sizes and orientations.

Let $\hat{\mathbf{s}}_1, \hat{\mathbf{s}}_2, \ldots, \hat{\mathbf{s}}_M$ be the M eigenshapes obtained from the PCA, where $\mathbf{s}_i \in \mathbb{R}^{2L}$ for $1 \leq i \leq M$. With these eigenshapes, any shape vector $\mathbf{s}$ of a person's face can be approximated by the following linear combination

$$\mathbf{s} = \bar{\mathbf{s}} + p_1\hat{\mathbf{s}}_1 + \cdots + p_M\hat{\mathbf{s}}_M, \tag{1}$$

for some coefficients p_1, p_2, ..., p_M. Usually the value M is much smaller than the original dimension of $\mathbf{s}$, i.e. $2L$, such that the the parameter vector $\mathbf{p} = [p_1, p_2, \ldots, p_M]^t$, called the shape parameter vector of $\mathbf{s}$, becomes a more compact representation of $\mathbf{s}$. The is the key parameter to synthesize the face shape $\mathbf{s}$.

Similarly, after performing the PCA on the 1D texture vectors collected from a number of the person's face images, the eigentextures, say $\{\hat{\mathbf{a}}_1, \hat{\mathbf{a}}_2, \ldots, \hat{\mathbf{a}}_{M'}\}$, can be derived. Afterward, every observed face texture of this person can then be approximated by

$$\mathbf{a} = \bar{\mathbf{a}} + \lambda_1\hat{\mathbf{a}}_1 + \cdots + \lambda_{M'}\hat{\mathbf{a}}_{M'}, \tag{2}$$

for some coefficients λ_1, λ_2, ..., λ'_M. The vector $\boldsymbol{\lambda} = [\lambda_1, \lambda_2, \ldots, \lambda_{M'}]^t$ is called the texture parameter vector of $\mathbf{a}$ which is a more compact representation.

3.2 Synthesizing of the Avatar Faces by AAMs

Before synthesizing the faces of avatars, we have to exploit an AAM to track the face of the speaker on the video frame. Using an AAM to track a face is through a model fitting process. The model fitting process iteratively updates the shape parameter vector and the texture parameter vector to reconstruct a face appearance that best matches the observed face appearance. For each observed face shape, two kinds of possible face deformation are considered. One kind of deformation is the deformation constituted by the local displacement of pixels on the mean face shape. The other kind of deformation is the global geometric transformation of the whole face. The global transformation can be assumed to be an affine transform. To deal with each kind of deformation separately, Matthews and Baker [5] formulated the AAM's fitting process as a process to minimize the following error residual

$$\sum_{\mathbf{x} \in \bar{\mathbf{s}}} [E(\mathbf{x})]^2 = \sum_{\mathbf{x} \in \bar{\mathbf{s}}} [\mathbf{a}(\mathbf{x}) - I(N(W(\mathbf{x}; \mathbf{p}); \mathbf{q}))]^2, \tag{3}$$

$$= \sum_{\mathbf{x} \in \bar{\mathbf{s}}} [\bar{\mathbf{a}}(\mathbf{x}) + \sum_{i=1}^{M'} \lambda_i \hat{\mathbf{a}}_i(\mathbf{x}) - I(N(W(\mathbf{x}; \mathbf{p}); \mathbf{q}))]^2 \tag{4}$$

where $\mathbf{a}(\mathbf{x})$ denotes the reconstructed intensity value of the pixel $\mathbf{x}$ on the face texture; $W(\mathbf{x}; \mathbf{p})$ denotes the local displacement of the pixel $\mathbf{x}$ which can be characterized by a shape parameter vector $\mathbf{p}$; $N(\mathbf{x}; \mathbf{q})$ denotes the global affine transform of the pixel $\mathbf{x}$ with respect to a parameter vector $\mathbf{q}$; $I(\mathbf{x})$ denotes the intensity value of the pixel $\mathbf{x}$ on the observed face image I. The goal of the AAM fitting process is to estimate the parameters including λ_i, $\mathbf{p}$, and $\mathbf{q}$ so that the error residual in Eq. (4) can be minimized. To this end, Matthews and Baker proposed in their paper an efficient algorithm, called the inverse compositional (IC) AAM algorithm which can converge to a locally optimal estimation for the parameters. As the derivations of the IC AAM algorithm are quite sophisticated, readers who are interested in the details should refer to the paper of Matthews and Baker.

For each AAM, two functions, the shape function $\mathcal{S}()$ and the texture function $\mathcal{A}()$, can be defined as:

$$\mathcal{S}(\mathbf{p} = [p_1, p_2, \ldots, p_m]^t; \bar{\mathbf{s}}, \mathbf{S}) = \bar{\mathbf{s}} + \sum_{i=1}^{m} p_i \hat{\mathbf{s}}_i \text{ and} \tag{5}$$

$$\mathcal{A}(\boldsymbol{\lambda} = [\lambda_1, \lambda_2, \ldots, \lambda_{m'}]^t; \bar{\mathbf{a}}, \mathbf{A}) = \bar{\mathbf{a}} + \sum_{i=1}^{m'} \lambda_i \hat{\mathbf{a}}_i, \tag{6}$$

with respect to the shape parameter vector $\mathbf{p}$ and the texture parameter vector $\boldsymbol{\lambda}$, where $\mathbf{S} = [\hat{\mathbf{s}}_1 \, \hat{\mathbf{s}}_2 \ldots \hat{\mathbf{s}}_m]^t$ and $\mathbf{A} = [\hat{\mathbf{a}}_1 \, \hat{\mathbf{a}}_2 \ldots \hat{\mathbf{a}}_{m'}]^t$. Thus, the local deformation of an observed face in shape and texture relative to the mean shape and the mean texture are

$$\Delta \mathcal{S}(\mathbf{p}; \bar{\mathbf{s}}, \mathbf{S}) = \sum_{i=1}^{m} p_i \hat{\mathbf{s}}_i = \mathcal{S}(\mathbf{p}; \bar{\mathbf{s}}, \mathbf{S}) - \bar{\mathbf{s}} \text{ and} \tag{7}$$

$$\Delta\mathcal{A}(\lambda; \bar{\mathbf{a}}, \mathbf{A}) = \sum_{i=1}^{m'} \lambda_i \hat{\mathbf{a}}_i = \mathcal{A}(\lambda; \bar{\mathbf{a}}, \mathbf{A}) - \bar{\mathbf{a}}, \tag{8}$$

respectively.

Let I and O be respectively the identities of the speaker and the avatar. The local deformation on the speaker's face, $\Delta\mathcal{S}(\mathbf{p}_I; \bar{\mathbf{s}}_I, \mathbf{S}_I)$, must be transferred in an appropriate manner to the local deformation, $\Delta\mathcal{S}(\mathbf{p}_O; \bar{\mathbf{s}}_O, \mathbf{S}_O)$, of the avatar's face. In doing this, we use the eigenshapes of the avatar's face to approximate the deformation on the speaker's face, obtaining

$$\sum_{i=1}^{m_O} p_{O,i} \hat{\mathbf{s}}_{O,i} \approx \sum_{i=1}^{m_I} p_{I,i} \hat{\mathbf{s}}_{I,i}, \tag{9}$$

Multiplying both sides of Eq. (9) with the transpose of the eigenshape $\hat{\mathbf{s}}_{O,i}$ and applying the orthogonality among eigenshapes lead to

$$p_{O,i} \approx \sum_{i=1}^{m_I} p_{I,i} \langle \hat{\mathbf{s}}_{I,i}, \hat{\mathbf{s}}_{O,i} \rangle, \tag{10}$$

where $\langle \mathbf{s}_1, \mathbf{s}_2 \rangle$ denotes the inner product of vectors $\mathbf{s}_1$ and $\mathbf{s}_2$. Thus, we obtain the shape parameter vector $\mathbf{p}_O = [p_{O,1}, p_{O,2}, \ldots, p_{O,m_O}]^t$ to approximate the scaled local shape deformation on the speaker's face. The final shape of the avatar's is then reconstructed as

$$\mathcal{S}(\mathbf{p}_O; \bar{\mathbf{s}}_O, \mathbf{S}_O) = \bar{\mathbf{s}}_O + \sum_{i=1}^{m_O} p_{O,i} \hat{\mathbf{s}}_{O,i}. \tag{11}$$

On the avatar's face, the transfers of shape deformation reflect mainly the variations of facial expressions, while the transfers of texture deformation exhibit the distinctions of the person identities. Similar to Eq. (11), the texture of the avatar's face can be reconstructed as

$$\mathcal{A}(\lambda_O; \bar{\mathbf{a}}_O, \mathbf{A}_O) = \bar{\mathbf{a}}_O + \sum_{i=1}^{m'_O} \lambda_{O,i} \hat{\mathbf{a}}_{O,i}, \tag{12}$$

where

$$\lambda_{O,i} \approx \sum_{i=1}^{m'_I} \lambda_{I,i} \langle \hat{\mathbf{a}}_{I,i}, \hat{\mathbf{a}}_{O,i} \rangle. \tag{13}$$

Eq. (11) and Eq. (12) defines the way to synthesize the avatar's facial appearance to have the same facial expression as the speaker at the speaking site. After the synthesis of facial expression, the avatar's face must be aligned to have the same head pose as the speaker, too. To this end, the global affine transform characterized by the parameter vector $\mathbf{q}$ which contains four parameter elements are applied to the synthesized avatar face. After the affine transform, both the facial expression and the head pose of the avatar face are synchronized to those of the speaker.

4 Multimedia Transmission and Synchronization between Networked Chatters

4.1 Multimedia Data for Transmission

As described in Section 3, the avatar's facial expression can be synthesized according to Eq (11) and Eq (12). The parameters involved in these two equations are $\bar{s}_O$, $\bar{a}_O$, $\hat{s}_{O,i}$, $\hat{a}_{O,i}$, $p_{O,i}$, and $\lambda_{O,i}$. Among these, the former four are derived after the training process. We can store them at the receiving site once the training process of the AAM is finished. Therefore, these four parameters need not to be transmitted on networks for each frame of visual data. The latter two coefficient parameters, $p_{O,i}$, and $\lambda_{O,i}$, acquired from the AAM fitting process are the parameters that need to be transmitted for every frame of visual data. These coefficients are all floating-point values, thus requiring a bandwidth of $S_c = \left[2 \times 4 \times (m_O + m_O') \right]$ bytes per frame. To align the head pose of the synthesized avatar with that of the speaker, the parameters of the global affine transform $\mathbf{q}$ are also required at the receiving site. These affine parameters contain four float-point values which take a bandwidth of $S_q = 16$ bytes per frame.

In addition to the above synthesizing parameters for visual transmission, the voice data must be also transmitted. The voices at the speaking site are usually recorded at the sampling rate of 8KHz, with each sample taking 8 bits. Thus, the bandwidth needed to transmit the uncompressed voice data per second is thus about $S_v = 8K$ bytes. If the voice data is compressed by MP3 or AAC encoding, the required bandwidth can be further reduced. In our current implementation, no voice compression is performed.

When packing the voices and the visual data for network transmission, it is necessary to precede each packet with a timestamp so that the receiving site can reassemble the received packets and to synchronize the voices with the visual data accordingly. The size of the timestamp is $S_t = 4$ bytes. One issue that should be concerned is the ways to pack the voices and the visual data. There are two different ways. One is to pack the visual data together with the voices, while the other is to pack these two types of data separately. The former one can prepare the synchronization information between the voices and the visual data in the packets at the speaking site and may ease the synchronization task at the receiving site. However, the disadvantage is that both the visual data and the voices of some frames may not be played at the receiving site if the packets get lost over networks. In contrast, the separately packed visual data and voices reduce the probability of simultaneously losing both types of data. Hence, the receiving site still may hear the voices even though the visual data gets lost, or vice versa. Nevertheless, packing the visual data and voices separately poses the burdens of synchronization between the visual data and the voices at the receiving site. In our design, we adopt this way to pack the multimedia data.

To sum up, supposing that the rate of playback at the receiving site is F frames/second and each voice packet contains voices recorded in a second, then the total bandwidth required for our AvPM per second amounts to

$$S = F(S_c + S_q + S_t) + (S_v + S_t) = F\left(8(m_O + m'_O) + 20\right) + 8004.$$

The above bandwidth is estimated with no compression of inter-frame redundancy. Actually, it is possible to employ some techniques like the differential coding for compressing the synthesizing parameters of the visual data of consecutive frames. With the differential coding, we can further reduce the bandwidth to a large degree.

4.2   Buffering Mechanism for Streaming and Audio-Visual Synchronization

When operating the AvPM over networks with poor quality of services (QoS), the required bandwidth and the reliability of networks could not always be guaranteed. The major side effects caused by the poor QoS are the discontinuity of multimedia streams and the unsynchronized lip motions and voices. To handle these two side effects, a buffering mechanism and a synchronization method are used in the proposed AvPM.

The discontinuity of multimedia streams results mainly from the delayed arrival of voice packets or visual packets at the receiving site. The playback at the receiving site would temporarily stop if no multimedia data is available. To prevent from the running out of multimedia data at the receiving site, we use two buffers, one for the visual packets and the other for the voice packets. At the speaking site, the voice recording module stores the recorded voice data every second. The stored voice data is immediately packed as a voice packet and then sent to the receiving site. At the same time, the AAM at the speaking site may have performed the fitting of the speaker's faces on F consecutive frames, where F is our frame rate. The fitting results are packed into F visual packets and sent to the receiving site. Whenever a packet arrives at the receiving site, the buffering mechanism stores this packet into the visual packet buffer or the voice packet buffer depending on the packet type of this packet. As the packet size of a voice packet is much larger than a visual packet in our design, the receiving rate of voice packets would dominate the playback at the receiving site. To reduce the probability of running out of voice packets in the voice packet buffer, our strategy for buffering the voice packets is to specify a size threshold , say θ_b, for the voice packet buffer. The playback module at the receiving site will not start to play the voices and the visual data until the number of voice packets in the voice packet buffer exceeds θ_b. Apparently, the value of θ_b affects the playback critically. If θ_b is too large, then it would cause a long delay to visualize and hear the avatar's visual and voice outputs at the receiving site. On the contrary, if θ_b is too small, then the buffering mechanism would lose its effect in preventing the running out of multimedia packets in the voice packet buffer. The appropriate value of θ_b depends on the current available bandwidth of networks. If the networks has higher bandwidth, then a small value of θ_b is better. Otherwise, the value of θ_b should be larger. In our design, we initialize the value of θ_b to 3. If the buffer runs out at a certain time point t_0, then we adapt its value to a value L_{avg} which is calculated by

$$L_{avg} = \lceil avg\left\{L_t | t_0 - T \le t \le t_0\right\}\rceil,$$

where T is a predefined time interval prior to the time point t_0 and $avg\{A\}$ denotes the average of the elements in A.

As to the synchronization between the voice data and the visual data, the timestamps associated with the voice and visual packets play an important role. Let t_i^a be the timestamp of the i-th voice packet A_i and t_j^v the timestamp of the j-th visual packet V_j. The receiving site structures the receiving voice and visual packets into several synchronization groups. Each synchronization group G_i contains the i-th voice packet and a set of visual packets subject to the following condition:

$$G_i = \left\{A_i, V = \{V_j | t_i^a \le t_j^v \le t_{i+1}^a - 1\}\right\}.$$

The playback of the structured synchronization groups is according to the order of the timestamp of the contained audio packets. For each synchronized group G_i, when the voice packet A_i is played, the set V of visual packets are rendered sequentially in the order of their timestamps.

5   Experimental Results

To assess the performance of the AvPM, we measure the transmitted data size over networks from a chatting session. The measured data is obtained from the NetLimiter, which is a network monitoring and management software. During the chatting session, the NetLimiter at the speaking site shows the size of data sent to the receiving site. For Microsoft MSN, the size of transmitted data fluctuates frequently depending on the head motions of the speaker. Larger motions cause larger sizes of data transmitted over the network. Fig. 2shows the curve that records the utilized bandwidth (in bits per second) during a 35-second chatting session for both the proposed method and Microsoft MSN. Since the Microsoft MSN cannot synthesize virtual avatars at the receiving site, we assign the synthesized avatar to be the speaker himself or herself, instead of any other person. Under this avatar designation, both Microsoft MSN and our method have the same visual outputs for comparison at the receiving site. In fact, the utilized bandwidth is independent of the avatar specification because the number of transmitted synthesizing parameters are the same for all avatars for the proposed AvPM.

In addition to the performance comparison with Microsoft MSN, we also compare the performance with that of the H.264 video streaming standard by using the JM software [1]. The H.264 can render different levels of video quality to adapt to different network bandwidths. Fig. 3 plots the curve that depicts the relation between the utilized bitrates and the attained quality levels. The PSNR is calculated from the residual between the compressed avatar face and the original avatar face. For the H.264, the higher quality of video is achieved at the cost of larger bandwidths. For the proposed AvPM, we do not perform any lossless or lossy compression on the synthesized avatar faces. Under such a

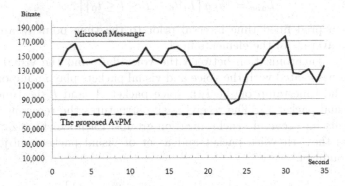

Fig. 2. The logged bitrates during a 35-second chatting session for the Microsoft MSN and the proposed AvPM

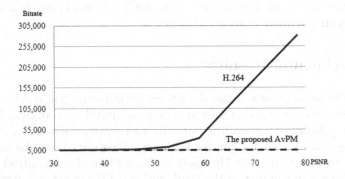

Fig. 3. Relationship between the PSNR and the bitrates for the H.264 and the proposed AvPM

condition, our AvPM transmits the original avatar faces at a bandwidth of 5,600 bits/sec. For the H.264, it requires a bandwidth of 282,652 bits/sec to transmit the highest-level quality (PSNR=80.446) of the avatar face obtained by setting the quantization parameter to 0. The frame rates of both the H.264 and our AvPM are kept as 5 frames/sec. Notice that in this comparison we do not include the voice data because the H.264 is only for video compression. In Fig. 4, we show the rendered avatar faces at the receiving site for different quality levels. One important note worthy of mentioning for the performance comparison is that both MSN and H.264 employ certain compression mechanisms on the transmitted multimedia, while the proposed AvPM does not. Even under this unbalanced condition, the proposed AvPM still outperforms both competitors in terms of the utilized network bandwidths for rendering the same multimedia quality. In Fig. 5, we show several snapshots of the synthesized avatar (Sherek) having the same facial expressions as the speaker. This figure also shows the tracked face by the AAM on each video frame.

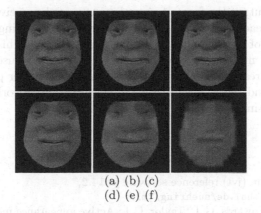

(a) (b) (c)
(d) (e) (f)

Fig. 4. The rendered avatar face of the proposed AvPM and the H.264 compression: (a) the proposed AvPM, (b) H.264 PSNR=65.365, bitrate=128,368 (c)H.264 PSNR=57.502, bitrate=33,716, (d) H.264 PSNR=51.049, bitrate=13,088 (e) H.264 PSNR=44.814, bitrate=7,172, and (f) H.264 PSNR=31.311, bitrate5,020

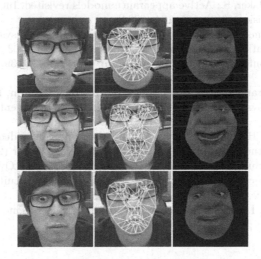

Fig. 5. Examples of synthesized avatars having different facial expressions synchronized with those of the speaker

6   Concluding Remarks

This paper presents the design of a novel avatar-based personal messenger, called the AvPM. Differing from the commonly used personal messengers, the proposed AvPM demands only a very low bandwidth from networks even though no compression techniques are employed. This prominent feature of the AvPM benefits from the proposed on-the-fly syntheses of visual outputs at the receiving site. Therefore, the data transmitted over networks contains no video frames, but a small amount of synthesizing parameters. Another key feature of the AvPM is its capability to output the faces of virtual avatars at the receiving site. The face expressions and head poses of the virtual avatar at the receiving site are synchronized with those of the real speaker at the speaking site. This kind of outputs makes the AvPM more attractive and more interesting to users. According to the experimental results, the proposed AvPM achieves better performance than Microsoft MSN and the H.264 in terms of the utilized network bandwidth and the rendered multimedia quality.

References

1. Joint video team (jvt) reference software jm14.2,
   http://iphome.hhi.de/suehring/tml/
2. Cootes, T.F., Edwards, G.J., Taylor, C.J.: Active appearance models. IEEE Trans. Pattern Analysis and Machine Intelligence 23(6), 681–685 (2001)
3. Goodall, C.: Procrustes methods in the statistical analysis of shape. Journal of the Royal Statistical Society. Series B (Methodological), 285–339 (1991)
4. Jolliffe, I.: Principal component analysis. Springer, Heidelberg (2002)
5. Matthews, I., Baker, S.: Active appearance models revisited. International Journal of Computer Vision 60(2), 135–164 (2004)
6. Persson, P.: Exms: an animated and avatar-based messaging system for expressive peer communication. In: GROUP 2003: Proceedings of the 2003 international ACM SIGGROUP conference on Supporting group work, pp. 31–39. ACM, New York (2003)
7. Rajan, V., Subramanian, S., Keenan, D., Johnson, A., Sandin, D., DeFanti, T.: A realistic video avatar system for networked virtual environments. In: Proceedings of IPT (2002)
8. Richardson, I.: H. 264 and MPEG-4 video compression: video coding for next-generation multimedia. John Wiley and Sons Inc., Chichester (2003)
9. Wiegand, T., Sullivan, G., Bjontegaard, G., Luthra, A.: Overview of the H. 264/AVC video coding standard. IEEE Transactions on circuits and systems for video technology 13(7), 560–576 (2003)
10. Wiley, J., Sons, I.: Avatars in Networked Virtual Environments

Virtual EZ Grid: A Volunteer Computing Infrastructure for Scientific Medical Applications

Mohamed Ben Belgacem[1], Nabil Abdennadher[2], and Marko Niinimaki[2]

[1] University of Geneva, Switzerland
mohamed.benbelgacem@unige.ch
[2] University of Applied Sciences Western Switzerland, Hepia Geneva, Switzerland
{nabil.abdennadher, markopekka.niinimaeki}@hesge.ch

Abstract. This paper presents the *Virtual EZ Grid* project, based on the XtremWeb-CH (XWCH) volunteer computing platform. The goal of the project is to introduce a flexible distributed computing system, with (i) a non-trivial number of computing resources infrastructure from various institutes, (ii) a stable platform that manages these computing resources and provides advanced interfaces for applications, and (iii) a set of applications that take benefit of the platform. This paper concentrates on the application support of the new version of *XWCH*, and describes how a medical image application MedGIFT utilises it.

1 Introduction

Nowadays, volunteer computing (VoC) and grid computing are a well-established paradigm of distributed computing. The term "volunteer computing" is used for all scenarios where a low priority guest application can run on unused remote resources without significantly impacting high priority host applications. In volunteer computing individuals donate unused or idle resources of their computers to distributed high performance computing applications.

On the other hand, Grid computing is the combination of computer resources from multiple administrative domains applied to a common application that requires a great number of computer processing cycles or the need to process large amounts of data.

There are several characteristics that distinguish the volunteer computing from Grid [1]:

- The number of volunteer nodes in VoC systems may range from less than 10 to hundreds of thousands.
- Volunteered resources are owned and managed by regular people, not by IT professionals
- Volunteers are anonymous, and those who misbehave cannot be fired or prosecuted
- Volunteered resources are often behind network firewalls that do not allow incoming connections
- Volunteer computing is asymmetric: volunteers supply resources, and not the other way round.

Grid and VoC platforms are organised with the help of middleware systems.

R.-S. Chang et al. (Eds.): GPC 2010, LNCS 6104, pp. 385–394, 2010.
© Springer-Verlag Berlin Heidelberg 2010

The most known grid systems are gLite [2], ARC [3], Globus [4], Unicore [5], Condor [6] and GridMP [7].

Berkeley Open Infrastructure for Network Computing (BOINC) [8] is the most widely used middleware in volunteer computing. XtremWeb (*XW*) [9] is a VoC middleware providing a framework and a set of tools to assist in the creation of volunteer computing projects.

XtremWeb-CH (*XWCH:* www.xtremwebch.net) [10], developed by the authors of this paper improves *XW* through the usage of peer-to-peer concepts. *XWCH* is an upgraded version of (*XW*). Major improvements have been brought to it in order to obtain a reliable and efficient system. Its software architecture was completely re-designed. The first version of XtremWeb-CH (*XWCH1*) is composed of three kinds of peers: the coordinator, the workers and the warehouses. Several applications have been deployed on *XWCH1* [11]. [12] details the limits of the *XWCH1* middleware. To overcome these drawbacks, a second version (*XWCH2*) was developed. This version is currently being used to deploy several desktop grid and VoC infrastructures such as *Virtual EZ Grid* [13] and *From Peer-to-Peer (From-P2P)* [14]. One of the main objectives of these two projects is to deploy scientific medical applications. Three applications are being gridified within these projects, but for the sake of brevity we only discuss one of them.

This paper is organised as follow: the next section presents the new features of *XWCH2*. Section 3 details the architecture of the *Virtual EZ Grid* infrastructure while section 4 presents one example of a medical application deployed on the *Virtual EZ Grid* platform: *MedGIFT*. Finally, section 5 gives some perspectives of this research.

2 XtremWeb-CH2 (XWCH2)

The new version of *XWCH* features improved support for parallel distributed applications. The extensions carried out are application driven. They were deduced from experiments carried out and lessons learned during the gridification and the deployment of several applications [15]. In more detail, the main improvements of *XWCH2* can be summarized as: dynamic task generation, flexible data sharing (data replication) and persistent tasks.

This paper will only detail the "dynamic task generation" aspect.

We shall also show improvements in the way the user communicates with the system, through its application programming interface (API) in section 2.2.

2.1 The *XWCH2* Architecture

Figure 1 illustrates the principal changes in the *XWCH2* architecture. Job submission is done by a flexible API, available for Java and C/C++ programs. The interfaces of the coordinator now contain user service and worker services, both of which are web services, implemented using WSDL [16].

Like in the earlier version of *XWCH*, the basic architecture of *XWCH2* consists of a coordinator, a set of worker nodes and at least one warehouse node [10]. However, contrarily to *XWCH1*, jobs are submitted to the coordinator by a "client node" which executes a client program that calls the services provided by *XWCH2*. The coordinator schedules jobs and pre-assign them to the workers. The workers retrieve the executable files and input files from warehouses (or other workers), compute the jobs, and store their outputs in the warehouses. The coordinator and at least one of the warehouses are assumed to be available to the workers involved in the execution of jobs created by the same client program. Communication between the coordinator and the workers is always initiated by the workers (*Work request, Work Alive* and *Work Result* in Figure 1); thus workers can receive tasks and send results even if they are run in "out-bound connectivity only" environments, like NAT sub-networks.

Since *XWCH2* can be used as a volunteer computing platform, it is not reasonable to assume that any two workers can always communicate directly with each other. Organizations have firewalls and NAT (Network Address Translation) sub-networks that protect the organization's network by limiting connectivity to/from the outside world. In *XWCH*, the workers can communicate directly with each other whenever it is possible, otherwise through a warehouse.

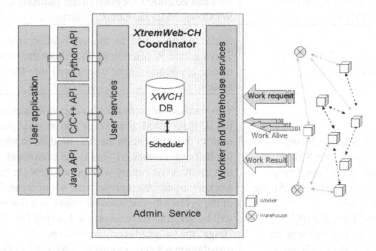

Fig. 1. *XWCH2* architecture

An *XWCH* application is composed of a set of communicating jobs and can be represented by a workflow. The number of jobs and the structure of the workflow cannot be known in advance. Jobs are created by the client program by calling a specific service of *XWCH2*.

2.2 Dynamic Tasks Generation

In what follows, we give a brief summary of the Java API functions (Table 1) that allows user to create *XWCH* jobs according to his/her needs. The entire API documentation is available at the *XWCH* web site www.xtremwebch.net.

Table 1. *XWCH2* Java API

XWCHClient (java.lang.String *serverendpoint*, java.lang.String *datafolder*, java.lang.String *clientID*)	This method creates a "connection" with the coordinator. *Serverendpoint* refers to the URL of the user services in Figure 1. *Datafolder* is a local folder (client node) where the binaries and input files exist.
AddApplication (java.lang.String *app_name*)	This method adds an application to the coordinator. It returns an *application_id*.
AddModule (java.lang.String *module_name*)*	This method adds a "module" to the coordinator and returns a *module_id*. A module is as set of binary codes having, in general, the same source code. Each binary code targets a specific (OS, CPU) platform.
AddModuleApplication (java.lang.String *module_name*, java.lang.String *binaryzip*, PlatformType)	Adds an executable binary file to a given module. This is "per platform" basis, i.e. different binary files can be added for each of the platform (MS Windows, MacOS, Linux, Solaris, etc.).
AddData (java.lang.String *app_name*)	Adds an input file to the application *app_name*. This method is often used to upload the input data of one application (one execution) into the *XWCH* system.
AddJob (java.lang.String *jobname*, java.lang.String *app_name*, java.lang.String *module_name*, java.lang.String *command_line*, java.lang.String *inputfiles*, java.lang.String *outfilespec*, java.lang.String *outfilename*, java.lang.String *flags*)	This method submits a job to the coordinator. A job ID is returned. *app_name* and *module_name* refer to the application and the module to which the job belongs. *command_line* is the command that invokes the binary with parameters (in the worker). *inputfiles* represent the set of input files of the given job. *outfilename* refers to a name that will be given to the compressed output file. By "flags" the programmer can pass specific distribution related options to *XWCH2* (replicate output data on several warehouses, execute a set of tasks on the same worker, execute one task on a given worker, etc.).
GetJobStatus (java.lang.String *Job_ID*)	Gets the status of the job.
GetJobFileOutName(java.lang. String *Job_ID*)	Gives the "reference" (identifier) of the Job's output file.
GetJobResult (java.lang.String *Job_ID*, java.lang.String *outfilename*)	Gets the output file (output data) of a given job.

An example of using the API to create and execute three communicating jobs: *Job1*, *Job2* and *Job3*. *Job2* and *Job3* are using the output of *Job1* as input data.

```
// Initialisation of the connection
c = new XWCHClient(ServerAddress, ".", IdClient,1,9);          c.init();


String appid = c.AddApplication("Hello World application");       String
ModuleId1 = c.AddModule("Module1");

String refWind = c.AddModuleApplication (ModuleId1,
BinaryPath_Module1_win, PlateformEnumType.WINDOWS); //Windows binary
String ModuleId2 = c.AddModule("Module2");
String refProcesswindows = c.AddModuleApplication(ModuleId2,
BinaryPath_Module2_win, PlateformEnumType.LINUX);   //Linux binary
. . .

String job0 = c.AddJob          ("First Job",          //Job description
                                appid,                 //Application ID
                                ModuleId1,             // Module identifier
                                CmdLine_for_job0,      //Command line
                                frefjob0.toJobReference(),
                                liste_files_out_job0,
                                file_out_id_job0,
                                "" );

//Wait until job0 ends
String status = "";
while (!status.equalsIgnoreCase("COMPLETE")) status =
                        c.GetJobStatus(job0).toString();

// Retrieve the reference of the output file of job0
String inputforJobs_1_and_2 = c.GetJobFileOutName(job0);

String job1 = c.AddJob          ("second Job",         //Job description
                                appid,                 //Application ID
                                ModuleId2,             // Module identifier
                                CmdLine_for_job1,      //Command line
                                inputforJobs_1_and_2,
                                liste_files_out_job1,
                                file_out_id_job1,
                                "");

String job2 = c.AddJob          ("Third Job",          //Job description
                                appid,                 //Application
```

```
                          identifier
                          ModuleId2,              // Module identifier
                          CmdLine_for_job2,       //Command line
                          inputforJobs_1_and_2,
                          liste_files_out_job2,
                          file_out_id_job2,
                          "");
//Wait until job1 and job2 end, by using "GetJobStatus" method (table 1)
String status = "";
while (!status.equalsIgnoreCase("COMPLETE")) status =
                          c.GetJobStatus(job1).toString();
status = "";
while (!status.equalsIgnoreCase("COMPLETE")) status =
                          c.GetJobStatus(job2).toString();

GetJobResult (job1, file_out_id_job1);
GetJobResult (job2, file_out_id_job2);
```

This client program does not show the different features supported by *XWCH2*. Nevertheless, it details how *XWCH2* handles communication and precedence rules between jobs. Although this program does not show it, calls to *XWCH2* services can take place in loops and tests controls. This means that the number of jobs and the structure of the graph representing the application are not known in advance.

3 The *Virtual EZ Grid* Project

This section presents a desktop Grid infrastructure called *Virtual EZ Grid* (http://www.xtremwebch.net/Projects/Virtual_EZ_Grid/EZ_Home.html). This platform, based on *XWCH2* middleware, is mainly used to deploy and execute three scientific medical applications. This section presents the architecture of the *Virtual EZ Grid* project while section 4 presents only one application: *MedGIFT*.

3.1 *Virtual EZ Grid* in Brief

The aim of *Virtual EZ Grid* is to establish a sustainable desktop Grid platform across several institutions. Three main goals are targeted by the project:

1. Construct a desktop grid infrastructure with non dedicated desktop PCs to provide harvested CPU power for scientific research projects.
2. Implement a reliable platform by using virtual environments to support secure computing and remote check-pointing. Virtual EZ Grid aims at providing a better control over environmental issues and energy consumption by running only the necessary PCs and shutting down unused PCs at night and during holidays. The proposed platform should give a non-intrusive experience to the PC users.

3. Evaluate the two first objectives in a real world setting with the several medical applications.

The *Virtual EZ Grid* architecture is shown in Figure 2.

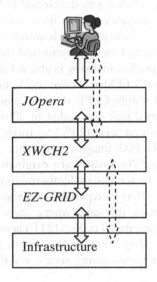

Fig. 2. The *Virtual EZ Grid* architecture

The three main supported tools of *Virtual EZ Grid* are: *XWCH2*, *JOpera* and *EZ-Grid*.

JOpera (http://www.jopera.org) is an open grid workflow management system. It provides a visual environment based on the Eclipse platform for modelling grid workflows as a collection of jobs linked by control and data flow dependencies.

EZ Grid: it's a PC grid infrastructure based on the concept of virtualization. On top of this fundamental layer, other functionalities are also considered, such as job check-pointing, restarting and migration. These features are necessary in order to offer a flexible environment with minimal disturbances for both the owner of the PC and the owner of the job.

The user can submit his/her application via the workflow management system *JOpera* or directly through the *XWCH2* middleware. *XWCH2* can be deployed natively or as a virtual machine (Figure 2).

4 The MedGIFT Application

One of the applications gridified and deployed on *Virtual EZ Grid* is MedGIFT. Content-based image retrieval is increasingly being used as a diagnostic aid in hospitals [17]. However, hospitals produce large amounts of images -- for instance the University Hospitals of Geneva radiology department produced about 70 000 images per day in 2007 [18]. Preparing these images in such a way that they can be used in diagnosis is a challenging task due to their volume. Content-based image retrieval systems typically use image features like properties of textures and colours [19]; here, we call the extracting features from images *indexing*.

The well-known GIFT, or Gnu Image Finding Tool, software is a content-based image indexing and retrieval package was developed at University of Geneva in the late 1990's. GIFT utilizes techniques common from textual information retrieval and uses a very large collection of binary-valued features (global and local colour and texture features) [19]. GIFT extract these features and stores them in an inverted file. In a typical desktop PC, the speed of indexing is about 1 or 2 images per second.

The history of the ImageCLEFMed image collection can be summarized as follows: ImageCLEF started within CLEF (Cross Language Evaluation Forum) in 2003. A medical image retrieval task was added in 2004 to explore domain-specific multilingual visual information retrieval [20]. The ImageCLEFMed2007 used in this report consists of about 50 000 images, originally from radiological journals Radiology and Radiographics. The images are originals used in published articles. Indexing a set of images can be seen as an "embarrassingly parallel" problem, i.e. "a problem in which little or no effort is required to separate the problem into a number of parallel tasks. This is often the case where there exists no dependency (or communication) between those parallel tasks." [21] Therefore indexing a large set (S) of images can be done by dividing S into small subsets, sending the subsets together with processing instructions into processing nodes, and then combining the output of the processing nodes.

The workflow for MedGIFT can be summarized as follow:

- Process PACKETGENERATOR runs in a client computer, using a directory of the ImageCLEFMed2007 sample as its input.
- PACKETGENERATOR generates packages that consist of the GIFT indexer program (executable), a batch file containing instructions of how to run it in the worker nodes, and an input zip file containing 1000 images (except for the last package).
- After each package has been generated, PACKETGENERATOR submits it to XWCH as a task.
- When all the tasks have been submitted, PACKETGENERATOR examines their statuses. When a status indicates that the task has been finished, PACKETGENERATOR downloads its output.

The process of executing PACKETGENERATOR (=the entire packaging/submission/ result retrieving process) took 4 hours 53 minutes 58 seconds (=17638 seconds). This figure is comparable with those achieved by the ARC Grid middleware in [18]. Individual execution for packages in the worker nodes are shown in Figure 3. The short execution time of the last package is because it contained only 25 images. The average of the execution times was 1006 seconds (=16 min 36 seconds) and the sum of the execution times 51316 seconds. The figure of 51316 seconds (ca 14 hours) would thus roughly correspond with executing the whole task on a single CPU.

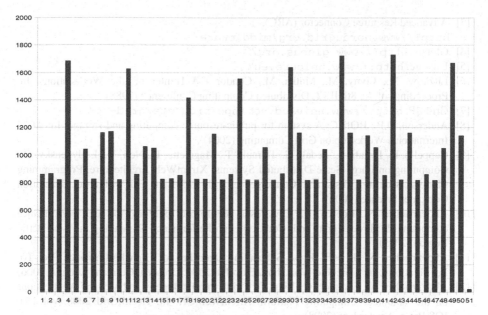

Fig. 3. MedGIFT package execution times

5 Conclusion

This paper has presented the new version of the volunteer computing environment *XtremWeb-CH* (*XWCH2*), used for the execution of high performance applications on a highly heterogeneous distributed environment. *XWCH2* is used in the *Virtual EZ Grid* project, where the computing nodes are provided from different institutes, and applications are built so that they utilise the *XWCH2* API directly, or by a JOpera workflow engine interface.

We have presented the details of the new features of *XWCH2*, in particular dynamic task creation. MedGIFT image indexing, a distributed application, is used as an example of a software that utilises the *Virtual EZ Grid* platform.

Acknowledgements

We gratefully acknowledge that:

- The *Virtual EZ Grid* project is in part funded via AAA/SWITCHand
- The right to use the ImageCLEFMed2007 was granted by Henning Muller on the basis that Marko Niinimaki was still a member of UNIGE's MedGIFT team in 2009.

References

[1] Anderson, D.P.: Opinion - Volunteer computing: Grid or not Grid? iSGTW newsletter (July 4, 2007)
[2] gLite, http://glite.web.cern.ch/glite/

[3] Advanced Resource Connector (ARC),
    http://www.nordugrid.org/middleware/
[4] Globus, http://www.globus.org/
[5] Unicore, http://www.unicore.eu/
[6] Litzkow, M., Livny, M., Mutka, M.: Condor - A Hunter of Idle Workstations. In: Proceedings of the 8th IEEE Distributed Computing Conference (1988)
[7] GridMP, http://www.univaud.com/hpc/products/grid-mp/
[8] Anderson, D.P.: BOINC: A system for public-resource computing and storage. In: ACM International Workshop on Grid Computing (2004)
[9] Cappello, F., Djilali, S., Fedak, G., Herault, T., Magniette, F., Neri, V., Lodygensky, O.: Computing on Large Scale Distributed Systems: XtremWeb Architecture, Programming Models, Security, Tests and Convergence with Grid. In: FGCS Future Generation Computer Science (2004)
[10] Abdennadher, N., Boesch, R.: Towards a peer-to-peer platform for high performance computing. In: Proc. Eighth Intl. Conf. on High-Performance Computing in Asia-Pacific Region (2005)
[11] Abdennadher, N., Boesch, R.: A Scheduling algorithm for High Performance Peer-To-Peer Platform. In: CoreGrid Workshop, Euro-Par 2006, Dresden, Germany (August 2006)
[12] Abdennadher, N., Evéquoz, C., Bilat, C.: Gridifying Phylogeny and Medical Applications on the Volunteer Computing Platform XtremWeb-CH. In: HealthGrid 2008, vol. 134. IOS Press, Amsterdam (2008)
[13] Virtual_EZ_Grid,
    http://www.xtremwebch.net/Projects/Virtual_EZ_Grid
[14] From-P2P, http://bilbo.iut-bm.univ-fcomte.fr/fromP2P/
[15] Abdennadher, N.: Using the Volunteer Computing platform XtremWeb-CH: lessons and perspectives. In: ACSE 2009, Phuket (Thailand) (March 2009)
[16] Chappell, D.A., Jewell, T.: Java Web Services. O'Reilly, Sebastopol (2002)
[17] Mueller, H., Michoux, N., Bandon, D., Geissbuhler, A.: A review of content-based image retrieval systems in medicine – clinical benefits and future directions. International Journal of Medical informatics 73, 1–23 (2004)
[18] Niinimaki, M., Zhou, X., Depeursinge, A., Geissbuhler, A., Mueller, H.: Building a Community Grid for Medical Image Analysis inside a Hospital, a Case Study. In: MICCAI Grid Workshop, New York University (September 2008)
[19] Squire, D.M., Mueller, W., Mueller, H., Pun, T.: Content-based query of image databases, inspirations from text retrieval: inverted files, frequency-based weights and relevance feedback. Technical Report 98.04, Computer Vision Group, Computing Centre, University of Geneva (1998)
[20] Müller, H., Kalpathy-Cramer, J., Kahn Jr., C.E., Hatt, W., Bedrick, S., Hersh, W.: Overview of the ImageCLEFmed 2008 Medical Image Retrieval Task. In: Peters, C., Deselaers, T., Ferro, N., Gonzalo, J., Jones, G.J.F., Kurimo, M., Mandl, T., Peñas, A., Petras, V. (eds.) Evaluating Systems for Multilingual and Multimodal Information Access. LNCS, vol. 5706, pp. 512–522. Springer, Heidelberg (2009)
[21] Foster, I.: Designing and Building Parallel Programs. Addison-Wesley, Reading (1995)

Towards Complex Negotiation for Cloud Economy

Kwang Mong Sim

Department of Information & Communications
Gwangju Institute of Science & Technology
Gwangju, South Korea
prof_sim_2002@yahoo.com

Abstract. In a Cloud computing environment, the dynamic configuration of a personalized collection of resources often requires Cloud participants (consumers, brokers, and providers) to establish service-level agreements (*SLAs*) through negotiation. However, to date, state-of-the-art approaches in Cloud computing provides limited or no support for dynamic *SLAs* negotiation. This position paper 1) presents the design of a complex Cloud negotiation mechanism that supports negotiation activities in interrelated markets: a Cloud service market between consumer agents and broker agents, and multiple Cloud resource markets between broker agents and provider agents, 2) specifies the negotiation protocols and strategies of consumer and broker agents in a Cloud service market, and 3) presents the design of the contracting and coordination algorithms for the concurrent negotiation activities between broker and provider agents in multiple Cloud resource markets. The complex Cloud negotiation mechanism is designed to support complex negotiation activities in interrelated markets in which the negotiation outcomes between broker and provider agents in a Cloud resource market can potentially influence the negotiation outcomes of broker and consumer agents in a Cloud service market. To the best of the author's knowledge, this work is the earliest proposal for a complex Cloud negotiation mechanism.

Keywords: Cloud economy, Cloud business model, Cloud negotiation, Grid economy, Automated negotiation, Complex negotiation.

1 Introduction

Cloud computing is an emerging and increasingly popular computing paradigm that aims at providing ubiquitous access to on-demand computing capabilities. A Cloud computing system consists of a collection of inter-connected and virtualized computers dynamically provisioned as one or more unified computing resource(s) through negotiation of service-level agreements (*SLAs*) between resource providers and consumers (or between resource providers and a third-party broker) [2]. In Cloud computing platforms, resources need to be dynamically (re-)configured and bundled (aggregated) via virtualization to provide different service profiles on demand [3]. Since consumers' requirements can potentially vary over time and amendments may need to be accommodated, supporting autonomous resource mapping and dealing

R.-S. Chang et al. (Eds.): GPC 2010, LNCS 6104, pp. 395–406, 2010.
© Springer-Verlag Berlin Heidelberg 2010

with changing requests accentuate the need for Cloud resource management systems that are capable of continuously managing the resource reservation process by autonomously adjusting resource prices and schedules via automated negotiation to accommodate dynamically changing resource demands. However, to date, the state-of-the-art approaches in Cloud computing provide limited support for dynamic *SLA* negotiations [2]. To this end, this position paper proposes a complex negotiation mechanism for bolstering negotiation activities among Cloud consumers, brokers, and Cloud providers, and to the best of the author's knowledge, this work is the earliest proposal for a Cloud negotiation mechanism. The novelty of this work is that the proposed complex Cloud negotiation mechanism is designed to support two kinds of negotiation activities: 1) the *multilateral negotiation between consumers and third-party brokers* for establishing contracts for brokers to provide services to consumers, and 2) *concurrent one-to-many negotiation between brokers and resource providers* for each broker to establish contracts with multiple providers to obtain a collection of resources to compose a service for sub-leasing to consumers. The impetus of this work is that the proposed complex Cloud negotiation mechanism supports concurrent negotiation activities in interrelated markets in which the negotiation outcomes between brokers and resource providers in one market can potentially affect and influence the negotiation outcomes of brokers and consumers in another market. The idea of conducting *Cloud commerce* [13] in *Cloud markets* [14] using negotiation agents is introduced in the next section.

2   Negotiation and Cloud Commerce

In a Cloud-based business model, users pay service/resource providers for consumption of their computing capabilities similar to the way that basic utilities such as electricity, gas, and water are charged [3], and it was noted that a market-oriented approach for managing Cloud resources is necessary for regulating their supply and demand through flexible and dynamic pricing [2]. [13] proposed the idea of an agent-based "Cloud commerce" model for controlling the allocation of resources in a Cloud computing environment. In recent years, there are increasingly strong interests in Cloud computing from IT providers (e.g., Amazon, Google, IBM, Sun Microsystems, and Microsoft – just to name a few), and it is envisioned that more Cloud computing infrastructures will be set up and consumer demands for Cloud computing capabilities will likely be increasing in the future as evident by the increasing number of web search queries submitted to Google [2]. The increasing popularity of Cloud computing among both the industry and the general public accentuates the need for autonomic Cloud resource management approaches for regulating the supply and demand of Cloud resources through dynamic and flexible pricing in a Cloud market consisting of Cloud resource providers competing to provide services and Cloud users with competing requests for Cloud resources.

Cloud Market: One of the possible market models for trading Cloud resources that is described in [2] consists of resource/service providers, IT consumers, and brokers that purchase resource capacities from providers and sub-lease these resources to IT consumers. In addition, there is a market directory that allows participants to locate providers or consumers with matching offers. A broker accepts requests from many consumers and each consumer can also submit its requirements and requests to multiple brokers. Consumers, brokers, and providers are bound to service contracts through *SLAs* that specify the details of the service to be provided agreed upon by all parties, and the penalties for violating the expectations. Such a market provides an infrastructure for 1) bridging disparate Clouds, 2) enabling consumers to select appropriate service providers that can satisfy their resource requirements, and 3) enabling providers to perform effective resource planning and resource pricing based on market conditions, user demand, and current level of resource utilization. Presently, even though providers have inflexible pricing for Cloud resources, it is envisioned that a market infrastructure described in [2] will enable variable Cloud resource pricing based on market conditions. This position paper suggests that automated negotiation is an appropriate economic model to facilitate flexible price setting of Cloud resources based on varying demand from consumers competing for resources and varying supply from providers competing to provide and lease their resources.

Agent-based Testbed: Figure 1 shows the design of an agent-based testbed for modeling the trading of resources in Cloud markets. It consists of provider agents and consumer agents acting on behalf of resource providers and consumers, respectively, and a set of broker agents. Broker agents accept service requests from consumer agents, purchase resources from provider agents, dynamically compose a collection of resources to satisfy consumer agents' requirements, then sub-lease the service to consumer agents. In doing so, broker agents need to carry out negotiation activities in two types of markets. In *Cloud service markets*, broker agents negotiate with consumer agents for mutually acceptable terms to establish *SLAs* for satisfying service requirements from consumers. In *Cloud resource markets*, broker agents negotiate with resource providers for reserving resources.

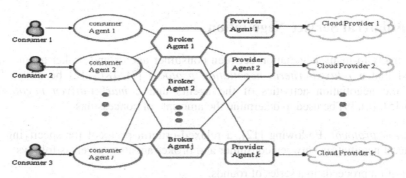

Fig. 1. An Agent-based Testbed

Cloud negotiation model: Figure 2 shows a Cloud negotiation mechanism for facilitating the negotiation activities 1) between consumer agents and broker agents and 2) between broker agents and provider agents. Since each broker agent can accept requests from multiple consumer agents and each consumer agent can also submit its requirements and requests to multiple broker agents, it is envisioned that a many-to-many negotiation model be adopted for negotiation between consumer agents and broker agents. Since a Cloud service may be dynamically composed using multiple types of Cloud resources, each broker agent can potentially negotiate in multiple types of Cloud resource markets with multiple groups of Cloud providers that provide different types of Cloud resources. Hence, it is envisioned that a concurrent one-to-many negotiation mechanism be adopted to facilitate concurrent negotiation activities between broker agents and different groups of provider agents.

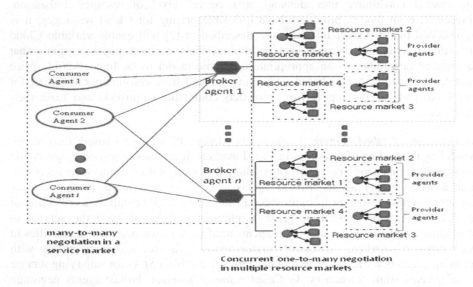

Fig. 2. A Cloud Negotiation Model

3 Multilateral Service Negotiation

For the many-to-many negotiation between consumer agents and broker agents, it is expected that a *relaxed-criteria negotiation protocol* [7], [8], [12] be adopted to specify the negotiation activities of the agents and a *market-driven negotiation strategy* [5], [6], [9] be used to determine the amounts of concessions.

Negotiation protocol: Following [12], a relaxed-criteria protocol for specifying the multilateral negotiation between consumer and broker agents is given as follows:

- Negotiation proceeds in a series of rounds.
- Adopting Rubinstein's alternating offers protocol [4], a pair of consumer and broker agents negotiates by making proposals in alternate rounds.
- Multiple consumer-broker agent pairs can negotiate deals simultaneously.
- When an agent makes a proposal, it proposes a deal from their space of possible deals (e.g., consisting of the most desirable price, the least desirable (reserve) price, and those prices in between). Typically an agent proposes its most preferred deal initially.

- If no agreement is reached, negotiation proceeds to the next round. At every round, an agent determines its amount of concession using the strategy described below.
- Negotiation between two agents terminates (i) when an agreement is reached, or (ii) with a conflict when one of the bargaining agents' deadline is reached.
- Agents follow one of the following rules for reaching an agreement:

R1: An agreement is reached if a consumer agent CA_t and a broker agent BA_t propose deals P_{CA}^l and P_{BA}^l, respectively, such that either 1) $U(P_{CA}^l) \geq U(P_{BA}^l)$ or 2) $U(P_{BA}^l) \geq U(P_{CA}^l)$, where P_{CA}^l and P_{BA}^l represent the buying and selling prices of a Cloud service, and U is a utility function.

R2: An agreement is reached if either 1) $\eta = U(P_{BA}^l) - U(P_{CA}^l)$, such that $\eta \to 0$ or 2) $\eta = U(P_{CA}^l) - U(P_{BA}^l)$, such that $\eta \to 0$, where η is the amount of relaxation determined using a fuzzy decision controller (*FDC*) and a set of relaxation criteria.

Relaxation criteria and FDC: In a relaxed-criteria negotiation protocol, consumer and broker agents will be programmed to slightly relax their bargaining criteria under intense pressure (e.g., when a consumer has a higher demand for computing services) with the hope of enhancing their chance of successfully acquiring the required service. The design of an *FDC* will generally follow that in [10], [11], [12], but differ in terms of the relaxation criteria, i.e., the inputs to the *FDC*. A consumer agent and a broker agent are both designed with an *FDC*: *FDC-C* and *FDC-B*, respectively. Two sets of relaxation criteria (for consumers and brokers, respectively) that are specific to Cloud service management are used as inputs to *FDC-C* and *FDC-B*, respectively.

Two criteria that can influence a consumer agent's decision in the amount of relaxation of bargaining terms are 1) recent statistics in failing/succeeding in acquiring Cloud services, i.e., *failure to success ratio* (*FSR*), and 2) *demand for Cloud services* (*DCS*). If a consumer agent is *less* (respectively, *more*) successful in acquiring Cloud services recently to execute its set of tasks, it will be under *more* (respectively, *less*) pressure to slightly relax its bargaining criteria with the hope of completing a deal. If a consumer has a *greater* (respectively, *lower*) demand for computing resources, it is *more* (respectively, *less*) likely to be under more pressure to slightly relax its bargaining criteria. Both *FSR* and *DCS* are inputs to *FDC-C* that a consumer agent uses to determine the amount of relaxation η.

Two criteria that can influence a broker agent's decision are: 1) recent *requests for Cloud services* (*RCS*) from consumers, and 2) the cost for acquiring the required Cloud resources to compose a service to satisfy the requests of a consumer, i.e., *cost of resource* (*CR*). If there are fewer recent demands from consumer agents for Cloud services, a broker agent is *more* (respectively, *less*) likely to slightly relax its bargaining criteria since it is under *more* (respectively, *less*) pressure to sub-lease resources it has acquired from Cloud resource providers. If a broker agent needs to pay a *higher* (respectively, *lower*) price for acquiring the Cloud resource required to compose a service for a consumer, then it is *less* (respectively, *more*) likely to slightly relax its bargaining terms. Both *RCS* and *CR* are inputs to *FDC-B*.

Novelty: The impetus and novelty of the relaxed-criteria negotiation protocol proposed above are as follows:

1) Whereas agents in previous works [5], [6], [9] negotiate only in one e-market, broker agents in the proposed relaxed-criteria negotiation protocol are expected to participate in negotiation in multiple (types of) markets, i.e., Cloud service markets and Cloud resource markets.

2) While agents in previous relaxed-criteria negotiation [7], [8], [10], [11], [12] adopted *FDCs* with a set of relaxation criteria determined by factors in only one market, the set of relaxation criteria of *FDC-B* in the proposed relaxed-criteria negotiation protocol are determined by factors from multiple markets – requests from consumers in a Cloud service market and costs of resources in one or more Cloud resource markets.

Negotiation Strategy: In a Cloud service market where consumers compete for computing services and brokers compete to provide services, a market-oriented approach for regulating the supply and demand of Cloud services is appropriate. To model dynamic pricing of Cloud services, it is anticipated that consumer and broker agents will adopt a *market-driven approach* when making concessions similar to that in [5], [9], [13]. In Sim's [5], [9], [13], a *market-driven agent* (*MDA*) determines the appropriate amounts of concessions using a combination of three negotiation functions: time (*T*) function, opportunity (*O*) function, and competition (*C*) function.

Time function: Since consumers are generally sensitive to deadlines in acquiring computing services, and deadlines may also affect brokers' scheduling and composition of services, it is intuitive to consider time when formulating the negotiation decision functions. A consumer agent's time-dependent concession making strategies can be classified into: i) *conservative* (maintaining the initial price until an agent's deadline is almost reached), ii) *conciliatory* (conceding rapidly to the reserve price), and iii) *linear* (conceding linearly) [5], [6], [9]. Let IP_{CA} and RP_{CA} be the initial and reserve prices of a consumer agent. Based on its time-dependent concession making function, the consumer agent's price proposal at negotiation round t is given as follows.

$$P_{CA}(t) = IP_{CA} + (\frac{t}{\tau_{CA}})^{\lambda_{CA}}(RP_{CA} - IP_{CA}) \tag{1}$$

where τ_{CA} is the consumer agent's deadline for acquiring a service, $0 < \lambda_{CA} < \infty$ is the concession making strategy. Three classes of strategies are specified as follows: *Conservative* ($\lambda_{CA} > 1$), *Linear* ($\lambda_{CA} = 1$), and *Conciliatory* ($0 < \lambda_{CA} < 1$). Details are given in [5], [9].

Opportunity function: Since a consumer agent can submit service requests to multiple broker agents and a broker agent also receives requests from many consumers, both consumer and broker agents should also be programmed to consider *outside options*. The *O* function in [5], [9] determines the amount of concession based on 1) trading alternatives (i.e., outside options) and 2) differences in utilities generated by the proposal of an agent and the counter-proposal(s) of its opponent(s). When determining opportunity, it was shown in [5], [9] that if there is a large number of trading alternatives, the likelihood that an agent's opponent proposes a bid/offer that is potentially close to the agent's own offer/bid may be high. For instance, if there is a large number of broker agents in the Cloud service market, then there may be a higher chance that one or more broker agents propose prices that are close to the proposed price of a consumer agent. Nevertheless, it would be difficult for an agent to reach a consensus if none of the so many options are viable (i.e., there are large differences between the proposal of the agent and the counter-proposals of all its opponents). On this account, the O function in [5], [9] determines the probability of reaching a consensus on an agent's own term by considering 1) trading alternatives (i.e., the outside options), and 2) differences between its proposal and the proposals of each of its opponent (i.e., the viability of each option). The general idea is that if the probability of reaching a consensus on its own terms is *high* (respectively, *low*), an agent should make a *smaller* (respectively, *larger*) amount of concession. Details for deriving the probability of reaching a consensus are given in [5], [9].

Competition function and market rivalry: Since *both* consumers compete for services and brokers compete to provide services, market rivalry and competition should also be modeled. Furthermore, different degrees of competition need to be considered since both demand for and supply of services may vary. However, in [5], [9], the C function determines the amount of competition of an *MDA* by considering the number of competitors and the number of available options in the market. For example, in a market with m buyers and n sellers, an agent B_j has $m-1$ competitors $\{B_2,..., B_m\}$ and n trading partners $\{S_1,..., S_n\}$. In a Cloud service market, whereas a consumer may have information about the number of providers providing the services it requires, it may not have knowledge of the number of consumers competing for the same type of service because consumers generally do not broadcast their requests to other consumers. Hence, a competition function that is different from that in [5], [6], [9] will be used for modeling market rivalry in a Cloud service market.

One of the possible ways to model market rivalry and competition in negotiation is to consider an agent's bargaining position B_p. In a *favorable market* (respectively, *unfavorable market*), a consumer agent is in an *advantageous* (respectively, *disadvantageous*) B_p because there are *more* (respectively, *fewer*) providers providing Cloud services and *fewer* (respectively, *more*) consumers competing for Cloud services. In a *balanced market*, a consumer is in a generally *neutral* B_p as the supply of Cloud services is not significantly more than the demand for services. Since a consumer agent does not know the number of its competitors, one method for estimating B_p at each negotiation round t is to consider the concession patterns of each broker agent. If broker agents are making relatively *larger* (respectively, *smaller*) concessions, then it is likely that the consumer agent is in a relatively *favorable* (respectively, *unfavorable*) B_p. Similarly, the B_p of a broker agent can also be estimated by considering the concession patterns of each consumer agent.

A consumer agent's B_p can be determined as follows. (A broker agent's B_p can also be determined in a similar way). Let $\Delta^i_{BA}(t) = P^i_{BA}(0) - P^i_{BA}(t)$ be the difference between the *initial* and the *current* proposals of each broker agent BA_i, and $\delta^i_{BA}(t) = P^i_{BA}(t-1) - P^i_{BA}(t)$ be the difference between BA_i's proposals in the *previous* and *current* rounds. Let $B_p(t)$ be a consumer agent's B_p at round t. $B_p(t)$ is derived by averaging the ratio of 1) the amount of concession in the current round $\delta_{BA}^i(t)$ and 2) the average amount of concession in the previous t rounds $\Delta_{BA}^i(t)/t$. More formally,

$$B_P(t) = \underset{i}{avg}\left(\frac{t \cdot \delta_{BA}^i(t)}{\Delta_{BA}^i(t)}\right) \tag{2}$$

If $B_P(t) \ll 1$, the consumer agent is more likely to be in a disadvantageous bargaining position (e.g., the consumer is in an *unfavorable market*). If $B_P(t) \ll 1$, it is likely that many broker agents are making smaller concessions at round t, i.e., the average of $\delta_{BA}^i(t)$ is likely to be relatively smaller.

If $B_P(t) \gg 1$, then there are generally many broker agents making larger concessions, and the consumer agent is more likely to be in an advantageous bargaining position (e.g., the consumer agent is in a *favorable market*).

4 Concurrent Cloud Resource Negotiation

For concurrent negotiation of multiple *SLAs*, it is expected that a concurrent negotiation protocol adapted from [15] be used. Figure 3 shows a concurrent negotiation mechanism of a broker agent for establishing multiple *SLAs* for a collection of Cloud resources. It consists of a *coordinator* which coordinates the parallel negotiation activities for acquiring n different types of Cloud resources in n different Cloud resource markets. In each Cloud resource market, a broker agent establishes an *SLA* by negotiating simultaneously with multiple provider agents for one type of Cloud resource. Furthermore, both broker and provider agents can be freed from a contract (i.e., an agent can decommit a contract) by paying penalty fees to their opponents. The reasons for allowing decommitments are as follows: 1) if a broker agent cannot acquire ALL its required resources before its deadline, it can release those resources acquired so that providers can assign them to other broker agents, and 2) it allows a broker agent that has already reached an intermediate contract for a resource to continue to search for better deals before the entire concurrent negotiation terminates. In negotiating for one type of Cloud resource in a resource market, there is a commitment manager that manages both commitments and decommitments of (intermediate) contracts. In summary, two algorithms are needed for the concurrent negotiation mechanism: 1) an algorithm for establishing *SLAs* and managing commitments and decommitments of contracts (see algorithm 1) and 2) an algorithm for coordinating the parallel negotiation activities (see algorithm 2).

Contracting and SLAs: At each negotiation round, the commitment manager determines whether to accept the proposed offers from the provider agents or whether to renege on an intermediate contract (to break an existing contract and take up a new and more favorable contract by paying a penalty fee). However, it is inefficient for a broker agent to simply accept all acceptable proposals from provider agents, and select the best proposal from them because it may be forced to pay a large amount of penalty fees for reneging on many deals. Since a Cloud resource can be requested by multiple broker agents simultaneously, a provider agent can renege on an intermediate contract established with a broker agent. A broker agent determines if each provider agent's proposal $P_j^i(t)$ is acceptable by first estimating the chance that a provider agent PA_j^i will renege on a contract, and compute the expected payoff of $P_j^i(t)$ taking into account the chance that PA_j^i may break a contract. The general idea in estimating the reneging probability of PA_j^i is that if a broker agent reaches a tentative agreement with PA_j^i at a price that is much *lower* (respectively, *higher*) than the average price of all provider agents, then there is a *higher* (respectively, *lower*) chance that PA_j^i will renege on the contract. Computing the expected utility of $P_j^i(t)$ considers *both* the outcomes that 1) PA_j^i will renege on a contract and 2) PA_j^i will abide by the contract. $P_j^i(t)$ is acceptable to a broker agent if it generates an expected utility that is higher than the utility of the broker agent's own price proposal for the resource. Algorithm 1 specifies the steps for commitment management.

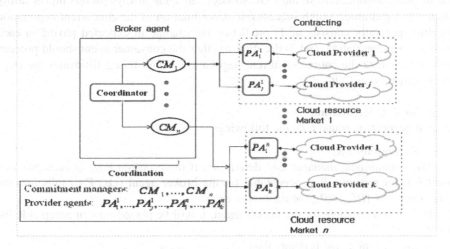

Fig. 3. Concurrent Negotiation of *SLAs*

Algorithm 1: **Commitment management**
At each negotiation round t, do the following:

1. Estimate the reneging probability of each provider agent PA_j^i
2. Compute the expected utility of each provider agent's proposal $P_j^i(t)$
3. Determine if each $P_j^i(t)$ is acceptable
4. If there are proposals that are acceptable then
    i. the broker agent sends a request for contracts to all corresponding provider agents
    ii. waits for the confirmation of contract from each PA_j^i
5. If the broker agent receives one or more confirmation of contracts then
    the broker agent accepts the contract that generates the highest expected utility
else
    the broker agent revises its proposal by making concession.

Coordination: In designing an algorithm for coordinating concurrent negotiations for establishing multiple *SLAs*, three factors are essential for a broker agent: i) successfully establishing all *SLAs* for the required set of Cloud resources needed for composing a service requested by a consumer agent, (ii) obtaining the cheapest possible price for the collection of resources, and (iii) establishing all *SLAs* rapidly. Since the dynamic configuration of a personalized collection of resources requires the establishment of *SLAs* between a broker agent and multiple Cloud resource providers, the failure of any one-to-many negotiation for establishing one *SLA* will result in the failure of the entire concurrent negotiation. Hence, ensuring a high negotiation success rate is most pertinent. This position paper proposes that a *utility-oriented coordination (UOC) strategy* [15] be adopted for coordinating concurrent multiple one-to-many negotiations. In the *UOC* strategy, an agent always prefers higher utility when it can guarantee a high success rate. Coordination of the concurrent negotiation activities generally consists of 1) predicting the change in expected payoff in each one-to-many negotiation, and 2) deciding whether the consumer agent should proceed with or terminate the entire concurrent negotiation. Algorithm 2 illustrates the steps for coordination in *UOC*.

Algorithm 2: **Coordination**
At each negotiation round t, do the following:

For each resource R_i,
1.   The commitment manager CM_i determines if the proposal $P^i_j(t)$ of each provider agent PA^i_j for resource R_i is acceptable for the broker agent (i.e., $P^i_j(t)$ falls into the *agreement zone* $[IP^i_{BA}, RP^i_{BA})$ of the broker agent)
2.   If $P^i_j(t)$ is acceptable for the broker agent, it will be placed into an acceptable list for R_i
3.   If any acceptable list is empty then
        the coordinator cannot complete the concurrent negotiation
     else
           i. **predict the change in utility** in each one-to-many negotiation in the next round $t+1$ using the information on negotiation status supplied by each CM_i
           ii. **decide whether to terminate or proceed** with the concurrent negotiation based on the prediction of the change in utility in $t+1$ for each one-to-many negotiation

5 Discussion and Conclusion

This position paper attempts to answer the following questions:

1) What would be an appropriate negotiation model for bolstering Cloud commerce?
2) What negotiation protocol and negotiation strategy should consumer agents and broker agents adopt in a Cloud service market?
3) What negotiation protocol and negotiation strategy should broker agents and provider agents adopt in a Cloud resource market?

Contribution: The contributions of this position paper include: 1) proposing and formulating a complex Cloud negotiation mechanism that supports negotiation activities in interrelated markets: i) the Cloud service market between consumer agents and broker agents, and ii) multiple Cloud resource markets between broker agents and provider agents, 2) specifying and formulating the negotiation protocols and negotiation strategies of consumer agents and broker agents in a Cloud service market, 3) designing the contracting and coordination algorithms for the concurrent negotiation activities between broker agents and provider agents in multiple Cloud resource markets.

Significance: The significance of this work is that it is believed to be the earliest work to consider a complex negotiation mechanism in which the negotiation outcomes in one market (i.e., a Cloud resource market) can potentially affect and influence the negotiation outcomes in another market (i.e., a Cloud service market). From the perspective of Cloud computing [3], this work is one of the earliest contributions to the field of Cloud resource management by providing a novel approach for facilitating the establishment of *SLAs* between consumers and brokers and between brokers and resource providers.   From the perspective of automated negotiation [1], this work attempts to introduce the application of agent-based negotiation techniques (in particular, relaxed-criteria negotiation [7], [8], [12], market-driven negotiation [5], [6], [9], and complex and concurrent negotiation [15]) to a new application domain requiring automated mapping of service requests to a collection of resources obtained through concurrent and parallel negotiation activities in multiple resource markets.

Challenges and future works: In the Cloud market infrastructure described in this work, brokers gain their utility through the difference between 1) the price paid by consumers for utilizing services composed by brokers and 2) the price that brokers paid to providers for leasing their resources. Since broker agents negotiate in a Cloud service market and multiple Cloud resource markets, their negotiation strategies must aim at maximizing revenues in the Cloud service market and minimizing costs in the Cloud resource markets. On this account, this position paper suggests that one of the research questions that need to be answered is: "What is an appropriate mathematical formulation for a broker agent's negotiation strategy that will take into consideration the pricing factors of 1) services in the Cloud service market and 2) resources in the Cloud resource markets?".

Ongoing work for designing and implementing the testbed described in this position paper are currently being carried out in the Multiagent and Cloud Computing Systems Laboratory (*MACCS Lab*) headed by the author at the Gwangju Institute of Science and Technology in South Korea. The ideas presented in this position paper are being tested in the Cloud servers in the author's *MACCS Lab* with nodes virtualized through hypervisor technologies such as *VMs*.

Acknowledgments. This work was supported by the Korea Research Foundation Grant funded by the Korean Government (MEST) (KRF-2009-220-D00092).

References

1. Rosenschein, J., Zlotkin, G.: Rules of Encounter: Designing Conventions for Automated Negotiation among Computers. MIT Press, Cambridge (1994)
2. Buyya, R., et al.: Cloud Computing and Emerging IT Platforms: Vision, Hype, and Reality for Delivering Computing as the 5th Utility. Future Generation Computer Systems 25(6), 599–616 (2009)
3. Foster, I., et al.: Cloud Computing and Grid Computing 360-Degree Compared. In: Proc. Grid Computing Environments Workshop, GCE 2008, November 12-16, pp. 1–10 (2008)
4. Rubinstein, A.: Perfect equilibrium in a bargaining model. Econometrica 50(1), 97–109 (1982)
5. Sim, K.M.: A market-driven model for designing negotiation agents. Comput. Intell. 18(4), 618–637 (2002)
6. Sim, K.M., Choi, C.Y.: Agents that react to changing market situations. IEEE Trans. Syst., Man, Cybern. B 33(2), 188–201 (2003)
7. Sim, K.M., Wang, S.Y.: Flexible negotiation agent with relaxed decision rules. IEEE Trans. Syst., Man, Cybern. B 34(3), 1602–1608 (2004)
8. Sim, K.M.: Negotiation Agents that make prudent compromises and are slightly flexible in reaching consensus. Comput. Intell. 20(4), 643–662 (2004)
9. Sim, K.M.: Equilibria, prudent compromises, and the 'Waiting' game. IEEE Trans. Syst., Man, Cybern. B 35(4), 712–724 (2005)
10. Sim, K.M., Ng, K.F.: A Relaxed-Criteria Bargaining Protocol for Grid Resource Management. In: Proc. of the 6th IEEE Int. Sym. on Cluster Computing and the Grid Workshops, Singapore, May 2006, p. 5 (2006)
11. Sim, K.M., Ng, K.F.: Relaxed-criteria Negotiation for G-commerce. Int. Trans. on Sys. Sci. and Appl., 3(2), 105–117 (2007)
12. Sim, K.M.: Evolving Relaxed-criteria Negotiation Rules. IEEE Trans. Syst., Man, Cybern. B 38(6), 1486–1500 (2008)
13. Sim, K.M.: Agent-based Cloud Commerce. In: Proc. of the IEEE Int. Conf. on Industrial Engineering and Engineering Management, Hong Kong (December 2009)
14. Sim, K.M.: Towards Agent-based Cloud Markets (Position Paper). In: Proc. 2010 Int. Conf. on e-CASE, and e-Technology, Macau (January 2010)
15. Sim, K.M., Shi, B.: Concurrent Negotiation and Coordination for Grid Resource Co-allocation. IEEE Trans. Syst., Man, Cybern. B 40(2) (to appear, 2010)

A Novel E-Newspapers Publication System Using Provably Secure Time-Bound Hierarchical Key Assignment Scheme and XML Security

Hung-Yu Chien[1], Ying-Lun Chen[2], Chien-Feng Lo[1], and Yuh-Ming Huang[1]

[1] Department of Information management, National Chi Nan University, Taiwan, R.O.C
[2] Department of Information management, Chaoyang University of Technology, Taiwan, R.O.C
hychien@ncnu.edu.tw

Abstract. A time-bound hierarchical key assignment scheme is a cryptographic key assignment scheme that organizes and encrypts the resources, according to the hierarchical tree relations and the time constraint, such that only authorized users can efficiently access the resources. This paper proposes a practical time-bound key assignment scheme, which is efficient and is proved secure. We, based on the time-bound hierarchical key assignment scheme and XML security, design and implement a new E-newspaper publication. The new system owns the practical merits: (1) the server can broadcast its publications with minimized communication overhead; (2) the subscribers, with only few set up data, can access to those authorized publications; (3) the system can efficiently manage and sell some of its backlogs, according to buyer's interests in specific categories of publications over a specific time periods. The experiment shows that the new system greatly improves both the efficiency of the server and the clients.

Keywords: time-bound hierarchical key assignment, access control, XML security, privacy.

1 Introduction

Internet is an excellent platform for sharing information. E-newspaper service is very popular and even crucial to our daily life. Usually, e-newspapers systems provide free services of some basic information and charge their customers for value-added services. To access the value-added services, the users have to navigate back to the server and authenticate themselves to the server to access the resources. Even though such conventional e-newspapers systems have several merits, they have several weaknesses and limitations. First, the server might be over-loaded when there are many subscribers simultaneously accessing value-added information on the server. Second, other systems could hardly share or process the huge, valuable information of e-newspapers, due to its non-sharable formats (for example, HTML and text). Third, the system could hardly manage its backlogs such that it can efficiently sell parts of its backlogs, according to users' interests. A user might be interested in only some categories of the publications within some specific time periods.

R.-S. Chang et al. (Eds.): GPC 2010, LNCS 6104, pp. 407–417, 2010.

Thanks to the technology of time-bound hierarchical key assignment [10] and XML security [13]-[15], we have new approaches to design and implement e-newspapers system. A time-bound hierarchical key assignment scheme allows the system to classify both the resources and the users into a set of classes $S = \{C_1, C_2, ..., C_m\}$ and organize these classes as a hierarchical tree, where the nodes in the tree denote the classes of users and resources, and the relation between nodes are defined by a partial order relation "$\preceq$". A relation "$C_j \preceq C_i$" means that the users in class C_i can access the resources owned by the class C_j. On the other hand, when $C_j \npreceq C_i$, it is illegal for users in C_i to access the resources in class C_j. The access is also restricted by a specified time periods. That is, a user can access the resources only if he has the corresponding privilege and the resources were generated during the specified time periods. The merits of time-bound key assignment schemes include flexibility and efficiency.

We can classify newspapers into different classes, according to the types of the news, or the value of the information, etc. The different classes of newspapers are encrypted using different keys. We then assign the users into these classes, according to their interest and the subscription fee, and assign them the corresponding keying material using the time-bound hierarchical key assignment scheme, such that a user can only access the authorized news published during the subscribed periods.

XML is a language to structure data and information such that applications can easily share these data and information. It has become a powerful tool to facilitate e-commerce on the Internet. To ensure the security of XML documents, W3C also defined XML security that consists of XML encryption, XML signature, etc. In this paper, based on time-bound hierarchical key assignment and XML security, we design and implement a newspapers publications system that has the merits: (1) the server efficiently broadcast its publications with minimized communication overhead *in broadcast environments*; (2) the subscribers, with only few set up data, can access to those authorized publications, according to both the users' privileges and the subscribed periods; (3) the system can efficiently manage and sell some of its backlogs, according to buyer's interests in specific categories of publications over a specific time periods. However, existing time-bound hierarchical key assignment schemes like [4]-[5], [7]-[12], [16] are either insecure or in-efficient. We, therefore, propose a new time-bound hierarchical key assignment which is efficient and is proved to be secure, under practical assumptions. The rest of this paper is organized as follows. Section 2 reviews the time-bound hierarchical key assignment and XML security. Section 3 proposes a new time-bound key assignment scheme. Section 4 presents our design of newspapers publication system. Section 5 states our conclusions.

2 Preliminaries

Time-bound hierarchical key assignment: In most of the cases, the resources in distributed environments can be classified, according the importance, into a number of disjoint classes C_i, $S = \{C_1, C_2, ..., C_m\}$. Likewise, according to the privileges in accessing the resources, users can also be classified into distinct classes. So, to control users' access to these resources, the conventional hierarchical key assignment schemes like [1]-[3] classify users/resources into a number of disjoint classes C_i , $S = \{C_1, C_2, ..., C_m\}$, and organize those classes into as a hierarchy tree, according to a partially ordered relation " $\preceq$ ", where " $C_j \preceq C_i$ " means that the privilege belonging to C_i is higher than or equal to the privilege belonging to C_j. Then, the conventional hierarchical key assignment scheme assigns distinct class keys K_i s to classes C_i s, and uses the key K_i to encrypt the resources in the class C_i. The users belonging to C_i are assigned the key K_i such that the users can derive K_j from K_i along with some public parameters if and only if $C_j \preceq C_i$. Thus, the users in class C_i can access the resources in class C_j, if $C_j \preceq C_i$. On the other hand, when $C_j \npreceq C_i$, it is infeasible for users in C_i to access the resources in class C_j.

The above conventional hierarchical key assignment schemes is efficient if the assigned keys are seldom updated. However, in many cases, it is likely that the class keys should be frequently updated for several possible reasons; for example, a user may be assigned to a certain class for only a certain period of time, and the key should be updated when the authorized time period expires [10]. In such cases, the system needs to assign distinct keys for every possible time periods. For such environments, the conventional hierarchical key assignment scheme should frequently update the class keys and frequently re-distribute the keys to the authorized users. It is not efficient. In 2002, Tzeng [10] proposed the first time-bound hierarchical key assignment scheme, where a user's access privilege is dependent on both the time constraint property and the hierarchical access property, and the generation of encrypting key is also dependent on the time period as well as the hierarchy of the classes. The system distributes the users the initial data only when they subscribe the services; and, the users can access the authorized resource during the whole authorized time periods, without receiving further control data afterwards. The system does not re-distribute the keys even though the encrypting keys are distinct for each time period. Once their authorized time periods expire, the users can on longer access the resources. The time-bound hierarchical key assignment scheme is, therefore, much more efficient than the conventional hierarchical key assignment approach. In Tzeng's scheme, the system lifetime is divided time into $z + 1$ parts (the time period begins at 0 and ends at z) and the data assigned to C_i at time period t would be encrypted by key $K_{i,t}$. So, a user who is assigned in C_i for the time periods from t_1 to t_2 can accesses those resources encrypted, using the key $K_{j,t}$, if it satisfies $C_j \preceq C_i$ and $0 \le t_1 \le t \le t_2 \le z$. However, Tzeng's scheme is very computational costly since the client must perform expensive computations in order to derive a legitimate key. Subsequently, Chien [4], based on tamper-resistant devices [6] and the concept of [3][10], proposed an efficient time-bound hierarchical key assignment scheme, where only simple hashing operations are required to derive the keys. Unfortunately, both Tzeng's scheme and Chien's scheme were shown to be vulnerable to collusion attacks [17][18], where a set of malicious users can co-operatively derive un-authorized keys. Following that, several related investigations have been published to enhance the security of time-bound key assignment schemes. These schemes can be divided, according to the computational cost, into two categories- the schemes with public key cryptography [5], [7], [10], [11], [12], [16], [21], and the schemes with tamper-resistant devices [4], [8], [9]. However, these schemes either suffer from security weaknesses [5], [16] or have poor performance in terms of public parameters/computations [5], [7], [10], [11], [12], [16]. The scheme [7] cannot fully support the time constraint property, because it can only specify the end time but not the start time, so all the users have the same start time. This paper, based on Chien's previous scheme [4], proposes a new time-bound hierarchical key assignment scheme. The new scheme is very efficient to be implemented on smart cards. We will prove the security of the proposed scheme in the random oracle model, and use the scheme to design and implement our E-news publication system.

XML and XML security: To consider its flexibility, scalability and inter-operability, our system adopts XML as newspapers format, and applies XML security [13-15] to ensure its security of data exchange. There are several related works like Miklau-Suciu's scheme [22] had applied XML and cryptographic keys to enforce the access control of published data, whereas these schemes did not consider the temporal constraints. Bertino et al. had also designed and implemented an XML document broadcasting scheme using an RSA-based time-bound hierarchical key assignment scheme [22]; however, they did not proved the security of their scheme, and did not provide any experiment result. Bertino et al.'s time-bound key assignment scheme is quite similar to that of Yeh [16], which we had reported the security weaknesses and had proposed an enhanced RSA-based version to improve both the security and the computational performance [5]. However, the computational performance of our previous RSA-based version is still not satisfactory [23]. We, therefore, shall propose a new scheme in this paper.

3 New Time-Bound Hierarchical Key Assignment Scheme

3.1 The New Scheme

Before presenting our E-news system, we first propose a new time-bound hierarchical key assignment scheme. The scheme has the following assumptions: (1) There is a secure one-way hash function $h()$ and a secure symmetric encryption scheme $E_k(m)$, where the encryption scheme should satisfy the in-distinguishability under chosen plain text attack (IND-CPA) property. Even though some collisions has been reported for those widely used hash functions, like MD5 and SHA-1, the pre-image to a given digest is still hard to find; it, therefore, will not endanger the security of our scheme; (2) tamper-resistant devices are available (even though several possible attacks on tamper-resistant devices have been reported, effective countermeasures to these problems have been proposed [19]) ; and, (3) there is a Trusted Agent (*TA*) in the system.

In the system, we further assume that a partial order set of disjoint classes ($C_1, C_2,..., C_n$) with respect to the binary relation " $\preceq$ " is available, and the lifespan of the system is divided into time periods, numbered as period 1, 2, ..., z. For example, if each time period represents a month, then $z = 1200$ means that the lifespan of the system is 100 years. Our scheme consists of four phases- initialization phase, user authorization phase, encrypting key generation phase, and decryption key derivation phase.

Initialization: TA randomly selects n secret class keys k_i's, $1 \leq i \leq n$, for the n disjoint classes, two random secret values a and b, and one symmetric encryption/decryption function $E(.)/D(.)$. For each directed edge "$C_j \preceq C_i$" in the hierarchical tree, TA publishes a public value r_{ij} defined in Eq. (1) on an authenticated public board, where $h()$ denotes a secure one-way hash function, R denotes a random value for this edge, x is TA's secret key, ID_i denotes the identity of C_i, $\|$ denotes the string concatenation, $\oplus$ denotes the bit-wise XOR operation, $E_x(...)$ denotes the encryption using the key x. Everyone can read the data on the board, but only TA can update the data.

$$r_{ij} = E_x(h(h(x \| ID_i) \| ID_j \| k_i) \oplus k_j \| R) \| E_x(k_j \oplus R) \tag{1}$$

User authorization: When a user is assigned to class C_i for the time period t_1 to t_2, TA distributes k_i to the user through a secure channel. TA also issues the user a tamper-resistant device, in which $E(\ )/D(\ )$, x, $h^{t_1}(a)$ and $h^{z-t_2}(b)$ are stored. $h^{t_1}(a) = h(h(...(h(a))...))$ denotes applying t_1 times hashing operations on the value a. *It is assumed that even the owners of these tamper-resistant devices cannot access and cannot update the values stored in the devices.*

Encrypting key generation: The data belongs to class C_i for time period t would be encrypted, using the key $K_{i,t}$. The encryption key $K_{i,t}$ is generated as Equation 2.

$$K_{i,t} = h(k_i \| h^t(a) \| h^{z-t}(b)) \tag{2}$$

Decryption key derivation: When a user, who is in class C_i for the time period t_1 to t_2, wants to decrypt the encrypted data in class C_i or in class C_j at time period t, where $C_j \preceq C_i$ and $t_1 \leq t \leq t_2$, his device can derive the decrypting key as follows.

For the class C_i, the user just enters k_i, and the device *secretly* computes $h^t(a) = h^{t-t_1}(h^{t_1}(a))$, $h^{z-t}(b) = h^{t_2-t}(h^{z-t_2}(b))$ and $K_{i,t} = h(k_i \| h^t(a) \| h^{z-t}(b))$. The values $h^{t_1}(a)$ and $h^{z-t_2}(b)$ are pre-stored in the device.

For the class C_j and $C_j \preceq C_i$ is a direct edge on the hierarchy, the user enters k_i, ID_j and r_{ij}, and the device decrypts the first part of r_{ij} to get $h(h(x \| ID_i) \| ID_j \| k_i) \oplus k_j \| R$, and then derives k_j and R. The device checks whether $E_x(k_j \oplus R)$ equals the second part of r_{ij}. If so, the device uses the local values to computes $h^t(a) = h^{t-t_1}(h^{t_1}(a))$, $h^{z-t}(b) = h^{t_2-t}(h^{z-t_2}(b))$, and $K_{j,t} = h(k_j \parallel h^t(a) \parallel h^{z-t}(b))$, where the key x is pre-stored in the device. If C_j is not directly connected to C_i but several edges distant from C_i, then the device iteratively computes the class keys along the path from C_i to C_j, and derives the decrypting key $K_{j,t}$ finally.

3.2 The Security Analysis and Performance Evaluation

Security analysis: The security of the proposed scheme is based on the security of tamper-resistant devices, the pre-image security of the one-way hash function and the security of the symmetric encryption. Our scheme can resist the collusion attacks that bother the previous schemes. Due to page limitation, we eliminate the detailed analysis and proof from this version.

Table 1. Comparisons among time-bound hierarchical key assignment schemes

	New scheme	Chien [4]	Chien-Tang-Chen[5]	Tzeng [10]	Tzeng [11]
Implementation requirements	Low-cost tamper resistant device	Low-cost tamper-resistant device	Public key cryptosystem	Public key cryptosystem	Public key cryptosystem
Number of public values	$n-1$	$n-1$	$n+z$	$n+6$	$n \cdot z$
Operations to generating/deriving the encryption keys	$L \cdot (2T_E + 2T_h) + (w+1) \cdot T_h$	$L \cdot T_h + (w+1) \cdot T_h$	$(N_i + w - 2)T_E$	$(n - N_i)T_E + (w)T_L$ (The worse case)	$(N_i \cdot w - 1)T_E$
Resistance to collusion attack	Yes	No	Yes	No	Yes
Provable secure	Yes	No	No	No	No

* In the table, n denotes the total number of classes; z denotes the total number of time periods; N_i denotes the number of classes C_j such that $C_j \preceq C_i$; w denotes the number of time periods between t_1 and t_2; that is, $w = t_2 - t_1 + 1$; L denotes the path from the user's class to the target class; T_h denotes the cost of one hashing operation; T_E denotes the cost of one modular exponentiations; T_L denotes that of one Lucas function operations .

Performance evaluation: We now examine the space requirement, the implementation cost, and the computational cost. Our scheme publishes one public value r_{ij} for each edge in the hierarchical tree; therefore, the total number of public values is n-1, while the number of public values of Tzeng's scheme [10] is $6+n$ and that of Chien's scheme [4] is also n-1, where n is the number of classes. On the user side, each authorized user remembers one key and keeps one simple tamper-resistant device that stores only the information (x, $h^{t_1}(a)$, $h^{z-t_2}(b)$, $h()$, $E()/D()$). The number of values on the user side is fixed and is independent of the number of classes and the number of time periods. On the TA side, the system only maintains the secret values x, ($k_1,...,k_n$), a, and b, and the public values r_{ij} s. The system dose not waste the bandwidth for key updating messages that the conventional hierarchical key assignment scheme does. To derive a time-bound encryption key $K_{j,t}$ of the user's class, our scheme involves only several hashing operations and two decryption operations for the key of the same class, while Tzeng's scheme requires many costly public key operations. The performance is summarized in table 1. From Table 1, we see that the proposed scheme is highly efficient in terms of computations, communications, and implementation cost. Although Chien's scheme [4] is also efficient, the scheme is vulncrable to the collusion attack and only the proposed new scheme is provably secure. Due to page limitation, the security proof is eliminated from this version.

4 The Proposed Newspapaers Publication System

System Architecture: This section proposes, based on the new time-bound hierarchical key assignment scheme and XML security, an E-news publication system design and implementation. Our system architecture is shown in Fig. 1. The server periodically generates its newspapers. These newspapers include several categories-art, TV, and sports, etc. These newspapers are generated in XML format. Each issue (say time period t) of a specific class (say class C_i) of the newspapers is encrypted by a class-time-bound key $K_{i,t}$. So, the XML-format newspapers are encrypted and its key-related data r_{ij} is embedded in the encrypted newspapers, applying the XML security technology. The server periodically publishes, via e-mails, the encrypted newspapers to its subscribers.

On the client side, each subscriber is equipped with an IC card (java card in our implementation) which is initialized with its initial key data, according to our time-bound hierarchical key assignment scheme. When accessing one's mailbox, the subscriber inserts his card, and the card computes the corresponding class-time-bound key, based on the information r_{ij} (of which the integrity is protected by the message authentication code $E_x(k_j \oplus R)$) in the e-mail, and finally decrypts the corresponding authorized sections of the encrypted newspapers.

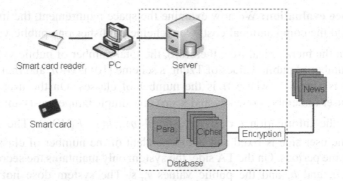

Fig. 1. Architecture of online newspaper publication system

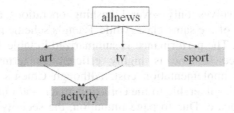

Fig. 2. The hierarchy of our newspapers

Classification of newspapers: We classify our newspapers into the hierarchy of classes as shown in Fig. 2. Our newspapers consist of several sections- the art section, the TV section, the sports section and the activity section, where the activity section is free for the subscribers in the "art" class and the "TV" class. The users corresponding to the "allnews" class have the highest privilege and can access all published newspapers, where the users of this class could be those subscribers who pay the highest subscription fee. The users in the "art" class, the "tv" class and the "sports" class can respectively decrypt their corresponding sections of the encrypted newspapers, and the users of the former two classes can access the activity section.

XML definition of Newspapers: Fig. 3 presents the structure of newspaper document. The decryption program will extract each element through the XML-related APIs (Application Programming Interface) and decrypts the authorized part of the cipher, according to user's privilege. All news in one newspapers document are generated at the same time period; therefore, they all share the same parameter t - the single TIME_PERIOD element. A newspapers document consists of zero or more NEWS elements, where a NEWS element corresponding to a class C_i contains a single piece of news and is encrypted using the key $K_{i,t}$ (shown in Eq. (2)).

```
<NEWSPAPER>
  <TIME_PERIOD>
    <NEWS>*
      <xenc:EncryptedData>
        <xenc:EncryptionMethod>
        <ds:KeyInfo>
          <ds:KeyName>
        </ds:KeyInfo>
        <xenc:CipherData>
          <xenc:CipherValue>
        </xenc:CipherData>
    </NEWS>
</NEWSPAPER>
```

Fig. 3. The structure of a newspapers document ("*" denotes zero or more occurrences)

In the ds:KeyName element, it includes the identity of a class node so that the decryption program can use this identity to search the corresponding public parameter r_{ij}. Since the public parameters r_{ij} s are for long-term-used (they would be updated only when the classes hierarchical tree is updated), we, therefore, arrange the r_{ij} document as a separate document and do not embed the document in each newspapers to save communication costs. All of the public parameters such as $r_{art,activity}$, $r_{tv,activity}$, etc. are embedded in one r_{ij} document as shown in Fig. 4. In the r_{ij} documents, each Para element presents one distinct public parameter, and each Para element has two attributes- ID_i and ID_j (the direct edge $C_j \preceq C_i$), the identities of security classes C_i and C_j respectively, and the value of r_{ij} (defined in Equation (1)). In Equation (1), x is TA's secret key, ID_i, ID_j denote the identities, k_i, k_j denotes the class keys of C_i and C_j respectively, and $\parallel$ denotes the string concatenation. To protect the integrity of public parameters, we add a message authentication code $E_x(k_j \oplus R)$.

```
<Rij_Document>
  <Rij>
    <Para IDi IDj>*
    <xenc:EncryptedData>*
      <xenc:EncryptionMethod>
      <ds:KeyInfo>
        <ds:KeyName>
      </ds:KeyInfo>
      <xenc:CipherData>
        <xenc:CipherValue>
      </xenc:CipherData>
    </xenc:EncryptedData>
  </Rij>
</Rij_Document>
```

Fig. 4. The structure of the r_{ij} document ("*" denotes zero or more occurrences)

When a user is assigned to the class C_i for time periods from t_1 to t_2, TA distributes the user the key k_i and a tamper-resistant device (a java card) which securely stores TA's secret key x, $h^{t_1}(a)$, $h^{z-t_2}(b)$, the identity ID_i of the class C_i, the time period t_1 and t_2. When the user accesses the newspapers in his mailbox, he inserts his card and inputs his secret key k_i, then the client software will retrieve the public values r_{ij} s from the r_{ij} document and compute the class-time-bound key $K_{j,t}$ defined in Equation (2); finally, the authorized sections of the newspapers can be decrypted for any sections $C_j \preceq C_i$ and $t_1 \le t \le t_2$. Due to page limitation, we eliminate the section of our implementation and field test evaluation from this version.

5 Conclusions

This paper has proposed a new time-bound hierarchical key assignment scheme, based on tamper-resistant device, symmetric encryption and one-way function. The proposed time-bound hierarchical key assignment scheme is efficient and is proved secure. Based on the proposed time-bound hierarchical key assignment scheme and the XML security, we have designed and implemented an E-newspapers publication system. The system has the following merits: (1) low server load and good convenience for the clients, since the users only access their local mailboxes when accessing the value-added information; (2) it is more powerful and flexible because the system can efficiently manage its publications and sell its backlogs, according to the classification and time constraint [10];   (3) it is more scalable and inter-operable because the documents are generated in standardized XML format such that the information can be easily shared and processed by other systems. The results show that the computational performance of the proposed scheme is much better than its RSA-based counterparts and the time-bound hierarchical key assignment provides a practical solution to secure distributed resource sharing, *especially for the broadcast environments*. We think it might provide a good solution to the digital TV broadcast problem. It deserves our further research.

Acknowledgements. This research is partially supported by National Science Council with project number NSC 97 - 2221 - E - 260 - 008 - MY2.

References

[1] Akl, S.G., Taylor, P.D.: Cryptographic Solution to a Problem of Access Control in a hierarchy. ACM Trans. on Computer Systems 1(3), 239–248 (1983)

[2] Chen, T.-S., Huang, J.-Y.: A novel key management scheme for dynamic access control in a user hierarchy. Applied Mathematics and Computation 162, 339–351 (2005)

[3] Chien, H.-Y., Jan, J.-K.: New hierarchical assignment without Public Key cryptography. Computer and Security 22(6), 523–526 (2003)

[4] Chien, H.-Y.: Efficient time-bound hierarchical key assignment scheme. IEEE Trans. on Knowledge and Data Eng. 16(10), 1301–1304 (2004)

[5] Chien, H.-Y., Tang, Y.-L., Chen, Y.-L.: A Secure and Efficient Time-Bound Hierarchical Key Assignment Scheme. In: Proc. of the 2007 IAENG International Conference on Communication Systems and Applications, Hong Kong, pp. 21–23 (2007)

[6] Gemplus, M.L.: Smart-Cards: A Cost-Effective Solution against Electronic Fraud. In: Proc. European Conf. Security and Detection, pp. 81–85 (1997)

[7] Huang, H.-F., Chang, C.-C.: A new cryptographic key assignment scheme with time-constraint access control in a hierarchy. Computer Standards and Interfaces 26(3), 159–166 (2004)

[8] Lee, W.-B., Li, J.-H., Dow, C.-R.: Efficient Date-Constraint Hierarchical Key Assignment Scheme. In: Proc. of the 2005 International Conf. on Security and Management, Las Vegas, Nevada, USA, pp. 51–57 (2005)

[9] De Santis, A., Ferrara, A.L., Masucci, B.: Enforcing the security of a time-bound hierarchical key assignment scheme. Information Sciences 176, 1684–1694 (2006)

[10] Tzeng, W.-G.: A Time-Bound Cryptographic Key Assignment Scheme for Access Control in a Hierarchy. IEEE Trans. Knowledge and Data Eng. 14(1), 182–188 (2002)

[11] Tzeng, W.-G.: Access control and authorization: A secure system for data access based on anonymous authentication and time-dependent hierarchical keys. In: Proc. ACM Symposium on Information, computer and comm. Security, Taiwan, pp. 223–230 (2006)

[12] Wang, S.-Y., Laih, C.-S.: Merging: An Efficient Solution for a Time-Bound Hierarchical Key Assignment Scheme. IEEE Trans. on Dependable and Secure Computing 3(1), 91–100 (2006)

[13] World Wide Web Consortium. Extensible Markup Language (XML) 1.0 (1998), http://www.w3.org/TR/REC-xml/

[14] World Wide Web Consortium. XML Encryption Syntax and Processing (2002a), http://www.w3.org/TR/xmlenc-core/

[15] World Wide Web Consortium. XML-Signature Syntax and Processing (2002b), http://www.w3.org/TR/xmldsig-core/

[16] [16] Yeh, J.-H.: An RSA-Based Time-Bound Hierarchical Key Assignment Scheme for Electronic Article Subscription. In: Proc. ACM Conf. Information and Knowledge Management, pp. 285–286 (2005)

[17] Yi, X., Ye, Y.: Security of Tzeng's time-bound key assignment scheme for access control in a hierarchy. IEEE Trans. on Knowledge and Data Eng. 15(4), 1054–1055 (2003)

[18] Yi, X.: Security of Chien's efficient time-bound hierarchical key assignment scheme. IEEE Trans. on Knowledge and Data Eng. 17(9), 1298–1299 (2005)

[19] Messerges, T.S., Dabbish, E.A., Sloan, R.H.: Examining smart-card security under the threat of power analysis attacks. IEEE Transactions on Computers 51(5), 541–552 (2002)

[20] Bellare, M., Rogaway, P.: Provably secure session key distribution: The three party case. In: 27th ACM Symposium on the Theory of Computing, pp. 57–66. ACM Press, New York (1995)

[21] Bertino, E., Carminati, B., Ferrari, E.: A temporal key management scheme for secure broadcasting of XML documents. In: ACM Conference on Computer and Communications Security, pp. 31–40 (2002)

[22] Miklau, G., Suciu, D.: Controlling Access to Published Data Using Cryptography. In: Proc. of the 29th international conference on Very large data bases, VLDB, pp. 898–909 (2003)

[23] Chen, Y.L.: Application and Design of Time-Bound Hierarchical Key Assignment Scheme, thesis, ChaoYang University of Technology, Department of Information Management (2007)

A Tree-Based Reliability Model for Composite Web Service with Common-Cause Failures

Bo Zhou[1], Keting Yin[1], Shuai Zhang[1], Honghong Jiang[1], and Aleksander J. Kavs[2]

[1] College of Computer Science and Technology, Zhejiang University, Hangzhou, China
{bzhou,yinketing,zhangshuai,zhejianghonghong}@zju.edu.cn
[2] State Street Corporation, Boston, MA, USA
ajkavs@statestreet.com

Abstract. Reliability is one of the most important quality dimensions for web services. Current reliability models for composite web service assume the statistical independence of its component web services, which is often not the case. In this paper, we research on the reliability correlation of component web services by identifying common-cause failures (CCF) and propose a tree-based reliability model for composite web service. We also present the method to estimate overall reliability of composite web service based on our reliability model. Evaluation shows that our method can improve the accuracy of reliability estimation for composite web service and is particularly valuable when designing fault-tolerant service-based system.

Keywords: composite web service, reliability model, common-cause failure.

1 Introduction

With the prevalence of web services [1] in recent years, more and more applications are developed based on Service-Oriented Architecture (SOA) [2]. Compared with the traditional software systems, service-centric systems are built upon bundles of web services, which could be developed by their own, or more commonly, provided by external parties and accessed over the Internet. Thus, the runtime environment for the web services-based system is prone to failure due to the uncertainty in the Internet and external parties. Meanwhile, business level applications have very stringent requirements on the reliability, for example, 99.99% requests should be processed correctly in a reasonable time. Not surprisingly, reliability of web services has been researched extensively and is still a hot topic.

Reliability is often defined as "the probability that it successfully responds within a reasonable period of time." [3]. For atomic web service, it can be measured using statistical method based on the history logs; while for composite web service, its reliability depends on the reliabilities of the underlying component services. Various methods has been applied to estimate the aggregated reliability for the composite web service, such as reduction method [4] [5] and Petri Net [6].

However, as far as the authors know, existing methods for reliability modeling of composite web services often assume the statistical independence between the component web services. While in real world environment, this assumption could be

R.-S. Chang et al. (Eds.): GPC 2010, LNCS 6104, pp. 418–429, 2010.
© Springer-Verlag Berlin Heidelberg 2010

often violated. Service providers tend to publish a series of web services that are closely related and they are potential candidates to be selected for the same web service composition; moreover, service consumers are likely to choose several component services from the same provider for reasons such as package discounts or trust in particular providers. If multiple component services are from the same provider or even deployed on the same server, accidents like system crash or regional power outage will lead to simultaneous failing of these services. Such correlations between component services are called Common Cause Failures (CCF) [7], which should be identified and modeled properly in order to estimate the reliability of composite web service more accurately, especially when developing fault-tolerant systems.

In this paper, we investigate the category of CCFs in the context of composite web service and propose a novel tree-based reliability model for composite web service that considers the presence of CCFs. We also present a recursive algorithm to compute the aggregated reliability. Our reliability model is more accurate and conforms to the reality better.

The rest of our paper is structured as follows. Section 2 introduces the preliminary knowledges. Section 3 presents our tree-based reliability model and the computing algorithm. Applications are demonstrated Section 4. Section 5 is the related work. Conclusion and future works are discussed in Section 6.

2 Preliminaries

Table 1 summarizes the reliability aggregation rules for four major composition patterns borrowed from existing literatures [8]. For sequence and parallel patterns, the aggregated reliability of the both is computed as the product of its component services' reliabilities.

Table 1. Reliability Aggregation Rules

Composition Pattern	Reliability Aggregation Rule	Comment
Sequential	$\prod_{i=1}^{n} Rel(ws_i)$	n: number of services in the pattern.
Parallel	$\prod_{i=1}^{n} Rel(ws_i)$	n: number of services in the pattern.
Conditional	$\min\{Rel(ws_1), ..., Rel(ws_n)\}$	Each service is on a branch in the pattern.
Loop	$Rel(ws_i)^k$	k: average number of cycles in the loop.

As we stated above, these aggregation rules only hold when the component services are statistically independent, but in real world, it is quite possible that some component services are correlated with each other in certain way. We observe that a web service could fail due to reasons in different levels. Table 2 categorizes the failures of web services into four levels and presents possible scenarios for each level. The listed scenarios are not comprehensive but should be sufficient for further discussions.

Table 2. Failures in different levels for Web Service

Level	Possible Scenarios
Service	logical errors in the implementation, binding fault, incompatibility issues
Host	system crash, unresponsiveness due to server overload, hardware failure
Provider	regional outage, closure of the operating company
Network	communication congestion, hardware failure

Service level failures will only affect a specific web service, i.e. failings of component services in this level are independent. Meanwhile, failures in the other three levels could cause multiple web services fail simultaneously, which are CCFs of these failed web services. Furthermore, service, host, provider and network are a list of levels of increasing coarse granularity, which can be organized using a tree structure:

Definition 1. Reliability Hierarchy Tree (RHT)
A Reliability Hierarchy Tree is used to model the reliability hierarchy for web services. It is a tree with four levels. We formally define it as RHT = (V, L, C, δ), where

- V is the set of all nodes in the RHT. It could represent a network, provider, host machine or web service depending on its located level.
- $L = \{N, P, H, WS\}$ is the set of levels in the RHT, which are network (N), provider (P), host (H) and service (WS) levels respectively from top (root) to the bottom (leaf). $\forall\ v \in V$, we use $L(v)$ to denote its level.
- $C = D \subset V \times V$ is the set of parent-child relations, where $\forall\ (x, y) \in C$, x is the parent node and y is the child node. Parent-child relations are identified by the following rules: (1) if a provider p is located in the network n, then add (n, p) to C; (2) if a host machine h is maintained by the provider p, then add (p, h) to C; (3) if a web service ws is deployed on the server h, then add (h, ws) to C.
- $\delta = V \times R^+$ associates each node with a positive real number denoting its reliability value. $\forall\ v \in V$, we use $Rel(v)$ to denote its reliability value.

Fig. 1 is an example of RHT. For the end user, the reliability of the web service is an integrated value of all levels. We use $RelU(ws_i)$ to represent the web service reliability from the user's perspective. For a single web service, its reliability from user perspective could be calculated easily given the RHT:

$$RelU(ws_i) = Rel(ws_i) * Rel(H_j) * Rel(P_m) * Rel(N_n) \tag{1}$$

where H_j, P_m, N_n are corresponding host, provider and network for this service.

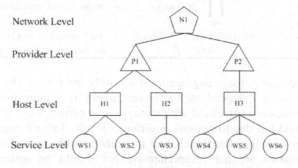

Fig. 1. An example of Reliability Hierarchy Tree

3 Tree-Based Reliability Model

In this section, we present the reliability model and aggregation method for the composite web service with common-cause failures. Four common composition patterns are discussed, which are sequential, parallel, conditional and loop.

3.1 Sequential Pattern

The sequential pattern is the most basic and common means to compose the web services, thus we use it as the starting point to present our method.

Definition 2. RelTree
RelTree is used to model the reliability relations of the component services in web service composition. Formally, given a composite web service cws = (ws$_1$, ws$_2$, ... ws$_n$), its RelTree = (V, L, C, δ) is a consolidated RHT where,

$\quad \forall$ v$\in$ V and L(V) = WS $\Rightarrow$ $\exists$ ws$\in$ cws, where ws is represented by the node v;

$\quad \forall$ ws$\in$ cws $\Rightarrow$ $\exists$ v$\in$ V, where L(V) = WS.

Definition 3. RelForest
The root node of RelTree represents a network. If a composite web service contains services from multiple networks, then its CCF-aware reliability model will contain several RelTree, which is called RelForest. Without loss of generality, we assume component services of a composite web service locate in only one network in the rest of this paper for simplicity.

RelTree can be constructed from RHT by pruning unrelated nodes and branches. Algorithm 1 shows the process.

Algorithm 1. RelTree Building

Input: RHT (denoted as *rht*), composite web service (denoted as *cws*)
Output: RelTree for *cws*
1 **foreach** component web service *ws* in *cws*
2 | find the corresponding node *s* in *rht*;
3 | **do**
4 | | mark *s* as visited;
5 | | **if** (*s* is root) **then break**;
6 | | set *s* = *s*.parent;
7 | | **if** (*s* is visited) **then break**;
8 | **repeat** from line 3;
9 **end for**
10 prune all the unvisited node;
11 **return** resulting RelTree;

Fig. 2 is an example of RelTree constructed from RHT, where the composite web service cws = {ws$_1$, ws$_4$, ws$_5$}. Each node in the resulting RelTree is annotated with the reliability value.

With the RelTree, we can answer the following questions about the reliability aspects of the composite web service accurately:

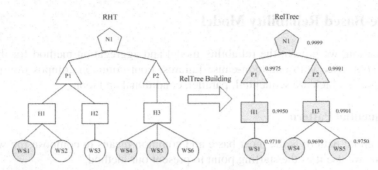

Fig. 2. Example of RelTree Building

- Q1: What is the reliability value of a component web service?
- Q2: What is the reliability value of the composite web service ignoring the CCFs?
- Q3: What is the reliability value of the composite web service when CCFs are considered?
- Q4: What is the probability that no more than n services failed simultaneously in the composition?

The answer for Q1 has been discussed above and the answer for Q2 is also straight-forward which is the product of reliability of each component web service as calculated in Q1. Q3 can be reduced to Q4 when n = 0 (i.e. all component web services are in good condition). Therefore, we give Algorithm 2 as the solution to Q4.

Algorithm 2. RelTreeCal

Input: the RelTree or subTree of RelTree for the composite web service (denoted as *relTree*), maximum number of failed nodes (denoted as *n*, and *n* should not be large than the number of leaves in the tree)

Output: the probability that no more than *n* services fail simultaneously in the service composition

1   initialize $rel \leftarrow 0$;
2   **foreach** *m* from 0 to *n*
3   initialize $t \leftarrow$ number of leaves in the *relTree*, $v \leftarrow$ root node, $p \leftarrow 0$;
4   **if** *v* is a leaf
5      $\mid$ $p = (m == 0)$? $Rel(v)$: $1 - Rel(v)$;
6   **else**
7   set $fn \leftarrow$ first child node of *v*,
8   set $on \leftarrow$ the set of child nodes of *v* except *fn*,
9   set $a \leftarrow$ number of leaves in the subTree *fn*, $b \leftarrow t - a$,
10   set $min \leftarrow (b >= m)$? $0 : (m - b)$, $max \leftarrow (a >= m)$? $m : a$;
11      $p = \sum_{i=min}^{max} pf * po$, where
12      $pf = RelTreeCal (fn, i)$, $po = RelForest (on, m - i)$;
13   **end if**
14   set $rel \leftarrow rel + p$;
15 **end for**
16 **return** *rel*;

The main steps of the algorithm are explained as follows:

- **Line 4, 5:** If v is a leaf, simply set its reliability or failure value depending on required number of failed node
- **Line 6-13:** Store first child node of v into fn and the rest child nodes (if any) into on, initialize a, b as the number of leaves in fn and on respectively, set min, max as the least and maximum number of failed services in the subTree fn respectively (Line 7-10). Enumerate all cases of distributing the number of failed services to fn and on (for fn, the number of failed services ranges from min to max) (Line 11), recursively invoke RelTreeCal and RelForest to calculate subTree probability (the algorithm for RelForestCal is similar and thus is omitted here due to limitation of the space).
- **Line 14:** Add up all subTree probabilities.

3.2 General Patterns

In this section, we discuss the tree-based reliability model for the other three composition patterns, namely, parallel, conditional, loop.

Parallel Pattern
Reliability of each component web service contributes equally to the overall reliability of the composite web service as in sequential pattern. Therefore, tree-based reliability model for the parallel pattern is the same as that for sequential pattern.

Loop Pattern
Assume the maximum number of cycles in a loop is known, then the loop can be represented by a sequence of conditional patterns. Fig. 3 is an example of loop unfolding, where p_i is the probability that the $(i+1)$th cycle will be executed after the ith cycle. Note $p_k = 1$. The value of maximum loop and the probabilities can be achieved from the historical record.

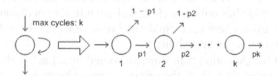

Fig. 3. Loop unfolding example

Conditional Pattern
Conditional pattern should be treated specially when evaluating the reliability. Each branch has its probability to be executed, and services on the frequent-visited branch have more impact than those on the rarely-visited branch. Therefore, aggregated reliability of conditional pattern could not be simply obtained as in sequential/parallel patterns. The basic idea is to transform the conditional pattern into other patterns, and then apply the above-mentioned approach to calculate its reliability.

Definition 4. Execution Path

A composite web service can have one or multiple execution paths, and all component services in an execution path will be executed in a run, i.e. execution path is free of conditional pattern. For complete definition of execution path, we refer interested readers to [9]. Each execution path is associated with an execution probability.

Fig. 4 is an example of a composite web service and its corresponding execution paths. By default, the split structure is conditional pattern while parallel pattern is annotated with the plus sign. Since the execution path only contains sequential and parallel patterns, we can apply the above the tree-based model and analysis method.

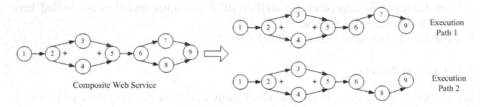

Fig. 4. Example of Execution Path

Zheng et.al [10] has proposed a rooted tree based approach to extract the execution path from composite web service, which could be applied in our context without much modification. For the detailed algorithms, interested readers could refer to the original paper; we just present the basic process as the following:

- **Step 1.** Reduce the parallel and loop patterns to the sequential and conditional patterns as described above. The resulting composition structure is free from parallel and loop patterns.
- **Step 2.** Then the composition structure is transformed into a rooted tree. Each node in the tree represents a component web service, and the root node represents the beginning component web service in the composition. The child nodes represent the component web services that will be executed after the current one. For sequential pattern, the node has only one child node, while for conditional pattern, multiple child nodes exist where each child node represents one branch. Each branch is annotated with the chosen probability.
- **Step 3.** Extract the execution path from the rooted tree. Each path in the rooted tree represents an execution path of the original composite web service. Starting from each leaf node, all execution paths can be identified and their corresponding execution probability can also be calculated.

For each execution path, we can build the RelTree and evaluate its reliability. A comprehensive example is presented in the next section to illustrate the whole process.

4   Application of Reliability Models

4.1   A Running Example

Fig. 5(a) is a composite web service with 14 component services. The parallel pattern is annotated with the plus sign to differentiate from the conditional pattern. Fig. 5(b) is the corresponding representation for the composite web service after the parallel and loop patterns are reduced. Note that the order of component services in the parallel patterns is not important after transformation. Then we apply the execution path extraction method to generate the rooted tree in Fig. 5(c). In Fig. 5(c) the conditional branches are annotated with the execution probabilities. Note the branches after the node 11 could have different execution probabilities depending on previous executed path. The execution paths can be generated by visiting each leaf node along to the root node. In Fig. 5(c), there are six execution paths for the composite web service, and their execution probabilities are also annotated, e.g. the first execution path (EP1) is (1, 2, 3, 4, 6, 11, 12, 14) with an execution probability of 0.21. By applying the RelTree Building algorithm, we get the RelTree for EP1 in Fig. 5(e) from the Reliability Hierarchy Tree in Fig. 5(d).

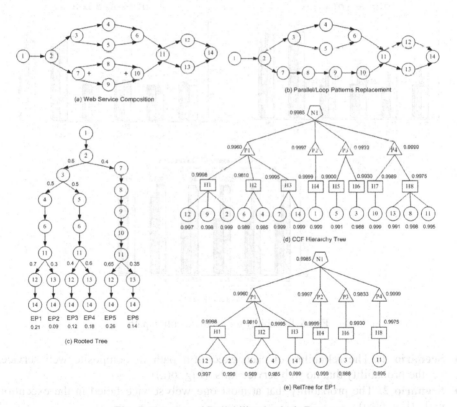

Fig. 5. Tree-based Reliability Analysis Process

Then the reliability of this execution path can be analyzed using our program developed in Java which is used to facilitate the tree-based reliability process. Table 3 shows the results.

Table 3. Reliability Analysis Result For EP1

Descriptions	Value
Reliability of the component web service 12	0.9913
Reliability of EP1 without considering CCF	0.8629
Reliability of EP1 considering CCF	0.9035
The probability that at most 2 component web services in EP1 fail simultaneously	0.9935

Fig. 6 shows comparison of reliability values computed using traditional and our CCF-aware approach for each execution path in different scenarios.

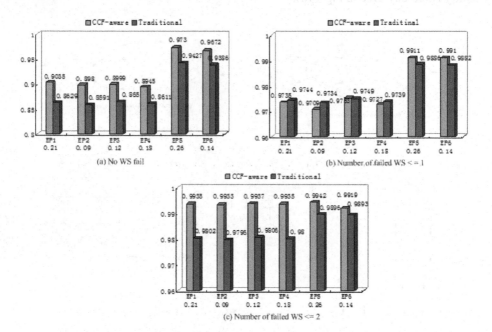

Fig. 6. Reliability for each execution path

- **Scenario 1:** The reliability of each execution path in composite web service, i.e. the probability that no web service fails. (Fig. 6(a))
- **Scenario 2:** The probability that at most one web service failed in the execution path. (Fig. 6(b))
- **Scenario 3:** The probability that at most two web service failed simultaneously in the execution path. (Fig. 6(c))

Also the execution probability is annotated under the corresponding execution path in the figure. The results indicate reliability values calculated by these two methods are different in all scenarios. Our method is superior to the traditional one in that it models the reliability hierarchy and is CCF-aware, which is guaranteed to estimate reliability values for the composite web service more accurately.

4.2 Evaluating a Fault-Tolerant System

The composite web service in Fig. 7 (a) improves its reliability by employing redundant web services. The component services 2 and 3 are invoked concurrently and the success of either one (or both) will be sufficient to continue the next step. If reliabilities of each component service in the composite web service are statistically independent, then the overall reliability can be calculated using the reliability value of each service (as annotated in Fig. 7 (a)), which is 0.9948 * (1 – (1 – 0.9261) * (1 – 0.9233)) *0.9881 = 0.9774, thus meets the overall reliability requirement. Unfortunately, in reality, reliabilities of the component services may correlate with each other in certain level.

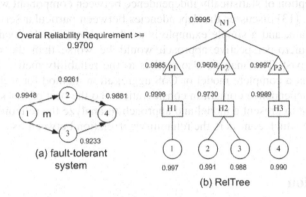

Fig. 7. Evaluating the Reliability of a Fault-tolerant System

Fig. 7 (b) is one possible RelTree for this composite web service, which indicates that WS2 and WS3 are deployed on the same machine. Thus they will fail simultaneously due to the common-cause failures in host, provider as well as network levels. Using our analysis program, the reliability of the composite web service is only 0.9194, which is far below the threshold. CCFs should be considered when designing the composite web service to get accurate reliability value, especially for those requiring high reliability and using fault-tolerant techniques.

5 Related Work

Reliability is one of the most important QoS metrics for the web service, which has been studied extensively. Tsai et al. [11] proposes a Service-Oriented software Reliability Model (SORM) which deals with both atomic and composite service. For the atomic service, group testing is used to evaluate its reliability efficiently. For the composite service, the overall reliability is evaluated using an architecture-based model. Grassi and Patella [12] focuses on the reliability quality metric for service-oriented applications and presents the RelServ service architecture to support reliability predict for composite service. His method only holds under the hypothesis that component services are independent. Zhong and Qi [6] propose a Petri net based approach to calculate the reliability of web service composition. In his approach, the web service composition specification is firstly transformed into Stochastic Petri Nets (SPN) model, then standard SPN methods and tools can be applied to analyze the reliability of web service composition. Cardoso et al. [4] models the reliability dimension of tasks in workflows by creating a mapping between reliability block diagrams (RBD) and workflow structures, and he develops the Stochastic workflow reduction (SWR) algorithm to compute QoS metrics (including reliability) for workflows based on task's QoS metrics. Xia et al. [5] proposes a reduction technique to simplify QoS (including reliability metric) of workflow systems based on GWF-net into tasks with qualitatively equivalent QoS metrics. Other structure-based reliability aggregation method for web service composition can be found in [8] [9]. However, all of these approaches do not consider the reliability correlation of the component services and take the assumption of statistically independence between component web services.

Jaeger et al. [13] discusses the dependencies between particular services using dependence domain, and a simple example is used to show that the availability calculated by the micro-perspective approach would be worse than the reality if such dependencies exist. The analysis also applies to the reliability metric, however, they does not present a complete model or QoS aggregation method for web service composition with dependence domain in consideration. To the best of our knowledge, our work is the first to present a model and approach to analyze the reliability of composite web service which considers the reliability correlation between its component web services.

6 Conclusion

In this paper, we propose a reliability model for composite web service considering CCF between component services in host, provider and network levels. RelTree is used to represent the correlation of component services and an analysis method is also presented to calculate the overall reliability. By replacing loop patterns with a sequence of conditional patterns and using execution path extraction technique to reduce the conditional pattern, our modeling and analysis approach are applicable to common composition patterns in the service composition. Our approach can achieve more accurate reliability value for the composite web service, and is especially useful for evaluating fault-tolerant mechanisms.

As the next step, we will research on considering CCF-aware reliability in the process of web service selection for the composition. In addition, we will study other aspects of correlation between component web services.

References

1. Curbera, F., Duftler, M., Khalaf, R., et al.: Unraveling the Web Services Web: An Introduction to SOAP, WSDL, and UDDI. IEEE Internet Computing 6(2), 86–93 (2002)
2. Papazoglou, M.P.: Service-Oriented Computing: Concepts, Characteristics and Directions. In: 4th International Conference on Web Information Systems Engineering, pp. 3–12. IEEE, Piscataway (2003)
3. Hwang, S., Lim, E., Lee, C., Chen, C.: Dynamic Web Service Selection for Reliable Web Service Composition. IEEE Transactions on Services Computing 1(2), 104–116 (2008)

4. Cardoso, J., Sheth, A., Miller, J., Arnold, J., Kochut, K.: Quality of service for workflows and web service processes. Web Semantics: Science, Services and Agents on the World Wide Web 1(3), 281–308 (2004)
5. Xia, Y., Zhu, Q., Huang, Y., Wang, Z.: A novel reduction approach to analyzing QoS of workflow processes. Concurrency and Computation: Practice and Experience 21(2), 205–223 (2009)
6. Zhong, D., Qi, Z.: A Petri Net Based Approach for Reliability Prediction of Web Services. In: Meersman, R., Tari, Z., Herrero, P., et al. (eds.) OTM 2006 Workshops. LNCS, vol. 4277, pp. 116–125. Springer, Heidelberg (2006)
7. Page, L.B., Perry, J.E.: A model for system reliability with common-cause failures. IEEE Transactions on Reliability 4(38), 406–410 (1989)
8. Jaeger, M.C., Rojec-goldmann, G., Muhl, G.: QoS aggregation for Web service composition using workflow patterns. In: Proc. Eighth IEEE International Enterprise Distributed Object Computing Workshop, pp. 149–159. IEEE, Piscatawy (2004)
9. Zeng, L., Benatallah, B., Ngu, A.H.H., Dumas, M., Kalagnanam, J., Chang, H.: QoS-aware middleware for Web services composition. IEEE Transactions on Software Engineering 30(5), 311–327 (2004)
10. Zheng, H., Zhao, W., Yang, J., Bouguettaya, A.: QoS Analysis for Web Service Composition. In: 2009 IEEE International Conference on Services Computing, pp. 235–242. IEEE, Piscataway (2009)
11. Tsai, W.T., Zhang, D., et al.: A software reliability model for web services. In: Proceedings of the Eighth IASTED International Conference on Software Engineering and Applications, pp. 144–149. Acta Press, Cambridge (2004)
12. Grassi, V., Patella, S.: Reliability Prediction for Service-Oriented Computing Environments. IEEE Internet Computing 10(3), 43–49 (2006)
13. Jaeger, M.C., Rojec-goldmann, G., Muhl, G.: QoS Aggregation in Web Service Composition. In: 2005 IEEE International Conference on e-Technology, e-Commerce and e-Service, pp. 181–185. IEEE, Piscataway (2005)

Efficient Astronomical Data Classification on Large-Scale Distributed Systems

Cheng-Hsien Tang[1], Min-Feng Wang[1], Wei-Jen Wang[1], Meng-Feng Tsai[1,*],
Yuji Urata[2], Chow-Choong Ngeow[2], Induk Lee[2], Kuiyun Huang[3],
and Wen-Ping Chen[2]

[1] Department of Computer Science and Information Engineering,
National Central University, Taiwan
[2] Institute of Astronomy, National Central University, Taiwan
[3] Academia Sinica Institute of Astronomy and Astrophysics, Taiwan

Abstract. Classification of different kinds of space objects plays an important role in many astronomy areas. Nowadays the classification process can possibly involve a huge amount of data. It could take a long time for processing and demand many resources for computation and storage. In addition, it may also take much effort to train a qualified expert who needs to have both the astronomy domain knowledge and the capability to manipulate the data. This research intends to provide an efficient, scalable classification system for astronomy research. We implement a dynamic classification framework and system using support vector machines (SVMs). The proposed system is based on a large-scale, distributed storage environment, on which scientists can design their analysis processes in a more abstract manner, instead of an awkward and time-consuming approach which searches and collects related subset of data from the huge data set. The experimental results confirm that our system is scalable and efficient.

Keywords: Classification, Support Vector Machine, Distributed System, Data Center.

1 Introduction

Classification of space objects is a common, important technique in many astronomy research areas. For example, analyzing the galaxies usually involves classification using each space object's appearance, magnitude, moving behavior, and many other characteristics. Most traditional classification methods focus on handling a small region of data store in one machine, and apply a single process to analyze the data. When those methods encounter an extremely large size of data, the analysis performance inevitably drops down dramatically. Unfortunately, we have already seen large data collections in terabyte-scale or even in petabyte-scale in the past decade, such as astronomy [1], high energy physics [2],

---

* Corresponding author.

R.-S. Chang et al. (Eds.): GPC 2010, LNCS 6104, pp. 430–440, 2010.

and aircraft engine diagnostics [3]. Thus scalable, efficient classification methods are very important to today's science research.

The Multiple Classifier System (MCS) [4] is one popular solution to divide data into small chunks, and then to classify the data chunks in parallel with multiple similar tools. Many dynamic classification selection methods, such as [5,6], only partially support MCS because some critical problems remain unsolved. First, these methods require gathering and combining different datasets into one complete set, and then use some static analysis processes to split the complete set into appropriate chunks. The splitting process should create diversity of chunks for better accuracy. This process is time-consuming because huge-size datasets are frequently exchanged and transferred among computing hosts and storage systems. Nowadays scientists have seen tera-byte or peta-byte of dataset constantly being transferred from one site to another site across different countries. Secondly, those dynamic classification selection methods are usually designed for face identification and brain wave measurement. The data characteristics can be very restrictive and thus they cannot be directly reused in other MCS applications.

The goal of this research is to provide a basic MCS platform for distributed, large-scale data storage systems. We provide a prototype of a decentralized MCS framework that supports classification with multiple classifiers. This design can reduce both data extraction time and computing loads in a distributed large-scale data center for astronomy research. The proposed approach uses LS-SVM [7] as the basic classifier, and applies a *Divide and Conquer Classifier Selection* method to train and select proper classifiers on a distributed environment. Our approach then combines the trained classifiers into one complete classification model. In comparison with other MCS systems, our framework can initiate local computation of dataset processing on each local site. In order to integrate the distributed information on each local site, we provide a portal that contains necessary metadata and query management tools for usability and interoperability. This allows the users to perform analysis on a more abstract level without learning data management on each local sites and the whole distributed environment.

The rest of the paper is organized as follows: In section 2 we provide the related work that has been done by other researchers. Section 3 presents our architecture, while in section 4 we discuss the methodology of the research. In section 5 we present our preliminary results. Conclusions and future work are described in section 6.

2   Related Work

Many researchers have proposed several kinds of multiple classifier systems (MCSs) for different problems in the literature. Zhu et al. design an attributed-oriented dynamic classifier selection method to mining stream data [6]. They use statistical information of attributes to split the evaluation set into disjoint subsets, and then evaluate the classification accuracy of each base classifier based on these subsets during training. Finally, they select the corresponding subsets using attribute values, and select the base classifier with the highest classification accuracy during tests. Woods et al. propose a dynamic classifier selection method based on local feature surrounding an unknowing test sample [5]. In this approach, the local accuracy estimation of individual classifier can help determine where a classifier performs most reliability in feature space. In [8], the dynamic classifier integration framework is proposed to overcome the diversity of application domains of pattern recognition. They consider the local expertise of each classifier, and combine the advantages of classification fusion and classifier selection to find the best single classifier. In order to provide an overview of MCS, Ranawana et al. explains the basic principles of MCS design [4].

Scalability is a serious problem for classifier systems using support vector machine (SVM) because the total number of used support vectors could be very large. Therefore, Tran et al. propose a clustering support vector machine method [9]. Their method is to assign all the data of each class to K groups using the K-means algorithm, and then train the SVM based on the central vectors of each group. Woodsend et al. also propose a SVM which supports parallel computing [10]. The method distributes full data sets evenly amongst the processors, use an interior point method to give efficient optimization, and utilize Cholesky decomposition to give good numerical stability. Hush et al. study the convergence properties of a general class of decomposition algorithms for support vector machines (SVMs) [11], develop a model algorithm for decomposition, and prove the necessary and sufficient conditions for stepwise improvement of the algorithm. Collobert et al. propose a parallel mixture method of multiple SVMs [12], in which a single set of SVMs is trained on subsets of the training set, and a neural network is used to provide a class prediction and to assign samples to different subsets. Due to the cost of the memory limitation and the computation time, Chang et al. develop a PSVM algorithm [13] to improve the scalability of SVMs. The approach loads the essential data to each machine for parallel computing, and usse matrix theory for memory reduction. Ali et al. develop a gird-based distributed SVM algorithm [14] which integrates data mining algorithm and Parallel SVM using MPI to improve the computing performance.

3   System Architecture

The proposed system is a general-purpose multiple SVM classifier system which is based on a cluster-based data center, where data are too huge to be stored at one single site (see Figure 1). Since data are inherently distributed, an integrated interface (portal) is required to simplify users' requests. The requests are then mapped into several independent query commands and issued to each site for preliminary processing. Then the computing results, such as classifier accuracy and rule models, are collected and filtered by middleware services, and finally formalized by the integrated interface. The functionality provided by the data center can be abstracted to four layers with several system sub-components (see Figure 2): the Virtual Observatory Portal Layer, the Query Management Layer, the Data Execution & Store Layer, and the Full Source Storage Layer.

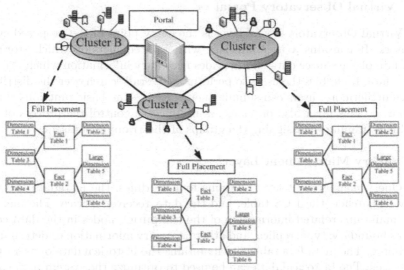

Fig. 1. A cluster-based data center which supports distributed classification

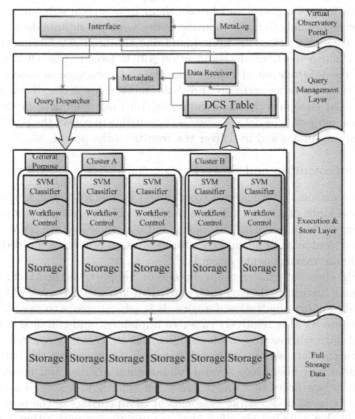

Fig. 2. The proposed system which can be abstracted to four layers with several system sub-components

3.1   Virtual Observatory Portal

The Virtual Observatory Portal layer is the entry point of the proposed system for users. It contains a user interface with related metalog which stores the metadata of the source data and provides necessary information which is related to the data. It enables the users to perform an overall search over the distributed data. Furthermore, users can submit queries with some basic functions through the portal. This layer also provides an interface to control the process of SVM classifiers training by assigning the groups of the training datasets.

3.2   Query Management Layer

The Query management layer contains four modules: the metadata table, the query dispatcher, the DCS table, and the data receiver service. The metadata table maintains related information of the computing nodes in the data center, such as boundary, type, replica, and other necessary information to determine job scheduling. The metadata table also maintains the historical data of user queries and status. The historical data can be used to optimize the system performance (e.g., adjusting the data replication strategy). The query dispatcher receives user queries from the portal and breaks them into several sub-queries. It then spreads the commands to the computing nodes with the desired data. The DCS (Dynamic Classifier Selection) table maintains the accuracy information of all classifiers when a distributed classification job is issued. The DCS table also maintains the information of proper classifiers of each groups based on some given criteria, such as an accuracy threshold and the top n classifiers. The rules of the selected classifiers are then combined into one complete model for the classification request. The data receiver is responsible to collect the partial results from computing nodes and to deliver the results to the portal.

3.3   Data Execution and Store Layer

The data execution & store layer is constructed by several clusters, which maintain different kinds of data for different purposes. There are three components in a computing node to perform local query and classification: the SVM classifier, the workflow control module, and the storage system built by a multi-dimension data warehouse management system [15].

The SVM classifier utilizes the technique of Support Vector Machine, a machine learning algorithm derived from statistical learning theory. SVM has been widely used in many application domains. It is advantageous to use SVM in our system because SVM is relatively easier to implement and can deal with different kind of data without too much modification. A workflow control module is provided for the data warehouse based management system on the bottom level which splits a user query into several fundamental queries, and rearranges the queries into a new order to improve execution efficiency. A special node, called the general-purpose node, works independent of all clusters in the proposed system. It provides a global classifier that communicates with other computing nodes, receives a subset of data of interest, and generates rules based on the data. The global classifier guarantees a lower bound of accuracy through global dataset.

The storage system uses a data warehouse architecture. It is derived from [15] of which the schema is designed for a centralized system. To improve the schema into decentralize schema, we use the data partitioning and allocation strategy in [16]. This approach enables parallel queries on a distributed multi-dimension data warehouse management system.

3.4 Full Source Storage

The full source storage system maintains the source data and provides data to the data execution & store layer when needed. Compared to the full source storage system, the storage system at the data execution & store layer only stores the data which researchers are interested in. In other words, the full source storage system is independent of the data execution & store layer, on which each computing node only maintains a subset of the source data. Notice that the cost of maintaining a full copy of source data in the system is high because it could consume too much space (in tera-bytes or even in peta-bytes) and network bandwidth. Therefore, the full source storage system only stores raw data. When the full source storage system receives a data request, it will extract, transform, and load the source data to the storage system at the data execution & store layer.

4 Methodology

The size of today's astronomical data is usually extremely large, and thus a single-processor classification method barely handles the scale of data. Therefore, we employ a parallel approach on a distributed storage system to deal with the data using a multiple SVM classifier system, as well as a distributed, dynamic classifier selection method called *the Divide and Conquer Classifier Selection (DC-CS)* service to find the best classifiers and rule models to improve classification accuracy.

The main procedure of the DC-CS service is shown as follows:

1. The user defines the criteria for training set selection from the portal.
2. When the query dispatcher receives a user request, it decomposes the request into several small sub-queries, and sends them to the computing nodes with the data of interest.
3. When a computing node receives a query, the workflow control module starts computing the best execution strategy by rearranging the execution order of sub-queries.
4. Once a computing node receives a query from the query dispatcher, the system extracts data from the local storage, puts the local training data sets into SVM classifiers, and generates a classification model.
5. All involved computing nodes randomly select n% (based on users' rules) of data from the training set, send them to the global classifier on the general-purpose computing node. The global classifier does not obtain any data from

the full source storage system. As soon as it receives all required data, it begins the same training procedure as what the other computing nodes do. Notice that the training procedure in Steps 4 and 5 can execute in parallel.

6. After the training and testing procedures finish, each computing node sends the accuracy information of each groups to the DCS table.

7. The DCS table maintains the accuracy information of all classifiers for each group, including the global classifier. After the accuracy information of each classifier is received, the DCS table chooses the best classifiers of each group defined based on users' selection criteria. The DCS table then combines the selected classifiers of each group into one complete classification model.

8. The system obtains the complete classification model and stores the selected classifiers for future use. Other training data sets can be used to refine the classification model to provide better classification accuracy.

The difference between the DC-CS service and other DCS algorithms is that the traditional algorithms (i.e. [5, 6]) need to: (1) collect all the training sets, (2) to do some static analysis in advance, and (3) to cut data into chunks. The large amount of data in each computing nodes thus could consume many resources if a traditional DCS algorithm is applied. On the contrary, the DC-CS service can have better efficiency by evenly distributing the workload and yet maintain acceptable classification accuracy. Furthermore, the global classifier can also provide a lower-bound accuracy in the worst case. The strategy makes the DC-CS service a practical solution in a large-scale, distributed environment.

A good data replication and replacement strategy can improve system performance, especially when the scale of data is huge. A bad method, on the other hand, could lead the system to an unrecoverable state when accidents happen (i.e. power failure). Our system uses the full-replica strategy (see Figure 3), which duplicates all the data in each node to some other nodes. Each dataset in the system has two replicas. The first replica will be placed at the neighbor node with the closest distance to the source dataset. The second one is placed at a randomly selected node in another cluster, if any. A node only communicates with the other nodes with replicas, thus reducing the communication overhead among computing nodes. Another reason for taking a full-replica strategy rather than using a block-interleaved approach (i.e., splitting data into several small blocks and duplicating the blocks) is that each computing node can have a larger continuous data set. Thus the SVM classifier could have more overlapped training data and test data if the size of each local training data set is too small to use. For example, we can use a threshold which is less than n% of the size of the total training datasets, where n is the total number of the computing nodes. To have better accuracy, the replica on the nearest node is activated to provide extra datasets.

5   Experimental Results

In this section, we evaluate the performance of the proposed system using two different kinds of real astronomical data: the *IPP diff image log* and the *MOPS data.* The expriments use ten Intel quad-core computers with 8G memory for parallel computing, and two storage servers to provide the source data. All computing nodes are connected via Fast Ethernet (100 MBit/s full duplex) switches. The IPP (Image processing pipeline) diff image log is generated from the Pan-STARRS project [17], in which telescopes scan the whole sky and create images. The diff image log provides difference data of related images within a month to show the magnitude variation in different bands for each observed sky object. The MOPS (The Moving Object Processing System) data is also produced by the Pan-STARRS project. It is a collection of datasets of moving objects (i.e. asteroids) in the sky. There are over 380,000 observed objects until now, and the size will grow up to six times as big as the current data size when the Pan-STARRS observatory starts working. To show the efficiency and accuracy of the proposed system, we use the single SVM classifier method as the comparison basis. The single SVM classifier method uses a simple greedy algorithm on a distributed environment. It selects the node with the largest local subset, acquires the missing part of data from other nodes, and performs a model training using the full training set.

Figure 4 shows the experimental results using different sizes of training sets of the IPP data. The astronomy experts mark the objects in diff image log based on magnitude and clarity of objects within 5 groups: good detections, possible good detections, unknown objects, possible bad detections, and bad detections. Figure 4(a) shows the total data transfer size between nodes during

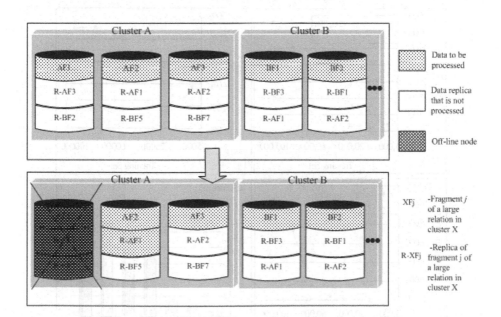

Fig. 3. The data replication and replacement strategy

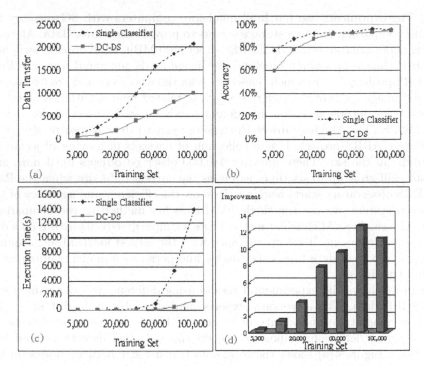

Fig. 4. Performance evaluation using the IPP data

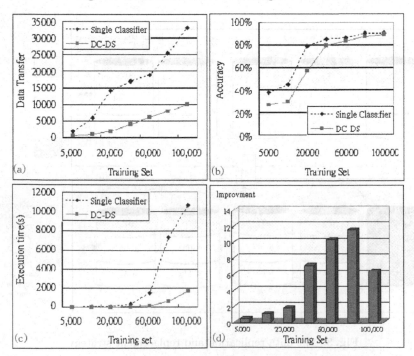

Fig. 5. Performance evaluation using the MOPS data

classification. It confirms that the single classifier needs to collect the whole data to a single computing node and requires more data migration. The DC-CS service, on the contrary, only needs to transfer randomly picked data to the global classifier and takes less bandwidth. Figure 4(b) shows that the accuracy of the proposed system is usually a little bit lower than the single classifier because the datasets are decomposed into smaller subsets. The figure also indicates that both methods can have the same accuracy if the data size is large. Figure 4(c) shows the total execution time from query submission to computation completion. The proposed DC-CS method is obviously a better choice because it is very scalable. Figure 4(d) shows the accuracy-time ratio, which is defined as follows:

$$\frac{Accuracy/Execution\,Time\,(using\,DC-CS)}{Accuracy/Execution\,Time\,(using\,Single\,Classifier)} \tag{1}$$

Figure 5 shows the results using different sizes of training sets of the MOPS data. Each moving object in the MOPS data contains 6 main attributes, which can be used to classify objects into different groups that have similar state [18]. The experimental results in Figure 5 are similar to the results in Figure 4, except that the average accuracy is lower because the data groups of MOPS data are more complicated.

All the experiments show that the accuracy using a single classifier could be a little higher than other classifier selection methods because it considers the full training sets. However, the accuracy of both methods is almost the same if the size of the datasets is large. The DC-CS method is obviously more efficient, and it can be ten times as fast as the single classifier method when the data size is large enough. The experimental results also show that our system can efficiently handle heterogeneous data.

6   Conclusions and Future Work

In this paper, we proposed and implemented a multiple classifier framework and system in a data center for astronomy research. We developed the DC-CS service, a multiple-classifier framework to provide fast and stable classification in a distributed environment. The global classifier of the DC-CS service ensures the classification accuracy in the worst case. We used real astronomical data to do several experiments, and the results showed that the proposed system is scalable, efficient, and accurate. The possible directions of our future work include: (1) expanding the system into a larger and more distributed storage system, (2) optimizing the system performance, and (3) integrating the services into a SOA architecture.

Acknowledgements

This research was sponsored by National Science Council, Taiwan under the grant 98-2219-E-002-022.

References

1. SDSS: Sloan digital sky survey (2009), http://www.sdss.org
2. PPDG: Particle physics data grid project (2009), http://www.ppdg.net
3. Austin, J., Davis, R., Fletcher, M., Jackson, T., Jessop, M., Liang, B., Pasley, A.: Dame: Searching large data sets within a grid-enabled engineering application. In: Proceedings of the IEEE, March 2005, pp. 496–509 (2005)
4. Ranawana, R., Palade, V.: Multi-classifier systems: Review and a roadmap for developers. International Journal of Hybrid Intelligent Systems 3(1), 35–61 (2006)
5. Woods, K., Kegelmeyer Jr., W.P., Bowyer, K.: Combination of multiple classifiers using local accuracy estimates. IEEE Transactions on Pattern Analysis and Machine Intelligence 19(4), 405–410 (1997)
6. Zhu, X., Wu, X., Yang, Y.: Effective classification of noisy data streams with attribute-oriented dynamic classifier selection. Knowledge and Information Systems 9(3), 339–363 (2006)
7. Suykens, J.A.K., Vandewalle, J.: Least squares support vector machine classifiers. Neural Processing Letters 9(3), 293–300 (1999)
8. Kim, E., Ko, J.: Dynamic classifier integration method. Multiple Classifier Systems, 97–107 (2005)
9. Tran, Q.A., Zhang, Q.L., Li, X.: Reduce the number of support vectors by using clustering techniques. Machine Learning and Cybernetics 2, 1245–1248 (2003)
10. Woodsend, K., Gondzio, J.: High-performance parallel support vector machine training. Parallel Scientific Computing and Optimization 27, 83–92 (2008)
11. Hush, D., Scovel, C.: Polynomial-time decomposition algorithms for support vector machines. Machine Learning 51(1), 51–71 (2003)
12. Collobert, R., Bengio, S., Bengio, Y.: A parallel mixture of svms for very large scale problems. Neural Computation 14(5), V1105–V1114 (2002)
13. Chang, E., Zhu, K., Wang, H., Bai, H., Li, J., Qiu, Z., Cui, H.: Psvm: Parallelizing support vector machines on distributed computers. In: Advances in Neural Information Processing Systems, vol. 20 (2007)
14. Meligy, A., Al-Khatib, M.: A grid-based distributed svm data mining algorithm. European Journal of Scientific Research 27(3), 313–321 (2009)
15. Tang, C.H., Yu, C.H., Shen, C.H., Tsai, M., Wang, W.J., Chang, Z.W., Chen, W.P.: A system design for terabyte-scale, distributed multidimensional data management and analysis in the taos project. In: Proceedings for the HPC Asia and APAN 2009, pp. 336–342 (2009)
16. Nguyen, T.M.: Complex Data Warehousing and Knowledge Discovery for Advanced Retrieval DevelopmentXInnovative Methods and Applications. Information Science Reference (2009)
17. pan STARRS: The panoramic survey telescope and rapid response system (2009), http://pan-STARRS.ifa.hawaii.edu
18. Bendjoya, Philippe, Zappal: Asteroid family identification. in asteroids iii, pp. 613–618. University of Arizona Press (2002)

Ontology-Based Personal Annotation Management on Semantic Peer Network to Facilitating Collaborations

Ching-Long Yeh, Chun-Fu Chang, Po-Shen Lin,
Yu-Peng Wang, and Yi-Chun Tsai

Department of Computer Science and Engineering, Tatung University,
40 Chungshan N. Rd. 3rd Sec., Taipei 104, Taiwan
chingyeh@cse.ttu.edu.tw, g9506019@cse.ttu.edu.tw,
jemmy1234@gmail.com, kitomu@gmail.com, wawa0927@hotmail.com

Abstract. The trend of services on the web is making the use of resources on the web collaborative. The Semantic Web technology is used to build an integrated infrastructure for the new services. In this paper, we develop a distributed knowledge based system using the RDF/OWL technology on peer-to-peer network to provide the basis of building personal social collaboration services for e-Learning. We extend the current tools accompanied with lecture content to become annotation sharable using the distributed knowledge base.

Keywords: Semantic Web, Web 2.0, e-Learning, Annotation, Peer-to-Peer Network, Ontology, RDF, Social Collaboration.

1 Introduction

Web sites provide effective intermediaries between instructors and learners to share lecture contents and exchange messages. From the course web site, learners choose to download lecture notes and slides used in class, lecture videos, etc., and study them offline either in printed form or on screen. During the course of reading, learner may want to take down notes, or annotations, about specific pieces of the contents as reminder that has been done. If learners have chance to share their annotations with each other, then it is possible to work out the collaborative intelligence according to the topics of the lecture content [1]. Instructor, on the other hand, may know learners' responses by collecting the annotations attached to lecture contents as an aid to future teaching. Yang, *et al.* summarize that this kind of personal annotation has the advantage in helping student in focusing and organizing learning content, and providing a place for discussion [2].

Web 2.0 services, for example, blogs, wikis, social web site, etc., provide collaborative environment by sharing content and response among authors and readers [1]. It has been investigated in e-Learning domain that the new services are helpful to enhance the interactions among instructors and learners [3][4][5][6][7]. Since the advent of Semantic Web, annotation mechanisms, for example, Annotea [8], CREAM [9][10], have long been developed for as means of knowledge sharing among users. Through browser, user adds annotations to web pages and the resulting

R.-S. Chang et al. (Eds.): GPC 2010, LNCS 6104, pp. 441–450, 2010.

ontology-based metadata in RDF [11] is either inserted in the web page document or stored in RDF server for others to use.

The Semantic Web technology has been employed to capture author-created wikitext in formal way, for example, Semantic Mediawiki [12], Semantic Wikipedia [13] and Rhizome [14]. The wikitext inserted with metadata in RDF makes the knowledge management of wiki content more efficient. Though the introduction of Semantic Web technology improves the collaboration and reuse of knowledge in Web 2.0 services, they however are isolated from each other and hence form disconnected communities and the valuable knowledge acquired from public effort, for example, Wikipedia, would be difficult to reuse [15]. For integrating the social web sites, the SIOC project develops an ontology describing entities found in Web 2.0 services as the infrastructure to build the integrated platform [15][16].

Yang, *et al.*, develops a personalized annotation management system as the basis to support collaborations in e-learning applications [2]. Documents and the associated annotations are stored in two relational data models, respectively. Annotations on the objects of documents are clustered according to their semantic similarities. User's query is first computed to determine the semantically related clusters and then further refine the search to obtain match result from the potential clusters. In their succeeding work [17], ontology technology is used to construct the context-aware environment for ubiquitous learning and peer-to-peer technology is employed to develop collaborative learning, including learning content access, personalized annotation management and discussion group.

In Web 2.0, the mechanism is naturally embedded in various kinds of services to support the multi-directional information flow among authors and readers. In Semantic Web context, the collaboration is further employed to create new knowledge to be reuse based on the exchange of knowledge on the distributed knowledge-based environment [18]. As mentioned previously, annotation taking and sharing is essential to facilitate knowledge management and collaborative learning. In this paper, we attempt to take advantages of both technologies, i.e., collaborative services in Web 2.0 and semantic integrated infrastructure in Semantic Web, to develop a platform for managing personal annotations. On this platform, user can annotate lecture contents and share the annotated results using Web 2.0 services, like wiki, blog, instant messaging, *etc.*, or reading tools, for example, MS PowerPoint, Adobe Acrobat. Under the platform is a distributed RDF store built on peer-to-peer network. Because of peer-to-peer network, user can keep the contents she creates in her peer node rather than disperse them all over different sites and pay attentions to manage them in different formats.

2   Semantic P2P Architecture for Social Collaboration

The technical architecture (see Figure 1) of the platform is built on a structured peer-to-peer network, where each node has the same function provides common collaborative services for user to perform social collaborations. Through the collaboration service interfaces user can access the services used to see in social software, including weblog, wiki, annotation, bookmark sharing, etc. In addition, personal reading tools, like MS PowerPoint, Adobe Acorbat Reader, plugged with annotation service can be used to do annotation taking and sharing as well. For example, User A takes notes on selected objects in PowerPoint slides and would like to share the annotation with other peer users. The annotation result is then stored as local RDF file and simultaneously published to the distributed RDF store by using the interface of the knowledge management layer. On the other hand, suppose user B wants to know what others have noted on the pieces of slides she is interested. User B may right click on the interested objects and select the request for notes from other peer nodes. The request is then carried out by querying the distributed RDF store and the result is presented to User B.

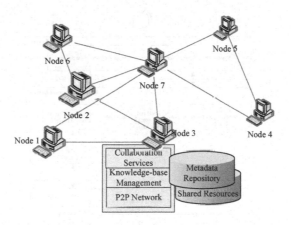

Fig. 1. Technical architecture of semantic peer network

In the peer-to-peer network, a distributed RDF store is maintained based the distributed hash technology (DHT) used in Chord [19]. The structure of Chord network is ring. In this paper, we employ the DHT for distinguishing the ontology of RDF triples and then the same technology is applied again to for distributing triples belong to the same ontology. The double application of DHT thus forms two-level ring structure. The nodes in each group are responsible for storing and routing triples of a specific ontology. Each node in a group connects to its inter-successors in other groups.

To support the above technical architecture, we design three-layered system architecture in each peer node, as shown in Figure 2. At bottom is the P2P Network Layer which is implemented using JXTA [20], which allows any device to join the network as a peer node to exchange messages with each other and collaborate independently of the underlying network topology. JXTA protocols are employed to communicate with other peers. In the middle is the RDF Management Layer which performs two tasks, the DHT topology management and distributed RDF store management. The former is carried out by the two-level Routing Module along with Intra- and Inter-finger tables. The latter is divided into management functions on distributed store and local RDF store.

Service Layer provides kinds of interface for user. One is for the system administration of the underlying distributed knowledge-base and the other is for user to access the social collaboration service on the semantic peer network. The system administration services consist of boot and configure the peer itself and access both the local and distributed RDF stores. The boot function is used for joining to the network. It starts up the two-level ring module and load RDF files to the memory and publishes the RDF triples to the network. Local RDF Management provides add, modify and delete function for users. Distributed RDF Management is use to managing the triples of other peer. Users can views the triples store in their distributed RDF store in Distributed RDF Management. The System Configure service is used to set up the system property.

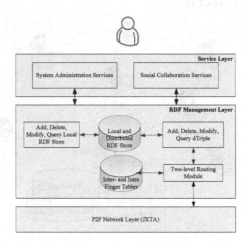

Fig. 2. Layered system architecture of peer node

3   Distributed RDF Store on the Two Level Ring Network

We extend the RDF ring mechanism in Chord-based RDFPeers [19][21] by distinguishing the ontology schema in RDF triples. The basic idea is that the RDF triples of a schema are distributed to the same ring. We therefore design a two-level ring on the P2P network, where the first level is based on the ontology schema and the next one is on the RDF itself. Each peer node is assigned two identifiers, GROUP_ID and PEER_ID, to recognize to which schema group the peer node belongs and identify itself within the belonging group. According to the concept of M-Ring [22], we treat the nodes of the same group as a virtual region or a "node" of the two-level ring. Thus, in each peer node we maintain two finger tables: the inter-finger table recording the connections to other groups, and the intra-finger table storing connection information of other peer nodes in the same group. According t the Chord mechanism, the entries in the intra-finger store the next 1, 2, 4…and 2^n-1 nodes in a group, where n is the bit-length of PEER_ID. The entries in the intra-finger table record the next 1, 2, 4…and 2^m-1 nodes on the group ring, where m is the bit-length of GROUP _ID.

Consider the case that if in two linking groups a specific node in each group is designated as the linking point, then either node being off would result in problem of missing link between both sides, a kind of hot spot problem. In this paper, we employ the concept of virtual region in M-Ring to avoid the above hot spot problem [22]. Instead of single linking point, each node in a group connects to its nearest successor in the succeeding group, or the inter-successor. For example, in Figure 3, the first entry of Nodes (0, 30) and (0, 3) point to their inter-successors (2, 0) and (2, 7), respectively.

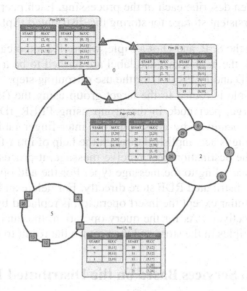

Fig. 3. Example of two-level ring

When a peer sends a message to other peer, it checks whether the target peer is in the same group. If not, the sending peer starts inter-group routine. Sender gets the nearest predecessor from the inter-finger table and forwards the message to the linking point in the predecessor group until the target group is reached. The intra-group routing is employed in order to pass the message to the target node. In Figure 3, for example, Node (0, 30) wants send a message to Node (2, 24). Node (0, 30) starts the inter-group routing, and find the nearest node, Node (2, 0). Then Node (0, 30) sends its message to Node (2, 0), and consign the sending process to it. Here, Node (2, 0) and the target node, Node (2, 24) belong to the same group. Node (2, 0) begins the intra-group routing. Because Node (2, 24) is in Node (2, 0)'s intra-finger table, the message is passed to Node (2, 24) by way of Node (2, 0).

Having developed the structured P2P network based on the two-level ring architecture, we then construct the distributed RDF store based on the structured P2P network. The basic idea is to deposit the triples in RDF files produced by peer nodes using the distributed hash computations. When an RDF file is newly created, modified, or deleted by a peer node, it is first of all parsed into the sequence of triples. The new, modified, and obsolete triples are computed to obtain their key which is formed by the GROUP_ID and PEER_ID as described previously. Then these keys are routed properly to be stored in the destination peer nodes. Noted that the destination peer may not exist in the network; we choose the successor to store the triple. When a query in the form of triple sequence is issued in a peer node, each triple is computed using the same distributed hash function, the resulting keys are used to route to the peers having the information about the triples in question.

Each of the above operations consists of three steps, hashing, routing, and processing. All the operations have the same hashing and routing steps, while each one has its own processing. In the following, we first of all describe the hashing and routing steps, and then describe each of the processing. Each peer node can nominate an RDF file in its persistent storage for storing the distributed triples.

- **Hashing.** Given the S, P, and O of a triple, where P is predicate and has the form, namespace:label, the namespace and label are hashed to be a pair of keys, which is the GROUP_ID and PEER_ID, for the use of routing step.
- **Routing.** The triple is routed to the target group using the GROUP_ID and then routed to the target peer node in the group using PEER_ID. The former inter-group routing is achieved by consulting the inter-finger tables, while the latter intra-group routing is accomplished through the help of intra-finger table.
- **Processing.** If the destination peer receive message, it process the add, delete or query function according to the message type. For the add operation, the triple is inserted into the distributed RDF store directly. For delete and modify operations, the process is similar except the insert operation is replaced by delete and modify operations, respectively. As for the query operation, the query pattern is used to match with the triples in the store and then return the result to original peer.

4 Collaboration Services Based on the Distributed RDF Store

As mentioned previously services interfaces are constructed upon the distributed RDF store, as shown in Figure 2, for system administration and for social collaborations, respectively. The former is descried in further details in the implementation section. In this section we describe the development of social collaboration services, including sharing of annotations on existing lecture notes reading tools, lecture video viewers, personal wikis, and instant messaging tools.

When viewing lecture videos and reading lecture notes, hereafter termed lecture content, the information flow is in general from producer to consumer, i.e., from instructor to learner only. In other words, learner can only read the content but is not able to express her opinions to the interested parts of the video or lecture notes. We argue that the collaboration among instructors and learners can be greatly improved by taking into of the structure of lecture content in the sharing of annotations. For example, learner may want to insert question about specific part of a lecture video and look for help from others. Learner may want to pause reading a learning content and take down her notes and share them with others of the lecture. Also instructor can have a look at the annotations about the lecture video to see the response from learners. In this paper we develop collaboration services for lecture content annotation taking and sharing to facilitate collaborations among instructors and learners. In this paper, the lecture contents are in various formats, including video, slide presentations in for example, Microsoft PowerPoint, and Adobe PDF.

The annotation plug-ins to existing tools, for example MS PowerPoint, provides user interface for the management of annotations on lecture content. The service programs deal with two kinds of objects. One is the physical files containing the knowledge sources, and the other is associated metadata, i.e., the annotations in RDF formats. Thus in a peer node the annotations are in RDF formats and stored as local files. We employ the SIOC (Semantically Interlinked Online Communities) ontology which is used describes the entities found in Web 2.0 services, including blogs, wikis, forums, social web site, etc., as the basis schema to develop the management functions of the knowledge produced by the annotation tools [15]. Each service program then extends the vocabulary according to their specific requirements.

In each service program, we construct three components, Content Manager, Annotation Manager, and Query Manager, which are in charge of the management of the learning contents.

- **Content Manager** is responsible for dealing with all information that is input from user, and it converts the resulting information into physical files and associated metadata in RDF format. When Content Manager detects newly created objects, it analyzes the in the objects and creates the metadata RDF file. Content Manager gathers information specific to the new objects, including creator, title and tags *etc.* from the lecture objects. With SIOC ontology, Content Manager stores the information as RDF files in the local repository. For example, the RDF file associated with a newly created article is shown as below.

- **Annotation Manager** is used to manage all the annotations user inserts into lecture objects. User inserts annotations to selected part of the lecture object, for example, some object in a PowerPoint slide, and indicate whether shares it with others. When inserting an annotation of the question type, it then sends off the question to the peer-to-peer network to ask for help. The annotations are stored as RDF file using SIOC schema. For example, a comment inserted to the article having the above metadata is represented as RDF as below.

- **Query Manager** is used to process the query issued by node user. When user wants to look for something interested to her, she enters the conditions through the user interface and the conditions are converted into SPARQL statement as input to the Query Manager. It then converts the SPARQL statement into triple patterns recognized by the query function of the search function in the underlying distributed RDF management system. It waits for the result returning from the query function and presents rendered result in the user interface for user to consume.

5   Implementation

The distributed RDF store is made up of the RDF management layer and the peer-to-peer network layer of the system architecture as shown in Figure 2. The later is implemented using an XML-based peer-to-peer network JXTA [20]. In this paper, we employ the JXTA peer ID as the basis to construct the peer ID in the two-level ring. We mainly use EndpointService protocol to exchange messages between peer nodes[1].

---

[1]   See [23] for details of implementation.

The RDF Management Layer performs two tasks, the DHT topology management and distributed RDF store management. The former is carried out by the Two-level Routing Module along with Inter- and Intra-finger tables. The latter is divided into management functions on dTriple and local RDF store. The former, dTriple, consists of the triples of distributed RDF store dispatched to a node according to of the DHT topology. The local RDF store consists of the RDF generated by the node. Both management functions support their user interfaces in the administration service of the service layer in Figure 2.

As shown in Figure 2, in the top layer of the system architecture provides of two kinds of services. One is for system administration and the other is for user's social collaborations. The former provides of a number of user interfaces: boot, local RDF management, distributed RDF management, and system configuration. The social collaboration services are implemented by using the application program interfaces when dealing with distributed RDF store. We have conducted experiments using these interfaces to measure the performance of the distributed RDF store. We set up an 8 peer node network to carry out the experiment. Each peer node is a personal computer commonly found in lab. We summarize the measuring results in Table 1.

To test the joining time, we divide the 8 nodes into two groups, DC and FOAF, and each node uses the same RDF file. At first, we create a boot peer, PEER 1.Then PEER2 to 7 join the network in turn by PEER 1. The result is of each peer join the network is shown in the row of Join with average 4.7 sec. For the test of publishing time, we employ an SIOC and a FOAF RDF file, each with 63 and 12 triples, respectively. The result is shown in the row of Publish. We perform two query tests using the following SPARQL statements, and the result is shown in the rows of Query1 and Query2, respectively.

```
PREFIX dc:<http://purl.org/dc/elements/1.1/>
SELECT ?r
WHERE { ?r dc:title ?z .}

PREFIX dc:<http://purl.org/dc/elements/1.1/>
SELECT ?r ?c
WHERE { ?r dc:title ?z .?r dc:creator ?c}
```

The performance measurement shows a preliminary success in building the prototype for the development of social collaboration services for e-learning. We develop a number of social collaboration tools based on the distributed RDF store. As described previously, each collaboration service has implemented three components, Content Manager, Annotation Manager, and Query Manager, for managing the annotations in RDF associated with the learning contents in various formats. We are developing annotation tools for HTML, video, slide, and instant messaging. They are under development at the moment of writing this paper; we therefore describe the current status of their implementations.

We employ, TiddlyWiki[2], a personal wiki tool using HTML with Javascript technology, as the tool for managing personal notebooks. We add annotation plug-in in TiddlyWiki. Behind the user interface, the associated annotations in RDF is created and stored as local file. The RDF file is then published to the distributed RDF store

---

[2] TiddlyWiki: A reusable non-linear personal web notebook. See http://www.tiddlywiki.com/

for other to share. After creating a new text, Content Manager adds the following associated attribute-values in the RDF file. The Annotation Manager then analyzes the annotations from the wiki-words in the wikitext and adds the attribute-value pairs of the annotations in the RDF file.

Table 1. Performance measurement for accessing an 8-node distributed RDF store (ms)

	Join	Publish	Qry1	Qry2
1	2266	625	516	1056
2	2251	6047	1801	1104
3	6938	1390	172	667
4	5094	5766	1280	1196
5	5390	3531	944	1045
6	4735	3953	797	856
7	5657	1406	612	944
8	5328	4719	1409	956
Avg	4707	3430	941	978

6 Conclusions

In this paper, we develop 3-layer system architecture on peer-to-peer network for building social collaboration services to facilitate collaborations in e-Learning. From bottom to top in the system architecture are peer network, distributed RDF management, and service layers. We combine the Semantic Web and Web 2.0 technologies to develop the distributed ontology-based RDF store of the system architecture. At the service layer, social collaboration services invoke the application program interfaces provided by the underlying distributed RDF management layer to make the annotation sharable to other user on the peer-to-peer network. We have implemented and tested the distributed RDF store and get preliminary success in operating the system. We extend tools used to be accompanied with lecture contents in various formats to make the consumption-only way of using lecture content to become collaborative among instructors and learners. We have implemented prototypes of extending TiddlyWiki, Microsoft PowerPoint, video player and Microsoft Live Messenger, and obtain promising results in sharing annotations on these tools. In the future, we will investigate how to make use of the in e-Learning and study the acceptability of using personal social collaborations tool in teaching.

Acknowledgments. Research for this paper was financed by National Science Council, Taiwan, under contract NSC 98-2221-E-036-042.

References

1. O'Reily, T.: What is Web 2.0: Design Patterns and Business Models for the Next Generation of Software. O'Reilly, Sebastopol (2005)
2. Yang, S., Chen, I., Shao, N.: Ontological Enabled Annotations and Knowledge Management for Collaborative Learning in Virtual Learning Community. Journal of Educational Technology and Society 7(4), 70–81 (2004)

3. Owen, M., Grant, L., Sayers, S., Facer, K.: Social Software and Learning, Futurelab, Bristol (2006)
4. Anderson, P.: What is Web 2.0? Ideas, Technologies and Implications for Education. JISC Technology and Standards Watch (2007)
5. Franklin, T., van Harmelen, M.: Web 2.0 for Content for Learning and Teaching in Higher Education. JISC Publications (2007)
6. Gillet, D., Ngoc, A., Rekik, Y.: Collaborative Web-Based Experimentation in Flexible Engineering Education. IEEE Transactions on Education 48(4), 696–704 (2005)
7. Gillet, D., Helou, S., Yu, C., Salzmann, C.: Turning Web 2.0 Social Software into Versatile Collaborative Learning Solutions. In: First International Conference on Advances in Computer-Human Interaction (2008)
8. Kahan, J., Koivunen, M., Prud'Hommeaux, E., Swick, R.: Annotea: an Open RDF Infrastructure for Shared Web Annotations. In: Proc. of the WWW10 International Conference, Hong Kong (2001)
9. Handschuh, S., Staab, S.: CREAM: CREAting Metadata for the Semantic Web. Computer Networks 42(5), 579–598 (2003)
10. Handschuh, S., Staab, S., Ciravegna, F.: S-CREAM - Semi-Automatic CREAtion of Metadata. In: 13th International Conference Knowledge Engineering and Knowledge Management Ontologies and the Semantic Web, pp. 358–372 (2002)
11. Beckett, D. (ed.): RDF/XML Syntax Specification (Revised), W3C Recommendation (2004)
12. Krötzsch, M., Vrandecic, D., Völkel, M.: Semantic MediaWiki. In: Cruz, I., Decker, S., Allemang, D., Preist, C., Schwabe, D., Mika, P., Uschold, M., Aroyo, L.M. (eds.) ISWC 2006. LNCS, vol. 4273, pp. 935–942. Springer, Heidelberg (2006)
13. Krötzsch, M., Vrandecic, D.: Semantic Wikipedia. In: Social Semantic Web, pp. 393–421 (2009)
14. Souzis, A.: Building a Semantic Wiki. IEEE Intelligent Systems 20(5), 87–91 (2005)
15. Bojars, U., Breslin, J., Peristeras, V., Tummarello, G., Decker, S.: Interlinking the Social Web with Semantics. IEEE Intelligent Systems 23(3), 29–40 (2008)
16. Bojars, U., Breslin, J., Finn, A., Decker, S.: Using the Semantic Web for Linking and Reusing Data across Web 2.0 Communities. Journal of Web Semantics 6(1), 21–28 (2008)
17. Yang, S.: Context Aware Ubiquitous Learning Environments for Peer-to-Peer Collaborative Learning. Journal of Educational Technology and Society 9(1), 188–201 (2006)
18. d'Aquin, M., Motta, E., Dzbor, M., Gridinoc, L., Heath, T., Sabou, M.: Collaborative Semantic Authoring. IEEE Intelligent Systems 23(3), 80–83 (2008)
19. Stoica, I., Morris, R., Liben-Nowell, D., Karger, D., Kaashoek, M., Dabek, F., Balakrishnan, H.: Chord: a scalable peer-to-peer lookup protocol for internet applications. IEEE Transactions on Networking 11(1), 17–32 (2003)
20. Oaks, S., Traversat, B., Gong, L.: JXTA in a Nutshell. O'Reilly Media, Sebastopol (2002)
21. Cai, M., Frank, M.: RDFPeers: a Scalable Distributed RDF Repository Based on a Structured Peer-to-Peer Network. In: WWW 2004, pp. 650–657 (2004)
22. Lin., T., Ho, T., Chan, Y., Chung, Y.: M-Ring: A Distributed, Self-Organized, Load-Balanced Communication Method on Super Peer Network. In: International Symposium on Parallel Architectures, Algorithms, and Networks (I-SPAN), pp. 59–64 (2008)
23. Chang, C.: Design and Implementation of an Ontology-based Distributed RDF Store Based on Chord Network. MSc Thesis, Department of Computer Science and Engineering, Tatung University, Taipei, Taiwan (2009)

On the Design of Semi-structured Multi-star Hybrid-Overlays for Multi-attribute Range Queries

You-Fu Yu, Po-Jung Huang, Quan-Jie Chen, Tian-Liang Huang, and Kuan-Chou Lai

Department of Computer and Information Science, National Taichung University
Taichung, Taiwan, R.O.C.
kclai@mail.ntcu.edu.tw

Abstract. In the past few years, resource discovery is an important mechanism in P2P applications. P2P networks could be categorized into structured and unstructured. In general, structured P2P networks (DHTs) provide efficient keyword search, but is difficult to offer a variety of search modes. Unstructured P2P networks are applied to highly churn P2P networks, but they are inefficient. In this paper, we propose a hybrid overlay to combine unstructured and structured P2P networks to provide multi-attribute range queries in the large scale P2P network. The proposed semi-structured overlay network which employs a structured multi-star overlay could provide efficient multi-attribute range queries with load balancing. The experimental results show that the proposed overlay performs well and could efficiently distribute the load.

Keywords: P2P, Overlay, Semi-structured, Range query, Multi-Attribute.

1 Introduction

In recent years, effective resource discovery is one of the key issues in developing P2P networks. Many previous studies have explored approaches to discover distributed resources in the large-scale P2P network. Structured P2P networks exploit distributed hash tables (DHTs) to construct the structured overlay for searching resources. Most of the DHT-based structured P2P networks hash the resource IPs or resource names as the resource IDs. Therefore, structured approaches could search the specified resource effectively. But, because of the resource ID cannot capture the original characteristics of the resource. These structured P2P networks are difficult to address the multi-attribute range query search. However, because the placement of nodes is completely unrelated to the overlay topology, unstructured P2P networks are more appropriate for highly churn P2P networks. Most of the unstructured networks employ the flooding approach to search resources. Flooding generates a lot of unnecessary traffic. Therefore, related studies mainly focus on improving the performance of flooding and on reducing the unnecessary traffic. Although unstructured P2P networks offer a variety of search modes, but they still have to address availability, scalability and persistence.

Since structured and unstructured P2P networks have their own advantages and disadvantages, some hybrid methods were proposed to overcome their shortcomings with retaining advantages. Therefore, we propose a semi-structured overlay network

R.-S. Chang et al. (Eds.): GPC 2010, LNCS 6104, pp. 451–460, 2010.
© Springer-Verlag Berlin Heidelberg 2010

which employs a structured multi-star overlay to provide efficient multi-attribute range query searches, and also to maintain unstructured attribute groups to achieve load balancing. This semi-structured P2P overlay groups the nodes with the same attribute to form one attribute-group, and then clusters attribute-groups with similar attributes to form one attribute-cluster. The attribute-cluster is constructed in the star fashion. These stellate attribute-clusters connect each other to form a structured multi-star overlay. This structured multi-star overlay provides efficient multi-attribute range queries. Nodes in the same attribute-group connect each other in the unstructured fashion to provide load balancing by regulating the number of connections between other attribute-groups.

This semi-structured P2P overlay aims to provide multi-attribute range queries in the large-scale P2P network. In the P2P network, each computing resource has some fixed attributes, for example, CPU speed, Memory size, bandwidth, etc. According to these attributes in the proposed overlay, the performance of the keyword searching could be improved; and the proposed overlay could support the multi-attribute search and the range query.

The rest of the paper is organized as follows: Section 2 discusses related works. Section 3 presents the design of our proposed semi-structured multi-star overlay. Section 4 discusses the multi-attribute range query search. Experimental results are presented in Section 5. We conclude the paper in Section 6.

2 Related Works

Many researches for the resource discovery focused on the effectiveness, flexibility and scalability. In the unstructured P2P networks, the search approaches like LightFlood [1] and pFusion [2], try to reduce the number of messages in broadcasting the queries. In the structured P2P networks, like Chord, CAN and Tapestry [3], construct the structured overlay to make the key-based search effectively.

Usually, the hierarchical overlays could reduce the search scope and unnecessary communication. The unstructured approaches like S-Club [4] and Gang et al. [5] construct the overlay-groups according to the service group and user's interest separately for reducing the search scope. Although these approaches reduce the search scope, they still cannot search effectively. Even some resources satisfy the query, they still may not be found. The structured SORD [6] approaches construct a two-tier architecture including the local ring and the global ring. The local ring is constructed by connecting the nodes which share the same attributes. The global ring is constructed by connecting the local rings in different regions. Although this two-tier architecture can provide the multi-attribute search, but the system need to send lots search messages to find the resources. James et al. [7] construct a structured overlay with the two-tier architecture. The lower tier is the context rings and the upper tier is the super ring. This structured overlay can provide contextualized keyword search, but each node need to maintain more connections. Therefore, the system is limited due to the lack of scalability.

In general, the DHT-based structured P2P networks could support the effective key-based search. However, to achieve the semantic search, they need to rely on other approaches. PIRD [8] defines the node ID by the node's attributes, and then constructs a structured multi-ring overlay according the node ID. Therefore, PIRD can support the semantic search. Ronaldo et al. [9] hash the attributes to matrixes. This system provides the semantic search by computing the matrixes and finding out the closest ones. However, this approach need more time for computing the matrixes. Simon et al. [10] propose a hierarchically structured P2P system which provides the range query. Due to the hierarchical architecture, the system need more traveled hops to route the search messages between different tiers. SARIDS [11] exploits the double-link architecture for the range query. But this system need more search messages for different attribute rings, and more computing time for filtering out the correct resource.

This paper proposes a semi-structured multi-star overlay to support range query searches. Its performance is evaluated by OMNet++ [12]. OMNeT++ is an event-driven simulator and described as a simulation environment with supporting GUI. OMNeT++ supply many components, modules and communication protocols for simulation.

3 Semi-structured P2P Network

3.1 System Design

This semi-structured P2P overlay consists of two parts: attribute-groups and stellate attribute-clusters. The attribute-group groups nodes with the same attribute vector.

3.1.1 Attribute Vector
In the P2P network, computing resources have static and dynamic attributes. For example, static attributes includes CPU speed, CPU number, memory size, and bandwidth, etc. Unless the hardware is updated, these attributes don't change. Dynamic attributes includes CPU utilization, free memory size, workload, etc. The values of these attributes may change in different time.

This proposed system uses a binary string to represent the attribute values of computing resources, namely the attribute vector. The scope of each attribute is different, so that attribute values have to be normalized. The hash function is defined as follow:

$$f(V_a) = \left\lfloor \frac{2^m \times (V_a - MIN_a)}{MAX_a - MIN_a} \right\rfloor, \tag{1}$$

where MAX_a and MIN_a are the maximum and minimum attribute values of attribute a respectively, V_a is the attribute value, and we use m bits to represent the attribute value. Assume that there are n kinds of static attributes. Each attribute hashes its attribute value in order. In addition, each computing resource maintains an attribute list to record dynamic attributes and to be updated periodically.

3.1.2 Attribute-Group
The similarity between two attribute vectors is the number of attributes with the same attribute value. We use $sim()$ to compute the similarity as follow:

$$sim(X_{av}, Y_{av}) = \text{the number of attribute value which is zero in } (X_{av} \oplus Y_{av}), \tag{2}$$

where X_{av} and Y_{av} are two attribute vectors. If the result of $sim()$ equals to n, it means that these two attribute vector are the same.

Computing resources with the same attribute vector are grouped into one attribute-group. Each attribute-group is represented by the attribute vector in which they are grouped. In the same attribute-group, computing resources connect each other by the unstructured approach.

3.1.3 Stellate Attribute-Cluster

After grouping computing resources into attribute-groups, there are a lot of different attribute-groups in the P2P network. The attribute-cluster is clustered with the attribute-groups in which the results of $sim()$ of any two attribute groups are n-1. In the attribute-cluster, the attribute-group with the smallest attribute vector becomes the central attribute-group which is surrounded by other attribute-groups. Therefore, there are at most $2^{n \times m}$ attribute-groups and $n \times 2^{m(n-1)}$ stellate attribute-clusters in the P2P network. Figure 1 demonstrates a stellate attribute-cluster.

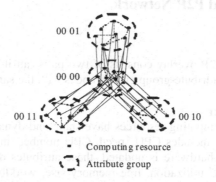

Fig. 1. A stellate attribute-cluster composed of four attribute-groups

Every computing resource maintains at least one connection between any two different attribute-groups in the same attribute-cluster. Because an attribute-group may be included in different stellate attribute-clusters, these stellate attribute-clusters are connected to form the multi-star overlay. Figure 2 shows the multi-star overlay.

3.2 Query Routing

This multi-star overly could be transformed into a hierarchical tree-like architecture as shown in Figure 3. Each central attribute-group is the parent node, others are children nodes. The query is hashed into an attribute vector by the formula (1), and then is routed to the attribute-group with the same attribute vector. Figure 4 illustrates the routing algorithm. G_{av}, Q_{av} and GC_{xav} are the attribute vectors of G, Q and GC_x respectively.

Because the children could connect with many parents, these computing resources may receive the same message over and over again in routing the range query. In order to reduce the traffic and to avoid the circular routing, the message is dropped after receiving.

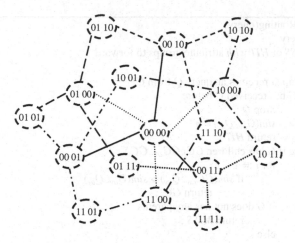

Fig. 2. The multi-star overlay with $n=2$, $m=2$

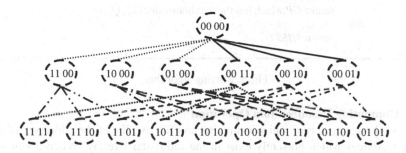

Fig. 3. The hierarchical tree-like architecture

3.3 Routing Cost

The proposed multi-star overlay is a hierarchical architecture with n layers. Queries are routing between attribute-groups in different layers. Therefore, the time required for resolving the search are $O(2n)$, and be unconcerned with the number of computing resources. As discussed in section 3.1.3, there are $2^{n \times m}$ different attribute-groups. In the structured P2P network, if the number of nodes is $2^{n \times m}$, the time complexity of resource discovery is $O(log\ 2^{n \times m}) = O(n \times m)$. Thus the multi-star overlay has a better time complexity of resource discovery when m is greater than 2.

3.4 Dynamic Operations

This section discusses the dynamic operations in the proposed multi-star overlay.

3.4.1 Initialization

When the first computing resource joins the multi-star overly, it becomes the central attribute-group of all the attribute-clusters. Therefore, the following computer resources connect with the first one, and then develop their own attribute-group and attribute-clusters.

```
Algorithm : Routing(query)
Input :   a query
Output : MISS or HIT with attribute groups to forward
begin
     when group G receives an query Q from GF
          if G has received Q before
               drop Q ;
          else if sim(G_av, Q_av) = n
               return HIT ;
          else if G has children GC_1, GC_2,...GC_x
               for i := 1 ~ x
                    if sim(GC_xav, Q_av) > sim(G_av, Q_av)
                         return GC_x ;
               if G does not has any parents
                    return MISS ;
               else
                    return GP which has the maximum sim(G_av, Q_av) ;
          else if G has parents GP
               return GP which has the maximum sim(G_av, Q_av) ;
          else
               return MISS ;
end
```

Fig. 4. Routing algorithm

3.4.2 Computing Resource Join Operation

There is a bootstrap server which maintains an effective list of the addresses of computing resources which presently exist in the multi-star overlay. When a new computing resource joins the multi-star overlay. The new computing resource firstly computes its attribute vector, and connects several computing resources which are provided by the bootstrap server randomly. And then, the new resource searches the attribute-group with the same attribute vector in order to join it. After joining the attribute-group, the new resource starts to find whether there are the other attribute-groups with the similar attribute vectors (i.e. $sim() = n$-1) and to connect with them.

3.4.3 Computing Resource Leave Operation

When a computing resource tries to leave actively, it sends the update messages to its neighbors in different attribute-groups. The update messages include a list of the addresses of its neighbors in the same attribute-group. When a computing resource receives an update message, it builds a new connection between one of the address list, and breaks the original one's connection. Besides, every computing resource sends the checking messages to its neighbors periodically to avoiding that the computing resource is left involuntary due to the failure. Every computing resource maintains at least one neighbors in each attribute-groups with $sim() = n - 1$. When there is no neighbor in a certain attribute-group, the computing resource forwards queries through the remaining neighbors to find one.

4 Multi-attribute Range Query Search

Although, most of the structured P2P networks provide efficient keyword searches, they need more queries or routing hops to support the range query search. The proposed multi-star overlay not only maintains efficient resource discovery, but also provide query searches without additional cost. In this study, when the query arrives at the attribute-group with the same attribute vector, it means query successfully due to that all of the computing resources in that attribute-group have the same attribute vector. Therefore, in the following section, we show the approach for the query which is routed between different attribute groups.

4.1 Multi-attribute Search

In this study, the proposed multi-star overly uses an attribute vector to preserve the resource's attributes. Client defines the computing resource's attribute values, and then generates a query with the attribute vector by the formula (1). Finally, the proposed approach could route the query to discover the satisfied resource.

4.2 Range Queries Search

There are two types of queries. One is the partial query and the other is the range query. User could issue the query with partial attributes without the remaining attributes. The randomly attributes is denoted by "*", and the results of exclusiveOR with any other values are zero (i.e. only the same attribute value). In addition, user can define the attribute values within a range.

Figure 5 illustrates the algorithm of a range query search. Where RQ denotes a range query and the attribute group G receives RQ from GF. TG is the results of Routing(RQ). GP and GC_x denote G's parents and children respectively. GP_{av} and RQ_{av} are the attribute vectors of GP and RQ respectively. The range query RQ will be packed into an attribute list RQ_l along with a target attribute vector RQ_t. RQ_l lists all of the combinations of RQ. RQ_t is similar to the partial query which set the attribute values within a range to "*".

4.3 Performance Analysis

In general, the procedure for performing the query search in the DHT-based structured P2P network consists of two steps. Step one is to find out the upper and lower bound nodes. Step two is to employ "one-hop" search to route the query node by node to find out all the nodes between the upper and lower bound nodes. Assume there are b nodes between the upper and lower bound nodes. Therefore, the time complexity is $O(\log N + b/2)$. It would spend more time in the step two when b is greater than $2 \times \log N$.

Figure 5 illustrates the procedure to perform the range query in the proposed multi-star overlay. The first step is to find out the central attribute-group of the attribute-cluster in which the attribute vector matches with the query. The second step is to employ the "radial" search which broadcasts the query star-by-star to find out all the resources which satisfy the query. Therefore, the time complexity of the range query in the proposed multi-star overlay is still $O(2n)$.

```
Algorithms : Range query search(range query)
Input :  a range query (an attribute vector list along with a target attribute vector)
Output : satisfied resource
Begin
    When G receives a range query RQ from GF
        if G has received RQ before
            drop RQ ;
        else
            TG := Routing(RQt) ;
            if TG = MISS
                return "There is no satisfied resource" ;
            else if TG = HIT  // it means TG = G and sim(Gav, RQtav) = n
                if G has a parent GP which sim(GPav, RQtav) = n and GP!=GF
                    forward RQ to GP ;
                if G has children GC1, GC2, ..., GCx
                    for i := 1 ~ x
                        if sim(GCxav, RQlav) = n and GCx != GF
                            forward RQ to GCx ;

                if sim(Gav, RQlav) = n
                    return G ;
            else
                if G has children GC1, GC2, ..., GCx
                    for i := 1 ~ x
                        if sim(GCxav, RQlav) = n and GCx != GF
                            forward PQ to GCx ;
                    if sim(Gav, RQlav) = n
                        return G ;
                else
                    forward RQ to TG ;
    end
```

Fig. 5. The algorithm for range query search

5   Experimental Results

The multi-star overlay is evaluated by the OMNet++ 4.0. OMNet++ is an overlay network simulator which could simulate all kinds of overlay networks. Figure 6(a) shows the average range searching time of Chord and multi-star overlay in 1024 nodes, where the query range is from 10 to 100. Because that Chord tries to find out all the matched peers by the one-hop search method after finding out the upper and lower bound nodes, the time arose from the one-hop search increases when the query range increases. However, the proposed multi-star overlay could keep a stable performance in different query ranges. Figure 6(b) shows the average search time for the keyword search when the number of nodes is from 256 to 16384. The attribute vector combinations are shown in Table 1. In Figure 6(b), the multi-star overlay preserves the efficiency of the keyword search in the structured overlay. The main reason of the increment of the average search time in the multi-star overlay is due to the increment of the number of attributes, which is independent of the number of nodes.

Table 1. Attribute vector combinations

Number of attribute-groups	256	1024	4096	16384
Attribute vector combination	$n=4, m=2$	$n=5, m=2$	$n=6, m=2$	$n=7, m=2$

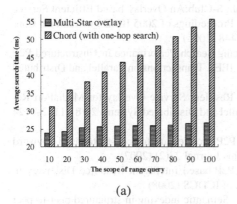

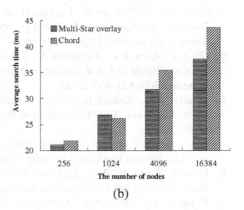

(a)   (b)

Fig. 6. (a) The average range searching time. (b) The average search time.

6 Conclusions

This study proposes a semi-structured multi-star overlay. The multi-star overlay preserves the characteristics both of structured and unstructured P2P networks. The attribute-groups are composed of computing resources with the same attribute vector by the unstructured approach to achieve load balancing. The stellate attribute-clusters are composed of attribute-groups with similar attribute vectors, and then connect each other to form the multi-star overlay. The multi-star overlay provides the efficient multi-attribute range query and is independent of the number of computing resources. The experimental results shows that the proposed semi-structured multi-star overlay performs well and could efficiently distribute the load.

Acknowledgements

This study was sponsored by the National Science Council, Taiwan, Republic of China under contract numbers: NSC 97-2221-E-142-001-MY3, NSC 97-3114-E-007-001- and NSC 98-2218-E-007 -005.

References

1. Song, J., Lei, G., Xiaodong, Z., et al.: LightFlood: Minimizing redundant messages and maximizing scope of peer-to-peer search. IEEE Transactions on Parallel and Distributed Systems 19(5), 601–614 (2008)

2. Demetrios, Z.Y., Vana, K., Dimitrios, G.: pFusion: A P2P Architecture for Internet-Scale Content-Based Search and Retrieval. IEEE Transactions on Parallel and Distributed Systems 18(6), 804–817

3. Stephanos, A.T., Diomidis, S.: A Survey of Peer-to-Peer Content Distribution Technologies. Comm. ACM 36(4), 335–371

4. Chunming, H., Yanmin, Z., Jinpeng, H., et al.: S-Club:An Overlay-based Efficient Service Discovery Mechanism in CROWN Grid. In: Proceedings of 2005 IEEE International Conference on e-Business Engineering, pp. 441–448 (2005)

5. Gang, C., Chor, P.L., Zhonghua, Y.: Enhancing Search Performance in Unstructured P2P Networks Based on Users' Common Interest. IEEE Transactions on Parallel and Distributed Systems 19(6), 821–835 (2008)

6. Ibrahim, A.O., Ahmed, K.: SORD: A Fault-Resilient Service Overlay for MediaPort Resource Discovery. IEEE Transactions on Parallel and Distributed Systems 20(8), 1112–1124 (2008)

7. James, S., Nick, A.: An optimized two-tier P2P architecture for con-textualized keyword searches. Future Generation Computer Systems Journal 23(2) (2007)

8. Haiying, S., Ze, L., Ting, L., et al.: PIRD: P2P-based Intelligent Resource Discovery in Internet-based Distributed Systems. In: Proc. of ICDCS (2008)

9. Ronaldo, A.F., Mehmet, K., Suresh, J., et al.: Semantic indexing in structured peer-to-peer networks. J. Parallel Distrib. Journal 68 (2008)

10. Simon, R., Bui, T.V., Klaus, W.: Range Queries and Load Balancing in a Hierarchically Structured P2P System

11. Yihsiang, L.: SARIDS: A Self-Adaptive Resource Index and Discovery System. Master thesis, National Tsing-Hua University (2009)

12. OMNeT++, OMNeT++ Discrete Event Simulation System, http://www.OMNeTpp.org

Distributed Island-Based Query Answering for Expressive Ontologies

Sebastian Wandelt and Ralf Moeller

Hamburg University of Technology, Hamburg, Germany
{wandelt,r.f.moeller}@tuhh.de

Abstract. Scalability of reasoning systems is one of the main criteria which will determine the success of Semantic Web systems in the future. The focus of recent work is either on (a) systems which rely on in-memory structures or (b) not so expressive ontology languages, which can be dealt with by using database technologies.

In this paper we introduce a method to perform query answering for semi-expressive ontologies without the limit of in-memory structures. Our main idea is to compute small and characteristic representations of the assertional part of the input ontology. Query answering is then more efficiently performed over a reduced set of these small represenations. We show that query answering can be distributed in a network of description logic reasoning systems to scale for reasoning. Our initial results are encouraging.

1 Introduction

As the Semantic Web evolves, scalability of inference techniques becomes increasingly important. While in recent years the focus was on pure terminological reasoning, the interest shifts now more to reasoning with respect to large assertional parts, e.g. in the order of millions or billions of triples. The first steps were done in [FKM+06]. The authors propose to extract a condensed summary graph out of the assertional part of an ontology, and then perform reasoning on that summary. [FKM+06] reports encouraging performance results. However, for avoiding inconsistencies due to merging, the summaries have to be rewritten in expensive *query-dependent* refinement steps. With increasing number of refinement steps necessary, the performance of the aproach degrades [DFK+09]. Moreover, the technical criteria for summarization (creating representative nodes by grouping concept sets), seems arbitrary. In [WM08], a method is proposed to identify the relevant *islands*, i.e. set of assertions/information, required to reason about a given individual. The main motivation is to enable in-memory reasoning over ontologies with a large ABox, for traditional tableau-based reasoning systems.

Given the island of an individual, we will make the idea of summarization more formal. In this paper we present an approach to execute efficient instant retrieval tests on database-oriented ontologies. The main insight of our work is that the islands computed in [WM08] can be checked for similarity and instance retrieval can then be performed over equivalence classes of similar islands. The query

R.-S. Chang et al. (Eds.): GPC 2010, LNCS 6104, pp. 461–470, 2010.
© Springer-Verlag Berlin Heidelberg 2010

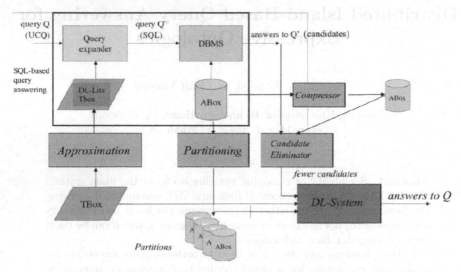

Fig. 1. Efficient query answering for expressive description logics ([KMWW08])

answering algorithm for instance retrieval over similar islands is implemented in a distributed manner. We report interesting scalability results with respect to our test ontology: increasing the number of nodes in the network by the factor of n almost reduces the query answering time to $\frac{1}{n}$. Moreover, we implemented our algorithm in such a way that the input ontology can be loaded in a offline phase and changed afterwards incrementally online.

Figure 1 is taken from [KMWW08] and shows the general structure of a reasoning system for expressive description logics. Our approach is situated in the modules *Partitioning* and *Candidate Eliminator*.

The remaining parts of the paper are structured as follows. Section 2 introduces necessary formal notions and gives an overview over Related Work. The main theoretical contribution of our work is in Section 3, the isomorphism criteria for islands. We show our implementation in Section 4 and provide initial evaluation results in Section 5. The paper is concluded in Section 6.

There is an extended verison of this paper available with proofs and further comments on the implementation and evaluation [WM10].

2   Preliminaries

For details about syntax and semantics of the description logic $\mathcal{ALCHI}$ we refer to [BCM+07]. Some definitions are appropriate to explain our nomenclature, however. We assume a collection of disjoint sets: a set of *concept names* N_{CN} , a set of *role names* N_{RN} and a set of *individual names* N_I. The *set of roles* N_R is $N_{RN} \cup \{R^- | R \in N_{RN}\}$. We say that a concept description is *atomic*, if it is a concept name or its negation. With $\mathcal{S}_{AC}$ we denote all atomic concepts.

Furthermore we assume the notions of TBoxes ($\mathcal{T}$), RBoxes ($\mathcal{R}$) and ABoxes ($\mathcal{A}$) as in [BCM+07]. A *ontology* $\mathcal{O}$ consists of a 3-tuple $\langle \mathcal{T}, \mathcal{R}, \mathcal{A} \rangle$, where $\mathcal{T}$ is a TBox, $\mathcal{R}$ is a RBox and $\mathcal{A}$ is a ABox. We restrict the concept assertions in $\mathcal{A}$ to only use atomic concepts. This is a common assumption, e.g. in [GH06], when dealing with large assertional datasets stemming from databases. With $Ind(\mathcal{A})$ we denote the set of individuals occurring in $\mathcal{A}$. Throughout the remaining part of the paper we assume the Unique Name Assumption (UNA), i.e. two distinct individual names denote distinct domain objects.

In Example 1 we define an example ontology, used throughout the remaining part of the paper to explain definitions. The example ontology is setting of universities. We evaluate our ideas w.r.t. to "full" LUBM [GPH05] in Section 5. Although this is a synthetic benchmark, several (if not most) papers on scalability of ontological reasoning consider it as a base reference.

Example 1. Let $\mathcal{O}_{EX1} = \langle \mathcal{T}_{EX1}, \mathcal{R}_{EX1}, \mathcal{A}_{EX1} \rangle$, s.t.

$\mathcal{T}_{EX1} = \{Chair \equiv \exists headOf.Department \sqcap Person, Prof \sqsubseteq Person,$
$\qquad\quad GraduateCourseTeacher \equiv Prof \sqcap \exists teaches.GraduateCourse\}$
$\mathcal{R}_{EX1} = \{headOf \sqsubseteq worksFor\}$
$\mathcal{A}_{EX1} = $see Figure 2

Next we discuss related work relevant to our contribution. In [SP08], the authors discuss a general approach to partition OWL knowledge bases and distribute reasoning over partitions to different processors/nodes. The idea is that the input for their partitioning algorithm is a fixed number of desired partitions, which will be calculated by different means (weighted graphs, hash-based distribution or domain specific partitions). The partitions are not independent from each other. Moreover, in some cases, the data is just arbitrarily spread over the different nodes in the networks. This leads to a noticeable amount of communication overhead between the nodes, because partial results have to be passed in between the nodes.

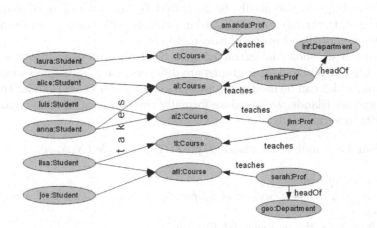

Fig. 2. Example ABox $\mathcal{A}_{EX1}$

The authors discuss rather small data sets, e.g. 1 million triples. These problems can already be solved with state-of-the-art tableau-based reasoning systems. Furthermore, their evaluation only talks about speed-up, without mentioning the actual run-time, or referring to some open/state-of-the art implementation. The work in [UKOvH09] proposes a MapReduce [DG04]-based technique, to compute the closure (set of all implications) over ontologies. Given the underlying MapReduce framework, their approach could scale in theory. The major difference to our work is that we focus on query answering, instead of brute force (bottom-up) generation of all possible implications of a given knowledge base. Moreover we focus on more expressive description logics and it is at least doubtful, whether their approach will work for non-deterministic logics (e.g. allowing for disjunctions). The authors of [BS03] discuss an approach to integrate ontologies from different sources in a distributed setting. They introduce so-called bridge-rules to identify, which parts of the ontologies overlap (and thus need to be communicated between the different reasoning nodes). The main focus of their work is rather on the integration of distributed ontologies, but not on scalable reasoning over large ontologies in general. There is additional work on distributed Datalog implementations (e.g. [ZWC95] and [GST90]) and on non-distributed reasoning optimizations/techniques for description logics, e.g. [GH06].

3   Similarity of Islands

In the following, we discuss how islands can be used for optimized instance retrieval tests and answering conjunctive queries. The main insight is that many of the computed islands are similar to each other. Especially in database-oriented scenarios, ontologies contain a lot of individuals, which follow patterns defined by a schema (i.e. the terminology of the ontology). If it is possible to define a formal notion of similarity for islands, and show that it is sufficient to perform reasoning over one representative island, instead of all these similar islands, then query answering can potentially be increased by several orders of magnitude (depending on the number dissimilar island classes). We consider an example to clarify the idea of island isomorphisms more clear.

In Figure 3 we show the extracted islands of all professors in our example ontology $\mathcal{O}_{EX1}$. While all four graphs are different, they have some similarities in common, which can be used to optimize reasoning over these islands. To define similarities over islands, we introduce formally the notion of an island and define a similarity criterion.

Definition 1. *A individual-island-graph IIG is a tuple $\langle N, \phi_n, \phi_e, root \rangle$, such that*

- *N is a set of nodes,*
- *$\phi_n : N \to 2^{\mathcal{S}_{AC}}$ is a node-labeling function ($\mathcal{S}_{AC}$ is the set of atomic concepts),*
- *$\phi_e : N \times N \to 2^{L_e}$ is a edge-labeling function*
- *$root \in N$ is a distinguished root node.*

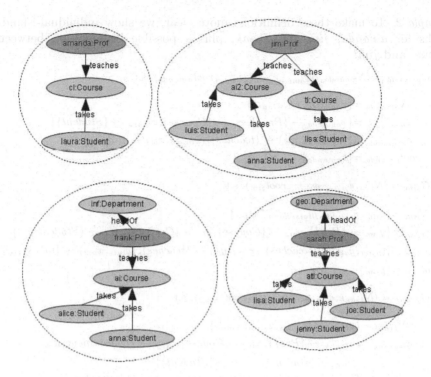

Fig. 3. Example: Islands of the four Professors in $\mathcal{O}_{EX1}$

If we have $\phi_e(a,b) = \rho$ and $\rho \neq \emptyset$, then we write $a \xrightarrow{\rho}_{IIG} b$. The definition of individual-island-graphs is quite straight-forward. In the following we define a similarity relation over two individual-island-graphs, based on graph bisimulations. Although the term *bisimulation* is usually used in process algebra to define similar processes, we use it here in the context of graphs.

Definition 2. *A* bisimulation *over* $IIG_1 = \langle N_{IIG_1}, \phi_{nIIG_1}, \phi_{eIIG_1}, root_{IIG_1} \rangle$ *and* $IIG_2 = \langle N_{IIG_2}, \phi_{nIIG_2}, \phi_{eIIG_2}, root_{IIG_2} \rangle$ *is a binary relation* $R_{IIG_1,IIG_2} \subseteq N \times N$, *such that*

- $R_{IIG_1,IIG_2}(root_{IIG_1}, root_{IIG_2})$
- *if* $R_{IIG_1,IIG_2}(a,b)$ *then* $\phi_{nIIG_1}(a) = \phi_{nIIG_2}(b)$
- *if* $R_{IIG_1,IIG_2}(a,b)$ *and* $a \xrightarrow{\rho}_{IIG_1} a'$ *then there exists a* $b' \in N_{IIG_2}$ *with* $b \xrightarrow{\rho}_{IIG_2} b'$ *and* $R_{IIG_1,IIG_2}(a',b')$
- *if* $R_{IIG_1,IIG_2}(a,b)$ *and* $b \xrightarrow{\rho}_{IIG_2} b'$ *then there exists a a'* $\in N_{IIG_1}$ *with* $a \xrightarrow{\rho}_{IIG_2} a'$ *and* $R_{IIG_1,IIG_2}(a',b')$

Definition 3. *Two individual-island-graphs* IIG_1 *and* IIG_2 *are called* bisimilar, *if there exists a bisimulation R for them.*

Example 2. To make these definitions more clear, we show individual-island-graphs for *amanda*, *jim* and *frank*, plus a possible bisimulation between *amanda* and *jim*:

- $IIG_{amanda} = \langle N_{amanda}, \phi_{n\,amanda}, \phi_{e\,amanda}, root_{amanda} \rangle$, s.t.

$$N_{amanda} = \{x_{amanda}, x_{cl}, x_{laura}\}$$
$$\phi_{n\,amanda} = \{x_{amanda} \rightarrow \{Prof\}, x_{cl} \rightarrow \{Course\}, x_{laura} \rightarrow \{Student\}\}$$
$$\phi_{e\,amanda} = \{(x_{amanda}, x_{cl}) \rightarrow \{teaches\}, (x_{laura}, x_{cl}) \rightarrow \{takes\}\}$$
$$root_{amanda} = \{x_{amanda}\}$$

- $IIG_{jim} = \langle N_{jim}, \phi_{n\,jim}, \phi_{e\,jim}, root_{jim} \rangle$, s.t.

$$N_{jim} = \{y_{jim}, y_{ai2}, y_{tl}, y_{luis}, y_{anna}, y_{lisa}\}$$
$$\phi_{n\,jim} = \{y_{jim} \rightarrow \{Prof\}, y_{ai2} \rightarrow \{Course\}, y_{tl} \rightarrow \{Course\}, y_{luis} \rightarrow \{Student\}, ...\}$$
$$\phi_{e\,jim} = \{(y_{jim}, y_{ai2}) \rightarrow \{teaches\}, (y_{jim}, y_{tl}) \rightarrow \{teaches\}, (y_{luis}, x_{ai2}) \rightarrow \{takes\}, ...\}$$
$$root_{jim} = \{y_{jim}\}$$

- $IIG_{frank} = \langle N_{frank}, \phi_{n\,frank}, \phi_{e\,frank}, root_{frank} \rangle$, s.t.

$$N_{frank} = \{z_{frank}, z_{ai}, z_{inf}, z_{alice}, z_{anna}\}$$
$$\phi_{n\,frank} = \{z_{frank} \rightarrow \{Prof\}, z_{ai} \rightarrow \{Course\}, z_{inf} \rightarrow \{Department\},$$
$$z_{alice} \rightarrow \{Student\}, z_{anna} \rightarrow \{Student\}\}$$
$$\phi_{e\,frank} = \{(z_{frank}, z_{ai}) \rightarrow \{teaches\}, (z_{frank}, z_{inf}) \rightarrow \{headOf\},$$
$$(z_{alice}, z_{ai}) \rightarrow \{takes\}, (z_{anna}, z_{ai}) \rightarrow \{takes\}\}$$
$$root_{jim} = \{z_{frank}\}$$

- $R_{jim,amanda} =$

$$\{(x_{amanda}, y_{jim}), (x_{cl}, y_{ai2}), (x_{cl}, y_{tl}), (x_{laura}, y_{luis}),$$
$$(x_{laura}, y_{luis}), (x_{anna}, y_{lisa})\}$$

It is easy to see, that $R_{jim,amanda}$ is a bisimulation for the islands (graphs) of the individuals *jim* and *amanda*. Furthermore, it is easy to see that there cannot be a bisimulation, for instance, between *jim* and *frank*.

The important insight is that bisimilar islands entail the same concept sets for their root individual, if the underlying description logic is restricted to $ALCHI$. This is shown in the following theorem.

Theorem 1. *Given two individuals a and b, we have* $\langle \mathcal{T}, \mathcal{R}, ISLAND(a) \rangle \vDash C(a) \iff \langle \mathcal{T}, \mathcal{R}, ISLAND(b) \rangle \vDash C(b)$, *if we can find a bisimulation* $R_{a,b}$, *for* $ISLAND(a)$ *and* $ISLAND(b)$.

The above theorem can be easily lifted to the case of more than two individuals, i.e. if we have n individuals, and for all of their islands one can find a bisimilarity relation, it is sufficient to perform instance checking on one island. In practice, especially in database-oriented ontologies, this can dramatically speed up the time for instance retrieval. To show this, we need to further introduce some mathematical notions.

Definition 4. *A* individual-island-equivalence $\sim_{ISL}$ *is an equivalence relation over individual islands, such that we have* $\sim_{ISL}(ISL, ISL)$, *if we can find a bisimulation* $R_{ISL,ISL}$ *between the two islands ISL and ISL. With* $[\sim_{ISL}]$ *we denote the set of equivalence classes of* $\sim_{ISL}$.

The main theoretical result of our work is summarized in the following theorem.

Theorem 2. *Given an ontology* $\langle \mathcal{T}, \mathcal{R}, \mathcal{A} \rangle$, *one can perform grounded instance retrieval for the atomic concept* C *over* $[\sim_{ISL}]$, *instead of all islands.*

Please note that our approach does not work directly for more expressive description logics, e.g. $\mathcal{SHOIQ}$. In the presence of cardinality restrictions we will need more sophisticated bisimulation criteria to identify similar nodes, since the number of related similar individuals matters. Nominals further complicate the bisimulation criteria, since individuals can be forced by the terminological axioms to refer to the same domain object, i.e. one might need to calculate all TBox-implications in the worst calse.

4   Distributed Implementation

We have implemented our proposal for Island Simulations in Java. For ontology access we use the OWLAPI 2.2.0[BVL03]. The general structure of our implementation, a description of each component and performance optimization insights can be found in [WM10]. Here we only give a short overview on the modules.

- (Server) OWL-Converter: converts OWL data to an internal representation
- (Server) Update Handler: determines changed islands in case of ontology updates
- (Server) Island Computor: computes the island for a given an individual and performs similarity computation
- *(Server) Node Scheduler*: determines the responsible node for the island: Round-Robin / capability-based
- (Server) TBox/ABox Storage: terminological/assertional part of the ontology.
- (Client) Query Manager: determines all active islands and uses the DL Reasoner module to find out which islands match the input query.
- (Client) DL Reasoner: implements an interface to a general description logic reasoner (in our case we used Racer [HM01]).

5   Evaluation

Our tests were run with respect to the synthetic benchmark ontology LUBM [GPH05]. Although some people claim that LUBM does not fully represent all the capabilities provided by the complete OWL specification, we think that it fits

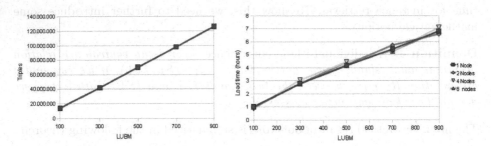

Fig. 4. Input size and load time

our constraint of database-oriented ontologies: rather small and simple TBox, but a bulk of assertional information with a realistic distribution with respect to numbers of professors, students, departments, etc. In our evaluation we compare three different measures, to determine the performance of our implementation:

- *Load time*: In Figure 4 we show the size of the assertional part in triples and compare the load time with different number of nodes in our network (1, 2 and 4 nodes). The load time only represents the time spent to traverse the input ontology one time and compute that bisimilarity relation over all islands of all individuals. It can be seen that the load time increases linearly with the number of triples in the assertional part. Please note that our loading algorithm is designed and implemented as an incremental algorithm. Thus, if we add a new assertion, we do not have to recompute all the internal structures, but only update the relevant structures.
- *Preparation time*: This measure indicates an initial preparation time after the ontology is fully loaded. Please note that this preprocessing step is query independent and only performed one time after the ontology was updated. The idea is that we can perform incremental bulk loading (measured in *load time*), without updating the (expensive) internal structures of the DL reasoner all the time.

  In the left part of Figure 5, we show the query preparation time for different numbers of universities and different numbers of nodes in the network. The number of nodes indeed affects the query preparation time. If we use 8 nodes, the preparation time is almost $\frac{1}{8}$ of the time needed for one node.

  In the right part of Figure 5 we compare the necessary number of islands to perform instance retrieval with the original work in [WM08]. It can be seen, that the number of islands increases linearly with the size of the input ontology for [WM08] (please note the logarithmic scale). Using bisimulation, the number of islands is almost constant for all input ontologies, since most of the newly introduced individual-islands are bisimilar to each other, e.g. professors who teach particular students in particular kinds of courses.
- *Query answering time*: The third measure indicates how long the actual query answering takes. In Figure 6, the query answering time (for instance retrieval) for the concepts *Chair*) are shown. This is the actual description-logic-hard task.

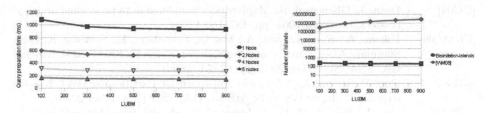

Fig. 5. Query preparation time and island count

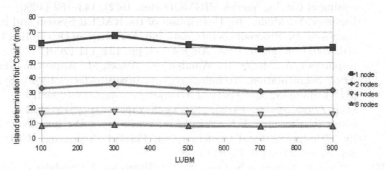

Fig. 6. Query answering time

6   Conclusions

We have proposed a method for instance retrieval over ontologies in a distributed system of DL reasoners. To the best of our knowledge, we are the first to propose instance retrieval reasoning based on similarity of individual-islands. The results are encouraging so far. We emphasize that our approach especially works for ontologies with a rather simple or average size terminological part. For future work, it will be important to investigate more ontologies and check the performance of our proposal. Furthermore, we want to extend our proposal to more expressive description logics, e.g. SHIQ or even SHOIQ.

References

[BCM+07]   Baader, F., Calvanese, D., McGuinness, D.L., Nardi, D., Patel-Schneider, P.F.: The Description Logic Handbook. Cambridge University Press, New York (2007)

[BS03]   Borgida, A., Serafini, L.: Distributed description logics: Assimilating information from peer sources. J. of Data Semantics (2003)

[BVL03]   Bechhofer, S., Volz, R., Lord, P.: Cooking the Semantic Web with the OWL API (2003)

[DFK+09]   Dolby, J., Fokoue, A., Kalyanpur, A., Schonberg, E., Srinivas, K.: Efficient reasoning on large SHIN Aboxes in relational databases. In: SSWS 2009 (2009)

[DG04]   Dean, J., Ghemawat, S.: MapReduce: Simplified data processing on large clusters. In: OSDI 2004, pp. 137–150 (2004)

[FKM⁺06]   Fokoue, A., Kershenbaum, A., Ma, L., Schonberg, E., Srinivas, K.: The Summary ABox: Cutting ontologies down to size. In: SSWS 2006, Athens, GA, USA, November 2006, pp. 61–74 (2006)

[GH06]   Guo, Y., Heflin, J.: A Scalable Approach for Partitioning OWL Knowledge Bases. In: SSWS 2006, Athens, GA, USA (November 2006)

[GPH05]   Guo, Y., Pan, Z., Heflin, J.: Lubm: A benchmark for owl knowledge base systems. J. Web Sem. 3(2-3), 158–182 (2005)

[GST90]   Ganguly, S., Silberschatz, A., Tsur, S.: A framework for the parallel processing of datalog queries. SIGMOD Rec. 19(2), 143–152 (1990)

[HM01]   Haarslev, V., Möller, R.: Description of the RACER System and its Applications. In: Proceedings International Workshop on Description Logics (DL 2001), Stanford, USA, August 1-3, pp. 131–141 (2001)

[KMWW08]   Kaplunova, A., Möller, R., Wandelt, S., Wessel, M.: Approximation and ABox Segmentation. Technical report, Institute for Software Systems (STS), Hamburg University of Technology, Germany (2008), http://www.sts.tu-harburg.de/tech-reports/papers.html

[SP08]   Soma, R., Prasanna, V.K.: Parallel inferencing for OWL knowledge bases. In: 37th International Conference on Parallel Processing, ICPP 2008, September 2008, pp. 75–82 (2008)

[UKOvH09]   Urbani, J., Kotoulas, S., Oren, E., van Harmelen, F.: Scalable distributed reasoning using MapReduce. In: Bernstein, A., Karger, D.R., Heath, T., Feigenbaum, L., Maynard, D., Motta, E., Thirunarayan, K. (eds.) ISWC 2009. LNCS, vol. 5823, pp. 634–649. Springer, Heidelberg (2009)

[WM08]   Wandelt, S., Möller, R.: Island reasoning for ALCHI ontologies. In: Proceedings of the 2008 conference on Formal Ontology in Information Systems, pp. 164–177. IOS Press, Amsterdam (2008)

[WM10]   Wandelt, S., Möller, R.: Distributed island simulation for reasoning over ontologies - technical report (2010), http://www.sts.tu-harburg.de/tech-reports/papers.html

[ZWC95]   Zhang, W., Wang, K., Chau, S.-C.: Data partition and parallel evaluation of datalog programs. IEEE Transactions on Knowledge and Data Engineering 7(1), 163–176 (1995)

An Extended Description Logic for Event Ontology

Wei Liu, Wenjie Xu, Jianfeng Fu, Zongtian Liu, and Zhaomang Zhong

School of Computer Engineering and Science, Shanghai University
Shanghai 200072, China
liuw@shu.edu.cn

Abstract. As a means of knowledge representation, event is close to the cognitive procedure of human beings. The reasonableness of event as the unit of knowledge, and the insufficiency of using description logic (DL) to act as logical foundation of event ontology language, are analyzed in this paper. According to the characteristics and requirement of the event ontology, this paper propose an event-oriented DL (EDL) to provide ontology languages (such as OWL) with well-defined semantics and inference service for supporting effective representation and reasoning of events.

Keywords: Event Ontology, Description Logic, EDL, Event Inference.

1 Introduction

Event-oriented knowledge representation method is reasonable based on the philosophical viewpoints that world is of material, material is of movement, movement is absolute and static is relative. Cognitive science has established that human beings perceive the real world through events. Events as the unit of human knowledge, has received more and more attention and high regards from the AI and Linguistics communities [1,2,3]. Events happened in the past world result in today's world. And events happening in today's world will result in tomorrow's world. So, to describe history is to describe a set of events and relationships among them. Human beings state a historical event by using discourse text. Discourse and text are linguistic representations of events and relationships. In order to understand these discourse texts, we must know their intended meaning. The intended meanings of discourse texts are always exist in brains of human beings as common knowledge. Event ontology is explicit specification of such common knowledge that can be understood by computers. In [4], we proposed an event-oriented ontology model to represent event structure of text.

The use of event ontologies needs a well-designed, well-defined ontology language, which is a language to represent event structures of specific domain, and these event structures can be described by using certain event classes and event factors. Event ontology is composed of a set of axioms that defined with such event structures. Because of DL's advantages in semantic representation, decidability and conceptual classification representation, most traditional ontology languages are built on the basis of DL, such as OWL[5]. DLs are now regarded as the formal foundation for ontology languages. Whereas, to construct event ontology for a specific

R.-S. Chang et al. (Eds.): GPC 2010, LNCS 6104, pp. 471–481, 2010.
© Springer-Verlag Berlin Heidelberg 2010

domain, we need to describe not only static concepts, but also dynamic features of the events, such as actions involved in events, time events happened and location where events happened. While modeling the event ontology with dynamic features, the capacity of DLs is insufficient, including i) DLs have no syntax and semantics to describe dynamic actions in an event. ii) DLs lack the expressivity to specify the temporal information of event. iii) DLs lack syntax and semantics for represent the non-taxonomic relations between event classes, such as follow relations between two events. iv) DLs provide inference service for static concepts, but could not support inference service on dynamic knowledge involved in events.

For the reasons above, this paper proposes an extension DL according to the characteristics and requirement of event ontology, called Event Description Logic (EDL). EDL aims at providing clear and well-defined semantics, as well providing decidable reasoning service to support effective representation and reasoning of events and events relations. The rest of the paper is organized as follows: In section 2, we propose several new definitions about event and event ontology; Section 3 discusses the extension of DL for event ontology, and introduces syntax and semantics of EDL in detail; Section 4 briefly discusses inference problems of EDL. Section 5 introduces related work and gives conclusions.

2   Related Definitions about Event Ontology

2.1   Definitions about Event

Definition 1 (*Event*). We define *event* as a thing happens in a certain time and environment, which some actors take part in and show some action features. Event e can be defined as a 6-tuple formally:

$$e ::=_{def} < A, O, T, V, P, L >$$

We call elements in 6-tuple event factors. A means an action set happen in an event. It describes the process of event happens. These actions executed in sequence or concurrently while event happens. O means objects take part in the event, including all actors and entities involved in the event. T means the period of time that event lasting. The time period includes absolute time and relative time. V means environment of event, such as location of event. P means assertions on the procedure of actions execution in an event. Assertions include *pre-condition*, *post-condition* and *intermediate* assertions. L means language expressions, including *Core Word Set*, *Core Words Expressions* and *Core Words Collocations*.

Definition 2 (*Event Class*). *Event Class* means a set of events with common characteristics, defined as

$$EC = (E, C_1, C_2, \cdots, C_6)$$

$$C_i = \{c_{i1}, c_{i2}, \cdots, c_{im}, \cdots\} \quad (1 \le i \le 6, m \ge 0)$$

Where E is event set, called extension of event class. C_i called intension of the event class. It denotes the common characteristics set of certain event factor (factor i). C_{im} denotes one of the common characteristics of event factor i.

Definition 3 (*Taxonomic Relations*). Suppose two event classes, $EC_1 = (E_1, C_{11}, C_{12}, \cdots, C_{16})$ and $EC_2 = (E_2, C_{21}, C_{22}, \cdots, C_{26})$. There exists taxonomic relation between EC_1 and EC_2 if and only if $E_2 \subset E_1$, or , $C_{2i} \subseteq C_{1i}$ (i=1,2,...,6) and there exists j (j=1,2,...,6) such that $C_{2j} \subset C_{1j}$. We call EC_1 hypernymy event class and EC_2 hyponym event class.

Definition 4 (*Parent-child Relations*). Suppose EC_1 is hypernymy event class of EC_2, if only if $EC_2 \subset EC_1$ and not exist such $EC_3 = (E_3, C_{31}, C_{32}, \cdots, C_{36})$ that $EC_2 \subset EC_3$ and $EC_3 \subset EC_1$, then EC_1 is the parent event class of EC_2 or EC_2 is the child event class of EC_1 .

2.2 Non-taxonomic Relationships of Event Classes

According to features of event, we define four kinds of non-taxonomic relationships of events.

Definition 5 (*Composite Relation*). If an event e can be decomposed to several events e_i(i>0) with smaller granularity. If all the smaller events e_i(i>0) have been finished means e is finished, then there exists composite relation between e and e_i(i>0). If each event instance of event class EC_1 is composed of one event instance of event class EC_2 and other event classes, then EC_1 composed of EC_2, denoted as $EC_1 \overline{\times} EC_2$.

Definition 6 (*Causal Relation*). If an event instance of ec_1 happens, event in ec_2 is more likely to happen at above a specified probability threshold, there is a causal relation between EC_1 and EC_2. EC_1 is cause and EC_2 is effect, denoted as $(\lambda EC_1 \rightarrow EC_2)$. λ is optional, it means the probability that event individual of EC_2 happens caused by an event individual of EC_1. We named λ as link degree of the causal relation. If λ equals 1, EC_1 will cause EC_2 necessarily. If λ is less than 1, $(\lambda EC_1 \rightarrow EC_2)$ means EC_1 will cause EC_2 probably.

Definition 7 (*Follow Relation*). Follow refer to events coming after in time or order, as a consequence or result, or by the operation of logic. If in a certain length of time, EC_2 follow EC_1 at above a specified probability threshold, there is a follow relation between EC_1 and EC_2, denoted as $(\lambda EC_2 \rhd EC_1)$. λ is link degree of the follow relationship.

Definition 8 (*Accompany Relation*). If EC_1 concur with EC_2 in a certain period of time, and the occurrence probability is above a specified threshold, there is an accompany relationship between EC_1 and EC_2, denoted as $(\lambda EC_1 \| EC_2)$. λ is the link degree of the accompany relationship.

2.3 Definitions of Event Ontology

Definition 9 (*Event Ontology*). An event ontology is a formal, explicit specification of a shared event model that exists objectively, denoted as *EO*.

Definition 10 (*Event Ontology Structure*). The structure of event ontology can be defined as a 3-tuple.

$$EO := \{ECs, R, Rules\}$$

Where *ECs* is the set of all events, *R* indicates all taxonomic and non-taxonomic relations between events. By using taxonomic relations, we can construct a hierarchy of event classes. While create a non-taxonomic relations, the relations name and the link degree are indicated, and the link degree can be valued from 0 to 1, which can be changed by learning or forgetting. *Rules* are expressed in logic languages, which can be used to describe the transformation and inference between events.

3 Extending DL for Event Ontology

Description logics (DLs) [6] are a family of knowledge representation languages that can be used to represent the knowledge of an application domain in a structured and formally well-understood way. A standard DL characterized by a set of constructors (i.e., conjunction, disjunction, negation, existential restriction and value restriction) that allow to construct complex concepts and role from atomic ones. We call these constructors $\mathcal{ALC}$ [6]. To represent event-oriented knowledge, we propose a new DL language by extending traditional DL, called EDL (Event Description Logics). EDL extends the expressiveness of traditional DL at three aspects as follows.

(1) Temporal information is an import factor of event ontology. There are two types of temporal information in event ontology, time properties of events and temporal relations among events. In EDL, we add temporal prepositions (such as at, during) and temporal connectives (such as before, after, among) to the $\mathcal{ALC}$ of DL.

(2) In the 6-tuple definition of event, *P* represents assertions of an event, it indicates predicates of actions involved in the event. In EDL, we improved DDL[7] to describe assertions of actions in an event.

(3) EDL combines temporal logic and modal logic to describe non-taxonomic among events class, such as causal relation, follow relation, etc.

In an EDL system, there are a set of constructors, a knowledge base including Event-TBox (for terminological knowledge) and Event-ABox (for assertion knowledge), and some inference rules on Event-TBox and Event-ABox. Based on $\mathcal{ALC}$ and the features of event, we extend some new constructors. These constructors are from temporal logic and modal logic partially. With these constructors, the temporal information of events and some non-taxonomic relations can be described explicitly. We name this extension version of $\mathcal{ALC}$ as $\mathcal{EALC}$.

Definition 11 (*$\mathcal{EALC}$ Event Syntax*). Let N_E be a set of event names, N_R be a set of role names and N_{CS} is a set of control structures. The sets of $\mathcal{EALC}$-event descriptions is the smallest sets such that:

(1) $\top$, $\bot$, and every event name $E \in N_E$ is an $\mathcal{EALC}$-event.

(2) If E and F are $\mathcal{EALC}$-events and $r \in N_R$, then $E \sqcap F$, $E \sqcup F, \neg E, \square E, \Diamond E, \exists r.E, \forall r.E$ are $\mathcal{EALC}$-events.

(3) If E and F are atomic $\mathcal{EALC}$-events, then a composite $\mathcal{EALC}$-event

$$ce ::= e \mid \varphi? \mid E \oplus F \mid E \parallel F \mid E \triangleright F \mid E^*, F^*$$

Where $e \in N_E$ and $\{\triangleright, \oplus, \parallel, *\} \in N_{CS}$, control structures are essential for building up complex composite events. In the production above, e represents an atomic event. $\varphi?$ represents testing action. $\oplus$ represents a choice control structure, $E \oplus F$ means only one of event E and event F happens. $\triangleright$ represents a sequence control structure, $E \triangleright F$ means event E and event F happens in sequence, and event F follow event E.

Based on these control structures above, we can construct more complex control structures. For example, the control structure "if φ then E else F" can be expressed as "$(\varphi? \rightarrow E) \oplus ((\neg\varphi)? \rightarrow F)$"; The control structure "while φ do e" can be expressed as "$(\varphi? \rightarrow e)^* \cup (\neg\varphi)?$"; The control structure "do e until φ" can be expressed as "$e \cup ((\neg\varphi)? \rightarrow e)^* \cup (\varphi)?$".

Definition 12 ($\mathcal{EALC}$ Action Syntax). Let $\mathcal{ET}$ be an acyclic Event-TBox, an atomic action involved in event is the form of

$A(x_1, \ldots, x_n) \equiv (Pre, Mid, Post)$ Where

(1) A is the action name.

(2) $x_1, \ldots, x_n$ are individual variables that denote the objects the action operate on.

(3) Pre is a finite set Event-ABox assertions, called pre-conditions, it specify under which conditions the action will be executed.

(4) Mid is a finite set of intermediate status of the action. A status in Mid is form of $C(a)$ or $r(a,b)$, with C primitive concept in $\mathcal{ET}$, r role name, and a, b objects name. All status in Mid set are in time sequence.

(5) $Post$ is a finite set of results, which denotes the post-conditions of the form φ / ψ, where φ is an Event-ABox assertion and ψ is a primitive literal for $\mathcal{ET}$.

(6) A composite action for $\mathcal{ET}$ is a finite sequence $A_1, \ldots A_n$ of atomic actions. The control structures in definition 11 can also be used to construct a composite action.

In comparison with the definitions of action in [7] [8], a Mid set is introduced to represent intermediate status and the process of status changing during the event happens, which improves the EDL's expressivity in describing the process of events.

Definition 13 ($\mathcal{EALC}$ Temporal Syntax). In $\mathcal{EALC}$, we define two types of temporal syntax, one type is for Event-TBox and another is for Event-ABox. Let $\mathcal{ET}$ be an Event-TBox, the temporal information for an event class can be described as:

(1) (in | at | during | am | before | after | since | until | from..to) T, and T is a periodic time noun, e.g. in autumn, from Monday to Wednesday.

(2) (in | at | during | am) every T, and T is a periodic time noun or a time unit, e.g. in every month, during every spring.

(3) (in | at | during | am) E, and E is an event class name to denote the occurrence time of this type of event, e.g. during World Cup, in war years.

Let AT be an Event-ABox, the temporal information for an event instance can be described as:

(1) (in | at | during | am | before | after | since | until | from..to) T, and T is a specific time of event happens, e.g. in 1970, from this Monday to Saturday.

(2) (in | at | during | am | before | after | since | until | from..to) E, and E is an name of specific event instance, e.g. after Indonesian tsunami.

Definition 14 ($\mathcal{EALC}$ Semantics). The language of $\mathcal{EALC}$ is interpreted in temporal models over T, which are triples of the form $\mathcal{I}=(\Delta^{\mathcal{I}}, \mathcal{E}^{\mathcal{I}}, \cdot^{\mathcal{I}(t)})$, where $\mathcal{E}^{\mathcal{I}}$ is non-empty set of events(the domain of $\mathcal{I}$) and $\cdot^{\mathcal{I}(t)}$ an interpretation function such that, for every $t \in T$, every event E, and every relation ER, we have $E^{\mathcal{I}(t)} \subseteq \mathcal{E}^{\mathcal{I}}$ and $ER^{\mathcal{I}}$ $^{(t)} \subseteq \mathcal{E}^{\mathcal{I}} \times \mathcal{E}^{\mathcal{I}}$. The main syntax and semantics of $\mathcal{EALC}$ can be summarized in table 1 below.

Table 1. The syntax and semantics (reduced) of $\mathcal{EALC}$

Constructors	Syntax	Semantics
non-empty event set	$\top^{\mathcal{I}(t)}$	$\top^{\mathcal{I}(t)} = \mathcal{E}$
empty event set	$\bot^{\mathcal{I}(t)}$	$\bot^{\mathcal{I}(t)} = \phi$
atomic event	E	$E^{\mathcal{I}(t)} \subseteq \mathcal{E}^{\mathcal{I}(t)}$
atomic event role	ER	$ER^{\mathcal{I}(t)} \subseteq \mathcal{E}^{\mathcal{I}(t)} \times \mathcal{E}^{\mathcal{I}(t)}$
event time	T	$\{t \in T \mid begin(t) < end(t)\}$
at time	$at\ T$	$\{t \in T \mid begin(t) = end(t)\}$
among time	$am\ T$	$\{t_1\ am\ t_2 \mid begin(t_1) < begin(t_2) \wedge end(t_1) > end(t_2)\}$
in time	$in\ T$	$\{t_1\ in\ t_2 \mid begin(t_1) = $
		$end(t_1) \wedge end(t_2) > begin(t_1) > begin(t_2)\}$
after time	$after\ T$	$\{t_1\ af\ t_2 \mid begin(t_1) > begin(t_2)\}$
before time	$before\ T$	$\{t_1\ bf\ t_2 \mid begin(t_1) < begin(t_2)\}$
For E,F events and ER an event role name		
foretells	$foretells\ E$	$\square E^{\mathcal{I}(t)}$
allows	$allows\ E$	$\lozenge E^{\mathcal{I}(t)}$
conjunction	$E \sqcap F$	$E^{\mathcal{I}(t)} \cap F^{\mathcal{I}(t)}$
disjunction	$E \sqcup F$	$E^{\mathcal{I}(t)} \cup F^{\mathcal{I}(t)}$
negation	$\neg E$	$\mathcal{E}^{\mathcal{I}(t)} \setminus E^{\mathcal{I}(t)}$
exist restrict	$\exists ER.E$	$\{x \mid \exists y. <x,y> \in ER^{\mathcal{I}(t)} \wedge y \in E^{\mathcal{I}(t)}\}$

Table 1. (*continued*)

value restrict	$\forall ER.E$	$\{x \mid \forall y. < x,y >\in ER^{I^{(t)}} \Rightarrow y \in E^{I^{(t)}}\}$
sub event class	$E \sqsubseteq F$	$E^{\mathcal{I}(t)} \sqsubseteq F^{\mathcal{I}(t)}$
compositeOf	$E \overline{\prec} F$	$\{f \in \varepsilon^{\mathcal{I}(t)} \mid \exists w \, am \, t. f \in F^{\mathcal{I}(w)} \Rightarrow f \in E^{\mathcal{I}(w)}\}$
restriction causal	$(\lambda \, E \rightarrow F)$	$\{e \in E^{\mathcal{I}(t)}, f \in F^{\mathcal{I}(t)} \mid P(\forall v \, am \, t.e \in E^{\mathcal{I}(v)} \Rightarrow$ $\exists w \, am \, t.after(w,v)) \, foretells \, f \in F^{\mathcal{I}(\omega)}) = \lambda\}$
necessarily causal	$E \rightarrow F$	$\{e \in E^{\mathcal{I}(t)}, f \in F^{\mathcal{I}(t)} \mid \forall v \, am \, t.e \in E^{\mathcal{I}(v)} \Rightarrow$ $\exists w \, am \, t.after(w,v)) \, allows \, f \in F^{\mathcal{I}(\omega)}\}$
restriction follow	$(\lambda \, E \triangleright F)$	$\{e \in E^{\mathcal{I}(t)}, f \in F^{\mathcal{I}(t)} \mid P(\forall v \, am \, t.e \in E^{\mathcal{I}(v)} \wedge$ $\exists w \, am \, t.after(w,v) \, fortells \, f \in F^{\mathcal{I}(\omega)}) = \lambda\}$
necessarily follow	$E \triangleright F$	$\{e \in E^{\mathcal{I}(t)}, f \in F^{\mathcal{I}(t)} \mid \forall v \, am \, t.e \in E^{\mathcal{I}(v)} \wedge$ $\exists w \, am \, t.after(w,v) \, allows \, f \in F^{\mathcal{I}(\omega)}\}$
restriction accompany	$(\lambda \, E \| F)$	$\{e \in E^{\mathcal{I}(t)}, f \in F^{\mathcal{I}(t)} \mid P(\forall v \, am \, t.e \in E^{\mathcal{I}(v)}$ $\wedge \exists w \, am \, v \, fortells \, f \in F^{\mathcal{I}(\omega)}) = \lambda\}$
possibly accompany	$E \| F$	$\{e \in E^{\mathcal{I}(t)}, f \in F^{\mathcal{I}(t)} \mid \forall v \, am \, t.e \in E^{\mathcal{I}(v)} \wedge$ $\exists w \, am \, t.after(w,v) \, allows \, f \in F^{\mathcal{I}(\omega)}\}$
trans role	ER^*	$(ER^{I^{(t)}})^*$

As mentioned above, an EDL knowledge base is the expansion of traditional DL knowledge base. Similar to traditional DL knowledge base [9], an EDL knowledge base contains a terminological part (called Event-TBox) and an assertional part (called Event-ABox), each part consists of a set of axioms.

Definition 15 (*Event-TBox*). A general event axiom is of the form $E \sqsubseteq F$, $E \overline{\prec} F$, $E \triangleright F$ or $E \rightarrow F$, where E, F are $\mathcal{EALC}$-events. An axiom of the form $E \equiv F$, where E is an event name, is called a definition. A finite set of general event axioms is called an Event-TBox. An interpretation $\mathcal{I}$ is a model that satisfies all definitions and axioms in Event-TBox $\mathcal{ET}$.

An Event-TBox $\mathcal{ET}$ satisfies following restriction that i) $\mathcal{ET}$ contains at most one definition for any given event name, ii) $\mathcal{ET}$ is acyclic, the definitions of any event E in $\mathcal{ET}$ does not refer (directly or indirectly) to E itself. In such an Event-TBox, the extensions of the defined events are uniquely determined by the extensions of the primitive events and the role names. In addition, $\mathcal{ET}$ contains definitions of all composite events.

Definition 16 (*Event-ABox*). An assertional axiom is of the form $x{:}E$ or $(x, y){:}r$, where E is an $\mathcal{EALC}$-event, r is an $\mathcal{EALC}$-role, and x and y are individual event names. A finite set of assertional axioms is called an Event-ABox. An interpretation $\mathcal{I}$

is a model of an assertional axiom x:E if $x^{\mathcal{I}} \in E^{\mathcal{I}}$, and $\mathcal{I}$ is a model of an assertional axiom $(x, y) : r$ if $<x^{\mathcal{I}}, y^{\mathcal{I}}> \in r^{\mathcal{I}}$; $\mathcal{I}$ is a model of an Event-ABox $\mathcal{EA}$ if it is a model of every axiom in $\mathcal{EA}$.

Definition 17 (*Event Knowledge Base*). An event knowledge base is a pair $(\mathcal{ET}, \mathcal{EA})$, where $\mathcal{ET}$ is an Event-TBox and $\mathcal{EA}$ is an Event-ABox. An interpretation $\mathcal{I}$ is a model of an event knowledge base $\Sigma = (\mathcal{ET}, \mathcal{ET})$ if $\mathcal{I}$ is a model of $\mathcal{ET}$ and $\mathcal{EA}$, denoted as $\mathcal{I} \models \Sigma \Leftrightarrow \mathcal{I} \models \mathcal{ET}, \mathcal{I} \models \mathcal{EA}$.

Now, we give an example of traffic accident that represented in EDL. We define atomic events related to traffic accident as follow: *emergency, traffic_accident, die, injure, call_police, rescue, come_to_scene, onsite_rescue, send_to_hospital, police_investigation*, and use four event roles, *Causal*($\rightarrow$), *CompositeOf*($\overline{\times}$), *Accompany*($\parallel$), *Follow*($\triangleright$), to construct events relations. An Event-TBox $\mathcal{ET}$ contains terminology axioms of events as follow:

> *traffic_accident* $\sqsubseteq$ *emergency*
> *serious_injure* $\equiv$ *injure* $\sqcap$ *send_to_hospital*
> *serious_traffic_acciden t* $\equiv$ *traffic_accident* $\sqcap$ (≥ 1 *Causal.die* $\sqcup$ ≥ 10
> *Causal.serious_injure*)
> *traffic_accident_handling* $\equiv$ *traffic_accident* $\sqcap$ *call_police*

The definitions above say: a *traffic_accident* belongs to *emergency*; *serious_injure* means that someone injured and need to be sent to hospital; A *serious_traffic_accident* is a *traffic_accident* that cause at least one person died or ten person injured seriously. *traffic_accident_handling* means that a *traffic_accident* happened and someone had called police. An Event-ABox $\mathcal{EA}$ contains assertional axioms of events as follow:

> $u \rightarrow (v \sqcup r) = \{$ *serious_traffic_accident*(u), *die*(v), *serious_injure*(r)$\}$
> $(x, y) \overline{\times} w = \{$ (*come_to_scene*(x), *onsite_rescue*(y), *rescue*(w))$\}$
> $r \parallel v = \{$*serious_injure*(r), *die*(v)$\}$
> $e \triangleright f = \{$ *call_police*(e), *police_investigation* (f)$\}$

Where the event u is an instance of *serious_traffic_accident*, the event v is an instance of *die*, the event r is the instance of *serious_injure*, and so are the events x, y, w, e, and f. Table 2 below gives the 6-tuple (which have been reduced) description of the event u, v, and e.

Table 2. Example Event Instances in $\mathcal{EA}$

Event	serious_traffic_accident(u)	die(v)	call_police(e)
Actions	{(ride(cyclist,bicycle) ∥ drive(driver, car)) $\triangleright$ collide(car, bicycle)}	die	call
Objects	cyclist, driver, bicycle, car	cyclist	someone, policeman

Table 2. (*continued*)

Time	am T$_1$	am T$_1$	at T$_2$
	T$_1$=(2009-01-01 15:00,	T$_1$=(2009-01-01 15:00,	T$_2$=(2009-01-01 15:00,
	2009-01-01 16:00)	2009-01-01 16:00)	2009-01-01 15:00)
Location	S1 Highway	S1 Highway	S1 Highway
Assertions	collide(car, bicycle)=	die(cyclist)=	call(someone, policeman)=
	({ ride(cyclist, bicycle),	({alive(cyclist)},	({unknow(police,accident)},
	drive(driver, car) },	{died(cyclist)})	{know(police,accident)})
	{stop(car), fall(bicycle)}})		
Language	collide, strike, dash	die, pass away	call, report, alarm

Suppose the following events have happened: *traffic_accident(u),die(v), serious_injure(r), call_police(e)*. Events *u*, *v*, *r* and *e* are instances of the relevant events. Firstly, we can infer that the *traffic_accident(u)* is a *serious_traffic_accident(u)*, because there are some person died and injured. Secondly, we can infer that the policemen and the ambulance came to scene, because someone had called the police, died and injured person need be sent to hospital. Thirdly, we can infer that the policemen investigated the accident after the serious traffic accident happened.

So, event instances *traffic_accident(u)*, *die(v)*, *serious_injure(r)* and *call_police(e)* will result in following event instances: *serious_traffic_accident(u)*, *rescue(w)*, *send_to_hospital(t)*, *traffic_accident_handling(u)* and *police_investigation* (*f*).

4 Inference Problems of EDL

We use an event knowledge base to define inference problems of EDL. An event knowledge base $\Sigma = (\mathcal{ET}, \mathcal{EA})$, contains some intension knowledge which can only be inferred through the extension knowledge.

4.1 Inference Problems of Event-TBox

Given an Event-TBox $\mathcal{ET}$, the most important inference problem is the satisfiability problem of the $\mathcal{ET}$. It also includes other inference problems such as subsumption problem and equivalence problem between the events.

Satisfiability problem: If there exists $\mathcal{I}$ and $\mathcal{I}$ is a model of $\mathcal{ET}$, and $\mathcal{E}^{\mathcal{I}}$ is non-empty set of events. We can infer that for every event $E^{\mathcal{I}} \subseteq \mathcal{E}^{\mathcal{I}}$ is satisfiability and $\mathcal{I}$ is model of event *E*.

Subsumption problem: If there exists $E_1{}^{\mathcal{I}} \subseteq E_2{}^{\mathcal{I}}$ while $\mathcal{I}$ is an arbitrary model of $\mathcal{ET}$. We can infer that E_1 is hyponym event, E_2 is hypernymy event. It can be written as $E_1 \sqsubseteq_{ET} E_2$ or $\mathcal{ET} \vDash E_1 \sqsubseteq E_2$.

Equivalence problem: If there exists $E_1{}^{\mathcal{I}}=E_2{}^{\mathcal{I}}$ while $\mathcal{I}$ is an arbitrary model of $\mathcal{ET}$. We can infer that E_1 and E_2 are the equivalent. It can be written as $E_1 \equiv_{ET} E_2$ or $\mathcal{ET} \vDash E_1 \equiv E_2$.

Subsumption problems and equivalence problems of events can be reduced to the satisfiability problem of events as follows:

(1) $E_1 \subseteq E_2 \Leftrightarrow E_1 \cap \neg E_2$ is not satisfiability;

(2) $E_1 \equiv E_2 \Leftrightarrow E_1 \cap \neg E_2$ and $\neg E_1 \cap E_2$ all are not satisfiability.

4.2 Inference Problems of Event-ABox

Given an Event-ABox $\mathcal{EA}$, the most important inference task is the instance checking problem of the $\mathcal{EA}$. But, firstly we need ensure that $\mathcal{EA}$ is consistent. So, the inference problems include consistency problem and instance checking problem.

Consistency problem: If $\mathcal{I}$ is a model of $\mathcal{ET}$, and also the model of $\mathcal{EA}$, we can infer that $\mathcal{EA}$ and $\mathcal{ET}$ are consistent or the knowledge base Σ is consistent.

Instance checking problem: (1) If the event e is the instance of the event E, $\mathcal{I}$ is an arbitrary model of a knowledge base Σ. We can infer that $e^{\mathcal{I}} \in E^{\mathcal{I}}$ or $\mathcal{E} \vDash e$; (2) If events x and y are the instance of the events E and F, and there are a relation r between the two events. $\mathcal{I}$ is an arbitrary model of a knowledge base Σ. We can infer that $<x^{\mathcal{I}}, y^{\mathcal{I}}> \in r^{\mathcal{I}}$ or $\mathcal{EA} \vDash (x, y) \in r$.

5 Related Work and Conclusions

Description Logics have been studied extensively in field AI over the last two decades. Especially, research works on extensions of DL make significant progress. A.Artale and E.Franconi [10] presented a class of interval-based temporal description logics for uniformly representing and reasoning about actions and plans, actions are represented by describing what is true while the action itself is occurring, and plans are constructed by temporally relating actions and world states. In [11], Frank Wolter constructed modal description logics with an expressive modal component, which allows applications of modal operators to all kinds of DL syntactic terms. Baader [8] presented a framework for integrating DLs and action formalisms into a decidable hybrid formalism, this framework allows the use of DL concepts for describing the state of the world, and the pre and post-conditions of actions. L Chang and Shi presented a dynamic description logic (DDL) [12] by combination of a typical action theory and the description logic ALCO@, it has been used to represent knowledge of dynamic application domains and as the logical foundation of semantic web. Research works above focus on representing one aspect (dynamic actions, temporal information, or uncertain information) of event features rather than regard event as a whole knowledge unit.

Event is a knowledge unit with bigger granularity than concept, it is dynamic and of state-changing, and there exists variety of uncertain relations between different events. So, it is necessary to integrate existing research results from DLs and construct an overall proposal for representing and reasoning event-oriented knowledge. In this paper, we have defined an event ontology framework and presented a first proposal for event-oriented description logic (EDL) by combining the research results from dynamic logics, modal logics and temporal logics with traditional description logics. A case showed that the proposed language is reasonable for modeling and reasoning event classes and non-taxonomic relationships of events. Our further study work will focus on extension of tableau algorithms for EDL's inference and construction of extended OWL language for event ontology.

Acknowledgement

This paper is supported by the Natural Science Foundation of China,No. 60975033 and Shanghai Leading Academic Discipline Project, No. J50103.

References

1. Nelson, K., Gruendel, J.: Event knowledge: structure and function in development. Erlbaum, Hillsdale (1986)
2. Zacks, J.M., Tversky, B.: Event structure in perception and conception. Psychological Bulletin 127(1), 3–21 (2001)
3. Filatova, E., Hatzivassiloglou, V.: Domain-independent detection, extraction, and labeling of atomic events. In: Proceedings of RANLP, Borovetz, Bulgaria, pp. 145–152 (2003)
4. Liu, Z., Huang, M., et al.: Research on event-oriented ontology. Computer Science 36(11), 126–130 (2009)
5. Bechhofer, S., van Harmelen, F., Hendler, J., Horrocks, I., et al.: OWL web ontology language reference (February 2004), http://www.w3.org/TR/owl-ref/
6. Baader, F., Calvanese, D., McGuinness, D., Nardi, D., Patel-Schneider, P. (eds.): The Description Logic Handbook. Cambridge University Press, Cambridge (2002)
7. Zhongzhi, S., Mingkai, D., Yuncheng, J., Zhang, H.: A logical foundation for the semantic Web. Science in China (Series F) 48(2), 161–178 (2005)
8. Baader, F., Lutz, C., Milicic, M., Sattler, U., Wolter, F.: Integrating description logics and action formalisms: First results. In: Proceedings of AAAI 2005, July 2005, pp. 572–577 (2005)
9. Baader, F., Horrocks, I., Sattler, U.: Description Logics. In: van Harmelen, F., Lifschitz, V., Porter, B. (eds.) Handbook of Knowledge Representation, Elsevier, Amsterdam (2007)
10. Artale, A., Franconi, E.: A Temporal Description Logic for Reasoning about Actions and Plans. Journal of Artificial Intelligence Research 9, 463–506 (1998)
11. Wolter, F., Zakharyaschev, M.: Modal Description Logics: Modalizing Roles. Fundamentae Informaticae 39, 411–438 (1999)
12. Chang, L., Shi, Z., Qiu, L., Lin, F.: Dynamic Description Logic: Embracing Actions into Description Logic. In: Proceedings of the 20th International Workshop on Description Logic (DL 2007), pp. 243–250 (2007)

An Empirical Analysis of Revisit Behaviors of Monthly Subscription-Based Mobile Video Services

Toshihiko Yamakami

ACCESS, CTO Office,
2-8-16 Sarugaku-cho, Chiyoda-ku, Tokyo, Japan
Toshihiko.Yamakami@access-company.com
http://www.access-company.com/

Abstract. The Mobile Internet is becoming a first-class citizen of the Internet in many advanced countries. It is also increasing its broadband capabilities with 3G penetration. As increased penetration and bandwidth leverage mobile application business opportunities, it is important to identify methodologies for serving mobile-specific demands. Regularity is one of the important means of retaining and enclosing *easy-come, easy-go* mobile users. It is known that users with multiple visits in one day and a long interval have a higher possibility of revisiting in the following month than others. The author applies this empirical law to his investigation of the mobile broadband services. The result shows that the method proposed for the text-based mobile services is also applicable to mobile video services in the mobile broadband context. The author shows that the method based with 2 bits per day can provide results that can be used for classifying monthly-scale regular users in the case study.

Keywords: mobile Internet, user behavior, revisit analysis.

1 Introduction

The "Mobile Internet" has become increasingly visible and continues to prove its penetration in real-world applications. Also, mobile broadband services starts to penetrate into real life. The percentage of 3G users reached 93 % of mobile subscribers in Japan in March 2009. Its any-time and any-place characteristics facilitate the addition of value to data services. The penetration of the mobile Internet continues to reveal new aspects of human behavior, with a large amount of access log data. It provides a new research question as to how the mobile broadcast service user's behavior differ from those of narrowband mobile users. Mobile handsets have small-sized screens even in the mobile broadband context, and therefore, it is difficult to retain and enclose end users due to the limited amount of information. It is crucial to increase end-user loyalty, and to enclose them in mobile services. For subscription-based mobile customers, it is more important to evaluate the long-term regularity of visits rather than the total number of visits. Past research in the mobile narrowband context indicates that users with multiple visits in one day, and a long interval, have a higher

R.-S. Chang et al. (Eds.): GPC 2010, LNCS 6104, pp. 482–491, 2010.

probability of revisiting possibility in the following month than other users. The author examines the applicability of this law to a mobile broadband service using commercial video service logs.

2   Background

2.1   Purpose of Research

The aim of this research is to identify the applicability of an empirical law which states that users with multiple visits in one day, with a long interval, have a higher probability of revisiting in the following month than the other users, to the mobile broadband context.

2.2   Related Works

The dynamics and volatility of mobile Internet services has prevented long-term observational studies. The first large-scale mobile Internet analysis was done by Halvey. He reported a positive correlation to the day of the week in the mobile clickstream [4]. Yamakami conducted a regularity study of mobile clickstreams and reported 80 % accuracy in the number of users that revisited the following month using statistical data on regularity [9]. It is still an active topic for researchers to study how many different types of regularity behaviors people show and how stable each behavior is over a long period of time.

Enclosing customers is the most crucial issue in e-commerce. The discussion about e-loyalty to Web sites started in the very early stages of e-commerce [8]. E-loyalty was discussed by Cyr for e-commerce [1] and [2]. Stickiness was argued by Li from a relationship perspective [6]. However, the question how to measure it in the mobile commerce context is still an unexplored field.

Mining data streams is a field of increasing interest due to the importance of its applications and the dissemination of data stream generators. Research dealing with continuously generated, massive amounts of data has caught the attention of researchers in recent days [3] [5]. Considering the fast growth of the mobile Internet, it is an important research topic to be covered.

Mobile clickstream analysis is a relatively unexplored field of research because there are still WML1.3-based mobile Internet sites used in many countries. The WML deck consists of multiple cards, where many user clicks are absorbed within the client and not available to servers.

Yamakami proposed an early version of the time slot method, to identify regular users with a long interval of sub-day web visits [11]. The method was coined on the conjecture that users who come to a web service twice in one day tend to return to the service the following month [10].

In stream mining, given the constraints of storage, it is desirable to identify the outcome in an on-the-fly manner. The modified method was proposed to incorporate the two major mobile constraints: distributed server environments and large data stream [9] [12].

The originality of this paper lies in its examination of the applicability of the previous method to the mobile broadband context.

3 Requirements

The following requirements exist:

Efficient Large-scale Mining Requirement. In order to cope with a large mobile user base, it is desirable to pack each item of user data into one-word (32-bit) memory in an efficient way. Assuming it to be process-able for one million users, 20 bits are required to store the ID. In order to get one-percent accuracy, it requires 7 more bits. This allows only 5 bits for the regularity mining work area.

One-path Constraint. With a large volume of data stream, it is realistic to perform an algorithm in a one-path manner. In other words, each click is processed only once during stream processing. There is no centralized server to sort and store all the click logs.

Distributed Server Configuration Requirements. In order to accomplish load balancing, it is common to use a distributed server configuration. In this distributed configuration, it is realistic to distribute clickstream among multiple servers. It is reasonable to assume that some of the server logs will have time lag when they arrive at an analysis system.

4 Method

The author performed a preliminary study of commercial mobile broadcast Internet users using clickstream logs. The patterns obtained indicated that users that return to a Web site after a certain length of time have a greater probability of returning to the same Web site the following month.

In order to capture this rule in an efficient method, Yamakami proposed a method called the *time slot count in a window method (TCW-method)* [11]. The author uses a 24 hour window size with 12-hour time slots in this paper to simplify analysis. The previous research using the TCW-method showed that a minimum bit count of 2 is usable and most efficient in storage utilization. The time slot is set to 12 hours and the time slot threshold value is 2, which means a user needs to visit during both 12-hour time slots in a day in order to be classified as a long-term regular user. 2 bits (bits A and B) are allocated for each user. For the initial state, these bits are set to 0. Bit B represents that the user is marked as a "long-term regular user". When a user visits a particular mobile Web site in the first half of a day, bit A is set to 1. If a user visits the same Web site in the second half of the day and bit A is 1, then bit B is set to 1. If bit A is 0, then nothing is done. If bit B is 0, when a day completes, then bit A is reset to 0. After repeating this process on all the days in a month, then the users with 1 at bit B are the users who are estimated to be long-term regular users. These users have a high probability of revisiting the site in the following month. This method is simple and easy to implement. There is a variation of this that uses more bits per day, however, the past research shows that using 2 bits for one day give the highest true positive ratio for this binary classification.

The processing flow is illustrated in Fig. 1.

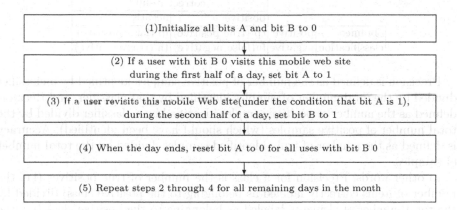

Fig. 1. Processing flow of the TCW method (24-hour window, 12-hour time slot, threshold 2)

This method is robust for distributed server configurations when there is an additional bit to allow delayed transfer of logs. When there are multiple servers and they transfer the user logs to the log analysis server in an asynchronous and unpredictable manner, this method requires one more bit to allow for when the first half of data arrives after some of the second half of daily data. If the extra bit is allowed, it also satisfies the one-path requirement. All the data can be processed in a one-path manner, without having to store the logs and process them in multiple paths.

When the above condition is met, the proposed method is efficient because it accommodates one-path process of random-order arrival of logs from distributed servers. It fits the mobile Internet log analysis requirements.

5   Case Study

5.1   Revisit Ratio

The author uses a revisit ratio to evaluate the classification of regular users. The revisit ratio $R(U, m)$ in month m for a group of users U is defined as follows where $A(U, m)$ are users in U that access content (any URL in a given Web site) in month m:

$$R(U, m) = \frac{\mid A(U, m) \cap A(U, m+1) \mid}{\mid A(U, m) \mid}$$

Where U_a is all users that access content in month m, $R(U_a, m)$ represents the total revisit ratio for month m active users. When the active users for month m are split into subgroups, $U_1, U_2, \ldots, R(U_1, m), R(U_2, m), \ldots$ denotes the revisit ratio for each user group.

The classification is defined as follows:

		correct result	
		positive	negative
obtained	positive	tp (true positive)	fp (false positive)
classification	negative	fn (false negative)	tn (true negative)

Precision is defined as the number of positive samples identified by a classifier divided by the total number of samples identified by that classifier, and Recall is defined as the number of positive samples identified by a classifier divided by the total number of positive samples (which should have been identified). Accuracy is defined as the number of truly identified samples divided by the total number of samples.

In other words, Precision for a class is the number of true positives (i.e. the number of items correctly labeled as belonging to the positive class) divided by the total number of elements labeled as belonging to the positive class (i.e. the sum of true positives and false positives, which are items incorrectly labeled as belonging to the class). Recall is defined as the number of true positives divided by the total number of elements that actually belong to the positive class (i.e. the sum of true positives and false negatives, which are items that were not labeled as belonging to the positive class but should have been). Accuracy is the sum of the true positives and true negatives divided by the total samples.

F-measure, which combines Precision and Recall, is the harmonic mean of precision and recall. Generally, F-measure is a weighted measure, however, we use F_1-measure where we apply the same weight to Recall and Precision.

$$Precision = \frac{tp}{(tp + fp)}$$

$$Recall = \frac{tp}{(tp + fn)}$$

$$Accuracy = \frac{tp + tn}{(tp + tn + fn + fp)}$$

$$F - measure = 2 * \frac{precision + recall}{(precision + recall)}$$

5.2 Data Set

The subject of observation is a commercial video service on the mobile Internet. This service was launched in 2007.

The user ID (UID), time stamp, command name, and content shorthand name are stored in the standard Apache log. The content is adult movies, which a user can enjoy in a stream mode or in a download mode. The commercial mobile service charges at monthly subscription fee to users, approximately 5 US dollars per month. Each channel charges this fee. There are 48 category channels. When a user subscribes to a category channel with the fee, he/she watches all the content in the category channel during the month.

There are 188,926 valid unique users in March 2009 and 182,230 in April 2009. There are 16,667,364 lines of log files in March 2009 and 17,708,308 in April 2009. The analysis is done only on the Web log without the user subscription database. An approximate classification of subscriptions was done from a log containing URLs that are accessible for only by subscribed users. From this approximation, the log contains 47,912 subscribed users, and 141,015 non-subscribed users. For subscribed users, the revisit ratio in April 2009 was 60.24 %. For non-subscribed users, it was 26.23 %. The log contains 0.5–0.7 million lines for each day. The peak access hours are around the midnight, 22:00-02:00. It should be noted that the system uses a Content Delivery Network for efficiency of image and video delivery. Images and videos are cached once they are accessed, and there is no successive log left in the Web server side. It is impossible to access images and videos directly, without prior web page access, therefore, this does not impact the revisit ratio analysis.

5.3 Result

The author performed Welch's t test for prediction and reality data. R is used to perform the test with t.test() [7]. The test summary is depicted in Table 1. The (0,1) vector of all users represents the revisit reality. The test examines how significant the proposed method's identification capability is for regular users, in other words, users with multiple time slot visits in a window are compared to all users that access content in the given Web site during the month.

Table 1. Welch's t test summary

Alternative hypothesis	True difference in means of two samples is not equal to 0
Sample 1	(0,1) vector of all users with multiple time slot visits in a window where 0 means no revisit in the following month 1 means a revisit in the following month
Sample 2	(0,1) vector of all users with news access in the month
Tool	R's t.test()

For subscribed users, the true positive ratio for binary classification of revisit users is 90.39 %. It is 47.40 % for non-subscribed users.

In the following tables, R(all) denotes the revisit ratio of all users the following month. The month is obvious from the month column, therefore, the second parameter month for R is omitted. R(TC) denotes the revisit ratio of users identified by the TCW method in the following month. The author performed a case study in March and April 2009 with 12-hour time slots. The users who visited the mobile site during the first and second half of one day are marked as the potential revisiting users.

The observed service is a mobile commercial video service in Japan.

The result is depicted in Table 2. The t test gives a 1 % confidence level of significance in all the cases.

For the charged user case, the true positive ratio is 90.39 % under the overall revisit ratio of charged users it is 60.24 %. Past research on a text-based news service during 2001-2002 showed a 85–95 % true positive ratio under a 50–70 overall revisit ratio. The results obtained from a recent mobile broadband service match the past results.

Table 2. Revisit Ratio in March 2009

Type	R(TCW)	R (all)	t-value	degree of freedom	p-value	significance
Total	81.03	34.86	-154.363	26416.3	0.0000	**
Subscribed	90.39	60.24	-90.644	39552.6	0.0000	**
Non-subscribed	56.86	26.23	-45.344	5890.8	0.0000	**

Note:
**: 1 % confidence level
*: 5 % confidence level

6   Discussion

6.1   Advantage of 12-Hour TCW Method

The proposed TCW method shows a promising true positive ratio, as well as a minimum storage requirement. This fits the daily user behavior patterns. With the 12-hour time slot, it gives the maximum storage efficiency using only 2-bits.

6.2   Advantages of the Proposed Method

The proposed method has the advantage that it does not depend on the final state. When the count of time slots with user visits reaches a certain threshold value, all the subsequent clickstream for the user can be safely discarded because the later results do not impact the final identification. The 2+1 bit TCW method maintains this advantage.

There is always a trade-off between a high true positive ratio and wide coverage. When a high true positive ratio is pursued, it will focus on the small group, therefore, the derived association rule can be applied to a small portion of the samples. When wide coverage is pursued, it is difficult to obtain the high true positive ratio of the derived rules. If a higher true positive ratio is required for applications, it will require the sacrifice of wide coverage.

This method can be applied to a wide range of mobile applications with time stamped logs. It is a key advantage of the proposed method.

6.3   Applications

It is important to identify what applications can use this measure to realize value-added services in the mobile Internet. For example, a high revisit ratio like 90 %

can be used as a measure of the impact of new services or new user interfaces. The revisit ratio can be used as a litmus test to measure the effectiveness of new services or new user interfaces.

It is difficult to capture user feedback on the mobile Internet because the user interface is limited and the user does not want to perform additional input to give service feedback. It is feasible for content providers to differentiate between users with high retention and others in their services. It could improve the user capture and retention rate of mobile services.

NTTDoCoMo enabled all content providers (both official carrier's and non-official Web sites) to use i-mode ID (their unique user identifier system) starting in March 2008. In the past, the use of a unique user identifier was restricted to only carrier-approved official sites. This new carrier movement increased the applicability of user-identifier-based research methods.

6.4   Implications for the Mobile User Behavior

It is interesting that the results are positive both in the 2001 context, and in the 2009 context. The network speed, content type, and mobile user experience are different, however, it still provides a positive result. The mobile handset screen still has a limited real estate. In order to enclose mobile users, it is crucial that the services maintain a certain mind share of a user over a certain range of time, e.g. 30 minutes. The rate of user mental recall on a sub-day time scale seems important for capturing and retaining end users.

The mobile business model shifted twice over the passed 9 years. In the early days, it was crucial to enclose the early adopters within the walled garden model. The number of mobile Internet users was limited, therefore, the payments were the major source of revenue for mobile content providers. In the middle stages, the services became open, and the ad-based business model emerged with social network services. It was difficult to call friends to join fee-based services. Some Japanese mobile social network services explored this direction. Then, there came the second shift. Free services attracted users with a high sensitivity to paying/purchasing. This was not good for advertisers. In order to compensate for this weakness, the newly emerged social network services customized their business model, e.g. with item purchasing. In the item purchase business model, end users will purchase specially featured items in their games and social network services.

This business model shift also leverages the importance of measuring user stickiness and loyalty to a mobile Web site.

It should be also noted that pull user behaviors persist over a long span of time even with drastic technology advances and accumulated mobile user experience. The text news services and on-demand video services are quite different, however, the importance of sub-day scale recall ability is still largely unchanged.

6.5   Limitations

Each service has its own characteristics. This research has limitations because it was performed on a single service. The limitations include (a) service-specific (the result came from news services), and (b) profile-specific (75 % of users were male).

This observation is based on a Japanese case study. In Japan, there is only one time zone. When this method is applied to a country with large time zone differences, it may need some refinement in order to define a one-day behavior time scale.

The detailed analysis of observed services are not covered in this paper. Even though the update interval of observed content is less regular than the content described in past literature (news services), this lack of analysis on content characteristics places a limitation of this paper.

The other intervals than 12 hours are not covered in this paper. From past literature, the length of the time slot had a minor effect on the true positive ratio. However, this lack of comparison is another limitation of this work.

7   Conclusion

The mobile Internet has become increasingly visible and continues to prove its penetration in real-world applications.

Mobile Internet business providers want to turn their raw data into new science, technology and business. The author conjectured that a user that show multiple visits to a mobile Web site on any day in a given month, has a high tendency to visit the site the following month.

Analysis of the mobile Internet needs to cope with its mobile-specific requirements: efficient large-scale data mining requirements, one-path requirements, and distributed server configuration requirements. Considering the stream-mining requirement of the mobile Internet, the author relaxed the time slot count method in order to match large-scale data in a distributed environment. The data should be processed with the one-path mechanism, allowing for the delay of log arrival.

In this paper, the author examined the TCW method in a mobile broad band service. The method that showed a good true positive ratio in the past for the text-based service also shows promising results for mobile broadband services. The 2 bits for one day method is effective in capturing day-based user behavior patterns in mobile services. The method is simple and reliable.

There is a growing trend of wireless carriers that are releasing their unique user identifier system to the open public. This will increase the importance and usability of user-behavior-based research methods for capturing mobile Internet user behaviors, which will facilitate and leverage improvements of mobile Internet applications.

Increasing visibility of device convergence, including mobile handsets, music players, digital TVs and digital cameras, leads to an increased importance for enclosing and retaining end users by mobile Internet services. The result in this paper provides a promising clue for service development in the device convergence era.

References

1. Cyr, D., Bonanni, C., ilsever, J.: Innovation, management & strategy: Design and e-loyalty across cultures in electronic commerce. In: Proceedings of the 6th international conference on Electronic commerce ICEC 2004, pp. 351–360. ACM Press, New York (2004)
2. Cyr, D., Head, M., Ivanov, A.: Design aesthetics leading to m-loyalty in mobile commerce. Information and Management 43(8), 950–963 (2006)
3. Gaber, M.M., Zaslavsky, A., Krishnaswamy, S.: Mining data streams: a review. ACM SIGMOD Record 34(2), 18–26 (2005)
4. Halvey, M., Keane, M., Smyth, B.: Predicting navigation patterns on the mobile-internet using time of the week. In: WWW 2005, pp. 958–959. ACM Press, New York (2005)
5. Jiang, N., Gruenwald, L.: Research issues in data stream association rule mining. ACM SIGMOD Record 35(1), 14–19 (2006)
6. Li, D., Browne, G., Wetherbe, J.: Why do internet users stick with a specific web site? a relationship perspective. International Journal of Electronic Commerce 10(4), 105–141 (2006)
7. R Development Core Team: R: A language and environment for statistical computing. R Foundation for Statistical Computing, Vienna, Austria (2005), ISBN 3-900051-07-0, http://www.R-project.org
8. Smith, E.R.: e-Loyalty: How to Keep Customers Coming Back to Your Website. HarperInformation, New York (2000)
9. Yamakami, T.: A 4+1 bit month-scale regularity mining algorithm with one-path and distributed server constraints for mobile internet. In: Takizawa, M., Barolli, L., Enokido, T. (eds.) NBiS 2008. LNCS, vol. 5186, pp. 232–241. Springer, Heidelberg (2008)
10. Yamakami, T.: A long interval method to identify regular monthly mobile internet users. In: AINA2008 Workshops/Symposium (WAMIS 2008), pp. 1625–1630. IEEE Computer Society Press, Los Alamitos (2008)
11. Yamakami, T.: A time slot count in window method suitable for long-term regularity-based user classification for mobile internet. In: MUE 2008, pp. 25–29. IEEE Computer Society Press, Los Alamitos (2008)
12. Yamakami, T.: A space-optimal month-scale regularity mining method with one-path and distributed server constraints for mobile internet. In: ICMB 2009, p. 42. IEEE Computer Society, Los Alamitos (2009)

A One-Seg Service Development Model: Ecosystem Considerations in the Context of Mobile Communication/Broadcast Convergence

Toshihiko Yamakami

ACCESS, CTO Office,
2-8-16 Sarugaku-cho, Chiyoda-ku, Tokyo, Japan
Toshihiko.Yamakami@access-company.com
http://www.access-company.com/

Abstract. Business model engineering is crucial in the context of convergence of mobile communications and broadcasting. The author presents a stage model of one-seg service evolution from lessons learned with one-seg in Japan. The author focuses awareness on the stages in the complicated relationship between stake-holders. With the examination of the transitions between stages, the author also proposes a three-dimensional fit model for mobile services. The author discusses the chronological order of fit identification during the stage transitions. This service transition with fit exploration and staged view is not specific to one-seg. Therefore, it can be applied to a wide range of mobile service development that incorporates new technological elements. It should be noted that the mobile technology brings a new perspective to service development using mobility. Mobile services require long-term incremental fit exploration which is crucial in mobile service development.

Keywords: one-seg, mobile service evolution.

1 Introduction

One-seg (1seg) is a mobile terrestrial digital audio/video and data broadcasting service in Japan, Brazil, Peru, Argentina and Chile. Experimental service began in Japan, in 2005 and commercial service began on April 1, 2006. In Brazil, broadcasting started in late 2007 in just a few cities, with a different transmission rate from Japanese 1seg: a 30 frames/sec transmission, while in Japan they use a transmission rate of 15 frames/sec. The first mobile phone handsets for 1seg were sold to consumers by KDDI in autumn 2005.

ISDB-T [2], the terrestrial digital broadcast system used in Japan and Brazil, is designed so that each channel is divided into 13 segments, with a further segment separating one channel from the next channel. An HDTV broadcast signal occupies 12 segments, leaving the remaining (13th) segment for mobile receivers. This is where the name, "1seg" or "One-Seg" is derived from.

Starting in 2009, Japan removed the obligation of simultaneous broadcasting and, therefore, one-seg can now distribute one-seg specific content. This is an important cornerstone for the development of one-seg business model.

R.-S. Chang et al. (Eds.): GPC 2010, LNCS 6104, pp. 492–501, 2010.

The author summarizes the lessons learned through 4 years of experience with one-seg services in Japan. Then, the author presents the implications it has for business model development in the context of mobile communication/broadcast convergence.

2 Purpose and Related Works

2.1 Purpose of Research

The purpose of this research is to identify a stage model of the convergence of broadcast/mobile communication services.

2.2 Related Works

One-seg is a standard developed in Japan [2]. One-seg has been successfully deployed in Japan, however, the many countries follow the other standards of DVB-H and MediaFLO. The past literature did not address one-seg based interaction either from a technical or a service perspective.

Some of the past one-seg literature did not address service development model in the emerging new interactivity model [6].

One-seg has relatively little visibility in the International studies, therefore, the business model research on this domain has been limited.

The fragmentations from having multiple international standards were discussed by Steen [9]. This is a clear obstacle to the successful proliferation of the mobile digital TV. However, we do not see any near-term solution to this fragmentation.

From the comparison of different digital mobile TV services, there is some existing literature from a technical perspective [7]. Also, a survey of usability study was presented by Buchinger to highlight open issues [3].

The convergence of communication and broadcasting attracted researchers' attention especially in terms of the business model development [5] [10]. Feijóo discussed the heterogeneous and fragmented nature of mobile content from the perspective of ecosystem [4].

On the human interface side, the discussions involve the TV viewing context [8] [11], and content customization [1].

Yamakami discussed a view of one-seg services as a mobile glue [12]. However, the one-seg based business model development was not been covered very well in past literature.

3 Method

The author uses the following methodology:

- analyze the launch of one-seg services, and
- analyze the launch of non-simultaneous one-seg content

The launch of one-seg services is analyzed with the following aspects:

- chasm analysis
- business conflicts among stakeholders
- lessons for coping with the chasms

The launch of non-simultaneous one-seg content is analyzed from what aspects have been highlighted in the departure from the simultaneous content.

4   Case Studies

4.1   Stake Holder Relationships in Mobile Services

TV is available in almost every households. This penetrates into everyday life in a deep manner. When we talk about mobile TV, we have to pay attention to the difficult relationships between stake holders. In any network-based service development, they have to be aware of the triangular relationship depicted in Fig. 1.

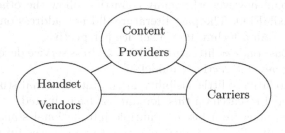

Fig. 1. Triangular relationship between stake holders in mobile services

In the mobile one-seg services, content is split into datacast content and web content. The datacast content is mostly distributed by the TV broadcasters.

Commercial TV broadcasters depend on advertisement revenue in Japan. The advertisement-based business model requires a certain critical mass, e.g. 10 million users in Japan.

4.2   Chasm Analysis

There are chasms for the all of stake holders in one-seg services. Without the penetration of TV-enabled handsets, it is difficult for datacast or web content providers to make any revenue predictions. For TV-enabled handset penetration, it is important that wireless carriers take risks to subsidize TV-enabled handsets. This is a challenge for wireless carriers because watching TV does not provide wireless carriers any new revenues. For datacast content providers, it is important to create new revenue models. Watching TV on handsets will not convince advertisers to pay extra for one-seg handsets.

From this analysis, the author proposes the following chasm model depicted in Table 1. The handset chasm is common to any mobile services that require new capabilities in the handset. The handset subsidy chasm is crucial when new capabilities introduce additional cost factors for handset manufacturing. When new costs are not covered by end users, this chasm is a clear obstacle for the

Table 1. Chasms

Type	Description
Handset chasm	The number of purchased TV-enabled and one-seg datacast-enabled handsets purchased does not form a critical mass.
Handset subsidy chasm	Wireless carriers do not take the risk to subsidize TV-enabled handsets.
Use chasm	Users simply watch TV, without making use of one-seg interactive features.
Datacast content chasm	Datacast content providers cannot identify appropriate business models.

handset chasm. The use chasm is common where user-adoption is a challenge. The datacast content chasm is unique to one-seg because it requires a special player for transmission.

The handset chasm can be overcome by making a cheap handset. This usually leads to a handset subsidy chasm because the advantage is clear to end users as far as the handset is being reasonably cheap. In one case in Japan, the standardization body agreed to prohibit one-seg handsets without one-seg browser function. Prior to this decision, we observed the following business conflicts between the two major stakeholders, wireless carriers and TV broadcasters, as depicted in Table 2.

Both players have some shared issues:

- Both are based on a regulatory business,
- Both have limited visibility of the emerging one-seg business models, and
- Both are nation-wide influential service business players.

This handset subsidy chasm is often solved when the wireless carriers take the risk in order to protect or expand their consumer base. When a wireless carrier does not see the value in bundling the one-seg functions into handsets, it will pose a significant obstacle to one-seg user acceptance.

4.3   Carrier and TV Broadcaster Relationship

In the following three stages, depicted in Fig. 2, the collaboration between wireless carriers and TV broadcasters is critical.

The basic standpoint of TV broadcasters is that they expect wireless carriers to ship (through subsidiary money) more one-seg enabled handsets with reasonable pricing. When wireless carriers agree to collaborate and share one-seg content business with TV broadcasters, it will provide forward motion. Also, when wireless carriers think their market share will be challenged by one-seg bundled phones, they will drive the shipment of one-seg empowered handsets. In the case in Japan, this view drove wireless carriers to increase shipment of one-seg handsets.

Table 2. Conflict of interests between wireless carriers and TV broadcasters

Players	Wireless carriers	TV broadcasters
Handset Cost	Sensitive	Out of scope
One-seg browser specs	Low to cut costs and increase carrier-specific differentiation	High to secure a rich user experience.
TV view time	Competes with time spend on communication	Longer, better
Motivation	Enclosing light data service users	Providing interactive TV experience
Weak point	Datacast is managed by TV broadcasters	No solid method to reuse audience rating-based core business
Ownership	Handset display is its own real estate	TV display is its own real estate
Influence on handset vendors	Strong	Weak
Authoring capability	Weak	Strong
Business change speed	Year-scale Service Competition	Same services and business models for passed 50 years

Fig. 2. Three stages of one-seg service adoption

There is a clear contrast between the two key players' business models, as depicted in Table 3.

Table 3. Business comparison between wireless carriers and TV broadcasters

Players	Wireless carriers	TV broadcasters
Service	Pull	Push
Type	Interpersonal	Mass media
Revenue model	Charged	Advertisement
Restriction	Regulation	Existing Sponsors
Position of TV	Trigger to communication services	TV anytime and anyplace

Also, there are some business trend position highlighted in Table 4. These trends are generally positive for wireless carriers.

Table 4. Business trend positions between wireless carriers and TV broadcasters

Players	Wireless carriers	TV broadcasters
Web 2.0	Community-based	Strong media influence on end users, but not quite active
Device convergence	Active player (camera, game console, TV, payment ...)	Passive player
Surrounding services	Strong services in payment, user profile, transaction, et al	Poor

4.4   Business Model Stage

Interactivity provides an advantage for integrated TV content. It facilitates user interactions like voting, blog, rating, user feedbacks and so on.

Mobile services have a strong affinity with communities. TV broadcasting can leverage content-focused community interactions.

It also facilitates leveraging new service platforms which integrate e-payment, location-aware content and so on.

This century is witnessing a drastic shift from synchronous real-time media to asynchronous media. The representative of asynchronous media is the Internet. However, the harmony of real-time and store-and-forward services is still the best match. The push capability of TV broadcasting and the pull capability of Internet provide the best service platform for end users.

One-seg was launched in Japan in April 2006. Currently, 90 % of the new mobile handsets sold have one-seg capability. The accumulated sales of one-seg enabled mobile handsets reached 60 million in Japan. This high penetration makes many end users service-ready for one-seg value-added services.

In the early stage of one-seg, TV broadcasters considered reusing full-seg content. This business model did not go smoothly however, because full-seg content has multiple business model constraints. For example, the originally full-seg content was paid-for by sponsors, which placed constraints on reuse.

In the second stage of one-seg, other business models were sought out. For example, DOCOMO and Tokai TV performed a region-specific marketing support field trial for troika, where a digital coupon was broadcast by one-seg.

In the third stage, the synergy of broadcasting and mobile communications will be targeted. Outside of one-seg broadcasting, BeeTV was launched in Japan in May 2009. BeeTV is new mobile customized video content, a joint venture between DOCOMO and Avex entertainment. It provides 3-8 minute mobile-friendly original video content via the mobile broadband network.

The differences are highlighted in Table 5.

Table 5. A staged business model

Stage	Initial	Second	Third
Content	Full-seg	E-coupon	Synergy
Key-player	TV broadcaster	Wireless carrier	Joint effort
Focus	Full-seg content	Technologies	Mobile-specific customization

5   A Three-Stage Model of Mobile Service Evolution

The lessons learned from the past evolution of the Japanese one-seg evolution are the followings:

- Conflicts in multi-use source strategy
- Chasms in technology-driven service development

Much of service development forms the following three stage evolution as depicted in Fig. 3.

In the context of any emerging technology, it is difficult to provide context-sensitive content, especially in a rapidly growing domain. The first common approach to dealing with this challenge is to have multiple-use of the existing content, in other words, content reuse. In order to bootstrap new services, it is necessary to convert existing content to fit the emerging contexts. It is usually difficult to identify the exact use context in the early stage, therefore, the chance of success is rather slim. After this stage, if there was not much success with the initial approach, it is common to explore technology-specific aspects.

In the case of one-seg, datacast are not restricted to the region-wide large-scale broadcasts. Area-focused narrow broadcasting is one examples of technology exploration. It is possible to broadcast electronic coupons to people in the region within a 300m by 300m targeted zone. This technology exploration may succeed in some cases. However, even in successful cases, it is necessary to make some match between technical capabilities and service requirements.

During these exploratory stages, content providers learn to use the technology and the exact user requirements in specific use scenes. After this period of learning, it is time to perform real service synthesis to deal with the previous challenges.

Fig. 3. A three-stage model of service development

6   Discussion

6.1   Stage-Specific Aspect

Content Reuse Stage: The reason why the initial stage is the content reuse stage is that every service needs content development in order to fit the new use contexts. At the initial stage, there is no measure to identify what fits the new use context. Therefore, the initial efforts by content providers are a combination of content reuse and content exploration.

Technology Exploration Stage: Identification of content fitness toward the new use context takes time. Therefore, the next exploration is to explore newly available technological features. The chance of identifying the right technology in the right context is not very high. Also, one of the reasons the technology exploration stage comes after the content reuse stage is that technology exploration directly impacts the manufacturing costs, which is not desirable at the early stage of production. As the number of users increases, the initial technology production cost decreases, which opens up a new opportunity to invest more advanced technical factor into the following devices.

Synthesis Stage: After content reuse and technical exploration, the accumulation of measures taken to fit the use context, testing of the newly introduced technologies and the findings of new user reactions follow. After this accumulation, it is possible to define and explore the new service contexts with the new service synthesis.

6.2   Service Fit Model

From the previous discussion, the author proposes the service fit model depicted in Fig. 4. Each dimension corresponds to the above mentioned stage model.

Content-Use fits correspond to the content reuse phase. In this dimension, content providers performs trials on content reuse.

Technology-Use fits correspond to the technology exploration stage. In this dimension, content providers analyze the gap between the expected technology use and the real use.

Use-Business Model fits correspond to the synthesis stage. In this dimension, content providers exploit the ways to provide effective synthesis for generation of revenues.

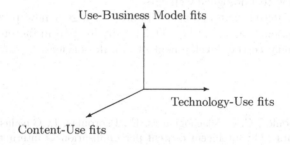

Fig. 4. The service fit model

This model is important because the mobile services bring a new perspective associated with mobility into the business landscape. It requires reexamination of use fits from the perspectives of content, technology and business models.

6.3   Advantages

The three-stage model from content reuse to service synthesis is applicable to a wide range of non-PC services. In particular, one-seg departs from the original TV use context, which is basically at home in a fixed location.

Also, the service fit model provides the three dimensions corresponding the three-stage model. The three-stage model provides the priority to explore the three dimensions.

6.4 Limitations

Limitation of this study includes, a) region-specific observations, and b) descriptive study without any quantitative measures. One-seg is a region-specific standard and further analysis is required to accommodate universal analysis without any region dependence. Also, this study is based on a qualitative description. Measures to be taken to identify chasms and stages remain for further studies.

7 Conclusion

Wide penetration of one-seg in Japan leveraged business opportunities for integrated broadcast/communication services. In order to facilitate mobile service development, it is important to identify the success factors in the one-seg context. The author proposes a three-stage service evolution model. With the examination of the transitions between stages, the author also proposes a three-dimensional fit model for mobile services. The author discusses the chronological order of fit identification during the stage transitions. These service transitions involving fit exploration with a stage view are not specific to one-seg. Therefore, they can be applied to a wide range of mobile service development which incorporates new technological elements.

It should be noted that mobile technology brings a new perspective to the service development using mobility. This is why long-term incremental fit exploration is so crucial to the development of mobile services.

References

1. Anagnostopoulos, C.N., Vlachogiannis, E., Psoroulas, I., Gavalas, D., Tsekouras, G., Konstantas, G.: Intelligent content personalisation in internet tv using mpeg-21. International Journal of Internet Protocol Technology 3(3), 159–169 (2008)
2. Asami, H., Sasaki, M.: Outline of ISDB systems. Proceedings of the IEEE 94(1), 248–250 (2006)
3. Buchinger, S., Kriglstein, S., Hlavacs, H.: A comprehensive view on user studies: survey and open issues for mobile tv. In: EuroITV 2009, pp. 179–188. ACM, New York (2009)
4. Feijóo, C., Maghiros, I., Abadie, F., Gómez-Barroso, J.L.: Exploring a heterogeneous and fragmented digital ecosystem: Mobile content. Telematics and Informatics 26(3), 282–292 (2009)
5. Funk, J.L.: The emerging value network in the mobile phone industry: The case of japan and its implications for the rest of the world. Telecommunications Policy 33(1-2), 4–18 (2009)
6. Maia, O.B., Vicente Ferreira de Lucena, J.: A communication infrastructure between the brazilian interactive digital tv and residential devices. In: EuroITV 2009, pp. 115–118. ACM, New York (2009)
7. Oksman, V., Tammela, A., Kivinen, T.: 'a tv in the pocket': an experimentation of mobile tv delivery technologies: Dvb-h, 3g and podcasting. In: Mobility 2007, pp. 507–511. ACM, New York (2007)

8. Saleemi, M.M., Björkqvist, J., Lilius, J.: System architecture and interactivity model for mobile tv applications. In: DIMEA 2008, pp. 407–414. ACM, New York (2008)
9. Steen, H.U.: The fragmentation of standards in mobile digital broadcast carriers. In: ICMB 2007, p. 11. IEEE Compuer Society, Los Alamitos (2007)
10. Tadayoni, R., Henten, A., Skouby, K.E.: Mobile tv as part of imt advanced: Technology, market development, business models and regulatory challenges. Wireless Personal Communications: An International Journal 45(4), 585–595 (2008)
11. Ursu, M.F., Thomas, M., Kegel, I., Williams, D., Tuomola, M., Lindstedt, I., Wright, T., Leurdijk, A., Zsombori, V., Sussner, J., Myrestam, U., Hall, N.: Interactive tv narratives: Opportunities, progress, and challenges. Transactions on Multimedia Computing, Communications, and Applications 4(4), 25 (2008)
12. Yamakami, T.: An interactivity model of mobile interactive tv: A one-seg case for mobile glue. In: ICIS 2009, pp. 212–217. ACM, New York (2009)

A Mechanism for Solving the Sequential Inconsistent Event in a Peer-to-Peer Network Virtual Environment

Jui-Fa Chen[1], Wei-Chuan Lin[2], Kun-Hsiao Tsai[1], Yu-Yu Cho[1], and Cheng-Yu Yu[1]

[1] Department of Information Engineering, TamKang University
alpha@mail.tku.edu.tw
[2] Department of Information Technology, Tak-Ming University of Science and Technology
wayne@takming.edu.tw

Abstract. As the prevailing of the Peer-to-Peer (P2P) computation recently, there are many applications had been proposed for P2P Networked Virtual Environment (NVE). However, there are still many problems in the P2P NVE such as event consistency, responsiveness, security, scalability, and reliability … etc. The event consistency can be divided into two problems such as causal and sequential consistency. In sequential consistency, when many avatars are competing for a resource and sending the allocating message to the server, who can get the resource? It is very important for these avatars to receive the consistent information. This paper proposes an information exchange mechanism to make sure that avatars can receive the event consistent information. When avatars are competing for a resource in a P2P NVE, the problem of sequential consistency can be solved by using the ACK packet and priority mechanism.

Keywords: Peer-to-Peer, Event Consistency, Sequential Consistency, Causal Consistency.

1 Introduction

As the prevailing of the distributed computing environment recently, there are many applications had been proposed based on the Peer-to-Peer (P2P) network virtual environment (NVE). The issues of P2P NVE include event consistency, bandwidth limitation, responsiveness, security, scalability, reliability … etc. The event consistency is more complicated than the others. Event inconsistency would happen when all players receive the packet of different orders because of network latency.

Event consistency can be divided into two problems such as causal and sequential consistent. Causal consistency is that operations which are causally related must be seen in causal order by all processes. For example, throws a stone into a pond, spray should be splashed up. If we see splashes happen first and have not seen the stone is thrown to the pond, this is the casual inconsistency. Sequential consistency means that the behavior of a set of operations would be as if the operations were performed in some serial order consistent with program order. When the event occurred did not follow the sequence of time, it is the sequential inconsistency. For example: if avatar A, B and C are competing for a resource in a P2P NVE, each avatar sends packet to the other two avatars. The order of the packets which each avatar receives might not be the same. For example, the order that the avatar A receives is A, B, C, and the

R.-S. Chang et al. (Eds.): GPC 2010, LNCS 6104, pp. 502–509, 2010.

order which avatar B receive is B, C, A, each avatar regards itself as the winner, this phenomenon is sequential inconsistency. This paper proposes an information exchange mechanism to solve the sequential consistent problem of competing for resources in a P2P NVE.

This paper is organized as follows: Section 2 is the related works. Section 3 describes the proposed system architecture. Section 4 shows the implementation results. Section 5 is the conclusion and future work.

2 Related Works

There are two problems of packet transmission in network such as packet delay and loss. If the packet is not arrived in time, we call it as packet delay. Packet delay might be caused by many reasons such as network bandwidth is not enough, a large size of packet, network latency... etc. If the receiver does not get the packet from the sender in a period of time, it is called as packet loss, and packet delay may also cause packet loss.

The event consistency problem can be divided into causal and sequential consistent. Causal inconsistent deriving from Lamport's [6][7] is known as the "happen before" relation. In [11], for causal consistent, Zhou proposed the "Causal-Receive Order Delivery" which is used in real-time system. Zhou classifies event into two types, one is a local event, and the other is a global event. Local events are listed in order, and mainly used to resolve global events. Based on the "happened before" relation, the causal history [9] of an event e includes all potential causal events happened to the event e. Thus, in order to preserve causality, when receiving a new event, a website should make sure that all the evens in the causal history of the received event had already been processed before processing the newly received event. This is called the causal relation.

Timed consistency which discussed in [10] mainly solves sequential consistency and causal consistency in real-time system. It proposed the time should be also considered in the event happened for preserving a consistent event model. For example, sequential consistency only cares about the operations executed in the distributed system sequentially [7]. Whereas, causal consistency cares about the causally related operations should be seen in the same order by all the websites of the system [1]. On the other hand, the time has been explored in memory systems that have a temporal consistency model (such as delta consistency [8]) and in several website cache consistency protocols [2][3][4]. Torres-Rojas proposes time consistency model which uses time stamp and buffer to let packet wait for a period of time instead of responding immediately (such as reader/writer problem).

3 System Architecture

Each avatar should login into a server and obtain three types of information such as system time, priority and unique ID. The system time is based on the time of login server; each avatar should have the same system time in NVE. Each avatar who has already logged in should also have the same priority and the priority would be set to zero. Each avatar should have different unique ID which is given from a unique login server. In such NVE, each resource would be set up a range which can be accessed, and the range of radius is M. The radius of avatar's Area of Interest (AOI) [5] should be greater and equal to 2M as shown in Fig. 1.

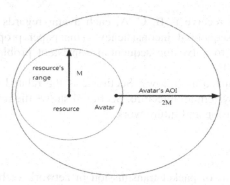

Fig. 1. The relation of avatar and resource

In this paper, we assumed the information exchange mechanism is by direct connection way [5]. A formula is proposed to calculate the numbers of avatar in AOI of a resource as shown in formula 1:

$$Q = N(N-1)*P \tag{1}$$

Q is the total bandwidth in NVE, N is the numbers of avatar in avatar's AOI (including avatar itself), and P is the packet size. The worst case is that if each avatar sends one packet to each others, there are N*(N-1) packets to be sent in each time. Assumed the total bandwidth in NVE is 1Mbytes, the packet size is 1K bytes, according to the formula 1, $N = \sqrt{1024 + N}$. Due to N should be an integer number, the maximum number of N is 32. It means that there are at most 32 avatars in the AOI of avatar A.

Before introducing the proposed information exchange mechanism, some keywords such as a competitor, time T, compete packet, competitor list, competitor list packet and real-competitor should be explained as listed followed:

Definition 1. The competitor is the avatar that wants to compete the resource with other avatars.

Definition 2. Time T is a period of waiting time and may be a constant. If α is Time to Live (TTL) for a packet, the time T for sending a packet and receiving the ACK packet is 2α, in the worst case, $T \geqq 2\alpha$.

Definition 3. When a competitor competes a resource, it should send a compete packet to other avatars which are in the range of resource (including the competitor itself.) Fig. 2 is the format of compete packet; the size of it is 48 bits. Bit 0-bit 23 is system time, bit 24-bit 31 is the priority and bit 32-bit 48 is the unique ID of the avatar.

0	24	32	48
system time		priority	unique ID

Fig. 2. The format of compete packet

Definition 4. The competitor would create a list to storing competitors' data when the competitor wants to send a compete packet. If the competitor received a compete packet from other competitor in a period of waiting time T, the other competitor should be joined to the competitor list.

Definition 5. After waiting for a period of waiting time T, the competitor will sent its own competitor list packet to other avatars which located in the AOI of the resource.

Definition 6. The real-competitors are derived from intersection of all competitor lists. They are avatars that are competing for resource. For example, the competitor list of A is {A, B, C, D}, the competitor list of B is {B, A, C}, the competitor list of C is {C, A, D}, and the competitor list of D is {D, A, C}, the real-competitors are {A, C}, and avatars B and D are not competitors any more.

The proposed information exchange mechanism is divided into four steps.

1.   If a competitor wants to compete for a resource, it should send a compete packet to other avatars within the AOI of the resource as shown in Fig. 3. After received the compete packet from the competitor, other avatars would return an ACK message to the competitor as shown in Fig. 4.
2.   After sending compete packet, the competitor would wait for a period of time. The competitor would compare the timestamp with all received compete packet from other avatars include itself. The waiting time should be the sum of the earliest received timestamp and time T as mentioned in Definition 2. In this way, it can guarantee that all avatars would receive the same consistent information.
3.   Whenever sends the compete packet, the competitor would set up a competitor list to store all competitors' data. As receiving a compete packet from other competitors during the period of the waiting time, the competitor puts the other competitors' data into its competitor list.
4.   After waiting a period of time, the competitor would send its competitor list to all other competitors in the AOI of the resource.

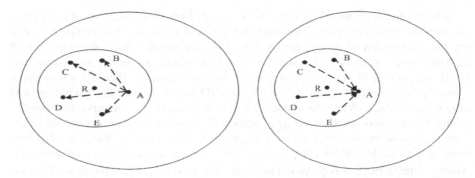

Fig. 3. Competitor A sends messages   **Fig. 4.** Competitor A receives ACK messages

According to the above steps, there are two cases of processing the information exchange to guarantee the information received among avatars is consistent. The main difference between these two situations lies in the waiting time is different. In Fig. 5, the avatar sends a compete packet later than other competitors, the waiting time T starting from the time of avatar sends the compete packet to avatar received other competitor's ACK. In Fig. 6, the avatar sends a compete packet earlier than other competitor, the waiting time T is starting from avatar sends the compete packet to other competitor received the avatar's ACK.

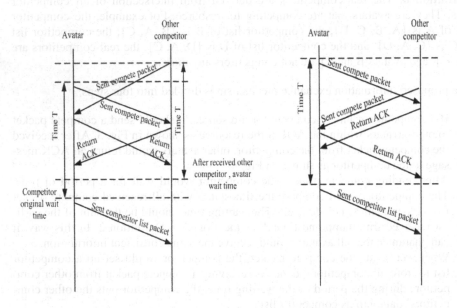

Fig. 5. Avatar sends a compete packet later than other competitor   **Fig. 6.** Avatar sends a compete packet earlier than other competitor

After waiting a period of waiting time T, competitors should receive all competitor list packets from each other. Each competitor would gather the real-competitors that are the intersection of all competitor lists. Each competitor elects the winner with highest priority from the real-competitors, and the winner has power to get resource. If all competitors of real-competitors have the same priority, their ID is compared secondly. The real-competitor with the largest ID would become the winner and can obtain the resource. When the winner obtains the resource, its corresponding priority would be set to zero and the priority of other real-competitors which cannot obtain the resource would be incremented by 1 to promote their priority. Because of packet delay and packet loss, if the compete and ACK packet were not be received during the waiting time, a method is proposed to fix it. Assumed that Δr is the time of packet that had been sent and received, when the competitor sent a compete packet, if the competitor did not receive ACK packet in $2\,\Delta r$, the competitor would send compete packet again every Δr time until the waiting time is over.

4 Implementation

The simulation environment is listed as table 1. The number in table 1 is calculated according to formula 1. Table 2 shows the attributes of the simulated avatars. Before competition resources, the priority of all avatars is set to zero initially. Simulation program runs three times to shown the competition result in Fig. 7. In Fig. 7, suppose that each avatar sends 1000 packets to compete for resources, the result shows each competitor gets 50-70 chances to obtain resources, and there is no avatar that is starved.

The proposed information exchange mechanism is to compare the avatar's priority first and then ID, and elect the winner with the highest priority and ID. From the simulation result, it shows that the chance for each avatar to obtain resources is fair, and also can avoid starvation happened. If the competing rate is increasing, the Fig. 8 shows that the unique ID cannot influence the chance to obtain the resource. This is because that the major concern of proposed information exchange mechanism is the priority of competitors not the unique ID. The factor of unique ID is influenced only when the competing rate is lower than or equal to 25%, the chance for the avatar to obtain resources is varying large.

Table 1. Simulated Environments

Bandwidth	240Kbytes
Packet size	1Kbytes
Avatar number	16
Resource number	1000
Compete rate	50%

Table 2. Avatar attributes

Avatar Name	Priority	Unique ID
A	0	100
B	0	102
C	0	103
D	0	105
E	0	107
F	0	110
G	0	130
H	0	160
I	0	180
J	0	190
K	0	200
L	0	240
M	0	255
N	0	261
O	0	270
P	0	294

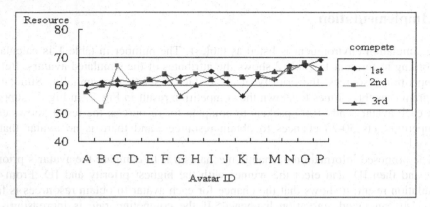

Fig. 7. Resource obtaining result by running 3 times

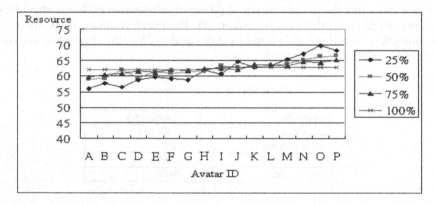

Fig. 8. Resource obtaining result by increasing competing rate

5 Conclusion and Future Work

In this paper, the problem to solve is the sequential event consistent issues of the competing resources among avatars. According to the proposed information exchange mechanism, each avatar could get the same information by sending compete and ACK packet while competing for the resources. From the simulation result, it shows that the avatar with larger unique ID number has the advantage to compete the resource when the competing rate is low. By using the priority mechanism, the resource competed by avatars can be assigned fairly to the avatar and prevented the starvation phenomenon. In this way, the competitors can judge which avatar should get the resource in a fair way and no starvation happened.

In the future, as the proposed information mechanism for guaranteeing avatars can obtain consistent information, each avatar when sent out the compete packet should wait for a period of time to receive the ACK message. As the bandwidth of internet grew larger and larger, the time T proposed by this mechanism can be reduce to react the message exchange quickly. The priority can also be improved by dividing the priority into several ranks to increase the chance of obtaining resource when some of the avatars with low priority.

References

1. Ahamad, M., Neiger, G., Burns, J., Kohli, P., Hutto, P.: Causal memory: definitions, implementation, and programming. Distributed Computing (September 1995)
2. Dilley, J.: The Effect of Consistency on Cache Response Time. IEEE Network 14(3), 24–28 (2000)
3. Cate, V., Alex: A Global File System. In: Proceedings of the 1992 USENIX File System Workshop, May 1992, pp. 1–12 (1992)
4. Gwertzman, J., Seltzer, M.: World-Wide Web Cache Consistency. In: Processing of the 1996 USENIX Technical Conference, San Diego, CA (January 1996)
5. Chen, J.-F., Lin, W.-C.: A Forwarding Model for Voronoi-based Overlay Network. In: International Workshop on Peer-to-Peer Network Virtual Environments, December 5 -7, pp. 77–82 (2007)
6. Lamport, L.: Time, Clocks, and the Ordering the Events in a Distributed System. Communications of the ACM 21(7), 558–565 (1978)
7. Lamport, L.: How to make a Multiprocessor Computer that correctly executes Multiprocess Programs. IEEE Transactions on Computer Systems C-28(9), 690–691 (1979)
8. Singla, A., Ramachandran, U., Hodgins, J.: Temporal Notions of Synchronization and Consistency in Beehive. In: Processing of the Ninth Annual ACM Symposium on Parallel Algorithms and Architectures (June 1997)
9. Schwarz, R., Mattern, F.: Detecting Causal Relationships in Distributed Computations: In Search of the Holy Grail. Distribute Computing 7(3), 149–174 (1994)
10. Torres-Rojas, F.J., Ahamad, M., Raynal, M.: Timed consistency for shared distributed objects. In: Proceedings of the eighteenth annual ACM symposium on Principles of distributed computing, Atlanta, Georgia, United States, May 04-06, pp. 163–172 (1999)
11. Zhou, S., Cai, W., Turner, S.J., Lee, F.B.S.: Critical causality in distributed virtual environments. In: Proceedings of the sixteenth workshop on Parallel and distributed simulation, Washington, D.C, May 12-15 (2002)

Enhanced Generic Information Services Using Mobile Messaging

Muhammad Saleem, Ali Zahir, Yasir Ismail, and Bilal Saeed

Hanyang University, Erica Campus, Ansan, South Korea
engr_saleemwazir@yahoo.com, alizahir@hanyang.ac.kr,
marwat_telecomm@yahoo.com, cse.bilal@yahoo.com
http://www.hanyang.ac.kr

Abstract. This paper proposes a new, efficient method of building a scalable generic application which can be used to provide various types of information services using mobile messaging. For specific information, mobile users send an SMS (Short Message Service) to the mobile gateway in a proper format which is then forwarded to the generic application. The generic application accordingly creates an automatic query and generates a prompt reply.

With this new architecture, the final query generating algorithm becomes fast, efficient and processing overhead is reduced. Consequently, user gets the information promptly without any long delay.

Keywords: SMS, SMS Gateway, Generic Information, Multiple Databases, Dynamic Query Generation.

1 Introduction

Globally, there are around 2.4 billion people that own cell phones and 80% of them carry their phone all the time. A text message to their cell phone is the perfect and cheaper way to provide useful information and transaction services such as mobile commerce and banking [8, 10], sales reporting [3] , billing information updates etc.

SMS technology already have been used in public transport services [2], mobile-quiz [4], SMS Blogging [9] and payments [5] but still there is room for where this technology can make a big impact.

It is not a trivial job to develop a stand alone system for every new SMS based information or transaction service. Rather, it could be a good idea to have a single system which can provide more than one services and also can take the extensibility and re-usability into consideration.

Authors [1] successfully developed a generic application which can be used to provide more than single service. The system administrator is able to register new messaging services in a very easy way without any programming or design changes. The generic application dynamically communicates with databases and extracts information based on the contents of the SMS. In order to get specific information, a user will send an SMS to mobile Gateway which will forward it to

R.-S. Chang et al. (Eds.): GPC 2010, LNCS 6104, pp. 510–521, 2010.
© Springer-Verlag Berlin Heidelberg 2010

the desktop application for necessary query execution. After collecting required information from a specific database, a prompt reply will be forwarded to the user in reverse order.

In this paper authors redefined the architecture and algorithm of [1] that lacks in terms of performance and processing overhead. Also the query generating algorithm generates some redundant information for every new user's SMS which slow down the processing and delays the information retrieval. In this new model, authors included the concept of skeleton query, due to which the redundancy in processing is removed and the final query generating algorithm becomes fast, efficient and short. In section V, authors compared new model and algorithm with previous work and proved that the new model is much better than old one in many aspects.

This paper is further organized as follows; section 2 shows an overview of the system, section 3 describes proposed design model for implementing this generic information system, section 4 describes an algorithm for generating a dynamic query, section 5 includes comparison of this model with the model discussed in [1], section 6 contains practical examples of information's systems for which this model can be used, and section 7 concludes future work.

2   Abstract View of the System

This section shows the abstract communication model of the system. The communication scenario of the system is same as described in [1]. The whole communication protocol of the system is divided into five steps as shown in Fig. 1. For commutation, each of the SMS Gateway and server contains and application developed in VB.Net.

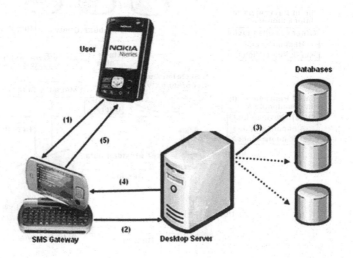

Fig. 1. SMS Messaging Service

1. For specific information, the user types an SMS in a proper format and sends to the SMS Gateway. The format of the SMS is predefined and conveyed to all users through some media like TV or internet.
2. After receiving the user SMS, the SMS Gateway application forwards it to the server application along with the user phone number.
3. Server application splits the SMS into sub-parts and read the semantic of it. After proper processing, the sever application generates a dynamic query and makes a dynamic link with the concerned database.
4. The result of the query execution is sent back to the SMS gateway along with the user number.
5. The SMS gateway then forwards the information to the concerned user as an SMS.

3 Proposed Model

Fig. 2 shows the detailed design model of the required system. This model works almost same as proposed in [1]. In this model authors focus on two main issues given as under;

- How to make the system scalable such that system administrator can register new messaging services without any programming changes.
- How the system is able to understand the semantic of the user SMS and extracts the required results.

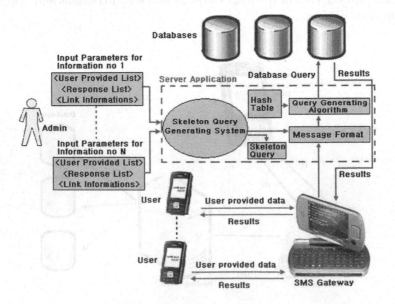

Fig. 2. Proposed Model

Server application is the intelligent entity in the whole system. Both of the above mentioned issues are solved by it. Before users can get any information, the system administrator must register new messaging services. For this Skeleton Query Generating System (SQGS) is used. The SQGS takes three database records as input and generates skeleton query, message format as output. The three input parameters are; *user-provided list, response list* and *link information*. These input parameters are provided by the system administrator using entity relationship diagram (ERD) of the concerned database. After generating the required outputs, the SQGS stored both of them into a specific table called *Hash Table*. Hash Table contains history of each messaging service provided by the system.

Typically *user-provided list* contains those tables attributes which user has to provide in sending SMS. The *response list* contains records which will be sent back to the user in reply. Both of the *user provided list* and *response list* only contain table attributes of a specific database. The third input parameter is the *joining conditions* between database tables. This parameter may be optional if all the records have to be extracted only from a single table. If the *user-provided list* or *response list* contains table attributes, selected from more than one table, then the administrator must provide this third input parameter.

For specific information, each of the users must follow the messaging format generated by the SQGS. The general format of the message is as under;

@ <Service No> <user-provided list>

Each of the available messaging services providing by the generic information system are uniquely identified by *Service No*. Typically *Service No* starts from 1 and increases by 1 for every new service added by the administrator.

Skeleton query is the template for the final query to be executed against a specific database for required information retrieval. Skeleton query contains some holes which must be provided by the user through sending SMS. For each of the hole, the user must provide a specific data in SMS. If the third input parameter is empty then the general format of the skeleton query is;

Select <response list> from <tables_used> where <user-provided attribute 1> = gap#1 and <user-provided attribute 2> = gap#2 and so on.

If the *link information* parameter is not empty then the general format of the skeleton query is;

Select <response list> from <tables_used> where <user-provided attribute 1> = gap#1 and <user-provided attribute 2> = gap#2 ... and <link information>

Where <*tables_used*> are the names of database tables from where *user-provided list* or *response list* is selected. The SQGS generates the skeleton query by the concatenation of the input parameters with specific SQL key words in a proper order. *Hash table* is used to store the history of all the messaging services proved by the generic information system. Table 1 shows the entries made by SQGS in *Hash table*.

For each of the new messaging service, the SQGS stores Service No, database name (which stores all information of the new messaging service), message format and skeleton query in the Hash Table.

In table 1, for service no 1 the *<response list>* is *Subject.Sub_name, Grade. Marks, Grade.Gpa, <tables_used>* are *Student , Grade , Subject* and *<user-provided attribute 1>* is *Student.St_id, <user-provided attribute 2>* is *Grade. Exam_name*. As more then one tables are used so the *<link information>* is *Student.St_id = Grade.St_id* and *subject.Sub_code = Grade.Sub_code*. In service no 2 and 3 only 1 table is used so there is no need of *link information*.

The records in *Hash table* are used by query generating algorithm for making the final query and a dynamic link with a specific database. For each of the new messaging service, the SQGS insert a single record into the *Hash Table*.

After adding new messaging service, the system administrator must convey the message format to all users. The system administrator can do this job by using website or some TV advertisement. Also user can send a query SMS to the server application, asking for the format of the SMS. The server application then replies with an SMS containing the exact format.

For each of the user SMS, the server application first split the SMS into subparts and then apply query generating algorithm to generate the final query. Query generating algorithm fills the gap in the skeleton query with proper user provided inputs. Hence skeleton query is once made and then used each time when new SMS message comes into the server application.

Table 1. Hash Table

Service No	Database Name	Message Format	Skeleton Query
1	Exam	@ <1> <St_id> <Exam_name>	Select Subject.Sub_name,Grade.Marks,Grade. Gpa from Student, Grade, Subject where Student.St_id=gap#1 and Grade.Exam_name = gap#2 and Student.St_id = Grade.St_id and subject.Sub_code = Grade.Sub_code
2	Exam	@ <2> <Sub_code>	Select Subject.Sub_name,Subject.crd_hrs from Subject where Subject.Sub_code = gap#1
3	Trans_ Services	@ <3> <Route_No>	Select Bus.Bus_No, Bus.Start_Stop,Bus.Dest_ Stop from Bus where Bus.Route_No= gap#1

4   Query Generating Algorithm

For specific information, the user SMS is forwarded to the server application. The server application applies query generating algorithm on the user SMS to generate the final query for required information extraction. This algorithm is divided into four steps given as under;

Input: User SMS in the general format(@ <*Service No*> <*user-provided list*
>), *Hash Table* which contains the history of all messaging services provided by
the system.
Output: An *SQL SELECT* query which executes against a specific database to
extract required information, sent back to the user in reply.

1. Make sub-parts of the received SMS by splitting the SMS using spaces.
   Store the subparts of SMS in an array named "SubFields" such that
   SubFields(0) contains "@", SubFields(1) contains "Service No",
   and so on.
2. Execute a query on "Hash Table" for the Service No("SubFields(1)")
   sent by user in SMS, to extract skeleton query and database name.
   The query is like;
     Select sekeleton query, Db name from Hash Table where Service_No
     = SubFields(1)

3. Store skeleton query in a variable "Skquery" and database name
   in a variable "Db_Name"

4. for i= 0 to UBound(SubFields())
   Skquery = Replace(Skquery,"gap#" & i+1, "'" & SubFields(i+2)&
   "'")
   end for

At the end of the algorithm the variable *Skquery* contains the final query to be
executed against the database stored in variable *"Db_Name"*.

Consider the skeleton query used for service no 1 in table 1, if the user SMS is
@ 1 2008553025 fall2009 then the final query after applying Query generating
algorithm is as under;

Select Subject.Sub_name,Grade.Marks,Grade.Gpa from Student,Grade,
Subject where Student.St_id = '2008553025' and Grade.Exam_name =
'fall2009' and Student.St_id = Grade.St_id and subject.Sub_code =
 Grade.Sub_code.

The above algorithm can also be implemented by constructing tree of the
skeleton query and filling the gaps during traversing of the tree. The general
tree of the skeleton query is shown in Fig. 3. The triangle represents sub trees
for each node.

This method works well if the skeleton query may contains some syntax errors
and we need to parse it for any syntax error. But in the given model, there is no
possibility of any syntax error so authors argue that the proposed algorithm is
short, fast and best fit for the required problem solution.

5   Comparative Analysis

In this section authors compare the new model with the model described in [1]
and analyze the performance, processing overhead and accuracy of the model.

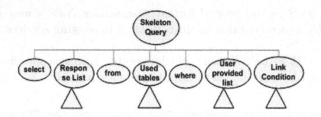

Fig. 3. General Tree of the Skeleton Query

In this new model, authors add a new concept of skeleton query due to which the query generating algorithm becomes very fast, efficient and short. Consequently the processing becomes very fast and users get information without any significant delay.

The main drawback in authors previous work [1] was that for each new SMS, the Query generating algorithm have to construct a new skeleton query and also fills the gap with proper user inputs. In this new model, SQGS only once construct the skeleton query and Query generating algorithm only fills the gap in it with proper data provided by the user in the sending SMS.

In our previous model, *user-provided list, response list, link information's* (if available), *message format, database name, Service No* and *tables used* are saved into the *Hash Table*. But with this new model, for each new messaging service, only *Service No, database name, message format* and *skeleton query* are saved. The columns entries into the *Hash table* are reduced from seven to four. Consequently it becomes easier to process the *Hash table* during query generating algorithm.

Other notable applications based on SMS technology are hospital search and appointments [11], Regional information services [12], Public Transport Service [2], Sales Reporting [3], Mobile-Quiz [4], and Payments [5]. Each of these applications provides specific information and did not take the extensibility and re-usability into consideration. Thus if system administrators want to add some new functionalities to an existing system, they have either to make changes to the existing system or rebuild the entire system from scratch [1].

Also for most of the SMS based applications like [11], [12], all the users are required to deploy an application to their mobiles. This application provides an easy interface for inputting required user data and can be used for security of the SMS. With this interface, it becomes easy for the users to provide required input data without following a strict SMS format. But it is not easy for every user to deploy a new application for each of the different services. Also these applications are device dependent and can only be dumped into specific high specification mobiles. Consequently this requirement limits the total number of users because only those users who have the required application in his/her mobile can get a specific service. But in our approach, we deployed a single application to the Gateway mobile only and all other users can simply get all the information by using a simple SMS interface without deploying any new application.

The only minor limitation to our approach is that all the users have to follow a fix SMS format. If the user SMS is not in the proper format then no information can be retrieved. But if the user SMS is not in the proper format, then a prompt reply is forwarded to the user providing the correct SMS format. So for the second time, the user can easily provide the correct SMS format.

As our system only provides information and cannot do any transaction ("insertion, deletion and Updation") to the databases so security of the SMS is not the key issue for only information services.

6 Case Studies

The new proposed system can be used for all the practical examples discussed in [1-3, 6-7, 11, and 12]. In this section authors show some practical examples for which how the system works.

6.1 Exam Results

As discussed in [1], suppose the administrator wants to add a new messaging service "Viewing Exam Results through SMS". In which a student provides *student ID* and *exam name/semester* and gets grades in response to his/her SMS. The administrator can use a database named "Exam" which contains the results of all the semesters. The ERD (Entity Relationship Diagram) of the database is shown in Fig. 4.

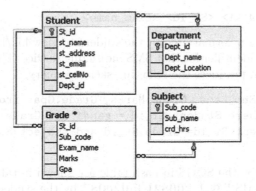

Fig. 4. ERD of the Exam Database

Fig. 5 show the screen shots of the Skeleton Query Generating System. The administrator selects three lists of attributes: one contains fields/attributes to be provided by the student in SMS and the other contains attributes to be provided in response to the user SMS/Query and the third input parameter is *link information* among tables, which is shown in Fig. 5.

As three tables are used during the selection for *user-provided list* and *response list* so all the three tables must be linked by some *join conditions*. Primary key of the tables are usually used for *join* between tables. For table *Student* and *Grade*, the *join condition* is *Student.St_id = Grade.St_id*. While for the *Subject* and *Grade* the *join condition* is *Subject.Sub_code = Grade.Sub_code*.

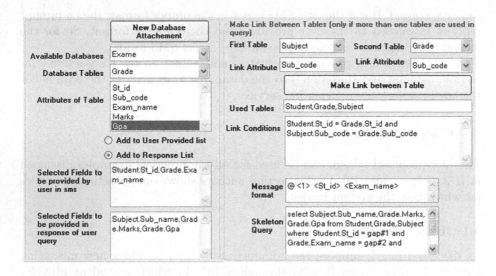

Fig. 5. Screenshot of SQGS for adding new information services

After the administrator provides all these three input parameters, the Skeleton Query Generating System produces the following message format;

@ <1> <St_id> <Exam_name>

This is the message format used by the student to view his/her results. Where <1> is the unique identifier for that SMS messaging service. The Skeleton Query Generating System produces the following skeleton query;

```
Select Subject.Sub_name, Grade.Marks, Grade.Gpa  from Student,
Grade,Subject where Student.St_id = gap#1 and Grade.Exam_name=
gap#2  and Student.St_id= Grade.St_id and subject.Sub_code =
Grade.Sub_code.
```

The entries saved by the SQGS in hash table are shown in table 1.

After sending SMS "@ **1 200821 fall2008**" by the student having student id **200821** and exam name **fall2008**, the query generating algorithm produces the following SQL Query;

```
Select Subject.Sub_name, Grade.Marks, Grade.Gpa  from Student,
Grade, Subject where Student.St_id = '200821' and Grade.Exam_name
= 'fall2008' and Student.St_id = Grade.St_id and Subject.Sub_code
= Grade.Sub_code.
```

This final query is exactly same as produced by the query generating algorithm described in [1]. After executing the above query on database **Exam** the message sent from student, and result from server application to SMS gateway application is shown in Fig. 6. The SMS gateway application then forwards the data received form the server to the student as an SMS.

Fig. 6. Screenshot of Gateway Application

The administrator can provide other messaging service using the same database like "viewing details of a subject", in which the user send *subject code* and in response the *subject name* and *total credit hours* are returned to him. The *user-provided list* contains *Subject.Sub_code* and *response list* includes *Subject.Sub_name* and *Subject.crd_hrs*. As the entire attributes belongs to a single table *Subject*, so there is no need of *link information*.

After providing these two input parameters, the format of the SMS to be provided by the user is: **@ <2> <Sub_code>**.The structure of the skeleton query is;

```
Select Subject.Sub_name, Subject.crd_hrs from Subject where
Subject.Sub_code = gap#1
```

After sending SMS " **@ 2 CSE545**" having subject code **CSE545**,the final query generated by the query generating algorithm is;

```
Select Subject.Sub_name, Subject.crd_hrs  from Subject where
Subject.Sub_code = 'CSE545'
```

In order to know the format of the SMS to view results, a student may sent an SMS **@ <query> <Service No>** to the SMS gateway, in a reply the correct message format is provided to the student.

6.2   Weather Information

Let the administrator wants to provide weather information to the users, in which the user send the *city code* and the system replies with the complete weather

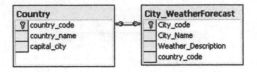

Fig. 7. Weather Information ERD

forecast of the city along with the country name. Fig. 7 shows the partial ERD of the system. After analyzing the ERD of the system, the system administrator selects table attributes *City_code* in *user-provided list,* and *country_name, City_Name* and *Weather_Description* in *response list.* As all these attributes are selected from two table so the third input parameter of the *join* condition between tables is like; *Country.country_code = City_WeatherForcast.country_code* After the administrator provides all these three input parameters, the Skeleton Query Generating System produces the following message format;

```
@   <3> <City_code>
```

The Skeleton Query Generating System produces the following skeleton query;

```
Select Country.country_name, City_WeatherForcast.City_Name,
City_WeatherForcast.Weather_Description  from  Country,
City_WeatherForcast where City_WeatherForcast.city_code = gape#1
```

After sending **SMS "@ 3 24789"** by the user having city code **24789**, the query generating algorithm produces the following SQL Query;

```
Select Country.country_name, City_WeatherForcast.City_Name,
City_WeatherForcast .Weather_Description from Country,
City_WeatherForcast  where City_WeatherForcast. city_code =
'24789'
```

7   Conclusions

In this paper, authors proposed a new architecture for a multi-purpose information system which can be easily used to provide different information in many firms. With this new architecture, the performance of the system becomes increased and processing overhead is reduced. The algorithm becomes very simple, fast and efficient. It is a cheaper way of providing useful information to users in those areas where there is no internet facility.

In future, authors will extend this system to an extend-able system which not only provides information but can also does transactions based on user SMS. The transactions could be like utility bills payments so that customer doesn't have to wait in long queues out side of the banks or other firms. With this new system, the user can make changes in the database records. But security is the main issue to such a system. The message must be sent in a secure way from user to the system.

Acknowledgments. This research work is sponsored by 'Higher Education Commission (HEC), Govt. Of Pakistan' under the scholarship program titled: MS Level Training in Korean Universities/Industry.

References

1. Saleem, M., Doh, K.G.: Generic Information System Using SMS Gateway. In: 4th international conference on computer science and convergence information technologies (ICCIT), South Korea, pp. 861–866 (2009)
2. Ching, L.T., Garg, H.K.: Designing SMS applications for public transport service system in Singapore. In: The 8th International Conference on Communication Systems, Singapore, vol. 2, pp. 706–710 (2002)
3. Wan, K.: An SMS-based sales reporting system for a fashion-clothes franchising company. In: Engineering Management Conference (IEMC), Managing Technologically Driven Organizations: The Human Side of Innovation and Change, New York, pp. 330–334 (2003)
4. Shahreza, M.S.: M-Quiz by SMS. In: Sixth international conference on advance Technologies, Tehran, pp. 726–729 (2006)
5. Aziz, Q.: Payments through Mobile Phone. In: 6th International Conference on emerging Technologies (ICET), Peshawar (2006)
6. Collins, C., Grude, A., Scholl, M., Thompson, R.: txt bus: wait time information on demand. In: Conference on Human Factors in Computing Systems, USA, pp. 2049–2054. ACM, New York (2007)
7. Aschoff, F.R., NovakT, J.: The mobile forum: real-time information exchange in mobile sms communities. In: Conference on Human Factors in Computing Systems (CHI), Italy, pp. 3489–3494. ACM, New York (2008)
8. Wang, H., Huang, X., Dodda, G.R.: Ticket-based mobile commerce system and its implementation. In: 2nd International Workshop on Modeling Analysis and Simulation of Wireless and Mobile Systems, Spain, pp. 119–122. ACM, New York (2006)
9. Prasad, A., Blagsvedt, S., Toyama, K.: SMSBlogging: Blog-on-the-street Public Art Project. In: 15th international conference on Multimedia, Germany, pp. 501–504 (2007)
10. Jamil, M.S., Mousumi1, F.A.: Short Messaging Service (SMS) Based m-Banking System in context of bangladesh. In: 11th International Conference on Computer and Information Technology (ICCIT 2008), Bangladesh, pp. 599–604 (2008)
11. Edwards, T., Sankaranarayanan, S.: Intelligent Agent based Hospital Search and Appointment system. In: 2nd international conference on Interaction Sciences: Information Technology, Culture and Human, South Korea, pp. 561–567 (2009)
12. Stenentt, D., Sankaranarayanan, S.: Personal Mobile Information System. In: 2nd international conference on Interaction Sciences: Information Technology, Culture and Human, South Korea, pp. 561–567 (2009)

A Focused Crawler with Ontology-Supported Website Models for Information Agents

Sheng-Yuan Yang

Department of Computer and Communication Engineering, St. John's University, 499, Sec. 4, TamKing Rd., Tamsui, Taipei County 25135, Taiwan
ysy@mail.sju.edu.tw

Abstract. This paper advocated the use of ontology-supported website models to provide a semantic level solution for an information agent so that it can provide fast, precise, and stable query results. Based on the technique, a focused crawler, namely, OntoCrawler, was developed, which can benefit both user requests and domain semantics. Equipped with this technique, we have developed an ontology-supported information agent shell in Scholar domain which manifests the following interesting features: ontology-supported construction of website models, website models-supported website model expansion, website models-supported webpage retrieval, high-level outcomes of information recommendation, and accordingly proved the feasibility of the related techniques proposed in this paper.

Keywords: Focused crawlers, Ontology, Website models.

1 Introduction

Along with popularity of application and use of Internet, how to search advantage information has become essential part in users. Current domain-specific search engines do help users to narrow down the search scope by the techniques of Query Expansion, Automatic Classification and Focused Crawling; their weakness, however, is almost completely ignoring the user interests [8]. New standards for representing website documents, including XML, RDF, and WOM, can help cross-reference of Web documents; they alone, however, cannot help the user in any semantic level during the searching of website information. OIL, DAML, and the concept of ontology stand for a possible rescue to the attribution of information semantics. In this paper, we proposed the use of ontology-supported website models to provide a semantic level solution for an information agent so that it can provide fast, precise, and stable query results. We also noticed that the concept of crawler is mostly used in the Web systems that work on information gathering or integration to improve their gathering processes or the search results from disparate resources, such as Dominos [4] and UbiCrawler [1]. In this paper, we developed an OntoCrawler using ontology and website models as the core techniques, which can help information agents to successfully tackle the problems of search scope and user interests. The Scholar domain was chosen as the target application of the system and will be used for explanation in the remaining sections.

R.-S. Chang et al. (Eds.): GPC 2010, LNCS 6104, pp. 522–532, 2010.

2 Domain Ontology

Ontology provides complete semantic models, which means in specified domain all related entities, attributes and base knowledge among entities owning sharing and reusing characteristics which could be used for solving the problems of common sharing and communication [10]. Protégé [3] was adapted in this paper, which supports two main ways of modeling ontologies via the Protégé-Frames and Protégé-OWL (adapted by us, shown in Fig. 1) editors; furthermore, knowledge workers could transfer to different formats of ontology such as RDF(S), OWL, XML or directly inherit into database just like MySQL and MS SQL Server (adapted by us and described later), which have better supported function than other tools [2].

Nowadays the research on ontology can be branched into two fields: one is to configure huge ontology in a specified field and through it to assistant the knowledge analysis in this field; the other is to study how to construct and express precisely with ontology [2]. In this paper, we adapted the former in which took advantage of built ontology database of some scholars to support OntoCrawler for querying webpage of related scholars, detailed in [16]. Briefly, we conducted statistics and survey of homepage of related scholars to fetch out the related concepts and their synonym appearing in the homepage. The second stage of ontology constructing of scholars is to transfer the ontology built with Protégé into MS SQL database.

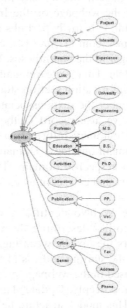

Fig. 1. The ontology structure of scholars in Protégé

3 Website Model Construction

The structure and example of a website model [17] was illustrated in Fig. 2. The webpage profile contains three sections, namely, basic information, statistics information,

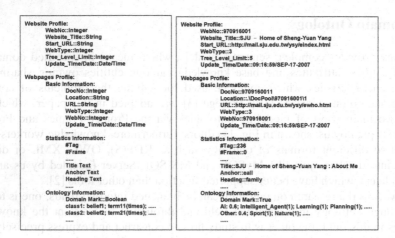

Fig. 2. Website model structure and example

and ontology information. The first two sections profile a webpage and the last annotates domain semantics to the webpage. DocNo is automatically generated by the system for identifying a webpage in the structure index. Location remembers the path of the stored version of the Web page in the website model; we can use it to answer user queries. URL is the path of the webpage on the Internet, same as the returned URL index in the user query result; it helps hyperlinks analysis. WebType identifies one of the following six Web types: com (1), net (2), edu (3), gov (4), org (5), and other (0), each encoded as an integer in the parentheses. WebNo identifies the website that contains this webpage. Update_Time/Date remembers when the webpage was modified last time. The statistics information section stores statistics about HTML tag properties. Specifically, we remember the texts associated with Titles, Anchors, and Headings for webpage analysis; we also record Outbound_URLs for user-oriented webpage expansion. Finally, the ontology information section remembers how the webpage is interpreted by the domain ontology. Domain_Mark is used to remember whether the webpage belongs to a specific domain. This section annotates how a webpage is related with the domain and can serve as its semantics, which help a lot in correct retrieval of webpages.

Let's turn to the website profile. WebNo identifies a website. Through this number, we can access those webpage profiles describing the webpages that belong to this website. Website_Title remembers the text between tags <TITLE> of the homepage of the website. Start_URL stores the starting address of the website. WebType identifies one of the six Web types as used in the webpage profile. Tree_Level_Limit keeps the search agent from exploring too deeply. Update_Time/Date remembers when the website was modified last time. This model structure helps interpret the semantics of a website through the gathered information; it also helps fast retrieval of webpage information and autonomous search of Web resources.

During the construction and expansion process of a website model, we need to extract primitive webpage information as well as to perform statistics. Website modeling involves three modules, detailed in [14]. Briefly, we use OntoExtractor to extract basic webpage information and perform statistics. We then use OntoAnnotator to annotate ontology information. Since the ontology information contains webpage classes, OntoAnnotator needs to call OntoClassifier (described later) to perform webpage classification. In order to facilitate these activities, we have re-organized the ontology structure into a two-layer structure (super and reference classes) [12], which stresses on how concept attributes are related to class identification. Each super class contains a set of representative ontology features for a specific concept, while each reference class contains related ontology features between two concepts. We have proposed an ontology-directed classification mechanism, namely, OntoClassifier [12] to make a decision of the class for a webpage or a website.

4 Website Models Application

4.1 Focused Crawler

A focused crawler namely OntoCrawler was proposed, as shown in Fig.3, which featured a progressive crawling strategy in obtaining domain relevant Web information. Inside the architecture, Web Crawler gathers data from the Web, detailed in Section 4.2. DocPool stores all returned Web pages from Web Crawler for OntoExtractor [14] during the construction of webpage profiles. It also stores query results from search engines, which usually contains a list of URLs. URLExtractor is responsible for extracting URLs from the query results and dispatching those URLs that are domain-dependent but not yet in the website models to Distiller. User-Oriented Webpage Expander pinpoints interesting URLs in the website models for further webpage expansion according to the user query. Autonomous Website Evolver autonomously discovers URLs in the website models that are domain-dependent for further webpage expansion. User Priority Queue stores the user search strings and the website model URLs from User-Oriented Webpage Expander. Website Priority Queue stores the website model URLs from Autonomous Website Evolver and the URLs extracted by URLExtractor.

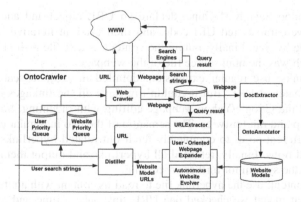

Fig. 3. Architecture of OntoCrawler

Distiller controls the Web search by associating a priority score with each URL (or search string) and placing it in a proper Priority Queue. We defined the ULScore as the priority score for each URL (or search string), detailed in [13]. Briefly, all search strings are treated as the top-priority requests, website model URLs are second-priority, and URLs extracted by URLExtractor are last-priority. This design prefers user-oriented Web resource crawling to website maintenance, since user-oriented query or webpage expansion takes into account both user interest and domain constraint, which can better meet our design goal than website maintenance.

4.2 Web Crawler

Fig. 4 showed the operation system structure of Web Crawler (developed with Java), and related techniques and functions of every part were described as below.

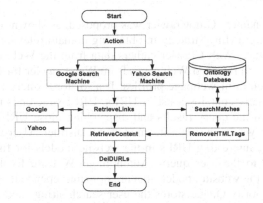

Fig. 4. System structure of Web Crawler

(1) Action: transfer internal query into URI code, and then embed into Google's query URL.
(2) Google/Yahoo Search Machine: declare an URL object and add Google query URL on well transferred URI code, and then used an iterative loop to read its content line by line. Finally, output the content as text file as final analysis reference, which was the html source file of the webpage.
(3) RetrieveLinks: use regular expression, detailed in [16], to search for whether there are matched URL. But it couldn't retrieve all the linkages in one time out because of the Google/Yahoo webpage editing with indenting. So we used an iterative loop and ran for twice. The semantic of the two in regular expression were slightly different so as to completely fetch out related hyperlinks corresponding to the conditions. Finally, returned all hyperlinks and output them into a text file to provide the system for further processing.
(4) RetrieveContent: use the hyperlink file to read its content with an iterative loop line by line, that meant we checked one URL link once a time and really linked the URL. After judging what kind coding of the webpage was, we read in the html source file of webpage with correct coding and output it as text file so as to let system conduct further processing. After completing all procedures mentioned above,

we could used SearchMatches method to judge whether the webpage was located in the range we hoped to query; supposed the answer was "yes", we would execute RemoveHTMLTags to delete the html label from source file and remained only the text content so as to let system conduct further processing and analyzing. Finally, we collected the number of queried webpage and divided with total of the webpage and the mean we got was the percentage of query processing.

(5) DelDURLs: proceed complete cross-comparison with URLs returned by Google and Yahoo for deleting duplication webpages to avoid duplicated operation of system backend and accordingly enhance its performance.

4.3 User- and Domain-Oriented Web Search

The basic goal of the website models is to help Web search in both a user-oriented and a domain-directed manner. We not only proposed a direct query expansion mechanism also proposed an implicit webpage expansion mechanism oriented to the user interest to better capture the user intention, detailed in [13]. Briefly, we proposed a strategy to select those hyperlinks, or URLs, that the users are strongly interested in according to the degree of domain correlation of a website with respect to the domain, which needs the parameter Domain_Mark in the webpage profile to determine it. We then employed an implicit webpage expansion mechanism which consulted the user models [19] for user interests and used that information to add more webpages into the website models by, for example, checking on how the anchor texts of the outbound hyperlinks of the webpages in the website models were strongly related with the user interests. We also employed a 4-phase progressive strategy to do website expansion, i.e., to add more domain dependant webpages into the website models, detailed in [13].

4.4 Webpage Retrieval

Webpage retrieval concerns the way of providing most-needed documents for users. Traditional ranking methods employ an inverted full-text index database along with a ranking algorithm to calculate the ranking sequence of relevant documents. The problems with this method are clear: too many entries in returned results and too slow response time. A simplified approach emerged, which employs various ad-hoc mechanisms to reduce query space, however, they need a specific, labor-intensive and time-consuming pre-process and; they cannot respond to the changes of the real environment in time due to the off-line pre-process. Another method called PageRank [6] was employed in Google to rank webpages by their link information. Google's high speed of response stems from a huge local webpage database along with a time-consuming, offline detailed link structure analysis.

Our solution ranking method takes advantage of the semantics in the website models, as shown in Fig. 5. The major index structure uses ontology features to index webpages in the website models. The second index structure is a partial full-text inverted index since it contains no ontology features. Since we require each query contain at least one ontology feature, we can always use the ontology index to locate a set of webpages. The partial full-text index is then used to further reduce them into a subset of webpages for users. Finally, we can employ the identified ontology features in a user query to properly rank the webpages for the user using the ranking method [15].

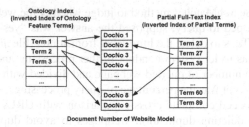

Fig. 5. Index structures in Website Models

5   System Evaluation

5.1   System Architecture

This paper have developed an Ontology-supported Information Agent Shell (On-toIAS) [18] based on the technologies described before, shown in Fig. 6. It contains the four main modules of information agents, including information crawling, information extracting, information classifying, and information presenting/ranking and orderly corresponding to OntoCrawler, OntoExtractor, OntoClassifier, and OntoRe-commender, respectively. The reason of the beginning word "Onto-" is all of module functions supported by ontology, which means the information agent shell is the core part of information agent separated from the domain ontology. The advantages of the approach are practicably the shell application areas based on the domain ontology and extensible its application areas according to assimilation and fusion processing from other related domain ontologies. Ontology Database is the key component, which stores both domain ontology and query ontology. Ontological Database (OD) is a stored structure designed according to the ontology structure, serving as an ontology-directed canonical format for storing webpage information processed by OntoIAS, which is separated from the shell. The approach not only can provide the basic operation semantic to the shell, but also can make the shell fast and precisely access information based on those semantic understanding. User Interface is responsible for singling out

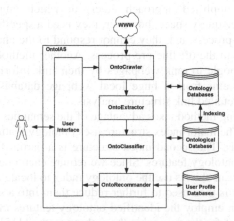

Fig. 6. Conceptual Architecture of OntoIAS

significant keywords from the user queries. Specifically, we use ontology, which defines the physical meanings of the important concepts involved in a given task, to successfully help the user interface develop a user profile to provide the personality functionality and store in User Profile Database through OntoRecommender.

5.2 System Experiments

In this experiment, we compared our query technique with the most popular query engines Google and Yahoo. Here, we used equations (1) and (2) to define Precision Rate, R_P and Recall Rate, R_R, in which NW_T meant the number of total returned web-pages; NW_C meant number of correct returned webpages; NW_R meant number of related returned webpages but they were not necessarily the correct webpage. The results in Table 1 were after comparing returned webpage one after another through domain experts, we can get the R_P and R_R of Google were 1% and 50.0% while Yahoo were 1% and 33.3%, respectively.

$$R_P = \frac{NW_C}{NW_T} \tag{1}$$

$$R_R = \frac{NW_C}{NW_C + NW_R} \tag{2}$$

Table 1. Comparison of the front 100 queries on Google and Yahoo

	NW_C	NW_R	NW_T	R_P	R_R
Google	1	1	100	1%	50.0%
Yahoo	1	2	100	1%	33.3%

When we used Google and Yahoo as base of webpage query, but on OntoIAS we keyed in the same set of keywords. The returned screen of the system was shown in Fig. 7 and comparison results were shown in Table 2. After comparing Tables 1 and 2, the query precision and recall rate for Google researching engine through assistance

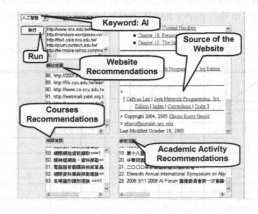

Fig. 7. Returned screen of OntoIAS

Table 2. Query result of the system

THRESHOLD=5	NW_C	NW_R	NW_T	R_P	R_R
OntoIAS	22	0	22	100%	100%

of OntoIAS has up-rise around 99% and 50% ($\dfrac{100\%-1\%}{100\%}$, $\dfrac{100\%-50\%}{100\%}$) while conditions of Yahoo were about 99% and 66.7% ($\dfrac{100\%-1\%}{100\%}$, $\dfrac{100\%-33.3\%}{100\%}$). From the above comparison, it indicated that OntoIAS offered more precision and recall rate than Google and Yahoo on webpage searching; in addition, the technique we proposed and verified has its availability and system performance.

The information query meant the best recommendations have chosen from a group of related information sets. That wonderfully possessed different approaches to the same purpose as whether sampling specimens can be on behaving of degree of sampling body in huge amount of datum. In the sampling survey domain, the reliability was usually employed to measure the degree of precision of sampling system itself, while the validity was emphasized whether it can be correct to reflect the properties of the appearance of things [9]. In other words, the former evaluates the stability of the measurement tool, while the latter focuses on the correctness of the tool itself. In 1979, J.P. Peter [7] had the aid of mathematic model to represent the definitions of the reliability and validity.

The recommending significant information of this experiment was asserted by the domain experts, including observed values, true values, error values, and related variances. Table 3 illustrates the reliabilities of some scholars' recommending information on "Courses" and "Academic Activities" which are 0.856 and 0.756 in average, respectively. Table 4 illustrates the validities of some scholars' recommending information on "Courses" and "Academic Activities" which are 0.856 and 0.756 in average, respectively. In the literatures, the regular-level values of reliability and validity are 0.7 and 0.5, respectively, which verify and validate our results are high-level outcomes of information recommendation. Finally, what merits attention is: the Professional Classification of each scholar can be accurately shown that prove the system structure we proposed in this paper has its accuracy and availability.

Table 3. Results of the reliability of classification information

Results / Domain Professor	Courses			Academic Activities			Professional Classification
	V_e	V_o	r_{tt}	V_e	V_o	r_{tt}	
C.S. Ho (何正信)	1	12	0.92	2	7	0.71	AI
T.W. Kuo (郭大維)	0	2	1	0	1	1	AI
S.Y. Yang (楊勝源)	0	5	1	0	1	1	AI
S.M. Chen (陳錫明)	7	11	0.36	3	7	0.57	Fuzzy
W.L Hsu (許聞廉)	0	1	1	2	4	0.5	AI
Average	0.856			0.756			

Table 4. Results of the validity of classification information

Results Domain Professor	Courses			Academic Activities			Professional Classification
	V_{co}	V_o	V_{al}	V_{co}	V_o	V_{al}	
C.S. Ho (何正信)	11	12	0.92	5	7	0.71	AI
T.W. Kuo (郭大維)	2	2	1	1	1	1	AI
S.Y. Yang (楊勝源)	5	5	1	1	1	1	AI
S.M. Chen (陳錫明)	4	11	0.36	4	7	0.57	Fuzzy
W.L Hsu (許聞廉)	1	1	1	2	4	0.5	AI
Average		0.856			0.756		

6 Conclusions

The paper has described how ontology-supported website models can effectively support Web search, which is different from website model content, construction, and application over our previous works [11]. The technique in this research has practically applied on Google and Yahoo searching engines and the experiment outcomes indicated that this technique could definitely up-rise precision and recall rate of webpage query. A website model contains webpage profiles, each recording basic information, statistics information, and ontology information of a webpage. We have developed OntoCrawler, which employs domain ontology-supported website models as the core technology to search for Web resources that are both user-interested and domain-oriented. Equipped with this technique, we also have developed an ontology-supported information agent shell in Scholar domain which manifests the following interesting features: ontology-supported construction of website models, website models-supported website model expansion, website models-supported webpage retrieval, high-level outcomes of information recommendation, and accordingly proved the feasibility of the related techniques proposed in this paper. In addition, our ontology construction is based on a set of pre-collected webpages on a specific domain; it is hard to evaluate how critical this collection process is to the nature of different domains. We are planning to employ the technique of automatic ontology evolution to help studying the robustness of our ontology. Finally, how to improve the webpage handling capability of our system is another course in the future, just like the techniques for processing free text information mentioned in [5], for handling all type of webpages and accordingly enjoys the highest user satisfaction.

Acknowledgments. The author would like to thank Chung-Min Wang, Yai-Hui Chang, Ssu-Hsien Lu, Ting-An Chen, Chi-Feng Wu, Hsieh-I Lo, and You-Jen Chang for their assistance in system implementation and experiments. The partial work was supported by the National Science Council, Taiwan, R.O.C., under Grant NSC-98-2221-E-129-012.

References

1. Boldi, P., Codenotti, B., Samtini, M., Vigna, S.: UbiCrawler: A Scalable Fully Distributed Web Crawler. Software: Practice and Experience 34(8), 711–726 (2004)
2. Chien, H.C.: Study and Implementation of a Learning Content Management System Search Engine for Special Education Based on Semantic Web. Master Thesis, MingHsin University of Science and Technology, HsinChu, Taiwan (2006)
3. Grosso, W.E., Eriksson, H., Fergerson, R.W., Gennari, J.H., Tu, S.W., Musen, M.A.: Knowledge Modeling at the Millennium: the Design and Evolution of Protégé-2000. SMI Technical Report, SMI-1999-0801, Stanford Medical Informatics, Stanford University, California, USA (1999)
4. Hafri, Y., Djeraba, C.: Dominos: A New Web Crawler's Design. In: Proc. of the 4th International Web Archiving Workshop, Bath, UK (2004)
5. Meng, I.H., Tseng, S.M., Yang, W.P.: Integrated Business Agents for Processing Free Text Information. Journal of Information Science and Engineering 20(2), 325–347 (2004)
6. Page, L., Brin, S., Motwani, R., Winograd, T.: The PageRank Citation Ranking: Bringing Order to the Web. In: Stanford Digital Libraries Working Paper of SIDL-WP-1999-0120, Department of Computer Science. University of Stanford, California (1999)
7. Peter, J.P.: Reliability: A Review of Psychometric Basics and Recent Marketing Practices. Journal of Marketing Research 16, 6–17 (1979)
8. Wang, C.M.: Web Search with Ontology-Supported Technology, Master thesis, Department of Computer Science and Information Engineering, National Taiwan University of Science and Technology, Taipei, Taiwan (2003)
9. Wu, T.X.: The Reliability and Validity of Attitude and Behavior Research: Theory, Application, and Self-examination. In: Public Opinion Monthly, Taipei, Taiwan, pp. 29–53 (1985)
10. Yang, S.Y., Ho, C.S.: Ontology-Supported User Models for Interface Agents. In: Proc. of the 4th Conference on Artificial Intelligence and Applications, Chang-Hua, Taiwan, pp. 248–253 (1999)
11. Yang, S.Y., Ho, C.S.: A Website-Model-Supported New Search Agent. In: Proc. of 2nd International Workshop on Mobile Systems, E-Commerce, and Agent Technology, Miami, FL, USA, pp. 563–568 (2003)
12. Yang, S.Y.: An Ontology-Directed Webpage Classifier for Web Services. In: Proc. of Joint 3rd International Conference on Soft Computing and Intelligent Systems and 7th International Symposium on advanced Intelligent Systems, Tokyo, Japan, pp. 720–724 (2006)
13. Yang, S.Y.: A Website Model-Supported Focused Crawler for Search Agents. In: Proc. of the 9th Joint Conference on Information Sciences, Kaohsiung, Taiwan, pp. 755–758 (2006)
14. Yang, S.Y.: An Ontology-Supported Website Model for Web Search Agents. In: Proc. of 2006 International Computer Symposium, Taipei, Taiwan, pp. 874–879 (2006)
15. Yang, S.Y., Chuang, F.C., Ho, C.S.: Ontology-Supported FAQ Processing and Ranking Techniques. Journal of Intelligent Information Systems 28(3), 233–251 (2007)
16. Yang, S.Y., Hsu, C.L.: Ontology-Supported Focused-Crawler for Specified Scholar's Webpages. In: Proc. of IEEE the Eighth International Conference on Intelligent Systems Design and Applications, Kaohsiung, Taiwan, pp. 409–414 (2008)
17. Yang, S.Y.: An Ontological Website Models-Supported Search Agent for Web Services. Expert Systems with Applications 35(4), 2056–2073 (2008)
18. Yang, S.Y., Hsu, C.L., Chu, Y.C., Wu, K.W.: A Study on Developing an Ontology-Supported Information Agent Shell. In: Proc. of 2008 International Computer Symposium, Taipei, Taiwan, pp. 444–449 (2008)
19. Yang, S.Y.: Developing of an Ontological Interface Agent with Template-based Linguistic Processing Technique for FAQ Services. Expert Systems with Applications 36(2), 4049–4060 (2009)

An Efficient Technique for OFDM System Using Discrete Wavelet Transform

W. Saad, N. El-Fishawy, S. EL-Rabaie, and M. Shokair

Dep. of Electronic and Communication Eng., Faculty of Electronic Engineering,
El-Menufiya University, Egypt
waleedsaad100@yahoo.com, nelfishawy@hotmail.com, srabie1@yahoo.com,
i_shokair@yahoo.com

Abstract. With the rapid expand of wireless digital communications, demand for wireless systems that are reliable and have a high spectral efficiency have increased too. Orthogonal Frequency Division Multiplexing (OFDM) has been recognized for its good performance to achieve high data rates. Fast Fourier Transforms (FFT) has been used to produce the orthogonal sub-carriers. Due to the drawbacks of OFDM-FFT based system which are the high peak-to-average ratio (PAR) and the synchronization, many works have replaced the Fourier transform part by wavelet transform. In this paper, an efficient technique for the OFDM system using wavelet transform is proposed. This system shows a superior performance when compared with traditional OFDM FFT systems through an Additive White Gaussian Noise (AWGN) channel. The system performance is described in Bit Error Rate (BER) as a function of Signal to Noise Ratio (SNR) and the peak-to-average ratio (PAR). Furthermore, the proposed system gives nearly a perfect reconstruction for the input signal in the presence of Gaussian noise.

Keywords: Orthogonal Frequency Division Multiplexing, Fast Fourier Transform, Discrete Wavelet Transform.

1 Introduction

OFDM is a multi-carrier transmission technique, which divides the available spectrum into many carriers, each one being modulated by a low rate data stream. To implement the OFDM transmission scheme, the message signal must first be digitally modulated. The carrier is then split into lower-frequency sub-carriers that are orthogonal to one another [1,2].

The message signal is first modulated using M-ary QAM. With the advent of cheap powerful processors, the sub-carriers can be generated using FFT. The FFT moves a signal from the time domain to the frequency domain. While the inverse FFT (IFFT) performs the reciprocal operation. The cyclic prefix (CP) is a copy of the last part of the OFDM symbol, and is of equal or greater length than the maximum delay spread of the channel. inter-symbol interference (ISI) [2]. The system model for FFT-based OFDM will not be discussed in detail in this paper as it is well known in the literature.

R.-S. Chang et al. (Eds.): GPC 2010, LNCS 6104, pp. 533–541, 2010.
© Springer-Verlag Berlin Heidelberg 2010

OFDM has been chosen for several current and future communications ys-tems all over the world such as asynchronous digital subscriber line (ADSL), digital audio broadcast (DAB), terrestrial digital videbroadcast (DVB-T) systems, WiMAX systems, etc....

OFDM has several advantages compared to other type of modulation techniques such as bandwidth efficiency, overcome the effect of ISI, and combats the effect of frequency selective fading and burst error. Nevertheless, the OFDM system has some weaknesses such as the high which means that the linear amplifier has to have a large dynamic range to avoid distorting the peaks. The other limitation of OFDM in many applications is that it is very sensitive to frequency errors caused by frequency differences between the local oscillators in the trasmitter and the receiver [2].

Due to the OFDM drawbacks, wavelet transforms have been considered as alternative platforms for replacing IFFT and FFT. In OFDM wavelet based, the spectral containment of the channels is better since it does not use CP and, hence throughput increases [3,4,5,6,7,8,9,10,11].

In this paper, an OFDM system based on wavelet transform is proposed. The proposed system is simply implemented by a one level Haar wavelet. The system is comed with the traditional OFDM systems using MATLAB simulink programs.

This paper is organized as follows; Section 2, gives an overview of the continuous and discrete wavelet transforms and its inverse definitions. Section 3, introduces a comprehensive discussion of the related previous works and the proposed OFDM based on wavelet transform architecture. The simulation results and the comison tests between the proposed and traditional systems are made in Section 4. Finally, conclusions are made in Section 5.

2 Discrete Wavelet Transform

In most Digital Signal Processing (DSP) applications, the frequency content of the signal is very important. The Fourier Transform is probably the most popular transform used to obtain the frequency spectrum of a signal. But the Fourier Transform is only suitable for signals whose frequency content does not change with time. The Fourier Transform does not tell at which time these frequency components occur. To solve this problem, the Wavelet transform, which was developed in the last two decades, provides a better time-frequency representation of the signal than any other existing transforms [12,6,4,13].

The Continuous Wavelet Transform (CWT) is provided by eq. 1.

$$X_{WT}(\tau, s) = \frac{1}{\sqrt{s}} \int x(t) . \psi^* \left(\frac{t - \tau}{s} \right) dt \tag{1}$$

Where $x(t)$ is the signal to be analyzed, $\psi(t)$ is the mother wavelet or the basis function, τ is the translation ameter, and s is the scaling parameter. There are a number of basis functions that can be used as the mother wavelet such as Haar,

Daubechies, Symlets and Coiflets. Haar wavelet is one of the oldest and simplest wavelet. While Daubechies wavelets are the most popular wavelets.

The DWT is just a sampled version of CWT. The signals are analyzed in CWT using a set of basis functions which relate to each other by simple scaling and translation. While in the case of DWT, a time-scale representation of the digital signal is obtained using digital filtering techniques.

The DWT is computed by successive lowpass and highpass filtering of the discrete time-domain signal as shown in figure 1.

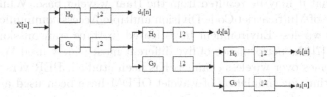

Fig. 1. Three-levels wavelet decomposition tree (DWT)

Where n is an integer. The low pass filter is denoted by G_0 while the high pass filter is denoted by H_0. At each level, the high pass filter produces detail information, d[n], while the low pass filter associated with scaling function produces coarse approximations, a[n].

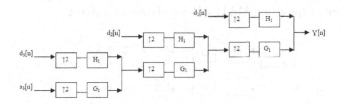

Fig. 2. Three-levels wavelet reconstruction tree (IDWT)

Figure 2 shows the reconstruction of the original signal from the wavelet coefficients or the inverse DWT (IDWT). Basically, the reconstruction is the reverse process of decomposition. In order to reconstruct the signal, a pair of reconstruction filters G_1 and H_1 are designed such that output signal y[n] is identical to the input x[n]. This is known as the condition for perfect reconstruction (PR) [13].

3   The Proposed Technique Description

Fourier based OFDM (OFDM-FFT) implementations have used conventional Fourier filters, and have accomplished data modulation and demodulation via the IFFT and FFT operations respectively. Wavelet based OFDM provides better performance due to superior spectral containment properties. In this paper, the IFFT and FFT blocks are simply replaced by IDWT and DWT wavelet filter blocks respectively. In OFDM-DWT data modulation and demodulation are accomplished via IDWT and DWT operations respectively.

Several works have been done in this field. In [6] the design of the transmitter and receiver for wavelet modulation and its performance in an AWGN channel have been outlined. It has showed that the BER performance of wavelet modulation as function of SNR in the AWGN channel is more accurate. In [8] different transmission scenarios concluded that DWT-OFDM performs much better than DFT-OFDM. But they observed an error floor in DWT- OFDM systems. They suggested that it may be resulted from the Haar wavelet base. While in [4] the performance of Multicarrier Code Division multiple Access communication (MC-CDMA) for wireless Environment investigated in three transmission scenarios. Whereas in [7] the performance of five different most widely used Wavelet bases OFDM schemes over wireless channels has been studied. BER versus SNR and an elapsed time for simulation of wavelet OFDM have been used as a measure of the system performance.

In this paper, the DWT process is simply implemented by a one level (2-band) reconstruction block as shown in figure 3. The input signal x[n] is split by two filters G_0 and H_0 into a low pass component and a high pass component respectively , both of which are decimated (down-sampled) by 2. In order to reconstruct the signal, a pair of reconstruction filters G_1 and H_1 are designed according to the perfect reconstruction condition. Haar 2-tap wavelet has been chosen for this implementation. That is because the Haar wavelet is the simplest type of wavelets, fast, and memory efficient. The filters coefficients corresponding to this wavelet type using MATLAB are shown in Table 1.

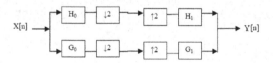

Fig. 3. The 2-band reconstruction block

Table 1. Haar 2-tap Wavelet Coefficients

H_0	G_0	H_1	G_1
$\frac{-1}{\sqrt{2}}$	$\frac{1}{\sqrt{2}}$	$\frac{1}{\sqrt{2}}$	$\frac{1}{\sqrt{2}}$
$\frac{1}{\sqrt{2}}$	$\frac{1}{\sqrt{2}}$	$\frac{-1}{\sqrt{2}}$	$\frac{1}{\sqrt{2}}$

The basic block diagram for wavelet based OFDM transceiver is shown in figure 4. At the transmitter, the random data bits are mapped into symbols to be modulated with Quadrature Amplitude Modulator (QAM). Afterwards, the complex symbols are modulated via IDWT instead of IFFT then it is transmitted through the channel.

At the receiver, the opposite operation is done. Firstly, the received symbols are demodulated using DWT then it is demapped by QAM demodulator. Finally, the symbols are converted to the bits.

As illustrated in figure 4, the OFDM-DWT modulator is implemented as follows; the incoming data symbols are separated into even and odd samples then they are applied to Haar 2-tap IDWT. While the OFDM-DWT demodulator is executed by Haar 2-tap DWT followed by sample interpolation (up-sampled) by 2. The delay unit by one sample time is inserted before the up-sampling unit to compensate the timing between even and odd samples. Subsequently, the two branches are added to reconstruct the original signal.

Instead of inserting high and low path filters before the IDWT to produce the detail and the coarse information respectively [6], samples separation into even and odd samples is employed. This simplifies the hardware implementation of the system. In addition, timing response is improved. Furthermore, the noise from the channel has less effect on the signal due to the signal higher instantaneous amplitude as in this case, the inputs to the IDWT are two coarse signals.

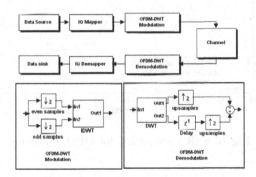

Fig. 4. OFDM-DWT transceiver

4   Simulation Results

In this section, the OFDM-DWT system behavior is studied through MATLAB simulink. In addition, comparisons between the OFDM-FFT systems and the proposed OFDM-DWT are done in terms of BER and.

The comparisons module between the OFDM-FFT without cyclic prefix (CP), OFDM-FFT with CP, and the proposed OFDM-DWT are shown in figure 5.

The data source produces frames of data bits. The frame consists of 64 samples each is converted into two bits per sample to be suited for QAM modulator. The IQ-Mapper converts the bits into samples and then performs QAM modulation. Afterwards, the complex data are generated which are the input to the three systems. Thereafter, the output from the OFDM modulator is transmitted through AWGN channel which adds Gaussian noise to the transmitted signals. Subsequently, the signals are received and OFDM demodulated, IQ-demapped, and converted to bits respectively.

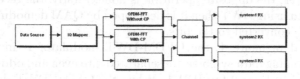

Fig. 5. The comparisons module between the three systems

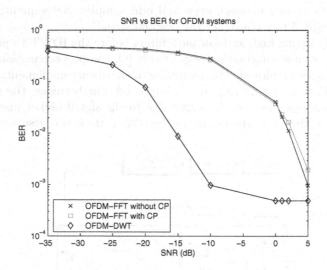

Fig. 6. SNR Versus BER for OFDM systems

Figure 6 displays BER performance as a function of SNR for all OFDM systems. The more SNR, the less BER for the systsm due to the reduction of the noise effect. The proposed system based on DWT shows better performance than the other traditional systems. This is because of the use of IDWT instead of IFFT. In addition, the samples separation implemented in the front of the modulator block gives more instantaneous amplitude to the transmitted signal and hence, it can immune the noise effect.

The two traditional OFDM systems base on FFT have nearly the same BER performance. This is because the effect of the CP to remove the inter symbol interference is expounded when multi-path propagation is tested. While the three systems behaves the same performance with higher SNR above 5 dB.

The output waveforms from the three systems compared with the input signal before bit conversion are shown in figure 7. These values are obtained at SNR=1 dB. The output from the proposed OFDM-DWT system gives nearly a perfect reconstruction for the input signal. This is because of the samples separations. Moreover, the filters are synthesized under the condition for perfect reconstruction in DWT system. While the two other systems behaves nearly in the same manner with worse performance compared with the proposed system.

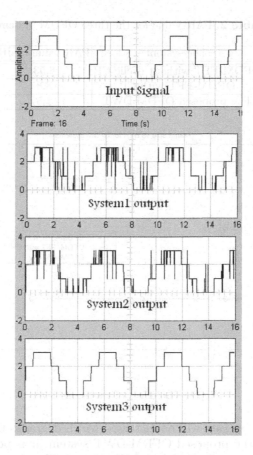

Fig. 7. The output waveforms compared with the input signal

The crest factor (CF) or peak-to-average ratio (PAR) or peak-to-average power ratio (PAPR) is a measurement of a waveform, calculated from the peak amplitude of the waveform divided by the Root Mean Square (RMS) value of the waveform $\left(CF = \frac{max|x(t)|^2}{x(t)_{rms}^2} \right)$. The definition of the PAR in dB should be $10log_{10}(CF)$. The PAR values for the three OFDM systems are shown in Table 2. It is cleared that the proposed system gives the best PAR value among the systems. This is because of the use of IDWT in place of IFFT. Then the average value of the transmitted signal for the proposed system is reduced. The reason for this is, the proposed system can nearly stabilize the amplitude of the transmitted signal due to the use of the sample separation in the front of the IDWT. The proposed OFDM-DWT has 7.03 dB and 7.3 dB better PAR performance than OFDM-IFFT without and with CP respectively.

The effect of the frame size on the three systems is revealed from figure 8. These values are obtained at SNR=1 dB for example. For OFDM-FFT based systems, the larger frame size, the more BER value and hence more system degradation. This is because that for larger frame size, the I/FFT size will be

Table 2. PAR Value for the three OFDM systems

The system	PAR value in dB
OFDM-FFT without cyclic CP	8.53
OFDM-FFT with CP	8.8
The proposed OFDM-DWT	1.5

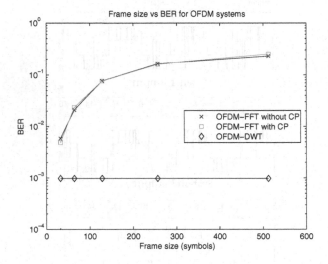

Fig. 8. The effect of the frame size

increased, and the bit rate will be increased which degrades the system performance. While for the proposed OFDM-DWT system, it is not affected by the
frame size. In this paper, Haar 2-tap I/DWT is used. Therefore, only two samples
are entered to the OFDM-modulator simultaneously unaffected with the frame
size. In addition, the BER performance for the proposed ODFM-DWT system
is better than other systems for all frame sizes.

At any other value for the SNR, the same relation will be the same. This is
because the proposed protocol is better than traditional system in all SNR as it
is obviously appeared from figure 6.

5   Conclusions

In this paper, an efficient technique OFDM-DWT system was proposed. Extensive
simulation programs were performed to investigate the efficiency of the proposed
system compared with traditional OFDM systems based on FFT. The proposed
system showed a superior performance. It was simpler and less hardware than traditional systems. In addition, it had less BER performance as a function of SNR
than traditional systems. Moreover, it donated a perfect reconstruction for the
input signal. Furthermore, it had less PAR value than traditional systems. In addition, the frame size had no effect on the proposed system performance.

References

1. Bahai, A.R.S., Saltzberg, B.R., Ergen, M.: Multi Carrier Digital Communications. Springer Science Business Media, Inc., Heidelberg (2004)
2. Andrews, J.G., Ghosh, A., Muhamed, R.: Fundamentals of WiMAX: Understanding broadband wireless networking. Pearson Education, Inc., London (2007)
3. Akansu, A., Duhamel, P., Lin, X., Courville, M.: Orthogonal tran multiplexers in communication: a review. IEEE Transactions on signal processing 46(4), 979–995 (1998)
4. Hailemariam, D.: Wavelet based multicarrier code division multiple access communication for wireless environment. Master's thesis, Addis Ababa University (2003)
5. Jamin, A., Mahonen, P.: Wavelet packet modulation for wireless communications. Wireless communication and mobile computing Journal 5(2) (March 2005)
6. Manglani, M.J.: Wavelet modulation in gaussian and rayleigh fading channels. Master's thesis, Faculty of the Virginia Polytechnic Institute and State University (July 2001)
7. Shiferaw, Y.: Comparative performance study on wavelet based orthogonal frequency division multiplexing (ofdm) using dierent wavelets. Master's thesis, Addis Ababa University (2007)
8. Zhang, H., Yuan, D., Jiang, M., Wu, D.: Research of dft-ofdm and dwt-ofdm on different transmission scenarios. In: The 2nd International Technology for Application, ICITA (2004)
9. Abdullah, K., Hussain, Z.M.: Studies on dwt-ofdm and fft-ofdm systems. In: International Conference on Communication, Computer and Power (ICCCP 2009), February 15-18 (2009)
10. Dilmirghani, R., Ghavami, M.: Wavelet vs fourier based uwb systems. In: 18th IEEE International Symposium on Personal, Indoor and Mobile Radio Communications (September 2007)
11. Mirghani, R., Ghavami, M.: Comparison between wavelet-based and fourier-based multicarrier uwb systems. IET Communications 2(2), 353–358 (2008)
12. Teolis, A.: Computational Signal Processing with Wavelets (1998)
13. Kingsbury, N., Magarey, J.: Wavelet transform in image processing. In: Signal Processing and Prediction. Eurasip, ICT press (1997)

Marginalized Particle Filter for Maneuvering Target Tracking Application

Fei Zhou[*], Wei-jun He[**], and Xin-yue Fan[***]

Institute of Wireless Location & Space Measurement
Chongqing University of Posts and Telecommunications,
No.2 of Road ChongWen in Nan-An Country, Chongqing, 400065, P.R. China
zhoufei@cupqt.edu.cn, raymond77511@163.com,
parrot2003@sohu.com, fanxinyue@cqupt.edu.cn

Abstract. This paper deals with the problem of maneuvering target tracking in wireless tracking service. It results in a mixed linear/non-linear Models estimation problem. For maneuvering tracking systems, these problems are traditionally handled using the extended Kalman filter or Particle filter. In this paper, Marginalized Particle Filter is presented for applications in such problem. The algorithm marginalized the linear state variables out from the state space. The nonlinear state variables are estimated by the Particle Filter and the rest are estimated with the result of the estimation of the nonlinear state variables by the Kalman Filter. Simulation results shows that the Marginalized Particle Filter guarantees the estimation accuracy and reduces computational times compare to the Particle filer and the Extending Kalman Filter in maneuver target tracking application.

Keywords: Marginalized Particle Filter; Kalman, Particle, maneuver target tracking.

1 Introduction

Wireless tracking service is one of the most important mobile services. The design of system model and tracking filter are the key technologies for such service. In recent years, as the wheel of research about the positioning and target tracking model turns with its accelerating velocity, kinds of state place models emerged toward to the complexity environment. For instance, Linear and Gaussian Models, Nonlinear and Gaussian Models, Nonlinear and Non-Gaussian Models and Mixed Linear/non-linear Models. Various filtering algorithm arises in view of the various types system model's

---

[*] Fei Zhou, Associate professor, Ph.D., his research is focused on wireless localization, digital signal process, and navigation algorithm.

[**] Wei-Jun He, Graduate student, M.S., his research is focused on mobile communication and wireless tracking.

[***] Xin-Yue Fan, Instructor, M.S., her research is focused on signal processing and radar image.

Sponsored by:
Natural Science Foundation of ChongQing Educational Committee (KJ080520);
Natural Science Foundation of ChongQing Science Committee (CSTC,2008BB2412).

R.-S. Chang et al. (Eds.): GPC 2010, LNCS 6104, pp. 542–551, 2010.

innate characteristic. Kalman filter(KF) is undoubtedly the optimal algorithm in solving the problem of Linear Gaussian Models. However, the assumption which is made by KF is failed in the situation of Nonlinear Non-Gaussian Models. So only approximate method can be used. There are two types of approximation of nonlinear filter. One is called Gaussian filter, such as Extended Kalman filter(EKF) and Unscented Kalman filter(UKF). However, the linearization process of the EKF is liable to large errors threatening the convergence of the algorithm, particularly for models with high nonlinearity. The other nonlinear filter is Particle filter (PF), a recently popularized technique for numerical approximation. The core idea behind the PF is to use samples (particles) to approximate the concerned distribution. It offers a general numerical tool to approximate the posterior density function for the state in nonlinear and non-Gaussian filtering problems. While the particle filter is fairly easy to implement and tune, its main drawback is the inherent computational complexity and it increases quickly with the state dimension. That may prevent the real time application of the particle filter. The defect of KF and PF is inevitable for Mixed Linear/non-linear Models, especially for the model which contains large number of linear states and fewer nonlinear ones. For instance, the states of linear and nonlinear coexist in aircraft navigation system (INS) or maneuver target tracking system. Generally speaking, the nonlinear states constitute only a small part of the whole state space and most are linear states[1]. So there is a serious need for a hybrid filter algorithm which provides a fusion and takes the advantage of KF and PF respectively. The computational times will have a large measure of decrease as soon as the linear state is marginalized out from the PF. By doing this, it requires much less computational, At the same time, the goal of improving the estimation precision and real time can be achieved.

Using Bayes' theorem we can then marginalize out the linear state variables from the whole state space. and estimate them using the KF, which is the optimal filter for this case. The nonlinear state variables are estimated using the particle filter. Marginalized Particle Filter(MPF) which is the filter using such idea[2,3] has been successfully used in several applications, for instance, in aircraft navigation, underwater navigation, communications, nonlinear system identification, and audio source separation[4].

In the paper, MPF has been successfully used in the maneuvering target tracking model, named Singer Model. The algorithm marginalized the linear state variables out from the state space. The nonlinear state variables are estimated by the Particle Filter and the rest are estimated with the result of the estimation of the nonlinear state variables by the Kalman Filter. Simulation results clearly show the superior performance of the MPF in estimation accuracy and computational times compare to the PF and the EKF in maneuver target tracking application.

2 The MPF Algorithm

Many problems in positioning and target tracking can be cast as mixed linear/non-linear estimation problem. The nonlinear filtering problem considered here consists of recursively estimating the posterior problem density function of the state vector in a general discrete time state space model and the observed measurements. Such a general model can be formulated as[5]:

$$\begin{cases} x_{k+1} = f(x_k) + u_k \\ y_k = h(x_k) + v_k \end{cases} \tag{1}$$

Where $f(\bullet)$ and $h(\bullet)$ are two arbitrary nonlinear function, u_k is the process noise. v_k is the measurement noise. x_k is the state of the system, y_k is the measurements of the system. Here the purpose is supposed to estimate the posterior probability density function(PDF) $p(x_{k+1}|y_k)$ [6] by the following equations according to the Chapman-Kolmogorov[7]:

$$p(x_{k+1}|y_{1:k}) = \int p(x_{k+1}|x_k y_{1:k}) p(x_k|y_{1:k}) dx_k \tag{2}$$

$$p(x_{k+1}|y_{1:k}) = \frac{p(y_{k+1}|x_{k+1}, y_{1:k}) p(x_{k+1}|y_{1:k})}{p(y_{k+1}|y_{1:k})} = \frac{p(y_{k+1}|x_{k+1}) p(x_{k+1}|y_{1:k})}{p(y_{k+1}|y_{1:k})} \tag{3}$$

Consider a state vector x_k, which can be partitioned according to[8]:

$$x_k = \begin{bmatrix} x_k^n \\ x_k^l \end{bmatrix} \tag{4}$$

Where x_k^n denotes the linear states and x_k^l denotes the nonlinear states, in dynamics and measurement relation. The explanation of how the marginalized particle filter works is started by considering the following model[4]:

$$\begin{cases} x_{k+1}^n = f_k^n(x_k^n) + A_k^n(x_k^n) x_k^l + u_k^n \tag{5a} \\ x_{k+1}^l = f_k^l(x_k^n) + A_k^l(x_k^n) x_k^l + u_k^l \tag{5b} \\ y_k = h_k(x_k^n) + v_k \tag{5c} \end{cases}$$

Here the target distribution is the posterior distribution $p(x_{k+1}|y_k)$, according to the Bayes' rule,

$$p(x_k|y_{1:k}) = p(x_k^l, x_k^n|y_{1:k}) = p(x_k^l|x_k^n, y_{1:k}) p(x_k^n|y_{1:k}) \tag{6}$$

can be achieved.

The estimation of Minimum Mean Squared Error (MMSE) is

$$\hat{x}_k = \int x_k p(x_k|y_{0:k}) dx_k = \int \left[\int (x_k^n, x_k^l) p(x_k^l|x_k^n, y_{0:k}) dx_k^l \right] \bullet p(x_k^n|y_{0:k}) dx_k^n \tag{7}$$

Therefore, the linear state $p(x_k^l|x_k^n, y_{1:k})$ and the nonlinear state $p(x_k^n|y_{1:k})$ can be estimated respectively after analytically marginalizing out the linear state variables from $p\left(x_k \mid y_{1:k}\right)$. According to Eq.(5c), if x_k^n is known, the measurement y_k is conditionally independent, Eq.(6) can be simplified as :

$$p\left(x_k^l \mid x_k^n, y_{1:k}\right) = p\left(x_k^l \mid x_k^n\right) \tag{8}$$

Eq.(5c) can't be the measurement equation because of none of information about nonlinear state in it. However, there is information about linear state in nonlinear state equation (Eq.(5a)). Accordingly, the nonlinear state x_k^n can be used to estimate the linear state x_k^l as its measurement in KF. The process model of Eq.(5a) and Eq.(5c) can be rewritten as:

$$\begin{cases} x_{k+1}^n = f_k^n\left(x_k^n\right) + A_k^n\left(x_k^n\right)x_k^l + u_k^n & (9a) \\ z_k = A_k^l\left(x_k^n\right)x_k^l + u_k^l & (9b) \end{cases}$$

Where $z_k = x_{k+1}^l - f_k^l\left(x_k^n\right)$.

If z_k is regarded as a measurement and x_k^l as the state, then Eq.(9) describes a linear Gaussian model, which enables the states to be optimized by the KF. The second density $p\left(x_k^n \mid y_{1:k}\right)$ in Eq.(6) will be approximated using the standard particle filter. It means that the KF's measurement update can be performed as soon as the estimation of $\hat{x}_{l+1}^n$ is known in the PF. In this way, a flow diagram of MPF is shown in figure 1:

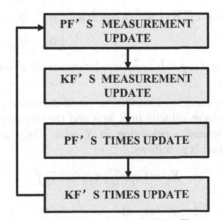

Fig. 1. Marginalized Particle Filter Flow

3   MPF for Singer

3.1   Singer Model

Singer Model is a typical maneuvering model. This model is flexible to describe the movement of targets[9].

Assume $a(k)$ is time correlation variable and the auto-correlation function is $R_a(\tau)$:

$$R_a(\tau) = E[a(k)a(k+\tau)] = \sigma_a^2 e^{-\alpha|\tau|} \quad \alpha \geq 0$$

By modeling the maneuver as a first-order autoregressive process, the maneuvering target dynamics can be derived to a standard form as follows[10]:

$$X_k = F_{k-1,k} X_{k-1} + W_{k-1}$$

Where $X_k = [x_k, \dot{x}_k, \ddot{x}_k]^T$, $x_k, \dot{x}_k, \ddot{x}_k$ are the position, velocity and acceleration respectively. Where the transition matrix $F_{k-1,k}$ is given by

$$F = e^{AT} = \begin{bmatrix} 1 & T & (\alpha T - 1 + e^{-\alpha T})/\alpha^2 \\ 0 & 1 & (1 - e^{-\alpha T})/\alpha \\ 0 & 0 & e^{-\alpha T} \end{bmatrix}$$

The parameters T and α are the data sampling time and the reciprocal of maneuver time constant respectively.

The process noise W_k is a vector of zero-mean white noise sequence as follows:

$$W_k = \int_{kT}^{(k+1)T} F_{(k+1)T,\tau} \tilde{W}(\tau) d\tau \tag{10}$$

The covariance matrix of W_k is given by

$$Q(k) = E[W(k)W^T(k)] = 2\alpha\sigma_m^2 \begin{bmatrix} q_{11} & q_{12} & q_{13} \\ q_{21} & q_{22} & q_{23} \\ q_{31} & q_{32} & q_{33} \end{bmatrix}$$

Where the elements $q_{ij}(i, j = 1, 2, 3)$ are functions of parameters α and T, that can be found in [11].

In the paper, Singer model is extended to multi-dimensional situation. One is non maneuvering with constant velocity in X axis and the other is maneuvering with constant velocity and constant acceleration in Y axis. They are independent and the mathematical description is as follows:

$$X_k = [x_k, \dot{x}_k, y_k, \dot{y}_k, \ddot{y}_k]^T$$

$$F = \begin{bmatrix} 1 & T & 0 & 0 & 0 \\ 0 & 1 & 0 & 0 & 0 \\ 0 & 0 & 1 & T & (\alpha T - 1 + e^{-\alpha T})/\alpha^2 \\ 0 & 0 & 0 & 1 & (1 - e^{-\alpha T})/\alpha \\ 0 & 0 & 0 & 0 & e^{-\alpha T} \end{bmatrix}$$

Marginalize the linear state x_{k+1}^l from X_k as Eq(11):

$$x_{k+1}^n = \begin{bmatrix} x_{k+1} \\ y_{k+1} \end{bmatrix} = \begin{bmatrix} 1 & 0 \\ 0 & 1 \end{bmatrix}\begin{bmatrix} x_k \\ y_k \end{bmatrix} + \begin{bmatrix} T & 0 & 0 \\ 0 & T & (\alpha T - 1 + e^{-\alpha T})/\alpha^2 \end{bmatrix}\begin{bmatrix} \dot{x}_k \\ \dot{y}_k \\ \ddot{y}_k \end{bmatrix} + \begin{bmatrix} u_{x_k} \\ u_{y_k} \end{bmatrix} \tag{11a}$$

$$x_{k+1}^l = \begin{bmatrix} 1 & 0 & 0 \\ 0 & 1 & (1-e^{-\alpha T})/\alpha \\ 0 & 0 & e^{-\alpha T} \end{bmatrix}\begin{bmatrix} \dot{x}_k \\ \dot{y}_k \\ \ddot{y}_k \end{bmatrix} + \begin{bmatrix} u_{\dot{x}_k} \\ u_{\dot{y}_k} \\ u_{\ddot{y}_k} \end{bmatrix} \tag{11b}$$

$$y_k = \begin{bmatrix} x_k \\ y_k \end{bmatrix} = \begin{bmatrix} \sqrt{(x_k-x_2)^2+(y_k-y_2)^2} - \sqrt{(x_k-x_1)^2+(y_k-y_1)^2} \\ \sqrt{(x_k-x_3)^2+(y_k-y_3)^2} - \sqrt{(x_k-x_1)^2+(y_k-y_1)^2} \end{bmatrix} + \begin{bmatrix} v_{x_k} \\ v_{y_k} \end{bmatrix} \tag{11c}$$

The TDOA(Times Difference Of Arrival) algorithm for localization is employed in the paper. The measurement matrix is given in Eq(11c) through TDOA. The measurement noise v_k is reference to the error model proposed by Bard in [12].

3.2 MPF for Singer

Eq.(11) is the complete form after separated from X_k in Singer model application. Compare to Eq.(5), $f_k^l(x_k^n)$ is zero. Then the model which is described in Eq.(5) becomes a triangular one as follows:

$$\begin{cases} x_{k+1}^n = f_k^n(x_k^n) + A_k^n(x_k^n)x_k^l + u_k^n \\ x_{k+1}^l = \qquad\qquad A_k^l(x_k^n)x_k^l + u_k^l \\ y_k = h_k(x_k^n) + v_k \end{cases} \tag{12}$$

Where $u_k^n \sim N(0, Q_k^n)$, $u_k^L \sim N(0, Q_k^l)$, $v_k \sim N(0, R_k)$.
Further more, x_0^l is Gaussian

$$x_0^l \sim N(\overline{x}_0, \overline{P}_0)$$

The MPF for Singer can be summarized in following steps:

Step 1: Initialization. *For* $i = 1, \cdots, N$,
    Take particles $x_{0|-1}^{n,(i)}$ from $p_{x_0^n}(x_0^n)$, and set $\{x_{0|-1}^{l,(i)}, P_{0|-1}^{(i)}\} = \{x_0^l, P_0\}$.
Step 2: PF's measurement update.
① Evaluate the importance weights

$$\tilde{\omega}_k^i \propto \tilde{\omega}_{k-1}^i \frac{p\left(y_k \big| x_k^{n,(i)}\right) p\left(x_k^{n,(i)} \big| x_{k-1}^{n,(i)}\right)}{q\left(x_k^{n,(i)} \big| x_{k-1}^{n,(i)}, y_{1:k}\right)}, \quad i=1,\cdots,N$$

② Normalize:

$$\omega_k^i = \frac{\tilde{\omega}_k^i}{\displaystyle\sum_{j=1}^{N} \tilde{\omega}_k^j}$$

③ Resampling。

Step 3: KF's measurement update.

For $i=1\cdots N$,

$$\hat{x}_{k|k}^{l*,(i)} = \hat{x}_{k|k}^{l,(i)} + L_k\left(z_k - A_k^n \hat{x}_{k|k}^{l,(i)}\right) \tag{13}$$

$$P_{k|k}^{*,(i)} = P_{k|k}^{(i)} - L_k N_k L_k^T \tag{14}$$

$$L_k = P_{k|k}^{(i)}\left(A_k^n\right)^T N_k^{-1}$$

$$N_k = A_k^n P_{k|k}^{(i)}\left(A_k^n\right)^T + Q_k^n$$

Step 4: PF's times update(prediction).

For $i=1\cdots N$, Predict new particles $\hat{x}_k^{n,(i)}$ from $x_{k-1}^{n,(i)}$.

Step 5: KF's times update.

For $i=1\cdots N$,

$$\hat{x}_{k+1|k}^{l,(i)} = A_k^l \hat{x}_{k|k}^{l,(i)} + L_k\left(z_k - A_k^n \hat{x}_{k|k}^{l,(i)}\right) \tag{15}$$

$$P_{k+1|k}^{(i)} = A_k^l P_{k|k}^{(i)}\left(A_k^l\right)^T + Q_k^l - L_k N_k L_k^T \tag{16}$$

$$L_k = A_k^l P_{k|k}^{(i)}\left(A_k^n\right)^T N_k^{-1}$$

$$N_k = A_k^n P_{k|k}^{(i)}\left(A_k^n\right)^T + Q_k^n$$

Step 6: Set $k = k+1$, and iterate from step 2.

It's worth noting that the second measurement update is called measurement update due to the fact that the mathematical structure is the same as a measurement update in the KF. However, strictly speaking, it is not really a measurement update, since there does not exist any new measurement. It is better to think of this second update as a correction to the real measurement update using the information in the prediction of the nonlinear state variables, as described in [4].

4 Simulation

In order to examine the effectiveness of MPF in Singer model tracking application, computer simulations are conducted. Estimation performance is compared with the EKF and standard PF.

In this section, Three Based Stations (BS) are used in the TDOA simulation. The coverage radius is 8-10 kilometers each. All results are based on 200 Monte Carlo runs. Computer configuration: Pentium(R) D CPU 2.80GHz, 512M. The parameter in the simulation is as Table 1:

Table 1. Parts of Parameters in Simulation

Parameter	Numerical value
X_{BS}	$[x_1, x_2, x_3]^T = [0, 5000, 10000]$
Y_{BS}	$[y_1, y_2, y_3]^T = [0, 10000\sqrt{3}, 0]$
T	200
σ_m^2	8
α	1/10
$W(k-1)$	$W_k = \int_{kT}^{(k+1)T} F_{(k+1)T,\tau} \tilde{W}(\tau) d\tau$
v_x	13.89m/s
v_{y0}	10m/s
a_{y0}	0
N	50

The following figure 2 shows the tracking trajectory of the algorithm:

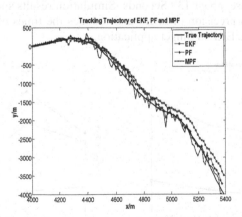

Fig. 2. Tracking Trajectory of EKF, PF and MPF

The tracking trajectory of MPF gives a better performance compare to EKF even with some vibration in tracking process according to figure 2.

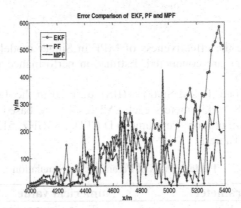

Fig. 3. Error Comparison of EKF, PF and MPF

Table 2. Comparison of RMSE of Error and tracking times

	$RMSE$ (m)	Times of Tracking (s)
MPF	86.0290	71.7136
PF	75.4784	210.5147
EKF	144.3814	2.9722

Figure 3 shows the error comparison of EKF, PF and MPF and Table 2 is the comparison of RMSE(Root Mean Square Error) and times of estimation. Where RMSE is calculated according to:

$$RMSE = \sqrt{\frac{1}{n}\sum_{i=1}^{n}\left(\hat{x}_i - x_i\right)^2 + \left(\hat{y}_i - y_i\right)^2}$$

The RMSE of MPF increases $10.55\,m$ compare to PF, but the computational times have a largely decrease, about 139 Seconds. Simulation results shows that MPF guarantees the estimation precision of target and reduces the times of computation compare to the PF and the EKF in Singer application.

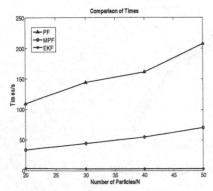

Fig. 4. Times Comparison of EKF, PF and MPF

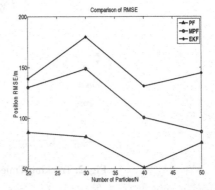

Fig. 5. RMSE Comparison of EKF, PF and MPF

Different particle numbers are used in the simulation, figure 4 shows the times comparison of EKF, PF and MPF and figure 5 shows the RMSE comparison of each. Figure 4 demonstrates that the reduction in times of computation is 67.45% in average. The main reason is that MPF marginalizes the linear states from the whole state space and estimate with KF. As a result, estimation accuracy is guaranteed and the computational demand is reduced.

5 Conclusion

In the paper, Marginalized Particle Filter has been successfully used in Mixed Linear and non-linear Models. It guarantees the estimation accuracy of target with smaller estimating delay compare to the PF and the EKF. In this algorithm, the nonlinear state variables are estimated by the standard Particle Filter. So if Gaussian Particle Filter or Regularized Particle Filter can be employed, the algorithm will give a better performance.

References

1. Yin, J.-j., Zhang, J.-q., Klass, M.: The Marginal Rao-Blackwellized Particle Filter for mixed linear/non-linear state space models. Chinese Journal of Aeronautics 20(4), 346–352 (2007)
2. Xue-yuan, Ma, G.-f., Hu, Q.-l.: Satellite attitude estimation based on marginalized particle filter. Control and Decision 22(1), 39–44 (2007)
3. Zhu, Z.-y., Dai, X.-Q.: Marginalized Particle Filter for maneuver target tracking. Journal of WuHan University of Technology 30(6), 118–121 (2008)
4. Schoh, T., Gustafsson, F., Nordlund, J.: Marginalized Particle Filters for mixed linear/nonlinear state-space models. IEEE Transaction of signal processing 53(7), 2279–2289 (2005)
5. Liang, J., Qiao, l.-y., Peng, X.-y.: Fault Detection Based on SI R State Estimation and Smoothed Residual. Chinese Journal of Electronics 35(12A), 32–36 (2007)
6. Gordon, N., Salmond, D.: Novel approach to nonlinear and Non-Gaussian Bayesian state estimation. Proc. of Institute Electric Engineering 140(2), 107–113 (1993)
7. Maskell, S., Briers, M., Wright, R.: Tracking using a radar and a problem specific proposal distribution in a particle filter. IEEE Proceedings, Sonar and Navigation 152(5), 315–322 (2005)
8. Kim, S., Holmstrom, L., Mcnames, J.: Multiharmonic tracking using Marginalized Particle Filters. In: 30th Annual International IEEE EMBS Conference, vol. 20(25), pp. 29–33 (2008)
9. Wang, L., Li, X.-b.: The improvement of antenna servo system of launcher based on Singer model. Tactical Missile Technology (1), 29–32 (2008)
10. Tafti, A.D., Sadati, N.: A novel adaptive tracking algorithm for fusion by neural network. In: The International Conference on Computer as a Tool, vol. 9(12), pp. 818–822 (2007)
11. Chen, X.: The algorithm research of Particle Filter location track for Wimax in high dynamic condition. Chongqing University of post and telecom, Chongqing (2007)
12. Bard, J.D., Ham, F.M., Jones, W.L.: An algebraic solution to the time difference of arrival equations. Proceedings of the IEEE 11(4), 313–319 (1996)

Business Independent Model of Mobile Workforce Management

Volker Gruhn and Thomas Richter*

Chair of Applied Telematics / e-Business, University of Leipzig
Klostergasse 3, 04109 Leipzig, Germany
{gruhn,richter}@ebus.informatik.uni-leipzig.de

Abstract. In this work we introduce a general model for the description of mobile workforce environments. In the context of Business Process reengineering projects such models are necessary to predict the outcome of the optimization efforts. The model we propose is designed to be domain independent and can thus be utilized in BPR projects for any business domain incorporating mobile workforce systems.

1 Introduction

Mobile business processes in workforce environments can be seen as processes, of which at least one activity takes place outside the organization's physical bounds [1,2] and mobile workers are scheduled to perform such activities. If we consider mobile processes in network based industries (e.g. utilities, telecommunications) we can state that indeed selected mobile processes can be seen as a combination of mobile activities, taking place at different locations. These processes consist of more than one mobile activity. The following section introduces such a business process originating in the utility industry. Additionally time restrictions apply as e.g. down-times have to be minimized. In such mobile environments numerous business processes are executed in parallel by different workers / teams. Based on their respective qualifications and locations workers may perform not all but just a few activities of a process, possibly even alternatingly for two or more processes. Additionally complexity increases by the possibility of emergencies (processes with high priorities) during operation which demand the immediate re-scheduling of closeby, adequately skilled workers.

Many organizations and enterprises with the according types of business processes are currently initiating or performing BPR projects of their mobile environment to introduce business process support with mobile workforce management systems [1]. Such projects usually include both the introduction of information systems to support the current processes and the examination of the whole process landscape which can lead to substantial process redefinition. The prediction of the outcome of process redefinition projects is (i) hard to achieve since many soft factors influence the costs of mobile processes and (ii) usually

---

* Corresponding author.

R.-S. Chang et al. (Eds.): GPC 2010, LNCS 6104, pp. 552–561, 2010.

of paramount importance for the approval of such projects by the management. Among the soft factors mentioned above are e. g. weather and traffic conditions, workforce scheduling methods, and the structuring of teams – just to mention a few. Many BPR projects are performed by external consulting firms, specialized on either certain IT-systems or certain business domains. To gain reliable calculations of the expected outcome of BPR projects such firms can apply simulation models of the mobile environment in question. Preliminary research on this topic is e. g. performed by Netjes et al. [3] who introduce a Colored Petri Net based [4] model for the analysis of resource utilization and perform several examinations regarding the skill balancing and resource allocation order in banking processes.

For the development of such simulation models we have designed a domain independent model of mobile workforce environments which will be presented in this article. The authors have demonstrated a simulation model for mobile environments utilizing this domain model [5,6]. This simulation system is feasible to be utilized independently from the business domain.

The remainder of this article is organized as follows. In the following section 2 we introduce the domain independent model. Related work is discussed throughout this section where appropriate. In the concluding section 4 we discuss possible applications of the model and motivate further research.

2   Process Model of Mobile Workforce Management

To develop a business independent domain specific model of mobility and the execution of mobile work it is necessary to understand (i) the differences and commonalities of mobile business processes and (ii) the entities usually involved in such processes.

Example Process. In the following we will illustrate the processes in question with an example from the utility industry. Figure 1a shows a typical situation after a new power substation was erected and needs to be connected to the existing power network. This is achieved by the insertion of a sleeve (tee branch) at location L3 into the power line between the stations at locations L1 and L2. For the necessary work security concerns demand that the power line between stations at L1 and L2 has to be turned off before and turned on again after the insertion. Fig. 1b shows the resulting process as a UML Activity Diagram.

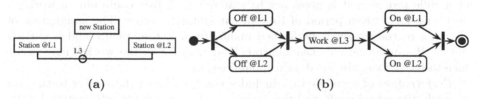

(a)   (b)

Fig. 1. Power line extension situation and according process

Since it is desirable to minimise the downtime of the line different workers should perform tasks at different locations to avoid downtimes of the line due to travel effort. For our example this means that different workers may turn the stations on and off while a third team works at the site to perform the sleeve insertion. As a result actually independent processes become interdependent due to the fact that one worker can be involved in several different processes. In this way delays that occur at a certain site may cause massive delays at completely different sites and processes. Additional types of processes for non-mobile workforce problems are discussed by Russell et al. who introduce a series of 43 Workflow resource patterns in [7].

Entities. Several different types of entities are involved with mobile workforce management. For the purpose of this work we will give a brief overview of the most important ones. For a broader and deeper insight we refer the reader to [5], [1], and [8]. Mobile work is performed by *workers* who are assigned with a current geographic location, skills, and a schedule. A group of co-operating workers is called a *team*. A *geographic location* is a position on the surface of the Earth. The *schedule* of a worker is an ordered list of tasks the worker has to perform. The period covered by a schedule can be any span of time and is not restricted to a day. The schedules of ground based long distance transportation, for instance, usually cover a week [9]. A *task* is an atomic unit of work to be performed assigned with a geographic location and a set of skills it demands. Workers or teams must have the adequate skills to be scheduled to perform a task. A task can be assigned with an *asset* which is a piece of equipment located at a geographic position. A *process* is an ordered set of activities defining how a business goal of a certain type can be achieved. Processes can be considered as templates for the operation of enterprises. A *case* instantiates a process. It is assigned with the concrete data for one execution of the process. In the same way tasks can be considered as instances of activities. Tasks are the work units of cases.

Abstract Model. Figure 2 gives an overview of the typical administrative parts of any mobile process.

Preparation of a mobile task includes the gathering and bundling of necessary information and material. It is carried out a the organization's headquarter. An example for the preparation of the inspection of a power network is the print-out of the list of all assets to be inspected.

Assignment of a mobile task to a worker appoints the worker to execute this task. To assign a worker to a task, the task's required qualifications must be in the set of the worker's skills. As traveling contributes considerably to the costs of mobile processes it is necessary to manage work lists containing a worker's activities for a given period of time in chronological order. The assignment of the task to the worker is performed manually or automatically and is carried out at the organization's headquarter. The transfer to the worker may occur face-to-face or via wireless data communication.

Performance of a mobile task includes the transfer of the worker to the site of work, the actual work, and the gathering of work-related information by the worker on-site. It is mainly carried out at the task's location.

Completion of a mobile task includes the analysis of the work results, the accounting, the updating of technical data, and the planning of further measures if necessary. It is typically executed at the headquarter.

The steps considered in this work are the assignment and the performance of the mobile task which are the process steps that are influenced by the properties of mobility (see Fig. 2).

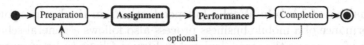

Fig. 2. Abstract mobile process

Assignment of Mobile Work. The primary goal of the assignment of mobile work is the minimization of the total process costs of the organization. The resulting secondary goals of the work assignment are the execution of the cases with the highest priority, the reduction of travel effort, and the avoidance of workers' idle times. The general assignment activities are depicted in Figure 3. The assignment can either be performed manually by a dispatcher or automatically by a workforce management system based on preset priorities, expected travel times, and interdependencies of the cases and tasks.

At the beginning of a working day for every case its tasks are inserted into the schedules of adequate workers. The next case is selected and inserted into the still incomplete schedules until all schedules are complete. A schedule is considered complete if it contains activities work for a whole working day – e. g. expected working and travel times sum up to eight or nine hours.

Algorithms for the solving of the respective mobile workforce scheduling problem are presented and discussed in [6]. If mobility is omitted from the problem domain the resulting can be interpreted as resource-scheduling and resource distribution in business process management. The foundations of resource scheduling research date back to the 1950ies and are summarized in [10]. Ursu et al. [11] present a distributed solution for workforce allocation based on independent agents. The workforce allocation is achieved by negotiation between agents utilizing a specialized communication protocol. In-depth Petri net based modeling and analysis of work distribution mechanisms of the Workflow Management Systems Staffware, FileNet, and FLOWer is presented in [12]. Further research by Pesic and van der Aalst focuses on the development of a reference model for work distribution in Workflow Management Systems [13]. They focus on the general lifecycle of work items and introduce a CPN based approach for the distribution of work items to resources at runtime. Though most of the work depicted above

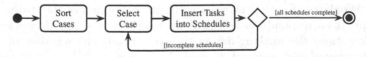

Fig. 3. Assignment of a mobile task

had creative influence on our work none covers the properties of mobile process environments. Resource allocation in mobile process environments has been in the focus of the following work. An automated resource management system (ARMS) for British Telecom is introduced in [14]. The system is intended for forecasting and analysis of resource demands and executes the dispatching of jobs to resources but does not handle precedence relations of chained tasks and process durations.

Performance of Mobile Work. Independently from the business objectives the performance of a mobile business process also follows a general scheme. For each task of a process the steps depicted in Figure 4 have to be executed.

Traveling is the transfer of the worker responsible for the execution of a task to the location of that task. It can start at the operational base of this worker (for the first task of the day) or at the location of another task that has been accomplished by the worker before. In this work traveling *towards* a task's location is considered to belong to that task.

Waiting may be necessary after the location of the task has been reached by the worker and either the time window of the task has not been reached yet or a preceding task of the case has not been finished yet. In the example of Fig. 1b "Work@L3" must not start until "Off@L1" and "Off@L2" are finished.

Execution of a task is the actual accomplishment of the business objective of this part of the process. The execution of tasks is considered as an economically weighted period of time which blocks a worker at a certain location with certain costs.

Finalization of a task includes the gathering of data describing the work results. This includes business data as e. g. the nature and amount of material consumed and administrative data as consumed time.

Further discussion of organizational aspects of resource management is e. g. accomplished in [15].

Fig. 4. Execution of a mobile task

3 State Models of Entities

Resulting from the characterization of abstract mobile processes as in Figure 2 and the assignment and performance of mobile tasks as in the Figures 3 and 4 state models for workers, tasks, and processes can be given.

Mobile Workers. Figure 5 shows a UML state diagram of the states a worker can adopt. It corresponds to a typical working day of a mobile worker. When the worker starts the working day in the state `Ready` the schedule of a worker is already created and assigned. Considering a typical daily routine the worker enters the state `Traveling` as soon as he drives to the site of the first task of his

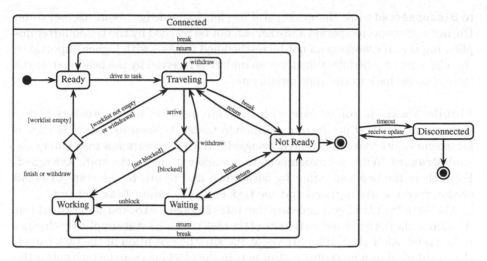

Fig. 5. State of a mobile worker with WFM-support

schedule. After reaching the working site the worker enters the state `Waiting` if the task is preceded by another task of the respective case *and* this other task has not been finished yet. Note that a preceding task can only block another task if they are assigned to different workers. For the example process in Figure 1b the blocked task could for instance be "Work @L2" while the blocking task could be "Off @L1". If waiting is over or not necessary the worker starts to work on the task and enters the state `Working`. If the schedule of the worker is empty after finishing the execution of the task the worker returns to state `Ready` and then finishes his working day via the state `Not Ready`. Otherwise the worker starts to travel to the next task by entering the state `Traveling` again. If emergency situations occur in the service area workers may be withdrawn from their current tasks. In such a situation a new task is added to the top of the worker's schedule and the worker interrupts his current activity to travel to the location of the newly added task. This is depicted in Figure 5 by the `withdraw` edges from the states `Traveling`, `Waiting`, and `Working`, by the `drive to task` edge from the state `Ready`, and by the `return` edge from the state `Not Ready`. From every state the worker can enter the state `Not Ready` via the `break` edges. This state may indicate a lunch break, or a traffic accident, for instance. Note that the nature of mobile work demands that a state change from the state `Not Ready` is only possible back to the preceding state of the worker.

All states of Figure 5 discussed above are substates of the superstate `Connected`. The state `Connected` is necessary because the states are declared with no respect to the knowledge the headquarter of the organization might have about a worker's state. Since the mobile workers operate in the field with unpredictable data or phone connections the current state of a worker may be unknown to the headquarter at any time during operation. The model introduced in this work assumes that every state change of a worker is reported to the headquarter via data communication. As soon as a timeout occurs the headquarter's state of a worker changes to `Disconnected` while the worker still has local knowledge about his real state. During a disconnected period a worker can not be reached by the headquarter implicating that the worker can not be rescheduled to cases with higher importance than his current schedule. Whenever an update is received by the headquarter the state changes back to the appropriate one.

Mobile Tasks. In conjunction with the state model of mobile workers Figure 6 shows the UML state diagram of mobile tasks. As soon as a case is chosen for execution its tasks are created alongside. With its creation a task enters the state `Created`. With the assignment to a worker it enters the state `Assigned`. From there the task can either be withdrawn and return to the state `Created` or the worker starts to travel and the task enters the state `Task Active`.

The state `Task Active` aggregates the states `Engaged`, `Blocked`, and `Execution`. As soon as the worker drives to the site of the task the task's state implicitly changes to `Engaged`. After the worker arrives at the site the execution of the task can either be blocked by a preceding task or not. In the blocking case the task enters the state `Blocked` and the state `Execution` otherwise. This complies with the worker entering either `Waiting` or `Working`, triggered by the same events. As soon as the task becomes unblocked it enters the state `Execution` and the work is performed. After finishing the work the task changes to the state `Finished`.

During all of the states aggregated by `Task Active` the task can be withdrawn from the worker and in turn re-enter the state `Created`. This implies that the worker immediately stops to travel, wait, or work and starts the next task in his schedule. A withdrawal is not possible after the task was finished. Instead the whole case must be considered at a higher level of process control. This situation will be discussed later. As for the state of a worker also the state of a task may be uncertain to the headquarter controlling the mobile operations due to the loss of data or phone connections. In addition to the task's state model discussed above a state `Unkown` is introduced indicating that the headquarter can not determine the current state of that task due to a connection timeout. Whenever the task is either in state `Assigned` or `Task Active` and the data connection to the worker is lost the headquarter assumes the task to be in state `Unknown`. Whenever an update from that worker is received the headquarter's

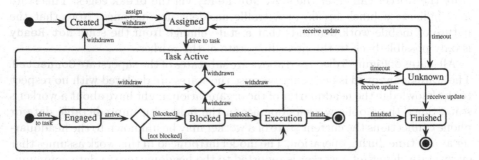

Fig. 6. State of a task

state model can be updated to the appropriate state. It is assumed that during a task being in the state Unknown this task might not be withdrawn from the worker to avoid unpredictable states of the whole case.

Mobile Cases. This leads to the state model for a case, depicted in Figure 7. As already stated above the tasks of a case are created alongside with the creation of the case itself. Since the state models of the two are quite similar the change of state of a task usually triggers a change of state of the appropriate case.

With its creation a case enters the state Created. With the assignment of the first task to a worker the case changes to the state Partly Assigned and with the assignment of the last unassigned task it changes to the state Assigned. If the case has just one task the state changes directly from Created to Assigned. Whenever a task is withdrawn from a worker as long as no worker started to work on one of the tasks of the case, the states change according to the assignment of tasks. If the case is in state Partly Assigned and tasks are withdrawn or assigned the case remains in the state Partly Assigned – see the looped edge of the state in Figure 7. After the assignment of the tasks the workers may start to drive to the locations of their respective current tasks. Since the processes considered here demand the completion of all activities all tasks must be assigned to workers. Thus the assignment of work takes place and is completed before the actual working day starts and thus no worker can start to drive before all schedules are complete. As soon as an arbitrary task of this case changes state to Engaged) the case changes state to Engaged accordingly. The case remains in the state Engaged until either the first task of the case is finished or all tasks of this case have been withdrawn. After the first task is finished the case changes state to Partly Finished. It is assumed that a case may or may not – corresponding to the organization's policy – be withdrawn after one of its tasks is finished. Thus the finishing of the first task of the case causes a change in the case's state. Note that Figure 7 depicts an organization where cases must be finished after their first task is finished. If the last engaged task has been withdrawn the state Case Active is left and the case re-enters the state Created demanding

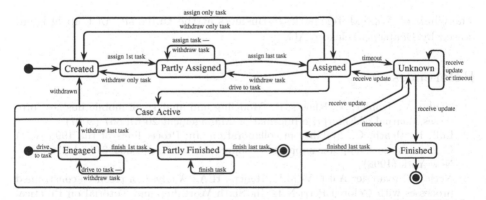

Fig. 7. State of a case

a completely new assignment turn. As soon as the last task has been finished, the case changes state to Finished. For the cases the same rules about the headquarter's knowledge of the case's state apply as for tasks and workers. Thus the state Unknown which is added. The meaning of the state Unknown is similar to the according state for tasks (see Figure 6). Whenever a case is in one of the states Assigned or Case Active and the connection to an arbitrary worker involved in this case times out the case changes state to Unknown. Additional timeouts and / or received updates keep the case remaining in the state Unknown until the states of *all* workers are known again – i. e. updates were received. The state of the case is then determined with respect to the according update messages.

4 Conclusion

The model introduced here was developed during a scientific consulting project performed for a German power and gas supply serving 500.000 customers and covering an area of 7000 km^2. The model covers both the static and dynamic properties of mobile workforce management systems and the uncertainty of data and phone connections. The model is independent from the business domain of dedicated organizations but represents the common attributes of centrally controlled mobile work in general. It further accounts not just for single mobile tasks but for processes that consist of an arbitrary number of mobile and non-mobile activities. Our model can be utilized for the requirements analysis of mobile workforce management systems, for the development of BPR simulations, or for the maintenance of a consistent nomenclature throughout any organization performing or dealing with the appropriate processes.

Further development of our model will cover different types of costs occurring in the mobile context (e. g. travel, waiting, equipment dowtimes). We will develop the model further collaterally with our simulation system for mobile organizations [5].

Acknowledgment

The Chair of Applied Telematics/e-Business at the University of Leipzig is endowed by Deutsche Telekom AG.

References

1. Gruhn, V., Köhler, A., Klawes, R.: Modeling and analysis of mobile business processes. Journal of Enterprise Information Management 20(6), 657 (2007)
2. Luff, P., Heath, C.: Mobility in collaboration. In: Proceedings of the 1998 ACM Conference on Computer supported cooperative work, pp. 305–314. ACM Press, New York (1998)
3. Netjes, M., van der Aalst, W.M.P., Reijers, H.A.: Analysis of resource-constrained processes with Colored Petri Nets. In: Sixth Workshop and Tutorial on Practical Use of Coloured Petri Nets and the CPN Tools (2005)

4. Jensen, K.: Coloured Petri nets: Basic concepts, analysis methods and practical use, 2nd edn., vol. 1. Springer, London (1996)
5. Gruhn, V., Richter, T.: A General Model of Mobile Environments: Simulation Support for Strategic Management Decisions. In: Proceedings of the 2nd International Workshop on Personalization in Grid and Service Computing, PGSC 2008 (2008)
6. Goel, A., Gruhn, V., Richter, T.: Mobile Workforce Scheduling Problem with Multitask-Processes. In: Rinderle-Ma, S., et al. (eds.) Komplexität von Entscheidungsproblemen. LNBIP, vol. 43, pp. 81–91. Springer, Heidelberg (2010)
7. Russell, N., van der Aalst, W.M.P., ter Hofstede, A.H.M., Edmond, D.: Workflow Resource Patterns. In: Pastor, Ó., Falcão e Cunha, J. (eds.) CAiSE 2005. LNCS, vol. 3520, pp. 216–232. Springer, Heidelberg (2005)
8. Gruhn, V., Köhler, A.: A Modeling and Analysis Approach for Mobile Information Systems. In: The First International Workshop on Mobility, Collaborative Working, and Emerging Applications, MobCops 2006 (2006)
9. Goel, A.: Fleet Telematics: Real-time management and planning of commercial vehicle operations. Springer, Heidelberg (2007)
10. Kolisch, R.: Serial and parallel resource-constrained project scheduling methods revisited: Theory and computation. European Journal of Operational Research 90(2), 320–333 (1996)
11. Ursu, M.F.: Distributed resource allocation via local choices: A case study of workforce allocation. International Journal of Knowledge-Based and Intelligent Engineering Systems 9(4), 293–301 (2005)
12. Pesic, M., van der Aalst, W.M.P.: Modelling work distribution mechanisms using Colored Petri Nets. International Journal on Software Tools for Technology Transfer (STTT) 9(3), 327–352 (2007)
13. Pesic, M., van der Aalst, W.M.P.: Towards a Reference Model for Work Distribution in Workflow Management Systems. Business Process Reference Models
14. Voudouris, C., Owusu, G.K., Dorne, R.J.H., Ladde, C., Virginas, B.: ARMS: An automated resource management system for British Telecommunications plc. European Journal of Operational Research 171(3), 951–961 (2006)
15. Zur Muehlen, M.: Organizational Management in Workflow Applications - Issues and Perspectives. Information Technology and Management 5(3), 271–291 (2004)

An Adaptive Job Allocation Strategy for Heterogeneous Multi-cluster Systems

Chao-Tung Yang[1], Keng-Yi Chou[1], and Kuan-Chou Lai[2]

[1] High-Performance Computing Laboratory
Department of Computer Science, Tunghai University, Taichung, 40704, Taiwan (ROC)
{ctyang,g97350007}@thu.edu.tw
[2] Department of Computer and Information Science, National Taichung University
Taichung, 403, Taiwan (ROC)
kclai@mail.ntcu.edu.tw

Abstract. In this paper, we propose a new job allocation system for multi-clusters environments, named the Adaptive Job Allocation Strategy (AJAS), in which a scheduler uses a self-scheduling scheme to dispatch jobs to appropriate distributed resources. Our strategy focuses on increasing resource utility by dispatching jobs to computing nodes with similar performance capacities to equalize job execution times among all nodes. The experimental results show that AJAS could indeed to improve the system performance.

Keywords: Multi-cluster, Job allocation, Loop scheduling, Load balancing.

1 Introduction

When single cluster is not sufficient to deal with complex large-scale applications, integrating multiple clusters via high speed Internet to provide high performance computing is proposed. The architecture of integrating clusters into a huge computing environment to improve computing power is called "Multi-clusters".

In the multi-cluster systems, clusters are heterogeneous due to the new-added powerful machines. Generally, MPI jobs are split evenly into several tasks of job for execution on clusters. However, different clusters have different computing capabilities; the even-spitted tasks would complete execution in different times. As a result, faster nodes of cluster have to wait for slower nodes; therefore, cluster resources are wasted. The worse management of multi-cluster environments can result in the inefficient utilization of cluster resources. Therefore, increasing resource utilization is an important issue in multi-cluster systems.

This study focuses on two important issues for heterogeneous cluster systems: the different job finishing time at different clusters and the utilization improvement for multi-cluster resources. In this paper, we introduce the Adaptive Job Allocation Strategy (AJAS) for multi-cluster environments to increase system efficiency. AJAS fetches needed information, e.g., CPU load, free memory usage, and network statuses, from running nodes. AJAS calculates each node's computing capability and assigns the nodes in different levels. Before dispatching, all jobs are partitioned via loop

R.-S. Chang et al. (Eds.): GPC 2010, LNCS 6104, pp. 562–572, 2010.
© Springer-Verlag Berlin Heidelberg 2010

self-scheduling for improving system performance. The scheduler then dispatches these jobs according to three AJAS policies. Decisions are made according to whether there are sufficient free nodes in the clusters, or co-allocation must be made to distribute jobs across multiple clusters. The experiment in our multi-cluster environment shows the feasibility of this job allocation strategy.

The remainder of this article is organized as follows. A review of relevant background and studies is presented in Section 2. Our new approach is outlined in Section 3. Experimental results are presented in Section 4. Section 5 concludes this research article.

2 Related Work

Recently, there are several ways to construct heterogenous clusters for new computational resources that yield better performance. This is the domain of Multi-Cluster Computing whose purpose is to provide the types of resources needed to resolve demanding problems[5]. In exploiting the potential computing power of computer clusters, an important issue is how to assign tasks to computers such that computer loads are well-balanced. The problem is how to assign the various parts of parallel applications to computing resources in ways that minimize overall computing times and make efficient use of resources. Loops are among them most important parallelizing devices in scientific programs, and considerable research work has been focused in this area.

Self-scheduling [3] refers to a large class of adaptive/dynamic centralized loop-scheduling methods. Self-scheduling schemes such as Pure [6], Chunk [7], Guided, Trapezoid, and Factoring have proven successful in shared-memory multiprocessor systems. Guided Self-Scheduling can dynamically change the numbers of iterations assigned to idle processors. More specifically, the next chunk size is determined by dividing the number of iterations remaining in a parallel loop by the number of available processors. The small chunks at the end of a loop partition serve to balance the workload across all working processors. Factoring Self-Scheduling (FSS) assigns loop iterations to working processors in phases. During each phase, only a subset of remaining loops iterations (usually half) is divided equally among available processors. Trapezoid Self-Scheduling (TSS) tries to reduce the need for synchronization while still maintaining reasonable load balances. This algorithm allocates large chunks of iterations to the first few processors and successively smaller chunks to the last few processors.

The major objective of scheduling in multi-cluster environments is to make the best use of resources. When a job arrives at the job queue, the scheduler is responsible for deciding which machine the job should occupy. Generally speaking, there are two scheduling schemes, static and dynamic [1]. Static scheduling, performed at compile time, allocates jobs to individual processors before execution, and the allocations remain unchanged during processing. Dynamic scheduling, conducted at run time, can support dynamic load-balancing and fault-tolerance. Although load balancing can share loads among nodes after job execution has begun[8][9], the practice introduces additional program execution overhead. Some works considers memory latency the main indicator for load sharing[11], or take memory and CPU power usage into account [10]. Others take additional measures such as queueing[9] and co-allocation method [12] into consideration. Previously, there was no need to consider co-allocation—allocation of jobs across clusters—in a single-cluster system, but it is necessary to implement it in multi-cluster environments.

3 Adaptive Job Allocation Strategy

Our system architecture provides two main functions, a monitoring service and a job manager. The user acquires node statuses before submitting any jobs to the system. As Figure 1 shows, users can browse the whole cluster via the monitoring service at any time and examine node states. The job manager watches over jobs in the job queue, which handles all user-submitted jobs. The scheduler uses a simple FCFS strategy and automatically chooses the node or cluster on which to run the first job in the queue.

Our hardware consists of four clusters, each with one head node and three tail nodes, except for the amd64-dua21 which has one head node and one tail node. Since we have few nodes, they are basically arranged hierarchically. Linux is installed on all nodes. The head nodes are responsible for providing services to their clusters and also play a part in computing. The tail nodes are the basic computational nodes. The master node is responsible for deploying jobs and offering monitoring services. As shown in Figure 2, clusters are composed of three layers, including master nodes, head nodes, and tail nodes.

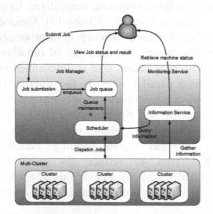

Fig. 1. System Architecture

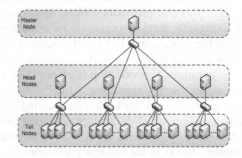

Fig. 2. System layers

The three layers function as follows.

- **Master Node:** The main system functions, the monitoring service and job manager, are in this node, which also holds the Ganglia monitoring server and web page, with RRD tool on it. Condor, which provides the queue system we need for our scheduler to function, is deployed on this node as well, along with the main scheduler system.
- **Head Node:** Each cluster's head node provides these services: the Network Information Service (NIS), Network File System (NFS), and the Message Passing

Interface (MPI) environment to enable the running of MPI jobs. Ganglia and Condor are implemented as well to provide information on cluster node statuses and to enable job scheduling.

- **Tail Node:** The bottom layer consists solely of these computational nodes. Their only tasks are to transmit their statuses and to run jobs. The working file systems for these nodes are mounted on NFS servers provided by the head nodes. Ganglia client-side services and Condor execute services are implemented on these nodes, along with MPI.

The main goal of a scheduling system is to make the best use of resources. Its main functions include Information-Gathering, System Selection, Job Partitioning and Execution. Information is gathered for the scheduler to make the best decisions in determining the nodes jobs leaving the queue are assigned to. Therefore, we propose the Adaptive Job Allocation Strategy (AJAS). Choosing the most efficient nodes on which to execute jobs is a great method for single jobs, but it does not always work out well in MPI environments because MPI jobs must be executed on multiple nodes, so choosing the most powerful nodes is not practical. It may be feasible for homogeneous and dedicated clusters since all their nodes are identical, but in heterogeneous environments, selecting nodes with similar performance capacities is more effective. And selecting similar machines to execute jobs can reduce idle times, and improve load balancing.

The AJAS allocation strategy has four main phases; Information gathering, Load balancing, Level classification, and Allocation policy application. The three allocation policies are Single Cluster, Cluster Pair, and Multi-cluster. Short descriptions of the tag meanings and steps in the simplified flowchart shown in Figure 3 are given below.

- job_i: The ith job dequeued from the queue, where i = 1~n. The program is usually a parallel program written by the MPI library and compiled by MPICH or LAM/MPI.
- NP_{req}: The number of processors required to execute jobi.
- NP_{all}: The total number of processors in the multi-clusters. If NPreq exceeds NPAll, the job is dropped.
- SC_{max}: The maximum number of processors in a single cluster on the same level.
- CP_{max}: The maximum number of processors in a cluster pair on the same level.
- MC_{max}: The maximum number of processors in all cluster pairs on the same level.
- CC_{max}: The maximum number of processors in all multi-cluster systems in idle states.

Jobs are dispatched from the master node's queue. The master node is responsible for making dispatch decisions, including fetching states and information on all nodes, and determining whether the number of processors requested is greater than the number of available processors in the whole cluster, which is the first decision made here. If the return is false, the job is abandoned and the user is informed that not enough processors are available to run the job. The scheduler then begins the Adaptive Job Allocation Strategy by calculating the performance capacities of all nodes.

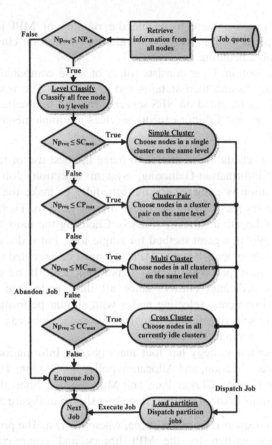

Fig. 3. AJAS flow chart

α % of the workload is then dispatched according to a performance weighting based on CPU clock speed and High Performance Computer Challenge (HPCC) [13][5] measurement of all nodes, after which the remaining workload is dispatched using some well-known self-scheduling scheme, such as GSS. To use this approach, we need to know the real computer performance as measured by the HPCC benchmark. We can then distribute appropriate workloads to each node, and achieve load balancing. The more accurate the estimation, the better the load balance.

HPCC is a useful computer benchmarking tool. It first examines HPC architecture performance using kernels with more challenging memory access patterns than High Performance Linpack (HPL).

"Level Classification" gathers information needed for classification by calculating each node's CP value while, the bandwidth is repeatedly measured. After sorting all nodes according to γ level, one of three policies is chosen for the job.

The "Single Cluster Policy" selects nodes in one cluster on the same level using the best-fit algorithm. If there are not enough free nodes to use this policy, the next is chosen.

The "Cluster Pair Policy" differs little from the "Single Cluster Policy", except that nodes are chosen from two clusters on the same level instead of from one. Cluster pairs able to supply the number of nodes the user requests are selected, and the BWnm values of all candidates compared; the cluster pair having the lowest latency is then chosen and the job is dispatched to the nodes for execution.

The "Multi-Cluster Policy" addresses situations in which users need huge numbers of nodes. This method attempts to use all the clusters on the same level. If this cannot meet job requirements, the job is sent back to the queue to wait in line for another try.

The "Cross-Cluster Policy" also addresses situations in which users need huge numbers of nodes, but where there are not enough nodes available on the same level. This method attempts to use all the clusters in the system.

We now discuss self-scheduling and how we evaluate the performance power of all nodes. The parameters and algorithms we use to partition workload and evaluate node performance are listed and explained below.

We propose to partition $\alpha\%$ of the workload according to a weighting based on CPU clock speed and HPCC performance measurement of all nodes, and dispatch the remaining workload via well-known self-scheduling scheme, such as GSS, FSS or TSS. To estimate node performance, we define the performance weighting (PW) for node j as PWj $(V1, V2, ..., VM)$, where Vi, $1 < i < M$, is a performance weighting variable. Our PW for node j is defined as

$$PW_j = \beta \frac{CS_i}{\sum_{\forall nodei \in S} CS_i} + (1 - \beta) \frac{HPL_i}{\sum_{\forall nodei \in S} HPL_i}, \; 0 \leq \beta \leq 1 \qquad (1)$$

where S is the set of all cluster nodes, CSi is node i CPU clock speed, and a constant attribute. HPLi is the HPCC HPL measurement analyzed above, and β is the ratio between 0 and 1.

Assume 24 loop iterations must be scheduled, the value of parameter α is 50%, and the PW values of the three nodes are 3, 2, and 1. Thus, the scheduler will assign 6 iterations to the first node, 4 to the second, and 2 to the third.

- $Load_i$: Sum of load1, load5, and load15 on Nodei, where Nodei is the ith Node and available for allocation; Loadi calculation is as follows:

$$Load_i = \frac{load^1 \times 15 + load^5 \times 5 + load^{15}}{21} \qquad (2)$$

- CP_i: Computing capacity of the ith node calculated as follows:

$$CP_i = \frac{HPL}{CPU_{num}} \times \frac{100 - Load}{100} \times (Mem_{free} + CPU_{freq}) \qquad (3)$$

- HPL: Site benchmarking value obtained using the benchmarking approach
- Cpu_{num}: Number of CPUs in a specified cluster
- Mem_{free}: Available node memory in gigabytes; if a node has 1.2GB of free memory, this value will be 1.2
- Cpu_{freq}: Node CPU clock rate in GHz; if a node has a clock rate of 1.8 GHz, this value will be 1.8

- *LS*: Since we sort γ levels according to computing power, this value is equal to the size of each level

$$LS = \frac{(CP_{max} - CP_{min})}{\gamma} \tag{4}$$

- γ: Number of levels nodes are sorted into; value depends on the number of clusters and their homogeneity; default value is the number of clusters in the environment, 4 in the present case
- CP_{min}: Lowest CP value among all nodes
- CP_{max}: Highest CP value among all nodes
- BW_{mn}: Average bandwidth between the master node in cluster m and cluster n in a given time period; k is the number of measurements computed to get the average bandwidth; default is 30. The bandwidth is constantly being measured, and the BWmn between two clusters is the bandwidth between them over the last two minutes.

$$BW_{mn} = \sum_{t=1}^{k} \frac{L_{mn}[t]}{k} \tag{5}$$

- *Lmn[t]*: Bandwidth between cluster m and cluster n at time t

All nodes are sorted into α levels from low to high according to performance capacity. The procedure below shows how this is done. The Level Classification function is responsible for sorting, as shown in Figure 4.

```
LevelClassify(CPi) {
if (CPi ≦ CPmin+ LS) then
Level1 = i
if (CPi ≦ CPmin+ LS × 2) then
Level2 = i
if (CPi ≦ CPmin+ LS × 3) then
Level3 = i
...
else
Levelγ = i
fi
fi
fi  }
```

Fig. 4. Level Classify Algorithm

After sorting all available nodes in our system, we now have a table showing which nodes belong on which levels. In other words, all nodes have been classified onto γ levels, the primary purpose for which is to equalize execution times. The γ value is dependent on the computing power of the specific multi-cluster system and differs in different environments. We recommend basing the value on the heterogeneity of the particular multi-cluster environment. When building clusters, we generally place nodes with similar computing capacities in the same clusters. Machines with the greatest capacity are grouped into one cluster, those with slightly less capacity into the next, and so on. In such cases it is feasible to simply set α equal to the number of clusters in your environment.

4 Experimental Results

In this section, we present our experiment enviroment, test programs, experiment results, and probe a few suspicious points.

Our experiments were conducted on a multi-cluster environment that includes five clusters, four consisting of one head node and three tail nodes, and one consisting of one head node and one tail node. Head and tail nodes all participate in job execution. The master node is responsible for dispathching jobs to these five clusters for performance estimation. The testbed hardware specifications are shown in Table 1.

Table 1. Hardware specification

Hostname	oct		quad		amd64-dual1		amd64-dual2		Amd64-dual3	
	Head	Tail	Head	Tail	Head	Tail	Head	Tail	Head	Tail
# of node	1	3	1	3	1	3	1	1	1	3
CPU	Intel Xeon E5410		Intel Core2 Quad Q6600		AMD Opteron 246		Dual-Core AMD Opteron 2212		AMD Opteron 246	
CPU clock	2327.512 MHz		2699.986 MHz		1992.128 MHz		2000.080 MHz		1992.387 MHz	
RAM	8GB		8GB		2GB		2GB		2GB	
HPCC (Gflops)	55.05 (N=30K)		33.65 (N=30K)		8,706 (N=15k)		13.68 (N=13k)		10.706 (N=15k)	
NIC	Gigabit				10/100M					
OS	Fedora Core 8				Fedora Core 7					
Lam	lam-7.1.41.fc8				lam-7.1.2-10.fc7					

Our experiments are divided into groups. Names in the first group end in –stat, indicating they use no scheduling, just static scheduling and do not adjust the computing method. Names in the second group end in –ngss, –nfss and –ntss, indicating they use loop self-scheduling to partition loops according to machine loading. Names in the third group end in -mach, indicating they use machine classification scheduling to assign computation jobs to machines with similar performance characteristics. The last group contains our proposed scheduling method combining loop self-scheduling and machine classification.

In this first experiment to determine how parameters α and β influence performance, we used the "matngss" , "mannfss" and "manntss" program for Matrix Multiplication with α and β, executing each program 100 times to ensure accuracy. The results are shown in Figure 5-6. We now know that setting α to 30 and β to 0.6 yields the best multi-cluster execution performance on Matrix Multiplication. We investigated parameter α, β values, as shown in Figure 5, and then used them in comparison with the other programs. We kept parameters α = 30 and β = 0.6.

Figure 5 show that our method required much less execution time than scheduling methods matmach and mangss, manfss and mantss on a 512 x 512 matrix. Our method also took less time than other programs when the classification level was set at 4. We thought more levels might give executable jobs more choices. The differences between AJAS and other programs are more obvious with 1024x1024 and 2048x2048 matrices, as shown in Figures 6.

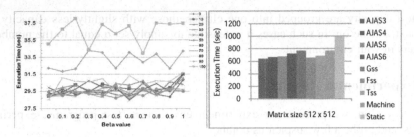

Fig. 5. The left Parameters α and β influence on Matrix Multiplication execution times for a 1024×1024 matrix. The right is Results for various programs on a 512×512 matrix.

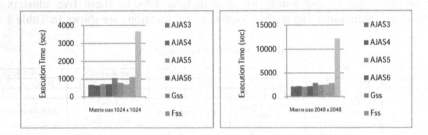

Fig. 6. Results for various programs on a 1024×1024 and 2048×2048 matrix

The Mandelbrot Set problem involves performing the same computations on various data points with different convergence rates. In this experiment, we were still investigating the influence of parameters α and β on performance. Here we ran the "manngss", "mannfss" and "manntss" program each one about 100 times to ensure accuracy. The result in left of Figure 7 shows that setting α to 50 and β to 0.5 yielded the best performance.

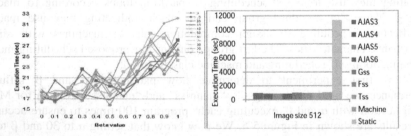

Fig. 7. The right is parameter α and β influence on Mandelbrot Set computation times for a 1024×1024 matrix. The right is results for various programs on a 512 x 512 matrix.

The results for parameter values of α = 50 and β = 0.5, shown in Figure 8. Figure 8, show that regardless of matrix size, AJAS, the method we propose, is reuse a bit and utilization for performance of multi-clusters, requires less execution time than methods such as manstat, which uses no scheduling, and manngss, mannfss, manntss and manmach, which use only one scheduling method.

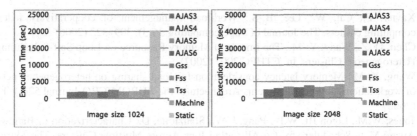

Fig. 8. Results for various programs on a 1024 x 1024 and 2048 x 2048 matrix

5 Conclusions and Future Work

Multi-clusters are another alternative to supercomputers for solving large-scale problems. This study proposes the Adaptive Job Allocation Strategy to handle machines in multi-clusters with similar computing characteristics on the same levels. This study also introduces a loop self-scheduling strategy for load balancing, thus improves performance. Experimental results show that our method is more efficient and better utilizes resources than other approaches. In the future, our work would enhance the scheduling strategy and handle the job-failure problem.

References

1. Cao, J., Chan, A., Sun, Y., Das, S.K., Guo, M.: A Taxonomy of Application Scheduling Tools for High Performance Cluster Computing. The Journal of Cluster Computing 9(3), 355–371 (2006)
2. Polychronopoulos, C.D., Kuck, D.: Guided Self-Scheduling: a Practical Scheduling Scheme for Parallel Supercomputers. IEEE Trans. on Computers 36(12), 1425–1439 (1987)
3. Chronopoulos, T., Andonie, R., Benche, M., Grosu, D.: A Class of Loop Self-Scheduling for Heterogeneous Clusters. In: Proceedings of the 2001 IEEE International Conference on Cluster Computing, pp. 282–291 (2001)
4. Hummel, S.F., Schonberg, E., Flynn, L.E.: Factoring: a method scheme for scheduling parallel loops. Communications of the ACM 35, 90–101 (1992)
5. Foster, I., Kesselman, C., Tuecke, S.: The anatomy of the grid: Enabling scalable virtual organizations. International Journal of Supercomputing Applications 15(3) (2001)
6. Hummel, S.F., Schonberg, E., Flynn, L.E.: Factoring: a method scheme for scheduling parallel loops. Communications of the ACM 35, 90–101 (1992)
7. Li, H., Tandri, S., Stumm, M., Sevcik, K.C.: Locality and Loop Scheduling on NUMA Multiprocessors. In: Proceedings of the 1993 International Conference on Parallel Processing, vol. II, pp. 140–147 (1993)
8. Werstein, P., Situ, H., Huang, Z.: Load Balancing in a Cluster Computer. In: Proceedings of the Seventh International Conference on Parallel and Distributed Computing, Applications and Technologies, pp. 569–577 (2006)

9. Xavier, P., Cai, W., Lee, B.-S.: Workload management of cooperatively federated computing clusters. The Journal of Supercomputing 36(3), 309–322 (2006)
10. Chen, D.-Z., Wang, Y.-M.: The Impact of Memory Resource on Loop Self-Scheduling for Heterogeneous Clusters. In: CTHPC 2007 (2007)
11. Wang, Y.-M.: Memory latency consideration for load sharing on heterogeneous network of workstations. Journal of Systems Architecture: the EUROMICRO Journal 52(1), 13–20 (2006)
12. Jones, W.M., Ligon III, W.B., Pang, L.W., Stanzione, D.: Characterization of Bandwidth-Aware Meta-Schedulers for Co-Allocating Jobs Across Multiple Clusters. The Journal of Supercomputing 34(2), 135–163 (2005)
13. HPC Challenge Benchmark, http://icl.cs.utk.edu/hpcc/

Privacy Protection of Grid Service Requesters through Distributed Attribute Based Access Control Model

Ali Esmaeeli and Hamid Reza Shahriari

Department of Computer Engineering and Information Technology
Amirkabir University of Technology, Tehran, Iran
{ali_esm,shahriari}@aut.ac.ir

Abstract. In Grid service environments, traditional identity based access control models are not effective, and access decisions need to be made based on service requesters' attributes. All of previous attribute based access control (ABAC) models are lacking in protection of users' privacy because in these models, access control decisions are made by providing the service provider with user attributes. This paper presents a Distributed Attribute Based Access Control (DABAC) model which protects users' privacy in Grid service environments. The DABAC model is based on XACML access control framework. In DABAC model, access control is distributed between home organization (service requester's organization) and destination organization (service provider's organization). In this model, user attributes are examined in home organization for which policy certificates are provided. This prevents service provider from accessing users' attributes. Therefore, users' privacy is protected. Moreover, distributed nature of this model, makes it more efficient comparing with previous models.

1 Introduction

Access control is an important protection mechanism in computer security. This mechanism can control the access of users to resources, and deny the access of inadmissible users. Access control mechanisms have evolved with the development of applications. Since the early 1970s, several kinds of access control models including Discretionary Access Control (DAC), Mandatory Access Control (MAC), and Role Based Access Control (RBAC) have been presented [1], [2], and [3]. In these models subjects and objects are identified by unique names, and access control is based on the identity of the subject, either directly or through roles assigned to the subject. DAC, MAC, and RBAC models are effective for closed and relatively static distributed systems where only a set of known users access a set of known services.

Nowadays, large-scale distributed open systems such as Grid have developed rapidly. A Grid system is considered as virtual organization consists of several independent autonomous domains that are working together to reach a common goal [4]. There are important differences between Grid systems and traditional systems. These differences make access control in Grid systems more complex than traditional ones. The most important difference is the type of relationship between users and resources. In Grid systems, the relationship between users and resources is ad hoc and

R.-S. Chang et al. (Eds.): GPC 2010, LNCS 6104, pp. 573–582, 2010.

dynamic. Moreover, service requesters and providers are in different security domains. In these environments, service requesters are usually identified by their characteristics or attributes, rather than predefined identities. It is clear that in such an environment, traditional identity based access control models are not useful. Thus, access control models based on user attributes are needed.

Since the late 1990s, with the development of large scale distributed systems, a new access control model –Attribute Based Access Control (ABAC) – has become increasingly important. In ABAC, access decisions are based on the attributes of users and resources, and it is not necessary to identify users before receiving their access requests for resources. This is the main advantage of ABAC access control models over previous models [1], [2], and [3]. Since users' attributes often contain private information about users, inappropriate mechanisms in ABAC models may result in exposure of users' privacy. There are several ABAC models which are offered for Grid systems [7], [9], [11], and [13], and we will review them in the next section. Almost all of these models have deficiencies in protecting users' privacy. The main reason is that access control decisions are made by providing the service provider with users' attributes. Due to private information about users which are included in these attributes, privacy of users may be violated. This paper presents Distributed Attribute Based Access Control (DABAC) model which can protect users' privacy. In DABAC model, access decisions are made in home organization. This prevents service provider (destination organization) from accessing users' attributes. Therefore, potential privacy deficiency of ABAC model is rectified, and users' privacy is protected.

The rest of this paper is organized as follows: In section 2 a brief overview of the most important ABAC models for Grid systems is presented. In section 3 we describe our new DABAC model. Section 4 describes the specifications of DABAC model and its differences with similar models. Finally in section 5, we conclude the paper and mention some future works.

2 Related Work

Since the early 1990s, with the development of Internet and Internet based distributed applications, public key infrastructure (PKI) and X.509 certificates have been widely used for user authentication. In 1996, the Simple Public Key Infrastructure (SPKI) was developed, which is a kind of PKI that emphasizes on authorization rather than authentication. This infrastructure was submitted in 1999, and now it is an internet standard [5]. In 1997, the Attribute Certificates (AC) was included in X.509 [6]. An attribute certificate may contain attributes that specify group membership, role, security clearance, or other authorization information associated with AC holder [15]. Almost all of the ABAC models appeared in recent years are based on X.509 attribute certificates. The most important ABAC models offered for Grid systems are as follows:

Akenti. The Akenti model consists of resources that are being accessed via a resource gateway (the Policy Enforcement Point - PEP) by users. These users connect to the resource gateway using the SSL handshake protocol to present authenticated X.509 certificates. Service providers express access constraints on the resources as a set of signed certificates. These certificates express the attributes a user must have in order to get specific rights to a resource [7] and [8].

PERMIS. PERMIS is a role based access control infrastructure that uses X.509 attribute certificates. Its detail specification is provided in [9] and [10].

Shibboleth. Shibboleth is an attribute authority service developed by the Internet2 community for cross organization identity federation. It asserts user's attributes between organizations. More precisely, it asserts attributes between the user's home organizations and organizations hosting resources that may be accessible to the user [11] and [12].

VOMS. VOMS, developed by the European Data Grid and DataTAG projects, runs in a virtual organization, manages authorization information about its own members, and supplies this information as a kind of attribute certificate [13].

Akenti, PERMIS, Shibboleth, and VOMS are kinds of ABAC systems and have been used in several Grid systems. There are two important issues related to these systems. First, in all of these systems, service providers have access to some user attributes for making access decisions. This is a security problem and may violate privacy policies of users. Second, all of decision making tasks are concentrated in one location (service provider organization) and this may result in efficiency or security problems. The DABAC model presented in this paper can eliminate both of these problems.

There are other research works and prototypes related to the negotiation of credentials such as TrustBuilder [16], XeNA negotiation framework [17], and the work done by Ljudevit Bauer [18]. Moreover, there exist some work on privacy based access model such as PuRBAC [19]. TrustBuilder supports automated trust negotiation between strangers on the internet. It lets negotiating parties disclose relevant digital credentials and access control policies and establish the trust necessary to complete their interaction [16]. XeNA is a new model for the negotiation of access within an eXtensible Access Control Markup Language (XACML) architecture. It enables trust management through a negotiation process and access control management within the same architecture [17]. PuRBAC is a purpose-aware RBAC extension which treats purpose as a central entity in RBAC. The model assigns permissions to roles based on purpose related to privacy policies [19]. Although these systems can be very useful, none of them are specialized for use in grid environments.

3 Distributed Attribute Based Access Control (DABAC) Model

The main advantage of Grid systems over traditional systems is their ability to facilitate communication between different organizations and enabling their users to access extensive set of resources and services. Virtual organizations are the main components of Grid environments, and users should access their required services through these organizations (they cannot directly access a service in another organization). Users usually have access to one organization as *home organization*. They can only access services maintained in other organizations *(destination organization)* through their home organization. From this point of view, each service requester is a user in an organization (source organization) who intends to access a service in another organization (destination organization). This is shown in Fig. 1.

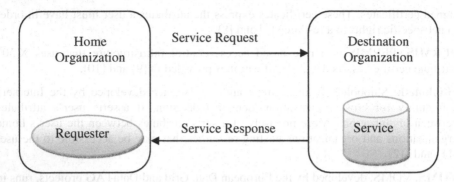

Fig. 1. Service requester and privider and their communications

In existing access control systems [7], [9], [11], and [13], the access decisions are usually made in the destination organization, which requires that the service requester sends its attributes to the destination organization. This will result in exposing service requester's attributes to privacy risks from destination organization. Thus, service requester privacy may be violated. In DABAC model, presented in this section, access decisions are made in home organization. Providing home organization with policy certificates enables it to make these decisions. A policy certificate expresses access constraints. This means that instead of sending user attributes from the home organization to the destination organization, policies are sent from the destination organization to the home organization. User attributes, resource attributes, and environment attributes are three kinds of attributes that the access control mechanism should consider them before allowing the user to access a service. User attributes (such as age, available credit, and nationality) contain information about a user. Resource attributes contain specific information about the resource (service) such as computational speed, maximum number of accepting requests, and cost of service (usually per unit of time). Environment attributes such as the number of current accesses to service (service load), contain information about environmental situation of service. User attributes, the most important attributes for authorization process, are kept in home organization. But resource attributes, and environment attributes are specified by destination organization during decision making process. In DABAC, access decisions in home organization are based on user attributes. Other attributes (resource and environment ones) are examined in destination organization. Therefore, the access control in DABAC is distributed between home and destination organizations, and there is no need to exchange attributes between them.

The model presented in this paper is based on XACML access control framework [14]. XACML is an OASIS standard which defines a policy language using the attributes of requestors, resources, and environment [15]. XACML is composed of 4 main components. These components are PEP (Policy Enforcement Point), PDP (Policy Decision Point), PIP (Policy Information Point), and PAP (Policy Administration Point). The PEP intercepts the access requests from users and sends the requests to the PDP. The PDP makes access decisions according to the security policy or policy set written by the PAP and using attributes of the subjects, the resource, and the environment obtained by querying the PIP [15]. Fig. 2 shows the data flow diagram of XACML [14].

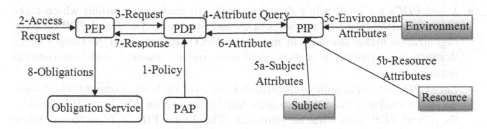

Fig. 2. XACML data flow diagram

PEP, PDP, PIP, and PAP, which are introduced in XACML, are the main components of our new model. Fig. 3 shows the components and data flow diagram of DABAC model.

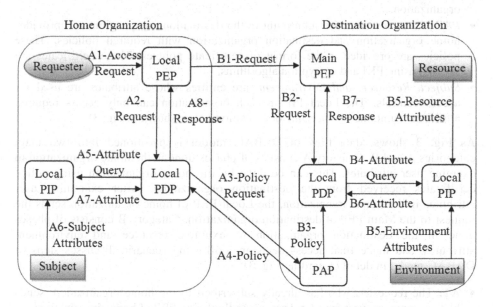

Fig. 3. Distributed Attribute Based Access Control model for Grid services

The components of this model are as follows:

- *Requester* is a user in home organization who wants to access a service in the destination organization (as was shown in Fig. 1, too). To become a member of the home organization, the user should subscribe to it, although it does not mean that he/she can have free access to services.
- *Local PEP* is a local policy enforcement point in the home organization. It receives access request from requester and sends the request to the Local PDP of home organization. Besides, if the access request is authorized in the home organization (after examining user attributes), then the Local PEP sends request to the destination organization.

- *Local PDPs* are local policy decision points (in each organization) which make access decision based on access policies and attributes. The Local PDP of home organization makes decisions using user (subject) attributes, and the Local PDP of destination organization makes decisions using resource and environment attributes.
- *Local PIPs* are local policy information points (in each organization) which have access to attributes maintained in the related organization. The Local PIP provides the Local PDP with required attributes. The Local PIP of home organization provides subject (user) attributes, and the Local PIP of destination organization Provides resource and environment attributes.
- *Main PEP* is a policy enforcement point in the destination organization. It receives an authorized access request from the Local PEP of home organization, and sends it to the Local PDP of destination organization. As mentioned before, only resource and environment attributes (not user attributes) are examined in the destination organization.
- *PAP* is a policy administration point in the destination organization, and provides home organization and destination organization with required policies. These policies are provided in the format of certificate policies. These certificates are secured using PKI and encryption algorithms.
- *Subject, Resource, and Environment,* are entities whose attributes are used for access controls. The Local PIP in each organization can only access required attributes maintained in the same organization (As is shown in Fig. 3).

As Fig. 3 shows, data flow in DABAC model is partitioned into two main categories A and B. Category A consists of phases done in the home organization to examine user attributes. This can be done by the home organization using policy certificates received from the destination organization. After examining user attributes in the home organization, the Local PEP of home organization sends the request to the Main PEP of destination organization. Category B consists of phases done in the destination organization to examine resource and environment attributes, and make final access decision. Following scenario discusses steps of DABAC model in detail (regarding Fig. 3).

- **A1:** The requester, who has already subscribed to the home organization, sends his/her access request for a Grid service to the Local PEP of home organization[1].
- **A2:** The Local PEP of home organization sends the access request of user to the Local PDP of home organization.
- **A3-A4:** The Local PDP of home organization requests necessary policy certificates from the PAP of destination organization. Subsequently, the PAP of destination organization sends necessary policies (in the format of policy certificate) to the Local PEP of home organization.
- **A5:** The Local PDP of home organization requests necessary user attributes from the Local PIP of home organization.

---

[1] The Local PEP of home organization may locate destination organization, where Grid service is located, in various ways. Although the specific method used for locating Grid services depends on Grid environment, usually "Grid information service" methods are used for this purpose [4].

- **A6-A7:** The Local PIP of home organization obtains required user attributes, and sends them to the Local PDP of home organization.
- **A8:** Using user attributes and policies, the Local PDP of home organization makes access decision and sends the result to the Local PEP of home organization. If the result is negative, the user request will be rejected and no more requests will be sent to the destination organization. However, if the result is positive, category B phases will initiate.
- **B1:** The Local PEP of home organization sends the authorized access request to the Main PEP of destination organization (authorization until this step is based on user attributes).
- **B2:** The Main PEP of destination organization sends access request to the Local PDP of destination organization where resource and environment attributes are checked.
- **B3:** The PAP makes policies available to the Local PDP of destination organization.
- **B4:** The Local PDP of destination organization requests necessary resource and environment attributes from the Local PIP of destination organization.
- **B5-B6:** The Local PIP of destination organization obtains required resource and environment attributes, and sends them to the Local PDP of home organization.
- **B7:** Using resource attributes, environment attributes, and policies, the Local PDP of destination organization makes access decision and sends the result to the Main PEP of destination organization. If the result is negative, the user request will be rejected. Otherwise, the user is authorized to access the service. The Main PEP of destination organization makes the access of user to the Grid service available.

In next section we will study security, privacy, and efficiency aspects of DABAC model. Moreover, a comparison study of DABAC and similar models is presented.

4 Discussion

The main distinction between the DABAC model and other similar models is that in DABAC, each organization has only access to the attributes maintained in it. Consequently, each organization can only examine and enforce some parts of access constraints. In other words, there is no exchange of attributes between different organizations. This will enable each organization to protect privacy of its users. The DABAC model presented in the previous Section is based on the following concepts:

- Only the service provider holds access control constraints. Other organizations can access these constraints through policy certificates received from the service provider.
- Local PIPs in each organization only have access to attributes stored in the same organization. It means that home organization has access to its users' attributes and destination organization has access to resource (service) and environment attributes.
- Access requests are sent to the destination organization only when the local PDP of home organization indicates that the user is authorized to access the service. In other words, unauthorized access requests are rejected by the local PEP of home organization.

- Service attributes and environmental attributes are examined in the destination organization. It is clear that only authorized access requests can reach this step.

Our presented model, DABAC, has many important privacy and efficiency properties compared to similar systems such as Akenti [7], PERMIS [9], Shibboleth [11], and VOMS [13]. Some advantages of DABAC model are:

- The most important advantage of DABAC over similar models such as Akenti, PERMIS, Shibboleth, and VOMS is its ability to protect privacy of service requesters. As mentioned earlier, this is possible because there is no need to exchange attributes between different organizations in this model.
- Grid systems consist of heterogeneous virtual organizations. Users of one organization in Grid environment may have access to services in other organizations. This will create a lot of security challenges. In DABAC, each organization examines attributes stored in the same organization. This distributed nature of DABAC model is completely compatible with heterogeneous specifications of Grid environments.
- In DABAC, an authorized access requests are rejected in home organization. This will prevent many attacks such as buffer overflow or denial of service attacks in destination organization. It will also reduce the traffic load on the network.
- In DABAC model, policy certificates are exchanged between different organizations instead of attribute certificates. This will lead to two good outcomes. First, the life time of policy certificate is usually more than life time of attribute certificate. It means that home organizations can use the policy certificate whose life time has not expired thus far. This will improve efficiency of system. Second, policy certificates are usually not confidential, and only their integrity is important for organizations. Therefore, the need to do complex encryption and decryption operations is lessen.
- Complex access control operations in similar systems (such as Akenti [7], PERMIS [9], Shibboleth [11], and VOMS [13]) may degrade the overall efficiency of system. Distributed nature of DABAC model reduces the high load on services and consequently improves efficiency.
- Destination organization in DABAC model should always trust to home organization which makes access decisions for service requesters. This is not an additional requirement for DABAC model in contrast to similar models such as Shibboleth [11], Akenti [7], PERMIS [9], and VOMS [13]. As in these models destination organization should also trust the home organization to sign an attribute certificate. It is clear that a malicious home organization can sign an invalid attribute certificate and send it to destination organization. Therefore, DABAC does not reduce usefulness of authorization model in contrast with other ABAC models.

5 Conclusion

Grid environments have new authorization and access control requirements which traditional access control models cannot satisfy. Attribute Based Access Control (ABAC) is an access control model which is applicable in Grid environments. In this model, access decisions are made based on user attributes. Akenti [7] and [8],

Shibboleth [11] and [12], PERMIS [9] and [10], and VOMS [13], are the most important models proposed for Grid environments. All of these models are based on attribute certificates. It means that service providers are provided with user attributes to make access decisions. This may have conflict with privacy policies of users. Distribute ABAC (DABAC) model which is presented in this paper, eliminates this problem by exchanging policy certificates (instead of attribute certificates) between different organizations. This model has many privacy, security, and efficiency advantages over similar existing models. It is also compatible with heterogeneous aspects of Grid environments.

This paper has only provided a brief specification of DABAC. Further analysis and investigation can be performed. Protocols between the requester and service provider must be formally specified in the next step. Specifying implementation details of DABAC and integrating it with Globus toolkit (which is the most important implementation of Grid) should be performed too. Afterwards, privacy properties of model can be proved formally and more deeply. Moreover, the model itself can be extended to provide more capabilities. Supporting local access control policies in home organizations is a sample extension of this model. This capability enables home organizations to define and enforce their own access control policies (independent of destination organization policies) when their users want to use resources located outside the organization. Enforcing these policies may be possible using local PEP.

References

1. Lampson, B.W.: Protection. In: 5th Princeton Conference on Information Sciences and Systems, Princeton, pp. 437–443 (1971)
2. Bell, D.E., LaPadula, L.J.: Secure Computer Systems: A Mathematical Model. Technical report, Mitre Corporation (1973)
3. Sandhu, R.S., Samaratiy, P.: Access Control: Principle and Practice. IEEE Communications 32(9), 40–48 (1994)
4. Foster, I., Kesselman, C., Tuecke, S.: The Anatomy of the Grid: Enabling Scalable Virtual Organizations. International Journal of High Performance Computing Applications 15(3), 200–222 (2001)
5. Ellison, C., Frantz, B., Rivest, R., Thomas, B., Ylonen, T.: SPKI Certificate Theory. IETF RFC 2693 (1999)
6. Park, J.S., Sandhu, R.: Smart Certificates: Extending X.509 for Secure Attribute Service on the Web. In: 22nd National Information Systems Security Conference (1999)
7. Thompson, M., Johnston, W., Mudumbai, S., Hoo, G., Jackson, K., Essiani, A.: Certificate-Based Access Control for Widely Distributed Resources. In: 8th Usenix Security Symposium (1999)
8. Thomson, M., Essiari, A., Mudumbaim, S.: Certificate-Based Authorization Policy in a PKI Environment. ACM Transactions on Information and System Security 6(4), 566–588 (2003)
9. Chadwick, D.: Authorization in Grid Computing. Information Security Technical Report 10(1), 33–40 (2005)
10. Chadwick, D., Otenko, A.: The PERMIS X.509 Role Based Privilege Management Infrastructure. Future Generation Computer Systems 19(2), 277–289 (2003)

11. Welch, V., Barton, T., Keahey, K., Siebenlist, F.: Attributes, Anonymity, and Access: Shibboleth and Globus Integration to Facilitate Grid Collaboration. In: 4th Annual PKI R&D Workshop (2005)
12. Barton, T., Basney, J., Freeman, T., Scavo, T., Siebenlist, F., Welch, V., Ananthakrishnan, R., Baker, B., Goode, M., Keahey, K.: Identity Federation and Attribute-based Authorization through the Globus Toolkit, Shibboleth, Gridshib, and MyProxy. In: 5th Annual PKI R&D Workshop (2006)
13. Alfteri, R., Cecchini, R., Ciaschini, V., Dellagnello, L., Frohner, A., Gianoli, A., Lorentey, K., Spataro, F.: VOMS, An Authorization System for Virtual Organizations. In: Fernández Rivera, F., Bubak, M., Gómez Tato, A., Doallo, R. (eds.) Across Grids 2003. LNCS, vol. 2970, pp. 33–40. Springer, Heidelberg (2004)
14. OASIS, Extensible Access Control Markup Language (XACML), V2.0 (2005)
15. Lang, B., Foster, I., Siebenlist, F., Ananthakrishnan, R., Freeman, T.: Attribute Based Access Control for Grid Computing. Technical Report, Argonne National Laboratory (2006),
    ftp://info.mcs.anl.gov/pub/tech_reports/reports/P1367.pdf
16. Winslett, M., Yu, T., Seamons, K.E., Hess, A., Jacobson, J., Jarvis, R., Smith, B., Yu, L.: Negotiating Trust in the Web. IEEE Internet Computing 6(6), 30–37 (2002)
17. Abi Haidar, D., Cuppens Boulahia, N., Cuppens, F., Debar, H.: XeNA: An Access Negotiation Framework Using XACML. Annals of Telecommunications 64(1-2), 155–169 (2009)
18. Bauer, L.: Access Control for the Web via Proof-Carrying Authorization. PhD theses, Princeton University (2003)
19. Masoumzadeh, A., Joshi, J.B.D.: PuRBAC: Purpose-Aware Role-Based Access Control. In: Meersman, R., Tari, Z. (eds.) OTM 2008, Part II. LNCS, vol. 5332, pp. 1104–1121. Springer, Heidelberg (2008)

Detecting and Resolving a Loop in the Tree-Based Mobility Management Protocol*

Trung-Dinh Han and Hoon Oh**

School of Computer Engineering and Information Technology, University of Ulsan,
(680-749) San 29, Mugeo 2-Dong, Nam-gu, Ulsan, South Korea
trungdinhvn@yahoo.com, hoonoh@ulsan.ac.kr

Abstract. A loop can take place in the process of managing tree topology for mobility management of mobile nodes in infrastructure-based mobile ad hoc networks. The formation of a loop degrades an effective bandwidth of the wireless network by passing the identical message repeatedly within the same loop. Therefore, the loop should be resolved quickly to revert the system back to the normal state. In this paper, we propose a simple and novel mechanism that detects and resolves a loop quickly by tracking the depth of trees. The performance of the proposed approach is compared with existing tree-based approaches as well as the hybrid approach. It is shown that the proposed approach shows the superiority of the new approach and far outperforms the other methods, and is robust against the rapid changes in network topology.

Keywords: Looping Problem, Mobility Management, Tree-Based.

1 Introduction

The mobility management is required to provide mobile nodes (MN's) with a global Internet service as well as a communication service via Internet gateway (IG) for the MN's in other mobile ad hoc networks. Since mobility management is usually accompanied by a high network overhead, various mechanisms that pursue efficiency of mobility management have been proposed for the last decade. Recently the tree-based mobility management approaches [1, 3, 5, 6] have been appealing due to its low network overhead and high scalability.

Despite that the tree-based approach has been studied in various ways for its successful employment, the looping problem has not been addressed yet that takes place in the process of maintaining tree topology. If a loop is formed in tree topology, network overhead increases rapidly, degrading an effective network bandwidth quickly. Therefore, an efficient mechanism to solve the looping

---

* This research was supported by Basic Science Research Program through the National Research Foundation of Korea(NRF) funded by the Ministry of Education, Science and Technology (2009-0076839).
** Corresponding author.

R.-S. Chang et al. (Eds.): GPC 2010, LNCS 6104, pp. 583–592, 2010.
© Springer-Verlag Berlin Heidelberg 2010

problem is required. However, solving the looping problem is not easy because of the *synchronization delay*[1] of link information between MN's in a tree.

In this paper, we propose a method to detect and resolve the looping problem by tracking and limiting tree depth. The proposed method not only reduces the possibility of loop formation greatly, but also resolves the loop quickly.

The tree-based approach that employs the proposed loop resolution scheme is evaluated by resorting to simulation, comparing with the original tree-based approach [1] and one traditional mobility management scheme, the hybrid approach [4] that combines the advantages of the proactive and the reactive mobility management schemes. According to our simulation results, the proposed loop resolution mechanism improves node registration, the latency, and jitter as well as reduces network overhead significantly.

Section 2 describes the network model, associated definitions, and looping problem. A method which detects and resolves the looping problem is described in Section 3. In Section 4, performance evaluation is presented by resorting to a simulation, followed by the conclusion in Section 5.

2 Background

2.1 Network Model and Definitions

In this paper, we consider an infrastructure-based mobile ad hoc network that consists of IG's and MN's. The considered network is maintained as a set of the trees, each originating from an IG and consisting of one IG and multiple MN's. We assume that nodes can overhear packets that are transferred between other nodes [2]. A node is said to be a *tree-node* if it belongs to any tree and to be an *orphan-node* if it does not have a parent (even though it has children). A link that represents a parent-child relationship in a tree is specially called a *tree-link*.

We define some messages where CT indicates the type of control message and HopToIG does the distance in hops from an MN to its IG.

- Hello(CT, HopToIG): IG broadcasts this hello message with HopsToIG = 0 periodically. A tree-node always unicasts this hello to its parent periodically.
- J-REQ(CT): MN sends this join request message to its neighbor to join.
- CR-REQ(CT): An orphan-node responds with this children release request message to its child that sends Hello.
- REG(CT, NodeID): A node sends this registration message to register with IG periodically. NodeID indicates IP address of the node. All intermediate nodes maintain tree information upon receiving this message.

2.2 Tree-Based Approach

In this section, we briefly describe the tree-based approach before identifying the problem to be resolved in this paper. An IG broadcasts Hello message periodically. An orphan-node that receives the Hello tries to join the IG by

---

[1] *Synchronization delay* indicates that if a link between any two nodes comes to being or is broken, the other nodes know the change only after some time interval.

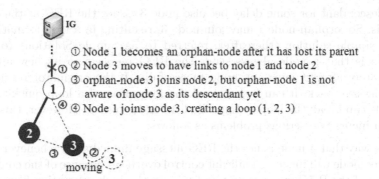

① Node 1 becomes an orphan-node after it has lost its parent
② Node 3 moves to have links to node 1 and node 2
③ orphan-node 3 joins node 2, but orphan-node 1 is not
  aware of node 3 as its descendant yet
④ Node 1 joins node 3, creating a loop (1, 2, 3)

Fig. 1. Loop formation in a tree maintenance

sending J-REQ to the IG. If the IG receives J-REQ, it takes the sender as its child. Upon receiving ACK (the acknowledgement message in the MAC layer), the orphan-node gets the IG as its parent and becomes a tree-node. Every tree-node sends Hello periodically to its parent to assure the link availability. An orphan-node that overhears Hello from any tree-node tries to join the sender by sending J-REQ. The tree-node that receives J-REQ takes the sender as its child. Upon receiving ACK for the Hello, the orphan-node gets the tree-node as its parent to become a tree-node. We name this process as *join hand-shaking* procedure. A tree-node becomes an orphan-node immediately when it fails to send Hello to its parent. Every tree-node registers with IG along tree paths periodically. The periodic registration makes sense in that any MN in the network can be requested for connection by other remote hosts or MN's via IG.

In order to reduce overhead, a node that becomes an orphan does not send a CR-REQ immediately to ask its children to *logically leave*[2] its parent. Instead the orphan-node just maintains all its descendants as if it has its own parent. If it receives Hello from any child, it responds with CR-REQ to ask that child only to logically leave the current orphan parent and join another tree-node. This is because the orphan-node may find another parent soon.

2.3 Problem Identification

Starting with an IG as a root node, the orphan-nodes join a tree-node such that their path length in hops to the IG is a minimum. A tree-node becomes an orphan-node when it loses connection to its parent. The orphan-node tries to join a tree-node. In this process, an orphan-node may join one of its descendants erroneously whom the orphan-node is not aware of due to the delay of information synchronization. A loop causes the involved nodes to deliver some messages repeatedly until it is broken, increasing network overhead substantially.

Fig. 1 shows that node 1 loses its parent and becomes an orphan-node, and then node 3 moves and joins node 2. However, node 1 is not aware of node 3

---

[2] The *logically leave* means that a node does not maintain a tree-link for its parent anymore, but a link as a neighbor.

as its descendant for some delay because node 3 issues the REG at the regular intervals. So, orphan-node 1 may join node 3, resulting in a loop formation.

One simple solution (thereafter, referred to as Simple Solution) to detect the loop is that a node always sends the REG message to its new ancestors immediately after it joins any node successfully. If the originator receives the REG message back, it can be aware of the formation of a loop quickly. Then, the node can break the loop by logically leaving its parent. However, this simple solution incurs two serious problems as follows:

- The way that a node issues the REG message immediately whenever it joins a tree-node will incur a significant control overhead because of the continuous relay of the REG message up to an IG and the high generation frequency of the REG in a high mobility network.
- The transmission delay of the REG message may cause the originator to break a *false loop* unnecessarily as follows. Referring to Fig. 1, suppose that node 1 has changed its parent to some other node in order to have the shorter HopToIG after it issued the REG message to its current parent, node 3. This change of parent breaks the loop naturally. If node 1 receives the REG message back later on, it will try to break the false loop that is not a loop anymore by logically leaving its new parent. In consequence, node 1 will be left as an orphan-node again.

3   Loop Detection and Resolution (LDR)

To detect and resolve the looping problem, we changes the join hand-shaking procedure as follows. If the joined child has its new HopToIG different from its old one, it immediately sends Hello to its parent, but only if it has at least one child, thus its children update their HopToIG quickly by overhearing the Hello.

A node determines that it is involved in a loop if its parent's HopToIG is equal to a specified value, DEPTH_LIMIT. Once a node detects a loop, it breaks the loop by becoming an orphan-node. The algorithm is detailed in Fig. 2.

We can prove that the LDR algorithm always detects and resolves a loop. Let us assume that an orphan-node does not join a tree-node whose HopToIG is equal to DEPTH_LIMIT. We consider two cases separately.

Case 1: Suppose that a node x has only one child. The node never joins its child since it does not overhear Hello from its child. So, it cannot create a loop.

Case 2: Referring to Fig. 3, suppose that a node v_1 has a descendant v_n that is $n - 1$ hops away from v_1 and v_1 has not received REG from node v_n yet that has joined v_{n-1} recently. Since node v_1 does not know v_n, it can join node v_n. Now, the group of nodes, $v_1, v_2, \ldots, v_{n-1}, v_n$, forms a loop. Since v_n joined v_{n-1} that is v_1's descendant, $H_{v_1} \neq H_{v_n} + 1$. Thus, according to line 6 and line 7 of the algorithm, $H_{v_1} = H_{v_n} + 1$ and v_1 would always send Hello. In line 15, node v_2 that is a child of v_1 overhears the Hello and changes its HopToIG: $H_{v_2} = H_{v_1} + 1 = H_{v_n} + 2$. Now, node v_2 will send Hello to its parent v_1 and now v_3 will overhear it: $H_{v_3} = H_{v_2} + 1 = H_{v_n} + 3$. In this way, for node v_i, $H_{v_i} = H_{v_n} + i$. Thus, HopToIG increases continuously.

//H_x : is the HopToIG of node x
//$x.P$: is the parent of node x
//$x.C$: is a set of children of node x
At a node x that detects disconnection to its parent:
1. IF node x overhears Hello from a tree-node y THEN
2.   IF H_y == DEPTH_LIMIT THEN return; ENDIF;
    // x is not an ancestor of node y or
    // x may not have received REG initiated by y
3.   IF x's descendant list does not include y THEN
4. x joins y;
5.   IF ($H_x \neq H_y + 1$) THEN
6. $H_x = H_y + 1$;
7. x immediately sends Hello to y if $x.C \neq \emptyset$;
8.   ENDIF;
9.   ENDIF;
10. ENDIF;
At a node x that overhears Hello from its parent:
11. IF $H_{x.P}$ == DEPTH_LIMIT THEN
12.   Node x breaks the loop by becoming an orphan-node;
13. ELSE
14.   IF ($H_x \neq H_{x.P} + 1$) THEN
15. $H_x = H_{x.P} + 1$;
16. x immediately sends Hello to $x.P$ if $x.C \neq \emptyset$;
17.   ENDIF;
18. ENDIF;

Fig. 2. LDR algorithm

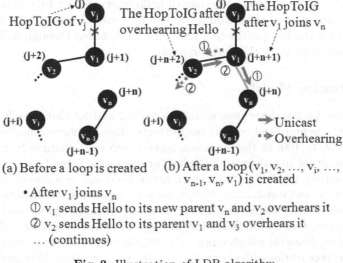

(a) Before a loop is created   (b) After a loop $(v_1, v_2, ..., v_i, ..., v_{n-1}, v_n, v_1)$ is created

• After v_1 joins v_n
  ① v_1 sends Hello to its new parent v_n and v_2 overhears it
  ② v_2 sends Hello to its parent v_1 and v_3 overhears it
  ... (continues)

Fig. 3. Illustration of LDR algorithm

During this process, a node that finds out the HopToIG of its parent which is equal to DEPTH_LIMIT breaks the loop by becoming an orphan-node itself in line 12 of the algorithm. In line 16, the existence of a loop implies that the node has at least one child and thus surely will issue Hello. Thus, the nodes in the loop continuously increase their HopToIG until any node breaks the loop after it satisfies the condition of the line 11.

We can quickly detect and resolve a loop by having a node generate Hello immediately if its HopToIG is different from its previous HopToIG. The DEPTH _LIMIT - $(j+n)$) number of Hello messages will be generated at maximum before breaking the loop where $j >= 0$ as the distance from the parent of the Hello initiator to an IG and $n >= 3$ as the number of nodes involved in a loop. Therefore, the bigger the $(j + n)$ is, the smaller the number of Hello messages generated to resolve a loop gets.

4   Performance Evaluations

We resort to simulation (use QualNet 3.9) to evaluate the tree-based approach that employs the LDR, named *TB-LDR*. This method is compared with the hybrid method [4] (*Hybrid*), and the original tree-based method [1] (*TB*).

4.1   Implementation of Hybrid and TB

Every registered MN and its associated IG manage their own *registration-timer* which is time-synchronized to prevent a stale registration of node. Thus, IG removes a registered node from its node registration list if the corresponding registration-timer expires. Also, every MN has to register with its IG periodically whenever its registration-timer expires. The registration-timer is set to 5 seconds for all the protocols. With the tree-based, hello interval is set to 3 seconds. Other parameters are also used to characterize the operation of each protocol. The values used for the key parameters were carefully chosen through multiple runs of simulation to produce the best outcome.

4.2   Evaluation Model

In simulation, we use three basic scenarios *S1*, *S2*, and *S3* that have IG locations in center, top center, and corner, respectively. The number of nodes (*nNodes*) varies from 50 to 100, or the maximum speed (*mSpeed*) changes from 0 m/s to 50 m/s. The other parameters and values are given in Table 1.

For evaluation, we use four metrics: *Control overhead, registration ratio, registration latency,* and *registration jitter*. Control overhead is obtained by summing up overheads of the control messages related to tree maintenance and a periodical node registration and dividing the sum by the number of nodes. This metric allows us to evaluate the effectiveness of LDR algorithm. Registration ratio is the ratio of the *registration-success* to the *registration-attempt*. This metric allows us to evaluate the stability of the paths from the MN's to IG. Also, based on the

Table 1. Simulation parameters and values

Parameters	Values	Remarks
Mobility Pattern	Random Waypoint	
Pause Time	30	
Number of Nodes	Varying density (1 fixed IG)	
Dimension	1000 x 1000	All protocols
Transmission Range	250 m	
Wireless Bandwidth	2 Mbps	
Registration Interval	5 seconds	
Simulation Time	600 seconds	
Advertisement Interval	2 seconds	
Advertisement zone (IG)	2 hops	Hybrid only
Increment in the expanding ring search (MN)	2 hops	

measured value, we can deduce which protocol can better deliver packets from MN's to IG or vice versus. Registration latency is the difference between the time that an MN issues a REG and the time that IG receives the same message. This metric also allows us to evaluate the relationship between network traffic and transmission delay. Registration jitter is the average difference of the latencies of two consecutive packets for all the registration packets that are issued by MN's. This metric allows us to evaluate path stability. All of metrics are affected by the looping problem in the tree-based approach or the flooding mechanism in the Hybrid approach.

4.3   Performance Evaluation

We compare the three mobility management approaches, TB-LDR, TB, and Hybrid according to the variations of IG deployment scenario, nNodes, and mSpeed. According to Fig. 4 - Fig. 7, the Hybrid approach shows the highest overhead of

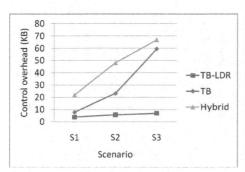
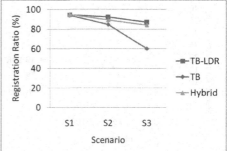

Fig. 4. Control overhead for different scenarios (nNodes = 50, mSpeed = 10 m)   **Fig. 5.** Registration ratio for different scenarios (nNodes = 50, mSpeed = 10 m)

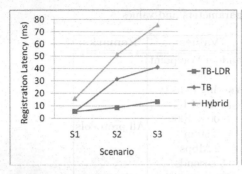
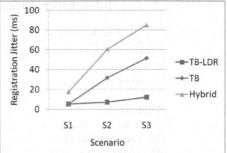

Fig. 6. Registration latency for different scenarios (nNodes = 50, mSpeed = 10 m)

Fig. 7. Registration jitter for different scenarios (nNodes = 50, mSpeed = 10 m)

all since it uses a flooding to discover a path to IG for registration. The overhead increases proportionally with the increase of average tree size from S1 to S3. Fig. 4 and Fig. 5 indicate that the TB suffers with the occurrence of a loop, showing a relatively high overhead and a low registration ratio. On the other hand, the

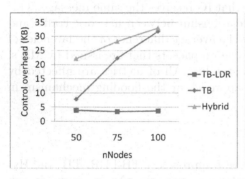
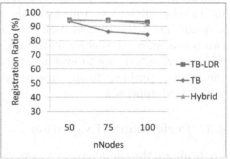

Fig. 8. Control overhead with varying node density (S1, mSpeed = 10 m/s)

Fig. 9. Registration ratio with varying node density (S1, mSpeed = 10 m/s)

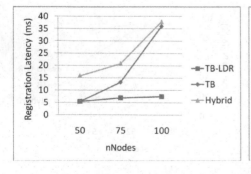
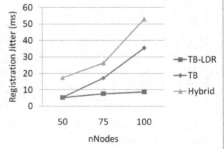

Fig. 10. Registration latency with varying node density (S1, mSpeed = 10 m/s)

Fig. 11. Registration jitter with varying node density (S1, mSpeed = 10 m/s)

TB-LDR shows the very competitive results for all the scenarios and metrics, even for the scenario S3 that tends to generate a loop more frequently.

Fig. 8 - Fig. 11 compare the protocols according to the variation of nNodes. Fig. 8 shows that the Hybrid has the highest overhead and the increasing overhead pattern with the increase in nNodes. This is because a flooding overhead is more sensitive to nNodes. The TB shows much more sensitivity to nNodes because the increased nNodes can put more registration messages into a loop that causes a message circulation. These values directly affect the other performance metrics. However, the TB-LDR remains very stable in overall ranges for all metrics by just resolving the looping problem. This means that the tree-based approach is very reliable unless a loop takes place.

Fig. 12 - Fig. 15 compare the approaches in terms of robustness against the increase of mSpeed. Furthermore, we use scenario S3 to effectively compare the scalability of the approaches against the size of tree. According to Fig. 12, the Hybrid and the TB shows higher sensitivity to mSpeed than the TB-LDR. The former experiences the more path explorations for registration due to the increased link failures while the latter experiences more loops due to the increased orphan-nodes transiently. However, overhead in TB-LDR is not very sensitive against the increasing speed, but control overhead at mSpeed of 50 m/s is almost twice as high as that at mSpeed of 0 m/s since the more J-REQ's are

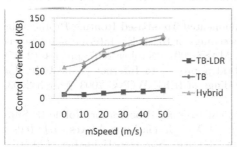

Fig. 12. Control overhead with varying mSpeed (S3, nNodes = 50)

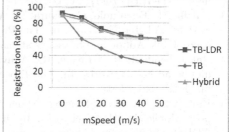

Fig. 13. Registration ratio with varying mSpeed (S3, nNodes = 50)

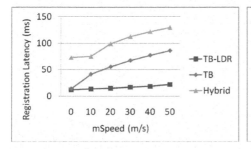

Fig. 14. Registration latency with varying mSpeed (S3, nNodes = 50)

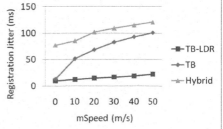

Fig. 15. Registration jitter with varying mSpeed (S3, nNodes = 50)

generated and some additional Hello messages are used to resolve a loop. The registration ratio of the TB-LDR is quite sensitive to the increasing mSpeed because of the increased possibility of link failure. The TB-LDR still maintains a good stability for the other metrics.

5   Conclusions

We identified a looping problem in the tree-based mobility management and presented a loop detection and resolution (LDR) method to solve the looping problem. We proved that the LDR method detects and resolves a loop quickly by tracking the depth of trees and then we justified its performance by resorting to simulation. The TB-LDR, the TB that employs the LDR method, was evaluated by comparing with the TB and the Hybrid. The simulation results show that the TB-LDR far outperforms the others and is highly scalable against the large size of trees and the high mobility of nodes.

References

1. Oh, H.: A tree-based approach for the Internet connectivity of mobile ad hoc networks. Journal of Communications and Networks 11(3), 261–270 (2009)
2. Jubin, J., Tornow, J.D.: The DARPA packet radio network protocols. The Proceedings of the IEEE 75(1), 21–32 (1987)
3. Caleffi, M., Ferraiuolo, G., Paura, L.: Augmented Tree-based Routing Protocol for Scalable Ad Hoc Networks. In: The Proceedings of the IEEE Internatonal Conference Mobile Adhoc and Sensor Systems, MASS 2007, October 2007, pp. 1–6 (2007)
4. Ratanchandani, P., Kravets, R.: A hybrid approach to Internet connectivity for mobile ad hoc networks. In: The Proceedings of IEEE WCNC 2003, March 2003, pp. 1522–1527 (2003)
5. Han, T.D., Oh, H.: A Topology Management Routing Protocol for Mobile IP Support Mobile Ad Hoc Networks. In: Ruiz, P.M., Garcia-Luna-Aceves, J.J. (eds.) ADHOC-NOW 2009. LNCS, vol. 5793, pp. 341–346. Springer, Heidelberg (2009)
6. Peng, W., Li, Z., Haddix, F.: A Practical Spanning Tree Based MANET Routing Algorithm. In: The Proceedings of the 14th International Conference Computer Communications and Networks, ICCCN 2005, October 2005, pp. 19–24 (2005)

Data-Centric Trust Framework for High Integrity Wireless Sensor Networks*

Mingming Li[1], Jianbin Hu[2], and Nike Gui[2]

[1] School of Computer Science,
Chongqing University of Posts and Telecommunications
Chongqing, China
applepig7744@hotmail.com
[2] School of Electronics Engineering and Computer Science,
Peking University, Beijing, China
{hjbin,guink}@infosec.pku.edu.cn

Abstract. Traditional wireless sensor networks (WSN) are entity-centric systems making Sybil attacks, collusion attacks, false data injection attacks etc. very effective attacks. These attacks are critical security threat to WSN. Although there are many security solutions to these attacks, such as cryptography, reputation, authentic consensus, none of them can well defense all these attacks respectively. In this paper, we address this challenge by combining classical security solutions and extending the traditional entity-centric trust to data-centric trust via Dempster-Shafer Theory (DST) and a new method: Proof-of-Reputation-Relevance (PoRR). Our data-centric trust framework gives a whole solution for those attacks. It is realized by our PoRR accomplished by collecting reputation weighted authentic consensus from witness nodes in a cooperative way. Event reports from attacks who fail to provide right PoRR are discarded or given low trust levels. Our simulation results show that our scheme is highly resilient to attackers and converges stably to the correct decision.

Keywords: data-centric trust, PoRR, DST, wireless sensor networks.

1 Introduction

As a novel generation technology, wireless sensor networks combine with wireless communication technology, sensor technology, and microelectronics technology. It will revolutionize information gathering and processing both in urban environments and in inhospitable terrain. Wireless sensor networks are quickly gaining popularity due to the fact that they are potentially low cost solution to a variety of real-world challenges. Their low cost provides a mean to deploy large sensor arrays in a variety of conditions capable of performing both military and civilian tasks. So the sensor networks security becomes

* This work is partially funded by NFSC project the Research of Data-Centric Security Mechanism in Wireless Sensor Networks (NO.60873239).
NSFC: National Natural Science Foundation of China.

R.-S. Chang et al. (Eds.): GPC 2010, LNCS 6104, pp. 593–602, 2010.
© Springer-Verlag Berlin Heidelberg 2010

one of the biggest challenges with large-scale prevalence. Sensor network is one of data-centric network [1] virtually which differs from other traditional networks. The priority of sensor networks is propagating data and collecting data in sensor network. Therefore we can say the core of network security is data security.

In all traditional notions of trust, data trust was computed by entity trustworthiness, such as certification authorities, cryptographic mechanisms, reputation systems, and so on. Cryptography presents an efficient mechanism for providing data confidentiality, data integrity, node authentication, secure routing and access control. There have been several proposals, all based on cryptography, to ensure security communication on sensor nodes such as SPINS[2], INSENS[3], TinySec[4]. However, cryptography alone is not sufficient for the characteristics and misbehaviors encountered in sensor networks. Besides malicious attacks, sensor nodes are also vulnerable to system faults. Reputation system (RFSN) [5] proposed by Ganeriwal-Srivastava can be used to solve the problem that internal adversarial nodes could have access to valid cryptographic keys. While trust in reputation systems was always established and evolved via fairly lengthy interactions among nodes. And it can't detect the malicious or non-malicious nodes which have good reputation but send the wrong data. These traditional trust systems are entity-centric trust which couldn't differentiate between what the nodes propagate and which nodes propagate.

It is analyzed that there are four main disadvantages in entity-based systems. Firstly, the data could be distorted by middleman or something wrong with the system-internal. Secondly, system resource will be wasted unnecessarily in false data dissemination. Thirdly, it is a lengthy interaction to establish and evolve security entity-based systems. Finally, none of these entity-based systems can defense various attacks independently. Network security needs all-in-one security solution, while few systems could propose an all-in-one solution.

1.1 Our Contributions

We propose a data-based trust framework for wireless sensor networks and a new notion of Proof-of-Reputation-Relevance (PoRR) to realize it. There are three improvements compared with traditional schemes in our system. First, our logic weighs each individual piece of evidence according to well-established rules and takes into account various trust parameters, such as event type and location relevance. Russell said *"All traditional logic habitually assumes that precise symbols are being employed. It is therefore not applicable to this terrestrial life, but only to an imagined celestial existence."* We use Dempster-Shafer Theory (DST) to realize it. So we can derive trust not only in data and entity but also from multiple pieces of evidence. DST has a good presentation in computing subjective probability [5]. Secondly, the sensor network is a data-based network making false data injection a very effective attack [6]. There are many constraints and characteristics in sensor networks. So the Proof-of-Relevance (PoR) [6] scheme used in Ad-hoc networks can't meet it. In this work, we borrow the idea of PoR to filter false data and introduce reputation to protect PoR from collusion attack. We call it Proof-of-Reputation-Relevance (PoRR) which will be prolifically addressed in the literature (Sec.2). The method of PoRR is the regeneration of the PoR scheme in sensor networks. Third, our framework is an all-in-one security model. We use cryptographic mechanism to provide node authentication and the PoRR scheme to filter false data. The data-centric trust will open up an information security era to protect what really need it.

The goal of our data-centric system: (1) Every node in sensor network is equal, but the same event reported by different nodes may have different trust levels (due to the distance to the event, timeliness of the report, nodes trustworthiness). (2) Different event reported by the same node may have different trust levels [8]. (3) The data-centric trust systems have intelligent decision logics. It can not only compute the trust value of nodes but also the message sent by each node. The decision logics can combine multiple pieces of evidence even from unreliable observers.

1.2 Related Work

There are many security solutions for sensor networks, such as cryptography, reputation, authentic consensus, while none of them can well protect networks respectively. These entity-centric systems would ignore system salient features, rendering applications ineffective and systems inflexible. So entity-centric systems make false attacks, Sybil attacks and collusion attacks very effective attacks. These attacks are based on the vulnerability of nodes. Data-centric systems bring a new notion to the WSN security. It makes WSN have enough power to defend these entity-based attacks.

Although lots of mathematical methods can be used in decision logics, many of them are not applicable to sensor networks. Because they could require prior probabilities for each question we interested [7] such as the Bayesian theory (BI). BI uses a prior probability to compute the posterior probability of an event. But it is difficult to derive the prior probability in sensor networks. The article [8] showed the contrast DST with BI. The major difference between BI and DST is that the latter is more suitable for cases with uncertain or no information. And DST has a good performance with low data trust. So we choose DST as the decision logics.

There are also many systems can filter false data such as RFSN, PoR, SEF [9] and IHA [10]. The trust establishment logics of RFSN are based on entities. Although trust logics in PoR SEF and IHA are all based on data, the performance of PoR is better [6]. PoR is not suit for sensor networks and can't be resilient to collusion attacks. RFSN isn't resilient to Sybil attacks. Our Proof-of-Reputation-Relevance scheme being different with the aforementioned work is designed for sensor networks. It can not only save energy compared with PoR, but also be resilient to Sybil attacks and collusion attacks.

2 Data-Centric Trust Framework

In this section, we first lay out preliminaries of our framework. Then the three parts of the scheme are described. Finally we analyze the security of our scheme.

2.1 Preliminaries

The kernel of our work is to deal a problem: how to generate reliable information in data-centric trust sensor networks. In other words, what is data trust? What does the kernel word "data" mean? *"Data trust is attributed to real data, including data report and the data-reporting entities"* [8]. Data-centric trust includes entity trust and the context trust. In this paper, reports are statements or information by nodes on events. We use reports as basic events. Trustworthiness of nodes and reports constitute data-centric trust. Hence, data trust builds on the information provided by source authentication and reputation systems without trying to supplant them. The kernel of data-centric trust is computing trustworthiness of reports. There are three components in our framework to realize data-centric trust: report generation unit, report verification unit and report decision unit.

Our preliminary work has three parts. First of all, we define a set $\Omega = \{\alpha_1, \alpha_2, ..., \alpha_N\}$ of mutually exclusive basic events. That is, the basic events list interested information which could be sensed by sensors, such as "the thickness of oil stain", "the current velocity", "wind force and velocity" and so on. These events come from one item of our lab as an example: oil stain monitoring system in the Lantsang River. Then the nodes are labeled. Let V be the set of nodes v_k, $V = \{v_1, v_2, ...v_k\}$. The location information of nodes v_k is assumed to be known. Finally, it is assumed that each node possesses an public/private key pair K_V^+ / K_V^- and a certificate $Cert_V$ issued by a trusted authority (which has a public key K_{CA}^+ trusted by all nodes). So we prepared basic events and basic nodes for generating reports.

2.2 Report Generation Unit

Once a node detects some event, it generates an event report of the following format $E_{ki} = \{d(v_k), \tau_{v_k}(\alpha_i), t\}$, where $d(v_k)$ is the node type of node v_k, $\tau_{v_k}(\alpha_i)$ is the task of node v_k, that is the event type, t is the event time. E_{ki} is the report of node v_k which detects a basic event α_i. Node type $d(v_k)$ equals to the attribute value of node. The node type value is between 0 and 1. The equality $d(v_k) = 1$ implies node v_k is legitimate and $d(v_k) = 0$ implies that the node is revoked or sleeping. Intermediate values can denote different trust levels or different levels of nodes. Event type $\tau_{v_k}(\alpha_i)$ is the event that node v_k detected in the time t. An event type is a query or an interrogation which specifies what a user wants. As an example, monitor oil stain, wind force, the current velocity and so on are the basic event types in our oil stain monitoring system.

Every node has a reputation table which stores neighboring nodes' reputations. The initial reputation is default (different systems could choose different initial values). Once nodes send package to its neighbors, the reputations will be increased or decreased, for applicable. We define the reputation table RT_k maintained by node v_k.

$RT_k = \{R_{ki}, ...\} ...$ R_{ki} is the reputation of node v_i at node v_k. The evolution of reputation is detailed in [5].

2.3 Report Verification Unit

In this section, we introduce the details of Proof-of-Reputation-Relevance (PoRR). PoR can prevent false data injection attacks in the danger warning system by providing the data authenticity via authentic consensus [6]. But it does not rule out the possibility of collusion attacks where more than T attackers collude to generate a false report. In the simulation of RFSN, the performance of BRSN is able to maintain its resiliency against collusion attacks on the premise of known some malicious nodes. While reputation-establishing need fairly lengthy interactions among nodes, so it isn't resilient to emergency which could happen in sensor networks. So we intend to do some work to protect the PoR from collusion attacks via adding reputation value.

We propose Proof-of-Reputation-Relevance (PoRR) to solve these problems. When detecting an event and before sending the warning message, the sensor node will spend some time collecting digital endorsements from the other witness nodes on the same event. Then reputations of these witness nodes will be changed. Every node has a reputation table which stores the reputations. When reputations change, the table will be updated.

Once collecting enough signatures and reputations, the node will generate the final warning message and accept it only if verification succeeds. We change the final report in PoR: $Report = \{E_{i1}, Cert_{i1}, Sig_{i1}, ..., E_{iT}, Cert_{iT}, Sig_{iT}\}$ to a new one and use reputation value as the weighted value for the signatures. The degree of reputation value will affect the weight of an event report. If an event detected by node v_k, this node will generate the final report with the following format:

$$E_{ki} = \{d(v_k), \tau_{v_k}(\alpha_i), t\}, i \in [1, T]$$

$$s_i = R_{ki} \times (E_{ki}, Cert_{ki}, Sig_{ki})$$

$$Report_{ki} = \{s_1, ..., s_T\}$$

The choice of the parameter T is a trade-off between detection power and overhead. Different sensor networks will choose different T [6]. The real-time systems need a smaller T and safety systems require a larger one.

When a node receives a *report*, it first examines whether there are enough signatures in the *report*. *Reports* with less than T signatures will be discarded. If there are T signatures, the node goes on to validate each signature in the report using the corresponding public key. If the T signatures are incorrect, the packet will be discarded. Then we check the reputation table of the receiver. If the reputation value is not beyond a constant (this number could be controlled by different systems), the packet will be discarded. If all conditions are satisfied, the node will accept the message and react according to the event type. Trust value will be computed in decision-making unit. Finally, reputation tables will be updated according to the trust value.

In this way the Proof-of-Reputation-Relevance compute trust about different pieces of evidence. Multi-evidence will be combined in the next part, the decision-making unit.

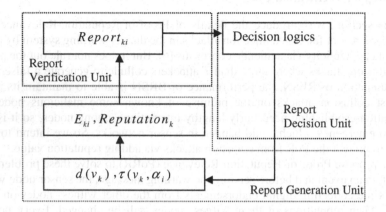

Fig. 1. Data-centric report trust establishment

2.4 Report Decision and Combination Unit

When we collect enough supporting evidence for event α_i, in this unit reports will be combined into one. We also can combine different events into one using the following formulas. First, we use e_k^i as the shortening of a $Report_{ki}$ of event α_i, generated by node v_k, $Report_{ki} = e_k^i$. Then we compute the trust value of a report e_k^i using DST.

In DST [7], the *frame of discernment* contains all mutually exclusive possibilities related to an observation. Hence, in this article, it is the set Ω defined previously. There are two main functions in DST: the belief function and plausibility function. The belief value corresponding to an event α_i and provided by $Report_{ki}$ is computed as:

$bel_k(\alpha_i) = \sum_{q:\alpha_q \subset \alpha_i} m_k(\alpha_q)$ which means it is the sum of all basic belief assign-

ments $m_k(\alpha_q)$, α_q being all basic events that compose the event α_i, In this case, only $\alpha_i \subset \alpha_i$ and hence $bel_k(\alpha_i) = m_k(\alpha_i)$. The plausibility value corresponding to event α_i represents the sum of all evidence that does not refute α_i and is computed as:

$pls_k(\alpha_i) = \sum_{r:\alpha_r \cap \alpha_i \neq \varnothing} m_k(\alpha_i)$. Belief and plausibility functions are related by

$pls(\alpha_i) = 1 - bel(\overline{\alpha}_i)$.

The combined trust level, corresponding to event α_i, is the belief function correspond-

ing to α_i: $d_i = bel(\alpha_i) = m(\alpha_i) = \bigoplus_{k=1}^{K} m_k(\alpha_i)$ where pieces of evidence can be combined

using Dempster's rule for combination: $m_1(\alpha_i) \oplus m_2(\alpha_i) = \dfrac{\sum_{q,r:\alpha_q \cap \alpha_r = \alpha_i} m_1(\alpha_q) m_2(\alpha_r)}{1 - \sum_{q,r:\alpha_q \cap \alpha_r = \varnothing} m_1(\alpha_q) m_2(\alpha_r)}$. As

above, using trust levels as weights of reports, the basic belief assignment that confirms α_i

is equal to the *trust level*: $m_k(\alpha_i) = F(e_k^i)$.

In Dempster-Shafer Theory [7], evidence evaluation is inspired by human reasoning. More specifically, the lack of knowledge about an event is not necessarily a refutal of the event. In addition, if there are two conflicting events, uncertainty about one of them can be considered as supporting evidence for the other. So $F(e_k^i)$ will show the applicable trust values.

2.5 Applicability

The scheme of data-based trust makes the network immune to false data injection attacks. Besides, the PoRR based on authentic consensus is immune to Sybil attacks where the nodes claim to have multiple identities, because Sybil nodes are unable to forge the authentic consensus without private keys even if they can claim to have multiple identities. PoRR also succeeds to the immunity of collusion attacks from reputation systems.

3 Simulation Evaluation

In this section, we will validate our analytical model and show the performance of our scheme.

We consider a network scenario where sensor nodes are scattered randomly to monitor oil stain of the Lantsang river. In this simulation, the neighbor nodes are labeled in sequence number according to physical location and we ignore the communications properties for simplicity. We simulate the environment of sensor networks. First, we establish the trust between a random node and one of its neighbors. We only study the trust evolution of good nodes and the bad ones are similar. The initial reputation is 0.5 in our simulation for comparison with RFSN. Comparison between PoRR and reputation is showed in Fig.2. The evolution of PoRR is faster than reputation due to using authentic consensus [6]. When a node haven't reputation value (that is $R_{ij} = 0.5$) about its destination nodes in its reputation table, it also can establish trust via collection signature.

Then we show some characteristics of data-centric trust scheme. The above mentioned that the same event reported by different nodes may have different trust levels and different event reported by the same node may have different trust levels in data-centric trust scheme. Fig.3 shows that different nodes have different trust with two sequence events. The evolution of reputation is much slower than PoRR. Real-time data-centric trust scheme via PoRR is showed in Fig.3.

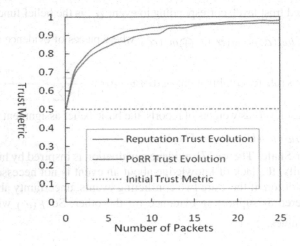

Fig. 2. Evolution of trust for Reputation scheme and PoRR

Finally, we simulate the false data attacks in wireless sensor networks. RFSN can prevent malicious or non-malicious insertion of data from internal adversaries or faulty nodes [5]. But it is not enough. Fig.4 shows the different performance between reputation and PoRR under different proportions of attackers. The performance of reputation is not very well because it can't identify false data packets of good nodes. Reputation scheme don't evaluate the trust of data but the trust of nodes. However, PoRR evaluate the report trust not only nodes trust. So PoRR makes a lower percentage of false decision under false data attacks.

In one word, the simulation results shows our scheme is resistant to false data attacks and has a good performance in trust evolution.

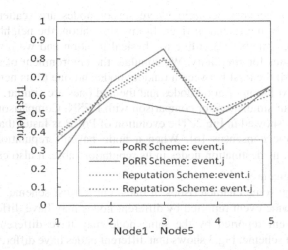

Fig. 3. Comparison of differents nodes trust about events in sequence

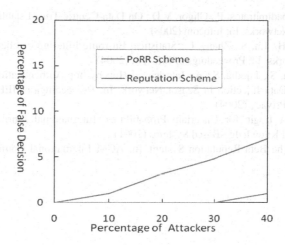

Fig. 4. Filtering false data comparison

4 Conclusion

In this paper, we propose data-centric trust framework which is an all-in-one security scheme. The data-centric trust scheme using PoRR can defense false data injection attacks in sensor networks. PoRR is a new method to defense collusion attacks and Sybil attacks. Our simulation results show the validity of the analytical results. Our plan for the next step includes optimizing our scheme and evaluation of our scheme in realistic application of wireless sensor networks. We thank the anonymous reviewers for their valuable comments.

References

1. Intanagonwiwat, C., Govindan, R.: Directed Diffusion for Wireless Sensor Networking. IEEE/ACM Transactions in Networking (2003)
2. Perrig, A., Szewczyk, R.: SPINS: Security Protocols for Sensor Networks. Mobile Computing and Networking (2001)
3. Deng, J., Han, R., Mishra, S.: A Performance Evaluation of Intrusion-Tolerant Routing in Wireless Sensor Networks. In: Zhao, F., Guibas, L.J. (eds.) IPSN 2003. LNCS, vol. 2634, pp. 349–364. Springer, Heidelberg (2003)
4. Karlof, C., Sastry, N., Wagner, D.: TinySec: Link Layer Encryption for Tiny Devices. In: ACM SenSys (2004)
5. Ganeriwal, S., Srivastava, M.B.: Reputation-based Framework for High Integrity Sensor Networks. ACM Transactions on Sensor Networks (2004)
6. Cao, Z., Kong, J., Lee, U.: Proof-of-Relevance: Filtering False Data Via Authentic Consensus in Vehicle Ad-hoc Networks. In: INFOCOM MOVE Workshop (April 2008)
7. Shafer, G.: A Mathematical Theory of Evidence. Princeton University Press, Princeton (1976)

8. Raya, M., Papadimitratos, P., Gligor, V.D.: On Data-Centric Trust Establishment in Ephemeral Ad Hoc Networks. In: Infocom (2008)
9. Ye, F., Luo, H., Lu, S., Zhang, L.: Statistical En-route Filtering of Injected False Data in Sensor Networks. In: Proceedings of Infocom (2004)
10. Zhu, S., Setia, S., Jajodia, S.: An Interleaved Hop-by-hop Authentication Scheme for Filtering False Data Injection in Sensor Network. In: Proceedings of IEEE Symposium on Security and Privacy (2004)
11. Jøsang, A.: A Logic for Uncertain Probabilities. International Journal of Uncertainty, Fuzziness and Knowledge-Based Systems (2001)
12. Jøsang, A.: The Beta Reputation System. In: ACM International Conference Proceeding Series (2006)

Shuffle: An Enhanced QoS Control by Balancing Energy Consumption in Wireless Sensor Networks

Rong-Guei Tsai and Hao-Li Wang

Department of Computer Science and Information Engineering,
National Chiayi University,
No. 300 Syuefu Rd., Chiayi City, 600, Taiwan
{S0970418,haoli}@mail.ncyu.edu.tw

Abstract. Recently, Wireless sensor networks (WSNs) are increasingly receiving attention in both industrial and academic areas. Most research on WSNs focus on routing and data aggregation; only a few papers discuss the quality of service (QoS). An earlier study introduced a QoS control approach based on the gur game. The gur game-based scheme can maintain the QoS without knowing total number of sensors. However, the lifetime of WSN is limited for the gur game-based scheme due to unbalanced power consumption. This paper proposes an enhanced QoS control scheme, namely Shuffle, periodically swapping active and sleep sensors to balance power consumption. This scheme uses the characteristic of gur game and extends lifetime with little modification. We evaluate Shuffle in various environments, showing that it significantly improves lifetime. The simulation result presents that Shuffle indeed compensates for the drawbacks and maintains the strengths of the Gur game-based method.

Keywords: Wireless Sensor Network, Gur Game, QoS Control, Lifetime.

1 Introduction

Advancements in sensor technology and a drop in their price have led to an increasing number of applications for wireless sensor networks (WSNs). WSNs consist of a large number of small sensors and a sink (BASE) station. The sensors are small devices with limited energy supply and low computational capability. They cover and monitor a sensing field to collect useful information.

Sensors are usually placed in sensor field randomly. To have high degree of reliability, the concept of redundancy is applied to WSN. One or more sensors may cover the same region and gather similar data. This ends up in many redundant data sent to the sink. To conserve energy in WSN, we have to avoid those redundant data collection. Sensors are scheduled to be active and idle periodically. Only part of all sensors are active in all period of time. This can keep high reliability and low data redundancy. Moreover, because sensor nodes usually have a limited life time, it is not reasonable to assume that the sensor network has a fixed number of nodes. Thus, we need to take into consideration additions and deletions of sensor nodes.

R.-S. Chang et al. (Eds.): GPC 2010, LNCS 6104, pp. 603–611, 2010.
© Springer-Verlag Berlin Heidelberg 2010

The question now arises: how to select a number of active nodes in all sensors which may be added or deleted randomly. This is known as the Quality of Service (QoS) control in WSNs. The definition of QoS is the number of active sensors, which should send information at any given time.

In QoS control design, we have two goals: (1) maximize the lifetime of the sensor network and (2) have enough sensors powered-up sending packets toward the sink. Herein, the lifetime of the sensor network is defined as the amount of time until the first sensor in the network runs out of energy.

A challenging point for a QoS control scheme is the unknown and unconstant number of total sensors. If the number of total sensors is constant and given, QoS control becomes an easy problem. A sensor can determine to be active in a fixed probability. In this paper, we propose an enhanced QoS Control scheme, named Shuffle, balancing the power consumption to extend the lifetime of WSN. Simulation results show that Shuffle has a longer lifetime than prior work.

This paper makes three contributions: (1) it recognizes the reason for limited lifetime for gur game-based scheme, (2) it enhances prior work by balancing the power consumption, and (3) it evaluates the proposed scheme in various environments, showing that Shuffle significantly improves lifetime.

The remainder of this paper is organized as follows: Section 2 surveys some of the previous work in QoS control for WSNs. In Section 3 we present the proposed QoS control scheme for WSNs. Section 4 shows the simulation results and section 5 concludes the paper.

2 Related Works

2.1 Previous Works on QoS Control in WSNs

This paper is motivated by an earlier work [1] which first proposed an QoS control approach based on the Gur game. We give a brief introduction to this gur game-based scheme later.

Some papers are concerned with energy conservation in QoS control scheme [3,4,5], but they do not focus on the problem of unbalanced power consumption. Some papers apply the QoS in the cluster structure [7,8,9]. Moreover, the goal of these papers is different from our goal. In [7,8,9], the definition of network lifetime is the duration for which the desired QoS is maintained, which is different from ours. To the best knowledge, this paper is the first attempt to solve problem of unbalanced power consumption in QoS control.

2.2 Using Gur Game in QoS Control

Herein, we introduce how to use the mathematical model of Gur Game to control the QoS. The principle of the Gur Game is based on biased random walks of finite-state automata. The automata describes a set of state with assigned meanings and a set of rules to determine how to switches from one state to the other. Figure 1 is a simple example of finite-state automata with 4 states for the gur game. Each state has its own meaning: state -1 and -2 mean sleep mode and state 1 and 2 mean active modes.

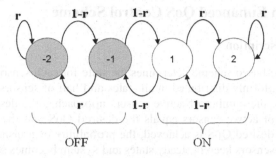

Fig. 1. An example of the automaton with 4 states for the gur game

The key in gur game is the reward function. The reward function is responsible to measure the performance of the system. An example of reward function is as followed:

$R*(t)=0.2+0.8exp(-0.002(K_t-n)^2)$, where K_t is the number of active nodes and n is the desired value of QoS. When Kt is close to n, the R value is approaching to the top value, 1. Fig. 2 shows an example of reward function with $K_t =35$.

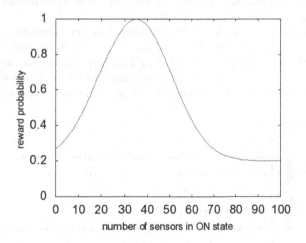

Fig. 2. An example of reward function with $K_t =35$

In a WSN, the sink (BASE) has the number of active sensors according to the number of received data from active sensors. Using the information and reward function, the sink has the reward value R and broadcasts R to all sensors. Based on the received R value from the sink, sensors can determine whether be active or be idle in next iteration. The decision is been made by each sensor based on the finite-state automata, current state, and the received R value. After a number of iterations, gur game can make the number of active sensors reach the target.

3 Shuffle: An Enhanced QoS Control Scheme

3.1 Problem Description

Initially, gur game-based scheme determines the state for each sensor node randomly. All sensors are uniformly distributed in all states and half of sensors are active. After a number of runs, the number of active sensors approaches the desired QoS. At the end, the number of active sensors equals the desired QoS and the whole system is stable. When the desired QoS is achieved, the probability of transition is equal to 1, which implies all sensors keep in steady states and system becomes stable.

Although the goal of QoS Control is achieved, there exists a potential problem. Since all sensors keep in steady states, active sensors are always an identical set of sensors and these sensors may die soon due to running out of energy. In contrast, sleep sensors always sleep in steady state. This unbalanced power consumption significantly cuts down the lifetime of WSNs.

To solve this problem, a straightforward way is to adopt the periodical sleeping mechanism. However, the periodical sleeping is not applicable to the gur game-based scheme. Moreover, a centralized scheduling scheme may control sensors quickly and effectively, but when the number of sensors increases, centralized scheme has scalability problem. Therefore, we desire to keep the characteristics of gur game and avoid the unbalanced power consumption.

Figure 3 shows an example of the unbalanced power consumption in gur game-based scheme. Fig.3(a) presents the initial states for all sensors, which are distributed uniformly in the four states (-2, -1 ,+1, +2). Fig.3(b) displays the node states at the 200th epoch. 97% of sensors are at the edge states, i.e. state -2 and +2. Fig.3(c) provides the node states at the 500th epoch, when almost all sensors are at the edge states.

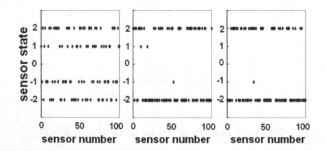

Fig. 3. States of sensors at different epochAn example of reward function with K_t =35 (a) 1st epoch, (b) 200th epoch, (c) 500th epoch

3.2 Shuffle: An Enhanced QoS Control Scheme

To avoid unbalanced power consumption, at first we think about exchanging active nodes for sleep nodes. In the beginning, we consider a simple and easy way. The BASE specifies some nodes to exchange states. However, it is not suitable when we are concern about the fairness and scalability.

Moreover, exchanging sensor states may cause system unstable. In particular, after a period of QoS vibration, QoS approaches to the target number and system becomes stable. However, stableness for a long time also implies unbalanced power consumption. Exchanging sensor states may help balance power consumption, but the stableness is destroyed.

To help system come back the stableness after exchanging sensor states, we think of gur game again. Due to the characteristic of self-optimization in gur game, QoS can automatically come back to desired QoS again after a period of QoS vibration.

Based on this idea, we propose an enhanced QoS control scheme, namely Shuffle, periodically applying gur game to maintain stableness after exchanging sensor states. To exchange sensor states, Shuffle swaps the state of sensor which is in the two edge states (i.e. -2, +2). In particular, all sensors in the two edge states swap. Then, Shuffle utilizes gur game to help system come back to stableness and achieve desired QoS. Shuffle attempts to modify the gur game-based scheme as less as possible and keeps the characteristic of gur game.

How long to trigger an exchange of sensor states is an important issue for Shuffle. If sensor state exchanges too often, there is not enough time to achieve stableness. In contrast, sensor state exchanges too long may lead to unbalanced power consumption. To determine the period of shuffle, we observe the QoS vibration. As shown if Figure 4, after about 450 epochs of QoS vibration, system becomes stable. Thus, we suggest the period of shuffle is larger than 500 epochs. In Figure 4, the period of shuffle is 1000 epochs. Clearly, after the second QoS vibration at the 1000th epochs, QoS reverts to desired QoS (i.e. 35) again.

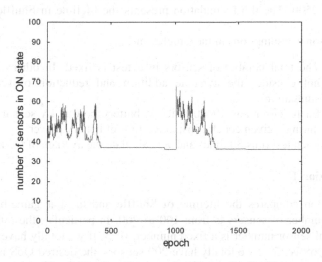

Fig. 4. Number of sensors in ON state for Shuffle

To show the benefit of Shuffle, Figure 5 present the residual energy of sensors at the end of lifetime for gur game based scheme and Shuffle. In Figure 5(a), many sensors in the gur game-based scheme still have high residual energy at the end of lifetime (10142 epochs) but the sensor #17 exhausts its power. The power consumption is extremely unbalanced. In contrast, most sensors in Shuffle have low residual energy at the end of lifetime (16923 epochs).

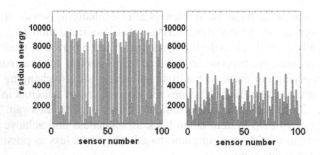

Fig. 5. Residual energy at the end of lifetime (a) gur game-based scheme (b) Shuffle

4 Simulations

We develop three simulations to compare Shuffle with the gur game-based scheme. The first simulation is to exam whether Shuffle has longer lifetime than gur game-based scheme when total number of sensors is from 100 to 200. The second simulation is to show the change of lifetime in Shuffle at when the period of shuffle changes from 500 to 2500. The third simulation presents the lifetime in Shuffle at different desired QoS.

We have some assumptions in the simulations.

1) The total number of sensors in a test is fixed. In other words, we do not consider the dynamic addition and reduction of sensors in the simulations.
2) Each sensor has 10000 units of battery power. IA sensor in ON state during a given epoch consumes a unit of battery power.
3) Each test runs 30 times and we calculate the average of the lifetimes.

4.1 Simulation 1

This simulation compares the lifetime of Shuffle and the gur game-based scheme when total number of sensors is from 100 to 200. In particular, the ratio of desired QoS and total sensor number is a fixed number, 0.35. If we totally have 100 sensors, the desired QoS is 35; if we totally have 200 sensors, the desired QoS is 70. The period of shuffle is 100 epochs. Figure 6 shows the lifetimes of Shuffle and the gur game-based scheme. The lifetime increases with the increasing total number of sensors. Clearly, Shuffle always have longer lifetime than gur game-based scheme. Specifically, Shuffle have 60% increase in lifetime when total number of sensors is 100.

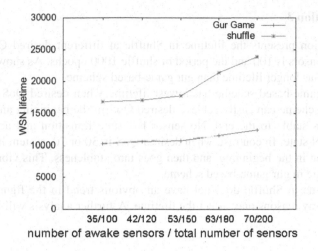

Fig. 6. Comparison of lifetime in different number of sensors

4.2 Simulation 2

The period of shuffle is an important parameter in Shuffle. This simulation shows the change of lifetime in Shuffle when the period of shuffle ranges from 500 to 2500. The total number of sensors is 100 and desired QoS is 35. As shown in Figure 7, the lifetime of Shuffle decreases with increasing period of shuffle. Since the gur game-based scheme does not shuffle, the lifetime is always the same.

When the period of shuffle grows up, fewer times of shuffle appear. Since fewer shuffles cause the unbalance power consumption, the lifetime decreases accordingly.

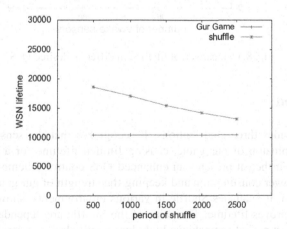

Fig. 7. Comparison of lifetime in different period of shuffle

4.3 Simulation 3

This simulation presents the lifetime in Shuffle at different desired QoS. The total number of sensors is 100 and the period of shuffle 1000 epochs. As shown in Figure 8, Shuffle still has longer lifetime than gur game-based scheme.

The gur game-based scheme has lowest lifetime when desired QoS is 50. This is because the scheme can easily achieve desired QoS in the beginning and then system always keeps stable to the end. No sensor has state transition and active sensor is always in ON state. In contrast, when desired QoS is 30 or 70, system has a period of QoS vibration in the beginning, and then goes into stableness. This vibration leads to longer lifetime in gur game-based scheme.

The lifetime in Shuffle does not have an obvious trend in the figure. This is because too many reasons may affect the lifetime. A further analysis will be done in the future.

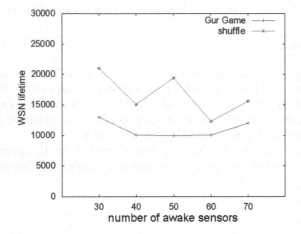

Fig. 8. Comparison of lifetime in different desired QoS

5   Conclusion

This paper provides three contributions. It recognizes that the sensors move to the edge in the automaton of gur game, causing limited lifetime for a prior gur game-based scheme. Further, it presents an enhanced QoS control scheme, named Shuffle, balancing the power consumption and keeping the strength of gur gamed scheme, like self optimization. It evaluates Shuffle in various environments, showing that Shuffle significantly improves lifetime. The gains of the Shuffle are dependent on the period of shuffle. A short period can achieve high degree of balance on power consumption, but frequent shuffles make the system unstable in a short period.

References

1. Iyer, R., Kleinrock, L.: QoS Control for Sensor Networks. In: IEEE International Communication Conference. IEEE Press, New York (2003)
2. Nayer, S.I., Ali, H.H.: A Dynamic Energy-Aware Algorithm for Self-Optimizing Wireless Sensor Networks. In: Hummel, K.A., Sterbenz, J.P.G. (eds.) IWSOS 2008. LNCS, vol. 5343, pp. 262–268. Springer, Heidelberg (2008)
3. Tsai, R.G., Wang, H.L.: Extending Lifetime of a QoS Control Scheme in Wireless Sensor Networks. In: Workshop of E-life Digital Technology, Tainan, Taiwan (2009)
4. Lo, H.J., Wang, H.L.: Power-saving QoS Control in Wireless Sensor Networks. In: Mobile Computing Workshop, Changhua Taiwan (2007)
5. Zhao, L., Xu, C., Xu, Y., Li, X.: Energy-Aware QoS Control for Wireless Sensor Network. In: IEEE Conference on Industrial Electronics and Applications. IEEE Press, New York (2006)
6. Chen, D., Varshney, P.K.: QoS support in wireless sensor networks: A survey. In: International Conference on Wireless Networks. IEEE Press, New York (2004)
7. Kay, J., Frolik, J.: Quality of Service Analysis and Control for Wireless Sensor Networks. In: 1st IEEE International Conference on Mobile Ad hoc and Sensor Systems. IEEE Press, New York (2004)
8. Liang, B., Frolik, J., Wang, X.: Energy efficient dynamic spatial resolution control for wireless sensor clusters. International Journal of Distributed Sensor Networks 5(4), 361–389 (2009)
9. Frolik, J.: QoS Control for Random Access Wireless Sensor Networks. In: IEEE Wireless Communications and Networking Conference. IEEE Press, New York (2004)

Scheduling of Job Combination and Dispatching Strategy for Grid and Cloud System

Tai-Lung Chen[2], Ching-Hsien Hsu[1], and Shih-Chang Chen[2]

[1] Department of Computer Science and Information Engineering,
Chung Hua University, Hsinchu 300, Taiwan
chh@chu.edu.tw
[2] College of Engineering,
Chung Hua University, Hsinchu 300, Taiwan
{ctl,scc}@sclab.csie.chu.edu.tw

Abstract. With the emergence of resource management and network techniques, the job scheduling has become an important issue in grid computing. In this paper, we present a job combination and dispatching strategy for scheduling jobs to client users which connect to data servers. Based on the job combination and dispatching strategy algorithm (*JCDS*), the optimization algorithm was proposed in this study; the *JCDS* with dynamic programming (*JCDS-D*). We both focus on the job allocating and the communication overheads minimizing in grid system. The significant improvement of our approach was increase the network and processors' utilization. The advantage of job combination strategy is that system throughput can be increased through job allocating to adaptive processors. To evaluate the efficiency of different techniques, we have implemented both methods and compare with the *FCFS*, *Min-Min*, and *Max-Min* algorithms. The experimental results show that the *JCDS* and *JCDS-D* provide obvious improvements in terms of performance.

1 Introduction

Grid and cloud system is important to integrate distributed data resources and establish a virtual platform to achieve network utilization and large-scale of data processing. Recently years, lots of researches provide users an infrastructure scheduling jobs and avoid the network traffic in high heterogeneous systems. The grid system construct by the collection of several data server and a lot of heterogeneous client users which connect to the system rely on web service. To investigate job allocating problem, the resource broker system need to be designed cautious for developing job scheduling technologies in grid and cloud system. In the high heterogeneous network environment, the communication ratio and job similarity are important to consider in design the job scheduling strategy. It is important to develop efficient job scheduling techniques that decrease network traffic and avoid too many duplicated jobs in grid computing.

R.-S. Chang et al. (Eds.): GPC 2010, LNCS 6104, pp. 612–621, 2010.

Figure 1 shows an illustration of the multi-site server paradigm which have multiple data server and the collection of client nodes connect to servers by heterogeneous network. A set of independent jobs in queue are scheduled by virtual machine and dispatched by job broker. Generally, the optimization of job dispatching problem has two phases. One is minimizing the makespan for sequential and non-identical jobs. The other one is maximizing total amount of finished jobs, namely maximize throughput.

In this paper, a combination strategy and parallel dispatching method for sequential and non-identical jobs in heterogeneous system is presented. The first main step of the proposed technique is the job broker according to the record table which have higher similar factor to combine jobs. Second, system dispatch jobs which had been combined to the client nodes which have low communication ratio.

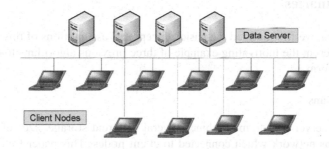

Fig. 1. The multi-site server paradigm

The rest of this paper is organized as follows. Section 2 describes the previous related researches in grid and cloud computing. Section 3 introduces the research definitions and notations which be used in this paper. In section 3.2, we present the motivating example of *FCFS*, *Min-Min* and *Max-Min* to demonstrate the heterogeneous model. In section 4, we illustrate the new scheduling algorithm of Job Combination and Dispatching Strategy algorithm (*JCDS*) and enhanced *JCDS* with Dynamic programming (*JCDS-D*). The performance comparisons and simulations results are discussed in section 5. Finally, section 6 is the conclusions and future work.

2   Related Work

Job scheduling research on heterogeneous processors can be designed in the virtual machine of job broker in Ethernet based cluster paradigm or grid and cloud computing. The main purpose of job scheduling is to achieve high performance computing and high system throughput. Cao *et al.* [9] presented the global grid load balancing in dynamic scheduling based on intelligent agents. Beaumont *et al.* [7, 8] introduced the master-slave paradigm with task scheduling in heterogeneous processors.

The computational grid becomes a widely accept paradigm for large-scale parallel systems. Angelo *et al.* [3] focused on developing the scheduling techniques to minimize makespan of a broadcast operation in grid environment. Beaumont *et al.* [5, 6] concentrated the broadcasting in heterogeneous platforms with one port model. To avoid contentions and schedule messages in minimal communication steps, Assuncao *et al.* [2] improve the resource allocating and scheduling performance of a virtual machine in cloud. The internet is 24 hours usable and supporting numerous services for users, Das *et al.* [10] report the architecture of Vijjana with semantic web operations. Aymerich *et al.* [1] concerns the analysis and design of a real time financial system on cloud computing technologies. Brandic *et al.* [4] present the autonomic computing of the self-adaptable services on grid and cloud. Evoy *et al.* [11] discuss the relationship between cloud computing technology and grid is important in the IT market.

3 Preliminaries

In this section, we first defined the basic concept and assumptions of this paper. Secondly, we present the motivating example of three previous algorithms to demonstrate the grid platform.

3.1 Definitions

A multi-site server paradigm combines several different storage sizes of servers and heterogeneous network which connected to client nodes. This paper follows next assumptions as listed.

- **Heterogeneous processors:** all clients node have different computation speed.
- **Non-identical jobs:** all jobs are different size.
- **Heterogeneous network:** communication costs between master and slave processors are of different overheads. This assumption justifies the situation of scheduling tasks on cluster based computational grid system in which the communication costs between clusters are different.
- **Multiple servers:** clients connect to different data server by different communication speed.

To simplify the presentation, we defined notations and terminologies.

Definition 1: In a grid system, the data server are denoted by $S_1, S_2, ..., S_m$, where m is the number of data storage servers.

Definition 2: In the grid system, the client nodes are presented by $P_1, P_2, ..., P_n$, where n is the number of processors.

Definition 3: Upon the assumption of non-identical jobs, those jobs are denoted by $J_1, J_2, ..., J_r$, where r is the job number.

Definition 4: The execution time of each one node to compute one task is different. We use P_{i_comp} to represent the execution time of the client i to complete one task.

Definition 5: The communication time of each one node to receive one task is different and every client connected to different server. We use $S_j P_{i\_comm}$ to represent the transmit time of the client i to receive one task from server S_j.

Definition 6: Given the jobs in queue content of different number of tasks and each job may have different set-theoretic intersection. The number of tasks in a job is denoted as J_{q_task}.

Definition 7: The communication cost of job from S_j to client node P_i is defined as

$$comm(P_{jiq}) = S_j P_{i\_comm} \times J_{q\_task}.$$

Definition 8: The computation cost of job in client node P_i is defined as

$$comp(P_{iq}) = P_{i\_comp} \times J_{q\_task}.$$

Definition 9: The heterogeneous *Communication Ratio* between server S_j and P_i is

defined as $CR_i = \dfrac{S_j P_{i\_comm}}{S_j P_{i\_comm} + P_{i\_comp}}$.

Definition 10: The *similar factor* (δ) of is defined as the task set-theoretic intersection between two jobs that joined the computation, means the number of tasks that involved in different jobs.

3.2 Computation Emphasized Job Scheduling

According to the related research, the *FCFS*, *Min-Min* based and *Max-Min* based heuristic algorithms will be discussed in this section. To simplify the presentation, there are many algorithms focus on the computation emphasized scheduling. We use example to represent the procedure of these three scheduling methods between data servers and the receiver nodes.

The common job scheduling of *FCFS* focus on sending job to available and faster processor first by order. Figure 2 shows the simple example of *FCFS* on two data servers and each has two jobs. According to Figure 2, the clients connect to data server by different bandwidth. The time for client nodes P_1 and P_2 to compute one task are $P_{1\_comp} = 2$, $P_{2\_comp} = 3$. According to definitions 5, the non-identical communication cost for slave processors to receive one task from server j is defined as $S_j P_{i\_comm}$. The communication overhead of $S_1 P_{1\_comm} = 1.5$, $S_1 P_{2\_comm} = 0.5$, $S_2 P_{1\_comm} = 0.5$ and $S_2 P_{2\_comm} = 1$. The *FCFS* of job scheduling policy are dispatching jobs to faster and available node first. As shown in Figure 2, the Job$_A$ is sent to faster node P_1, Job$_B$ is sent to the available node P_2 when P_1 is receiving Job$_A$. By the order, the Job$_C$ is allocated to P_2 and the fourth job is allocated to P_2.

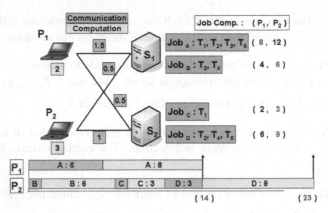

Fig. 2. The *FCFS* job scheduling on heterogeneous network

In the same example, we discuss the *Min-Min* algorithm of job scheduling on multi-site data server system. *Min-Min* algorithm is an intuitionally approach which faster and available node receives small jobs first. In the other words, the slower nodes will allocate larger job. This method enable the fast nodes receive jobs first, but decrease the load balance because of large job allocated to slower nodes may waste much time period in executing. Figure 3 shows the job scheduling of the *Min-Min* algorithm. As the respectively rules of *Min-Min*, the order of four jobs from small to large is Job_C, Job_B, Job_D, and Job_A.

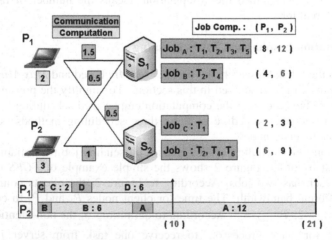

Fig. 3. *Min-Min* job scheduling on heterogeneous network

Max-Min algorithm is contrary to *Min-Min* that the faster and available node receives large jobs first. Another example of *Max-Min* job scheduling with multi-site data server is given in Figure 4. In this example, $J_{A\_task} = 4$, $J_{B\_task} = 2$, $J_{A\_task} = 1$, and $J_{D\_task} = 3$. The fast node P_1 receives and processes the largest Job_A, and second Job_B is sent to the available node P_2 and so on.

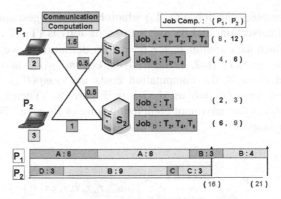

Fig. 4. *Max-Min* job scheduling on heterogeneous network

Min-Min method may let fast node accessing many small jobs frequently when the number of jobs is numerous, and make slower node cause higher loading because of processing large jobs usually. It is obviously that *Max-Min* method enabled the fast node have higher utilization in the same makespan of 21. However, the infrastructure on the purpose of minimizing execution time about how these servers dispatching jobs to clients should be considered in various phases.

4 Job Combination and Dispatching Strategy with Dynamic Programming

Grid and cloud system include datacenter and provide services for client users. The virtualization services enable the cloud computing to release resources and access large parallel jobs. It is important to improve the system efficiency and to maximize the usage of computing nodes. The designed strategy is a flexible platform by setting the bounds of *similar factor* (δ) which can decide the ratio of job combining and dispatching.

According to the definitions, both job combination and dispatching strategy algorithm (*JCDS*) and enhanced *JCDS with Dynamic programming* (*JCDS-D*) algorithms will be discussed in this section.

JCDS is performed according to the following three principles.

1. Jobs will be combined according to the largest bound of *similar factor* (δ).
2. The combined job will be dispatched to the client nodes which is available.
3. If there have more than one client nodes are available, system will dispatching larger jobs to the node that has shortest *Communication Ratio* (CR_i).

Figure 5 demonstrates an example of *JCDS* with two data servers and two client nodes in heterogeneous network. The communication cost of server sites to client nodes are assumed as $S_1P_{1\_comm}$ = 1.5, $S_1P_{2\_comm}$ = 0.5, $S_2P_{1\_comm}$ = 0.5 and $S_2P_{2\_comm}$ = 1. The computation time for client nodes P_1 and P_2 are P_{1_comp} = 2, P_{2_comp} = 3. The number of tasks in each job is J_{A_task} = 4, J_{B_task} = 2, J_{A_task} = 1, and J_{D_task} = 3. Job combination is according to the principles and present in Figure 5, the task set of Job$_B$

is (T_2, T_4, T_6) combine with $Job_D (T_2, T_4)$ which have the largest *similar factor* $\delta = 2$ of set-theoretic intersection, and the other tasks of Job_A is (T_1, T_2, T_3, T_5) combine with $Job_C (T_1)$ which have *similar factor* $\delta = 1$. By definition 7, we have the communication costs are $comm(P_{121})=2$, $comm(P_{112})=3$, $comm(P_{223})=1$ and $comm(P_{214})=1.5$; according to definition 8, the computation costs are $comp(P_{21})=12$, $comp(P_{12})=4$, $comp\ (P_{23})=3$ and $comp(P_{14})=6$ as shown in Figure 5. Therefore, we have the makespan of *JCDS* is the maximum completion time of $P_2 = 18$. Namely, the *JCDS* minimizes the makespan.

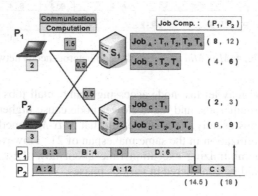

Fig. 5. *JCDS* job scheduling on heterogeneous network

Because of the joined clients and sequential jobs in cloud system, the scheduling strategy *JCDS-D* with constructing *Processed Task Recording Table* (*PTRT*) to reduce the processing time is necessary. The *PTRT* record the tasks which had been processed in each client nodes. Each entry of *PTRT* is with the form $< \alpha, b_1, b_2, ... >$, where α is the number of tasks that had been processed, b_1 is the first task, b_2 is the second and so on.

Table 1. An example of *Processed Task Recording Table*

Client Node ID	Task ID
P_1	<3,2,4,6>
P_2	<4,1,2,3,5>
...	...
P_n	-

The *JCDS-D* is a dynamic programming without replicate jobs frequently to many nodes, and dispatching jobs to the client node which have highest bound of similar factor. The strategy of *JCDS-D* is a hybrid scheme which will record the job allocating and processing flow. The services can decide and setup the parameter of δ let the clients to reduce the loading and overhead.

JCDS-D is performed according to the following principles.

1. Jobs will be dispatched to the node which have highest bound of *similar factor* (δ) according to *Processed Task Recording Table* (*PTRT*).
2. Jobs will be dispatched to the client nodes which is available.
3. If there have more than one client nodes are selected and available, system will dispatch jobs to the node that has shortest *Communication Ratio*.

Figure 6 presents the sequential job example of *JCDS-D* in heterogeneous network. Job allocating is according to the *JCDS-D* principles and shown in Figure 6. In the first step, the task set of Job$_A$ can be allocated to the available node of P_1 or P_2. According to the *JCDS-D* principles, Job$_A$ is dispatched to the shortest communication ratio node of P_2 and the *PTRT* record the processing tasks P_2: <4, 1, 2, 3, 5>. The Job$_B$ is dispatched to the available node of P_1 and the *PTRT* record the processing tasks P_1: <2, 2, 4> feedback to data servers. Before dispatching Job$_C$, the services check the *PTRT* and discovered the record in P_1, and then transmit Job$_C$ to P_1.

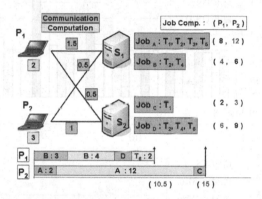

Fig. 6. *JCDS-D* job scheduling on heterogeneous network

We have the makespan of *JCDS* is the maximum completion time of $P_2 = 15$. Therefore the client do not executing the same tasks again if P_1 still have the result data. *JCDS-D* method will increase the client nodes' utilization when the jobs become numerous and high heterogeneous. *JCDS-D* achieves the dynamic programming scheduling and avoids the frequency of data translation. In the *JCDS-D* method shows the scheduling results which have the high processor utilization and minimum makespan than other methods. Compare to the *JCDS* results, the makespan is accelerated from 18 to 15 in the *JCDS-D* scheme.

5 Performance Evaluation

In this section, we have implemented the *FCFS*, *Min-Min*, *Max-Min*, *JCDS* and *JCDS-D* algorithms. To evaluate the performance of these techniques, several parameters of the number of client nodes, network heterogeneity, job size and similarity are including in our experiments.

Figure 7(a) is the system throughput within different number of jobs in job queue. The *JCDS-D* and *JCDS* algorithms have considered the communication ratio and similar factor that perform better than the other methods when job is numerous. *FCFS*, *Min-Min*, and *Max-Min* have almost the same throughput when job increasing. Similarly, the *JCDS-D* method has higher throughput as shown in Figure 7(b) with the high heterogeneity environment. The theoretical analysis in section 4 is matching the simulation result.

The first performance comparison is five job scheduling algorithms on grid paradigms with 8 client nodes. Figure 7 presents the simulation results of the experiment setting with ±5~±10 client processing speed variation and ±5 communication cost variation. The variation of job size is ±10 in five data servers.

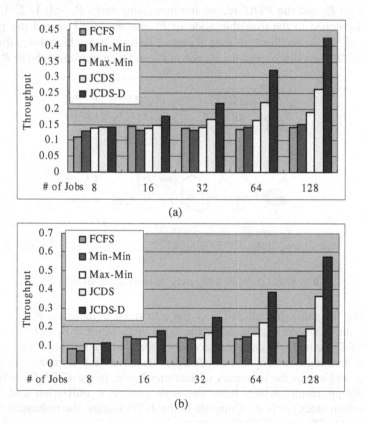

(a)

(b)

Fig. 7. Simulation results for different number of jobs in 100 cases (a) performance comparison for $0 < P_{i\_comm} \leq 5$ and $0 < S_j P_{i\_comp} \leq 5$ (b) performance comparison for $0 < P_{i\_comm} \leq 5$ and $0 < S_j P_{i\_comp} \leq 10$

According to the above simulation results, we conclude that the *JCDS-D* scheduling technique has higher system throughput, stable load balance, and better processor utilization.

6 Conclusions

The cloud computing is need to be designed to provide the services of efficient resource management, system rebalancing, or job allocations in virtual or physical machines. The problem of job scheduling platform design has been main challenges in cloud computing. In this paper, we have present combination strategy and parallel dispatching services of *JCDS* and *JCDS-D* for clouds and grid computing. In order to avoid unnecessary replica of jobs in client nodes, a processed task recording table is constructed after the execution of each client node. Simulation results indicate that the *JCDS-D* scheduling outperforms others method in terms of, higher average throughput and higher client nodes' utilization. Our proposed method can be applied to the services of virtual platform in cloud system.

References

1. Aymerich, F.M., Fenu, G., Surcis, S.: A Real Time Financial System based on Grid and Cloud Computing. In: Proceedings of the 2009 ACM Symposium on Applied Computing, pp. 1219–1220 (2009)
2. Assuncao, M.D., Costanzo, A.D., Buyya, R.: Evaluating the Cost-Benefit of Using Cloud Computing to Extend the Capacity of Clusters. In: Proceedings of the 18th ACM International Symposium on High Performance Distributed Computing, pp. 141–150 (2009)
3. Angelo, L., Steffenel, B., Mounié, G.: Scheduling Heuristics for Efficient Broadcast Operations on Grid Environments. In: Proceedings of International Parallel and Distributed Processing Symposium (2006)
4. Brandic, I., Music, D., Dustdar, S.: Service Mediation and Negotiation Bootstrapping as First Achievements towards Self-adaptable Grid and Cloud Services. In: Proceedings of the 6th International Conference Industry Session on Grids Meets Autonomic Computing, pp. 1–8 (2009)
5. Beaumont, O., Legrand, A., Marchal, L., Robert, Y.: Complexity Results and Heuristics for Pipelined Multicast Operations on Heterogeneous Platforms. In: Proceedings of International Conference on Parallel Processing, pp. 267–274 (2004)
6. Beaumont, O., Legrand, A., Marchal, L., Robert, Y.: Pipelining Broadcasts on Heterogeneous Platforms. IEEE Transactions on Parallel and Distributed Systems 16(4), 300–313 (2005)
7. Beaumont, O., Boudet, V., Petitet, A., Rastello, F., Robert, Y.: A Proposal for a Heterogeneous Cluster ScaLAPACK (Dense Linear Solvers). IEEE Trans. Computers 50(10), 1052–1070 (2001)
8. Beaumont, O., Boudet, V., Rastello, F., Robert, Y.: Matrix-Matrix Multiplication on Heterogeneous Platforms. In: Proc. Int'l. Conf. Parallel Processing (2000)
9. Cao, J., Spooner, D.P., Jarvis, S.A., Nudd, G.R.: Grid load balancing using intelligent agents. The International Journal on Future Generation Computer Systems 21, 135–149 (2005)
10. Das, A., Reddy, R.Y.V., Wang, L., Reddy, S.: Information Intelligence in Cloud Computing-How can Vijjana, a Collaborative, Self-organizing, Domain Centric Knowledge Network Model Help. In: Proceedings of the 5th Annual Workshop on Cyber Security and Information Intelligence Research, vol. 35 (2009)
11. Evoy, G.V.M., Schulze, B.: Using Clouds to Address Grid Limitations. In: Proceedings of the 6th International Workshop on Middleware for Grid Computing, vol. 11 (2008)

The Routing Mechanism with Interference Aware and Congestion Aware for IEEE 802.16j Networks

Wei-Hang Liang, Horng-Twu Liaw, Li-Lin Hsiao, Jyun-Fu Chen,
and Ming-Huang Guo[*]

Department of Information Management, Shih-Hsin University
No. 1, Lane 17, Sec. 1, Muja Rd., Wenshan Chiu, Taipei, Taiwan, 116, R.O.C.
praise740@yahoo.com.tw, htliaw@cc.shu.edu.tw,
hsiao@cc.shu.edu.tw, m97663002@cc.shu.edu.tw,
mhguo@cc.shu.edu.tw

Abstract. In this paper, we introduce a new routing mechanism for IEEE 802.16j. The proposed mechanism can avoid interference between nodes, stabilize the efficiency of transmission, and also provide backup path. According to the simulation results, our mechanism provides better performance than other researches on the theme of functional integrity. Also, the proposal greatly improves stability of transmission, packet delay time, and throughput.

Keywords: IEEE 802.16j Networks, Interference Aware, Congestion Aware, Routing Mechanism.

1 Introduction

In the network of IEEE 802.16j, RS (Relay Station) often deployed inside or on the coverage of base station to enhance the signal or extend the coverage of base station [9,11] . There can be one or many RS inside a base station, and every MS (Mobile Station) has many paths connected. Furthermore, the amount of RS, the handling capability and the quality of wireless media on the path are likely different, and interference even may occur due to the overlap of signals between each RS. Therefore, how to select a proper routing path in such environment is a crucial issue. To manage above problems, this research will develop a new routing mechanism for IEEE 802.16j. The proposed mechanism can avoid interference between nodes, stabilize the efficiency of transmission, and also provide backup path.

The outline of this paper is organized as follows. In Section 2, we briefly review some researches related to the routing mechanisms with interference aware or congestion aware. In Section 3, we introduce the routing mechanism with interference aware and congestion aware in IEEE 802.16j network. In Section 4, the analysis of our mechanism and other related works are presented. Finally, the conclusion of this research is given in Section 5.

---

[*] Corresponding author.

R.-S. Chang et al. (Eds.): GPC 2010, LNCS 6104, pp. 622–631, 2010.

2 Related Works

IEEE802.16j is a created standard to ameliorate IEEE802.16e; thus, these two networks are compatible with each other. At present, IEEE802.16e provides secondary services for the users who locate on the fringe of signal range considering the signal declines with the expanding distance. Consequently, IEEE802.16j adds RS technique to manage the problem of insufficient intensity of signal of remote areas.

Currently, IEEE802.16 network can be divided into two modules, which are PMP (Point to Multi-Point) and mesh modes [2]. Regarding the technique of scheduling, it can be classified into Centralized Scheduling [5,6,8] and Distributed Scheduling [4,6,7]. There are many researches related to the issue of interference aware routing or congestion aware routing [3,10,12,13-17]. However, in wireless networks, the selected path must avoid interfering links when the source node transmits data to the destination node. The congestion aware mechanism ought to be established in order to diminish packet loss rate and low latency. Accordingly, this research proposes a mechanism which comprises interference aware, congestion aware and backup path for the purpose of locating a better transmission path when transmitting date from the source node.

3 The Proposed Mechanism

In this paper, we develop the mechanism with path interference aware and congestion aware on mesh topology. The proposal establishes several MS paths to transmit to base station via RS. In figure 1, the route from MS to MMR-BS either passes through RS1→RS2→MMR-BS or RS1→RS3→MMR-BS. Additionally, this research determines a better transmission path by the numeric data concluded from path interference and congestion aware.

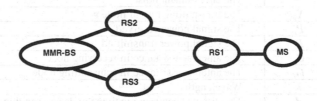

Fig. 1. The demonstration of the multi-path design in IEEE 802.16j [1]

3.1 The Interference and Congestion Aware Algorithm

In order to select a better routing path, every node in the network must collect the *LI* (Link Interference) from the nodes of 1-hop distance, compare the summation of every path, add the *LI* of every link on the path as *PI*, and finally select the path with the lowest *PI* to transmit data. The path with the second lowest *PI* is taken as the backup path of source node. During the process of transmitting data, every node on the path will detect occurrence of congestion of link; should there be any congested, backup path will be applied to continue the transmission of data.

3.2 Congestion Aware and Congestion Detection Algorithm

3.2.1 Routing Algorithm Based on Path Interference

This research is developed based on AODV routing algorithm. It will primarily check if there is a transmission path to the destination node in the routing table when transmitting data from the source node to the destination node. If there is no such route information, the AODV algorithm will activate the route detecting mechanism to find the proper route. When the source node transmits data, it firstly collects the interfering numeric from the node of 1-hop distance and calculates *LI*. The *LI* will be written into the path request packet and transmit to the connected nodes. When the connected nodes receive packets, they also collect the *LI* from the node of 1-hop distance, added to the previously received request packet, transmitted to the next node, and so on. This transmitting mode will continue until the packets are completely transmitted to the destination node. At last, destination node receives the path request packet from every route, and it will calculate the *PI* of every path and compare it on every route, so as to identify the lowest *PI* and the lowest path interference. At the final stage, two routes with the lowest and the second lowest *PI* will be selected as the main and backup transmission paths. The destination node will finally transmit a path with the lowest *PI* to the source node and this path will be the main path for transmitting data. Table 1 shows the definition of notations used in the proposed mechanism.

Table 1. The definition of notations used in the proposed mechanism

Notation	Description
ETT	The expected transmission time
$P_r(v)$	The strength of received signal for node v
v	The interfering node
V'	The interfering node set
α	Weight（0~1）
N	The environment noise
X_v	The transmitting rate of node v
P_r	The signal power received
P_t	The signal power transmitted
G_r	The antenna assistance in receiving node
G_t	The antenna assistance in transmitting node
λ	Wavelength
d	The distance between receiving node and sending node
ARPN	The average number of packets received
R	The number of packets received
t	The time period
i	The node umber

In the paper, *LI* of node i is calculated by $\alpha \times \left(\dfrac{N + \sum_{v \in V'} P_r(v) \cdot X_v}{ETT_i} \right)$. After *LI* on

the path of all the links are obtained, they are summarized and used as the basis of path selection. Then the signal power $P_r(v)$ received by node is determined by $P_t G_r G_t \lambda^2 / 4\pi d^2$.

As shown in figure 2, there are three optional paths between the source node (s) and the destination node (d), which are Path (1), Path (2) and Path (3). The *LI* and *PI* collecting processes are described as above, and the destination node receives *PI* 12 from Path (1), *PI* 11 from Path (2) and *PI* 9 from Path (3). According to the proposal, Path (3) will be opted as the main transmitting path for its lowest *PI*; while the path with the second lowest *PI* will be the backup path of the source node.

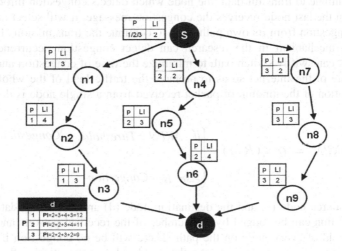

Fig. 2. The demonstration for the path selecting process with interference aware

When a node is added into the network, the *LI* of other nodes on the path will thus be changed, so the path tree construction of the whole network will be crashed by the newly added nodes. Consequently, the *LI* on the whole network must be recalculated, and the *LI* must be reorganized whenever there are new nodes add to the network. The figure 3 shows a situation that Node 4 (n4) adds to the network. If the *PI* of Path s→n4→n3→d is lower, the transmitting path will switch from Fig. 3 (a) (s→n1→n2→d) to Fig. 3 (b) (s→n4→n3→d) for a better transmitting path.

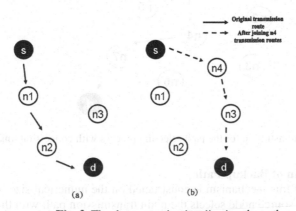

Fig. 3. The demonstration in adjusting the path

3.2.2 Congestion Aware Detection Based on Traffic

The congestion aware mechanism in this research will calculate the amount of packet received in every node. Once the receiving node receives an amount of packet which is lower than the threshold, it suggests there is no congestion occurs. On the contrary, when receiving node receives a number of packets which is higher than the threshold, the congestion occurs because the receiving node is unable to process the traffic. In order to continue to transmit data, the node which detects congestion informs the last node. When the last node receives the congestion message, it will select another path without congestion from its own path table to continue the transmission. The congestion aware mechanism in the research can detect congestion occurrence between every node, can swiftly switch path to minimize the time of congestion and minimize the overhead of the Internet so as to promote the traffic load of the whole network. The calculation of the amount of packet received from a single node is demonstrated as follows.

$$ARPN_i = \alpha \times (R/t) \begin{cases} if \quad ARPN > Threshold \quad, \; Congestion \\ \\ else \; No \; Congestion \end{cases}$$

When the source node (s) and the destination node (d) are processing data transmission, congestion can be judged by the number of the received packets and the upper limit threshold of every node on the path. There will be no congestion if the packet amount is lower than or equals to the threshold; while congestion will occur if the amount is higher than the threshold. At this time, the node will be blocked and cannot transmit any data until the congestion is over, and later on it will select a new path for transmission. Basing on the path with the lowest *PI* as the main transmission route, as shown in the figure 4, the original transmission path is s → n1 → n4 → n6 → d, and the transmission path switches to s → n1 → n4 → n7 → d when congestion occurs.

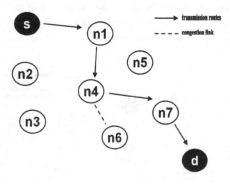

Fig. 4. The demonstration for the path selecting process with congestion link aware

3.2.3 Construction of Backup Path

The backup path of this mechanism is constructed on the numerical size of *PI*. At the initial network, the source node selects the main transmission path with the lowest *PI*, for the sake of immediately switching to another path once damage occurs on the path. Therefore, there should be nodes on the main path and backup node. Owing to every node calculates its own and neighboring *LI* when receiving path request packet, the backup node is selected by the second lowest *LI* of the neighboring nodes. The advantage of this backup mechanism lies in that path does not need to relocate the path when damage occurs, and node can immediately react and handle the congestion or damage occurs on the path. On account of the above, node does not need to report to the source node step by step. This can lower the overhead of network and enhance capacity of network.

The figure 5 shows the selected procedure of the backup path. During the transmission of data, the source node (s) and the destination node (d) will notify its own path node and backup node. The main path node is selected from the neighboring nodes with the lowest *LI*, and the backup node is selected from the neighboring node with the second lowest *LI*. Once the damage occurs on the main path, the backup path will be activated to continue the data transmission. In the figure, the column inside the form near every node represents the detected *LI* of every node, the next node and the backup node.

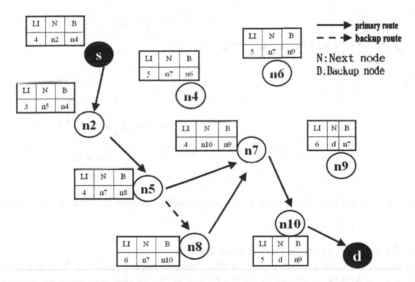

Fig. 5. The demonstration for the backup path construction

4   Simulations and Analysis

The simulating environment of this research is fundamentally on NS-2 to simulate the network environment of IEEE 802.16j, the sending node and the receiving node are stable during the simulation. The research will conclude a better path to provide information transmission and will compare it with the AODV routing protocol. In the simulation, the nodes are distributed randomly in the range of 1000m*1000m and there are 12 RS nodes in the network. In addition, the transmission radius of every RS node is 250m. In the process of simulation, the source node will locate the nearest RS when processing transmission, and transmit data to the source node via other RS.

4.1 Simulation Result

4.1.1 Analysis of Throughput Performance

The figure 6 (a) and figure 6 (b) show the analysis of average throughput and the standard deviation of throughput between our mechanism and AODV mechanism, respectively. In the figures, the paths which selected by AODV have unstable throughput performance. The main reason is there is no interference and congestion detection toward path when selecting a proper path, so it is uncertain to select a proper path. In addition, the AODV mechanism will relocate a new path when the path is damaged. This may affect the transmission performance due to the packet delay. As a consequence, these factors may affect the throughout performance of network. The proposal considers interference as well as congestion and it switches path as soon as it is congested, damaged or unable to transmit data. As a result, the throughput performance in the proposal is more valuable than that of AODV's.

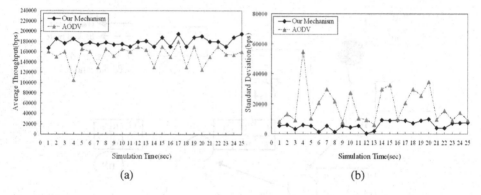

(a)   (b)

Fig. 6. The comparisons of the throughput performance between the AODV mechanism and ours

4.1.2 Analysis of Average Packet Loss Rate

The figure 7 shows the comparison of the average packet loss rate between the proposal and the AODV mechanism. In the figure, it shows that our mechanism provides better performance than the AODV one. The main reason is the AODV algorithm selects differently among node and path, it does not consider either interference or congestion occurrence of network. Thus, transmission path usually is built on the path which passes fewer nodes. Applying this method, however, is a poorer way to select a transmission path and it causes the AODV algorithm has higher rate of packet loss. The proposed mechanism has better quality of transmission and path because of the consideration of every incident during network operation. Besides, our proposal provides backup path mechanism to support a more stable transmission, refrain from disconnection of the Internet and cause unnecessary loss. Above results indicate our mechanism is able to select a better transmission path and has lower packet loss than the AODV algorithm.

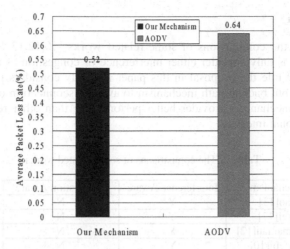

Fig. 7. The comparison of the average packet loss rate between the AODV mechanism and ours

4.1.3 Analysis of Average Delay Time

The figure 8 shows the comparison of the average delay time between the AODV mechanism and ours. In the figure, it shows the proposal provides better performance than the AODV one regarding the topic of average delay time. The main reason is AODV relocates a new path when congestion or disconnection occurred on the path, which causes data fail to transmit to the destination node, more time cost relocating the new path and increase of delay time of packet. The proposal, nevertheless, provides a mechanism which automatically detects congestion of the node on the path and immediately switches to the backup path once congestion or disconnection occurs. Therefore, it greatly minimizes the delay time of packet and reaches a better performance of network.

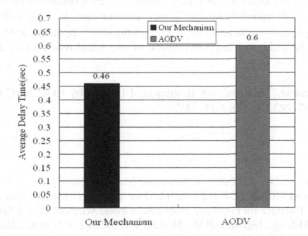

Fig. 8. The comparison of the average delay time between the AODV mechanism and ours

4.2 Discussion

Table 2 shows the comparisons of some related works [10,12,13-17]. In the table, most mechanisms only consider either interference or congestion as the basis but not both of them. While the proposal in this paper not only considers path interference and congestion but backup path mechanism to avoid disconnection of network. Consequently, our mechanism provides better performance than other researches on the theme of functional integrity.

Table 2. The comparisons of some related works

Year	Mechanism	Interference Aware	Congestion Aware	Route Backup
2005	Tao[13]	Y	N	N
2005	Wei[17]	Y	N	N
2006	Subramanian[12]	Y	N	N
2007	Kortebi[10]	Y	N	N
2008	Vo[14]	N	Y	Y
2008	Wang[15]	Y	N	N
2008	Wang[16]	N	N	N
2009	Our mechanism	Y	Y	Y

Note: N suggests no consideration of this item, Y suggests with consideration of this item.

5 Conclusion

In this paper, we provide a mechanism constructed on IEEE 802.16j module, and the transmission aims to select a better transmission path among many transmission paths for the purpose of offering the lower path interference, low latency and enhancing the throughput of wireless Internet. According to the simulations, the proposal greatly improves stability of transmission, packet delay time and throughput. In the near future, WiMAX will become the main stream of metropolitan wireless Internet with the features of high transfer rate and longer transfer distance. Also, WiMAX can be used in notebook computers and mobile communication apparatus to receive and send data in the future and boost the convenience of users and reach a facilitating network society.

Acknowledgement. This research is supported in part by ROC NSC under contract numbers NSC97-2221-E-128-005 -MY3.

References

1. IEEE, http://ieee802.org/16/relay/docs/80216j-06_015.pdf
2. IEEE Standard 802.16-2004: IEEE Standard for Local and Metropolitan Area Networks. Part 16: Air Interface for Fixed and Mobile Broadband Wireless Access Systems (2004)
3. Campista, M.E.M., Esposito, P.M., Moraes, I.M., Costa, L.H.M.K., Duarte, O.C.M.B.: Routing Metrics and Protocols for Wireless Mesh Networks. IEEE Network 22, 6–12 (2008)

4. Chieh, T., Tsai, Wang, C.Y.: Routing and Admission Control in IEEE 802.16 Distributed Mesh Networks. Wireless and Optical Communications Networks, 1–5 (2007)
5. Cao, M., Raghunathan, V., Kumar, P.R.: A Tractable Algorithm for Fair and Efficient Uplink Scheduling of Multi-Hop WiMAX Mesh Networks. In: The 2nd IEEE Workshop on Wireless Mesh Networks, pp. 93–100 (2006)
6. Cheng, S.M., Lin, P., Huang, D.W.: A Survey on Radio Resource and Mobility Management for Wireless Mesh Network. In: The 12th Mobile Computing Workshop, pp. 223–231. Taiwan University (2006)
7. Cao, M., Ma, W., Wang, X.: Modeling and Performance Analysis of the Distributed Scheduler in IEEE 802.16 Mesh Mode. In: ACM MobiHoc 2005, pp. 78–89 (2005)
8. Du, P., Jia, W., Huang, L., Lu, W.: Centralized Scheduling and Channel Assignment in Multi-Channel Single-Transceiver WiMAX Mesh Network. In: Wireless Communications and Networking Conference, pp. 1734–1739 (2007)
9. Esseling, N., Walke, B., Pabst, R.: Fixed Relays ForNext Generation Wireless Systems. The Journal of Communications and Networks 7, 104–114 (2005)
10. Kortebi, R.M., Gourhant, Y., Agoulmine, N.: On the of SINR for Interference-aware Routing in Wireless Multi-Hop Networks. In: The 10th ACM Symposium on Modeling, Analysis, and Simulation of Wireless and Mobile Systems, pp. 395–399 (2007)
11. Pabst, R., Walke, B., Schultz, D.: Relay-Based Deployment Concepts for Wireless and Mobile Broadband Radio. IEEE Communication 42, 80–89 (2004)
12. Subramanian, A.P., Buddhikot, M.M., Miller, S.: Interference Aware Routing in Multi-Radio Wireless Mesh Networks. Wireless Mesh Networks, 55–63 (2006)
13. Tao, J., Liu, F., Zeng, Z.: Throughput Enhancement in WiMAX Mesh Networks Using Concurrent Transmission. Wireless Communications, Networking and Mobile Computing 2, 871–874 (2005)
14. Vo, H.Q., Yoon, Y.Y., Hong, C.S.: Multi-Path Routing Protocol Using Cross-Layer Congestion-Awareness in Wireless Mesh Network. In: The 2nd International Conference on Ubiquitous Information Management and Communication, pp. 486–490 (2008)
15. Wang, B., Mutka, M.: Path Selection for Mobile Stations in IEEE 802.16 Multi-Hop Relay Networks. World of Wireless, Mobile and Multi-media Networks, 1–8 (2008)
16. Wang, J., Jia, W., Huang, L.: An Efficient Centralized Scheduling Algorithm for IEEE 802.16 Multi-Radio Mesh Networks. In: The 2nd International Conference on Ubiquitous Information Management and Communication, pp. 1–5 (2008)
17. Wei, H.Y., Ganguly, S., Izmailov, R., Haas, Z.J.: Interference-Aware IEEE 802.16 WiMAX Mesh Networks. In: Vehicular Technology Conference, vol. 5, pp. 3102–3106 (2005)

A Handover Scheme in Heterogeneous Wireless Networks

Yuliang Tang[1], Ming-Yi Shih[2], Chun-Cheng Lin[3], Guannan Kou[1],
and Der-Jiunn Deng[2],*

[1] Dept. of Communication Engineering, Xiamen University, Fujian, China
[2] Dept. of Computer Science and Information Engineering,
National Changhua University of Education, Changhua, Taiwan
djdeng@cc.ncue.edu.tw
[3] Dept. of Computer Science, Taipei Municipal University of Education, Taipei, Taiwan

Abstract. In order to achieve seamless handover for real-time applications in the IP Multimedia Subsystem (IMS) of the next-generation network, a multi-protocol combined handover mechanism is proposed in this paper. We combine SIP (Session Initiation Protocol), FMIP (Fast Mobile IPv6 Protocol) and MIH (Media Independent Handover) protocols by cross-layer design and optimize those protocols' signaling flows to improve the performance of vertical handover. Theoretical analysis and simulation results illustrate that our proposed mechanism performs better than the original SIP and MIH combined handover mechanism in terms of service interrupt time and packet loss.

Keywords: Vertical handover, MIH, IMS, FMIP, NS2.

1 Introduction

In next-generation wireless system, *access networks* can be carried out by different technologies, such as WiFi, WiMAX and UMTS, while the *core network* infrastructure is established on an all-IP based network. There have existed a variety of applications for next-generation wireless system, in which the IP Multimedia service is one of main applications. The IP Multimedia Subsystem (IMS) is an architectural framework for delivering IP multimedia services, which applies Session Initiation Protocol (SIP) to controlling multimedia communication sessions. SIP can provide IP mobility by the RE-INVITE signaling. However, SIP has a longer end-to-end signaling delay which may cause frequent disruption for real-time applications in node motion. Therefore, as the nodes move among heterogeneous wireless networks, one of the greatest challenges is how to provide fast and seamless mobility support.

Media Independent Handover (MIH) standard [1] was proposed for solving the above problem. Some research (e.g., see [2]) had been done by using MIH to improve the SIP-based node mobility handover process in vertical handover. In addition, MIH is also used to assist the Mobile IP (MIP) based handover process. Fast Mobile IPv6

---

* Corresponding author.

R.-S. Chang et al. (Eds.): GPC 2010, LNCS 6104, pp. 632–641, 2010.
© Springer-Verlag Berlin Heidelberg 2010

Protocol (FMIP) which is an extension to MIPv6 designed for eliminating the standard MIP handover latencies [3], and it is a combined SIP+MIH handover architecture by cross-layer design. However, in fact, the improvement of the handover performance for the previous approaches is limited when only one or two kinds of protocols are combined to solve the handover problem. Hence, a better way to solve the problem is a combination of more layer protocols by cross-layer design. In this paper, our interests focus on how to accelerate the handover process.

Handover occurs when a communicating node moves from one network to another. It can be classified into two modes: *make-before-break* and *break-before-make*, in which the former connects to the new network before the node tears down the current connected network, while the latter just does the other way. The make-before-break mode is more complicated to be implemented, but may have a better performance on end-to-end delay and packet loss. In this paper, we propose an integrated scheme of combining FMIP, SIP and MIH signaling to optimize the performance of vertical handover on make-before-break mode.

2 Background

2.1 Relevant Protocols

SIP is a signaling protocol, widely used for controlling multimedia communication sessions such as voice and video calls over IP. It supports terminal mobility when a mobile node (MN) moves to a different location before a session establishment or during the middle of a session. Before the SIP RE-INVITE signaling, the correspondent node (CN) can send data to the MN prior to the MIP registration. However, even though working with MIP, SIP still needs a new care of address (NCoA) whose configuration costs more time.

IEEE 802.21, a.k.a., Media-Independent Handover (MIH), is designed to optimize the handover between heterogeneous networks so that transparent service continuity comes true. The MIH consists of a signaling framework and triggers that make available information from the lower layers (MAC and PHY) to the higher layers of the protocol stack (network to application layer). Furthermore, MIH is responsible for unifying a variety of the L2-specific technology information used by the handover decision algorithms so that the upper layers can abstract the heterogeneity that belongs to different technologies.

The core idea of MIH is the introduction of a new functional module Media Independent Handover Function (MIHF) which operates as a glue of L2 and L3 (see Figure 1). MIHF accesses various MAC layers in heterogeneous networks, controls them through different service access points (MIH_LINK_SAP), and provides to up-layer users a media independent service access point (MIH_SAP), such as FMIP, SIP, etc. It is accomplished through three services: media-independent event service (MIES), media independent information service (MIIS), and media-independent command service (MICS).

In MIES, the MIH user can be notified a certain event by local or remote MIHF. The MIH events are made available to upper layers through the MIH_SAP, such as MIH_Link_Up (L2 connection is established, and link is available for the user);

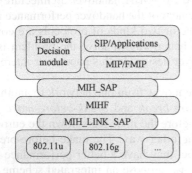

Fig. 1. Multi-protocol Stack   **Fig. 2.** The simulation model

MIH_Link_Going_Down (L2 connection loss is imminent); MIH_Link_Down (L2 connection is lost). The MIIS is a function for MIHF which discovers available neighboring network information to facilitate the network selection and handover. It provides mostly static information. The MICS gathers information on the status of connected links and the connectivity decision to the lower layers by offering commands to the upper layers (e.g., scanning of available networks). Therefore, the MICS commands control, manage, and send actions to lower layers, and can be issued by both local and remote MIH users. There is an IETF workgroup MIPSHOP that addresses an L3 transport mechanism for the reliable delivery of MIH messages between different access networks.

MIPv6 was designed to enable MNs to maintain connectivity when they move from one network to another. However, the latency caused by MIPv6 operation is unacceptable for real time applications. To overcome this problem, fast handovers for Mobile IP protocol have been proposed by the Mobile IP working group of the IETF, which enables an MN to connect to a new point of attachment more rapidly. Fast Mobile IPv6 (FMIP) applies an unclearly-defined link layer event to triggering the mobile node beginning handover process while the MN still connects to the previous link. The MN exchanges the RtsolPr/PrRtAdv (Router Solicitation for Proxy Advertisement and Proxy Router Advertisement) message with the previous access router (PAR) to obtain the target access router's MAC, IP addresses, and valid prefix.

2.2 Related Work

In [4] and [5], some schemes of integrating SIP and MIP have been proposed to optimize the mobility management. For achieving the fast handover procedure, cross-layer schemes have been investigated widely. In those schemes, some of them use MIH to facilitate handover while others do not. In [6], the author proposes an integrated mobility scheme that combines the procedures of FMIP and SIP. But without MIH, the real-time requirement of L2 trigger is still an unresolved problem. The scheme in [7] suggests a scheme that combines MIH and SIP, but, even if it claims to make handover before breaking the link, it does not consider the packet loss while the old link quality becomes poor. The schemes in [8] and [9] use existing MIH services to optimize the FMIP. MIH is used to reduce the time of discovering Access Router (AR) by using

MIIS to retrieve necessary information of neighboring network without using RtSolPr/PrRtadv messages. Especially in [9], ARs control the data forwarding (to MN) with subscribed triggers of MIH events (MIH_Link_Up and MIH_Link_Down). However, additional MIHF operations in handover may increase the system signaling load. Without simulation, it is hard to say that these schemes indeed improve the performance of handover. In [10], the authors proposed a mechanism combining SIP, FMIP and MIH. However, the work is limited in 802.16 networks, and there is no comparable simulation result either.

2.3 The OSM

In next-generation wireless networks, the network infrastructure is heterogeneous and all-IP. There are multiple protocols and functional modules to support the handover (see Figure 1). Note that the conventional approaches for improving the handover performance are combined by SIP and MIH, while our proposed handover approach is a combination of SIP, FMIP and MIH. For comparison, we briefly descript the *original SIP and MIH combined handover mechanism* (OSM), which is a make-before-break handover mechanism. Recalling that IP mobility is achieved by the SIP RE-INVITE signaling, the MN sends the RE-INVITE signaling to its corresponding node (CN) to re-establish the communicational session with the new IP address. Before the handover process begins, the MN retrieves the prefix of the NAR through the IS in advance. In order to complete handover process before previous link down, the new IP address configuration and the SIP RE-INVITE signaling are triggered by MIH's link going down event (LGD) in OSM. After exchange Router Solicitation (RS) and Router Advertisement (RA) signaling, the MN connects to the NAR.

3 Our Proposed Mechanism

In order to achieve seamless handover for IP multimedia subsystem in heterogeneous networks, we propose the *FMIP-auxiliary SIP and MIH handover mechanism* (FASM), which is based upon the architecture of Figure 1. The idea behind the FASM is to introduce the FMIP to the SIP and MIH combination architecture. In [11], a handover decision module (HDM) was proposed to handle the network management, which decides a handover target network. Through the MIH_SAP interface, the HDM registers with the local MIHF to become an MIH user. When the link layer event happens, the HDM can obtain the event notification from MIHF. Different from [11], our main concern in FASM is on how to use the cross-layer information to achieve a fast handover, rather than how to select a handover target network any more. Therefore, we assume that the link layer handover decision is always valid and the HDM takes charge of choosing the target network.

3.1 Handover Process

In FASM, the fast handover process is achieved by the following three main steps. See also Figure 3 which illustrates the signaling process in FASM. In the first step, the LGD (MIH_Link_Going_Down) event is used to trigger the handover action, while the MIIS is used to tackle the issues related to the radio access discovery and candidate AR discovery. The second step is started after the HDM chooses out the target network. In the second step, the FMIP operation is triggered by the LUP (MIH_Link_Up) event. The operations of HI, HAck, FBack, UNA signaling are used not only for the MN to configure its NCoA in advance but also for the ARs to buffer the packets that are forwarded to NCoA. After the NAR receives the UNA signaling, it can serve the MN immediately. The third step is the mixed MIP Bind Update operation with SIP, including SIP RE-REGISTER and SIP RE-INVITE signaling. In FASM, the SIP proxy server and the MIPv6 home agent (HA) are mixed together as an integrated logical entity which is the SIP Server (SS) in Figure 3.

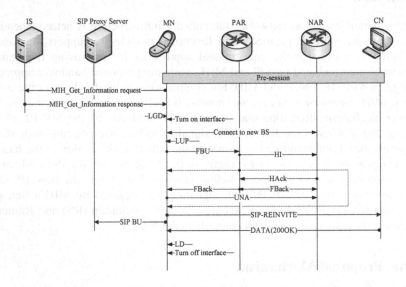

Fig. 3. Signaling flows of the FASM. Dotted line depicts buffering and forwarding packets

3.2 Details of Signaling Flows

Event Registration. At the early beginning, the HDM registers an interesting MIH Event (i.e., L2 triggers) to the local MIHF. This task can be done by MIH_Event_Subscribe.request/response primitives. According to different MIH Event triggers, the HDM will control the FMIP and SIP in different ways as follows: LGD will trigger the HDM to turn on the interface to connect the target network; LUP will trigger the HDM to tell the FMIP to send FBU to PAR and begin the other FMIP handover process sequentially; LD will tell the HDM that the make-before-break handover is over, and the previous interface can be closed.

Retrieval of Neighboring Network Information from the IS. In FASM, the functions of RtSolPr/PrRtAdv messages in standard FMIP are replaced by MIH¬¬_Get_Information request/response messages, so the RtSolPr/PrRtAdv messages can be deleted in FASM, and thereby the signaling load can be reduced. The MN obtains the network's neighbor information by the MIH_Get_Information request/response messages, and stores the information about the networks in its cache.

The MIH_Get_Information request/response can be done much before the L2 trigger (i.e. MIH_Link_Going_Down), unlike the original FMIP in which the RtSolPr/PrRtAdv only occurs after L2 triggers.

Network Selection and Switching Link. When the signal strength of Base Station (BS) becomes poor, the HDM will be notified that the current connecting link is going down (i.e., LGD event). Then the HDM chooses the target handover network by using the neighbor network information in the MN's cache, and turns on the corresponding interface. Hence, the MN can connect to the target network rapidly in the L2 layer. After the L2 connection is completed, the HDM is notified by LUP. The target network information stored in the MN's cache will be used to auto-configured the NCoA. In the FMIP protocol operation, the FBU is sent to the PAR from the pre-link. After sending FBU, the MN waits to receive FBack from the pre-link. As soon as the MN receives FBack, it sends UNA to the NAR. UNA can be sent successfully because this operation is done after the LUP trigger. After receiving FBU from the MN, the PAR completes the HI/HAck operation to obtain a valid NCoA, and sends it to the MN via FBack. The proposed mechanism implements a bi-casting buffering and forwarding policy in which the PAR buffers and forwards the data packet to MN's PCoA and NCoA simultaneously.

SIP and MIP Bing Update. After sending UNA to the NAR for announcing its existence, the MN, as an SIP user client, will continue the handover procedure by sending a SIP RE-INVITE message to the CN. The RE-INVITE message carries the updated SDP (Session Description Protocol) parameters to the CN. As a result, call parameters are renegotiated on an end-to-end basis. Meanwhile, SIP BU is send to the MN's SIP server to update the relation between URI and CoA (care of address) as well as the binding of CoA and HA.

3.3 Mechanism Analysis

In OSM, during LGD and 200OK signaling, the link quality of pre-link is too poor to receive the packets (see Figure 4). Assume that the data packet loss distribution is $P(x)$, where x is the ratio of the receive signal power to the BS send power of the pre-link. During LGD to 200OK, the data packet loss is L_{loss}, which can be determined as follows: $L_{loss} = \int_{R_{lg d}}^{R_{200OK}} P(x)dx$, where R_{200OK} is the ratio when the MN receive the 200OK

signaling, and $R_{lg d}$ is the ratio when the MN receives the LGD event.

The above weakness can be overcome by our proposed mechanism (see Figure 5). During FBU and 200OK, the data packets arrived will be buffered and forwarded to both the MN and the NAR simultaneously, and thus the data packet loss L_{loss} is reduced. When the data packets are bi-casted, the MN may receive some packets twice. But the duplicate packets can be handled by the higher layer, e.g., the duplicate packets can be found out by a sequence number of the RTP in the higher layer. As soon as the PAR receives FBU, it sends HI to the target NAR specified in the FBU. The NAR serves as the DAD for the NCoA auto-configured by the MN, and sends an available address to the PAR. The PAR delivers the available NCoA to the MN in the FBack signal. Hence, compared with the OSM, the probability of successfully using NCoA is improved.

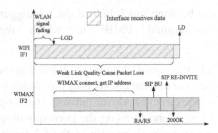

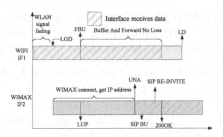

Fig. 4. Network switching in OSM   **Fig. 5.** Network switching in FASM

4 Simulation

4.1 Simulation Design

The NIST mobility packet is used in the NS-2.29 simulator. Note that the NIST mobility packet can support the vertical handover as well as the MIH protocol, but not SIP and FMIP. Hence, the SIP and FMIP modules are implemented in our simulator based on the NIST mobility packet and the NIST WIMAX module. For evaluating the performance, we focus on the data packet loss and service interrupt time from CN to MN when the MN hands over between 802.11 and 802.16 networks.

An error model is used in the simulation, which expresses a relationship of the data packet loss and link quality. The impact of the error model can be observed in Figures 6 and 7, in which the handover occurs when the time when the MN receives the RTP packet sequence is 6000 to 7000, and the jitter means the time interval of the successive received packet. Therefore, if there is no error model, when the quality of the previous link is poor, there is still no packet loss. On the contrary, the simulation result with error model added reveals the relationship of the packet loss and the link quality more practically. The bigger packet sequence leads to the poor previous link quality. The greater jitter leads the more packet loss.

The simulation topology is shown in Figure 2. To evaluate our proposed mechanism, we set up a 2000 × 2000 simulation area where there is a WiMAX BS and a

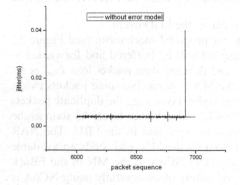

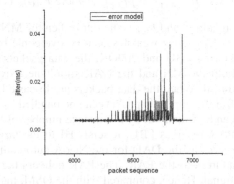

Fig. 6. Simulation result without error model   **Fig. 7.** Simulation result with error model

WiFIi BS. The WiMAX BS has a power radius of 1000 m which covers the WiFi BS that has a power radius of 50 m partly (see Figure 2). The CN connects to the backbone with 100 mbps data transport rate. The WiMAX BS and WiFi BS connect to the backbone also with 100 mbps. The IS and SIP proxy servers connect to the backbone with 10 mbps data transport rate, respectively. Except that the link delay between BSs and the router RT is 15 ms, the other links' delay is 30 ms. The MN is initialized in the 802.11 BS and moves to the 802.16 BS area in random at the beginning of the simulation. A RTP application data flow is build between CN and MN that starts at 5 s and ends at 40 s with a rate of 1 mbps.

4.2 Simulation Results

Jitter. In the simulation, the jitter indicates the time interval of the two successive packets. A large jitter is caused by a large packet loss (see Figure 8). The FASM scheme shows a remarkable improvement of performance in jitter, compared to the OSM scheme (see Figures 8 and 9). The improvement is attributed to the FMIP buffer and forwarding mechanism. When the previous link quality is poor, the LGD trigger comes out indicting the beginning of the handover process. Then, the PAR receives FBU and forwards packets to the MN's NCoA in FASM. When the NAR receives UNA, it begins to forward packets to the MN. The MN begins to receive packets when the packet sequence number is 6840. In comparison, in OSM scheme, the MN receives the packets from the PAR until the SIP 200OK is received, hence some packets are lost, and the jitter is larger than that of the FASM scheme. The large jitter between the 6900 and 7000 in Figure 9 is caused by the SIP RE-INVITE signaling.

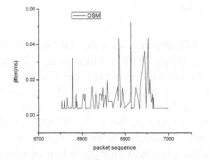
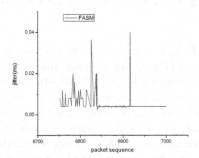

Fig. 8. Simulation model with error model   **Fig. 9.** Simulation model with error model

Packet Loss. In Figure 10, the Pr is the ratio of the MN's receiving power of LGD to that of LD which indicates the time interval between LGD and LD. Larger ratio also means better link quality. The smaller Pr leads to the bigger packet loss, because smaller Pr means that the handover process will begin under poorer link quality and there might be not enough time to complete the FMIP signaling in pre-link. While the $Pr \geq 1.45$, the data packet loss of OSM and FASM is almost same. This is because the handover begins when the pre-link quality is very good so that no packet will be lost. In Figure 10, the data packet loss is reduced from 110 to 41 when Pr is 1.25.

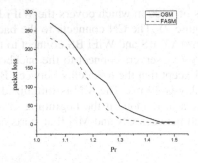

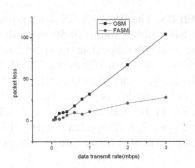

Fig. 10. Packet loss in OSM and FASM

Fig. 11. Data transmition rate of the CN versus packet loss

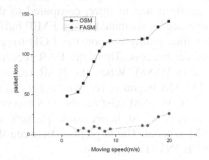

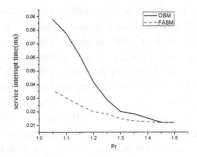

Fig. 12. Movement speed of the MN versus packet loss

Fig. 13. Service interrupt time in OSM and FASM

Figure 11 shows the effect of the different RTP data rates on the data packet loss. The RTP data rate is varied from 0.1 mbps to 3 mbps. With the increasing RTP data rate, both OSM and FASM suffer increasing packet loss. However, the OSM experiences more severe packet loss than the FASM. This is because the FASM employs the FMIP for reducing the packet loss when the handover begins. Figure 12 shows the influence of the movement speed of the MN on the data packet loss. The MN's speed is varied from 1 m/s to 20 m/s. The OSM scheme is severely affected by the increase in speed, whereas, the FASM scheme suffer a relatively small change. When increasing movement speed of the MN, the quality of the link becomes poor more quickly, so, the packet loss increases from 48 to 141 in OSM scheme. In FASM, the average packet loss is 10. This result is also attributed to the FMIP's buffer function. When the packet is buffered by the NAR, no matter how the movement speed changed, packets will ultimately be forward to the MN, so the packet loss is avoided.

Service Interrupt Time. The influence of the Pr on handover service interrupt time is investigated as follows. The Pr is varied from 1.05 to 1.5. Both FASM and OSM are severely affected by the increase in Pr. Smaller Pr leads to the bigger service interrupt time, because the smaller Pr means that the handover process will begin under poorer link quality and there might be not enough time to complete the FMIP signaling in pre-link. While the Pr ≥ 1.45, the service interrupt time of OSM and FASM is almost same.

This is because the handover begins when the pre-link quality is very good. In Figure 13, the service interrupt is reduced from 77 ms to 30 ms when Pr is 1.1. It is obvious that the FASM reduces the service interrupt time almost half than the OSM when Pr is smaller then 1.4. The FASM benefits from the FMIP's UNA signaling so that the MN can connect to NAR more quickly. Although the Pr is 1.05, the service interrupt time is still less then 100 ms. The phenomenon is caused by not only the make-before-break handover mechanism but also by the imperfect of the simulation in NS2.

5 Conclusion

In this paper, we propose an integrated handover mechanism FASM combined with SIP, FMIP and MIH protocols in IMS (IP Multimedia Subsystem) to achieve seamless handover in heterogeneous networks. In this scheme, FMIP is introduced into SIP and MIH combination architecture. By using FMIP, the NCoA can be obtained in advance, and data packets are buffered and forwarded to both NCoA and PCoA while previous link quality is poor. Hence, our scheme can significantly reduce data packet loss and service interrupt time. Moreover, simulation results obtained by the NS2 simulator show that the proposed FASM has better handover performance than OSM, e.g., the service interrupt time is reduced about fifty percent when the ratio of the receiving power of LGD to that of LD is 1.1. The proposed mechanism has the ability to achieve the handover of "seamless end to end services" in heterogeneous networks.

References

1. IEEE P802.21: IEEE Standard for Local and Metropolitan Area Network: Media Independent Handover Services (2009)
2. Huang, C.-M., Lee, C.-H., Tseng, P.-H.: Multihomed SIP-Based Network Mobility Using IEEE 802.21 Media Independent Handover. In: Proc. of ICC 2010. IEEE Press, Los Alamitos (2010)
3. Koodli, R.: Mobile IPv6 Fast Handovers IETF. RFC 5568 (2009)
4. Karl, A., Muslim, E., Christer, Å.: A new MIP-SIP interworking scheme. In: Proc. of MUM 2008, pp. 117–120. ACM Press, New York (2008)
5. Prior, R., Sargento, S.: SIP and MIPv6: Cross-layer mobility. In: Proc. of ISCC 2007, pp. 311–318. IEEE Press, Los Alamitos (2007)
6. Nursimloo, D.S., Kalebaila, G.K., Chan, H.A.: A Two-layered Mobility Architecture Using Fast Mobile IPv6 and Session Initiation Protocol. Hindawi Publishing Corporation (2008)
7. Choong, K.N., Kesavan, V.S., Ng, S.L., de Carvalho, F., Low, A.L.Y., Maciocco, C.: SIP-based IEEE802.21 media independent handover: a BT Intel collaboration. BT Technology Journal 25(2), 219–230 (2007)
8. Mussabbir, Q.B., Yao, W.: Optimized FMIPv6 handover using IEEE802.21 MIH Services. In: Proc. of MobiArch 2006, pp. 43–48. ACM Press, New York (2006)
9. Mohammed, B., Hossam, A.: MIH-based FMIPv6 optimization for fast-moving mobiles. In: Proc. of ICPCA 2008, pp. 616–620. IEEE Press, Los Alamitos (2008)
10. Huang, H.H., Wu, J.S., Yang, S.F.: A multiple cross-layers explicit fast handover control using MIH in 802.16e Networks. In: Proc. of WOCN 2008. IEEE Press, Los Alamitos (2008)
11. Yoo, S., Cypher, D., Golmie, N.: Timely effective handover mechanism in heterogeneous wireless networks. In: Proc. of WOCN 2008. IEEE Press, Los Alamitos (2008)

A 3D Video Rendering and Transmission Mechanism Based on Clouding Computing System

I-Ju Liao, Hua-Pu Cheng, Tin-Yu Wu, and Wei-Tsong Lee

Dept. of Electrical Engineering, Tamkang University, Taipei, Taiwan, ROC
ericwahahaha@gmail.com, voyoage@msn.com, tyw@mail.tku.edu.tw,
wtlee@mail.tku.edu.tw

Abstract. The purpose of this paper is to provide a 3D and real-time video system for monitoring the status of the residences through the Internet anytime and anywhere. With the traditional method, many monitors are usually needed simultaneously to display different corners but it is inconvenient for users whose devices are cell phones only. Therefore, to integrate the mobile communication system with the algorithm of 3D image system, we design a system to monitor the status of the residences. By rotating the monitor, this system allows users to monitor different corners and nooks in a house by one single monitor and ensure the safety of the residences.

Keywords: 3D video, Free viewpoint, clouding computing.

1 Introduction

Owing to the development and evolvement of cloud technology and video communication system in recent years, to provide readily available network resources becomes the major purpose of the current information industry, in which cloud technology plays a very important role. At present, the development of high-definition televisions have achieved almost the peak and all kinds of new high-definition playback systems and transmission methods are proposed. With the maturity of high-definition video communication systems, our proposed mechanism aims to bring a whole new experience to the public by integrating 3D display technology and free viewpoint to enhance the visual effects and to apply them to the academic filed. Up to now, the main problem of portable devices is the lack of efficiency. Therefore, to allow the public to experience images of higher sense of reality, this paper proposes to integrate cloud technology with 3D technology: by using the random accessibility of cloud technology to obtain information, and the distributed processing to attain 3D imaging, portable devices finally can access to free viewpoint video systems anytime and anywhere.

2 System Architecture

The architecture of the proposed mechanism is chiefly established at the access points and clients with lower computing capabilities. The system architecture is shown as the following Figure 1.

R.-S. Chang et al. (Eds.): GPC 2010, LNCS 6104, pp. 642–651, 2010.
© Springer-Verlag Berlin Heidelberg 2010

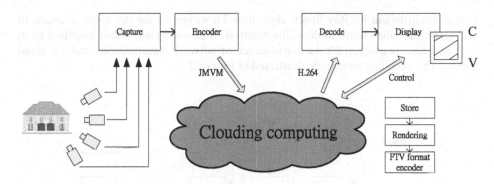

Fig. 1. System overview

2.1 Image Processing Flow

The proposed mechanism mainly focuses on the free viewpoint video transmissions, and the processing diagram is given as Figure 2. First of all, through a simple embedded system, our designed system captures the needed images from several video cameras, compresses the data and hands it over to the cloud system. Finally, we can establish a 3D environmental model and determine the rendering method according to the clients' devices after the image is accomplished.

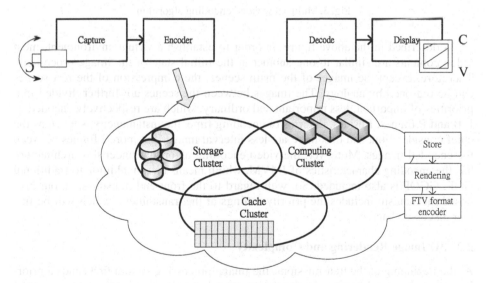

Fig. 2. Image processing diagram

2.2 Image Capture and Encode

As far as the image capture is concerned, in order to set up a virtual visual environment, we establish many video cameras to capture the light information to create a virtual environment by Ray Space algorithm. However, as for the video sources, to accelerate the video transmissions, the multi-view encoding algorithm modified from JMVM codec is adopted for the convenience of network transmissions and the cloud access. The encoding strategy is illustrated in Figure 3.

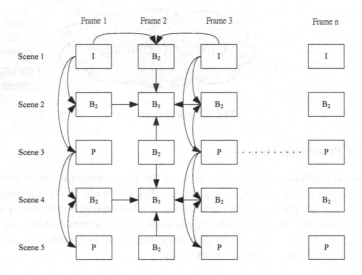

Fig. 3. Multi-view video encoding algorithm

As described in the above figure, in order to establish a virtual environment, most video contents are similar to one another at the initial state of the image processing. Therefore, except the images of the main scenes, the compression of the rest scenes can be reasoned by analogy. The images between the scenes are further divided into priorities of important, less important and ordinary, which are respectively encoded as I, B and P frames. Besides, in terms of encoding time, the instantaneity is taken as the chief consideration, and thus there are less interval images but more I frames between the encoded images. Moreover, the video encoding algorithm under this architecture has the encoding characteristics of JMVM, which means that in addition to traditional GOP, GGOP is also included. So, with regard to the front-end transmission, our proposed mechanism includes the priority settings at the transmitters, which will be further discussed later.

2.3   3D Image Rendering and Complexity

At the beginning of the transmissions, the image processing system first sends a priority list to the cloud system. As for the front-end transmission, our system gives the cloud system the priority rules, in which I frames with the top priority are followed by P, B2, and B3 frames. After the transmission is completed, our system recalculates the priority by the angles of the cameras. If the user chooses the images of the angle θ, this system processes the images captured by two cameras nearest to the angle θ with the highest priority. Finally, we calculate the values of SD and SSD, while the priority of SSD is higher than SD.

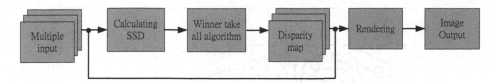

Fig. 4. 3D rendering flowchart

The image based rendering method is used to establish 3D images. First, by using the information stored in the ray-space, we draw the horizontal scan-line of the images of the same vertical coordinates as the epipolar line, and store the images as epipolar plane images (EPI), as shown in Figure 5.

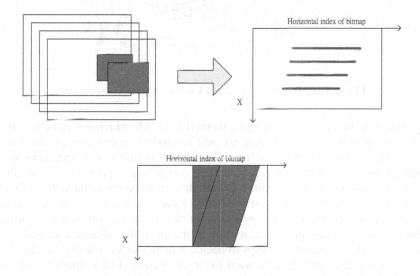

Fig. 5. Ray-space: made RPI from image first and combine it into RPI

2.4   The Job Distribution System and Images Rendering

The cloud is responsible for computing and transmitting data. The overall architecture of cloud computing and transmission as given in Figure 6 can be roughly divided into three parts: the computing, the transmission and caching, and the search and adjustment of the imaging data.

2.4.1   The Job Distribution System and Job Pool

In the first part, the upper application layer classifies the data streaming into several jobs of different attributes in the job pool. Our job scheduling system selects the jobs from the job pool and assigns the jobs to the lower computing modules. In order to put the job pool into practice as shown in Figure 7, since the data we transmit and compute is real-time, we must consider whether the data is valid or not. Invalid data must be deleted from the job pool to avoid that the job distribution system allocates invalid data to execution nodes and wastes the computing resources and network

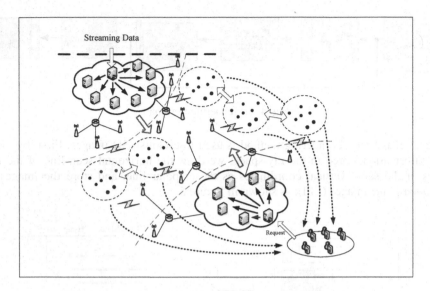

Fig. 6. The Architecture of Cloud Computing and Transmission

bandwidth. For this reason, we design a method to decide which job can enter the job distribution system first. In addition, we add an update mechanism of cache to enhance its utility rate. On the other hand, the job scheduling system evaluates several aspects of the present execution nodes. The computing capacity of the execution nodes is first estimated to determine whether the execution nodes have the abilities to process the jobs. Second, the system evaluates the execution time of an execution node while processing certain job and the accuracy of this estimation will influence the image quality. The third concern aims at the possible influences caused by the packet loss, and this estimation helps to decide whether to use the error correction or compensation mechanism, like Forward Error Correction (FEC). Furthermore, every execution node in our system has to communicate with the job distribution system periodically, reports its own condition, and hand in the progress report.

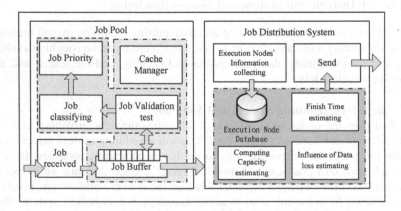

Fig. 7. The Job Pool and the Job Distribution System

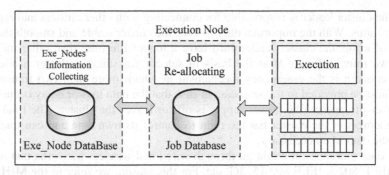

Fig. 8. The Execution Node

2.4.2 The Principle of Execution Node

This section introduces the principle to implement an execution node. In our system, every execution node can communicate with one another and exchange the information. Therefore, with the support of one another, the nodes can cooperate together to get the work done quickly. As shown in Figure 8, in order to achieve the above-mentioned purpose, every execution node must collect its neighbors' information in its database. While a node's workload is too heavy and other nodes are relatively free, the node can re-allocate the job to others to enhance the work efficiency. After receiving the data, the execution node stores the data in its cache memory temporarily and waits for the order of the CPU to process the data. Figure 8 reveals that only when the execution node does not receive the CPU's order will the job be stored in the job database or re-allocated to others. The job database also records some meta-data of jobs, like the destination, TTL and the attribute of the data.

2.5 Data Transmission and Storage

2.5.1 Building a Virtual Cluster

The focus of this part is how to establish a virtual cluster and to manage the transmission path. According to the connection quality and the types of the received data, different clusters are established. In the cluster, every node can store data but the cache of the node is limited. Therefore, a node is responsible for one part of the whole job. It would be beneficial to store data serially to avoid the network disconnections. To establish a cluster, we must consider several concerns and the first is the steadiness of the connection quality. To store real-time data streaming, it is necessary to avoid the data loss and delay, and to maintain the connection quality among the nodes. The second concern is the power supply. Members of the cluster might only have portable devices like notebooks or mobile phones that do not have stable power supply, and how to extend the life time of a cluster by distributing the power becomes an important consideration [16].

Third, how to select the cluster leader is crucial because the leader has to handle the data transmission, coordination, and the modification of the transmission path.

Also, the cluster leader is responsible for connecting with other clusters and reporting its own status. With the important duty to keep the cluster stable and smooth the processing of a job, the cluster leader must have a longer life time than other members. Thus, we refer to Figure 9 as the basis of selecting a suitable cluster header. The fourth concern is the emergency mechanism in which more than two transmission paths must be provided to transmit data in case that the data loss or delay occurs when a member disappears (the power supply is off) or leaves the cluster. The final is that every member of the cluster has the right to control its own data and can transfer or delete the data when necessary.

The data transmission might go through wired and wireless networks that may include IEEE 802.3, IEEE 802.15, 3G, etc. For this reason, we refer to the MIH protocol to solve the handoff problem in the diversified network environment, as shown in Figure 10.

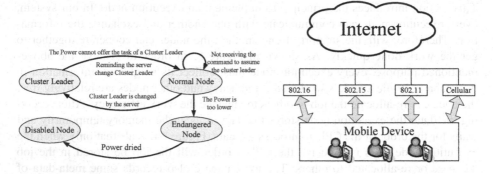

Fig. 9. Status of cluster leader   **Fig. 10.** WLAN architecture

2.5.2 Data Storage

Another transmission problem is where the data should be sent to. Every virtual cluster is given a Cluster ID (C_ID) and every C_ID refers to certain part of the data. When a task is completed by an execution node, the execution node transmits the data to a virtual cluster that stores the data with the same type of C_ID. According to the C_ID, the nodes check what is stored in each cluster. The C_ID is set by the job distribution system. As shown in Figure 11, every user will be supported by different virtual cluster.

Figure 12 shows that every user has its own virtual cluster to process different jobs and store data. Through a searching server, a user can obtain useful information from his cluster, complete the task and hand the result to the user. In such a mechanism, every node provides its own cache to store data streaming and every smaller cluster stores different types of data that waits to be requested by users. Moreover, every member checks whether the data is invalid or not, and deletes the invalid data to improve the utility rate of cache. In our opinion, every member should have the cache management strategy to handle the data storage.

Fig. 11. Users and clusters   **Fig. 12.** v-cluster and single user

2.6 Data Searching and Error Correction

2.6.1 Data Searching and Caching

The focus of the final section is data searching and error correction or compensation mechanism of images. As far as the data searching is concerned, the searching server records the cluster where the data is currently located at the beginning of data transmission. However, since every member of a cluster is possible to move, we manage these nodes by a binary tree structure. Every node manages and connects to two nodes below only. Before the data is input, based on the power of the nodes, the cluster establishes the Max-heap, which is used to transmit and search for data. The data is stored from the left to the right and from the top to the bottom. This structure allows us to use methods like Breadth First Search (BFS) to search for data, and to save not only the searching time but also the power of the whole cluster. However, the problem of the Max-heap is that members of the left sub-tree consume more power than that of the right sub-tree. Therefore, in order to prolong the life time of a cluster, we permit two brother nodes in the tree to exchange their positions when a node's power is less than his brother's child. After finding out the data, the node that owns the data must transmit the data to the root, and the root will transmit the data to the user directly. Also, the node broadcasts a message to notify the brothers and sons that the data has been found out to stop the search. The message keeps being broadcasted until all nodes stop searching. In addition, owing to the continuity of data streaming and the regular data storage, we can predict the position of the data and the data searching thus can be accelerated. As illustrated in Figure 13, when a user requests the data from a cluster, the cluster searches for the data from the top to the bottom until the data is found out. Next, the node that stores the data broadcasts the message to ask the nodes to stop searching. The neighboring nodes help to transmit the message in both horizontal and vertical directions so that the power will not be wasted.

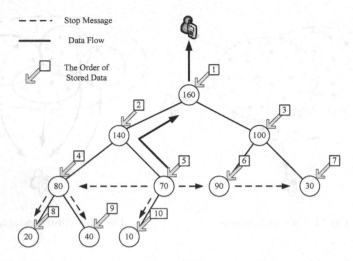

Fig. 13. Data search and transmission

2.6.2 Error Correction

The data might be lost because of the network congestion or the departure of the members. At present, there are two kinds of mechanisms that can improve the packet loss: send-based repair, and receiver-based error concealment. Our system uses the first one and adopts the Forward Error Correction (FEC), which transmits redundant information or data (or called redundant packet), and attaches it to the original trans-mitted data. When part of the data is lost, the receiver can recover the correct data by the redundant information.

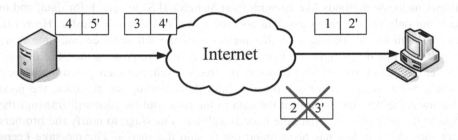

Fig. 14. Forward Error Correction

3   Conclusion

When 3D images and video are more and more popular nowadays, we still need some powerful graphic computing devices to render and establish 3D videos. In this paper, we thus proposed a 3D image and transmission system based on cloud computing system. Since 3D images costs lots of computing power to render, we use the cloud computing mechanism for users to watch 3D videos and even free viewpoint videos with mobile devices. In our architecture, all computing of the image is finished in the

Internet by using the store computing and cache clusters. With our proposed architecture, users who want to watch 3D videos by mobile devices surely can enjoy the entertainment more smoothly. Our future target is to enhance the cache performance and the rendering speed of 3D images.

References

1. Liu, C., Wu, J.: Adaptive Routing in Dynamic Ad Hoc Networks. In: WCNC 2008 (2008)
2. Fujii, T., Tanimoto, M., Furo-Cho, Chikusa-ku: Free-Viewpoint TV System Based on Ray-Space Representation. In: Proceedings of SPIE, vol. 4864, pp. 175–189 (2002)
3. Fan, L.-Z., Yu, M., Jiang, G.-y., Wang, R.-d., Kim, Y.-d.: New Ray-Space Interpolation Method For Free Viewpoint Video System. In: Sixth International Conference on Parallel and Distributed Computing Applications and Technologies (PDCAT 2005), pp. 684–688 (2005)
4. Kanade, T., Okutomi, M.: A Stereo Matching Algorithm with an Adaptive Window: Theory and Experiment. IEEE Trans. PAMI 16(9), 920–932 (1989)
5. Anantrasirichai, N., Nishan Canagarajah, C., Redmill, D.W., Bull, D.R.: Dynamic Programming for Multi-View Disparity/Depth Estimation. In: ICASSP 2006, pp. II-269–II-272 (2006)
6. Daniel, S., Richard, S.: A Taxonomy and Evaluation of Dense Two-Frame Stereo Correspondence Algorithms. International Journal of Computer Vision, 7–42 (2001)
7. Shao, F., Jiang, G., Chen, K., Yu, M., Choi, T.: Ray-Space Data Compression Based on Prediction Technique. In: International Conference on Computer Graphics, Imaging and Visualization, pp. 347–350 (2005)
8. Kobayashi, T., Fujii, T., Kimoto, T., Tanimoto, M.: Interpolation of Ray-Space Data by Adaptive Filtering. In: Corner, B.D., Nurre, J.H. (eds.) Proceedings of SPIE, Three-Dimensional Image Capture and Applications III, vol. 3958, pp. 252–259 (2000)
9. Faugeras, O.: Three-Dimensional Computer Vision a geometric viewpoint (1993)
10. Scharstein, D., Szeliski, R.: High-accuracy stereo depth maps using structured light. In: IEEE Computer Society Conference on Computer Vision and Pattern Recognition, vol. 1, pp. 195–202 (2003)
11. Palmieri, F.: Network-aware scheduling for real-time execution support in data-intensive optical Grids (November 28, 2008)
12. Gravvanis, G.A., Morrison, J.P., Stockinger, H.: Special Section: Defining the grid, experiences and future trends (November 5, 2008)
13. Papazachos, Z.C., Karatza, H.D.: The impact of task service time variability on gang scheduling performance in a two-cluster system. Department of Informatics, Aristotle University of Thessaloniki, 54124 Thessaloniki, Greece
14. Namjoshi, J., Gupte, A.: Service Oriented Architecture for Cloud based Travel Reservation Software as a Servic. In: IEEE International Conference on Cloud Computing (2009)
15. Xu, R. (Student Member, IEEE), Wunsch II, D. (Fellow, IEEE): Survey of Clustering Algorithms. IEEE Transaction on Neural Networks 16(3) (May 2005)

Executing Multiple Group by Query Using MapReduce Approach: Implementation and Optimization

Jie Pan[1], Frédéric Magoulès[1], and Yann Le Biannic[2]

[1] Ecole Centrale Paris, Grande Voie des Vignes,
92295 Châtenay-Malabry Cedex, France
jie.pan@ecp.fr, frederic.magoules@hotmail.com
[2] SAP BusinessObjects, 157-159, rue Anatole France,
92309 Levallois-Perret Cedex, France
yann.lebiannic@sap.com

Abstract. MapReduce model is a new parallel programming model initially developed for large-scale web content processing. Data analysis meets the issue of how to do calculation over extremely large dataset. The arrival of MapReduce provides a chance to utilize commodity hardware for massively parallel data analysis applications. The translation and optimization from relational algebra operators to MapReduce programs is still an open and dynamic research field. In this paper, we focus on a special type of data analysis query, namely, multiple group by query. We first study the communication cost of MapReduce model, then we give an initial implementation of multiple group by query. We then propose an optimized version which addresses and improves the communication cost issues. Our optimized version shows a better accelerating ability and a better scalability than the other version.

1 Introduction

Along with the development of hardware and software, more and more data are generated at a rate much faster than ever, and processing large volume of data is becoming a challenge for data analysis software. People look for solutions based on parallel model. For instance, the parallel database, which is based on the *share-nothing* design, allows data table to be partitioned, and the computations are proceeded in parallel on each piece of data [8]. MapReduce is a new parallel programming model which turns a new page in data parallelism history. MapReduce model is a parallel data flow system that works through data partitioning across machines, each machine running the same single-node logic [9]. MapReduce initially aims at supporting information pre-processing over a large number of web pages. It has good scalability load balancing and fault tolerance. However, compared with SQL, MapReduce is not good to support relational algebra operators and query optimization. A combination of MapReduce and SQL is expected for data analysis applications in a near future. The combination between MapReduce and SQL consists in realizing and optimizing each relational

R.-S. Chang et al. (Eds.): GPC 2010, LNCS 6104, pp. 652–661, 2010.

algebra operator is becoming a dynamic research field. It is more complex to realize it with MapReduce. In this paper, we address a special type of group by query namely multiple group by query. In addition, in a MapReduce-based implementation, the processing over input data, intermediate output and final output should also be handled. This paper is organized as follows. In Section 2, we introduce the related work. Then, we discuss issues about MapReduce model in Section 3. In Section 4, we describe the multiple group by queries. We present our initial implementation of MapReduce-based and optimized implementation based on MapCombineReduce in Section 5. Finally in Section 6, we present a set of experimental results performed in a grid platform, Grid'5000. Then we analyze the computation costs of these two implementations. Section 7 summarizes our work.

2 Related Work

The paper [1] firstly introduced MapReduce model. Then, [3] gives a rigorous description of this model in Google's domain-specific language, Sawzall. Hadoop[5] and GridGain[4] are two different open-source implementations of MapReduce. Hadoop is bound with the Hadoop distributed file system (HDFS), each data reading/writing operation concerns data searching and location, which results in a long latency. On the contrary, GridGain is a MapReduce computational tool, and it is not bound with a file system. As data analysis applications involves a large amount of data reading/writing, and requires short response time. For these reasons, we choose GridGain in our work for its low latency feature. Apart from MapReduce model, people proposed some extensions. An improved MapReduceMerge was put forward in [2] for efficient merge of data already partitioned and sorted. In the reference [12], the author used an extended MapReduceReduce model to realize Parallel Genetic Algorithms (PGA). In our work, we use a MapCombineReduce structure, where we propose to use Combiner to locally reduce intermediate aggregating results in order to decrease communication cost. Cascading[11] is based on Hadoop[5]. It allows users to define and compose predefined workflow tasks into workflow for processing data. [13] tried to combine the stream processor and MapReduce to process distributed web data indexing and index searches. Hive[15] and PigLatin[16] are two attempts on data query language. They are both built over Hadoop. Hive support queries written in HiveQL, while PigLatin is a language between high declarative SQL and low-level procedural MapReduce. HadoopDB[14] combined these two parallel databases and MapReduce to utilize both of the high-performance and scalability. In their work, they experimented with select query, join query, simple group by query. In contrast, in this paper, we focus on multiple group by query, which is a typical data analysis query. This type of query is time and resource consuming. We initially use a MapReduce approach and we propose an original optimization on the top of the initial implementation.

3   MapReduce and MapCombineReduce

MapReduce is a parallel programming model proposed by Google. It aims at supporting distributed computation on large datasets by using a large number of computers with scalability and fault tolerance guarantees. During the map phase, the master node takes the input, and divides it into sub-problems, then distributes them to the worker nodes. Each worker node solves a set of sub-problems and sends the sub-results back to the master node. During the reduce phase, the master node combines all the sub-results to generate the final result of the original problem. MapCombineReduce model is an extension of MapReduce model. In this model, an optional component, namely the **combiner**, is added. This combiner component is proposed and adopted in Hadoop project. At the end of the processing procedure of the mapper, the intermediate key-value pairs are already available in memory. For the sake of efficiency, we sometimes need to execute a reduce-type operations on each worker node. The combiner collects the key-value pairs from the memory. Therefore, the key-value pairs produced by the mappers are processed by the combiner instead of being written into the output immediately.

3.1   Communication Cost Analysis of MapReduce

The following points are considered as the main factors which influence the communication cost. (i) The amount of intermediate data to be transferred, from the mappers to the reducers (case without a combiner component) or from the combiners to the reducers (case of a combiner component). (ii) The physical locations of the mappers the combiners and the reducers. If two communicating components are on the same node, the communication cost is low; otherwise the cost is high. (iii) The number of mappers, combiners and reducers respectively. Usually, the number of mappers is defined according to the problem's scale and the hardware's computing capacity. The number of combiners is usually equal to the number of computing nodes. Whether or not the number of reducers is user-definable depends on the MapReduce supporting tool. For example Hadoop allows the user to specify the number of reducers. Opposite, GridGain fixes the number of reducers to one. (iv) The existence of a direct physical connection between two communicating components. A direct connection between two components means that tow nodes which hold the component are physically connected to each other. (v) The existence of contention over the communicating path.

4   Multiple Group by Query

In this paper, we are specially interested in the case where a set of group by queries use the same select where clause block. They have the form as `select X, SUM(*), from R where condition group by X`, where X is a set of columns on relation R. X can include several different columns, for example, in the following form:

```
select sum(A),B,C,D from R where I>i group by B;
select sum(A),B,C,D from R where I>i group by C,D;
select sum(A),B,C,D from R where I>i group by D;
...
```

Some commercial database systems support a similar **group by** construct named **grouping sets**, and it allows the computation of multiple group by queries using a single SQL statement [6]. The number of records in the relation can be very large and the number of columns and column set can be large also, then this kind of group by queries can be time and resource consuming. In our approach, we partition the large relation table into smaller data fragments. Accordingly, we run the entire set of group by queries on all data fragments, then we merge the results. We realize this approach by using MapReduce model, in which the detailed specifications will be given in the next section.

5   Initial and Optimized Implementations

Intuitively, group by queries could match with MapReduce model. The selecting phase corresponds to the mapping phase in MapReduce model, and the aggregating phase corresponds to the reducing phase. As in a multiple group by query, the selecting phase concerns multiple group by clauses, having the same *select where clause*, we propose that the mapping phase performs the calculations of filtering data according to the where condition. The aggregating phase corresponds to a set of reduce-type operations. We simply use the reducer to implement the aggregating phase at first, then we propose an optimization based on the extended MapCombineReduce model.

5.1   Initial MapReduce Model-Based Implementation

The data table used in our tests is a relation table of 15 columns. We divide this table into several fragments. We use a horizontal partitioning method [10] to equally divide the data table. All the data fragment files are replicated on every worker node. In the implementation, the mappers perform the selecting operations, and the reducer performs multiple aggregating operations. In order to realize the selecting operations, each mapper first opens and scans a certain data fragment file locally stored on the node, and then selects the records which meet the where conditions. Thus, each mapper filters out a group of records. After that, all the records filtered by the mappers are then sent to the reducer as intermediate results.

The reducer realizes the aggregating operations as follows. Firstly, the reducer creates a set of aggregate tables to save the aggregate results. Each table corresponds to a group by clause. The table has two columns: distinct value column and aggregate value column. Secondly, the reducer scans all intermediate results, and simultaneously the reducer updates the aggregate tables by adding the new arriving aggregate column value onto some records in the aggregate tables. The final result obtained by the reducer is a group of aggregate result tables, each table corresponding to one group by clause.

5.2   MapCombineReduce Model-Based Optimization

In the initial implementation, all the intermediate results produced by the mappers, i.e. all the records matching the *where clause*'s condition, are sent to the reducer over the network. If the selectivity [1] of the *select where clause* is relatively small, for instance 0.01, the output of mapping phase will be moderate, and the initial implementation is suitable. However, if the selectivity of the *select where clause* is big, for instance 0.09, then the number of records will be great and the volume of data to be transferred over the network will become large. This will cause a higher communication cost. As a consequence, the initial implementation is not suitable anymore.

In order to reduce the network overhead caused by the intermediate data transmission, we propose a MapCombineReduce model-based implementation. As **combiner** is not available in GridGain software,we propose to realize MapCombineReduce task by two successive GridGain MapReduce tasks. We illustrate this approach in the Figure 1. The mappers of the first MapReduceact as MapCombineReduce's mappers; its reducer acts as a trigger to activate the second MapReduce task. The the second mappers act as the combiner; the second reducer acts as the MapCombineReduce's reducer.

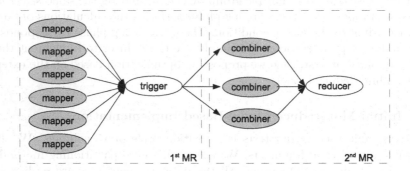

Fig. 1. Create the task of MapCombineReduce model by combining two GridGain MapReduce tasks

Concerning the multiple group by queries, the combiner's work is to pre-aggregate at each worker node. In our optimized implementation, the mappers perform the selecting operations as in the initial one. However, the results of the selecting will be put into the local cache. The mapper sends a signal when it finished it work. The combiners (i.e. mappers of the 2nd MapReduce) do the local pre-aggregations locally on worker node. Each of the combiners generates the partial aggregates. Then they send the partial aggregates to the reducer. After merging all the partial aggregates, the reducer generates the final aggregate

---

[1] A selectivity of a select query means the ratio value between the number of records satisfying the predicate defined in the select where clause and the cardinality of the relation.

result of the multiple group by query. Thus, the volume of data to be transferred is reduced during the pre-aggregation phase.

6 Experiments

We use a real grid platform, Grid'5000[7],which is composed of 9 sites geographically distributed in France featuring a total of 5000 processors. For our experiments, we choose one cluster in the Sophia site. In this cluster, all the computers are of model IBM eServer 325. The total number of nodes in this cluster is 49 and each node is composed of 2 CPUs of AMD Opteron 246 with the following characteristics: 2.0 GHz, 1 MB of cache, 333 MHz. The total memory of one node is 2 GB. The network is composed of 2xGigabit Ethernet and 49 cards Myrinet-2000. We launch an instance of GridGain on the master node andeach worker node. We configure the JVM's maximum heap size of each GridGain instance as 1536MB.

6.1 Speedup

We use a data table of 640000 records which contains 15 columns, including 13 columns of *text* type and 2 columns of *numeric* type. Each record is stored as a different line. We partition this table with 5 different fragment sizes:1000, 2000, 4000, 8000 and 16000. Several multiple-group-by queries with different selectivities (0.0106, 0.099, 0.185) are executed on this table. Each query includes 7 group bys. In order to test the speedup, we firstly run a sequential test on one machine in the cluster, then we launch the parallel tests realized with GridGain on 5 machines, 10 machines, then on 15 machines, and finally on 20 machines. Figure 2 shows the execution time in milliseconds of the initial and of the optimized version of the multiple group by query implementation.

As we can see from the above results, the parallel implementations reduce a lot the execution time comparing with the sequential implementation. An obvious acceleration can be observed when using larger fragment size like 2000 4000, 8000, 16000. The smallest fragment size, i.e. 1000, brings many job startup and closure overhead, for that, we do not obtain an optimal speedup with the small fragments. The job startup includes receiving data or parameters from the calling node (usually, master node), etc. The job closure consists in establishing a connection with the master node to send back the job results. When the fragment size is equal to 1000 or smaller, the number of jobs is large and the startup cost becomes important. We can see also that the for small selectivity 0.0106 (first 2 small figures in Figure 2), the output of the mappers is not large enough, and the optimized version does not clearly exhibit its advantage. However, with the augmentation of selectivity, the intermediate data being transferred considerably large. As a consequence, the optimized version shows a better accelerating ability than the initial version.

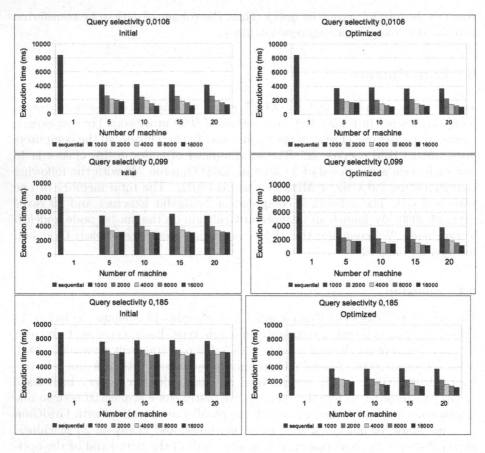

Fig. 2. Execution time versus the number of machines and the fragment size (1000, 2000, 4000, 8000, 16000)

6.2 Scalability

For the scalability, we use several data tables having the same columns, but containing several times more records than the one of the speedup tests. We use several tables composed of 640000, 1280000, 1920000 and 2560000 records respectively. The experiments performed using a table of 640000 records are run on 5 machines, those using 1280000 records table are run on 10 machines, those on 1920000 records table are run on 15 machines, and those over 2560000 records table are run on 20 machines. We use the fragment of 16000, and adopt the queries with the same selectivities as in speedup tests. Figure 3 shows the results obtained. These figures show that our optimized method has very good scalability. On data tables with an increasing scale, the executions spend almost the same time (the difference is smaller than 1 seconds). As we can see from the first small figures (selectivity=0.0106), the workload is relatively small and both optimized and initial version give an acceptable execution time (within

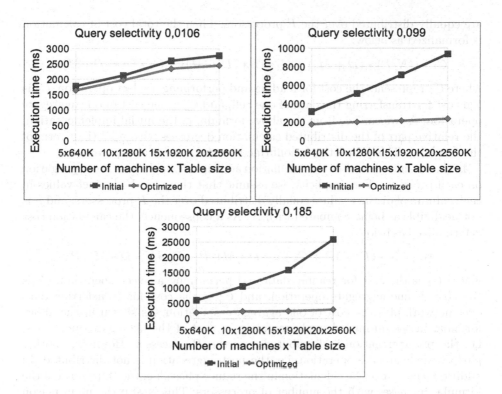

Fig. 3. Comparison of the execution time upon the size of the table and the query selectivity

3 seconds). Note that when selectivity is small, the communication cost is not dominant and the pre-aggregation work does not help so much. In the other figures, the selectivities are larger. More records are selected out. As a consequence, the optimized version shows better performance than the initial versio. This behavior is clearly outlined for a query selectivity equal to 0.099 and 0.185.

6.3   Computational Cost Analysis

Assume a table with N records, D columns of string data type (dimensions) and M columns of numeric data type (measures). The query runs over this table and allow to select n records from all the N records. The calculation is assumed to be performed over P processors. In the initial implementation, the calculations consists of:(i) The processors iterate over the whole table composed of $(N*(D+M)$ cells, and each processor generates $(n/P)*(D+M)$ cells; (ii) The data of $n*(D+M)$ cells is sent from each of the P processors towards the reducer node; (iii) The reducer node iterates over the $n*(D+M)$ cells.

For simplicity, we assume that the cost of group by and aggregation is almost linear upon the number of numeric cells to be aggregated, and that the n records are equally distributed over the P processors. Then the total cost of calculation is formalized as below:

$$C_1 * ((N/P) * (D + M)) + C_2 * (n * (D + M)) + C_3 * (n * (D * M))$$

where C_1 represents the cost for reading and performing a select operation, C_2 is the cost for transferring the data of one cell, and C_3 is the cost of one aggregate operation. As we can see from the above formula, in the initial implementation, the relative part of the distributed calculation decreases with n/N (first term of the formula). This properties is confirmed by the numerical experiments.

In the optimized version, the calculation additionally includes a pre-aggregation on each processor. For simplicity, we assume that there are V distinct values in each column of distinct values equally distributed over the P processors, and n is not negligible as being compared with N. As a consequence, the calculation cost is formalized as below:

$$(C_4 * N * (D + M) + C_5 * n * D * M)/P + C_6 * V * D * M * P$$

where C_4 is the cost for reading data and performing a select operation, C_5 is the cost of one aggregate operation, and C_6 is the cost for transferring data over network plus the cost of one aggregate operation. As shown in the above formula, in the optimized implementation, a part of the aggregate operations, i.e. the pre-aggregation is distributed over the P processor. However, another part of the aggregate operation, i.e. the post-aggregation is not distributed. In addition, the cost of the calculation in the reduce phase, i.e. the third term of the formula, increases with the number of processors. This is also the main reason that our optimized implementation does not reach the linear speedup. We will focus on this point in our follow-up work.

7   Conclusion and Future Works

In this work, we analyzed the MapReduce model, and its communication cost. We gave out an implementation of multiple group by query. We used GridGain as the lower MapReduce supporting layer because of its low latency. The initial version of our implementation of the multiple group by query is based on MapReduce model, which implements selecting by mappers and aggregating by reducer. As GridGain does not support a combiner component, we improved our initial implementation by adding an optional combiner constructed through merging two GridGain's MapReduces. The combiner act as a pre-aggregator which aggregates at node level. With the combiner, we reduce the amount of intermediate data transferred over the network. We run the experiments on a public academic grid platform named Grid'5000. Our experimental results showed that the optimized version has better speedup and scalability for a reasonable selectivity. However, our implementation only realizes a simple multiple group by query, in the sense that each group by query contains only one column in its group by clause. Further improvements will be investigated in order to work on more general multiple group by query where each group by query contains more than one column.

Acknowledgments

This work was supported by the SAP BusinessObjects Chair in Business Intelligence at Ecole Centrale Paris. The authors wish to thank the SAP Business Objects ARC (https://www.sdn.sap.com/irj/boc/arc).

References

1. Jeffrey, D., Sanjay, G.: MapReduce: Simplified data processing on large clusters. Communications of the ACM, 107–113 (2008)
2. Hung-chih, Y., Ali, D., et al.: Map-reduce-merge: simplified relational data processing on large clusters. In: SIGMOD 2007, pp. 1029–1040 (2007)
3. Lämmel, R.: Google's MapReduce programming model. Sci. Comput. Program, 208–237 (2007) (revisited)
4. GridGain, http://www.gridgain.com/
5. Hadoop, http://hadoop.apache.org/ (accessed, April 2009)
6. Zhimin, C., Vivek, N.: Efficient computation of multiple group by queries. In: SIGMOD 2005, pp. 263–274 (2005)
7. Grid'5000, https://www.grid5000.fr/
8. Dewitt, D.J., Gray, J.: Parallel database systems: the future of high performance database systems. Communications of the ACM, 85–98 (1992)
9. Hellerstein, J.: Parallel programming in the age of big data (2008)
10. Stephano, C.A., Mauro, N., et al.: Horizontal data partitioning in database design. In: SIGMOD 1982, pp. 128–136. ACM, New York (1982)
11. Cascading, http://www.cascading.org/
12. Chao, J., Christian, V., et al.: MRPGA: An Extension of MapReduce for Parallelizing Genetic Algorithms. In: ESCIENCE 2008, pp. 214–221 (2008)
13. Dionysios, L., Kenneth, Y., et al.: Ad-hoc data processing in the cloud. In: Proc. VLDB Endow., pp. 1472–1475 (2008)
14. Azza, A., Bajda-Pawlikowski, et al.: HadoopDB: An Architectural Hybrid of MapReduce and DBMS Technologies for Analytical Workloads. In: VLDB (2009)
15. Thusoo, A., Sarma, J.S., et al.: Hive - A Warehousing Solution Over a Map-Reduce Framework. In: VLDB (2009)
16. Christopher, O., Benjamin, R., et al.: Pig latin: a not-so-foreign language for data processing. In: SIGMOD 2008, pp. 1099–1110. ACM, New York (2008)

A Fully-Protected Large-Scale Email System Built on Map-Reduce Framework

Duy-Phuong Pham, Shyan-Ming Yuan, and Emery Jou

Department of Computer Science and Engineering,
National Chiao Tung University, Taiwan
pdphuong.cs97g@nctu.edu.tw, smyuan@cs.nctu.edu.tw,
emeryjou@cs.nctu.edu.tw

Abstract. Running an email system with full protection from spam and viruses has always been a pain for any system administrator. The problem becomes more severe for those who are responsible for large number of mail-boxes with huge amount of data in a large-scale email system. By using MapReduce framework, which is designed for distributed processing of large data sets on clusters of computers, this paper proposes a solution of building a large-scale email system with complete protection from spam and viruses.

Keywords: MapReduce, large-scale email system, anti spam.

1 Introduction

Running an email system in a large-scale environment which has hundreds thousands or millions of mailboxes with data size ranges from tens of thousands GBs to a few TBs a day is not an easy task. Decision of how to combine individual components of an email system to guarantee efficiency and robustness should be made wisely and carefully. Moreover, these systems also require spending significant budget on dedicated hardware. At the moment, most of production email systems require investment on high-class dedicated servers (e.g. SAN, NAS...). Finally, expanding these system to cope with growth of business is not as simple as plugging a newly-purchased server to the network.

MapReduce framework, first described by Google [1], has gained significant attention of both industry and academic community. Running on cluster of commodity computers, MapReduce framework is specifically designed for distributed processing of large datasets. By splitting whole large data set into smaller pieces and distributing these small data pieces among compute nodes, MapReduce has been proved to be efficient for dealing with large data set [1]. MapReduce framework goes together with a specialized distributed file system which provides data availability and reliability.

The features of MapReduce framework listed above fit perfectly with the requirements of a large-scale email system. Spam and virus scanning has a lot to do with

R.-S. Chang et al. (Eds.): GPC 2010, LNCS 6104, pp. 662–669, 2010.
© Springer-Verlag Berlin Heidelberg 2010

large volume of data which consists of messages small in size, and dealing with data of this type is what MapReduce is designed for. Resource consuming flexibility of MapReduce framework makes resource adjustment of the system easy and seamless. This is especially meaningful when people are in the hype of moving their things to the Cloud. Needless to say, availability and reliability of MapReduce framework is crucial for a production email system.

In the following sections, we will present a novel email system built on facilities provided by Map Reduce framework. The remainder of this paper is organized as follows: Section 2 will analyze the issues related with a large-scale email system, especially the problem of spam scanning. In terms of building an email system, MapReduce will be investigated in Section 3. Details about the proposed model will be presented in Section 4. Finally, conclusion is given in Section 5.

2   Issues of a Large-Scale Email System

The most obvious problem in a large-scale email system is that there is large amount of data to process (scanning messages for viruses and spam) and store. Handling this amount of data requires cooperation of multiple computers. There have been several solutions targeting on orchestrating these computers. The earliest and simplest solution is using features provided by Domain Name System (DNS) server [2]. Multiple Mail Exchange (MX) records or multiple Address (A) records are associated with a single domain name. Upon receiving a query, DNS server will return to the sender the list of all mail servers it knows. It is up to the sender to choose one server to send the message. Recently, Cao et al. [3] have built an email system on a Grid-computing environment. The broker of the Grid system assigns appropriate scanning workload to individual member nodes. The workload distribution is based on current capacity of member nodes. The scanned messages are then stored in a data-grid.

In terms of load balancing, these methods generally perform pretty well. However, how an email system should be designed to efficiently perform spam scanning has not been touched yet.

Kim et al. [4] point out that an effective spam scanning engine requires user-specific preference data. One message is spam of a person but it can be ham of another. The quality of a spam scanner is not only justified by how it minimizes the number of negative false (spam mail is marked as normal) but also how it minimizes the number of positive false (normal mail is marked as spam). Allowing scanners to use user-specific filters and rules is a simple yet effective approach to achieve good quality of spam scanning. DSPAM [5], a well-known open-source spam scanner, has been successful with this method.

Unfortunately, using user-specific filters or rules raises another issue. An email system with user-specific preference data consumes much more storage than by common filters and rules. Typical deployment of DSPAM put user-specific preference data in a centralized database. Thus, accessing this information will somehow suffer from I/O overhead. This shortcoming will become more serious as the number of mailboxes grows[1].

In this paper, we will introduce an email system model that is not only capable of storing and processing huge amount of data but also effective in solving spam scanning. This system is based on MapReduce framework. Therefore, before going into details of the system, we will first briefly introduce MapReduce framework and the features from which we will take advantages.

3 MapReduce

MapReduce is a software framework intended to provide developers utilities to quickly writing distributed computing applications. The framework runs on a cluster of computers. Among these computers, one plays the role as master, others act as slaves. It is the master computer to be responsible for assigning tasks to slaves. Before assigning a specific task to a specific slave, the master needs some considerations to be sure that overall overhead is minimized.

Basically, an application built upon MapReduce framework is composed of Map operation and (optionally) Reduce operation. Input of Map-Reduce application, which is the list of $<key0, value0>$ entries will be split into smaller chunks. The slave computers are then assigned a number of Map tasks to process these chunks. Output of Map operation also has the format of $<key1, value1>$ entries. Values of $key1$ and $key0$ are not necessarily in the same domain. Output from all Map nodes, $<key1, and value1>$ entries, are grouped by $key1$ values before being distributed to Reduce operation. It is the turn of Reduce operation to combine value1 values according to a specific $key1$. Product of Reduce operation may be in format of a list, $<value2>$ or just a single value, $value2$.

Word occurrence counting is a 'Hello, world!' example of MapReduce. Let's assume that we need to count the occurrence of every single word in a very large set of documents. Input of our program is $<key0, value0>$ entries, in which $key0$ is the name of a document, $value0$ is the content of a document. This large set of document is split into smaller parts and fed to Map operation. Map operation goes through the documents assigned. For each word it encounters, Map operation produces an intermediate $<key1, value1>$ entry, $key1$ is the word itself, $and value1$ is an integer number of 1. The framework then puts all entries having the same value of key (word) into one group and invokes Reduce operation. Reduce operation adds up all $value1$ associated with a single word and produces the final output. Figure 1 illustrates phases and dataflows of MapReduce framework.

---

[1] National Chiao Tung University runs several email domains for its faculties, employees, students. One typical domain of these has 2.000 mailboxes and receives 40.000 messages per day on average. After entering NCTU's email system, a message is scanned by ClamAV for viruses. The virus-free message is then scanned by SpamAssassin for spam using common rules and filters. SpamAssassin can remove about 70% spam mails. A message can pass SpamAssassin scanning need to be scanned again with user-specific rules and filter by DSPAM. Finally, clean messages are then stored in a Network Attached Storage (NAS). After 1.5 year of operation, DSPAM generates more than 2GB of user-specific data for 2.000 mailboxes.

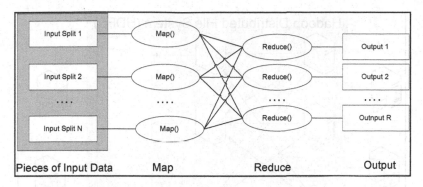

Fig. 1. Operation and Data-flows in MapReduce framework

A program once expressed by Map and Reduce operations can operate in parallel. All a developer need to do is providing MapReduce framework a map function and a reduce function, specifying the input data, and desired location of output data. MapReduce framework will be in charge of the rest. Details about assigning tasks, maintaining balance among slave computers, monitoring status of tasks, re-submitting task if it is failed, etc... are kept under the hood by the framework. To guarantee efficient task assignment, the master needs:

- **Current capacity of the slaves:** An agent running in each slave computer will periodically reports slave's health to the master. This information will be taken into account to make sure that none of slave computer is overloaded.
- **Data locality:** MapReduce framework goes together with a distributed file system. Not only computing but also data storing is distributed among computers. In current implementations [6, 7], storing data and processing it are handle in the same set of computers. Because of running on commodity computers, Map-Reduce framework is designed with frequent-failure-resistant in mind. The pieces of a large input file may have several replicas distributed among slave computers. Task assignment will use this information of data locality to bring computing as close as possible to the data.

4   Design Model

In order to build a prototype for experimental purpose, Hadoop [6], an open-source implementation of MapReduce framework is employed. All features of Map-Reduce framework listed in section 3 are available in Hadoop. At the time of writing, Hadoop is still growing up.

This section shows how the features listed in section 3 fit the requirements of a large-scale email system. Components of this email system and their associated Map-Reduce framework's components are shown in Figure 2.

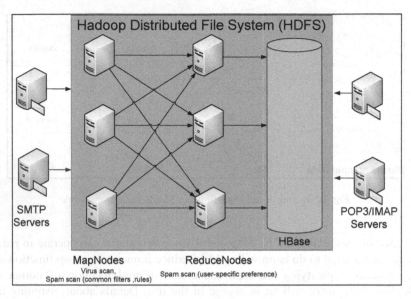

Fig. 2. Email System built on Map-Reduce framework

4.1 Distributed File System

HDFS (Hadoop Distributed File System) is the built-together DFS of Hadoop. Large files are split into pieces, multiple replicas of each piece are distributed among DataNodes (term used by Hadoop to refer slave computers serve data storage function). This storage strategy, though consumes more storage space, gains high degree of data availability and reliability. Moreover, the fact that MapReduce framework runs on a large number of commodity computers which benefits from low-cost hardware is a good excuse for this redundancy. In our design, HDFS is used to store both raw and processed messages (processed message are store on a database built on HDFS). HDFS is mounted to SMTP servers as local folders, messages received by SMTP server will be immediately written to HDFS. At this stage, each SMTP server creates its own folder in HDFS to store messages it received. This means, one message destined to a specific address can be accepted by any SMTP server in the system and stored in different folders in HDFS. This highly improves availability of the whole system. No longer do the messages have to stay too long in waiting queue or even be dropped when the queues are full.

4.2 Doing Message Scanning in MapNodes

JobTracker (term used by Hadoop to refer to master computer that coordinates computers serving computing functions) assigns Map tasks to slave computers (Map nodes). Map nodes will scan messages for viruses and spam using filters and rules common to all users. Map task assignment uses information about current status of slave computer and data locality to make sure none of slave computers is overloaded and the possibility of moving input data around is minimized. What makes the fact that scanning for viruses and scanning for common spam is put in Map task is that: messages destined to a specific address are randomly resides in several DataNodes. Therefore, messages destined to one address can be processed by any MapNode and each MapNode should be able to scan messages of any user.

4.3 Doing Message Scanning in ReduceNodes

A message after passing scanning procedure at Map node needs going through another "spam-detecting-door" in a Reduce node. Spam rules and filters used in ReduceNodes are user-specific. It is the inner feature of Map-Reduce framework makes it reasonable to put user-specific filters and rules in Reduce nodes. As mentioned above, $<key1, value1>$ output entries of Map nodes will be grouped by $key1$ values. Then, those entries associated with one specific key will be processed by only one Reduce task running on a certain Reduce node. By taking advantage of this feature, user-specific preference data can be distributed and cached locally in Reduce nodes. This greatly reduces IO overhead suffered by traditional systems and, therefore, enhances the overall quality and performance of spam scanning. In steps 4.2 and 4.3, a found infected message is eliminated, whether a message found as spam is be eliminated or marked as spam depends on configuration and the rating the engine assigned to the message.

4.4 Using MapReduce Framework's Statistical Data to Achieve Finer Load Balancing Granularity

With the design described so far, the workload carried out in slave computers is fairly distributed. We can, however, make some customization to Hadoop to achieve finer load balancing granularity. Because raw messages storing is fairly distributed among DataNodes, scanning workload is also evenly distributed among MapNodes. Nevertheless, the workload distribution might not be that fair for ReduceNodes. Those ReduceNodes responsible for busier mailboxes will handle more messages.

Counter is one of Map-Reduce framework's optional facilities suggested in [1]. Counter is mainly used for counting occurrence of certain events, e.g. number of total entries processed by Map-Reduce application. With this feature, we can easily obtain statistical data about number of messages passed to ReduceNodes and their associated mailboxes. This information gives us some foundation to divide workload from busy mailbox more evenly between ReduceNodes.

In order to make this work, we need certain control to which ReduceNode the output of a MapNode is passed. Originally, a MapNode partitions its output into R (which is the number of ReduceNodes) partitions. Partitioning is based on a default hash function, $partitionID=hash (MapNode's output key) mod R$. Following instructions in [8], we can take control over how to partition output data of a MapNode. Combining this technique with statistical information above, we can effectively balance the workload assigned to each ReduceNode. Moreover, the assignment can be changed dynamically. This is especially useful at the beginning of system's operation. The reason is: at the beginning, statistical figures are not stable or even unavailable.

4.5 Using HBase to Solve the Big Problem of Small Files

Normal email messages after passing through scanning procedures are now ready to be stored in recipients' mailboxes[2]. These messages can be pushed to traditional storage system (e.g. SAN, NAS...). Another option is using MapReduce framework's DFS for messages storage to take advantages of low cost hardware and storage reliability. MapReduce's DFS, however, is designed for large file storage and it is also not optimized for low-latency data access. This makes DFS of MapReduce not suitable for a very large number of messages which are very small in size. Moreover, unlike raw messages which are read sequentially, messages in mailboxes are accessed in a random manner. As suggested by [9], there are a few solutions offered by Hadoop, i.e. archives files, sequence files, map files, HBase. Among them, HBase, the open-source, distributed, column-oriented database, providing random, real-time access to our big data, is the appropriate answer for this problem of small files.

5 Discussion and Further Work

In this paper, we have introduced a novel design for a large-scale email system based on MapReduce framework. Large-scale email systems, with a very large number of messages to be stored and scanned for viruses and spam, require significant computing and storage resource. MapReduce framework which is designed for efficiently processing large datasets is a potential environment to build this kind of email system on. Especially when MapReduce framework runs on virtual machines in cloud-computing environment, this email system will be highly scalable. It can be easily reconfigured to run on more or less computers when the system become busy or idle.

One shortcoming of this design is that the system runs in intervals. Messages, once enter the system, need to wait in DFS awhile before being processed. The reason is that the original MapReduce framework, and its implementation Hadoop, are designed for batch-processing. Although it is acceptable for a message not to be delivered in real-time, but this limitation can be eliminated and the responsiveness of the whole system can be improved if an online version [12] of MapReduce framework is employed as [10, 11] suggest.

References

1. Dean, J., Ghemawat, S.: MapReduce: Simplified Data Processing on Large Clusters. ACM Column 51, 107–113 (2008)
2. Aitchison, R.: Pro DNS and BIND. Apress Inc. (2006)
3. Cao, T.D., Pham, P.D., Le, S.N., Le, T.D., Vu, T.M., Dao, T.A., Pham, S.T.: A Grid-Based Anti-Virus And Anti-Spam System For Emails. In: ACOMP 2008: International Workshop on Advanced Computing and Application, Ho Chi Minh city, Vietnam (2008)
4. Kim, J., Dou, D., Liu, H., Kwak, D.: Constructing a User-Preference Ontology for Anti-spam Mail Systems. In: Kobti, Z., Wu, D. (eds.) Canadian AI 2007. LNCS (LNAI), vol. 4509, pp. 272–283. Springer, Heidelberg (2007)

---

[2] In some configuration. A spam message may be also put to user's mailbox but marked as spam.

5. DSPAM project, http://www.nuclearelephant.com/
6. Hadoop project, http://hadoop.apache.org/
7. Disco project, http://discoproject.org/
8. Venner, J.: Pro Hadoop. Apress, Inc. (2009)
9. White, T.: Hadoop: The Definitive Guide. O'Reilly Media, Inc., Sebastopol (2009)
10. Ekanayake, J., Pallickara, S.: MapReduce for Data Intensive Scientific Analyses. In: IEEE Fourth International Conference on eScience (2008)
11. Logothetis, D., Yocum, K.: Ad-hoc Data Processing in the Cloud. In: Proc. of 34th International Conference on Very Large Data Bases, Auckland, New Zealand (August 2008)
12. Condie, T., Conway, N., Alvaro, P., Hellerstein, J.M., Elmeleegy, K., Sears, R.: MapReduce Online. EECS Department, University of California, Berkeley, Technical Report No. UCB/EECS-2009-160 (2009)

Agent-Based Immunity for Computer Virus: Abstraction from Dendritic Cell Algorithm with Danger Theory

Chung-Ming Ou[1] and C.R. Ou[2]

[1] Department of Information Management, Kainan University, Luchu 338, Taiwan
cou077@mail.knu.edu.tw
[2] Department of Electrical Engineering, Hsiuping Institute of Technology,
Taichung 412, Taiwan
crou@mail.hit.edu.tw

Abstract. Biologically-inspired artificial immune systems (AIS) have been applied to computer virus detection systems (CVDS). An agent-based CVDS based on danger theory of human immune system is proposed. The intelligence behind such system is based on the functionality of dendritic cells in human immune systems. This paper embeds multiple agents into AIS-based virus detection system, where each agent coordinates one another to calculate mature context antigen value (MCAV). According to MCAV, computer host met with malicious intrusion can be effectively detected.

1 Introduction

Recently the Internet has become a powerful mechanism for propagating malicious codes. Internet worms (which is a type of computer viruses) spread through computer networks by searching, attacking and infecting remote computers automatically. The very first worm is the Morris worm in 1988; while Code Red, Nimda and other Internet worms have caused tremendous loss for the computer industry every since. In order to defend against future computer virus, one efficient way is to understand various properties of viruses, which include the impact of patching, awareness of other human countermeasures and the impact of network traffic, even the ways how these viruses reside in a certain hosts, etc.

Artificial immune systems (AIS), based on human immune systems, have been applied to anomaly detections. AIS has been developed based on the negative selection algorithm [1]. However, Aickelin et al. [2] suggested that the negative selection algorithm could not work since it was based on a simplified version of the immunological *self-nonself* theory. Such theory has been challenged within immunology domain and some alternative theories have been proposed, for example, the danger theory (DT). This theory postulates that the immune system responds to the presence of molecules known as danger signals, which are released as a by-product of unplanned cell death. DCs can combine the danger and safe signal information to decide if the tissue environment is in distress or

R.-S. Chang et al. (Eds.): GPC 2010, LNCS 6104, pp. 670–678, 2010.

is functioning normally. The danger theory states that the immune system will only respond when damage is indicated and is actively suppressed otherwise. Dendritic cells are antigen presenting cells (APC) that provide a vital link between the innate and adaptive immune system, providing the initial detection of pathogenic invaders. The Dentritic Cell Algorithm (DCA) is a biologically inspired technique developed for the purpose of detecting intruders in computer networks [3].

There are several researches related to anomaly detections based on AIS. [2] outlined a project describing the application of the danger theory to intrusion detection systems. The basis for discrimination was not centered around self or non-self, but to the presence or absence of danger signal. Fu et al. [4] proposes a four-layer model based on DT and AIS. King et al. [5] describe functionality of intelligent agents such as H-cells and S-cells in biological-inspired immune system.

The major purpose of this paper is to facilitate agent mechanisms with AIS based on danger theory. It is feasible to improve AIS-based anomaly detections. Agent is an entity that has the ability of consciousness, solving problems and communication. Agents equipped with dentritic cell functionality can "detect" danger signal issued by computer hosts being attacked or suspiciously being attacks. The computer threats come from Internet, which is very similar to that of pathogens to our bodies. The central challenge with computer security is how to discern malicious from benign activity.

The arrangement of this paper is as follows. In section 2, background of this research, such as AIS, DCA and danger theory, will be described. Section 3 will focus on agent-based computer virus detecting systems with DCA.

2   Preliminary Knowledge

2.1   Immunity-Based Anti-virus

Human immune system can be categorized as innate and adaptive immune system. Adaptive immune response is orchestrated by DCs. For example, anti-virus software has recently adopted some features analogous to the innate immune system, which can detect malicious patterns. However, most commercial products do not yet have the adaptive immune system's ability to address novel threats.

2.2   Computer Security and Immune System

Boukerche [6] provides a mapping between computer security and immune system. For example, major Histocompatibility Complex (MHC) stimulates APC (antigen presenting cell) to activate, which helps cells identifies antigens. This mechanism is also important in our agent-based CVDS (see data processing in algorithm 2).

Another important aspect is the following: a computer security system should protect a host or network of hosts from unauthorized intruders, which is analogous in functionality to the immune system protecting the body from invasion by foreign pathogen.

2.3   Dendritic Cell Algorithm (DCA)

The Dentritic cell (DC) is an antigen presenting cell which captures antigen protein from the surrounding area and process it by ingesting and digesting the antigen. DCs are also innate immune cells. Once activated, they migrate to the lymphoid tissues where they interact with T cells and B cells to initiate the adaptive immune response.

DCs are the first defense line for human immune systems which will arrive at the location where an antigen intrudes and then swallow the latter to the pieces. These pieces will be attached to APC and present it to the T-cells. DCs can be regarded as the commander for human immune systems. Therefore they represent the key element to initiate the upcoming immune reaction. DCs activate immune systems when its Toll-like receptor (TLR) is ignited. Immune cells rely on some receptors in order to detect intrusion cells.

The Dentritic Cell Algorithm (DCA) is an AIS algorithm which is particularly developed for anomaly detection. It provides information how anomalous a group of antigen is. This is achieved through a generation of an anomaly coefficients valued namely, mature context antigen value (MCAV). It is believed that a DC is better performed by agent technology while considering its adoption to network environment. This antigen-plus-context information is passed on to a class of responder cells, termed T-cells.

Semimature implies a safe context and mature implies a dangerous context. This is a pivotal decision mechanism used by the immune system and is the cornerstone of this DCA. When DCs are in semimature or mature state, they produce costimulation (CSM) signals, which generate suppressive and activated effects for semimature states and mature states respectively.

2.4   Danger Theory

Matzinger [7] proposed the danger theory, which has become more popular among immunologists in recent years for the development of peripheral tolerance (tolerance to agents outside of the host). This theory proposes that APCs, (in particular, DCs), have danger signal receptors (DSR) which recognizes signals sent out by distressed or damaged cells. These signals inform the immune systems to initiate an immune response. The APCs are activated via the danger signals. These activated APCs will be able to provide the necessary signal to the T helper cells which control the adaptive immune response. This theory postulates that the immune system responds to the presence of molecules known as danger signals, which are released as a by-product of unplanned cell death.

The danger signals are generated by ordinary cells of the body that have been injured due to attack by pathogens. These signals are detected by DCs. There are three modes of operation: immature, semi-mature and mature. In the dendritic cell's immature state it collects antigen along with safe and danger signals from its local environment. The dendritic cell is able to integrate these signals to decide whether the environment is safe or dangerous. If it is safe, the dendritic cell becomes semi-mature. Upon presenting antigen to T-cells, the dendritic cell will cause T-cell tolerance. If it is dangerous, DCs becomes mature and causes the T-cell to become reactive on antigen-presentation.

2.5   Agent-Based Models (ABM)

Agent is an entity that has the ability of consciousness, solving problem, self-learning and adapting to the environment. To have the agents learn, we may use artificial immune system methods: the immune system response attributes of specificity, diversity, memory and self/non-self recognition are needed. It may be used to optimize the agent's responses to human opponents. Functionalities of the biological immune system (e.g., content addressable memory, adaptation, etc.) are identified for use in intelligent agents.

According to [8], ABM is an appropriate method for studying immunology. As computers became more powerful and less expensive, the ABM became a practical method for studying complex systems such as the immune system.

3   Computer Virus Detection Mechanism with Agent-Based AIS

Different from traditional self-nonself paradigm, CVDS will detect danger signals emitted by computer hosts. These danger signals are based on security threat profile, which defines by system calls generated by running processes. According to [10], threat profile may be composed by excessive CPU, memory load at the host, bandwidth saturation, high connection number of the host, etc.

3.1   Agents in AIS

Antigens are binary strings extracted from the IP packets, which include IP address, port number, protocol types, etc. Our protocol, which is different from that of [11], is based on the danger signal rather than self-nonself paradigm. Therefore, we design antigen agent, DC agent, T Cell agent and Responding agent to perform the so-called DCAs.

Antigen Agent (Ag Agent). Antigen agents, which are installed at the proxy server (i.e. firewall or gateway) represent data item of the data set. They extract and record selected attributes from the data items. As one Ag agent samples multiple times in the DCA, each antigen agent then randomly selects certain amount of DC agents and sends those DC agents a picked message. When the Ag agents receive the complete mature context from the DC agents, it calculates the MCAV. This data is classified according to this MCAV and MCAV threshold.

Dentritic Cell agents. DC agents are complex compared to other agents. Similar to nature DC, each DC agent has three stages, namely immature, semimature and mature. The DC agents installed at hosts, start from the immature stage. When a picked signal issued from an Ag agent, DC agent executes data processing function such as DCA. When a DC agent is on either semimature state or nature state, it returns the mature context to each Ag agent it sampled.

T-cell agents. TC agent accesses Ag agent to get every MCAV corresponding to each antigen. Compared with the low level dangers caused by the change of users' behaviors or the wrong operations, the low level dangers caused by computer viruses are concentrative and successive. When the (danger) value exceeds the activated threshold, which indicated that a high level danger occurs. TC agents are installed at the Security Operating Center (SOC); therefore it has all these resources to compare the output category with the original category of each Antigen, to calculate the overall true positive or accuracy of the virus detections.

Responding Agents (RP agents). Ag Agents, DC agents and TC agents are coordinating each other to perform DCA. After some danger signals are determined by TC agents, the latter will inform RP agents, which is installed at SOC. Danger signals represents an infected host is found, RP agents will activate some control measure to corresponding data (i.e. computer virus). Two measures are considered [11]:

1. Reporting to the SOC or security manager, for example, patches downloaded, activate relevant anti-virus software on this infected host and removes virus.
2. Disruption of intrusion, discards a suspicious packets, kill the related process, cut-off infected sub-network, this can prevent large-scale spreading of computer virus, in particular internet worm, which has high spreading rate by its nature.

3.2   Agent-Based Computer Virus Detection System (CVDS)

The agent-based antigen processing, whose purpose is to improve the steps of efficient process of antigen identification, has been proposed in [8]. We may propose such identification scheme based on danger theory, namely, computer hosts will issue some danger signals according to the threat profile.

Greensmith et al. proposed DCA [3][12]. The purpose of DCA is to correlate data in the form of antigen and signals, then identify groups of antigens as normal or anomalous. DCA is based on the observed function of natural dentritic cells. DCs are natural intrusion detection agents, who monitor the host tissue for evidence of damage. DC agents in this CVDS will evaluate antigens and corresponding signals according to DCA to determine whether antigens are malicious nor not. Now the architecture of agent-based CVDS is illustrated as Fig 1.

The "context" means the classification for antigen. If an antigen is collected in an environment of danger, the context of this antigen is anomalous and such antigen collected by the DC agent is potential an intruder. While in the immature state, DC agent has the following three functions, which are performed each time a single DC is updated:

1. **Sample antigen:** DC agents collect antigen from an external source (in this case, from the computer hosts) and places the antigen in its own antigen storage data structure

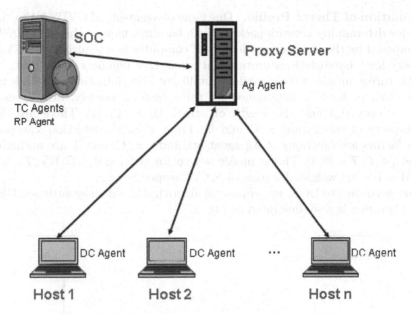

Fig. 1. Agent-based Computer Virus Detection System

2. **Update input signals:** DC agent collect values of all input signals present in the signal storage area.
3. **Calculate interim output signals:** At each iteration, each DC calculates three temporary output signal values from the received input signals, with the output values then added to form the cell's cumulative output signals.

Algorithm 1. DCA

```
input : Sorted antigen and signals
output: Antigen and their context (0 for safe/1 for danger)
Initialize DC agents;
While CSM output signal < migration threshold do
        get antigen;
        store antigen;
        get signals;
        calculate output signals;
        update cumulative output signals;
end
if semi-mature output > mature output then
        Ag context is assigned as 0;
        State of DC=semi-mature;
else
        Ag context is assigned as 1;
        state of DC=mature;
end
```

Calculation of Threat Profile. One issue of agent-based CVDS is the "baseline" for determining network packets. Such baseline, namely *Ag agent attribute*, is composed by the environment factors of computer hosts, such as CPU usage, memory load, bandwidth saturation and connection numbers of the host.

The threat profile, which provides intelligent determination of attack types of network packets, is determined by three factors, namely, attack severity (S), certainty (C) and the length of attack time (T) [4]. There are different aspects of estimating S, C and T. From network detection viewpoints, these factors are functions of Ag agent attribute. S, C, and T are normalized, namely, $S, C, T \in [0, 1]$. Threat profile is a vector $\langle W_S, S; W_C, C; W_T, T \rangle$, where W_S, W_C, W_T are weighted factors of S, C, T respectively.

Now according to DCA, we propose an algorithm based on agent-based CVDS. This algorithm is also illustrated as Fig. 2.

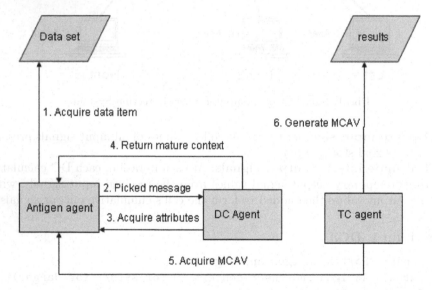

Fig. 2. Diagrammatic Illustration of Agent-based Computer virus detection system

For the step 4, each antigen gets a binary string of mature contexts which can be calculated to get the its MCAV through the number of context "1" divided by the number of all contexts. According to [9], it is similar to a voting system, where the antigen is the candidate and the DC agents are the voters. If the context is "1" ("0"), it means the DC agent determines this antigen is malicious (benign). The MCAV is actually the probability of that this antigen is being malicious.

The passive reaction is initiated by sending some alarm signal such as an e-mail to the administrator and a strategy proactive is defined through mobile agents that implement the characteristics of the reaction. According to [6], an applied reaction is defined for each of the following monitors such as DNS, FTP, HTTP, POP3 and SMTP.

Algorithm 2. Agent-based CVDS

```
Input: Antigen and Signals
Output: Antigen Types
1.  Data Processing:
    Ag agent extracts antigen from network
    traffic signal according to threat profile.
2.  Agent response:
    2.1 DC agent returns context value according to
        Ag agent attribute; also according to the
        policy of the SOC.
    2.2 DC agents will response to such antigen by
        updating its state (see DCA).
3.  Danger Signal processing:
    3.1 if this DC agent returns mature values to Ag
        agent, Ag agent transfers it to the SOC.
    3.2 SOC categorize such signal according to the
        (updated)threat profile.
4.  MCAV generation:
    4.1 TC agent generates MCAV, which is sent to the
        Ag agent.
    4.2 Ag agent determines if the corresponding
        antigen is malicious or not.
```

This agent-based CVDS can adapted into cloud computing environment, as TC agents installed at SOC will collect information from hosts and proxy server to calculate MCAV and also update threat profile. Fig. 3 illustrates the agent

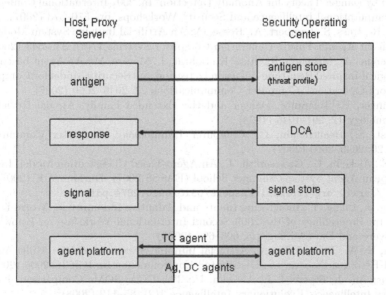

Fig. 3. Agent Interaction for Agent-based Virus Detection

interactions between SOC, computer hosts and proxy server. This can be regarded as a Security mechanism based on cloud computing.

4   Conclusions

We propose an agent-based computer virus detection system. The intelligence behind such system is based on the danger theory of dendritic cells in human immune systems. In particular Computation of MCAV by utilizing DCA can reduce the false positive rate of danger signals issued by computer hosts. Three agents, namely, Ag agent, DC agent and TC agents are coordinated to exchange information of anomaly detections. Due to the paragraph limitations, simulations of agent-based CVDS is not included. Algorithms presented in this paper is more conceptual, numerical simulations for refining these algorithms is for the future work.

References

1. Hofmeyr, S., Forrest, S.: Immunity by Design. In: Proc. of the Genetic and Evolutionary Computation Conference (GECCO), pp. 1289–1296 (1999)
2. Aickelin, U., Bentley, P., Cayzer, S., Kim, J.: Danger Theory: The Link between AIS and IDS. In: Timmis, J., Bentley, P.J., Hart, E. (eds.) ICARIS 2003. LNCS, vol. 2787, pp. 147–155. Springer, Heidelberg (2003)
3. Greensmith, J., Aickelin, U., Cayzer, S.: Detecting Danger: The Dendritic Cell Algorithm, HP Laboratories, HPL-2008-200
4. Fu, H., Yuan, X., Wang, N.: Multi-agents Artificial Immune System (MAAIS) Inspired by Danger Theory for Anomaly Detection. In: 2007 International Conference on Computational Intelligence and Security Workshops, pp. 570–573 (2007)
5. King, R., Russ, S., Lambert, A., Reese, D.: An Artificial Immune System Model for Intelligent Agents. Future Generation Computer Systems 17(4), 335–343 (2001)
6. Boukerche, A., Machado, R., Juca, K., Sobral, J., Motare, M.: An Agent based and Biological Inspired Real-time Intrusion Detection and Security Model for Computer Network Operations. Computer Communications 20, 2649–2660 (2007)
7. Matzinger, P.: Tolarance, Danger and the Extended Family. Annual Review in Immunology 12, 991–1045 (1994)
8. Forrest, S., Beauchemin, C.: Computer Immunology. Computer Communications 20, 2649–2660 (2007)
9. Gu, F., Aickelin, U., Greensmith, J.: An Agent-based Classification Model. In: 9th European Agent Systems Summer School (EASSS 2007), Durham, UK (2007), http://arxiv.org/ftp/arxiv/papers/0910/0910.2874.pdf
10. Zhang, J., Liang, Y.: Integrating Innate and Adaptive Immunity for Worm Detection. In: Proceedings of the 2009 Second International Workshop on Knowledge Discovery and Data Mining, pp. 693–696 (2009)
11. Yeom, K.-W., Park, J.-H.: An Artificial Immune System Model for Multi Agents based Resource Discovery in Distributed Environments. In: ICICIC 2006 (2006)
12. Greensmith, J., Feyereisl, J., Aickelin, U.: The DCA: SOMe Comparison, Evolutionary Intelligence. Evolutionary Intelligence 1(2), 85–112 (2008)

A Metadata Classification Assisted Scientific Data Extraction Architecture

Yue-Shan Chang and Hsiang-Tai Cheng

Dept. of Computer Science and Information Engineering, National Taipei U.
151, University Road, Sanhsia, Taipei County, 237, Taiwan
ysc@mail.ntpu.edu.tw, edisoncheng3918@gmail.com

Abstract. Data extraction and information retrieval from a great volume of data set always is a tedious and difficult work. Therefore, an effective and efficient technology for searching for desired data becomes increasingly important. Due to metadata with certain attributes characterizing the data files, to extract data with help of metadata can be expectably to simplify the work. In our previous work, we have proposed a Metadata Classification (MC) to improve significantly the performance of scientific data extraction. In this paper, we will propose a scientific data extraction architecture that is based on the assistance of classified metadata. The architecture is built by utilizing mediator/wrapper to develop a scientific data extracting system to help oceanographer to analyze the ocean's ecology by means of temperature, salinity and other information. The result shows that the architecture with the help of metadata classification can extract user's desired data effectively and efficiently.

Keywords: Metadata, Metadata Classification, Data Extraction, Argo, Ocean Data.

1 Introduction

Many large scientific data archives manage and store huge quantities of data, deal with this data throughout its life cycle, and focus on particular scientific domains. Therefore scientists can utilize these data in the relevant research. Data extraction from a great volume of data set always is a tedious and difficult work. Therefore, an effective technology for searching and extracting desired data becomes increasingly important. There were representative research had been proposed in last decade [1-5]. Most of proposed approaches utilized mediator/wrapper architecture to access various information sources. These work offered excellent technologies and tools for extracting user desired data.

It is well-known that metadata is "data about other data", of any sort in any media. An item of metadata may describe an individual datum, or content item, or a collection of data including multiple content items and hierarchical levels, for instance a database's schema. Metadata, in general, can be used for assisting data extraction.

R.-S. Chang et al. (Eds.): GPC 2010, LNCS 6104, pp. 679–688, 2010.
© Springer-Verlag Berlin Heidelberg 2010

Using metadata to represent the file system also minimizes required processing to handle operations. In our previous work, we have proposed a Metadata Classification (MC) to improve significantly the performance of scientific data extraction [6]. The approach has been applied to an international ocean-observatory project, named Argo, which has a global array of 3,000 more free-drifting profiling floats in the recent years.

Many existing systems [1, 7-9] provided the similar functionalities for data extraction. Most, however, share one or more of the following problems:

1. They do not support flexible query and extraction interface for users.
2. They do not provide flexibility, extensibility, and scalability architecture for scientific data extraction.
3. They do not provide metadata management and offer the help for data extraction based on metadata management.
4. They do not support faster data extraction mechanism for scientific data.

In this paper, we will propose a scientific data extraction architecture that is based on the assistance of classified metadata and management. Currently, the architecture is applied to the Argo project and builds an Argo data extraction system. The architecture is built by utilizing mediator/wrapper to develop a scientific data extracting system to help oceanographer to analyze the ocean's ecology by means of temperature, salinity and other information. Additionally, in the proposed architecture and system, we provide a flexible SQL-based query interface to users for inquiring desired data. We also conduct experiment for evaluating the performance. The result shows that the architecture with the help of metadata classification can extract user's desired data effectively and efficiently.

The remainder of the paper is organized as follows. Section 2 presents related work. Section 3 introduces the Argo database structure that involves content of metadata file and Argo floats. Section 4 depicts proposed architecture, its operations of components, and shows the implementation. Section 5 evaluates the performance of proposed architecture and makes a comparison with existing approach. Finally, we give concluding remarks in Section 6.

2   Related Work

Here we survey some related literatures.

Teng et al. [7] designed architecture to deal with Argo data retrieving and analyzing via internet. Visualization based GIS and massive data management based on Oracle are also introduced in this paper.

In addition, there are other websites, such as USGODAE Monterey site [8] and Coriolis site [9], also provide easily a web interface for accessing the Argo data. USGODAE Monterey provides user interface and a set of display tools including a profile location plot for all profiles returned by the query (may be plotted with or without float ID for queries returning many profiles), Download of selected profiles (in NetCDF Multi-Profile format) as a TAR file, Plots of T-P and S-P for individual profiles, and Plots of float tracks for individual floats, etc.

Coriolis site [9] also provides user friendly interface and a set of display tools. The user interface with a subsetting tool allows selection by profile type, time and lat/long windows, measured parameter, platform type, and real time or delayed mode QC data, etc.

Song et al. [1] presented a Grid-enabled Information Integration System based on mediator/wrapper, called Dynamic Mediation Service Management System (DMSMS). DMSMS searches data sources needed by users at run-time through Data Source Registry, and provides a GUI-based Mediation Schema Designer tool to help users to create mediation schemas easily and conveniently. The system also provides a mediation service over virtual data sources (mediation schemas) and a notification service to actively deal with the changes of data sources.

3 Metadata Classification

This section introduces briefly the files set of Argo, which are presented in a tree hierarchy, and explains simply the metadata classification approach. Details please refer to [6].

3.1 Data Structure of Argo Data Set

Argo's files collected by Argo's float can be stored in a tree hierarchy, the folder are named sequentially in Year, Month, Day. Each leaf folder contains the files named in date cascading the float ID and a metadata file that depicts what the folder have. Each metadata file recorded all files' name, longitude, latitude, and max pressure in the folder. Obviously, if we would like to search data from the folder, the content of metadata file can be used to assist the data search.

As mentioned above, in the metadata file, a record represents data related to a certain float. For example, a record "20081001_19000922.ios, -36.088, 18.465, 2008" means the float 19000922 rose to surface and transmitted collected data back to GDAC on the date 2008/10/01 at the location longitude equals to -36.088 and latitude equals to 18.465. The 20081001_19000922.ios is the file name of float data. The metadata can help oceanographer to find the float's file at a certain location. Details please refer to [6]. The content of the file can help oceanographer to analyze the ocean's ecology by means of temperature, salinity and other information.

While an oceanographer wants to analyze the ocean data, he can easily access what he desired is from these files. Even though, it is also a complicated work if we want to retrieve data from a longer period and a larger geographical range. We give an example to demonstrate the problem and scenario of data search in the Argo's data set.

For example, in a query "SELECT TEMPERATURE , SALINITY WHERE -45 < LONGITUDE < 45 AND 30 < LATITUDE < 45 AND 20081001 < DATE < 20081130" , the first task of process is to open each metadata file in the date folder from date 20081001 to 20081130, and to discover those floats located in desired geographical range. The second task is to open those files met the criteria and retrieves the temperature and salinity data. Obviously, the first task is not an easy work. We call this search method in that way as *Raw* approach, this is a time-wasting work.

3.2 Metadata Classification

The basic idea of the Metadata Classification is to classify the float's file according to float's position (longitude and latitude) every day and create a year-level metadata per year, as shown in Fig. 1. In other words, we create another metadata in the upper level. The structure of the metadata is mainly classified by year, and then next layers are ocean, month, and day respectively.

The metadata classification is executed by a component named *Metadata Classifier* (*MCr*) and is constructed as a classified grid that is a two dimensions array, called *GridMap*. The idea is that the MC executes classification process for each metadata file every day in a year. The classification process is to retrieve float's file name according to the location stored in a record and save the filename to relevant cell of the *GridMap*. The filename saved in the same grid cell represents that these floats respond their data in a certain geographic range, as shown in Fig. 2. The processes can be depicted simply as follows:

1) MCr will scan each metadata file of a year and compute the range of longitude and latitude.
2) MCr computes the bias of two dimensions array for the longitude and the latitude. The bias can be used for calculating the size of *GridMap* and obtaining the shift value.
3) The *GridMap* can be declared
4) MCr searches all of metadata files of the year, retrieves each record in metadata file, and then puts the filename of a float into the related grid cell.

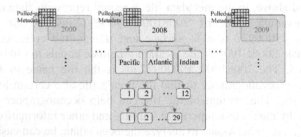

Fig. 1. Layer-promoted Metadata

After the GridMap constructed, a query algorithm is necessary for discovering the desired target files. The algorithm does not inquire all of metadata file instead of inquiring the new generated metadata (GridMap) with a desired geographical range. The algorithm can easily compute the longitude bias and latitude bias, and then map the location of *GridMap* according to the two biases. Finally, the query can get directly the target file list from the *GridMap*.

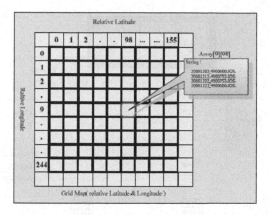

Fig. 2. The *GridMap*

4   Design and Implementation

Here we present the proposed architecture. The entire system architecture is divided into six components, as shown in Fig. 3, and next we will depict the main task and responsibility of each component in details. This section we also give an example to represent the workflow in the architecture. Since the system needs to provide a variety of query, a good presentation for various queries is necessary. We also introduce an xml-based formation mechanism for extracted data.

4.1   Architecture and Components

There are six components in the architecture. They are Application UI, Mediator, Query Parser, MC Wrappers, Result Formatter, and System Metadata respectively.

As shown in Fig. 3, Mediator is the core component and is responsible for mediating and coordinating the request and result between user UI and the system components. The mainly work of Mediator is to transmit the user's SQL-based query to Query Parser, to collect the result from wrappers, and to merge the results for user. The other task is to coordinate communication of each component in this system.

Query Parser is responsible for parsing the user's query according to three SQL-based keywords, SELECT, FROM, and WHERE, to obtain target, range, and condition respectively and then returns the parsing results to Mediator. MC Wrappers are the run-time processes that are responsible for retrieving the target data from the files according to the criteria sent from the Mediator. Each wrapper is to process one year of Argo data files. After a wrapper receives the request from Mediator, it first parses the request and query the *GridMap* constructed by metadata classifier mentioned last section to obtain the target files. Then it extracts user desired data stored in the target files. And finally it returns result to Mediator. System Metadata is a repository and is responsible for storing system metadata of the entire system. It allows Mediator to acquire the reference of MC Wrapper, so as it can invoke the corresponding MC Wrappers to extract desired data.

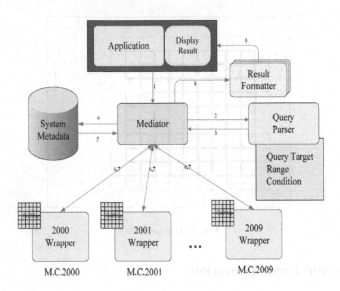

Fig. 3. System Architecture

Result Formatter is responsible for formatting the extracted results for users according to the context of user query. Since the proposed system needs to provide a variety of display, we utilize well-known XML to format the results. Fig. 4 shows an xml file's content after processing user's query. We use this file to explain the xml format briefly. The tag *ArgoSelect* is the root of this xml file, and there are some meaningful children nodes belong to *ArgoSelect*, they are *Date, Pres,* and *DataList* respectively. The tag *Date* represents the range of date in searching data. The tag *Pres* represents pressure, which fulfill the conditions as well as means the query. The tag *DataList* represents data list that conform to the searching condition in which it has an attribute named as *filename*, the rest are geographical data. Finally, the Application UI will invoke a Java Applet to show the results for user.

4.2 Workflow of Components

This section will give an example to explain the operation and scenario of the proposed system. Fig. 5 shows the operation workflow in our system while a user sending a request from the Application UI. And next we will explain how to proceed with this workflow step by step.

For example, while user send a query request, "SELECT TEMP, PRES FROM -43 < LONGITUDE < -23, 24 < LATITUDE < 44 WHERE 20081204 < DATE < 20081204，PRES = 500.0", first the Application UI redirects the request to Mediator. The Mediator then invoke Query Parser to parse the query that is a SQL clause and retrieve the criteria from three keywords, SELECT, FROM, and WHERE to obtain the range is "-43 < LONGITUDE < -23，24 < LATITUDE < 44", the condition is "20081204 < DATE < 20081204，PRES = 500.0" and the target is "TEMP，PRES".

```
<?xml version="1.0" encoding="UTF-8" standalone="no" ?>
- <ArgoSelect>
    <Date>20081204~20081204</Date>
    <Pres>200.0</Pres>
  - <DataList>
    - <Data FloatFile="20081204_4900782.IOS">
        <Lat>35</Lat>
        <Long>-34</Long>
        <Temp>15.078</Temp>
      </Data>
    - <Data FloatFile="20081204_6900410.IOS">
        <Lat>32</Lat>
        <Long>-33</Long>
        <Temp>36.476</Temp>
      </Data>
    - <Data FloatFile="20081204_1900637.IOS">
        <Lat>35</Lat>
        <Long>-31</Long>
        <Temp>14.982</Temp>
      </Data>
    </DataList>
  </ArgoSelect>
```

Fig. 4. Xml file format

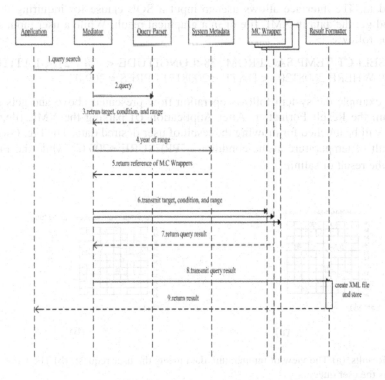

Fig. 5. Workflow of System Components

We referred [3] to implement the Query Parser that keep some metadata about the query for verifying the correctness of query string. Therefore the Query Parser will first check the validation of the query. And it will return processed results, including target, range, and condition clause, to Mediator if validation is ok. Then the Mediator will, according to the clause "20081204 < DATE < 20081204", inquire the System Metadata to find out what MC Wrappers should be invoked.

Here, because the range of date is only in 2008, there is one MC Wrapper for 2008 will be invoked. If the range is across different years, more than one MC Wrappers will be invoked for different years to deal with the request from Mediator. MC Wrapper will first retrieve target files from *GridMap* mentioned in Section 3 and then extract desired data from the retrieved files according to the criteria from the Mediator. And then MC Wrapper returns the result to Mediator. The next step is that the Mediator will merge the results from MC Wrappers if necessary, and then forwards merged result to Result Formatter. Result Formatter stored result in xml file format that is similar to Fig. 4.

4.3 Implementation

Based on the architecture and scenario presented above, we implement an ocean data extracting system. The system provides a flexible interface for user to extract desired ocean data. The interface allows user to input a SQL clause for inquiring the Argo data and get the data in XML file or in a graphical result. While a user input a query string as follows:

— "SELECT TEMP,SAL FROM -38<LONGITUDE < -28 , 29 < LATITUDE < 39 WHERE 20081204 < DATE < 20081214,PRES = 200.0"

The example the system follows operation flow presented above and gets a XML file from the Result Formatter. After Application UI parsing the XML file, a Java Applet will be lunched for drawing the result of user desired data. The Fig. 6(a) shows the result of temperature at the condition "PRESURE =200.0" while the Fig. 6(b) shows the result of salinity.

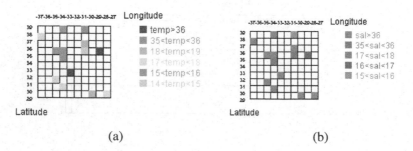

(a)   (b)

Fig. 6. Results. (a) The view of temperature data meets the user request. (b) The view of salinity meets the user query

5 Performance Evaluation

To evaluate the performance of the system, we conducted two experiments, one is to evaluate the algorithm of metadata classification; the other is to evaluate the implemented system. These two experiments were run on the Notebook that with an Intel Core 2 Due 1.4GHz CPU and 1GB RAM.

Fig. 7(a) shows the comparison between the *RawQuery* algorithm and classified metadata Query algorithm (*MM_Query*). The *MMQuery* algorithm only takes about 50ms for most round of measurement, and the latency only slightly increase while the number of days increasing. The reason is that the *MMQuery* only take the time to computing the retrieve the target filename from cascaded file string of grid map. The latency of *RawQuery* algorithm is obviously increasing with the number of days increased. Obviously, the proposed approach has a significant performance enhancement in finding the target files.

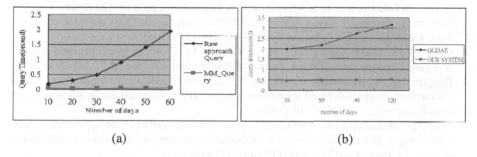

(a)   (b)

Fig. 7. (a) Comparison with Raw Approach (b) Performance comparison with GODAE

In addition, we also conduct an experiment to evaluate the performance of our system, and compare with other similar systems, USGODAE [8]. Fig. 7(b) shows that our system is superior to USGODAE in terms of query time about 4~6times. Although, the comparison is unfair to the USGODAE because a little extra round trip time is needed to the USGODAE, in general is around thousands millisecond. According to performance evaluations, it has shown that the system has a significant performance enhancement in finding the target file than the USGODAE.

6 Conclusion and Future Work

In this paper, we have proposed a scientific data extraction architecture that is based on the assistance of classified metadata and management. Currently, the architecture is applied to the Argo project and builds an Argo data extraction system. The architecture is built by utilizing mediator/wrapper to develop a scientific data extracting system to help oceanographer to analyze the ocean's ecology by means of temperature, salinity and other information. According to the result of our measurement, it clearly shows that such system can reduce the latency of data search. The evaluation shows that metadata classification can help the data search and retrieval in effective and efficient way.

In the future, we will aim at implementing the entire system of Argo project to grid platform environment, just like utilizing Globus Toolkit.

Acknowledgement

This work was supported in part by the Nation Science Council of Republic of China under grant NSC98-2221-E-305-006.

References

1. Song, J., Yoo, S., Park, C.-S., Choi, D.-H., Lee, Y.-J.: The Design of a Grid-enabled Information Integration System Based on Mediator/Wrapper Architectures. In: International conference on Grid Computing & Application, Las Vegas, USA, pp. 114–120 (2006)
2. Wohrer, A., Brezany, P., Tjoa, A.M.: Novel Mediator architecture for Grid information systems. Future Generation Computer Systems 21, 107–114 (2005)
3. Chang, Y.-S., Liang, K.-C., Cheng, M.-C., Yuan, S.-M.: Prototyping an integrated information gathering system on CORBA. Journal of Systems and Software 72(2), 281–294 (2004)
4. Bouguettaya, A., Benatallah, B., Hendra, L., Ouzzani, M., Beard, J.: Supporting dynamic interactions among web-based information sources. IEEE Transactions on Knowledge and Data Engineering 12(5), 779–801 (2000)
5. Mena, E., Illarramendi, A., Kashyap, V., Seth, A.P.: OBSERVER: an approach for query processing in global information systems based on interoperation across pre-existing Ontologies. In: Parallel and Distributed Databases (1999)
6. Chang, Y.-S., Lai, H.-J., Cheng, H.-T.: Improving Scientific Data Extraction using Metadata Classification. In: GridCAT 2009, Taiwan, December 2009, pp. 669–673 (2009)
7. Teng, J., Liu, Z., Sun, M., Sun, C., Xu, J.: Development of Online Argo Data Service Platform Based on GIS. In: IEEE International Conference on Geoscience and Remote Sensing Symposium, July 31-August 4, pp. 1316–1318 (2006)
8. http://www.usgodae.org/cgi-bin/argo_select.pl
9. http://www.coriolis.eu.org/cdc/argo_rfc.htm

Price Differentiation All-Pay Auction-Based Incentives in BitTorrent

Yan Pang and Zongming Guo

Institute of Computer Science and Technology
Peking University
{pangyan,guozongming}@icst.pku.edu.cn

Abstract. Free riding, the behavior of attempting to benefit resources contributed by others while sharing their own values as minimum as possible, is one of the key problems in many P2P systems. Incentive mechanisms are proposed to solve the problem. In this paper, we introduce an all-pay auction model to study the resource distribution process in BitTorrent-like P2P system. Based on this model, the advantages and disadvantages of original BitTorrent incentives are presented. To improve the BitTorrent system-wide performance, we propose a price differentiation all-pay auction based incentive mechanism considering the long-term share ratio and the short-term predicted upload bandwidth comprehensively. Our simulation results verify the effectiveness of the new incentive mechanism to prevent free-riders and strategic peers.

Keywords: Incentive mechanism, all-pay auction, price differentiation.

1 Introduction

Peer-to-Peer (P2P) systems have played a major role in the Internet. According to Sandvine's research report in 2009 [1], P2P file sharing traffic accounts for 20% of total bytes, and BitTorrent is still the dominant P2P file sharing application. In a typical P2P file sharing system, numerous peers collectively form a self-organizing, self-maintaining network without central authority. Being operated by an independent user (person or organization), each peer interact with one another with varying degrees collaboration and competition. Rational users always attempt to maximize their own utilities; they may refuse to contribute their fair share of resources. Free riding or strategically selfish, a rational user acted in P2P system, causes system-wide performance degradation and has become one of the key problems. Incentive mechanisms are employed in P2P systems to encourage contributions. Existing incentive mechanisms prevented free riders and self-strategic peers to a certain degree, but some mechanisms adopted short-term history lack of robustness when the bandwidth fluctuated and others employed long-term history might miss the high-capability newcomers.

This paper discusses the impact of free riders and selfish-strategic peers in BitTorrent, and then proposes an incentive mechanism employing a neighbor selection policy

R.-S. Chang et al. (Eds.): GPC 2010, LNCS 6104, pp. 689–697, 2010.
© Springer-Verlag Berlin Heidelberg 2010

with price differentiation. The main contributions could be summarized in the following respects:

- We discuss an all-pay auction model to describe the resource distribution process of BitTorrent and analysis pros and cons of the incentive mechanism in BitTorrent.
- We propose a novel incentive mechanism considering the long-term share ratio and the short-term predicted upload bandwidth comprehensively. The mechanism includes neighbor selection policy with price differentiation which encourages peers to contribute their service as more as possible.

The remainder of this paper is structured as follows. Section 2 shows the related work. In Section 3, we propose an all-pay auction model to describe the resource distribution process of BitTorrent. Based on this model, we analysis the incentive mechanism in BitTorrent. The novel incentive mechanism with price differentiation based neighbor selection policy is designed in detail in Section 4. Section 5 describes the simulation result. Finally, we describe future work in Section 6.

2 Related Work

BitTorrent is still the dominant P2P file sharing application. With the free riding and the related problems of selfish-strategic behavior becoming one of its most significant threats, more research has been done on detecting, modeling, and proposing strategies to this problem. One solution to resolve the problem of free riding in P2P networks is incentive mechanism that aims to influence node's behaviors in a certain manner in order to increase the utility of the system.

B. Cohen describes the BitTorrent protocol, the technical framework, and the choking algorithm in [2]. He relates the BitTorrent to the iterated prisoner's dilemma (IPD) and uses tit-for-tat (TFT) strategy to optimize BitTorrent peers' download speed and also to be an incentive mechanism to prevent free riding.

Subsequently, the BitTorrent incentive mechanism is discussed in some literatures. [7] claims that the optimistic unchoking promote the system's robustness by giving leechers chances to connect to other fast leechers or seeders. On the other hand, [8] evaluates the choking algorithm in BitTorrent and questions its efficiency in providing reasonable reciprocation in balancing upload and download rates. [5] suggests that the Tit-for-Tat mechanism is not efficient enough in deterring unfairness; and relates this inadequacy to the heterogeneity of peers' bandwidths. Moreover, [6] argues that BitTorrent lacks fairness: It does not punish freeriders effectively neither it does reward users who contribute properly. [9] presents an experimental study on the behavior of BitTorrent. The results show that a freerider can perform better than a compliant peer.

Several modified BitTorrent clients [3, 4] have been developed which exploit different strategies to achieve better performance at the expense of users running unmodified BitTorrent. BitThief [3] is a free riding client which could download from BitTorrent swarms without contributing any resources. A BitThief peer opens as many connections as possible and continuously pretends to be a newcomer to get more optimistic unchoke slot. The BitThief peer also pretends being a great uploader in sharing communities by announcing bogus information to cheat the tracker and get a higher sharing ratio without ever uploading a single bit. BitTyrant [4] strategically tries to maximize its download rates by dynamically adapting and shaping the upload bandwidth allocated to its neighbors. It minimizes upload bandwidth to keep the position in other peer's unchoking set and maximize the number of active connections with other peers. A BitTyrant peer reaches relatively high download rates and, in some conditions, even a 70% speed improvement [4].

Much work has been done to prevent the free riders and especially the selfish strategic peers [11, 12, 14, 15, 16]. PropShare [11] attempts to improve original TFT of BitTorrent by using the Proportional Response algorithm [13] to split the peer's upload bandwidth in proportion to the contribution received from its neighbors in the previous round. Because peers' allocations change and PropShare uploads to and estimates rates of only a small subset of neighbors in each round, it fails to create an accurate view of the current rate allocations of a larger neighborhood. FairTorremt [14] proposed a deficit based distributed algorithm that accurately rewards peers in accordance with their contribution. A FairTorrent peer simply uploads the next data block to a peer to whom it owes the most data. Unlike existing incentive mechanisms, we propose an enhanced choking algorithm based on short-term predicted upload bandwidth and long-term share ratio, which enables to not only restrain the free riding of selfish peers but also improve the performance of benign peers.

3   BitTorrent Is an All-Pay Auction

All-pay auction is an auction in which all players pay the amount of their bids in advance, but only the person who bids the highest wins the prize. It is different from the normal auction that only winners need to pay the amount of their bids. We find that the resource distribution process including choking algorithm in BitTorrent maps to an all-pay auction process better.

3.1   Choking Algorithm

The choking algorithm contains neighbor selection and bandwidth allocation policies. It determines to whom the uploading service should be provided and how much bandwidth is provided to each peer.

Neighbor Selection Policy. In order to provide a fairly good uploading service to requesting peers, each peer is limited to upload to a small number of peers concurrently. Assume that a peer can potentially connect to any of the other $(n-1)$ peers in the system. Each peer selects a subset of other peers as neighbors to provide uploading service to them as well as obtain downloading service from them. Regular unchoking and optimistic unchoking are adopted in BitTorrent.

Regular unchoking: A peer will provide uploading service to n_u neighboring peers in every unchoking period, and these neighboring peers are the top n_u peers based on their observed average upload rates to this particular peer.

Optimistic unchoking: A peer will provide uploading service to n_o neighboring peers, independent of their upload rates to this particular peer. This is implemented in the BitTorrent protocol to discover neighbors who can provide the best download rates and to enable the newcomers get the data as soon as possible.

Bandwidth Allocation Policy. After selecting the neighbors, the peer assigns its bandwidth to its neighbors.

Equal sharing: The original BitTorrent mechanism is to equally split the uploading bandwidth BW among all neighboring peers. When there are (n_u+n_o) competing neighboring peers requesting file download, the source peer p_s transmits a file to a competing peer p_i with an assigned bandwidth u_i, where $u_i = \dfrac{BW}{n_u+n_o}$.

3.2 All-Pay Auction Model

The BitTorrent could be described as a top-k all-pay auction as Algorithm 1. Based on this economic model, we could figure out the advantages and disadvantages of original BitTorrent's incentives.

Algorithm 1. At round t, peer p_s runs an all-pay auction for its upload bandwidth.

While peer p_s has not finished download the file
begin
    (1) Receives average bandwidth of $(t-1)$ and $(t-2)$ from every interested peer p_i as p_i's payment for the bid of this round;
    (2) Sends $1/(n_u+n_o)$ fraction of its total upload bandwidth to each of the highest n_u interesting bidders;
    if ($t\%3==0$)
        (3) Sends $1/(n_u+n_o)$ fraction of its total upload bandwidth to other n_o interested peers at random;
    $t=t+1$;
end;

From the Algorithm 1, we could find that only the top n_u uploading peers could be assigned the bandwidth from the peer p_s. This incentives all peers to bid for the top n_u positions. But we also find that each of the top n_u uploading peers wins the same prize, $1/(n_u+n_o)$ of p_s's bandwidth. The first highest interesting peer receives the same bandwidth as the n_uth interesting peer. Uploading more can not obtaining more. The equally allocation of bandwidth provides no service differentiation among the competing peers. Therefore, rational users have no incentive to provide their service, resulting in the tragedy of the common. Further more, each peer only bids (n_u+n_o) auctions. Once a highly-capability peer wins all of the (n_u+n_o) auctions in which it bids, it has no incentive to bid more in these auctions.

The original neighbor selection policy based on short-term observed bandwidth is wasteful, and often leads to sub-optimal use of bandwidth. There are several reasons: (1) a peer commits its bandwidth for a whole choking period. (2) it uses the observed download rate from a peer as a prediction of future contribution. Such predictions are often erroneous. Especially in a dynamic environment peers often change their allocations or may stop reciprocating all-together. (3) Discovery of better peers is quite slow in real networks. Especially high-capability peers may waste a lot of bandwidth and time before they can find other high-capability peers to exchange data with.

BitTyrant strategically exploits those loopholes to maximize its download rates by dynamically adapting and shaping upload bandwidth to win the short-term observed bandwidth contest. At the same time, considering the short-term bandwidth alone makes some peers always being beaten by BitTyrant and waste their optimistic unchoke bandwidth. PropShare utilizes the short-term observed bandwidth as the proportion to split the source upload bandwidth to peers. As the number of peers increasing, the bandwidth is spitted less and less, and then the performance of system will decrease. FairTorrent use the long-term contribution to deal with BitTyrant, but it will miss high-capability newcomers when the newcomer's first contribution is less than some weaker peers which have a large accumulated contribution. Some strategic peers will also play tricks on FairTorrent by providing good service in the beginning and accumulating a large deficit and then enjoying the service without providing any service.

4 Novel Incentive Mechanism in BitTorrent

By analyzing the all-pay auction model of BitTorrent and some existing incentive mechanisms, we find that the incentive mechanism in BitTorrent needs to improve. We propose a novel incentive mechanism including neighbor selection policy with bandwidth price differentiation which considering the long-term share ratio and short-term predicted upload bandwidth.

Figure 1 shows an interested peer p_i's choking policies in the contiguous three choking periods. In BitTorrent, the duration of a choking period of all peers is same as 10 seconds, but the beginning time is different. The choking periods of p_i are t_i-2, t_i-1 and t_i, and the choking periods of source peer p_s are t_s-2, t_s-1 and t_s. We could see the asynchronous choking period between the source peer p_s and the interested peer p_i. The gray denotes that p_i unchokes p_s in that choking period. At the beginning of round t_s, the original BitTorrent client p_s exploits the average bandwidth of duration of (t_s-1) and (t_s-2) as p_i's predicted contribution of this round. They are often incorrect. A more accurate prediction is needed. For simplicity, we could regard the higher average upload bandwidth in the contiguous two previous choking periods as the predicted upload bandwidth. Further more, we could divide five seconds as a sampling

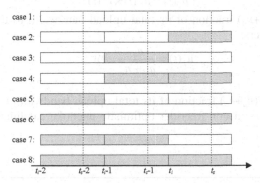

Fig. 1. The choking periods of a peer

unit and regard the highest value among the contiguous four units as the predicted value. The more accurate prediction will be studied in our future work.

The cumulative data in a long-term could revise errors introduced by short-term dynamic data. We propose a novel neighbor selection policy using metrics of long-term share ratio and short-term predicted upload bandwidth. The long-term share ratio denotes the peer's altruistic degree to the source peer and the short-term predicted upload bandwidth is based on the current service capability. In general, a peer with a good share ratio for a long time will keep the altruistic attitude in the future. In the auction model of BitTorrent, we consider the long-term share ratio as the unit price of each peer's upload bandwidth to the source peer instead of using the uniform price of the bandwidth to discriminate the altruistic degree. The higher the share ratio is, the higher the unit price is. The bid of a peer in the auction is the unit price multiplying the amount of predicted upload bandwidth. We still consider the fixed n_u unchoke slots and n_o optimistic unchoke slots, and each slot is allocated equal upload bandwidth. All the initial received data and sent data is set to 1 byte.

The proposed neighbor selection policy could be described as Algorithm 2.

Algorithm 2. At round t, peer p_s runs an all-pay auction with price differentiation for its upload bandwidth.

While peer p_s has not finished download the file
begin
    (1) Predicts the upload bandwidth according to the higher average bandwidth of $(t-1)$ and $(t-2)$, $\tilde{u}_i^s(t)$, from every interested peer p_i as p_i's amount for the bid of this round;
    (2) Increments the total received data from peer p_i and the total sent data to p_i by the number of bytes received and sent in the $(t-1)$ round, and calculates the share ratio of previous $(t-1)$ rounds of each interested peer p_i as p_i's unit price for the bid of this round:
$$r_i^s(t) = \frac{\sum recv_i^s + recv_i^s(t-1)}{\sum sent_s^i + sent_s^i(t-1)};$$
    (3) Calculates the (amount×price) as p_i's payment for the bid of this round:
$$b_i^s(t) = \tilde{u}_i^s(t) \times r_i^s(t);$$
    (4) Sends $1/(n_u+n_o)$ fraction of its total upload bandwidth to the highest n_u interesting bidders;
$$u_s^i(t) = \frac{n_u}{n_u + n_o} \cdot BW_s;$$
    if $(t\%3==0)$
        (5) Sends $1/(n_u+n_o)$ fraction of its total upload bandwidth to other n_o interested peers in non-freerider optimistic unchoke candidate set at random;
    $t=t+1$;
end;

The new auction's bid takes account of the service capability (by the bandwidth) and the altruistic degree (by the share ratio), thus competing peers who provide the high upload bandwidth and high share ratio will win the auction and the source peer could obtain the faster and better service. If a selfish-strategic peer exploits a smallest bandwidth to win one round auction, this small value will reduce its cumulative share ratio, then if it wants to win the next round auction, it should provide a higher bandwidth. This reduces the impact of the BitTyrant client. At the same time, some peers with low-capability optimistic unchoke peers with high-capability frequently, but high-capability peers do not unchoke them for their low upload bandwidth, then the upload bandwidth devoted to optimistic unchoke is waste in the original BitTorrent. Using the novel neighbor selection policy, low-capability peers' optimistic unchoking will raise their share ratio quickly because there is no reward data, and then they could acquire one unchoking chance after several optimistic unchoke for its high share ratio. This reduces the waste of the low-capability peers' upload bandwidth. Further more, a good peer sent little data in one round because the network congestion or other accidents, however, it is likely to get the high bid in the bandwidth auction for its high long-term share ratio, and the source peer will still unchoke it. This promotes the stability of the neighborship in the dynamic environment just like the Generous-Tit-for-Tat (GTFT) strategy dose.

5 Performance Evaluation

In this section, we assess the performance of our incentive mechanism based on experimental evaluation.

We design a discrete event driven simulator of BitTorrent based on OMNeT++, INET framework, and OverSim. In the application layer, we implement a BitTorrent protocol including tracker and original BitTorrent client, selfish strategic client (BitTyrant), and enhanced client with our proposed incentive mechanism. We vary the number of peers from 50 to 300. One initial seed peer with 10MBps upload bandwidth is set to never sleep in any of the cases and the rest of the entering peers initially contain no pieces. The upload bandwidth of free riders is zero and download bandwidth is same as other ordinary peers. In underlay network, the number of routers is configured proportion to the number of peers. Table 1 shows the simulation parameters of BitTorrent.

Table 1. BitTorrent simulation parameters

Number of total peers	50, 100, 300
Number of initial seeds	1
Peer arrival time	Poisson
Number of unchoke neighbor peers	5
Regular choking period	10 Second
Optimistic unchoke period	30 Second
Seed choking period	10 Second
Size of shared file	50MB
Size of chunk	256KB
Downlink bandwidth	2MBps
Uplink bandwidth	512KBps

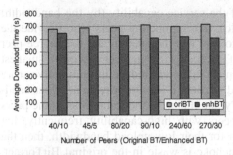

Fig. 2. Download time of a single enhanced BT

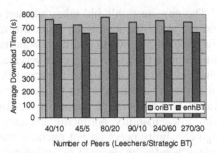

Fig. 3. Average download time

Figure 2 depicts the average download time in the scenario of different total number of peers with the fraction of 10% and 20% enhanced BT client mixed. Enhanced BT clients maintain low average download time when run against original BT clients.

Figure 3 shows the average download time of an original BT swarm and an enhanced BT swarm mixed with 20% or 10% selfish strategic clients separately. The average download time decreases in enhanced BT swarm in each group of peers. This means that the enhanced BT client could reduce the impact of selfish strategic peers effectively.

6 Conclusion and Future Work

In this paper we propose an all-pay auction model to describe the resource distribution process of BitTorrent-like systems. Within the model, we show that the original BitTorrent provides some local incentive mechanisms, but there are still many defects that could be utilized or have been utilized by free riders and strategic peers.

We design an incentive mechanism based on a price differentiation all-pay auction model. The neighbor selection policy with price differentiation is proposed to incentive the peers that "the more you give the more you get" and save the upload bandwidth of the low-capability peers. The novel incentive mechanism is robust to the dynamic environment and could be merged into BitTorrent easily.

There are many interesting areas of future work. The problem of seeder's bandwidth allocation is very important. Some strategy peers utilize the altruistic nature of seeders to obtain services without contributing to the system. We will complement the incentive mechanism with the seeder's unchoking algorithm.

We also plan to verify the effectiveness of our proposed incentive mechanisms by realistic deployments, and to improve the algorithm's effectiveness under extreme conditions by considering more limitations.

Acknowledgment

This work is supported by National Development and Reform Commission High-tech Program of China under contract No. 2008-2441 and National Basic Research Program (973 Program) of China under contract No.2009CB320907.

References

1. Sandvine: Global Broadband Phenomena (2009),
   http://www.sandvine.com/downloads/documents/
   2009GlobalBroadbandPhenomena-FullReport.pdf
2. Cohen, B.: Incentives Build Robustness in BitTorrent. In: Proceedings of the Workshop on Economics of Peer-to-Peer Systems (2003)
3. Locher, T., Moor, P., Schmid, S., Wattenhofer, R.: Free Riding in BitTorrent is Cheap. In: Proceedings of HotNets (2006)
4. Piatek, M., Isdal, T., Anderson, T., Krishnamurthy, A., Venkataramani, A.: Do incentives build robustness in BitTorrent? In: Proceedings of NSDI, pp. 1–14 (2007)
5. Bharambe, A.R., Herley, C., Padmanabhan, V.N.: Analyzing and Improving a BitTorrent Network's Performance Mechanism. In: Proceedings of INFOCOM (2006)
6. Jun, S., Ahamad, M.: Incentives in BitTorrent Induce Free Riding. In: Proceedings of the Workshop on Economics of Peer-to-Peer Systems (2005)
7. Liogkas, N., Nelson, R., Kohler, E., Zhang, L.: Exploiting BitTorrent for Fun (but not Profit). In: Proceedings of IPTPS (2006)
8. Legout, A., Urvoy-Keller, G., Michiardi, P.: Rarest First and Choke Algorithms are Enough. In: Proceedings of IMC, pp. 203–216 (2006)
9. Sirivianos, M., Han Park, J., Chen, R., Yang, X.: Free-riding in BitTorrent Networks with the Large View Exploit. In: Proceedings of IPTPS (2007)
10. Nisan, N., Roughgarden, T., Tardos, E., Vazirani, V.: Algorithmic Game Theory. Cambridge University Press, Cambridge (2007)
11. Levin, D., LaCurts, K., Spring, N., Bhattacharjee, B.: BitTorrent is an Auction: Analyzing and Improving BitTorrent's Incentives. In: Proceedings of ACM SIGCOMM, pp. 243–254 (2008)
12. Fan, B., Lui, J.C., Chiu, D.M.: The Design Trade-Offs of BitTorrent-like File Sharing Protocols. IEEE/ACM Transactions on Networking 17(2), 365–376 (2009)
13. Wu, F., Zhang, L.: Proportional Response Dynamics Leads to Market Equilibrium. In: Proceedings of ACM Symposium on Theory of Computing (2007)
14. Sherman, A., Nieh, J., Stein, C.: FairTorrent: Bringing Fairness to Peer-to-Peer Systems. In: Proceedings of ACM Conference on the Emerging Networking Experiments and Technologies (2009)
15. Chen, X., Chu, X., Chang, X.: Incentive framework using Shapley Value for BitTorrent-like Systems. In: Proceedings of ICICS, pp. 1–5 (2009)
16. Satsiou, A., Tassiulas, L.: Reputation-Based Resource Allocation in P2P Systems of Rational Users. IEEE Transactions on Parallel and Distributed Systems (2009)

Author Index